The Literature of *Lashkar-e-Tayyaba*

The Literature of *Lashkar-e-Tayyaba*

Deadly Lines of Control

C. CHRISTINE FAIR AND SAFINA USTAAD

Oxford University Press is a department of the University of Oxford. It furthers the University's objective of excellence in research, scholarship, and education by publishing worldwide. Oxford is a registered trade mark of Oxford University Press in the UK and certain other countries.

Published in the United States of America by Oxford University Press
198 Madison Avenue, New York, NY 10016, United States of America.

© Oxford University Press 2023

All rights reserved. No part of this publication may be reproduced, stored in a retrieval system, or transmitted, in any form or by any means, without the prior permission in writing of Oxford University Press, or as expressly permitted by law, by license, or under terms agreed with the appropriate reproduction rights organization. Inquiries concerning reproduction outside the scope of the above should be sent to the Rights Department, Oxford University Press, at the address above.

You must not circulate this work in any other form
and you must impose this same condition on any acquirer.

CIP data is on file at the Library of Congress
ISBN 978-0-19-888393-7

DOI: 10.1093/oso/9780198883937.001.0001

To Jeff, who makes everything possible. And my ever-evolving pack of canine associates who make life bearable.
C. Christine Fair

Contents

Notes on Transliteration and Translation	ix
Foreword	xiii
Acknowledgements	xvii

1. Introduction to This Volume   1

2. What is the *Lashkar-e-Tayyaba*?   19

3. Islamic Sources Used in This Volume   31

4. 'Why Are We Waging *Jihad*?' With a Foreword by Abdus Salam bin Muhammad   43

5. 'In Defence of *Jihad*' by Ubaidurrahman Muhammadi   79

6. 'The *Mujahid*'s Call' by Naveed Qamar   177

7. *We, the Mothers of the* Lashkar-e-Tayyaba by Umm-e-Hammad   213

8. Fighter Biographies   231

9. *Highway to Heaven* by Amir Hamza   335

10. The Problem with *Takfir* by Abul Hassan Mubbashir Ahmed   375

11. *Destination Kashmir is Nigh* by Ali Imran Shaheen   449

12. *Noble Warriors and Battlefronts* by Muhammad Tahir Naqqash   487

Notes	593
References	619
Index	627

Notes on Transliteration and Translation*

Due to its nature and content, we make frequent use of non-English words throughout this book. We made several decisions about how to render the myriad foreign words that merit brief explanation. First, where possible, we chose to use the simplest and, where applicable, most common English transliterations over the more phonetically correct—but less accessible—versions. For example, we use *jihad* instead of *jihād* for 'جهاد'. In doing so, we privilege simplicity and accessibility over orthographic rigor.

Second and more substantively, the orthographic rules for Arabic and Urdu vary. While this volume presents English translations of LeT's Urdu publications, within those publications, LeT's authors often present lengthy excerpts from Arabic sources. Usually, the authors we translate provide their own translations of these sources. For this reason, we do not replicate the original Arabic in our translation. If for some reason the authors of this volume did not translate the source into Urdu, we relied upon canonical publications of that work and cites them appropriately.

Because this volume is primarily a presentation of translations of LeT's Urdu- materials, we will use Urdu orthographic variations rather than those of Arabic. This distinction is important because there are both differences in pronunciation, and in some cases, orthography and transliteration between the two languages. One such common class of words involves the Arabic character 'ة'. When a word from Arabic is brought into Urdu, the character is usually rendered into the Urdu character 'ت', which is pronounced as a 't'. This occurs frequently for words that recur in this book. For example, a common word is 'شریعة', which is pronounced as *shariʾah* in Arabic with the '̕' indicating a glottal stop. However, in Urdu, this word is written as 'شریعت' and pronounced as *shariat*, omitting

---

* This note reproduces with some modification Appendix 1 in Fair, C. Christine. *In Their Own Words: Understanding the Lashkar-e-Tayyaba* (New York: Oxford University Press, 2019): 215–217.

X NOTES ON TRANSLITERATION AND TRANSLATION

the glottal stop which is not used in colloquial Urdu. Another common word that occurs in the Urdu source materials that we use in this book is the Arabic- origin word for prayer, 'صلاة', pronounced as *salaah* in Arabic but rendered 'صلا ت' and pronounced as *salaat* in Urdu. It should be noted that very few people use the word *salaat* for prayer in Pakistan, with most persons still preferring the Persian- origin word *namaz* (نماز), despite the ongoing Arabization of Urdu consistent with the growing importance of Saudi Arabia as a religious authority. The word for education or training offers yet another example of this type. Arabic speakers will spell the word 'تربية' as pronounce it as *tarbiya*, while Urdu speakers will spell it 'تربیت' and pronounce it as *tarbiyat*. In some cases, the organization prefers to use the Arabic spelling (i.e. *Jamaat ud Dawah* instead of *Jamaat ud Dawat*). In those cases, we use the Arabic transliteration consistent the organization's own revealed preferences.

Another character that introduces differences in pronunciation (but not orthography) is 'ض', which is pronounced as a 'd' in many Arabic dialects but as a 'z' in Urdu. Thus, the word common 'رمضان' is often transliterated as *Ramadan* in Arabic but as *Ramazan* in Urdu. A third character that is written identically in both Urdu and Arabic but pronounced differently is 'ث', which is pronounced similar to the consonantal cluster 'th' in Arabic but as a sibilant 's' in Urdu. Therefore, common word 'حدیث' is pronounced as *hadeeth* in Arabic but as *Hadees* in Urdu.

Finally, one transliterates some Arabic and Urdu words differently because the same word is pronounced differently despite being written identically. Perhaps the most common example of this difference is in the word *jihad*. While Arabic speakers will often pronounce this word as *jehad*, with the 'e' taking on a sound similar to that in the English word 'egg', Urdu speakers tend to pronounce it as *jihad*, with the 'I' taking on the sound similar to the 'I' in 'it'. As noted above, we prefer to use the most common transliteration where possible instead of using formal diacritics. This has some import for how vowels are written and pronounced. If I were to transliterate 'مجاهدین' formally we would do so as *mujahidīn*, to indicate the long 'I' sound in the word. However, we use *mujahideen* instead. (We do not use the other common variant *mujahidin* because it introduces confusion about the correct pronunciation.) In all cases, unless we are quoting an Arabic source, citing a text with a different spelling,

NOTES ON TRANSLITERATION AND TRANSLATION   xi

or quoting text with an alternate, we use the simplest transliteration of the Urdu variant throughout.

In addition to these transliteration choices, we also tend to use the appropriate Arabic or Persian plurals rather than Anglicized plurals. For example, the word for religious seminary is *madrassah*. We prefer the Persian plural for this word, *madaris*, rather than *madrassahs*.

The transliteration of individuals' names required us to make similar choices. We use the transliteration employed by the author in question when they are writing in English. When the author has no history of writing in English, we apply the same rules as above to select the easiest translations: Rabani is preferred to Rabaani. We make no effort to standardize spellings even for names that are pronounced identically but have different spellings (i.e., Ahmad vs. Ahmed, or Muhammad vs. Mohammad). The only exception to this rule is that we have standardized the spelling of Muhammad when referring to the Muslim prophet, unless we are quoting an English source that uses a different spelling.

As non-theists, we do not capitalize the words for 'god', 'gods', 'prophet', 'goddesses', and the likes unless they are used as a proper noun. While we will use the expression the prophet Muhammad, we will not generally capitalize the word prophet on its own. Similarly, Allah is a specific name for a god and thus we will capitalize that word as we would Kali or Ram, which are proper names referring to a specific (Hindu) goddess and god respectively.[1]

Foreword

In this volume, C. Christine Fair and Safina Ustad have painstakingly gathered and translated a representative collection of innumerable writings of the *Lashkar-e-Tayyaba* (The Army of the Pure). Documents such as *Hum Jihad Kyon Kar Rahen Hain?* ('Why Are We Waging *Jihad*?') and *Difa-i-Jihad* (*In Defence of Jihad*) clearly lay out the organization's understanding of *jihad*, and when it must be fought and by whom. Other publications translated in this volume, such as *Mujahid ki Azaan* (*The Mujahid's Call*), *Ghaziyan-i-Saf-Shikan* (*Noble Warriors and Battlefronts*), and *Hum Ma'en Lashkar-e-Tayyaba Ki* (*We, the Mothers of Lashkar-e-Tayyaba*), provide insight into how the organization recruits adherents to its cause and what kind of operations they claim to conduct.

Many of the texts in this volume explain the root of the organization's opposition to other religious traditions in the country. *Shahrah-i-Bahisht* (*Highway to Heaven*) by Amir Hamza is dedicated to revealing the heterodox practices associated with popular mystical traditions in Pakistan, while *Masalah-yi takfir aur is ke usul o zavabit* (*The Problem of Takfir and its Principles and Regulations*) takes aim at organizations which engage in the dangerous practice of *takfir*, by which they declare Muslims to be apostates and subsequently subject them to lethal violence. *Kashmir Manzil Dur Nahin* (*Destination Kashmir is Nigh*) by Ali Imran Shaheen typifies the organization's approach to the history of the region, the narratives it propagates about the nature of the Kashmir dispute as well as what it wants its readers to believe about Indian Hindus, and the nature of the Indian state itself.

Fair and Ustaad's volume is timely. *Lashkar-e-Tayyaba* (The Army of the Pure) remains the most important Pakistan-based *jihadi* organization operating in South Asia. Scholars believe it enjoys the fullest support of the Pakistani establishment, something conceded by Pakistan's former president and army chief, Pervez Musharraf. Despite the insistent demands of the international community that Pakistan shut down the organization and arrest and try its leaders for important terrorist attacks

xiv FOREWORD

such as the November 2008 attack on Mumbai, *Lashkar-e-Tayyaba* and its various front organizations flagrantly operate freely in the country while continuing to expand its membership and bases of support.

The reasons for the Pakistan state's unstinting support for the *Lashkar-e-Tayyaba* are found in this volume, which provides the first ever attempt to make the organization's seminal work accessible to the larger analytical community. As the authors argue, there seem to be two over-arching motivations of the Pakistani state to protect this group at all costs. The first reason is generally well known, if incompletely understood, namely, the organization sustains a capacious and unquenchable agenda for violence. Its ideology is based upon the Quranic verse that says, 'You are obligated to fight even though it is something you do not like' (*Surat al-Baqarah* 2:216). Extrapolating from this verse, the group asserts that military *jihad* is a religious obligation for all Muslims. The group then defines the endless conditions under which that obligation must be carried out, which is described in the author's translation of the organization's central treatise, *Hum Jihad kyun Kar rahe hain?* ('Why Are We Waging *Jihad?*'). For the *Lashkar*, *jihad* is essential to ensure the ascendancy of Islam and a true Islamic state. The conclusion that one draws from this booklet is that the organization can justify a state of permanent *jihad*.

Lashkar-e-Tayyaba's efficacy in conducting brutal operations in India as well as in Afghanistan is only one reason it enjoys the unflinching support of the Pakistani state. The second reason is that the organization is also an important partner in enhancing peace and security within Pakistan itself. Whereas the various Pakistan-based Deobandi militant groups espouse similar beliefs about *jihad* and its utility, *Lashkar* does not attack the Pakistani state itself or its citizens. It even cautions against public demonstrations that seek to destabilize the government, whether civilian or military led. Pakistan's various Deobandi militant groups attack political and even military leaders they consider to be behaving like apostates as well as Pakistan's other sectarian and communal populations. In contrast, *Lashkar* preaches strict nonviolence within the state itself.

With the rise of the Islamic State in Pakistan and revivification of the *Tehreek-e-Taliban-e-Pakistan* (Pakistani Taliban), *Lashkar* has become ever more invaluable as is evident in the authors' translation of *Masalah-yi takfir aur is ke usul o zavabit* (*The Problem of Takfir and its Principles and Regulations*). *Lashkar* has drawn the ire of other *jihadi* groups because it refuses to declare Muslims to be non-Muslims much less subject them to murderous violence upon doing so. *Lashkar*, mobilizing Islamic history and Quranic interpretation, argues that very few jurists are adequately qualified to engage in *takfir* and the evidentiary requirements for doing so are high. *Lashkar* condemns those who make frequent use of *takfir* as engaging in a grave sin. Ultimately, *Lashkar* argues that anyone who recognizes the primacy of Allah cannot be declared apostates and the only recourse is peaceful rehabilitation through proselytization and education. It even condemns violence against non-Muslims in Pakistan arguing that they should instead be invited to convert.

As a testament to the group's importance to the Pakistani state, Pakistan has steadfastly refused to move against *Lashkar-e-Tayyaba* or other so-called *jihadi* assets designated by the United Nations Security Council. In doing so, it has courted international ignominy and a seemingly permanent grey listing by the Financial Action Task Force (FATF), which aims to compel countries to comply with international norms on terror financing and money laundering. Presumably, no country aspires to join Iran and North Korea on the FATF's blacklist, which enjoins sweeping sanctions that restrict access to the global financial system. Most countries, upon receiving a grey listing, shut down access to funds for terrorist groups. This is not the case with Pakistan. For Pakistan, securing a position on the grey list remained a diplomatic victory that dodged the catastrophic economic consequences of a blacklisting for several years, while thwarting international demands that it prosecute terrorist leaders for accessing illicit funds and to tighten laws and banking security regulations relating to terrorist groups. Pakistan was removed from the grey list in October 2022, likely in effort to shore up Pakistan's decrepit economic state.

Pakistan has long honed this stratagem of playing a cat and mouse game with the international community since 1992, when the Americans first warned Pakistan about harbouring and nurturing *jihadi* groups targeting India. Then, after the kidnapping of an American tourist by a group called *Harkat-ul-Ansar* (HuA), Pakistan banned the group, only to allow it to resurface as *Harkat-ul-Mujahideen* (HuM). Since then, this current familiar pattern has emerged. Pakistani officials minimally satisfy a checklist of actions to evade immediate pressure without permanently shutting down its favoured *jihadi* groups. While Pakistan fears financial sanctions, it acts to minimally satisfice legal and technical requirements of the moment while retaining its *jihadi* options. Pakistan seemingly takes one step forward to mitigate exigent international pressure while bounding two steps back to protect its *jihadi* assets once the immediate pressure is off.

For the near and far term this organization will remain an important instrument for securing state's domestic and foreign agendas. While Pakistan can rightly claim victory in Afghanistan, that victory has come at a high cost. Pakistan's own Taliban are enjoying a comeback with the Afghan Taliban's return to power. The Pakistani state will work hard to encourage the Pakistani Taliban and other Deobandi *jihadis* either to go to Afghanistan to aid the still nascent Taliban state or to join groups like *Jaish-e-Muhammad* and fight in India. *Lashkar-e-Tayyaba* will put important competitive pressure on so-called Kashmiri groups like Jaish while also discouraging *jihadi* groups from operating within Pakistan. Having secured its bona fides as being too dangerous to fail, Pakistan remains confident that it can continue to play and win the game of cat and mouse it has perfected over the last thirty years.

Anyone who seeks to seriously understand this organization and its relationship with the Pakistani state must grapple with the contents of this volume.

Husain Haqqani

Acknowledgements

This volume is the culmination of more than thirteen years of work. The authors first met in 2010 in the context of a project on Pakistani political violence with Ethan Bueno de Mesquita, Jacob Shapiro, C. Christine Fair, and Jenna Jordan. After the project's completion, we began focusing on the large collection of materials which Fair began collecting as a student in Pakistan during the 1995–1996 academic year while studying Urdu at the Berkeley-Urdu Language Program in Pakistan and during numerous trips to Pakistan until August 2013.

We collected the materials presented here through a combination of visits to Pakistan over several decades, as well as the inter-library loan facilities at Georgetown and Harvard Universities and the Library of Congress. Georgetown University's Edmund A. Walsh School of Foreign Service generously provided substantial resources for this effort for which we are profoundly grateful. Without this financial support over many years, this project would not have been possible. To this end, we thank the recently deceased James Reardon-Anderson and Anthony Arend in particular. Additionally, we are extremely indebted to the Security Studies Program within the School of Foreign Service which provided research assistant support as well. The substantial funding from the School of Foreign Service also made possible the book *In Their Own Words: Understanding Lashkar-e-Tayyaba*, which draws extensively from the publications included here.[1] In this sense, this current book can be seen as the source material for *In Their Own Words*.

We remain obliged to C.M. Naim (lovingly known as Naim Sahab) at the University of Chicago for imbuing Fair with a love of the Urdu language, despite being untalented in its use. We also thank Jayant Prasad, Rumel Dahiya, and Ashok Behuria at IDSA in New Delhi, Don Rassler and the Combating Terrorism Center (CTC) at West Point, Nadia Shoeb, Daniel Byman, Bruce Hoffman, Keir Lieber, Jacob Shapiro, Praveen Swami, Ashley Tellis, Arif Jamal, Ali Hamza, Maryum Alam, the late Mariam Abou Zahab, Jaideep and his colleagues, and numerous others who met with us over the years in India, Pakistan, Afghanistan, and Bangladesh. Seth Oldmixon also deserves a special mention. He is one of the most undervalued assets in the community of South Asia analysts in the United States or elsewhere. With his vigilant monitoring of social media feeds and publications of militant organizations as well as the vastly diverse South Asian press, he is more well informed about the minutiae of South Asia and their significance than many intelligence analysts. He has patiently tracked down individuals and references when questions have arisen. I hope one day he too will write a book. We also owe a debt of gratitude to Dr. Mohammad Taqi, Ambassador Husain Haqqani, Ismael Royer, and Professor Jonathan Brown for entertaining frequent requests for help in translating something peculiar to this organization and/or understanding a foundational concept propounded by this organization as well as ideologically affiliated organizations.

Closer to home and to heart, Fair wants to express her abiding gratitude to her husband, Jeffrey Dresser Kelley and their ever-evolving pack of canine companions, who have patiently, and at times, less patiently, abided long absences with grace and aplomb. They also endured long periods of her inattention while finishing this book and its companion. They forewent vacations and grew ever-more tufts of grey hair wondering when—or if—it would ever conclude.

Ustaad would like to thank Mariam for providing her with the office and mental space to complete the translations included in this volume. She is also indebted to Noor Ali for offering access to online scholarly resources without which the foreword for this book would not have been possible. Most importantly, she is grateful to Dr. Fair for giving her an opportunity to contribute to a project that is becoming ever more relevant in today's politically volatile world.

We are both extremely indebted to Barun Sarkar at Oxford University Press, who has been equally patient, generous, and supportive of this project. Without his belief in this project, there would have been no project at all. We also owe a huge debt of gratitude to Mr. Prateek Chadha, who provided important pro bono technical advice.

1
Introduction to This Volume

Lashkar-e-Tayyaba (LeT, also known as *Jamaat ud Dawah*, JuD), a terrorist organization based in Pakistan, is the deadliest Islamist militant organization operating in India, Afghanistan, and elsewhere in South Asia and beyond. While former Pakistani President Pervez Musharraf admitted repeatedly that the state explicitly used groups like LeT and other groups operating in Kashmir, the Pakistani state denies such support.[1] Although there is considerable scholarship on its history and operations, few scholars have exploited the organization's vast publications.[2] This volume is the first scholarly effort to curate a sample of LeT's Urdu-language publications and then translate them into English for the scholarly community studying this group and related organizations. The original texts were written and published by Dar-ul-Andlus (which exclusively publishes LeT's books, pamphlets, posters, speeches, etc.) with the explicit intention of diffusing the group's ideology, raising funds, and cultivating volunteers for the organization. It is our hope that by rendering this group's materials more accessible we can contribute to the myriad efforts to combat such groups and the violence they perpetrate.

What's in a Name?[3]

While international attention to LeT is relatively new, the organization itself is not. It coalesced in the late 1980s in Afghanistan when Zaki-ur-Rehman Lakhvi merged his *Ahl-e-Hadees* militant group with another *Ahl-e-Hadees* organization, *Jamaat ud Dawah* (JuD, Organization for Proselytization), which Hafiz Muhammad Saeed and Zafar Iqbal established. The organization that ensued from this merger was known as the *Markaz-ud-Dawah-wal-Irshad* (MDI, Centre for Preaching and Guidance). Within a few years of MDI's founding, Hafiz Saeed established

2 THE LITERATURE OF *LASHKAR-E-TAYYABA*

LeT as MDI's armed wing. The exact date of LeT's formation is not known but scholars generally assess that it was established in 1989 or early 1990.[4]

Reflecting American indifference to the group and the lack of threat it posed to US interests, Washington did not designate the group as a Foreign Terrorist Organization (FTO) until December 2001 and did so only after another militant group, *Jaish-e-Muhammad* (JeM), attacked India's parliament in December of that year. This attack garnered American attention because it both precipitated the largest Indian military mobilization along the Pakistani border since the 1971 war and because this mobilization had adverse impacts for US military operations in Afghanistan, which began on 7 October 2001. Washington was relying on Pakistan's army to capture or kill Taliban and Al Qaeda forces fleeing into Pakistan as the Americans moved from north to south in their offensives. Pakistan, offering the justification of India's deployment along its eastern border, swung some of its troops from the western Afghan front to the east permitting thousands of Taliban, Al Qaeda, and allied fighters to ensconce themselves in various parts of Pakistan—including the Federally Administered Tribal Areas (FATA), as well as prominent cities in Balochistan, Sindh, Punjab, and Khyber Pakhtunkhwa—from where they would continue fighting for some twenty years as of this writing in 2023.

The United States, eager to broker a path to de-escalation such that Pakistan could re-orient its force posture back towards Afghanistan, prosecuted vigorous diplomatic efforts largely intended to persuade India to stand down and Pakistan to take palliative moves which would permit India to do so. To appease India, the United States proscribed LeT and JeM among other Pakistan-based and Pakistan-backed terrorist organizations. At the same time, the President George W. Bush administration insisted that Pakistan's military dictator and president, General Pervez Musharraf ban the LeT and other organizations, which the United States had recently designated. The Bush administration also persuaded Musharraf to make a series of public statements that would ameliorate Indian concerns and prevailed upon him to curtail Pakistan's dispatch of Islamist terrorists into India for a limited time after the events of September 2011.[5]

As is well known, Musharraf's bans were merely subterfuge: Pakistan's intelligence agencies warned its so-called '*jihadi* assets' of the impending

INTRODUCTION TO THIS VOLUME 3

bans, giving them ample time to transfer their financial assets to new bank accounts and expeditiously re-emerge under new names. Saeed, for his part, declared that MDI had been dissolved and replaced by JuD. Saeed also resigned as LeT's *emir* and took over the helm of JuD. Yahya Mujahid, spokesperson for LeT cum JuD and one of the founding members of MDI announced: 'We handed *Lashkar-e-Tayyaba* over to the Kashmiris in December 2001. Now we have no contact with any *jihadi* organization.'[6] In practice, the vast majority of LeT's assets and personnel were subsumed into JuD while the organizational nodes and operatives outside of Pakistan continued to serve under the banner of LeT. Despite his ostensible resignation from LeT, Hafiz Saeed remained the leader of both organizations; the placard above LeT offices was merely replaced with that of JuD. In the organization's various publications, Saeed is still referred to as the 'Commander of the *Mujahideen*'. One high-ranking US official summarized the farce by noting that: 'LeT's old offices merely changed the name on the door.'[7]

In the intervening years, JuD raised a number of related organizations, including the *Idara Khidmat-e-Khalq* (IKK, Organization for Humanitarian Assistance), which it ostensibly established in 2004 to provide humanitarian assistance to the victims of the Asian Tsunami.[8] In April 2006, the US Department of Treasury declared the IKK an FTO.[9] Later, in 2009, JuD founded another humanitarian front, Falah Insaniat Foundation (FIF, Foundation for Welfare of Humanity). The FIF garnered attention when Pakistani and international media reported that it was taking a lead in humanitarian relief during the 2010 massive monsoon-related floods. Shortly thereafter, in 2010, Washington designated FIF as an FTO and the United Nations did so in 2012 in accordance with UN Security Council Resolutions 1267 (1999) and 1989 (2011).[10]

In addition, JuD has participated in several umbrella organizations with other militant and right-of-centre political groups, including the *Tehreek-e-Tahafuz Qibla Awal* (Movement for the Safeguarding of the First Centre of Prayer), the *Tehreek-e-Tahafuz-e-Hurmat-e-Rasool* (Movement to Defend the Honour of the Prophet), and the *Difa-e-Pakistan Council* (Defence of Pakistan Council). It also organized the *Pasban-e-Harmain-Sharifain* (Defenders of the Sacred Sites in Mecca and Medina) and argued that the Yemeni Houthi rebels aimed to invade Saudi Arabia and assault the *harmain*—the Grand Mosque in Mecca, which surrounds the Ka'ba, and the prophet's mosque in Medina.[11]

4 THE LITERATURE OF *LASHKAR-E-TAYYABA*

Notably, unlike the many other militant groups organized under the banner of Deoband (e.g. the Pakistan Taliban, the *Sipha-e-Sahaba-e-Pakistan/Lashkar-e-Jhangvi, Harkat-ul-Ansar*, among others), as of June 2023, JuD has experienced a meagre single rift. This brief fissure occurred in July 2004 when elements of the group's leadership became vexed that Hafiz Saeed was posting his own relatives to top positions and enjoying excessive access to the widows of *jihadi* activists. Lakhvi, in particular, was perturbed by Saeed's blatant nepotism in making these appointments because he believed that he was being side-lined in the organization. Given that Lakhvi was a foundational member of MDI as well as the founder of the militant group that combined with JuD to form MDI, these developments were intolerable. Lakhvi briefly parted ways with Saeed and formed the *Khairun Nas* ('Good People', a reference to the companions of the prophet). This fissure was temporary, and the organization soon merged back to JuD, likely due to the active intervention of Pakistan's Inter-Services Intelligence Agency (ISI).[12] For these varied reasons, I use JuD, LeT, and MDI more or less interchangeably unless I specifically state otherwise both because doing so is accurate, and because I hope to remind the reader of this fact, irrespective of what the Pakistani government or the organizations says to the contrary.

In early August 2017, JuD opened a new front when it formed a political party named the Milli Muslim League ('National Muslim League', MML) with the aim of rendering Pakistan a 'real Islamic and welfare state'.[13] The organization wasted no time entering the political fray: after Prime Minister Nawaz Sharif was forced to resign on 16 August 2017 and thus vacate his seat in the national assembly for the NA 120 constituency,[14] JuD quickly fielded a candidate under the MML banner for the 17 September 2017 by-election to fill that vacancy. Because the MML had not yet been registered as a political party, the candidate (Muhammad Yaqoob Sheikh) filed his nomination papers with the Election Commission of Pakistan (ECP) as an independent candidate.[15] Despite being in existence for a mere four weeks, it received four times as many votes as did the Pakistan People's Party (PPP) in that by-election. This is most certainly due to the fact that it enjoyed the explicit backing and support of the security establishment.[16] Curiously, despite the fact that the July 2018 general election was massively engineered by Pakistan's intelligence agencies to ensure that Imran Khan's *Pakistan Tehreek-e-Insaf* would prevail, foisting Mr.

INTRODUCTION TO THIS VOLUME 5

Khan into the seat of prime minister, the MML did not win a single race. Given the closeness of this party to the establishment, this is a curious outcome of what many call the 'General Selection of 2018'.[17]

In this volume, we generally use the monikers JuD, LeT, FIF, and MML interchangeably, reflecting our opinion that this proliferation of appellations has little if any meaningful impact upon the organization and acknowledging the active collusion of the Pakistani state and the organization to continue to use the group even as rebranded fronts of the organization are proscribed by international actors. We will indicate, where appropriate, when and if a particular item specifically uses one of these appellations.

Brief Note on Curation Methodology[18]

This book comprises English translations of a curated sample of Urdu-language foundational texts from the vast body of literature produced and disseminated across Pakistan and beyond by local militant organization *Lashkar-e-Tayyaba* (LeT) through their in-house Lahore-based publisher, *Dar-ul-Andlus* (House of Andalusia). This name is a reference to the Iberian peninsula, which was conquered in 711 AD by Al-Walid I of the Umayyad dynasty (661–750), and subsequently ruled by various caliphs and emirs over seven centuries, until the last stronghold of Granada was relinquished by Muhammad XII of the Nasrid dynasty (1230–1492) to the Catholic Monarchs, Queen Isabella I of Castile and King Ferdinand II of Aragon in 1492; this was also the year Columbus took off for the Caribbean in search of India, and Jews were exiled from Spain.

Putting together a volume of this scale forces one to think of issues of: representativeness (i.e. 'how representative is this particular work relative to the entirety of LeT publications?'); importance (i.e. 'how important is this book in explaining LeT, even if it is not representative or even unique?'); popularity (i.e. which publication is more popular and thus possibly more salient?); among other pertinent questions. In an ideal world, we would have wanted to assemble all LeT's published items, which is tantamount to a census or a universe, from which we could draw a well-characterized sample as this is the most scientifically robust way of drawing a sample. For myriad reasons, this option simply is not achievable because the organization has not made a complete listing of its oeuvre available. Necessarily, we adopted a second-best approach, which other scholars could presumably replicate. We first used WorldCat—a master catalogue of library materials drawn from 16,131 partner institutions in 120 countries—to develop a master list of all Dar-ul-Andlus publications.[19] A search on WorldCat for '*Dar-ul-Andlus*' (also spelled as Dārulandlus) produced 117 items that were published from 1999 to 2020, including books and non-circulating items such as audio recordings and posters the vast majority of which are in the Urdu language. Second, working through the interlibrary loan facilities at Georgetown University and Harvard University to acquire the books, we augmented Fair's original sample of materials which had been collected over numerous trips to Pakistan from 1995 to 2013. In addition, Ustaad made several trips to Pakistan during the course of this project and visited their bookstores looking for germane materials. (Note: We did not evaluate non-circulating items such as recordings because they were not available through interlibrary loan.)

It turns out that American libraries house many of LeT's most important writings thanks to a programme that began in 1962: the so-called PL-480 programme, named after the eponymous public law which allowed the US Library of Congress to use rupees from Indian purchases of American agricultural products to buy Indian books. Through this programme, libraries throughout the United States have acquired books from South Asia. A few years later, in 1965, a field office was opened in Karachi to oversee the acquisition of Pakistani publications. While the PL-480 programme was discontinued long ago, the Library of Congress in Washington DC continues to employ the same institutional infrastructure to acquire publications from Pakistan and India under the rechristened South Asia Cooperative Acquisitions Program. We are extremely grateful to the Library of Congress, the Regenstein Library at the University of Chicago, and the other libraries across the United States which purchased these publications through this programme and made them available to us and other scholars through our institutions' interlibrary loan programmes. We are particularly grateful to Georgetown University's Lauinger Library, which never failed to produce a book we requested through interlibrary loan.[20] As one US government official quipped when we explained the sources of our materials, 'there is no

INTRODUCTION TO THIS VOLUME 7

better way to keep terrorist literature out of the hands of would-be terrorists than putting it in a library'.[21]

Once we assembled the collection, we next examined the volumes to determine which texts best addressed the overarching questions posed for this and a related scholarly effort.[22] Specifically, we looked for volumes that delineate what LeT/JuD says it does as an organization, what external and internal political imperatives shape the organization's behaviour in and beyond Pakistan, how the organization recruits and retains fighters, and how it cultivates a larger community of support. We also sought volumes that discussed the fighters of LeT, what motivates them, and who the families are that empower and enable them. Once we selected the critical texts, we perused the volumes and identified key sections within them for translation. Unless noted elsewhere, Ustaad translated the works while Fair edited and annotated them as required for context or clarity.

Note that we also had to make a number of decisions regarding transliteration for non-Latin alphabets, namely, Arabic and Urdu as well as translation decisions, all of which are described in a detailed note in the prefatory materials of this book.

Plan of *The Literature of the Lashkar-e-Tayyaba*

The most recurring and pressing theme that emerges from LeT's literature is the twin obligation of *jihad* (literal war) and *dawah* (proselytizing), with added emphasis on the former as a religious obligation mandated by Allah and his prophet, Muhammad, as the key to political dominance in this world, and salvation in the world hereafter. While *jihad* is not considered one of the five so-called pillars of Islam (i.e. belief in Allah's oneness, prayer, fasting, charity tax, and pilgrimage), the literature invariably elevates warfare to the status of an obligation of faith. Buttressed by theological and historical references, much of LeT's literary estate is split between establishing the *jihad* imperative and detailing exactly how war is to be conducted (i.e. legitimate and illegitimate targets, rules of engagement, short- and long-term objectives, and issues of leadership and authority). Lesser, but clearly identifiable, themes include proselytizing as a way to organize one's personal life, distinguishing between asceticism and piety, rejection of *jihad* as an internal struggle against the ego,

8 THE LITERATURE OF *LASHKAR-E-TAYYABA*

rejection of revolt against an Islamic government, rejection of mysticism, and rejection of cricket, music, films, and political activism as meaningless Western influences.

The rest of this volume is organized as follows. While this book is principally intended to offer scholars and analysts translations of what we assess to be some of the most important texts published by LeT and JuD, Chapter 2 provides a brief overview of the group and why we care about it. Readers who are familiar with this group can skip this chapter as it is intended for the uninitiated. Chapter 3 provides a brief overview of the kinds of sources from which LeT's various literatures derive legitimation and credibility, including through consistent references to the Quran, the *Seerat* (biographical literature about Muhammad), the *Sunnat* (reported actions of Muhammad), the *Hadees* (quotations attributed to Muhammad), and traditional narratives about Islamic history that prevail in Pakistan. This chapter situates the sources and references employed by the various authors in an effort to understand the meta-narrative they chart for their readers and the credibility they establish through frequent deployment of these sources.

The next several chapters form the most important contributions of this volume: translations of our curated sample of some of LeT's most salient and explanatory writings. Chapters 4, 5, and 6 respectively present, in full, complete translations of 'Why Are We Waging *Jihad?*', 'In Defence of *Jihad*', and 'The *Mujahid*'s Call'. The first two titles, namely, 'Why Are We Waging *Jihad?*' and 'In Defence of *Jihad*', are pamphlets which counter anti-*jihad* sentiment by offering an itemized list of arguments in simple, straightforward, colloquial language against the most mainstream political and theological opponents of *jihad*. Both titles employ a question–answer format in varying styles (the first, as a letter to the publisher, and the second as a dialogue between a *mujahid* and an 'inquirer'); and both titles resort to bullet points to present major themes, making it easier for readers to contextualize the issues and memorize the riposte. Here, we find, in categorical terms, the desire to restore the early Islamic empire across 'Andalusia, Hindustan, Israel. Bulgaria, Hungary, Cyprus, Sicily, Africa, Russian Turkistan and Lower Chinese Turkistan, up to Kashgar';[23] the importance of disregarding *jihad* as an internal struggle;[24] the assertion that war is a way of life mandated by Muhammad;[25] and the perception of

INTRODUCTION TO THIS VOLUME   9

Muhammad and the Muslim community as inheritors of a militant tradition embodied by the pre-Islamic Judaic prophets.[26]

In these pamphlets, and elsewhere in LeT's writings, Sufis (or Barelvis) are never referred to by name; rather, they are usually referred to as stone-worshippers or grave-worshippers. Similarly, when the authors refer to Shī'a, they rarely if ever do so explicitly and instead describe them as 'those who ridicule the (prophet's) companions'.[27] More interestingly, the literature repeatedly calls for a non-violent, non-confrontational attitude when dealing with ideological opponents and non-Muslims, as long as they are citizens of Pakistan. Consequently, all violence is to be directed beyond the borders of the Pakistani state, while dissidents within the state, be they corrupt bureaucrats, misguided politicians, grave-worshipping mystics, heretical Shī'a, or local Christians and Hindus, are only to be proselytized and debated, but never attacked. Conspicuously absent from the list of minorities who are not to be attacked specifically identified are Ahmadis. This is noteworthy for two reasons: first, the Ahmedi sect is perceived as the most heretical of all non-Sunni sects, so the fact that they are not mentioned could only mean LeT sanctions their persecution (which, in Pakistan, is particularly violent, ongoing, and without repercussion). More importantly, a cornerstone of Ahmedi faith is the absolute rejection of violent *jihad*, limiting the 'struggle' to an intellectual endeavour, which sets them apart from all other Islamic sects (including Sufis, who do not categorically reject violence despite problematizing it) as LeT's chief ideological opponents in context of warfare.

Compared to the first two pamphlets, '*The Mujahid's Call*' directly addresses college students attending secular schools and their parents, as it reaffirms, predicts, and encourages the social isolation a student should expect when he decides to live his life 'righteously'. By page 20, the author has assumed the reader is a committed proselytizer so without wasting much time on converting him, the text elaborates how he must organize his daily life, shifting from the second-person to a first-person narrative: 'You must ask yourself: how can I, as an individual, fulfil this obligation? First of all, my life must change: a proselytizer cannot maintain a regular routine or hold on to certain friendships and social activities while preaching Allah's word'. Further along, the text explicates the twin obligation of *jihad* and proselytizing. 'The battlefield of truth and falsehood will test our progress in two realms: one is the battlefield of proselytization,

10   THE LITERATURE OF *LASHKAR-E-TAYYABA*

which we enter armed with knowledge and evidence; the second is the literal battlefield which we will storm with advanced weapons to wage *jihad*; two civilizations will clash, and one will dominate the other. Allah will aid His followers in humiliating the disbelieving enemy.'[28]

While rhetorically superior to the earlier two titles, this tract clearly addresses a more educated and self-reflective audience, while offering some cogent critiques of the educational system and the gaps it leaves in character building. *The Mujahid's Call* draws a direct link between a student, who might be ostracized for a sanctimonious attitude, and the legendary persecution Muhammad had to deal with in Mecca, according to the traditional accounts: 'Arise and Warn! These were the words with which the prophet was instructed to spread the divine message he received at the cave of Hira. It is necessary to inspire every individual at every academic institution to proselytize and wage *jihad* in order to universalize the message of *tawheed* (oneness of Allah) and *Sunnat*. No doubt, there will be hurdles, for this is the path of humiliation, poverty, and strife but, if we tread this thorny road with fortitude, Allah's favour and approval await us in the afterlife.'[29]

Chapter 7 presents a selection of introductory essays from a three-volume hardcover collection titled *We Are the Mothers of Lashkar-i-Tayyaba* (Vols. 1–3). While a good portion of these volumes comprise several hundreds of biographies of young men in their early to mid-twenties who have died in *fidayeen*, or high-risk missions in Kashmir, we present selected biographies in Chapter 9, which focuses exclusively on fighter biographies.

In Chapter 8, we present a sample of fighter biographies spanning many decades. These biographies are presented from various points of view, including the perspective of commanders and colleagues of the fighter. The most emotive of these points of view are those of the deceased's family members, usually the mother. These family members' accounts often trace the transformation of both mother and son from ordinary individuals to paragons of virtuous suffering; for instance, when LeT workers arrive at the house of a young man recently killed in an operation to deliver the news of his 'martyrdom', the way this exchange takes place is crucial to determining the mother's character: 'Abu Sohaib Shaheed's mother is a woman who struck such a bargain with eternity. When *Lashkar-e-Tayyaba's mujahideen* arrived at

INTRODUCTION TO THIS VOLUME 11

her doorstep to give her news of her son's martyrdom, she asked them only one question from behind the door, "Where did the fatal bullet hit my son?"[30] Notice how the mother, in a moment of extreme grief, is presented as having the presence of mind to converse from behind the door, without revealing her face, and her only concern is whether her son died an honourable death or not.

Due to the repetitive nature of these biographies, we provide a handful of samples in addition to the introductory essays to the first two volumes. The lead writer for this project, a woman who identifies as Umm-e-Hammad, once thought of LeT as a criminal organization but is now the mother of a 'martyr' herself, travelling the length and breadth of Pakistan compiling stories about other women who gave their sons permission to fight and die. This literary graveyard uses romantically charged language and constant references to iconic women from Islamic history, to reassure the mothers of 'martyrs' they made the right decision by letting their sons sacrifice themselves for the cause (operatives cannot participate in battle without their parents' permission): 'A new chapter of martyrdom and valour was being written in the history of our nation. The unrivalled sacrifices of our women remind one of Khaula, Hafsa, Ammara, Safia and countless other blessed women whose lives were the embodiment of perseverance and strength. Funerary wreaths consumed more flowers than wedding bouquets. Schools were empty and graveyards were full. Shrines of martyrdom sprung up across the valley like orchards but the women who bore these brave young men did not so much as wince. Their radiant faces put the terrified tyrants to shame.'[31]

What is most disorienting about this title, and impossible to translate into English, is the way the 'martyrs', all young men in their early to mid-twenties, are referred to with respectful pronouns and terms specifically reserved for the elderly. For example, *Abu Abdullah Shaheed Din Pur Sharif se taaluq rakhtay thay* (as opposed to *taaluq rakhta tha*), or, *yeh jab bhi ghar atay* (as opposed to *yeh jab bhi ghar ata*).[32] It is odd for a mother to use these terms for her son, particularly in the socio-economic class from which the families belong. Additionally, the name of the 'martyr' appears with a diacritic that translates to 'May Allah's mercy be upon him', usually reserved for classical scholars and religiously renowned personalities from history. All this is to emphasize that age has no bearing on the status of a martyr.

12   THE LITERATURE OF *LASHKAR-E-TAYYABA*

In Chapter 9, we translate illustrative excerpts from Maulana Amir Hamza's 2004 volume *Shahrah-e-Bahisht* (*Highway to Heaven*), a book that aims to undermine local mystical traditions and beliefs. Amir Hamza himself is the founding ideologue of LeT/JuD and is one of the most influential persons in the organization. He is currently the convener of an LeT front organization called the *Tehreek-e-Hurmat-e-Rasool* (Movement for the Sanctity of the Prophet), which, since at least 2011, has opposed any reforms to Pakistan's noxious 'blasphemy law'.[33] *Highway to Heaven* is unarguably the most linguistically and referentially rich and textured work included in this compilation. Its audience comprises those who are confounded or offended by local mystical traditions such as the veneration of relics and shrines. However, its intention is not as unambiguous. For the most part, it sets out to mock local traditions, while affirming the readers' biases against these practices, and offering material to argue against 'corrupting innovations' in faith. The content varies from a 'scholarly' socio-historical analysis of mystical practices, tracing them to Christian and Hindu rituals, to a farcical account of the author indulging in these practices himself only to realize they are hoaxes orchestrated by charlatans and witch doctors to exploit the uneducated masses. By and large, *Highway to Heaven* does not attack the great mystics of the past themselves, whose shrines and mausoleums have a metonymical relationship with the towns and cities in which they stand; rather, the author excoriates those who build and venerate these shrines and organize religious festivals around the venues. This should be seen within the organization's adamance about the doctrine of the oneness of god (*tawheed*). In LeT's various writings, the practices of mystics are heavily criticized for their similarity to Hindu rituals, such as the use of prayer beads, talismans, propitiation of saints, and prescribed rituals and potions to heal any variety of physical, mental, and emotional ailments. In LeT's literature such practices are tantamount to *shirk* (sometimes translated as idolatry, but which also includes ascribing the attributes of Allah to others) or even polytheism.

Chapter 10 presents translated selections from *The Problem with* Takfir which contends with the theological issues of *takfir* (i.e. the juridical process of declaring a self-proclaimed Muslim a *kafir*, or infidel, based on his or her actions, statements, or beliefs). In contrast to the virulent, violent, and formidable tone and content of the preceding titles, *The Problem with*

INTRODUCTION TO THIS VOLUME   13

Takfir is surprisingly gentle, flexible, and, at times, even progressive. This may have less to do with a liberal outlook and more to do with a state-driven agenda that aims to maintain the status quo within Pakistan. This is evident from a subsection in the introduction, beginning on page 27, devoted entirely to the problem of declaring Pakistani political leaders infidels, where a popular local cleric explains in great detail why this is unacceptable.

The Problem with Takfir is arguably the most difficult text in this compilation to translate, primarily because the author himself struggles with elucidating complex theological arguments while trying to balance an uncharacteristically compassionate tone within the framework of an uncompromising moral outlook. The following lines in the preamble sum this up: 'The purpose of this brief preamble is to elaborate on the issue of *takfir*, an issue that plagues our world today. Certain organized youths have displayed alarming rigidity when it comes to this issue. On one hand, this rigidity can be seen as a manifestation of their passion and zeal for Islam but on the other hand it embodies sanctimony and arrogance. Where the former is worth appreciating, it is important to highlight and condemn the latter.'[34] This tension is present throughout the text, such as where the author talks about women's inheritance rights in context of *takfir*: 'Consider the fact that most Muslims completely ignore the laws of inheritance regarding women, filching the latter of their rightful share. Should all those who ignore this law be declared infidels and sent to hell or should we let Allah decide their fate ... ?' In all this, the author sporadically reminds the reader that, despite the stringency of its application, *takfir* is undoubtedly a part of *shariat*, and it is crucial to recognize *kufr* and wrongdoing, vigorously defending himself and LeT from the charge of being modern-day *murjiya*, a term he defines on page 49: 'Certain sects that are misguided, such as *murjiya*, believe that faith solely means heartfelt belief and the declaration thereof; according to them, *kufr* occurs only in the realm of belief. This is wrong! According to this logic, even Pharaoh cannot be termed an infidel considering he never denied Allah's lordship and godliness and only disobeyed His command.'

Chapters 11 and 12 respectively present excerpts from the last two titles, *Kashmir Manzil Dur Nahin* (*Destination Kashmir is Nigh*)[35] and *Ghaziyan-i-Saf-Shikan* (*Noble Warriors and Battlefronts*)[36] respectively. Both are similar in format in that they open with elaborate introductory

14 THE LITERATURE OF *LASHKAR-E-TAYYABA*

essays on history and segue into episodic chapters and subsections that are largely repetitive and formulaic. On the other hand, in content, the two are mutually reflective. The bulk of the material in *Destination Kashmir is Nigh* deals with alleged atrocities committed by the Indian Army in Kashmir, however, the introductory chapters included in this compilation outline a stylized history of the Kashmiri resistance that accords with the problematic Pakistani government's preferred narrative, and, more importantly, the posited enduring relationship between the so-called local resistance and LeT. This explains why the language in the introductory chapters is noticeably more eloquent and idiomatic, compared to the language employed in the sample episodes of violence that are simpler and more colloquial. In describing the purpose of this title, the author states on page 27: 'This manuscript presents only a fraction of the sacrifices made in the six months from 11 June 2010 to 11 December 2010. If every single instance of aggression were documented, countless volumes would fill endless stacks in the libraries of justice. Every effort has been made to cover all aspects of the struggle; additionally, the history of the movement and the geography of the region have also been examined in considerable depth.'

Kashmir Manzil Dur Nahin (*Destination Kashmir is Nigh*) is quite lengthy at 350 pages and comprised seven major sections each with numerous brief chapters dilating upon the main themes of the section. In this volume, we present translations of important and illustrative sections, which include all of the extensive prefatory material, a brief note by Hafiz Muhammad Saeed himself, the Emir JuD/LeT as well as another short preface by Amir Hamza,[37] a founding ideologue of JuD/LeT, who currently is the Convener of the *Tehreek-e-Hurmat-e-Rasool* (Movement for the Sanctity of the Prophet, another LeT front organization). We next present an excerpt from Chapter 1, which is titled 'Get out of Kashmir,' which contains eleven chapters on the title theme. We present translations of five sub-sections from Chapter 2, titled 'Every Wound is Kashmir'. From Chapter 3, 'We Will Never Submit', we present translations of four sections and three sections from Chapter 4, titled 'Never Forget the Blood We Spill'.

In contrast, and in response to the helplessness and oppression described in *Destination Kashmir is Nigh*, the last title, *Noble Warriors and Battlefronts* targets young men seeking adventure and spoiling for war. In

INTRODUCTION TO THIS VOLUME   15

a 600-page tome to militancy, the LeT gloats extensively over their presence and operations in India, in general, and in Kashmir, in particular. It traces the history of LeT's presence in Kashmir and the rest of India, beginning with their first attack on Indian military personnel and concluding with their attack on the Red Fort in 2000. Each chapter reads like an action-packed film script, replete with oppressive soldiers, victimized villagers, dramatic dialogue, and heroic LeT operatives, part Rambo part Robin Hood, who emerge from the forests of the valley to restore dignity and peace among brutalized populations. According to the author, this title documents a living *jihadi* struggle: 'With Allah's blessings, I have attempted to document the rise of *Lashkar-e-Tayyaba* as this organization ravages disbelief through fire and sword. I have done this precisely so our narrative does not befall the same fate as other movements, and so future generations won't have to speculate or debate the truth of this struggle for they will have a reliable resource and a ready reference at hand.'

Two themes which feature prominently in earlier titles but find practical expression in *Noble Warriors and Battlefronts* are the justification for collaboration with non-Muslims, and the legitimacy of non-combatants as targets of violence. Throughout LeT's literature, the groups assert that it is perfectly acceptable to work in collaboration with non-Muslims, particularly polytheists, in various situations.[38] However, in earlier titles, this is mentioned hypothetically, and the references used to back this claim date back to Muhammad's lifetime. In *Noble Warriors and Battlefronts*, this is manifest in the friendly, at times familial dynamic between LeT militants operating in Kashmir and local Hindu villagers, often collaborating against the oppression of the Indian Army.[39] Hindu women not only refer to LeT militants as brothers, but they also house them, feed them, and watch over them, in the face of manhunts and crackdowns. All this is explained in the voice of an old Hindu man who claims the Indian Army rapes and plunders everyone indiscriminately, which is why the locals, irrespective of religion, welcome LeT militants to counter the aggressors.[40] Tellingly, this subsection ends with the old Hindu man almost converting to Islam but ultimately holding back, to the chagrin of his LeT friends. The author seeks to convince his readers that Muslim warriors are not out forcibly converting anyone, even though the fighters hope they can inspire non-Muslims to embrace Islam. The author also wants to dilate upon the dedication with which the LeT *mujahid* fights

16 THE LITERATURE OF *LASHKAR-E-TAYYABA*

all forms of oppression against Muslims and non-Muslims alike. As the author states in the introduction to this title: 'Our *jihad* is by no means limited to Kashmir; we intend to take this fight to every region of the world where Muslims are being persecuted and oppressed. We will travel to these lands with our heads on silver platters the way Tariq bin Ziyad[41] landed on the shores of Spain to defend the honour of a Christian girl.'[42]

Since November 2008, LeT has been notorious for the terrorist attacks in Mumbai against civilian targets that left over one hundred and fifty people dead, and over three hundred injured. However, in *Noble Warriors and Battlefront*, the author asserts that targeting non-combatants is *verboten* and that fighters must only combat Indian soldiers and paramilitary forces. This theme is highlighted most clearly in the concluding chapter of this title. Setting the bulk of the episodic encounters in the wildernesses of Kashmir, where certain Hindu villagers are presented as collaborators and junior officers of the Indian Army are portrayed as victims of high-ranking Brahmin majors, the book builds up to the grand finale of the Red Fort attack in Delhi in 2000, a daring operation executed at a historical venue in the heart of India's capital that left twelve soldiers dead. The venue, according to the author, is as symbolic as it is strategic: it is the last fortress from where the Muslim Mughal king Bahadur Shah Zafar ruled over India before being dethroned and exiled by the British; at the same time, certain military regiments like the Rajputana Rifles are stationed inside the fort. For these reasons, it is presented as the ideal target. Intriguingly, the attack took place during a light show that allowed the militants to make their way into the fortress among civilians. This fact also allows the author to highlight the fact that, despite the presence of so many people, the militants were careful only to target the soldiers on the premises: 'Then, the *fidayeen* go hunting... two civilians appear before them but their lives are spared for we are at war only with Hindu soldiers... the occupiers and oppressors... as soon as the civilians disappear a military car arrives on the scene; the two soldiers inside are instantly shot dead... The *mujahideen* were not interested in attacking civilians; their targets included Rajputana Rifles' headquarters as well as the prison where, according to the Indian Army, high value terrorists and *mujahideen* are interrogated.'[43]

The chapter about this attack anthropomorphizes the heritage site as delighted to have LeT operatives walk among its passageways. Presented as a dilapidated prisoner of war first taken by the Christians (the English) and then held hostage by the polytheists (Hindus), it is portrayed as having waited for centuries for Muslims to reclaim its lost glory. The descriptions include the identities of the LeT operatives, the towns they hailed from, the inaccuracies in media reports about them, as well as their tactical and ethical considerations in the course of executing their mission. The final chapter of this book is a fitting conclusion to the body of literature translated.

Analytically, this volume is a challenge. After all it is an empirical fact that the organization targets civilians. One explanation for this text is that it is intended largely for propaganda purposes to convince Pakistanis of the legitimacy of the organization's violence. Clearly, once a potential recruit is prepared for operations, they are instructed that targeting civilians is valid. Despite our best efforts, we were unable to find more operational literature that closes the gap between these aspirations and propagandistic writings that may garner financial and human support for the organization and the actual training that operatives receive in advance of being deployed for operations.

2
What is the *Lashkar-e-Tayyaba*?*

Although the exact year in which *Lashkar-e-Tayyaba* (LeT, Army of the Righteous)[1] coalesced is unknown,[2] scholars generally contend that it began when Zaki-ur-Rehman Lakhvi gathered several Pakistani *Ahl-e-Hadees*[3] adherents to wage *jihad* against the Soviets in Afghanistan at the very end of that conflict (1979–1989).[4] A year later, in *circa* 1985, Hafiz Muhammad Saeed and Zafar Iqbal, two professors from the Islamic studies department of Lahore Engineering University, founded *Jamaat ud Dawah* (JuD, Organization for Proselytization), which was initially a small group engaged in *tabligh* (proselytization) and *dawah* (missionary work) with the intent of promulgating the *Ahl-e-Hadees* creed. In *circa* 1986, Lakhvi's LeT amalgamated with Saeed and Iqbal's JuD to form the *Markaz-ud-Dawah-wal-Irshad* (MDI, Centre for Preaching and Guidance), which had three preoccupations: *jihad*, proselytization of the *Ahl-e-Hadees maslak*, and the creation of a new generation of Muslims committed to its ideology.[5]

Within a year of its formation, MDI established its first militant training camp, *Muaskar-e-Tayyaba*, in the Afghan province of Paktia, which does not border Pakistan. It established another camp, *Muaskar-e-Aqsa*, in Kunar, which abuts the Pakistani tribal agencies of Bajaur and Mohmand in Pakistan's Federally Administered Tribal Areas (FATA).[6] Kunar is distinct from much of Afghanistan because it is home to numerous *Ahl-e-Hadees* whereas many Afghans tend to be associated with different Sufi orders (e.g. Naqshabandi). This feature made Kunar an attractive safe haven for Wahhabi Arabs in Afghanistan, despite the fact that Wahhabis are technically distinct from Salafis.[7]

After the Soviets withdrew from Afghanistan, MDI reoriented towards Indian-administered Kashmir because, as Hafiz Saeed explained, the group wanted to distance itself from the internecine in-fighting among

---

* This chapter draws from C. Christine Fair, *In Their Own Words: Understanding the Lashkar-e-Tayyaba* (New York: Oxford University Press, 2019): 67–109.

20 THE LITERATURE OF *LASHKAR-E-TAYYABA*

different so-called *jihadi* groups. LeT relocated its training facilities to Pakistan-administered Kashmir where it established numerous camps in the mountains. The organization's decision to eschew warlord infighting reflects partly MDI's preference to abjure participating in Muslim-on-Muslim violence. The decision also reflects its belief that Kashmir is the most legitimate open front in the region, and that it entered the fray there before it became Pakistan's proxy of choice.[8]

MDI's headquarters (*Markaz*) was built on a sprawling, 200-acre campus in Muridke, in Pakistan's Punjab province, 30 kilometres from Lahore. The Punjab, unlike the FATA, is one of the most militarized provinces in Pakistan. Of the nine regular Pakistan Army corps, six are in the Punjab as well as the Army Air Defence Command and Strategic Forces Command, which are treated as corps. The MDI *Markaz*, which is now the headquarters for JuD, hosts numerous amenities and profit-making activities, including: a *madrassah* (seminary), a large *jamia* mosque, a hospital, a market, a large residential area for scholars and faculty members, a garment factory, an iron factory, a woodwork factory, a stable, a swimming pool, a fish farm, and agricultural tracts.[9]

On 25 January 1990, MDI staged its first militant mission in Kashmir when its operatives ambushed a jeep that was carrying Indian air force personnel travelling towards Srinagar Airport. One squadron leader and three pilots were killed.[10] In the early 1990s, MDI segmented its activities and organizational structure. While MDI continued the mission of proselytization and education, it hived off LeT as a tightly related militant wing of MDI.[11] However, Hafiz Saeed was the leader (*emir*) of both organizations, which attests to the degree to which it was nearly impossible to distinguish MDI and LeT.[12] Hafiz Saeed explained the continuity between the two organizations as follows: 'Islam propounds both *dawah* and *jihad*. Both are equally important and inseparable. Since our life revolves around Islam, therefore both *dawah* and *jihad* are essential; we cannot prefer one over the other.'[13]

The Inter-Services Intelligence Agency (ISI) had hoped that LeT, with its demonstrable superior capabilities, would intensify the conflict in Kashmir and expand the geographical expanse of the insurgency. In the early 1990s, the ISI and the Pakistan army began providing support to the organization. The army helped to build LeT's military apparatus specifically for use against India as opposed to Afghanistan, Chechnya, or other theatres where LeT activists fought periodically. The Pakistan army

WHAT IS THE *LASHKAR-E-TAYYABA*?   21

helped design the organization's military training regime and has long co-located army and ISI personnel at LeT training bases to help oversee the regimen and to lead the organization's trainers.[14] Pakistan's investments paid off: within a few years, LeT became the biggest challenge to the Indian security forces in Kashmir, prior to the introduction of *Jaish-e-Muhammad* (JeM) many years later.

In 1999, LeT introduced a new tactic in Indian-administered Kashmir: namely, the *fidayeen* attack. By doing so, the LeT and its Pakistani handlers hoped to reverse a three-year decline in militant activity in Indian-administered Kashmir. The first such mission involved two LeT operatives, who attacked the headquarters of the Border Security Force (BSF, an Indian paramilitary organization) in Bandipura with grenades and gunfire. The BSF Deputy Inspector General perished in that attack. These attacks embarrassed Indian security forces and helped to burnish LeT's reputation for being the most formidable of the various militant groups operating in Kashmir.[15] Since then, these kinds of attacks have become a hallmark of LeT's operations, which resemble high-risk missions in which well-trained commandos engage in fierce combat during which dying is preferable to being captured. Hafiz Abdul Rehman Makki, a key LeT leader, explained in the pages of *Mujallah-ul-Dawah* that the *fidayeen* commanders are killed only by the hands of their attackers, not their own.[16] Thus, while martyrdom is in some sense the ultimate objective of a LeT *fidayeen* operation, the organization selects missions where there is a possibility—howsoever remote—that the assailants will survive to kill more of the enemy in the future. This stands in firm contrast to the suicide attacks popularized by Deobandi terrorist groups such as the Afghan Taliban, Pakistan Taliban, *Lashkar-e-Jhangvi*, and JeM, in which the death of the attacker is the *sina qua non* of a successful suicide attack even if the attacker kills no one else other than himself in the assault.

In December 2001, Pakistan banned LeT, along with several other militant groups, after JeM attacked the Indian parliament earlier that month, bringing India and Pakistan close to the brink of war. These bans deceived no one. Pakistan's intelligence agencies alerted the soon-to-be banned organizations of the upcoming proscriptions, providing them ample time to transfer their assets to new accounts and to reorganize and relaunch under new names. In the case of LeT, Hafiz Saeed announced

22 THE LITERATURE OF *LASHKAR-E-TAYYABA*

the organization had been restructured and would operate as JuD, separate from LeT, which would strictly be a Kashmiri organization led by Maula Abdul Wahid al-Kashmiri. Saeed dissolved MDI and replaced it with JuD, which was the name of the original organization he founded in 1985 and which was still registered as a Pakistani charity. He resigned as LeT's *emir* and became the *emir* of JuD, which was described as an 'organization for the teaching of Islam, politics, [and] social work'.[17] According to Yahya Mujahid, 'we handed *Lashkar-e-Tayyaba* over to the Kashmiris in December 2001' to be led by al-Kashmir.[18] This purported division was merely a reorganization: JuD subsumed the vast majority of LeT's human, financial, and material assets, while the organizational nodes and operatives outside of Pakistan continued to serve under the banner of LeT. As further evidence of the organizational continuity between the various groups, Hafiz Saeed, Zafar Iqbal, Hafiz Abdul Rehman Makki, and Zaki-ur-Rehman Lakhvi were in charge of the new organization, while al-Kashmiri was merely a figurehead.[19] Those who could no longer fight in Kashmir were either retained in so-called reserve forces or remained active by participating in social work or preaching under the guise of JuD or other organizations under Saeed, such as the *Falah Insaniat* Foundation (FIF, Foundation for Welfare of Humanity).[20]

By 2005, the organization formally began sanctioning and supporting its cadres going to Afghanistan to fight with the Afghan Taliban where they engaged American, International Security Assistance Force (ISAF), Afghan, and Indian targets.[21] However, the LeT was chary about becoming extensively involved in the Afghanistan insurgency and the degree to which it would be required to work with and through the various Deobandi groups who were at war with the Pakistani state.

Ultimately, the organization opted to enter the Afghan insurgency for several reasons. First, Pakistan was forced to restrict Kashmir operations after the Indian parliament attack and that on Indian military families in Kaluchak (in Kashmir) in May 2002. Under significant US pressure, Musharraf adopted the so-called 'moderated *jihad*' strategy (which denied LeT and other *jihadi* groups' easy access to this prized theatre of operations).[22] The organization, seeking to retain fighters as well as experienced commanders who were anxious for active combat, found Afghanistan a welcoming theatre. Second, the LeT's donors believed that Afghanistan was a more important objective than Kashmir after the ouster of the Taliban and Al Qaeda and the subsequent occupation of the country by American and ISAF forces. Third, under the American security umbrella, India established a robust presence in Afghanistan which was a perennial irritant to Pakistan.[23] Fourth and most importantly, the ISI sanctioned the organization's expanded role in Afghanistan where it, along with the Haqqani Network, became Pakistan's most important assets with which it could attack Indian and international military targets in Afghanistan. However, for LeT, the Afghan theatre was of secondary importance to that of Kashmir and is a theatre of compulsion rather than a theatre of preference.[24]

The organization came under considerable pressure again in 2007 when some members—including senior leaders—considered dumping 'its ISI paymasters, [to] join forces with al Qaeda and shift its theatre of activity from fighting Indian forces in Kashmir to launching the attacks against coalition forces in Afghanistan.'[25] In January 2006, Deobandi militants under the leadership of two brothers, Maulana Abdul Aziz and Abdul Rashid Ghazi, took over and fortified the Red Mosque in Islamabad and a nearby women's *madrassah*, which they used as a base for vigilante violence and criminal activities such as violent demonstrations, destruction of property, armed clashes with security forces, and kidnapping. The final straw was their abduction of ostensibly Chinese prostitutes. At long last and under Chinese pressure, the Pakistan armed forces launched Operation Silence in July 2007. During the conflict, more than two hundred people died. Ghazi was killed and his brother was captured, while trying to abscond in a *burqa*.[26]

Some of the notable LeT attacks in Afghanistan included the 2008 assault on an American base in Wanat, Nuristan.[27] In that attack, insurgents came close to overrunning the American base. LeT attacks on Indian targets included the July 2008 car bombing of the Indian Embassy,[28] the February 2010 *fidayeen* attack on Kabul guesthouses hosting Indians,[29] and the May 2014 attack on the Indian consulate in Herat.[30]

David Coleman Headley (also known as Daood Gilani) came to LeT at a propitious moment when the organization was struggling to remain relevant and to retain its fighters who sought to wage *jihad* on a wider landscape. Headley, an American Pakistani, worked as agent of both the ISI and the LeT as well as an informant for the US Drug Enforcement Agency (DEA).[31] Headley first tried and failed to secure support from

24 THE LITERATURE OF *LASHKAR-E-TAYYABA*

the ISI, LeT, and Al Qaeda to attack a Danish newspaper which published offensive cartoons of prophet Muhammad.[32] Headley encouraged both the ISI and the LeT to attack multiple targets in Mumbai. Lakhvi found this appealing as he was worried that the organization would not remain coherent under the varying pressures to join Al Qaeda in Afghanistan or even to fight against Pakistanis, a position the organization abjured from the beginning. Major Iqbal, Headley's handler within the ISI, called him to Lahore explaining that he was 'under tremendous pressure' to prevent the *Lashkar* from fracturing.[33]

Until that point, LeT and the ISI were considering Headley's Mumbai mission but were not convinced by it. Now things had changed. The ISI and LeT were 'compelled to consider a spectacular terrorist strike in India' that would 'sate the desire of some factions to attack the enemies of Islam—Americans, Israelis and Europeans—as well as India'.[34] Headley's Mumbai plan fit the bill. After receiving substantial training in spy craft by the ISI, Headley carried out the reconnaissance for the 2008 Mumbai assault.[35] Pakistan deployed government forces outside LeT's Qadisiya mosque in Lahore and ISI agents 'rode shotgun' to protect Hafiz Saeed. Similarly, government forces provided security to the complex at Muridke, while 'plain-clothed agents, hair cropped, cradling machine guns, patrol[ed] the faux Greek villas of the movement's leaders'.[36]

The suggestion to attack Chabad House came from sixteen Indians whom LeT had recruited in Mumbai to help develop a list of potential attack sites. A late addition to the target list, it was a Jewish welfare centre staffed by an American rabbi. Rather than catering to the needs of Mumbai's Indian Jewish community, Chabad House principally served Israelis—many of whom travel to India after completing their compulsory military service. While the attacks on the Taj, the Trident-Oberoi, and the Chhatrapati Shivaji Terminus (CST) were not controversial within the LeT, attacking Chabad House was widely debated. Some within the old guard objected to its inclusion, noting that it was beyond LeT's brief and would result in the organization becoming the target of global counter-terrorism efforts. However, those who were more swayed by Al Qaeda convinced Lakhvi to push the organization in this new direction.[37] Ironically, while the expansion of the target set beyond Indians caused some analysts to interpret the move as LeT cosying up to Al Qaeda, it was, in fact, a move to prevent such a robust embrace.[38] Headley

WHAT IS THE *LASHKAR-E-TAYYABA*? 25

is currently serving a thirty-five-year prison sentence for his pivotal role in the Mumbai 2008 attacks.

Despite being operational since 1990, the US government did not recognize the group as a Foreign Terrorist Organization (FTO) until December 2001, largely because the group did not pose a serious threat to American interests narrowly defined. Washington only did so after another militant group, *Jaish-e-Muhammad* (JeM), attacked India's Parliament in December of that year, precipitating the largest Indian military mobilization along the Pakistani border since the 1971 war. (Regrettably, many media accounts of this attack claim erroneously that it was jointly executed by JeM and LeT and this fallacy perdures in the scholarly and policy analytical literature to date.) The United States was motivated to act because India's military mobilization complicated US operations in Afghanistan: as US forces and their Afghan partners drove the fleeing Taliban and their Al Qaeda associates south and towards the Pakistan border, Pakistan's army was supposed to kill or capture those crossing into Pakistan. After the Indian deployment on its western border, Pakistan's forces swung many of its troops from its border with Afghanistan to the Indian border. Consequently, fleeing Taliban, Al Qaeda, and allied fighters were able to establish sanctuaries in various parts of Pakistan—including the Federally Administered Tribal Areas (FATA), as well as prominent cities in Balochistan, Sindh, Punjab, and Khyber Pakhtunkhwa—from which they would continue operating.

Both to preclude an Indo-Pakistani war and re-concentrate Pakistani focus towards its Afghan border, Washington spent considerable political capital persuading India to stand down. As a part of these diplomatic efforts, the United States proscribed LeT and JeM among other Pakistan-based and Pakistan-backed terrorist organizations. At the same time, the administration of President George W. Bush pressured Pakistan's military dictator and president, General Pervez Musharraf, to impose the afore-noted ban on LeT and other organizations which Washington had designated. Washington also press-ganged Musharraf to make a series of public statements aimed at mitigating Indian concerns and even persuaded him to curtail sending terrorists into India for some time after the events of the 2001 parliament attack.[39]

Despite the so-called ban, the organization has spawned numerous related organizations since 2001. The *Idara Khidmat-e-Khalq* (IKK,

26 THE LITERATURE OF *LASHKAR-E-TAYYABA*

Organization for Humanitarian Assistance) was set up in 2004 to provide relief to the victims of the Asian Tsunami.[40] At that time, the organization collected and dispatched considerable supplies to Sri Lanka.[41] In April 2006, the US Department of Treasury declared IKK a FTO.[42] Later, in 2009, JuD set up another humanitarian front, *Falah Insaniat* Foundation (FIF, Foundation for Welfare of Humanity), which raised its profile by providing relief during and after Pakistan's massive monsoon-related floods in 2010. The United States also designated FIF as an FTO in 2010, and the United Nations followed suit in 2012 by designating FIF pursuant to UN Security Council Resolutions 1267 (1999) and 1989 (2011).[43]

Under the banner of JuD, the organization has been a part of several umbrella organizations with other militant and right of centre political groups. For example, in January 2009, JuD was involved in a group called the *Tehreek-e-Tahafuz Qibla Awal* (Movement for the Safeguarding of the First Centre of Prayer), which held anti-Israel protests in Lahore. (LeT/JuD attendees are easily identified by the organization's distinctive black and white flag.) Similarly, in 2010, JuD had a noticeable presence in the *Tehreek-e-Tahafuz-e-Hurmat-e-Rasool* (Movement to Defend the Honour of the Prophet), which organized protests against the Danish cartoons of the prophet Muhammad. Later in 2012, JuD was prominent in the *Difa-e-Pakistan Council* (Defence of Pakistan Council), which organized large rallies in Lahore, Rawalpindi, Karachi, and elsewhere to protest American policies in Pakistan as well as the US/International Security Assistance Force (ISAF) activities in Afghanistan. In the spring of 2015, JuD also generated popular support for Pakistani military assistance to the Saudi-led alliance in Yemen. To do so, JuD formed the '*Pasban-e-Harmain-Sharifain*' (Defenders of the Sacred Sites in Mecca and Medina) and argued that the Yemeni Houthi rebels aimed to invade Saudi Arabia and assault the *harmain*—the Grand Mosque in Mecca, which surrounds the Ka'ba, and the prophet's mosque in Medina.[44]

While many of Pakistan's myriad militant groups have experienced numerous splits, as of December 2018, JuD has only experienced one such split, which occurred in July 2004, when elements of the group's leadership became dismayed that Hafiz Saeed was appointing his relatives to top positions. This fissure was temporary, and the organization soon merged back with JuD, likely due to the intervention of Pakistan's Inter-Services Intelligence Agency (ISI).[45] For these reasons, I use JuD, LeT, and MDI more or less interchangeably, unless stated otherwise, because doing so is accurate, and because I hope to remind the reader of the fact, irrespective of what the Pakistani government or the organizations say to the contrary.

In early August 2017, JuD formed a political party named the *Milli Muslim League* (the 'National Muslim League', MML) with the objective of reconfiguring Pakistan as a 'real Islamic and welfare state'.[46] While Saeed initially said that this party was separate from JuD, like many of his pronouncements, this too ultimately proved to be fiction. Upon Saeed's release from 'house arrest' in late November 2017, the MML leadership opined: 'Mr Hafiz Saeed will soon start planning out our membership strategy and getting others on board through networking'.[47] Saeed dropped the façade in early December when he announced that JuD is 'planning to contest the 2018 general elections under the banner of *Milli Muslim League*'.[48] The MML, headed by Saifullah Khalid, a close aide of Saeed and a foundational member of JuD, fielded several candidates in the 2018 general election but won no races.

Pakistan has weathered considerable international scrutiny in recent years for its ongoing support of the LeT and other proscribed Islamist militant groups such as the *Jaish-e-Muhammad*, the Haqqani Network, among others led by the Financial Action Task Force (FATF). The FATF is an obscure international watchdog that monitors those countries suspected of taking inadequate action to crack down on terrorist groups operating in their country. Critically for Pakistan, its FATF ranking is tied to the distribution of multilateral assistance, such as funding through the International Monetary Fund (IMF).[49] Should Pakistan receive a 'black listing' by FATF, it would no longer be eligible for IMF lending.[50] Because Pakistan would be financially devastated without such funding, it is unlikely that the FATF will ever give Pakistan the much-deserved black-rating and instead has issued it a 'grey listing'. In fact, this grey listing was perfectly acceptable to Pakistan as it allowed Pakistan to continue supporting its *jihadi* assets while still being able to access important IMF funds.[51]

To this end, Pakistan has continued to engage in its various Kabuki-style theatre antics to appease international observers. Consistent with this long-standing modus operandi, LeT has once again changed names. The organization now operates under the moniker 'The Resistance Group'

28 THE LITERATURE OF *LASHKAR-E-TAYYABA*

or TRF. This change is more curious than the previous name changes: this time the organization has dropped its long-standing logo.[52] In a perverse disregard of facts, in October 2022, Pakistan was removed from the grey list as the country, once again, teetered on the brink of financial collapse with a soaring current account deficit, inflation in excess of 20% and currency depreciation. FATF president T. Raja Kumar explained this decision in Paris: 'After a lot of work by the Pakistani authorities, they have worked through two separate action plans and completed a combined 34 action items to address deficiencies in their anti-money laundering and counter-terrorist financing systems'.[53] With this reputational fillip, foreign investors presumably would be less wary of the country. As of June 2023, these expectations have not materialized.

What Makes LeT Different?

There are numerous militant groups based in Pakistan over which the Pakistani military and intelligence agencies enjoy varying degrees of command and control.[54] While there are different ways of understanding and categorizing these groups, the basic difference among them is their sectarian affiliations, which is determined by the *maslak* (school of Islamic thought derived from the Arabic *salaka*, which means to walk or walk on a path) that an individual or group embraces.[55] In Pakistan, there are five *masalik* (pl. of *maslak*): four of which are Sunni while the fifth is Shīʿa. Shīʿa Islam itself has many fissures in Pakistan which are beyond the purview of this volume. The four Sunni *masalik* in Pakistan are: Barelvi, Deobandi, *Jamaat-e-Islami* (JI), and *Ahl-e-Hadees*. All but the *Ahl-e-Hadees* follow the Hanafi school of Islam, despite their myriad differences. The *Ahl-e-Hadees*, while often confused with Wahhabism which follows the Hanbali school of *fiqh* (jurisprudence), follows no such school and for this reason is often referred to as 'ghair muqallid'.

While many scholars are wont to describe Pakistan-based terrorist groups as 'Salafi' or 'Wahhabi', the vast majority of such groups are Deobandi, including: the Pakistani Taliban, *Lashkar-e-Jhangvi/Sipah-e-Sahaba, Jaish-e-Muhammad*, among numerous others. A smaller number of groups are overseen by *Jamaat-e-Islami* such as *Hizb-ul-Mujahideen, Al Badr*, and *Al Shams*.[56] While Barelvi militancy is often overlooked in

Pakistan, it has been present and often materializes most blatantly and violently over so-called 'blasphemy' issues. This is because Barelvi ascribe to the prophet attributes which other *masalik* believe are reserved only for the prophet.[57]

LeT is the most prominent *Salafi* terrorist organization in Pakistan. And it is distinctive for several reasons that will become clear in this volume. First and foremost, LeT has never attacked any target within Pakistan. It exclusively kills in Kashmir and elsewhere in India as well as Afghanistan since the US invasion of Afghanistan in October 2001. Second, as documents we translate here show, LeT is vigorously anti-communal and anti-sectarian within the confines of Pakistan. LeT is adamant that no one who recognizes the sovereignty of Allah should be murdered no matter how wayward they may be in their practice of Islam. The only way of dealing with such persons is through prayer, teaching, and inviting them to become better Muslims through *jihad*. This creates some problems for the organization regarding the Ahmadis, who are widely reviled as apostates throughout Pakistan and subject to violence. LeT believes that while they should not be treated violently, they should not call themselves Muslims either.[58]

Within Pakistan, LeT also discourages violence against other religious minorities such as Christians and Hindus. The only way to contend with these disbelievers in Pakistan is again through proselytization, generosity, and the provision of social services. The Pakistani state has allowed LeT to establish vast social work networks in communities where religious minorities live in oppressive conditions lacking water, sanitation, health, and school facilities to better enable LeT to do its work converting them. This means that while LeT's cadres murder Hindus, Sikhs, and even other Muslims *outside of Pakistan*, within Pakistan, its behaviour must be peaceful.

LeT is also virulently pro-state. LeT asserts without equivocation that the only permissible solution to shortcomings in government leadership is education (*tarbiyat*) and proselytization (*dawah*) of such wayward leadership. Permissible responses exclude 'rebellion or processions or protests; on the contrary, in administrative matters, they [leaders] ought to be obeyed, while turning to Allah for help'.[59] This philosophy is at the heart of the organization's domestic political utility in Pakistan

30 THE LITERATURE OF *LASHKAR-E-TAYYABA*

and explains in considerable measure why the Pakistani state invests so heavily in its organization and activities at home and abroad.

Another important distinction is that LeT abjures the practice of *takfir* (declaring a Muslim to be non-Muslim [*kafir*]), which is also often associated with lethal violence. Often the debate over *takfir* is seen among Salafi groups, but Deobandi groups in Pakistan also do it. This reticence to declare someone a *kafir* puts LeT at considerable odds not only with some of Pakistan's most important proxies such as the Afghan Taliban but also with some of the most dangerous groups killing Pakistanis such as the *Lashkar-e-Jhangvi*. It also puts LeT at odds with other Salafi militant groups whose origins are beyond Pakistan, such as the Islamic State. This schism over the use of *takfir* is rooted in Islamic scholars' differing views regarding the most apposite course of action towards Muslim leaders who fail to impose *shariat*, and the proper conduct of *takfiri* (the practice of declaring a Muslim to be a *kafir* [non-believer] and thus subject to the death penalty).

One strand of Salafis, known as quietists, impugn those whom they consider to be cavalier in their application of *takfir* to be *Khawarij* or neo-*Khawarij*, referencing the early rebels in Islamic history who believed in violent rebellion against unworthy leaders. In turn, the Salafi jihadists denounce these quietists as *Murji'i* or neo-*Murji'i*, alluding to a defunct group of early Muslims who believed that no matter how horrendous a Muslim leader may be, rebellion is forbidden unless they commit *kufr* (an act of unbelief), and therefore meets their rigorous process of evaluating the facts and concomitant evidentiary standards for being declared a *kafir*. *Khawarij* literally means seceders, derived from the Arabic verb, *kharaja* (to secede or move out), while *Murji'i* literally means one who postpones or defers, derived from *irjah* (to postpone of defer). The implications of this schism are important for understanding the ties that bind the LeT to its state sponsors: Al Qaeda, the Islamic State, and various sectarian groups and parts of the Pakistani Taliban have declared war on the Pakistani state and many of its inhabitants based upon political and sectarian differences; LeT abjures such violence against Pakistanis.

Pakistan's disciplined overseas operations at the behest of the state, along with these important domestic political perquisites, render LeT as one of Pakistan's most important partners in helping the state manage the blowback from its time-worn policy of using Islamist militants as tools of state policy while seeking to prosecute its policies in India and Afghanistan.

3

Islamic Sources Used in This Volume

When we began working with *Lashkar-e-Tayyaba* (LeT) written materials, one of the first things we observed is their internal consistency, sophistication, logic, and repeated appeal to and deployment of a variety of Islamic historical sources, namely, the Quran (scripture), *Hadees* (quotations attributed to Muhammad), and *Seerat* (the biography of Muhammad). The Quran, and the traditional Islamic narratives about Muhammad in the *Seerat* and *Hadees* have had a universal and spiritual hold on Muslims through the ages, evidenced by the extent to which they are invoked for political, social, and religious legitimation, no less in *jihad* narratives. Within these sources, LeT locates the *jihad* imperative, proselytization as a way to organize one's personal life, distinction between asceticism and piety, rejection of the notion that *jihad* is an internal struggle against the ego, and rejection of rebellion and political activism against an Islamic government. Given the cultural valence of these Islamic sources, it is necessary to contextualize them in order to understand the narrative LeT charts for their literary audience.

In this chapter, we discuss each of these three sources within its historical context in order to give the reader a clear idea of its content and weight. To conclude this chapter, we will highlight how each of these sources is used in one of LeT's foundational texts, namely, 'Why Are We Waging *Jihad*?'

Quran: The Word of Allah

Islamic traditions universally believe the Quran to be the literal word of Allah transmitted orally to Muhammad through the archangel Gabriel over a period of twenty-three years that started in Mecca in 609 CE, when Muhammad was forty years old, and ended in Medina close to the time

32 THE LITERATURE OF *LASHKAR-E-TAYYABA*

of his death in 632 CE. While scholars dispute when the Islamic scripture was codified into a closed canon of text, contemporary historians agree, based on linguistic forensics and thematic analysis, that what we refer to as the Quran today came to exist in its current form sometime around the mid-seventh century, a few decades after Muhammad's death.[1]

The Quran, in its traditional form, comprises approximately 6,200 verses divided into 114 chapters that are neither organized thematically nor chronologically, but rather, for the most part, according to their length; within each chapter, clusters of thematically linked verses are stitched together to produce a voice that is allusive, liturgical, meta-textual (explaining, interpreting, and justifying itself), and authoritative. The overarching concern throughout the text is belief in the oneness of god (i.e. *tawheed*) and fear of an impending Day of Judgement, with about one-third of the content directly related to achieving salvation in the hereafter. The one message the Quran hammers in repeatedly is *taqwa*, or piety, defined as mindfulness of god and the last judgement; all other injunctions regarding ritual and law such as prayer, fasting, pilgrimage, inheritance, warfare, marriage, and divorce relate to an inherent sense of righteousness and modesty that stem entirely from this notion of piety. Although piety was practised in a variety of forms in other monotheistic traditions of Late Antiquity (Christian spiritual athletes performed extreme forms of self-abnegation while Jewish piety aimed at the affirmation of life led in obedience to the Torah[2]), the Islamic notion of piety adds the crucial dimension of militant piety, based on the Quranic injunction of 'enjoining what is good and forbidding what is evil' (*al-amr bi-l-ma'ruf wa-l-nahy 'an al-munkar*), variations of which occur at least a dozen times in the book (*Surat al-Imran* 3:104; *Surat al-A'raf* 7:157; *Surat Luqman* 31:17).[3]

While the Quran's primary concerns are monotheism and salvation, as a living document revealed at a specific time in history, over a period of twenty-three years, at various moments it directly responds to events in the life of Muhammad and the early monotheistic community he founded; for instance, the punishment for slander in the Quran derives from a scandal involving one of Muhammad's wives, and the ruling around adoption comes from Muhammad marrying his foster son's ex-wife. It is important to keep in mind that the characters in these specific instances are not mentioned by name; much like the stories about biblical prophets, the context of the revelation in these cases is a result of extensive exegetical inquiry

ISLAMIC SOURCES USED IN THIS VOLUME   33

that has yielded an area of study unto itself, known as *Asbab al-Nuzul* or circumstances of revelation. Recognizing the Quran as a living interactive body of verses revealed over the course of two decades is important to the subject matter at hand since a bulk of LeT's Quranic references are directly linked to the scripture addressing issues of war and peace as they pertain to the existential dilemmas of the early community of believers.

Sunnat: Muhammad's Way of Life

The most strident refrain throughout LeT's literature is the need for Muslims to live their lives 'according to the Quran and *Sunnat*'. In Islamic jurisprudence, the Quran and *Sunnat* make up the two primary sources of Islamic law. It is important to understand what the term *Sunnat* refers to within an Islamic context, and how it relates to *Hadees* (quotations attributed to Muhammad enshrined in six canonical texts) and *Seerat* (Muhammad's biography).[4]

In its most generic sense, the Arabic word *Sunnat* means 'a path, a way, a manner of life'. On the other hand, *Sunnat* in the conventional sense refers specifically to the customs, habits, and actions of Muhammad, including statements he uttered and his explicit and tacit responses to specific situations. The Quran gives no biographical information about the prophet. Traditional Islamic literature about Muhammad proliferated over a century after his death and was derived from oral sources known as *akhbar* (reports). Conspicuously absent from Islam's first century are any records pertaining to the founder of the religion or his earliest companions. As Donner notes: 'As for those sources that are truly contemporary documents—consisting, for the most part, of archaeological and epigraphic information—they have been, and remain, exceedingly scarce, and most important events and figures in the story of Islamic origins (including the prophet Muhammad and the first four caliphs, for example) are completely "un-documented" in the strict sense of the term.'[5] Quotes attributed to Muhammad, as well as biographical information about the events in his life were derived entirely from the plethora of *akhbar*, or reports about Muhammad transmitted orally from one generation to the next in Islam's first century. It is important to note here that while *Sunnat* as a category is repeatedly invoked in LeT texts and Islamic jurisprudence,

34 THE LITERATURE OF *LASHKAR-E-TAYYABA*

there is no distinct body of canonical texts that comprise this category; all *Sunnat* are derived from *Hadees* (i.e. quotes attributed to Muhammad).

Hadees: Muhammad's Words

Hadees refers to quotes attributed to Muhammad, compiled in six canonical texts each of which contains thousands of quotations categorized according to their subject matter and relative authenticity. Every *Hadees* consists of two parts: the *isnad*, or the chain of narrators who transmitted the report; and the *matn*, the main text and content of the report attributed to Muhammad. In LeT's writing, often various *Hadees* are referenced by listing at least one name from the chain of transmitters (e.g. Abu Huraira reported the prophet once said ...) followed by the actual words attributed to Muhammad, concluding with the name of the canonical text(s) that contain(s) said *Hadees*.[6]

The late ninth century, two and a half centuries after Muhammad's death, saw the founding fathers of *Hadees* compilation, namely, Imam Bukhari (d. 870), Muslim bin al-Hajjaj (d. 875), Abu Dawood (d. 888), and al-Tirmidhi (d. 892), organize their *Hadees* collections into categories of relative authenticity, ranging from *sahih* (sound) *Hadees* to *zaeef* (weak) *Hadees*, based on exhaustive methodologies that yielded tens of thousands of quotations. While the Quran is an ostensibly ancient liturgical text codified in the mid-seventh century, *Hadees* literature is the product of an empire; what began as imperial inquiry by an Umayyad caliph eventually grew into a body of literature that dominated Islamic jurisprudence and social life thereafter. When comparing the text of the Quran to *Hadees* literature, what is most striking is the difference in their content and concerns, as well as the degree to which the *Hadees* narratives reflect the salient political rivalries and debates raging in the Muslim community in the first two centuries after Muhammad's death. Subject to forgery on a massive scale in early and medieval Islam, it comes as no surprise that *Hadees* literature abounds with semantic and historical anachronisms absent from the classical text of the Quran.[7]

Despite these obvious discrepancies, *Hadees* literature has a significant place in Muslim societies. As a body of text comprising diverse fragments of information with extended chains of transmitters passed down over

ISLAMIC SOURCES USED IN THIS VOLUME   35

two hundred and fifty years, its content covers a broad range, that is, legal injunctions, rituals, the virtues of individuals or tribes, eschatology, ethical conduct, biographical fragments, Muhammad's expeditions, correct manners, admonitions, and homilies; also, the body of the text is rife with contradictions. Trained religious scholars resolve these contradictions through rigorous modes of assessment, however, in the public consciousness, a *Hadees* has weight by its mere association with Muhammad; when a *Hadees* is quoted, it has already had the impact it seeks, especially with a chain of transmitters and/or a reference to the canonical text in which it is presented, even before the recipient has had a chance to check its authenticity or place in a judicial ruling.

Notably, jurists (*faqih*) in the ninth century did not give much weight to the methodologies employed by the *Hadees* collectors.[8] They viewed these methodologies as inferior to the jurists' far more rigorous system for determining the probabilistic authenticity of particular *Hadees*. This juridical method yielded only a dozen or so very generic reports,[9] compared to the tens of thousands *Hadees* traditions recorded by the compilers. However, despite these methodologies of varying rigor, religious scholars of the time unapologetically employed weak, unfounded, and categorically false reports if they suited a particular agenda.[10] Ibn Hanbal (d. 855), one of the most renowned classical Islamic jurists, is reported by his student al-Khallal to have passed by a mosque where a storyteller was invoking forged reports attributed to Muhammad to curse heretical Muslims. The famed jurist remarked: 'How useful these preachers are to the masses, even if the mass of what they narrate is untrue.'[11] The admission of *zaeef Hadees*, or even false ones, is not uncommon; as is seen in this anecdote—the mere attribution of a statement to Muhammad lends the statement weight, its lack of authenticity notwithstanding.

In addition to semantic and thematic discrepancies between the Quran and *Hadees* traditions, the Quran is devoid of anachronistic references to people, groups, or events dating to periods long after the lifetime of Muhammad, another fact that speaks to the earlier dating of the Quran. The *Hadees* literature, on the other hand, is full of such anachronisms, ranging from references to specific personalities (references that are extremely important to debates on political legitimacy), references to specific tribes whose rivalries exploded in the eighth century, as well as references to Muhammad himself, whose person and prophethood are

36 THE LITERATURE OF *LASHKAR-E-TAYYABA*

very much in the background in the Quran where he is presented as a mortal devoid of the miraculous powers bestowed upon earlier prophets, but who, in the *Hadees* (and *Seerat*) narratives, becomes a veritable miracle-worker healing the sick with his spittle, procuring water from the ground with his heel, and splitting the moon with the stroke of his index finger. The *Hadees*'s image of Muhammad does not align with his appearance in the Quran but rather with that of earlier prophets, whose biblical careers came to be more fully known through intimate post-conquest encounters with Jewish and Christian communities.

Contemporary historians are able to identify a plausible date for particular traditions, and, at times, even the individual most likely responsible for initially placing a *Hadees* into circulation, by correlating chains of transmission as well as by interrogating the content.[12] Consider the supposed utterances of Muhammad where one finds descriptions of how the black banners will come from Khurasan, and that someone named 'al-Saffa' will appear during a period of political schism, and a tyrant from the Umayyad house will ascend Muhammad's pulpit. It is evident that these 'predictions' ascribed to Muhammad reveal the later origin of the sayings, when the Umayyads (661–750), who were identified with white banners, were overthrown by the first Abbasid caliph Abul Abbas (r. 750–754); he flew black standards and his title was al-Saffa.[13] With good cause, modern scholarship on Islamic origins has intensified the Islamic tradition's own internal scepticism of prophetic traditions in its attempts to reconstruct the beginnings of Islam.

Seerat: Muhammad's Biography

In Arabic, the word *Seerat* literally means, 'to travel' or 'to journey', and in context of a particular individual, it refers to their life journey. In conventional parlance, *Seerat* refers to the life of Muhammad, or his biography. As mentioned earlier, the Quran offers scant information about Muhammad's life and person. The bulk of what is believed about him comes from oral reports (*akhbar*) transmitted over the first two centuries after his death that were then organized in *Hadees* compilations and used to derive a biography of the prophet. Some scholars contend that the *Seerat* is a subset of *Hadees* literature, although the most significant

ISLAMIC SOURCES USED IN THIS VOLUME   37

difference between them and is that the *Hadees* generally convey a religious doctrine without much concern for any particular event while the *Seerat* deals with Muhammad's biography and the chronology and significance of important events that transpired over the course of his life. (To reiterate, *Sunnat* refers to Muhammad's customs, habits, and reactions as derived from *Hadees*).[14]

The traditional accounts of Muhammad's life vary in detail, but the basic structure of his biography is relatively consistent, particularly with regard to his military career. According to the traditions, the earliest community of believers formed in Mecca around 610 as a peaceful yet brutally persecuted monotheistic movement launched by a forty-year-old Muhammad. In 622, Muhammad made *hijra* (migration) to Medina where he launched his career as a political leader and a military commander. The rest of his life (622–632) was largely taken up by warfare; he started out by dispatching raiding expeditions against Meccan trade caravans that quickly evolved into a series of full-blown, military confrontations that continued, intermittently, over the next five years; meanwhile, he also orchestrated military campaigns against internal existential threats posed by the various Jewish tribes of Medina. Eight years after the *hijra*, in 630, Mecca capitulated and Muhammad entered his native town in triumph, only to return to Medina from where he continued his military activity, dispatching raiding expeditions northwards against Byzantine frontier fortresses, personally leading one such expedition in 631 at Tabuk. He may have been planning a large-scale campaign against Byzantine Palestine and Syria but, according to the traditions, he died peacefully in Medina, in 632. Contrary to the traditional narrative, some contemporary scholars, as well as the earliest non-Muslim sources to reference Muhammad indirectly (Doctrine Jacobia 634), claim that he led the conquest into Jerusalem in 634 and died far from Medina.[15]

The earliest biography of Muhammad that exists today is a document based on the manuscript written by Ibn Ishaq (d. 767) some one hundred and twenty years after Muhammad's death. This was by no means the first attempt at compiling Muhammad's biography except all earlier manuscripts known to have existed are lost. Interestingly, Ibn Ishaq's manuscript did not survive either; it is known only through later recensions by Ibn Hisham (d. 833) and even later by Tabari (d. 923), both of whom confess to editing and emending Ibn Ishaq's work at will. Evidence shows that

38 THE LITERATURE OF *LASHKAR-E-TAYYABA*

the original title of Ibn Ishaq's work was not *al-Seerat* (*The Biography*) but rather *Kitab al-Maghazi* (*Book of Military Campaigns*). The importance of warfare in early perceptions of Muhammad's life become even clearer in the second best-known work in the genre, which was also called *Kitab al-Maghazi*; this book, devoted entirely to the campaigns and raids supervised by Muhammad, was composed by the famous scholar al-Waqidi (d. 823).[16] These early manuscripts were not biographies as we might understand the genre, but were a recounting of Muhammad's military campaigns; they use the words *Seerat* and *maghazi*, or biography and military career, largely interchangeably.

The foreword to LeT's foundational text on *jihad*, the first text in this compilation, namely, 'Why Are We Waging *Jihad*?', opens with the line: 'countless blessings upon the prophet who, along with demonstrable proofs, was sent with a sword to make Islam dominate all other faiths'.[17] This brazen identification of Muhammad as primarily a sword-brandishing prophet sits perfectly well with the earliest accounts we have about his life, however, it is unusual in a South Asian context where he is more commonly referred to by benevolent epithets, such as *Rehmat-al-il-Alameen* (Mercy upon the Two Worlds) or *Habib Allah* (Allah's Beloved) rather than as a warrior, his military credentials notwithstanding.

It is important to note here that while *Hadees* are usually cited with reference to the chain of transmitters and the canonical text in which it is enshrined, references to events in Muhammad's life are less specific. The broad brushstrokes of Muhammad's life are largely agreed upon universally, such as his life in Mecca, his migration to Medina, his relationship with his clan, his military career, and his relationships with his wives and his children. When referencing any of these aspects of his life, it is not common to cite a particular biographer's *Seerat*. As will be seen in the next section, *Seerat* is usually referenced as a universally accepted narrative that does not demand a specific citation, unlike the Quran and *Hadees*.

An Example: LeT's Use of Quran, *Hadees*, and *Seerat*

'Why Are We Waging *Jihad*?' by Abdussalam Bin Muhammad is an example of how LeT employs the Quran, *Hadees*, and *Seerat*, as is discussed

ISLAMIC SOURCES USED IN THIS VOLUME   39

in Chapter 4. This foundational LeT text lays out the most important organizational imperatives for waging *jihad*, who may wage it and when, and who are legitimate targets of *jihad*. For justification, Bin Muhammad mobilizes all three Islamic sources.

In this text, the author begins by establishing the imperative to fight, tracing it to Muhammad's migration and relying upon curated selections from the Quran:

> As long as the prophet lived in Mecca, he was forbidden from fighting the infidels; when he migrated to Medina and the infidels continued harassing him, Allah gave him permission to wage war.
>
> أُذِنَ لِلَّذِينَ يُقَاتَلُونَ بِأَنَّهُمْ ظُلِمُوا وَإِنَّ اللَّه عَلَى نَصْرِهِمْ لَقَدِيرٌ
>
> Sanction is given unto those who fight because they have been wronged; and Allah is indeed Able to give them victory.
>
> (*Surat al-Hajj* 22:39)
>
> After this, Allah made fighting compulsory for Muslims.
>
> كُتِبَ عَلَيْكُمُ الْقِتَالُ وَهُوَ كُرْهٌ لَكُمْ
>
> Warfare is ordained for you, though it is hateful unto you.
>
> (*Surat al-Baqarah* 2:216)
>
> Thus, fighting infidels was made compulsory to achieve the following objectives ...

While the opening paragraph of the cited above is only a few lines, it touches upon the most significant aspect of the *Seerat*, that is, Muhammad's migration from Mecca to Medina, and his corresponding transformation from a mere apocalyptic prophet to a military commander and statesman. This turning point is repeatedly mentioned throughout LeT texts (note: it is referenced without any citation since it is a universally accepted event) because this is when Allah specifically commanded Muhammad and his followers to take up arms. Interestingly, while the narratives of Muhammad's biography are universally accepted, how these

40 THE LITERATURE OF *LASHKAR-E-TAYYABA*

events are interpreted varies widely. For instance, LeT view god's command to fight as an injunction to wage an eternal battle against infidels, while the contrary opinion views this event in the *Seerat* as evidence that *jihad* can only be waged when an Islamic state has been established.

To counter the latter view, the author of 'Why Are We Waging *Jihad*?' asserts that those who believe *jihad* can only be waged after the establishment of an Islamic state are either disingenuous or engaging in logical fallacy. The author cites numerous Islamic injunctions that were mandated after the prophet migrated to Medina, such as 2.5 per cent charity tax on wealth, the sacrificial obligations of cattle owners, the 10 per cent tax on land revenues, fasting in the month of Ramazan, prohibition on temporary marriages, prohibition on usury, the call to prayer, prohibition on fornication etc.; the author goes on to argue that if *jihad* can only be waged with the establishment of an Islamic state, based on the fact that Muhammad was commanded to fight only after he established a state in Medina, are Muslims relieved of all the aforementioned obligations as well until the creation of said Islamic state? Since such a line of argument would be considered absurd, the author asserts that it is just as absurd to suggest *jihad* cannot be waged without an Islamic state.

The author goes on to cite yet another important event in the *Seerat*, the story of Abu Baseer, which is further disputed in its interpretation. The historical context for the story of Abu Baseer begins with the Treaty of Hudaybiyyah. According to the traditions, some years after Muhammad's migration to Medina, he and his followers decided to make a pilgrimage to Mecca. When they arrived at the sacred city, they were stopped outside by the Meccans who would not let them through. Tensions between the Meccans and Muhammad almost climaxed into conflict before a peace agreement was reached between the two parties. This agreement came to be known as the Treaty of Hudaybiyyah. Some crucial terms of this agreement, and their subsequent breach by the Meccans, ultimately led to Muhammad conquering Mecca. The story of Abu Baseer concerns an ostensibly unfair clause of the treaty, according to which any Meccan who accepted Islam and defected to Medina would have to be returned to Mecca while a Muslim in Medina who travelled to Mecca would never be returned to Medina. This, among many other clauses, was seen as inherently unfair to the believers; nonetheless, the terms were signed, and Muhammad and his men returned to Medina.

In time, a Meccan from the Quraysh tribe, namely, Abu Baseer, accepted Islam and defected to Medina whereupon the Meccans dispatched two men to Medina to retrieve him. As per the terms of the accord, the prophet handed Abu Baseer over to the Meccans. During the journey back to Mecca, the two escorts, along with Abu Baseer stopped at a place called Zulhalifa where Abu Baseer turned on his captors. He managed to kill one of them while the other fled and ran back to Medina with Abu Baseer hot on his heels. When the Meccan reached Medina, he ran straight to Muhammad and told him what had transpired. When Abu Baseer arrived shortly thereafter, Muhammad cried: 'May Abu Baseer's mother be lost on him, for he will surely incite fighting.' Abu Baseer immediately understood that Muhammad would again return him to Mecca, so he fled to the seacoast. Meanwhile, in Mecca, another man known as Abu Jandal also converted to Islam but, instead of trying to flee to Medina, he joined Abu Baseer by the sea. Thereafter, converts to Islam who escaped Mecca continued to join Abu Baseer. Over time, the numbers of assembled defectors formed a sizable group (*asaba*) and began attacking and plundering Meccan caravans en route to Syria. Exasperated, the Meccans appealed to the prophet and asked him to recall Abu Baseer and his men to Medina so that they would cease their attacks upon trade caravans. Subsequently, Muhammad dispatched a message to the converts commanding them to return to Medina. The author narrates this account by referencing *Sahih Bukhari* (one of the *Hadees* compilations) and *Mashkawa Kitab-ul-Sulah*. The author claims that, in this *Hadees*, several things are evident.

First, he asserts that Abu Baseer began his fight against the infidels through his own initiative and, after assembling other converts from Mecca, they commenced guerrilla warfare in accord with god's command as given in *Surat an-Nisa* 4:84:

فَقَاتِلْ فِي سَبِيلِ اللَّه لَا تُكَلَّفُ إِلَّا نَفْسَكَ وَحَرِّضْ الْمُؤْمِنِينَ

So, fight (O Muhammad) in the way of Allah Thou art not taxed (with the responsibility for anyone) except for thyself and urge on the believers.

(*Surat an-Nisa* 4:84)

42 THE LITERATURE OF *LASHKAR-E-TAYYABA*

While his initial operation against the infidels was in self-defence, he later began offensive operations using guerrilla tactics.

Second, the author observes Abu Baseer conducted these operations without the command of a caliph, despite being ordered by Muhammad to return to Mecca after the prophet remanded him to the Meccans. While initially Abu Baseer was his own *emir*, he became the *emir* for the entire group of converts.

Third, Abu Baseer did not demand an Islamic state as a base for his anti-infidel operations. Indeed, the world's first Islamic state rejected him due to its truce with the very infidels he sought to fight. Despite being unable to form an Islamic state on his own, he continued fighting, both to preserve his own life and also to ensure that his camp was a refuge for other converts to Islam escaping Mecca. By attacking these infidels, he aimed to coerce them to amend the terms of their treaty with Muhammad.

Fourth, the author observes that Muhammad did not condemn any of Abu Baseer's operations and even gave him his tacit approval by remaining silent. The author summarizes the account of Abu Baseer as evidence that there are no preconditions for fighting infidels, particularly in matters of self-defence. Moreover, the author claims that those who wait for such conditions jeopardize their freedom, wealth, honour, and may even imperil their lives.

A drastically contrary interpretation of the Abu Baseer story contends that Muhammad did not give his tacit approval to Abu Baseer to wage warfare as a rebel. The fact that Muhammad cursed Abu Baseer when the latter returned to Medina with an infidel's blood on his hands can be read as an explicit renunciation of the convert's tactical escape. What is more, according to tradition, when Muhammad finally recalled Abu Baseer and his men so they would stop attacking Meccan trade caravans, Abu Baseer died the night before he and his men were to return to Medina. Muhammad's reaction to Abu Baseer, and the fact that he died before he could ever set foot in Muhammad's city, suggests that the kind of guerrilla warfare waged by Abu Baseer is categorically unacceptable. In contrast, LeT authors see this exact same event in Muhammad's life as evidence for waging *jihad*, with or without the establishment of an Islamic state.

4

'Why Are We Waging *Jihad*?'

With a Foreword by Abdus Salam bin Muhammad

Here we present a translation of *Lashkar-e-Tayyaba*'s foundational document titled *Hum Jihad Kyon Kar Rahen Hain* ('Why Are We Waging *Jihad?*'), written by Bin Mohammad.[1] We know that this publication has been republished countless times over many years, but we have not been able to discern when it was published for the first time. This document lays out not only the external parameters of the organization's commitment to violence, but also its commitment to domestic tranquillity within Pakistan itself. Bin Muhammad wrote this pamphlet in a Socratic style in which a quester first poses a query, which the narrator proceeds to answer through a combination of a selective recounting of events in the Quran, *Sunnat*, and *Hadees* as well as historical and contemporary events that give salience to the textual references that he mobilized. At first blush, the pamphlet addresses the efforts of so-called pious Muslims who refute the necessity of waging *jihad* under various pretences. However, in advancing these arguments, bin Muhammad makes a very specific case about waging *jihad* outside of Pakistan. In this pamphlet, he identifies specifically who should be the object of *jihad*, and why and—most importantly—who should not be the object of *jihad* and the reasons for their exemptions.

This pamphlet argues that no matter how questionable or even wrong a person's practice of Islam may be, if the individual in question is *kalima-go* (one who has uttered the *kalima* or affirmation that there is no god but Allah and Muhammad are his prophets), he or she should not be killed. The author argues that anyone who has said the *kalima* will never deny the supreme authority of Allah. Therefore, such persons should be rehabilitated through *dawah* rather than be murdered. This puts the organization in direct opposition to the *Deobandi* groups and

44 THE LITERATURE OF *LASHKAR-E-TAYYABA*

Islamic State which practice *takfir*, and which believe that once one is declared a *kafir*, they are worthy objects of violence.[2] (N.B: *Deobandis* are not doctrinally '*takfiri*', although they behave as if they are through their frequent use of declaring persons to be *kuffar* and thus deserving violence or death.)

This raises the interesting question of whether or not Ahmadis are *kalima-go*. Ahmadis continue to endure a campaign of deadly violence against them, mostly perpetrated by Deobandi militant groups as well as individuals motivated by the belief that killing them will confer upon them spiritual rewards to the murder owing to their '*wajib ul qatal*'[3] status.[4] Despite the widespread antagonism against Ahmadis and the prominent campaign of violence against them, we found no mention of Ahmadis in any of the numerous LeT publications reviewed for this effort. Given LeT's political savvy and the evermore salience of this matter in Pakistan's domestic politics, this silence strikes us as strategic rather than accidental. If one considers Ahmadis to be *kalima-go* and accept the supremacy of Allah, this should provide some justification for not murdering Ahmadis and treating them as others who behave deviantly in Pakistan, principally through *dawah* and *tabligh*. The problem with Ahmadis is that while they do say the textual-equivalent *kalima*, many Pakistanis believe that they are committing an act of apostasy with said utterance. In fact, Ahmadis are not permitted to use the terms '*namaz*' to describe their prayer, '*masjid*' to describe their place of worship or even the word 'Quran' to describe their holy book. They do so at the risk of being charged with blasphemy and/or being murdered by vigilantes.[5]

This discontinuity between what Ahmadis say they do and what ordinary Pakistanis believe about their claims opens up an obvious ambiguity about what LeT means when the organization counsels Pakistanis against murdering anyone who claims to be '*kalima-go*'. Unfortunately, the organization publicly obfuscates this matter and refuses to clarify this question even when asked pointedly. (One of the authors specifically asked JuD spokespersons for clarification on this issue dozens of times over at least two years. On each occasion, the organization deflected the question and refused to answer it.) The organization likely prefers this ambiguity because it neither wishes to encourage violence against Ahmadis nor does it wish to incur the wrath of the myriad Pakistanis who believe that Ahmadis are apostates and thus 'wajib ul qatal'. On the one hand, a reasonable Muslim may consider Ahmadis to be *kalima-go* or at least concede that Ahmadis recognize the supremacy of Allah even if they do not share the mainstream view of the ordinal finality of the prophet. On the other hand, such ordinary reasonable Muslims may in fact be offended that Ahmadis could say the *kalima* and engage in other Muslim rituals. It is likely that the organization remains silent on this exigency, preferring this ambiguous situation to prevail, because LeT's leadership likely believe Ahmadis to be *wajib ul qatal*; however, because the *tanzeem* serves at the pleasure of the Pakistani state it must maintain its position of neither committing nor advocating violence against anyone in Pakistan. This is yet another example of how LeT circumscribes its organizational convictions within the hard demands of its sponsors in Pakistan's deep state.

In this (and other translations), we retain the organization and structure of the original. This pamphlet has several sections, many of which can be read on their own without reference to the other sections. It begins with a foreword by the author, Abdus Salam bin Muhammad. Bin Muhammad, at the time of writing, was an employee with LeT's educational branch in Muridke. In it, he explains how this pamphlet came to be. In the first major section of the pamphlet, the author exposits eight objectives that motivate *jihad*. This is followed by assessment of whether or not these objectives have been achieved, which the author concludes in the negative. The next seven sections address in turn whether *jihad* can be waged in the absence of an Islamic state; whether *jihad* is mandated until the day of judgement; argues that the Islamic State and the Caliph are themselves created through *jihad* itself; exposits the nature of the obligation to fight *jihad*; the intentions to fight; the conditions under which the obligation to fight *jihad* evolves; explains why one does not fight *jihad* in Pakistan even though, at first blush, it seems warranted by the force of the logic established elsewhere in this pamphlet. The document concludes with an inventory of the various excuses not to wage *jihad* and a consequent rebuff to each. While each of the major sections of this pamphlet are well argued, there is little overarching

46 THE LITERATURE OF *LASHKAR-E-TAYYABA*

logic to the structure of the pamphlet reflecting its origins as a speech that was subsequently adumbrated in various written fora prior to its current form.

Foreword

Unbounded gratitude to Allah for bestowing us with love for those who wage *jihad* in His path; countless blessings upon the prophet who, along with demonstrable proofs, was sent with a sword to make Islam dominate all other faiths. After the victory against the communists in Afghanistan, the spirit of *jihad* was rekindled in the Muslim world and *jihadi* movements were launched across the globe, raising hopes of humiliating disbelievers and promulgating Islam.

Under these circumstances, fighting disbelief would not have proved difficult at all had it not been for certain Muslim sages who expend the wealth of their knowledge and zeal in trying to delegitimize *jihad* against the infidels of our times by claiming such militancy categorically goes against the Quran and *Sunnat*. They proffer restrictive terms and preconditions for waging *jihad* that simply cannot be met; subsequently, they would rather have us all live as slaves. In truth, infidels have not affected *jihadi* movements as adversely as the 'esteemed' Muslims who breed dissonance and doubt.

In addition to waging militant *jihad*, all brothers associated with *Markaz-ud-Dawah-wal-Irshad* actively work to eliminate such doubts. In my capacity as a worker at *Jamiat-ul-Dawat-al-Islamiya*, the educational branch of the *Markaz*, I am blessed with plenty of opportunities to counter such dilemmas. Thanks to Allah, in response to certain questions, I recently drafted an essay in *Mujallah-ul-Dawah* titled 'Why Are We Waging *Jihad*?' This essay outlines the objectives of *jihad* in detail and responds to its most common objections.

Upon the insistence of some friends, a revised and edited version of this essay is now being republished, independently.

A speech delivered at a *Markaz-e-Tayyaba* conference of scholars in Muridke, titled 'Excuses For Not Waging *Jihad*', has also been added to this publication. This speech originally appeared as an article in *Mujallah-ul-Dawah*.

I am convinced by my faith in Allah's beneficence that whosoever memorizes this essay will gain incredible insights into *jihad* and will be better equipped to enlighten those who are curious about the struggle, while eliminating all doubt from the minds of those who oppose it.

May Allah infuse our actions with propriety, and may He cleanse and accept our efforts.

Abdus Salam bin Muhammad
Worker *Jamiat-ul-Dawat-al-Islamiya*
Markaz-e-Tayyaba. Muridke
Ph: 799448–799497

Why Are We Waging *Jihad*?

Question: Is *jihad farz-i-ayn* (compulsory for every individual) at this time? If so, what proof can you offer, considering no prophet waged militant *jihad* until taking practical steps to establish an Islamic state? Currently, an Islamic state does not exist.

If we assume *jihad* is compulsory, then the barbarism and cruelty in Kashmir and other countries is just as pervasive in our own backyard— why do we not wage *jihad* in Pakistan? Please prove your point with references. Even if we strengthen our Islamic state by waging *jihad* internationally, what good is it if we are hollow from within? Please elaborate.

Basim Sharif Pasruri
Rana Iftikhar Ahmed Pasruri

Answer: As long as the prophet lived in Mecca, he was forbidden from fighting the infidels; when he migrated to Medina and the infidels continued harassing him, Allah gave him permission to wage war.

Sanction is given unto those who fight because they have been wronged; and Allah is indeed Able to give them victory[6]

(*Surat al-Hajj* 22:39)

48 THE LITERATURE OF *LASHKAR-E-TAYYABA*

After this, Allah made fighting compulsory for Muslims.

Warfare is ordained for you, though it is hateful unto you.

(*Surat al-Baqarah* 2:216)

Thus, fighting infidels was made compulsory to achieve the following objectives:

First Objective: Ending Civil Strife Among Muslims (*Fitna*)

Fighting[7] is compulsory as long as disbelievers have the power to inhibit a person from accepting Islam through fear of pain or persecution, or a person who accepts Islam is subjected to cruelty or torture, anywhere in this world. It is mandatory to wage *jihad* until all obstacles to accepting Islam are categorically eliminated. Allah says:

And fight them until persecution is no more, and religion is for Allah. But if they desist, then let there be no hostility except against wrongdoers.

(*Surat al-Baqarah* 2:193)

Second Objective: Dominance of Islam

Fighting disbelievers is mandatory until Islam dominates the entire world and Allah's law reigns supreme everywhere.

And fight them until persecution is no more, and religion is for Allah. But if they desist, then let there be no hostility except against wrongdoers.

(*Surat al-Anfal* 8:39)[8]

The prophet himself said:

I have been commanded to fight them until they bear witness that none other than Allah is worthy of worship and Muhammad is the Messenger of Allah, and (until) they establish prayer and pay *zakat*; when they do this, their property and lives are safe from me while in matters of faith in Islam, their reckoning is with Allah.

(Bukhari and Muslim)

Third Objective: *Jizya* Collection

Fighting infidels is compulsory until every disbeliever (who does not wish to convert to Islam) of the world is subdued and wilfully offers *jizya* (non-Muslim tax) to Muslims.

> Fight against such of those who have been given the Scripture as believe not in Allah nor the Last Day, and forbid not that which Allah hath forbidden by His messenger, and follow not the religion of truth, until they pay the tribute readily, being brought low.
>
> (*Surat at-Tawbah* 9:29)

Fourth Objective: Defending the Defenceless

As long as anyone in the world is being persecuted, it is compulsory to fight until injustice ends.

> How should ye not fight for the cause of Allah and of the feeble among men and of the women and the children who are crying: Our Lord! Bring us forth from out this town of which the people are oppressors! Oh, give us from Thy presence some protecting friend! Oh, give us from Thy presence some defender!
>
> (*Surat an-Nisa* 4:75)

Fifth Objective: Avenging Murder

If an infidel murders a Muslim, avenging the crime is mandatory. If a Muslim murders a fellow Muslim, religious compassion may prevail

50 THE LITERATURE OF *LASHKAR-E-TAYYABA*

and the crime may be pardoned or compensated with blood money. But murder at the hands of an infidel must be avenged, unless the infidel converts to Islam. Allah says:

> O ye who believe! Retaliation is prescribed for you in the matter of the murdered.
>
> (*Surat al-Baqarah* 2:178)

In 6 AH, the prophet travelled to Mecca with the express intention of performing a pilgrimage. The infidels of Mecca confronted him, but he did not engage them militarily. Instead, he sent Hazrat Uthman to Mecca as an envoy. The Meccans refused to send Hazrat Uthman back and it was rumoured he had been killed. When the prophet heard of this he refused not turn back without a fight and he proceeded to take a pledge of allegiance from fourteen hundred of his companions. When the infidels got wind of this pledge, they returned Hazrat Uthman (brief *Seerat* of the prophet and *Seerat* of Ibn Hisham).

It is obvious this pledge was taken with the prospect of retributive justice for Hazrat Uthman. Allah approved of this pledge in the following verse:

> Allah was well pleased with the believers when they swore allegiance unto thee beneath the tree.
>
> (*Surat al-Fath* 48:18)

In 8 AH the prophet dispatched Haris bin Umair Azadi with a letter for the ruler of Basra. On the way, Haris was captured and killed by Sharhabeel bin Amr al-Ghassani, the governor of Balqa, Syria, in the service of Caesar. News of the assassination profoundly upset the prophet; he assembled an army three thousand strong (short of the Battle of Khandaq,[9] an army of this size had never been assembled before) and told Zayd bin Harisa, its appointed *emir*, to march to the place where Haris bin Umair had been killed. First, Zayd was to invite the people into the fold of Islam; should they accept, he was to let them be, but if they rejected the message, with Allah's help, he was to wage war. This event led to the Battle of Mu'tah[10] in which three thousand Muslim soldiers battled two hundred thousand infidels, and lost three *emirs*, until Saifullah Khalid took command and led the Muslim forces to victory (*Ar-Raheeq al-Makhtum*).

Before passing away, the prophet appointed Zayd bin Harisa's son Arjumand Usama the *emir* of a campaign against the people of the same region to further punish them; Hazrat Abu Bakr Siddiq executed the prophet's command.

Sixth Objective: Punishment for Breaking a Treaty

If a nation breaches a treaty made with Muslims, it is compulsory to fight the offending nation.

> And if they break their pledges after their treaty (hath been made with you) and assail your religion, then fight the heads of disbelief Lo! they have no binding oaths in order that they may desist.
>
> (*Surat at-Tawbah* 9:12)

Allah has foretold six auspicious consequences of battling a nation that has breached its treaty with Muslims:

> Fight them! Allah will chastise them at your hands, and He will lay them low and give you victory over them, and He will heal the breasts of folk who are believers. And He will remove the anger of their hearts. Allah repenteth towards whom He will. Allah is Knower, Wise.
>
> (*Surat at-Tawbah* 9:14–15)

In 6 AH, the prophet made a ten-year truce with the Quraysh of Mecca, despite certain blatantly inequitable terms. In 8 AH, when the Quraysh breached this truce by participating in a campaign against Banu Khaza'a, a tribe under the prophet's protection, the prophet attacked and conquered Mecca with ten thousand soldiers.

The prophet signed peace treaties with the Jewish tribes of Medina but when they broke these treaties, the prophet exiled Banu Qaynuqa and Banu Nazir, and slaughtered all the adult males of Banu Qurayza, and took their women and children as concubines and slaves.

Seventh Objective: Fighting in Self-Defence

When a nation attacks Muslims, it is compulsory to fight in self-defence.

Fight in the way of Allah against those who fight against you but begin not hostilities. Lo! Allah loveth not, aggressors.

(*Surat al-Baqarah* 2:190)

When the infidels attacked Medina in the Battle of Khandaq, the prophet commanded every Muslim to participate in the fight; during the Battle of Tabuk[11] when he got wind of the enemy's impending attack, he commanded every able-bodied male to meet the enemy on the battlefields beyond the Arab frontiers even though those were trying times.

Eighth Objective: Freeing Occupied Lands

If infidels occupy a Muslim territory, it is compulsory to expel them by force in order to restore Muslim control. Allah says:

And slay them wherever ye find them, and drive them out of the places whence they drove you out.

(*Surat al-Baqarah* 2:191)

The battle mentioned in *Surat al-Baqarah*, waged against the Bani Israel [reference to Jews] under Talut's [Goliath] command, in order to win back Muslim lands. Allah quotes these brave soldiers:

Why should we not fight in Allah's way when we have been driven from our dwellings with our children?

(*Surat al-Baqarah* 2:246)

Allah aided the Muslims despite their dismal numbers; the Prophet David slaughtered the infidel commander Talut and defeated the infidels. In addition to a breach of a treaty, Mecca was conquered because Muslims had been driven out of the city.

Consider your question: has *jihad* been made compulsory in these times; if so, what is the proof?

Whether *jihad* is *farz-i-ayn* (a duty compulsory for every individual) or *farz-i-kifaya* (a duty a few members of the community can perform on behalf of the entire community) is discussed further on, but first we must determine if *jihad* is even obligatory in these times.

Have We Achieved Our Objectives?

I have stated eight objectives from the Quran that make *jihad* mandatory, as ordained by Allah. One by one, let us consider if any of these objectives has been met.

1. Fighting is mandatory as long as perfidy exists. Is there any region on the planet where those who wish to adopt Islam can do so without any hindrance from disbelievers? Can the untouchables of Hind (India) find refuge in Islamic social justice and convert without fear? They have declared their intention of converting to Islam en masse, on numerous occasions, but every time Hindu thugs terrorize them into changing their decision. Can Muslims living in China, Russia, and other communist countries practise their faith? Can they proselytize where they live? Is a communist living in any of these places allowed to convert to Islam? Do Muslims in various Christian lands face persecution because of their faith? If so, and it is certainly so, then is there any doubt about the *jihad* imperative?

2. Fighting is mandatory until Allah's religion dominates the globe. Is Allah's religion the only dominant system in the world? Is the current world order aligned with Islamic principles or run with godlessness? Do global markets operate within Allah's usury-free economic system; under pressure from infidel regimes, aren't even Muslim countries trapped in this usurious network? Have Allah's proscriptions been established across the globe? Considering Islam does not dominate unbelief anywhere in the world, is there any doubt about the obligation to wage *jihad* for the sake of Islamic domination?

54 THE LITERATURE OF *LASHKAR-E-TAYYABA*

3. Until every infidel government is disbanded and every disbeliever pays *jizya*, fighting is mandatory. Is there any place on earth where infidels live as *dhimmi*s relative to Muslims; is there any place where they declare their inferior status by paying *jizya* to Muslims? You will notice, the current global order is quite the opposite—infidels collect *jizya* from Muslims through organizations like the IMF and World Bank, which suck Muslims nations dry. Is *jihad* not necessary to end this humiliation as well as to humiliate the infidels?

4. Fighting is mandatory as long as the weak are being oppressed and persecuted. Is there any place on earth where Muslims are not subjected to cruelty? Aren't Muslim men, women, and children in Hindustan, Kashmir, the Philippines, Chechnya, various states in Russia and China, and Bosnia pleading for help? Considering this situation, in light of the Quran's categorical explication, what further proof does one need for the *jihad* imperative?

5. *Jihad* is obligatory to avenge the murder of a Muslim at the hands of an infidel. Has no Muslim been killed in Hindustan? How many Muslims have been raped and killed in Kashmir? We are responsible for avenging the murder of 5 million Muslim deaths from 1947. Who will avenge the Muslim women who are currently giving birth to Hindu and Sikh children? How many Muslims have been slaughtered in China, Russia, Albania, and Yugoslavia in the name of revolution? How many were forced to become communists? Only a few months ago, twenty-three thousand Muslims were slaughtered every single day in Bosnia.

6. When a nation violates a treaty with Muslims, fighting that nation becomes mandatory. Is there any nation on earth that has not committed such a violation with Muslims? Has Hindustan honoured the post-partition Liaquat–Nehru Pact by protecting the lives and property of Muslims and safeguarding the sanctity of mosques? Muslims in Hindustan are subjected to a bloodbath under the veneer of sectarian violence. Their factories and shops are burnt with impunity. Pakistani embassies are attacked regularly. In addition to Babri Mosque, countless other mosques have been martyred.

Did Hindustan honour its pledge to let Kashmiri Muslims hold a plebiscite?

'WHY ARE WE WAGING *JIHAD*?' 55

7. When a nation attacks Muslims, fighting in self-defence is obligatory. Currently, seven hundred and fifty thousand Hindus have attacked Kashmiri Muslims with the backing of India's armed forces.

In Burma, Buddhists are attacking and displacing Muslims indiscriminately.

In Bosnia, barbaric Serbs slaughter Muslims with impunity, backed by the Christians and communists of the world. Russians have declared war on Chechen Muslims fighting for their survival.

Israel has plunged the dagger of its existence into the heart of the Arab world.

Filipino Christians have made life unbearable for their Muslim countrymen.

Even animals risk their lives in defence of their young—if a dog or a cat takes off with a helpless chick, the mother hen does not go seeking a *fatwa* (opinion) from a *mufti* (the one who issues *fatwa*s) but charges the attacker without any concern for its own life—we, on the other hand, are still caught up in arguing over the legitimacy of *jihad*.

8. When infidels occupy Muslim lands, fighting is mandated in order to drive out the disbelievers and restore Islam's authority.

   a. Muslims ruled Andalusia (Spain) for eight hundred years after which Christians conquered the region and exiled every single Muslim resident. We are responsible for taking back this land.

   b. All of Hindustan, Northern Kashmir, Hyderabad, Assam, Nepal, Burma, Bihar, and Junagadh were Muslim sultanates that fell to foreigners because we terminated *jihad*.

   c. Jews rule Palestine and *Bayt-ul-Muqaddis* (Sacred House in Jerusalem), the first *qibla* (centre of worship) for Muslims. Many other countries such as Bulgaria, Hungary, Cyprus, Sicily, Africa, Russian Turkistan, and Lower Chinese Turkistan, up to Kashgar, were under Muslim control. It is our duty to wrest these lands from the infidels. Muslims once ruled the landscapes of Switzerland and marched up to within 90 kilometres of Paris; today, all this land belongs to infidels.

56 THE LITERATURE OF *LASHKAR-E-TAYYABA*

One hopes I have sufficiently explained all the factors that mandate *jihad* in our times and that I have cleared all doubts regarding its legitimacy.

Jihad in the Absence of an Islamic State

Now I shall address the second part of your question. You wrote that no prophet waged *jihad* with the sword before establishing an Islamic state and that currently, an Islamic state does not exist.

We do not have sufficient information about the earlier prophets so one cannot make credible assertions about their lives. Regardless, other prophets are not our concern because we belong to the *ummat* of the Prophet Muhammad. For us, his life is a guiding light, and I will use him as my reference.

No doubt, Islam was revealed over a span of twenty-three years. Muslims followed Islamic injunctions as they were revealed. Some of those commandments were revealed in Mecca, others in Medina. After Islam's revelation in its entirety, its commandments have to be obeyed in their entirety till the Day of Judgement. Allah alone can allow for exceptions, such as when He states:

Allah tasketh not a soul beyond its scope.

(*Surat al-Baqarah* 2:286)

Also:
So keep your duty to Allah as best ye can.

(*Surat at-Taghabun* 64:16)

But this exception cannot be used to excuse oneself from fulfilling certain obligations simply because they were mandated after the creation of the Islamic state. According to your reasoning, one could say *azaan* (call to prayer), praying, and congregational prayers were not mandated until the creation of an Islamic state either.

The 2.5 per cent charity tax on wealth, the sacrificial obligations of cattle, and the 10 per cent tax on land revenues were also mandated only after the creation of the Islamic state.

Fasting in the month of Ramazan was mandated eighteen months into the creation of the Islamic state. Alcohol was prohibited in the sixth or eighth year after the establishment of said Islamic state (Reference: Fath ul Bari; *Kitab-ul-Ashraba*).

It was six years after the creation of the Islamic state that the prophet prohibited temporary marriages at Khaybar. The ban on consuming the meat of the domestic mule was made around the same time (*Sahih Bukhari* and *Sahih Muslim*).

The verse prohibiting usury was not revealed until all other commandments had been established in the Islamic state. This was around 10 AH *Sahih Bukhari* quotes Ibn Abbas: 'The last verse to be revealed to the prophet was regarding usury.'

According to what you claim, until the establishment of an Islamic state, we are under no obligation to call out the *azaan*, pray, or congregate for prayer.

Until the establishment of an Islamic state, we need not pay the charity tax.

Until then, we need not fast in Ramazan.

Until the creation of an Islamic state alcohol should be legal and there ought to be no prohibition on drinking.

Until the establishment of said state, we ought to indulge in temporary marriages and consume the meat of domestic mules.

And until then, usury ought to be legal as well.

To take your point to its logical conclusion, alcohol, temporary marriages, and the flesh of mules ought to be legal for six years after the establishment of an Islamic state, and usury ought to be allowed for ten. And prohibitions on extra-marital sex, theft, slander, etc. should also be enforced at corresponding moments of their revelation after the creation of the prophet's Islamic state.

These are the kinds of arguments proffered by those who suggest we do away with the punishment for extra-marital sex until a social reformation, or, who suggest a thief's hand ought not to be amputated in the face of wealth disparity.

No, brother, this reasoning is flawed. Regardless of when a commandment was revealed, whether it was before or after the establishment of an Islamic state, makes no difference; it is mandatory till the Last Day. And obligations must be honoured, the moment one is capable of doing so.

58 THE LITERATURE OF *LASHKAR-E-TAYYABA*

Similarly, regardless of when a prohibition was revealed, before or after the establishment of an Islamic state, it holds till the end of time.

This applies to *jihad* as well. Initially, fighting was prohibited and restraint was urged. In Medina, this prohibition was first lifted, and eventually, it was mandated; and it shall remain obligatory till the Last Day.

Those who want to escape this obligation make all sorts of excuses. They say *jihad* with the sword is not permitted until the creation of an Islamic state.

Or, *jihad* is not permitted in the absence of a caliph.

Or, *jihad* is not permitted if we are weak in numbers.

But none of these excuses are valid.

Jihad is Mandated till the Day of Judgement

Jabir bin Samurah reports that the prophet said, 'This religion will exist forever; one *asaba* (group) of Muslims will continue fighting for it until the Last Day.'

The Arabic dictionary's *Kitab-al-Qamus* states: '*Asba* refers to a group of men, horses, or birds ten to forty members strong. *Asaba* has the same meaning.'

Whether an Islamic state exists or not, *jihad* will continue, come what may!

This obligation will be honoured, whether by a standing army or a small group of ten to twenty men. If an Islamic state or a caliphate is a prerequisite for *jihad*, and currently, according to you, there is neither caliphate nor state, then, by your reasoning, one must conclude *jihad* cannot be waged. Should one, then, consider the prophet's prediction false or what?

One need not go so far as to invoke an Islamic state; one can even fight as a lone warrior. Allah says:

So fight (O Muhammad) in the way of Allah Thou art not taxed (with the responsibility for anyone) except for thyself and urge on the believers.

(Surat an-Nisa 4:84)

In 6 AH, the prophet signed a ten-year peace treaty with the Meccans. According to one of the terms of this treaty, if a Meccan converted to Islam and defected to Medina, he had to be returned to Mecca. Once all the terms of the treaty were forged, and the two sides returned to their respective cities, a Meccan by the name of Abu Baseer, of the Quraysh tribe, converted to Islam and managed to escape to Medina. The Meccans sent two men to Medina to bring him back. As per the agreement, the prophet handed him over. On their way back, as the party of three stopped to rest at a place called Zul Halifa, Abu Baseer tricked one of his escorts into handing over his sword and proceeded to kill his gullible captor. The second Meccan panicked and ran all the way back to Medina, where he went straight to the prophet and told him what had transpired. Meanwhile, hot on the Meccan's heels, Abu Baseer arrived in Medina as well. Upon seeing him, the prophet said, 'May Abu Baseer's mother be lost on him; he's a rabble-rouser.' Abu Baseer instantly understood the prophet was going to return him to Mecca, so he immediately took off for the seacoast. Meanwhile, in Mecca, a person by the name of Abu Jandal converted to Islam and joined Abu Baseer. Thereafter, every convert from the Quraysh who skipped Mecca went straight to Abu Baseer. Gradually, these defectors grew into a sizable group (*asaba*). I swear upon Allah, they attacked and plundered every caravan of the Quraysh heading to Syria. Finally, the Quraysh pleaded with the prophet, invoking their kinship with him, to recall Abu Baseer and his men to Medina (so they would stop attacking Quraysh's caravans).

Subsequently, the prophet sent word to the converts to return to Medina (*Sahih Bukhari* with reference to Mashkawa, *Kitab-us-Sulah*).

This *Hadees* makes evident that:

1. Abu Baseer started fighting the infidels independently, without waiting for assistance. When he was joined by other men, they started guerrilla warfare and this was in accord with Allah's command:

   Abu Baseer's initial operation against the infidels was in self-defence but later he acted aggressively and conducted guerrilla warfare.

60 THE LITERATURE OF *LASHKAR-E-TAYYABA*

2. Abu Baseer did not execute his operations under the command of a caliph. The prophet was determined to have him returned to Mecca; in fact, he literally handed Abu Baseer over. In the initial operation (when he slaughtered his captor), Abu Baseer was his own *emir*; in later operations, he became the *emir* for his entire group of fellow converts.
3. He did not seek an Islamic state as a base for his operations. The first Islamic state in the world had to reject him due its treaty with the infidels and Abu Baseer was unable to form an Islamic state of his own. As he continued fighting alone, he not only saved his own life but also became a point of refuge for other Muslims fleeing the Quraysh. He proceeded to attack and humiliate the infidels to the point of forcing them to erase their unjust clause from their treaty with the prophet.
4. The prophet did not condemn any of Abu Baseer's operations; in fact the prophet gave his tacit approval through his silence on the matter. It is unfortunate that recently an elderly philosopher tried to devalue Abu Baseer's noble mission by branding him a rabble-rousing vandal.

To sum up, Abu Baseer is proof that there are no preconditions for fighting infidels, especially in matters of self-defence. Numbers do not matter; neither does the establishment of an Islamic state nor the presence of a caliph. In the absence of an *emir*, every person is his own *emir* and those who wait for certain conditions to be met end up losing their freedom, wealth, life, and face.

The Islamic State and Caliph are Created Through *Jihad*

In Muharram 656 AH, Tartars razed Baghdad to the ground and assassinated Caliph Musta'sim Billah. For the next three and a half years, until Rajab 659 AH, Muslims were without a caliph. Had Muslims terminated *jihad* at this time, Islam would have been wiped off the map but small, seemingly insignificant, rebel militias continued to wage a militant struggle, in whatever form possible, until they gradually defeated the Tartars and restored the caliphate. Sheikh Ibn Taymiyyah says the rebels who defeated the Tartars were the fulfilment of the prophet's prophecy in which he predicted that his *ummat* would always include a group of Muslims who will uphold the truth and will remain unharmed and undefeated until the Last Day (*Compilation of Sheikh al-Islam Ibn Taymiyyah*, 414 and 531).

The truth of the matter is that in the absence of a caliph and, heaven forbid, with the abolishment of every single Islamic state, instead of terminating *jihad*, it is crucial to understand that *jihad* is the very blessing that gives hope of restoring the caliphate and re-establishing an Islamic state.

Currently, Is *jihad Farz-i-Ayn* or *Farz-i-Kifayah*?

At the start of this essay, I stated eight objectives from the Quran that mandate *jihad*. You asked me to prove that *jihad* is *farz-i-ayn* (obligatory for every single individual).

First, it is important to understand what *farz-i-ayn* and *farz-i-kifayah* mean. Ibn Qadamah states:

> *Farz-i-ayn* are obligations that are mandatory for every single Muslim, for example, prayer, fasting.
>
> *Farz-i-kifayah* are obligations a certain number of Muslims can perform on behalf of the entire community, but if the requisite number of Muslims does not perform these obligations, then the entire community is considered to have sinned. Initially, all Muslims are commanded to perform these obligations, like *farz-i-ayn*, but the difference between the two is that a certain number of Muslims can perform the *farz-i-kifayah*, subsequently freeing the rest of the community of their obligation. On the other hand, each and every individual is responsible for *farz-i-ayn*.
>
> (*Wa-al Sharah-al-Kabir*, Ibn Qadamah, *Kitab-al-jihad*)

Religious scholars cite the funeral prayer and funerary rites as examples of *farz-i-kifayah*; every Muslim is obligated to perform these for the deceased but if a few Muslims take care of the task, the rest of the

62 THE LITERATURE OF *LASHKAR-E-TAYYABA*

community is relieved of its duty. However, if no one performs these last rites, then the entire community is responsible.

It is abundantly obvious that *jihad* is mandatory for Muslims; I proved this point with references to the Quran, which state eight objectives that must be achieved through *jihad*.

The question, however, remains whether *jihad* is *farz-i-ayn*, which, like prayer and fasting, must be performed by every single individual, or if it is *farz-i-kifayah*, which, when performed by a certain number of individuals relieves the rest of the community of its obligation.

Some scholars consider *jihad farz-i-ayn*; they put forth the very Quranic verses quoted in this essay as proof. The Quranic interpretation offered by Qurtabi states:

> Burdi claims that Saeed bin Musaib said, '*jihad* is eternally *farz-i-ayn* for every individual Muslim'.
> (*al-Jama-al-Ahkam-al-Quran-al-Qurtabi* 38:3 and 201:2)

On the other hand, many scholars claim *jihad* is *farz-i-kifayah*, that is, if some Muslims are engaged in it others are relieved of their obligation. There is sound evidence for this perspective.

1. Allah states:
And the believers should not all go out to fight. Of every troop of them, a party only should go forth, that they (who are left behind) may gain sound knowledge in religion, and that they may warn their folk when they return to them, so that they may beware.
(*Surat at-Tawbah* 9:29–122)

This makes it clear that not every Muslim is obligated to march into the battlefield; even if one contingent goes into battle, the rest of the community is relieved from this obligation.

2. Allah states:
Those of the believers who sit still, other than those who have a (disabling) hurt, are not on an equality with those who strive in the way of Allah with their wealth and lives. Allah hath conferred on those who

strive with their wealth and lives a rank above the sedentary. Unto each Allah hath promised good, but He hath bestowed on those who strive a great reward above the sedentary.

(Surat an-Nisa 4:95)

This verse clearly states that the ones who stayed back in their homes were also blessed but the ones who marched into the battlefield had a higher status than the former. If *jihad* was *farz-i-ayn*, how could the ones who stayed back, be blessed?

3. Abu Huraira claims that the prophet said: 'He who believes in Allah and His prophet, and prays, and fasts in Ramazan, has the right to be let into paradise, whether he wages *jihad* in Allah's cause or remains in the land where he was born.' People wondered if they ought to spread word of these glad tidings to the rest. 'Absolutely,' said the prophet, 'paradise has one hundred levels which have been prepared by Allah for *mujahideen*. The distance between two levels is equivalent to the distance between the earth and the sky. So when you beg Allah, beg for *firdous*, for that is the highest and most blessed level; right above it lies the realm of god and it is the fountainhead of the rivers of paradise.'

This *Hadees* makes it clear that if a Muslim does not wage *jihad* and decides to stay back at home fulfilling all their other obligations, he can still enter paradise. If *jihad* was *farz-i-ayn*, how could the prophet's glad tidings be true?

It appears both perspectives are accurate in their own right, without being mutually exclusive for their essence is the same.

Battling the infidel is an expansive operation that requires the participation of all sectors of society. Although the most eminent actors are the *mujahideen* who face the enemy in the battlefield, to think they are the only ones fighting the enemy is a misconception. In fact, those who prepare and deliver ammunition to the front lines, those who deliver food and various other supplies, and those who protect the homes of the ones on the battlefield are very much involved in the struggle. Similarly, intending to fight the enemy, being ready to be called upon for this task,

64   THE LITERATURE OF *LASHKAR-E-TAYYABA*

inspiring others to participate in *jihad*, and receiving and passing on weapons training are foundational aspects of *jihad*. In this context, consider a few *Hadees*:

1. Zayd bin Khalid reports that the prophet said, 'whoever prepares a warrior on his way to fight in Allah's cause is part of the fight, and whoever takes care of the warrior's family is part of the fight'.
2. Abu Saeed reports that the prophet dispatched an army to Bani al-Haiyyan and said for every two men, one should stay back, but both shall reap the reward.
3. Ans reports that the prophet said: 'Fight the polytheists with your wealth, your lives, and your tongues.'
4. Sahal Bin Hanif reports that the prophet said, 'he who sincerely begs Allah for martyrdom will be ranked among the martyrs even if he dies in his bed'.
5. Ibn Abbas reports that the day Mecca was conquered, the prophet said, 'after the conquest of Mecca there is no *hijrat* (sacred migration) but there is *jihad* and its intention, so when you are called (to action), respond' (*Sahih Bukhari* and *Sahih Muslim*).

These *Hadees* prove that the one who prepares the recruit going into battle in Allah's cause is also participating in battle, and the one who cares for the families of those in the battlefield is also part of the fight, and between two brothers, the one who stays back to manage the business of the one going off to war is also waging *jihad*.

One can fight polytheists with one's wealth, life, and tongue. One can join the fight and die a martyr simply by intending to do so, sincerely.

In short, *jihad* is *farz-i-ayn* when the *emir* commands everyone to fight, in which case only those who are ordered to stay back are excused from battle but even they are considered part of the war; when commanded, every able-bodied person must join the fight, as was the case in the Battle of Tabuk when everyone was commanded to join the battle and only a few men were left behind to manage the city (of Medina). Allah rebuked the ones who stayed back out of sheer laziness. On the other hand, if the *emir* does not order everyone to fight, then *jihad* is *farz-i-kifayah*, simply because it is impossible for every individual to join the fight; also, it is unwise for all members of society to abandon their cities and homes for the battlefield. As long as there is a sizeable force confronting the enemy, more need not join the war; however, if someone decides to fight despite all this, he will have a right to the one hundred levels of paradise that Allah has promised those who wage *jihad*.

This is what لَا يَسْتَوِي الْقَاعِدُونَ (those of the believers who sit still... 4:95) and مَا كَانَ الْمُؤْمِنُونَ لِيَنفِرُواْ كَآفَّةً (and the believers should not all go out to fight... 9:122) refer to, as does the *Hadees* about staying in the place one was born.

But if *jihad* refers to the intention of fighting, preparing to fight, weapons training and stockpiling, preparing *mujahideen* for battle, caring for and protecting the households of those in the battlefield, in short being involved in the war in some way or the other, then this *jihad* is *farz-i-ayn* and no one can escape this obligation.

So is the case with *amr bil-maruf wa nahi an-al-munkar* (enjoining good and forbidding evil). Abu Saeed Khadri reports that the prophet said:

> Prevent evil by force when you witness it, but if you do not have the strength to stop it then speak up against it, and if you cannot speak then know it is wrong in your heart, for this is the least manifestation of faith.

Scholars have declared forbidding evil *farz-i-kifayah*; if a certain number of people do so, the entire community is relieved of this duty, but everyone is obligated to discourage one another from wrongdoing and at the very least, must intend to forbid evil in his or her heart, for without this intention nothing will remain of faith. Similarly, *jihad* is mandatory for all Muslims in some form or the other and he who has no intention of fighting infidels is a hypocrite.

> Abu Imama reports the prophet said: 'He who has not participated in a war, or prepared someone ready to participate in a war, or cared for the household of someone participating in a war, Allah will ensure that person suffers greatly, before the Last Day.'
>
> (Abu Dawood)

Abu Hurairah reports that the prophet said, 'He who dies without having fought in battle and without ever intending to fight in battle has died on the lip of hypocrisy' (*Sahih Muslim*).

66 THE LITERATURE OF *LASHKAR-E-TAYYABA*

Manifest Intention to Fight

The above *Hadees* prove that every Muslim is obligated to fight infidels in some form or another, and if nothing else, every Muslim must at least intend to wage *jihad*. Allah himself has stressed the importance of making manifest such intent. In *Surat at-Tawbah*, Allah says of the hypocrites:

> And if they had wished to go forth, they would assuredly have made ready some equipment.
>
> (*Surat at-Tawbah* 9:46)

Thus, it is apparent that he who refuses to fight infidels, acquire any military training, learn how to use weapons, own weapons, learn how to ride a horse, or try to deliver military supplies, is disobeying Allah and is patently a hypocrite.

When *Farz-i-Kifayah* becomes *Farz-i-Ayn*

Certain people excuse themselves and others from *jihad* by arguing it is *farz-i-kifayah*, not *farz-i-ayn*, hence it is not a universal obligation. This is precisely why the Muslim *ummat* has stopped waging *jihad* all over the world, despite being globally humiliated by infidels. Until the requisite number of individuals perform *farz-i-kifayah*, this duty falls upon every able-bodied person.

For instance, every doctor in a city is obligated to heal the sick and wounded but if a few doctors are able to take care of those in need, then the rest of the doctors are relieved of this duty; if no one tends to the sick then all doctors are held responsible.

Everyone who knows how to swim is obligated to save a person who is drowning. Only one person is needed to complete the task, so whoever goes ahead and saves a drowning man has fulfilled everyone's obligation to act. But no one can excuse himself from diving in to help on the pretext that the action was *farz-i-kifayah* and not *farz-i-ayn*. Neither can one excuse oneself because his father forbade him from saving a life.

Imam Shokafi states: The Quran and *Sunnat* contain so many proofs about *jihad* being mandatory they cannot all be listed here; however, *jihad* is only obligatory as *ala-al-kifayah*. When some people fulfil this obligation, others are relieved of their responsibility, but if enough people aren't fulfilling this obligation, it is *farz-i-ayn*.

Reread the eight objectives and their Quranic references at the start of this essay. Are enough Muslims fighting for these objectives? Have all Muslims been relieved of their obligation to wage *jihad*?

Is there a *jihadi* outfit that can end all treachery and perfidy in this world singlehandedly?

Is there a *jihadi* outfit that can establish an Islamic world order all by itself?

Is there a single group that is able to collect *jizya* by force from all the infidels in the world?

Are there enough *mujahideen* in the world who can protect the weak and vulnerable singlehandedly?

Is there a *jihadi* outfit that can avenge the deaths of all the millions of innocent Muslims who have been killed in various countries over the past few centuries?

Is there a single Muslim group that can confront the infidels of the world about all the pacts and treaties that they have broken with Muslims?

Are sufficient numbers of *mujahideen* busy reconquering all the Muslim lands stolen by infidels? Are there enough *mujahideen* engaged in a war to win back Andalusia, Hindustan, Russia, Chinese Turkestan, *Bayt-ul-Muqaddis* (Dome of the Rock) etc.?

Infidels are attacking Muslims in various regions across the globe; are there sufficient people defending these Muslims?

If not, and certainly there are not, is there any doubt about the accountability of every single able-bodied Muslim who is not actively engaged in *jihad*? We must all take stock of our apathy, and we need to stop using the debate over *farz-i-kifayah* and *farz-i-ayn* as an excuse to shy away from our obligations.

68 THE LITERATURE OF *LASHKAR-E-TAYYABA*

Why Don't We Wage *jihad* in Pakistan?

In context of *jihad*, you state that the kind of barbarism and cruelty rampant in Kashmir occurs in Pakistan and various other countries; you ask why we do not wage *jihad* in Pakistan.

It is unfortunate that you do not see the difference between the cruelty in Hindustan and the injustices in Pakistan.

Pakistan was founded on the principle of *La ilaha il la-Allah* (there is no god but Allah), while Hindustan's flag bears the *veer* wheel which is a Hindu symbol.

We can appeal to Pakistan's leaders to make good on their promises to apply Islam because they do not deny its supremacy even though they sometimes act like hypocrites, but leaders in Hind are self-declared infidels. Do you not know the difference between a Muslim hypocrite and an infidel? During the prophet's time, even when the hypocrites were increasingly disobedient and the prophet's companions sought permission to kill them, the prophet said let them be or else people will say Muhammad kills his own men. Do you want us to fight our Muslim brothers instead of infidels?

If there are instances of unrest in Pakistan, they are the result of various Muslim groups contending for power. This is not a fight between idolatry and Islam, and besides, these scuffles are fomented by Hindustan. In Hindustan, Muslims are killed for being Muslims. They are robbed and raped. Do you not see any difference between oppressing someone for the crime of being Muslim, and oppression in general?

Do you not know Bal Thackeray has publicly declared that Muslims in Hindustan have three options: 1. leave the subcontinent; 2. convert to Hinduism; and 3. die. Are Muslims in Pakistan in a similar predicament? In Hindustan, the Babri Mosque, an architectural symbol of Islam, was razed to the ground by a mob; many other mosques have been similarly destroyed. Are mosques in Pakistan also destroyed to make room for Hindu temples? Muslims do not dare slaughter a cow in Hindustan because Hindus worship cows. Do Muslims in Pakistan face the same dilemma?

In Hindustan the Muslim prayer-call causes Hindus and Sikhs to riot. Making these calls on a loudspeaker is prohibited. Do we have similar prohibitions in Pakistan?

In Hindustan and Kashmir, Muslims are under attack from the Hindu Army. Six hundred and fifty thousand soldiers are stationed in Kashmir. Are there any Hindu soldiers or foreign soldiers stationed in Pakistan to punish us for being Muslim? Do you not understand the obvious: in order to free the Muslims caught in the grip of infidels, it is imperative for Muslims to unite regardless of their differences. When infidels come to rape and plunder, they are not concerned with the school of Islamic jurisprudence you adhere to or your political affiliation—they won't let you be until you convert to Hinduism. Allah says:

> And the Jews will not be pleased with thee, nor will the Christians, till thou follow their creed.
>
> (*Surat al-Baqarah* 2:120)

Do you not know the only way to end infighting and oppression in Pakistan is to begin fighting infidels? If we do not fight infidels, we will never stop fighting among ourselves, neither will we stop oppressing one another.

One hopes you see the difference between waging *jihad* against fellow Muslims in Pakistan (where we live, by Allah's grace, in peace) and waging *jihad* against Hindus in Hindustan (where Muslims are slaughtered for being Muslims, where we have yet to settle the scores of 1947 and 1971).

I am deeply saddened when a Muslim brother declares Pakistan and Hindustan equally legitimate for *jihad*. These are precisely the kinds of things Hindus want Muslims to think and say. May Allah grant all brothers wisdom.

And now, regarding your last statement: 'even if we strengthen the state of Islam by waging *jihad* in foreign lands, what good is it if we are hollow from within? Please elaborate.'

Brother, it is through *jihad* with the enemy that we can strengthen ourselves from within. Those with a sense of Islamic honour are the ones who wage *jihad*. See for yourself; when Muslim rulers are devoid of dignity, they cannot stand up to infidels. The true Muslim man will always fight infidels because they are infidels, and it is through such a man that Allah will grant the country stability and inner strength. Therefore, make every attempt to continue *jihad* against infidels and inspire others to fulfil this sacred obligation.

70 THE LITERATURE OF *LASHKAR-E-TAYYABA*
Excuses for Not Waging *Jihad*

When a person is reluctant to act, instead of admitting his failure, he deceives himself in order to guard his ego. Those who object to *jihad* in Kashmir or to *jihad* anywhere around the world are being disingenuous. They claim to be in favour of *jihad* but when asked why they do not participate in the struggle, they come up with a million excuses while expressing their superficial support for militancy.

The Quran speaks of such suspect individuals in the following words:

> And if they had wished to go forth, they would assuredly have made ready some equipment, but Allah was averse to their being sent forth and held them back and (it was said unto them): Sit ye with the sedentary!
>
> (*Surat at-Tawbah* 9:46)

Tell me, do these esteemed people know how to disassemble a Kalashnikov? Can they hit their target with a weapon? It is obvious they are all talk; they are insincere. Allah is true and everyone else is false. As Allah says, if they intended to fight, they would be in a training camp; they may have an excuse for not going into the battlefield but if they are not even training for battle then it is obvious they have no intention of joining the fight. They are all liars.

No *Jihad* in the Absence of a Caliph

First Excuse

It is said that *jihad* cannot be waged without an *emir*. If there is no caliph how can there be *jihad*?

In response, keep one thing in mind: in *Sahih Muslim*, Jabir bin Samrah reports in Mashkawa's book *Al-Jihad*, that the prophet said:

> This faith will last forever ...
> ... one group of Muslims will continue fighting for it ...
> The word he used was not *jihad* it was *yaqatul*, which literally means, 'fight'.
> '... until the Last Day is established'.

Allah's prophet said fighting will continue till the Last Day, and it is because of the aforementioned group's militancy that Islam will last forever. The caliphate was abolished in 1924. According to the logic of the naysayers, we ought to make peace with our status as bootlickers to the infidels and continue living our lives under the protection of their governments. You have your excuse conveniently etched out for you: without a caliph there can be no *jihad*... so sit pretty, complacent in the knowledge that Allah has not mandated war.

Brothers, this is wrong! In fact, in these times, it is essential to fight for the sake of re-establishing the caliphate. Islam demands this from us. The prophet predicted one group would always fight for truth. Those who oppose them and abandon them will not matter.

Jihad with the Assistance of Polytheists: Second Excuse

Some people cite the following incident from the prophet's life as proof that help from polytheists cannot be employed. During the Battle of Badr,[12] a person offered assistance to the prophet. When he was asked about his faith, he denied being a Muslim to which the prophet said: 'Return. You are a polytheist, and I will not be aided by your ilk.'

Brothers, a closer look at the prophet's life reveals that a polytheist's help must be denied when such a person cannot fully be trusted, or if this person is not an ally, or if there is no need of assistance. But if the polytheist is an ally, and both of you have a common goal, then it is perfectly reasonable to accept his assistance. The prophet's entire life is testament that Allah consistently sent him help through polytheists.

1. Consider Abu Talib. He was a polytheist who said to the prophet: 'I swear, until they bury me in the earth, I will not let anyone harm you.' Did Allah's Messenger say: 'Uncle, you are a polytheist so back off; I do not want your protection'?
2. When the prophet was boycotted by the infidels and exiled to the Valley of Abu Talib, Muslims as well as the polytheists of the tribes of Banu Hashim and Banu Mutalib joined him. Did the prophet say to the polytheists: 'Go brother, I do not need your help... leave this place for I will not accept the support of a polytheist'? He did not.
3. Disappointed by the response he received from Mecca, the prophet sought support from the people of Taif, who were also polytheists.

72 THE LITERATURE OF *LASHKAR-E-TAYYABA*

4. On his way back from Taif, the prophet's life was under threat by the residents of Mecca. The prophet's companion Zayd asked him how they were going to make it back into the city. The prophet told him Allah would find a way. The prophet sent Muta'am, a polytheist, a plea for help and protection in order to re-enter the city. Muta'am had many sons with whom he escorted the prophet into Mecca, publicly announcing that the prophet had his protection. Abu Sufyan asked Muta'am if he had converted to Islam to which Muta'am said: 'No, I have not converted, but I give him (the prophet) my protection.' Abu Sufyan replied: 'Very well then, we respect your protection. No one will hurt him.'

5. When the prophet was migrating from Mecca to Medina he hired a guide who, according to *Sahih Bukhari*, was a polytheist. Had there been a confrontation with the enemy on the way, this polytheist would have sided with the prophet; do you think the prophet would have said, 'you should leave; I do not want your help because you are a polytheist'?

The Prophet Sought Help from Polytheists after the Battle of Badr: Third Excuse

Some insist that all the events listed above occurred before the Battle of Badr. However, according to the Treaty of Hudaybiyyah, the Muslims and the Quraysh of Mecca were free to give their protection at will. Subsequently, Bani Khaza'a allied with the prophet, while Banu Bakr allied with the infidel Quraysh. The Quraysh stressed its alliance with Banu Bakr when the latter attacked Banu Khaza'a. A *Hadees* reported by Ahmed states the prophet retaliated and Banu Khaza'a, whose members were mostly polytheists with the exception of a few converts to Islam, joined him in the fight. The very fact that they were allies proves they had not converted as a tribe; and as polytheists, they fought alongside the prophet.

In *Masnad Ahmed* (Vol.1:179), Abdullah bin Emir reports that when the prophet conquered Mecca, he prohibited the use of weapons but made an exception for Banu Khaza'a whose men were allowed to slaughter any man from Banu Bakr because the latter had acted treacherously. By the time of 'Asr, the prophet is reported to have said: 'Enough, Banu Khaza'a have had their revenge, now no one is allowed to use their weapon.'

Notice this event took place after the Battle of Badr. This proves that even after the Battle of Badr, the prophet made alliances with polytheists.

Why Not Wage *Jihad* in Pakistan Instead of Kashmir? Fourth Excuse
Some say, why fight in Kashmir when there are battles to be fought within Pakistan. Why take help from the Pakistani government, which is an un-Islamic establishment that perpetrates idolatry within the country? Is *jihad* in Kashmir more important than combatting the growing polytheism within our borders? This is the gist of many objections. Let us consider these questions thoroughly.

Brothers, infidels come in all forms. There are infidels who have not uttered the *kalima* (declaration of the oneness of god and acceptance of the prophet as his messenger) and there are those who have made this declaration of faith. Those who have not declared the *kalima* antagonize us primarily because we are Muslims. This is the basis of their animosity. However, infidels who have recited the *kalima* will never fight us because of our faith; they have simply gone astray and we will try to guide them back into the light; we will never fight them until they attack us. We will consider them misguided and misinformed; we will point out to them their pagan ways but we will not war with them because, if we wage war against those who declare their Islamic faith, we cannot conscientiously war against those who reject Islam.

According to a tradition reported in *Sahih Bukhari*, the prophet was once distributing wealth when a man (who had declared his Islamic faith) said (various traditions report numerous inappropriate terms uttered by this fellow but, in short, he said): 'Oh Muhammad, by Allah you have not been just.' The prophet's companions sought permission to behead him there and then but the prophet said, 'Let him be, otherwise it will be said that Muhammad kills his own men, and if we start killing our own men how will we kill our enemies?'

Many people are uncomfortable with this reasoning and accuse us of accepting everyone as Muslim regardless of whether they worship graves or ridicule the companions (of the prophet); we are accused of accepting all sorts of un-Islamic attitudes. We do not accept any of

74 THE LITERATURE OF *LASHKAR-E-TAYYABA*

these attitudes, but we believe it is wrong to make enemies of those who bear allegiance to the prophet. We have no doubt that those who pray to anyone other than Allah are acting like polytheists, but they say the *kalima*, and they would never reject the Quran; even though some of their clerics may say as much, they never make such declarations publicly. The *Khawarij* declared Hazrat Ali and Hazrat Uthman infidels even though the prophet had himself said Hazrat Ali would enter paradise. Now, anyone who contradicts the prophet's words is an infidel, so the *Khawarij* were infidels who called themselves Muslim. This is why Hazrat Ali said to the *Khawarij*, 'you will receive your pensions, you will receive your share of loot, and you are free to enter our mosques, but if you cause mischief, we will not spare you'. Then, when they killed Hazrat Khabbab and his bondwoman, Hazrat Ali commanded them to hand over Hazrat Khabbab's murderer. They said they were all his murderers, so Hazrat Ali proceeded to slaughter them all, and only ten of them survived.

Considering we would go as far as honouring a truce with infidels, how could we possibly fight our brothers in faith with whom we have no conflict? But those of you who feel it imperative to fight them, by all means, why don't you take up arms? We are already engaged on one front. Why don't you take up this one? We consider it categorically unethical to fight those who declare themselves Muslim. We are obligated to guide them; we were the ones responsible for letting them go astray in matters of faith in the first place because we were too busy sloganeering... Long Live So-and-So... Death to So-and-So ... !

If the Government Assists Victims, We Need Not Wage *Jihad*: Fifth Excuse

Should we give up supporting the victims in Kashmir simply because the government of Pakistan is assisting them? What utter nonsense! Hafiz Saeed Sahib was once questioned by a foreign fighter about fighting with the aid of the devil. Hafiz Sahib said if your house is on fire and the devil's fire brigade shows up will you stop trying to extinguish the flames simply because the satanic government's firefighters are there to help? By Allah, the foreign fighter was speechless.

If the government wants to extinguish the fire in our house, let it try; we ought to help the government. If the government wages war with

Hindustan because mosques are being razed to the ground there and because Muslims are being slaughtered indiscriminately, should we withdraw from the battlefield simply because the government has not yet fully implemented Islamic law in Pakistan?

Mujahideen Provoke Hindus to Rape and Plunder: Sixth Excuse
Some object to *jihad* because they claim it provokes Hindus to rape women in Kashmir. They say while *mujahideen* execute their operations and make good their escape, innocent Muslim civilians in the valley are left vulnerable to interrogations, rape, murder, and crackdowns.

Brothers, this is what is known as being more loyal than the king, for if this accusation were true, Kashmiris would be *Lashkar-e-Tayyaba*'s worst enemies. On the contrary, we have their utmost love and support. They adore our *mujahideen* more dearly than they love their own children. (*Mujallah-ul-Dawah* is full of such testimonials.) Brothers, women are undoubtedly raped, but only in areas where our fighters do not have bases. Civilians obviously suffer brutal crackdowns in the areas where we are embedded but no one dares rape a woman there because Hindus know that the minute they attempt such barbarism, *mujahideen* will avenge the crime before its culmination.

First Wage *Jihad* Against the Ego, Then Against Satan, Then Against Worldly Desires, and Finally, Against the Enemy: Seventh Excuse
Some levy all kinds of preconditions for waging *jihad*. They say first one must wage *jihad* against the ego, then against Satan, then against worldly desires (never mind that there is no way to gauge or claim ones success in such a combat), and only then, against the enemy.

But did the prophet state such preconditions for waging *jihad*? Absolutely not! Consider the conquest of Mecca when the prophet had ten thousand warriors at hand and the force grew to twelve thousand within a matter of hours; the fresh recruits did not even know how to pray properly yet they were commanded to march onto Mecca. Were they first required to wage *jihad* against their egos, or against Satan, or against their worldly desires? What preconditions do the critics speak of?

The truth of the matter is that the focus on meditation at hermitages and shrines was fostered precisely to terminate *jihad*. This is why the

76 THE LITERATURE OF *LASHKAR-E-TAYYABA*

government's educational curriculum is geared so heavily towards mysticism. This is what the poet Iqbal sarcastically refers to when he says:

> Keep them engrossed in their chanting
> So they never leave their monasteries

When it is time to fight the enemy, you suggest a *jihad* against the ego. Iqbal says:

> Some dandy scrawled on the mosque's wall
> 'Idiots prostrate when it's time to stand'.

It is time to stand up, so why prostrate now? Get up! Prostrate at the appointed hour.

Satan has gotten the better of those who think that militant *jihad* must necessarily preclude a *jihad* against the ego, or against Satan, or against temptation, and that these *jihad*s can only be waged in a cloister through incantations and meditation. With Allah as my witness, I have seen young warriors at the training camp of Umm-al-Qura weep heavier tears than have ever been shed in a cloister. Among these men are landowners, educated men, men who have the means to fulfil all kinds of worldly desires, men with loved ones and parents back home—they have abandoned everything to sacrifice their lives by way of *jihad*. Is it possible to make such sacrifices without having fought against the ego, or against Satan, or against temptation? Absolutely not! (And the young warriors who have grown full beards and wear the hems of their *shalwars*[13] well above their ankles and fulfil every *Sunnat* of the prophet—have they not waged *jihad* against their egos as well?) The only way one can war against the ego and Satan is on the battlefield.

A tradition from Nasai[14] states that when the son of Adam was about to convert to Islam, Satan beckoned him to reconsider before giving up the religion of his forefathers. The man said, 'Be gone! I will not heed you!' After converting, when it came time to migrate in Allah's cause, Satan reappeared and urged him to reconsider before abandoning his motherland and the community that had sheltered him all his life. Again, he said, 'Be gone! I will not heed you!' After migrating, when it came time to wage *jihad*, Satan blocked his path and reminded him he could be killed (in Nasai, Ahmed reports the specific word used is 'killed'), that someone else might marry his widow, while his children are orphaned. The prophet said this man paid Satan no heed and carried on; whoever acts this way, Allah is responsible for opening for him the gates of paradise. Whether this person is martyred on the battlefield, or dies of some sickness, or drowns, or dies in an accident, Allah will grant him paradise.

Hence, we ought to stop making excuses and join the *jihad* as soon as possible. If it is not possible for you to wage *jihad*, at least support those who do. Do not pay heed to Satan's whispering. Do not compromise your afterlife for this world. May Allah guide us all. Amen.

And the conclusion of my prayer: Praise be to Allah, Lord of the Worlds.

5
'In Defence of *Jihad*'
by Ubaidurrahman Muhammadi

In this chapter,[1] we present a translation of the 1998 treatise, *Difa-i-Jihad* ('In Defence of *Jihad*') by Ubaidurrahman Muhammadi.[2] This book also contains a publisher's note from the then-editor of Dar-ul-Andlus, Muhammad Saifullah Khalid, as well as a foreword by Hafiz Saeed himself. Saeed's imprimatur upon this volume is extremely important because it demonstrates his linkages to LeT's violent mission even though he and Pakistani authorities deny these connections.

This volume resembles *Hum Jihad Kyon Kar Rahen Hain* ('Why Are We Waging *Jihad?*') in that it is generally structured around questions posed by an anonymous inquirer and the answers to those questions are ventriloquized through a posited, learned *mujahid*. While there is considerable overlap between the texts, they both have distinct foci. *Hum Jihad Kyon Kar Rahen Hain* ultimately advances an argument that a good Muslim should abjure violence within Pakistan against anyone who recognizes the ultimate sovereignty of Allah and instead should wage *jihad* on Pakistan's external enemies. The reason for this is straightforward: when Pakistanis stop fighting their external enemies, they will turn their guns upon Pakistan and Pakistanis. This text specifically focuses upon *jihad*, who must wage it, under what circumstances and for what reasons, while also maintaining the argument that any problem within Pakistan should be handled through education and proselytization (*dawah*), tasks which LeT under its various guises have long undertaken.

While seeking to make Pakistan a non-violent place where social, cultural, and political challenges are remediated through education and proselytization of LeT's interpretation of the *Ahl-e-Hadees* creed, *jihad* is posited not only as the singular means of achieving parochial objectives such as 'liberating Kashmir' and breaking up India upon communal lines, but *jihad* is the means of restoring glory and political significance to the *ummat*. This text argues

80 THE LITERATURE OF *LASHKAR-E-TAYYABA*

that the Muslim world was at the peak of power and influence when it was actively waging *jihad*. Once it ceased doing so, it began a steady decline that culminated in the subservience of Muslims to the conniving great powers. Thus, per this text, one should wage *jihad* not only because it advances local objectives but, more significantly, because it is the only means of restoring the grandeur and triumph of Islam and the entirety of the Muslim *ummat*.

In this chapter, we present a complete translation of 'In Defence of *Jihad*'. Thus, a note about its structure is in order as we retained the organizational structure of the document. The pamphlet begins with publisher's note penned by Muhammad Saifullah Khalid, the editor of Dar-ul-Andlus, which is followed by a Foreword by Hafiz Saeed. Ubaid-ur-Rahman Muhammadi introduces his treatise with a section titled 'Reason for Writing', in which the author describes his own experiences training in Afghanistan and then fighting *jihad* in Kashmir. Upon returning from the fight, he was dismayed to learn that intellectuals were casting aspersions upon the *jihad* in Kashmir. He wrote this pamphlet to interrogate the arguments of these intellectuals. The remainder of the text is comprised of ten rambling chapters, with numerous concatenated subsections that advance the overall goal despite a paucity of organizational logic. In the first chapter, titled 'The Rise and Fall of the Islamic Nation', the author explains that the Islamic Nation rose through the conduct of *jihad*, and it is abjuring of *jihad* which explain the fall of this same nation. The chapter argues that the Islamic Nation can be revivified only through *jihad*. Chapter 2, 'Bounties of the Afghan *jihad*', begins with the naïve inquirer explaining to the learned *mujahid* that his friends see no benefit of the Kashmir *jihad* and recalls LeT's own demurral's from fighting in Afghanistan after the Soviets withdrew and the country was plunged into civil war. The inquirer challenges the learned *mujahid* to explain why LeT refused to aid fellow *Ahl-e-Hadees mujahideen* when they tried to establish their own emirate in Kunar. Here the author explains these early decisions and describes the various benefits that accrued from the Afghan theatre. In Chapter 3, 'The Conspiracy to Ensnare Muslims in Civil War', the author adumbrates a global conspiracy to ensure that Muslims are divided among themselves in effort to prevent the rise of a great Islamic Nation. In Chapter 4, 'Significance of the Sequence of the Meccan and Medinite Periods', the author takes on the often-repeated argument that *jihad* was mandated during the Medina period and thus should only be waged under the auspices of an Islamic State. This is one of the most important arguments advanced by Muslim *jihad* opponents which he convincingly undermines. Chapter 5, 'Significance of Lack and Abundance in *jihad*', to motivates outnumbered *mujahideen* to fight a much larger Indian force. To do so, he analyses various battles from the times of the prophet to show that the faithful fighters prevailed over much larger infidel forces.

In Chapter 6, 'The Kashmir *Jihad* According to *shariat*', the author turns his power of logic upon the Kashmir theatre. Here the author mobilizes arguments rooted in *shariat* to motivate this struggle while also making political arguments about the nature of the Indian state and the posited struggles of Indian Muslims among several other topics that the author things are relevant to this conflict. Chapter 7, 'Why Do You Ignore the Principle of *Qisas* (Retributive Justice)?' addresses the common belief that LeT is a government tool, that it fights an asymmetric war at the government's behest, and this is why the organization does not criticize the corruption and other maladies of the Pakistani state. The learned *mujahid* explains to the ingenue that the organization will take any help it can get to fulfil its obligations of *jihad*, even assistance from non-Muslims. He explains to the inquisitive questioner that the organization will advance moral arguments to the government to encourage it to conduct itself in accordance with the principles of *shariat*. In Chapter 8, 'How Is *Jihad* Possible without a Caliph?', the author continues to undermine a belief held by Muslim critics of *jihad*: that it can only be waged by a rightful Caliph. Chapter 9, '*Jihad* Upon US Command', seeks to undermine the popular conspiracy theory that the organization wages *jihad* at the behest of the United States. The final chapter, Chapter 10, 'Muslim Lands Occupied by Disbelievers', rehearses histories of so-called Muslim states that are currently occupied by non-Muslims. This chapter is intended to motivate Muslims to rectify this by undertaking *jihad*.

Publisher's Note

Allah says:

And if they had wished to go forth, they would assuredly have made ready some equipment, but Allah was averse to their being sent forth

82 THE LITERATURE OF *LASHKAR-E-TAYYABA*

and held them back and (it was said unto them): Sit ye with the sedentary! Had they gone forth among you they had added to you naught save trouble and had hurried to and from among you, seeking to cause sedition among you; and among you there are some who would have listened to them. Allah is Aware of evil doers.

(Surat at-Tawbah 9:46–48)

In the verses above, Allah criticizes those who make highhanded declarations of faith but cannot stop quibbling over *jihad*. Every era has had its share of procrastinators who have hindered *mujahideen* wherever and whenever *jihad* was waged in Allah's cause.

The prophet himself had to deal with such prevaricators. Objections were raised regarding the Afghan *jihad* as well, and today, the *jihad* in Kashmir is under similar scrutiny.

On one hand are those who sacrifice life and limb in Allah's cause as they march towards paradise, irrigating the alpine meadows of Kashmir with their blood. On the other hand are the armchair critics who argue this is not *jihad*, this is a fight for land, this is suicide, there aren't enough resources to fight, there is no *jihad* without a caliph, *jihad* is the army's responsibility, parental approval is necessary, Kashmir's *jihad* should be waged by Kashmiris, *mujahideen* are causing problems for Kashmiri Muslims, etc.

Our respected brother Maulana Ubaid-ur-Rahman Muhammadi responds to all these objections in *Difa-i-jihad* ('In Defence of *Jihad*'). By adopting the format of a dialogue, he makes his points with remarkable clarity. His manuscript is replete with citations from the Quran, quotations from the *Hadees*, and references to the military career of the prophet.

This book is a treasure trove of information as well as a rejoinder to any doubt about the subject.

Dar-ul-Andlus is honoured to make this available with the latest composition and design techniques. May Allah bless us with the capacity to comprehend the value of *jihad* and the fortitude to tread the path to martyrdom. Amen!

In Search of Salvation,

Muhammad Saifullah Khalid
Editor, Dar-ul-Andlus

Foreword

Jihad-i-Hind has begun. In Kashmir, *mujahideen* are writing a glorious chapter of our times in blood; with absolute faith in Allah, they advance well into enemy frontiers. Devoted mothers dispatch obedient sons to the battlefield for the freedom of Kashmir; the end of disbelief is near. Divine Providence showers victories. The gathering strength of this *jihad* and the march of the *mujahideen* have shattered the enemy who falters and flails and consequently resorts to propaganda, presenting these noble warriors as terrorists to the world. But *mujahideen* pay no heed to propaganda; they march to their martyrdom upon Allah's will. The unwavering sacrifices of the martyrs add momentum to the struggle as the gates of victory and providence are thrown open.

In these trying times, those who are dutiful and blessed sacrifice their blood, their wealth, and their progeny for the struggle; but then there are those who fall prey to insidious propaganda and scepticism. They give hollow excuses to shirk their obligation. They present fallacious arguments to hinder the struggle. They say *jihad* in Kashmir goes against *shariat*. Furthermore, they say there is a lack of resources to combat the infidels. They insist it is wiser to focus on our Muslim leaders than waste time in Kashmir. These people are unconsciously aiding the enemy. The times call for a concerted effort to unify the Islamic nation in order to glorify the name of Allah and obliterate the hubris of disbelief for it is time to free the Muslim victims of conniving Hindus, eradicate the Jewish conspiracies against the *ummat* (Islamic nation), free *Bayt-ul-Muqaddas* (Dome of the Rock) from occupiers, end global Christian domination, and make the true faith overpower all other false ideologies.

A global *jihad* is underway to achieve these goals. The first sign of victory was Allah's dissolution of the Soviet Union. Now, *mujahideen* are assembling in Hindustan and sacrificing their lives in Kashmir.

In this context, brother Ubaid-ur-Rahman Muhammadi elaborates the importance of *jihad* in the text *Difa-i-jihad* with references from the Quran and *Hadees*; his presentation is highly agreeable as he supplements citations with rational arguments and affectionately addresses those who have doubts about the matter. Stylistically, 'In Defence *of Jihad*' is comprehensible, accessible, and memorable. It is crucial to disseminate this

84 THE LITERATURE OF *LASHKAR-E-TAYYABA*

work to inspire the nation. May Allah bless the writer's efforts and benefit his cause. (Amen)

The Lord's Lowly Servant

Professor Hafiz Saeed
Emirate *Jamaat ud Dawah* Pakistan

Reason for Writing

When *jihad* was launched in Kashmir by Allah's will, I was inspired to partake in the struggle. As I arranged to attend a military training camp, I convinced some friends to join me. One of my 'learned' friends backed out a day before our planned departure. He made numerous excuses that concluded with the blanket statement: 'There is no *jihad* underway; people are simply being fooled in the name of *jihad*.' Taken aback, I said, 'Allah has blessed us with discerning minds, so instead of heeding propaganda, let us go see what is happening for ourselves; then, we can authentically answer anyone who asks us about this so-called *jihad*.' After considerable deliberation, my friend agreed to join me once again. We travelled through Afghanistan where we first toured *Muaskar-e-Tayyaba* and ended up in *Muaskar-e-Aqsa*.[3]

We were so profoundly moved by the moral and physical training at these camps that we never turned our backs on the struggle again! I am the first to admit, the kind of muscle this *jihad* deserves is not yet being supplied; therefore, I pray:

> Our Lord! Forgive us for our sins and wasted efforts, make our foothold sure, and give us victory over the disbelieving folk.
>
> (*Surat al-Imran* 3:147)

This was a brief description of how I came to be associated with the movement.

Later, I came to know of well-renowned intellectuals who publicly opposed the *jihad* in Kashmir. I set about engaging them; I soon realized that some merely wished to amend certain aspects of the struggle (to them I am grateful); others, never having made the effort to find out about it themselves, were relying on hearsay—when they discovered the true nature of the *jihad* (in Kashmir) they joined in the effort wholeheartedly (thank Allah!); finally, there were those who were obstinate in their opposition to *jihad* itself. Below is my encounter with one such individual.

An encounter with a friend:

Once, while arguing with me about the *jihad* in Kashmir, a friend of mine said: 'You go around accusing the Indian Army of excessive force against Kashmiri Muslims whereas you are the ones wreaking havoc in Kashmir.'

Surprised, I asked, 'Sir, how can you call us aggressors? Kindly elaborate. Perhaps you are accusing me in the heat of the moment.'

He said: 'Had you read the Quran you would have seen this verse:

Fight in the way of Allah against those who fight against you, but begin not hostilities. Lo! Allah loveth not, aggressors.'

(*Surat al-Baqarah* 2:190)

After quoting this verse, my friend continued: 'You force Indian soldiers into battle by ambushing them. They kill one or two of your men, but you kill them by the dozen! Is this not transgression? Is this not the kind of transgression the Quran prohibits?'

I was deeply saddened by my friend's narrow-mindedness and his obvious misunderstanding. I said: 'According to your reasoning, when the prophet of Allah slaughtered seven hundred of Banu Qurayza's unarmed Jews and inflicted grave losses on the infidels in numerous battles, he acted in contradiction to this verse. Tell me, did the prophet not grasp the meaning of the verse or did he intentionally act against it?' (May Allah forgive me for even suggesting so).

My friend had no response, so he changed the subject. In an attempt to save face, he even expressed remorse for those killed in the line of duty.

86 THE LITERATURE OF *LASHKAR-E-TAYYABA*

This time, I was the one who suggested we turn to the Quran. I asked my friend's student to bring us a copy, which I opened to *Surat Muhammad* to the following verse:

> ... And those who are slain in the way of Allah, He rendereth not their actions vain.
>
> (*Surat Muhammad* 47:4)

I said, 'Brother, you ought to worry about yourself instead of worrying about the martyrs. Despite all your learning, you expend your faculties delegitimizing *jihad*. How will you justify this before Allah? Think about it; after all, one day you will stand before your Lord.'

How is *Jihad* delegitimized?

Consider: Some people verbally oppose *jihad* by creating doubt and disseminating misinformation while others publish their opposition in various magazines and newspapers. One particular pamphlet, reputed to be indisputable, was distributed in the thousands. One day, Brother Abu Nauman Saifullah Khalid Kasuri asked me to respond to this work. When I set about writing my rebuttal, I discovered over a hundred objections to *jihad* issued by various organizations and groups. Only a few of these objections are intellectually engaging; most of them are based on propaganda and misinformation.

On one hand I was acutely aware of my limitations, on the other hand the struggle was under attack. In helpless submission, I turned to god:

My Lord, help me, guide me, open my heart, make my words comprehensible and accessible; give me the strength to present the truth and defend *jihad*; give my pen the power to obliterate false ideologies, as You claim:

> Nay, but We hurl the true against the false, and it doth break its head and lo! it vanisheth. And yours will be woe for that which ye ascribe (unto Him).
>
> (*Surat al-Anbiya* 21:18)

I proceeded to draft a dialogue between an inquirer and a *mujahid* (singular of *mujahideen*), which takes the form of a series of questions and answers. I also cite verses from the Quran, references from

Hadees, and quotations of the prophet's companions, in defence of *jihad*.

It falls to the reader to determine how successfully I have obliterated the polemic of false and anti-*jihad* ideologies with evidence from the Quran and *Sunnat*. I hope to hear back from my readers, Allah-willing.

An Overview of '*In Defence of Jihad*'

This book answers questions in light of the Quran, the *Hadees*, and the lives of the prophet's companions. Errors made in the first edition have been rectified. In addition to certain edits and amendments, the book has also been organized anew. 'In Defence of *Jihad*' is divided into ten chapters—it opens with a list of these chapters as well as a list of subjects discussed in each chapter.

Readers ... ! Every effort has been made to create an error-free book with accurate references, and one that is perfectly formatted using the latest technology. But due to the inevitability of human error, all readers, in general, and all scholars, in particular, are requested to point out scholarly and hermeneutical errors for the sake of future editions.

May Allah make this book a source of inspiration for thought and action; may it strengthen the *jihad* movement, and may it be a source of salvation for me in this world and the world hereafter.

Ubaid-ur-Rahman Muhammadi
8 Rajab-ul-Murajab 1419AH/ 29 October 1998

Chapter 1: The Rise and Fall of the Islamic Nation

INQUIRER: *Assalam-u-Alaikum*
MUJAHID: *Walaikum Assalam*
INQUIRER: I am here to have some questions answered.
MUJAHID: Please continue. What would you like to know?
INQUIRER: I want to know why Muslims aren't united.
MUJAHID: Muslims are divided and weak because *jihad* has been disregarded.

88 THE LITERATURE OF *LASHKAR-E-TAYYABA*

INQUIRER: Some say that Muslims are downtrodden because they have stopped proselytizing.

MUJAHID: This is not true. Proselytizing continues through Friday sermons and various organized congregations. If there's one thing that is missing, it is *jihad*.

INQUIRER: Some say that Muslims lag in education whereas infidels have made remarkable advances in this field so it seems uneducated Muslims cannot compete with more advanced nations.

MUJAHID: This, too, is untrue. Millions of Muslims are enrolled in modern universities but despite this, their problems multiply; they are downtrodden, poverty stricken, and trapped in the infidel's death-grip. Consider what Allah says:

Faint not nor grieve, for ye will overcome them if ye are (indeed) believers.

(3: 139)

Allah clearly states *jihad* is the only way for the Islamic nation to gain dominance, as long as we march into battle with the full force of our faith.

INQUIRER: We lack resources and manpower; in these circumstances one cannot wage *jihad* unprepared. We ought to confront the enemy on political, economic, industrial, and educational platforms.

MUJAHID: This is wishful thinking. No matter how much progress you make in these fields, the enemy will always be far more advanced than you. Prepare yourself, by all means, but do not invoke 'preparation' as an excuse. Instead, actively participate in *jihad*; Allah will bestow his beneficence and make Muslims dominant, Allah-willing.

INQUIRER: Is *jihad* permissible without a caliph?

MUJAHID: Absolutely! *jihad* can be waged without a caliph.

INQUIRER: What is the *shariat*'s take on *jihad* in the absence of a government?

MUJAHID: *jihad* is permissible in the absence of a government or an organized congregation.

INQUIRER: What about *jihad* waged by small factions and groups?

MUJAHID: Factions can wage *jihad* as well.

INQUIRER: Can *jihad* be waged in the absence of an emirate?

MUJAHID: *jihad* can be waged without an organized congregation. For example, if a Muslim is trapped behind enemy lines, he does not need to join an organization or seek out an emirate; he will wage *jihad* all alone. When Syedna Abu Baseer found himself in such a situation he killed the disbeliever who held him captive and escaped to spend the rest of his days waging *jihad*.

INQUIRER: Is *jihad* imperative in our times or is it better to resolve problems through peaceful dialogue?

MUJAHID: *jihad* will continue till the end of time. It has always earned the Islamic nation respect and glory whereas dialogue has cost Muslims many victories. Dialogue is not the solution; *jihad* is the only answer.

INQUIRER: Can *jihad* be waged for any land or region?

MUJAHID: Yes, the world belongs to Allah, and his people have the right to rule it.

INQUIRER: Do infidels have no right over any region in the world?

MUJAHID: If infidels govern the world there will be rebellion, chaos, and mischief, but if Muslims govern the world, they will uphold Allah's *kalima* (declaration that there is no god but Allah and Muhammad are His Messenger).

INQUIRER: Kindly elaborate ...

MUJAHID: Infidels forever contradict Allah's commands; this gives rise to mischief and chaos in the world. But Allah describes Muslims as follows:

Those who, if We give them power in the land, establish worship and pay the poor due and enjoin kindness and forbid iniquity.

(*Surat al-Hajj* 22:41)

This is why it is essential that Muslims govern, while emasculating infidels ...

... until they pay the tribute (jizya) readily, being brought low.

(*Surat at-Tawbah* 9:29)

Brother, the path of *jihad* will make the world a peaceful place free of mischief, Allah-willing.

90 THE LITERATURE OF *LASHKAR-E-TAYYABA*

INQUIRER: It is strange that you are unwilling to grant infidels an inch of land to establish their government on this vast planet while in reality the situation is quite the opposite: infidels dominate; they are resourceful, militarily advanced etc. while Muslims are scattered, helpless, and leaderless; *jihad* is not permissible without a caliph while Muslim governments are weak and split up into sectarian factions. They are disorganized and in a state of crisis. In such circumstances, who will wage *jihad* and how?

MUJAHID: Do not fear, mothers dispatch their sons to the battlefield to this day. Contact any one of the nation-wide offices of *Markaz-ud-Dawah* and you will discover *mujahideen* heading to Kashmir from every corner of the country. Point is, when the Islamic nation lacks resources we should look to the life of the Prophet, the model of excellence and a guiding light for us all. The Islamic nation needs to be reminded of the importance and centrality of *jihad* by recalling the time the Prophet lacked resources, yet he confronted and defeated a mighty enemy.

INQUIRER: But the Prophet launched his mission by proselytizing, yet you talk of *jihad*.

MUJAHID: Today, Muslims are obligated to proselytize and wage *jihad* simultaneously. Let us take a cursory look at some successes in the Prophet's life.

There was a time when the infidels of Mecca considered the prophet too weak to be paid any mind. When they forced the prophet to migrate, he left Mecca for Medina where he launched proselytizing and *jihadi* missions to the four corners of the world in service of the true faith. Within a mere decade Mecca was conquered, after which followed a series of military triumphs. The Prophet personally led twenty-seven military expeditions... he bore battle scars on his body... his companions wrote the history of Islam with their blood.

Allah blessed the companions' sacrifices in war and made Muslims victorious; in a short duration the banner of Islam waved over a large portion of the world.

This brief sketch reveals that *jihad* was the solution then, and it is the only solution now.

INQUIRER: What was the condition of Muslims after the Prophet's death?

MUJAHID: During the reign of the pious caliphs, and many years after, *jihadi* missions were dispatched across the globe; nations fell before the might of Islam by Allah's grace, and the Islamic empire expanded in the east and in the west.

INQUIRER: How did these campaigns end and why did *mujahideen* return to the comfort of their homes?

MUJAHID: The downfall began when *jihad* was terminated; the enemy marched into Muslim territory, stole their lands, and subjected them to a bloodbath. And so the gates of Providence were closed. Muslims were no longer victorious because their leaders came to love the luxuries of this world and grew to fear the glories of death on the battlefield. Consequently, lands that had been conquered by Muslim generals fell to the enemy. Below is a brief description of these events:

1. The Negro Bilal belonged to what is today called Eritrea, which was ruled by King Negus during the prophet's era. Negus was the first Muslim ruler upon whose death the prophet offered absentia funerary prayers. For many years after Negus' demise this region was ruled by Muslim kings. When *jihad* was terminated, Muslims lost control in the region to Christians who maintain their authority there till today.
2. Syedna Umar Farooq conquered Palestine; the Jews personally handed him the keys to *Bayt-ul-Muqaddas* (Dome of the Rock). Muslims ruled this region for twelve hundred and sixty years. Because *jihad* was terminated, Jews pose as rulers of this region today.
3. Burma ...
4. Thailand ...
5. and Nepal were ruled by Muslims. Because *jihad* ended, these regions are under the control of Buddhists.
6. Bulgaria ...
7. Russia
8. and vast swathes of China were under Muslim control but because there was no more *jihad*, these places are now governed by communists.
9. Hindustan, Kashmir
10. and Assam had been won by Muslims who governed these regions for twelve hundred years. Then, *jihad* came to an end; today Hindus have made life hell for the Muslims who live there.

92 THE LITERATURE OF *LASHKAR-E-TAYYABA*

11. Cyprus was conquered during Syedna Uthman Ghani's rule but today, because *jihad* was terminated, it is ruled by Europeans.
12. The famous Muslim general Tariq bin Ziyad conquered Spain (Andalusia) where Muslims ruled for seven hundred years. Today the region is governed by Christians.
13. Italy...
14. Philippines...
15. Portugal...
16. Poland
17. Romania...
18. Yugoslavia
19. and Greece etc. were conquered by Muslims. For many years the banner of Islam flew over these lands that today, are controlled by Europeans.

Infidels rule over vast territories of the world. By listing the regions above, we have invited thinkers to become actors, in order to strengthen and expand the esteemed enterprise of *jihad* and prepare the Muslim nation for its march into the battlefield.

INQUIRER: These shocking facts, set beside humiliating defeat, make it seem like Muslims have lost their most treasured territories to thieving infidels—what do Muslims have left?

MUJAHID: Despite these defeats Allah has bestowed Muslims with limitless wealth. Muslims rule some of the most important regions of the world. Below is a brief geographical context of the Muslim world. Pay close attention.

Geographic Significance of the Muslim World

Losing vast areas of Islamic territory is certainly humiliating. (May Allah bless us with the will to wage *jihad* and follow the footsteps of our forebears.) Despite this, many regions under Muslim control today are bounteous. Currently, there are over fifty-five Muslim countries spread over two and a half million square miles of land.

Muslims still control many of the international land and sea routes.

The strategic importance of Muslim regions can be gauged by the fact that most of the land, sea, and air routes connecting South Asia, Africa, Europe, and Australia pass through Muslim areas.

The coasts of Africa and Asia, as well as the Mediterranean, all of which are the lifeline of international trade, are located in the Muslim world.

While Muslims have the upper hand in controlling all global trading routes, there is no dearth of natural and material resources either. We have been blessed with a majority of the world's agricultural and mineral resources with a monopoly over raw steel, natural gas, gold, silver, uranium, aluminium, copper, coal, petrol, and oil.

In addition, Allah has bestowed us with mosques, advanced centres of learning, learned scholars, cultural institutions, health, industrial resources, trade, etc. and there is no dearth of talent either. Every year, millions of pilgrims visit the Sacred House, the mosques are full of worshippers, and our populations are blessed with numerous pious personages. Charity and endowments ensure that religious institutions, hospitals, and social organizations operate smoothly. Various trusts have been set up by the wealthy for these purposes. Despite all this, why is the Muslim nation in a state of humiliation and despair?

The answer to this question can be found in a *Hadees*:

> When you engage in usurious trade, and are led by the tails of cattle, and are content with agricultural pursuits, and terminate *jihad*, Allah will oppress you with humiliation which will not ease until you return to your faith (*jihad*).
>
> (Abu Dawood Ahmed[4])

Four Hundred Million Muslims Enslaved?

According to the prophet, as long as Muslims shirk their obligation to wage *jihad*, they are doomed to despair. Muslims do not heed the prophet's truthful words. What's more, 400 million Muslims in the world go on living helplessly as slaves.

INQUIRER: This means that if Muslims reignite *jihad* they can break the enemy's back.

94 THE LITERATURE OF *LASHKAR-E-TAYYABA*

MUJAHID: Absolutely! The arrogance of infidels can easily be obliterated but it is tragic that despite having all the resources in the world, Muslims are clueless. They consider themselves weak and helpless. The enemy has conspired to destroy their will; they have lost control of their resources and wealth. Muslims are persecuted, their women are raped, their sanctified spaces are defiled; they are being slaughtered and their rights are being violated right, left, and centre.

Six Million Powerless Muslim Soldiers

Infidels have disempowered 6 million uniformed Muslim soldiers across the globe. Imagine the psychological despair that plagues the Muslim world. There is an utter lack of will. Divisiveness has weakened the ranks. Many religious scholars have not lived up to their role of inspiring the nation, a role they naturally inherited from the prophets.

Muslim leaders are too focused on retaining personal power. Many intellectuals have denied the importance of *jihad* altogether; the literate idiots among us are busy trying to prove that *jihad* is unnecessary and redundant. There is a segment of society that insists on labelling *jihad* terrorism and equating it with treachery.

Our enemies have taken full advantage of the situation by dividing the Muslim world into ever-smaller factions while some unconscionable Muslims are acting as their agents. Our solution for these troubled times is based on the prophet's recommendations.

Jihad is the Only Solution to Our Problems and the Only Means to Achieve Peace

INQUIRER: What should we do in this situation? What is the solution? How can we regain our dignity? How is *jihad* to be waged? Please elaborate.

MUJAHID: If we want to free Muslims from the oppressive yoke of the infidel, and take back our stolen lands, and protect the rights of Muslims all over the world, then we must:

- Wage *jihad*
- Blockade air routes
- Restrict traffic on sea routes
- Remove all safety measures from land routes; we must lie in ambush, and much like Syedna Abu Baseer, attack every trade caravan of the infidels that passes through our territory

Unfortunately, Muslim rulers no longer have the power to take such bold and radical steps. Muslims no longer realize the importance of confronting the enemy and reaping the benefits of *jihad*.

Allah commands Muslims to remain forewarned, and aware through *jihad*.

Allah says:

Warfare is ordained for you, though it is hateful unto you; but it may happen that ye hate a thing which is good for you, and it may happen that ye love a thing which is bad for you. Allah knoweth, ye know not'
(*Surat al-Baqarah* 2:216)

The prophet stressed the importance of *jihad* in the following words: 'Undoubtedly, paradise lies in the shade of swords' (Bukhari). Hence, *jihad* leads to victory, success, and dignity; it is the only path to paradise.

Questioning the Afghan *Jihad*

For a long time, *jihad* had been all but forgotten; paradise was no longer sought in the shade of the sword, and the commandment to kill had long been disavowed. Then, Russians invaded Afghanistan and ordinary Afghans confronted the invaders. Arab scholars legitimized this struggle so *mujahideen* from around the world joined the *jihad*. But in Pakistan, scholars and laypersons alike began debating whether this *jihad* was in line with the *shariat*, even though Afghans began their *jihad* once their country had already been stolen from them. In those days, the following issues were raised in Pakistan:

96 THE LITERATURE OF *LASHKAR-E-TAYYABA*

1. *jihad* can only be waged under a caliph's authority while Afghans do not have a caliph.
2. If nothing else, there must at least be an established Islamic state to wage *jihad* whereas the Afghans do not possess one.
3. *jihad* can only be waged to uphold the word of Allah; Afghans are only fighting to free their land.
4. All sorts of different ideological groups have joined the Afghan *jihad*.
5. *mujahideen* in Afghanistan lack the resources, technological skills, advanced weaponry, and sheer manpower to confront the superpower of the time.

It was concluded that *jihad* in Afghanistan was not in line with *shariat* and should therefore be terminated; the land ought to be left to the Russians and proselytizing was the only obligation that needed to be fulfilled.

The Beginning of a Difficult Journey

To counter these doubts, religious scholars and muftis the world over declared this *jihad* legitimate and obligatory; *fatwas* were given confirming that those who die in the course of this fight will be martyrs (Allah-willing), and that supporting this struggle, both financially and militarily, will gain Allah's favour. Esteemed sheikhs of the Arab world met Pakistani scholars to convince them of the importance of said *jihad*. At this time, *Markaz-ud-Dawah-wal-Irshad* officially began work on preaching and rejuvenating *jihad*. After Afghanistan, Kashmir and Bosnia were next. Gradually, what started as a national movement gained an international following. Thousands of workers are embedded in all corners of the world, preaching, and inspiring *jihad*, and the movement now beats in the hearts of millions of Muslims.

Because there is a difference between words and action, this rapidly growing movement immediately drew criticism from the armchair scholars. Initially, the criticism was muted but gradually it gained a voice further amplified by propaganda, accusations, and misrepresentation. The critics thought the movement hot air but instead it has been soaked in the selfless sacrifices of those who are dedicated. Critics are busy trying to delegitimize and misrepresent this struggle, in an attempt to terminate *jihad* through their writings and their speeches. They spend generously on their propaganda and call this diabolical activity *jihad-bil-qalam* (*jihad* by the pen) and *jihad-bil-maal* (*jihad* by wealth).

This is nothing but a lame attempt to excuse oneself from the kind of *jihad* waged by the prophet, the sword and hammer, hammer to head kind, in which your friends fall dead around you. Critics demoralize those who wish to follow the prophet's *Sunnat*. We ask those who seek the truth to compare the lives of those who ramble against *jihad* with the lives of those *mujahideen* who have dedicated themselves to this struggle; visit the training camps and assess the curriculum; observe the way these young warriors live; see how they spend their days and how they manifest their dedication; meet the ones who have spent years camped out in Kashmir. Then, decide for yourself which path you would rather take.

Chapter 2: Bounties of the Afghan *jihad*

INQUIRER: *jihad* has been a rallying call for some time now. My friends say nothing will come of the *jihad* in Kashmir, much like the Afghan *jihad* in which thousands of Muslims lost their lives over thirteen years but which ended in civil war.

MUJAHID: Why do your friends not recognize the victory and benefits of the Afghan *jihad*? Even disbelievers recognize the glory, victory, and dignity that resulted from this *jihad*.

INQUIRER: My friends won't tire of listing all the disadvantages of this *jihad*. They trace all of Afghanistan's current problems back to it.

MUJAHID: Brother, share some of these disadvantages. Allah blessed Muslims generously, well beyond anyone's expectations.

INQUIRER: Let us start with *Markaz-ud-Dawah-wal-Irshad*. My friends say that your organization refused to cooperate with the Islamic Emirate of Kunar [a province in Afghanistan] when they faced trying times, despite the fact that they were sincerely trying to establish an Islamic state based on the principles of the Quran and *Sunnat*.

98 THE LITERATURE OF *LASHKAR-E-TAYYABA*

Some Questions

MUJAHID: Those who deny the benefits of the Afghan *jihad* and look for reasons to criticize it are blind.
You tell me, was this Islamic state established because of the *jihad* or did it exist prior to the war?

INQUIRER: There is no doubt this state was established because of *jihad* but now all of Afghanistan is a source of humiliation for Muslims which means the Afghan *jihad* was a mistake.

MUJAHID: May Allah bless those who deny the bounties of the Afghan *jihad* with perspective. Really, let those who are ignorant of the benefits of this *jihad* know that while the *jihad* restored a sense of dignity among common Muslims it proved to be a great asset in terms of the Quran and *Sunnat*. For example:

1. Arab *mujahideen* travelled to Afghanistan and helped realign the locals' beliefs with the authentic principles of Islam, opening the path for proselytization.
2. Earlier, the *madaris* in Afghanistan only taught a narrow form of Islamic jurisprudence but now millions of *madaris* offer expertise in Quran and *Sunnat*. Thousands of Afghan students travel to Pakistan to join Salafi *madaris*. By conservative estimates, this year (1997) alone saw some five thousand students from the province of Badakhshan travel to Pakistan for this purpose.
3. Rampant missionary work in Kunar has inspired countless people in the region to live their lives according to the Quran and *Sunnat*.
4. The province of Nuristan has also experienced the prevailing authority of the Quran and *Sunnat*. Tell me, was the *jihad* in Afghanistan beneficial or not?

Questions for Those Who Oppose *Jihad*

1. Before Afghanistan, Russians invaded Samarkand and Bukhara and various other Islamic states. Pray tell:
2. Was there any chance of Russians withdrawing their troops from these regions before the Afghan *jihad*?

'IN DEFENCE OF *JIHAD*' 99

3. Did Russians alter the Islamic character of these states?
4. Did Russians allow Muslims to worship, pilgrimage to Mecca, pay charity tax etc. once they invaded the Islamic states?

INQUIRER: Absolutely not.

MUJAHID: After invading various Muslim countries, and establishing their control over Afghanistan, what country would Russians have invaded next?

INQUIRER: Pakistan.

MUJAHID: Think over the issue in light of these facts. At the time of the Russian invasion, Afghans were poor and weak, but they paid no mind to their shortcomings and decided to confront the Pharaonic superpower. At the time, those who opposed *jihad*, lamented the Afghans for recklessly taking on this fight. What happened next? Soon, Russians turned tail and ran so fast they left their atom bombs behind; even their air power proved futile; their tanks and canons were sold as scrap metal in market squares.
: Did Russians not run away?

INQUIRER: Indeed, they were defeated, and they left.

MUJAHID: In addition to Afghanistan, did five other states not gain their freedom?

INQUIRER: Absolutely.

MUJAHID: Is it not true that Muslim citizens of these nations were free to pilgrimage to Mecca after seventy years?

INQUIRER: Absolutely. After seventy years they were free to perform the pilgrimage.

MUJAHID: Muslims were not allowed to teach their children the Quran or *Hadees*. Anyone caught reciting the Quran was executed or imprisoned. Is this not true?

INQUIRER: It is true. Reciting the Quran was a crime.

MUJAHID: Did the Afghan *jihad* not allow people to study the Quran and *Hadees*? Isn't it true that they are now able to publish the Quran and make pilgrimage?

INQUIRER: No doubt. Millions of blueprints of the Quran have been shipped there from Pakistan and Saudi Arabia and Saudis have borne the expense of thousands of Muslims traveling to Mecca from this region. Also, mosques, once converted into stables, resonate again with the call to prayer.

100 THE LITERATURE OF *LASHKAR-E-TAYYABA*

MUJAHID: Mosques had been shut down and were used as stables and breweries.

The Afghan *jihad* restored the dignity of prayer-houses. At any given time, tens of thousands of worshippers now bowed before Allah. Quranic recitation echoed in every home. How was all this possible?

INQUIRER: No doubt, Allah made all this possible due to the Afghan *jihad*.

MUJAHID: Now answer this: aren't the ones who say the Afghan *jihad* was pointless and that our warriors in Kashmir should return, conspiring with, or inadvertently defending, the enemy?

INQUIRER: This, indeed, is foolish. They are benefitting the enemy.

Why Were You Silent?

MUJAHID: Consider the fact that those who expend their resources trying to prove that the Afghan *jihad* is pointless were silent when:

- Mosques were being used as taverns.
- Mosques were converted to stables for mules and horses.
- Muslims could not even imagine going on a pilgrimage.
- Muslims were forced to recant their faith in Allah and deny His existence altogether.
- Muslims, forbidden from sanctioning their marriages before Allah, were forced to produce illegitimate children.
- Brothels were established to promote vice, obliterating all sense of modesty.
- Shameless communists transgressed all sexual mores; incest was rampant.
- Any Muslim caught promoting Islam was tortured and locked up forever.

These facts are known the world over. Decide for yourself, what kind of person would silently watch Muslims being humiliated and object to their freedom.

'IN DEFENCE OF *JIHAD*' 101

The Martyrdom of Sheikh Jamil-al-Rahman

INQUIRER: When the martyr Sheikh Jamil-al-Rahman's Islamic state in Kunar was being disbanded, why did *Markaz-ud-Dawah-wal-Irshad* refuse to cooperate with the sheikh and why did your organization consider his fight treacherous and barbaric when it was being waged to guard an Islamic state? Please elaborate.
MUJAHID: This is one of numerous rumours that are part of a smear campaign against *Markaz-ud-Dawah-wal-Irshad*.

Sir, it is necessary to comprehend certain facts regarding the attack on the Islamic emirate to guard oneself from insidious misconceptions.

When *Hezb-e-Islami* assembled its forces in Kunar, Sheikh Jamil-al-Rahman and his men were tricked into believing a massive attack was being launched against the Russians. The sheikh was caught off guard when *Hezb-e-Islami* attacked his Islamic emirate. Instead of retaliating, the kind-hearted sheikh prohibited the members of his *Jamaat al Dawah ila al Qur'an wa Ahl al-Hadees* from fighting back because he despised infighting. As a result, the people in Kunar did not confront their attackers.

In the same spirit, he refused help from respected Zaki-ur-Rehman in Bajaur when the latter offered to assist him in this fight.[5] After consulting his comrades, the sheikh told Zaki-ur-Rehman that his assistance was neither needed nor appropriate—this message was sent to our training camp *Muaskar-e-Tayyaba* in Afghanistan, which is why our warriors never joined the battle in Kunar.

The sheikh acted like Syedna Uthman; he sacrificed his life but refused to permit civil war and treachery between Muslim factions. He relentlessly tried to resolve issues through peaceful negotiations, but his enemies were hungry for war while the sheikh was determined not to fight them. Many of his men sought permission to retaliate but he would not have the blood of fellow Muslims on their hands.

Having commanded his men to maintain peace, he relocated to Bajaur. He was certain he would gain a stronghold in the region through peaceful negotiations and with the support of Arab *mujahideen*. The enemy was determined to keep Muslims engaged in civil war even though the sheikh

102 THE LITERATURE OF *LASHKAR-E-TAYYABA*

refused to compromise his values. So, conspirators assassinated him. His martyrdom is testament to his sincere attempts at uniting Muslims.

Even today, there are those who want to fan the flames of discord between Muslims to keep them in a state of civil war. May Allah help us recognize such conspiracies and protect us. Amen.

INQUIRER: Are you not responsible for re-establishing an Islamic state once it has been dissolved? You will probably argue that you were busy fighting the aggressors in Kashmir but wasn't the dissolution of the Islamic state (in Kunar) an act of aggression as well?

MUJAHID: I have already stated the sheikh's policy for his state. But one ought to ask those who want to make this issue the basis of their attacks against my organization what they sacrificed for this cause. Why did they not lend their support? This world is full of naysayers. Because the *jihad* movement is gaining momentum, it makes such people nervous and they try their best to undermine our efforts. They are neither sincere about the Salafis in Kunar nor do they have any intention of helping them in their struggle.

Russia's Anti-Islamic Objectives in Afghanistan

INQUIRER: Was there really an end to treachery in Afghanistan? Did Allah's faith end up reigning supreme there? Was your decision to focus your struggle on Kashmir justified?

MUJAHID: Indeed. For the most part, all kind of treachery in Afghanistan had been eliminated which is why we returned. Do you know why Russians invaded Afghanistan? I will tell you:

- v Russians invaded Afghanistan to lay waste the mosques.
- v Russians invaded Afghanistan to end *La ilaha Ill-Allah* (there is no god but Allah).
- v Russians invaded Afghanistan to spread disbelief.
- v Russians invaded Afghanistan to establish a satanic government.
- v Russians invaded Afghanistan to turn religious schools into brothels.
- v Russians invaded Afghanistan in order to capture Pakistan.

'IN DEFENCE OF *JIHAD*' 103

They were the source of treachery in the land and we went to eliminate them. We were able to cleanse the region for the most part, before moving on to Kashmir, thanks to Allah!

INQUIRER: Afghanistan is ravaged by civil war. Were the sacrifices of one hundred and fifty thousand martyrs in vain?

MUJAHID: My brother, one must accept some harsh realities. Why blame *jihad* for the discord between Afghan Muslims? Look at it this way: twenty-four hundred thousand Muslims sacrificed their lives for the establishment of the Islamic state of Pakistan but today the country is a mess; law and order is an issue, no one is safe, bombings are rampant, and worshippers are killed in mosques, but would you say creating Pakistan was pointless and therefore, we should reunite with Hindustan?

INQUIRER: We will not reunite with Hindustan, but we can certainly mourn the state of our country and commiserate over our plight.

MUJAHID: We too are aggrieved by what's going on in Afghanistan, but it is important to keep in mind *jihad* has nothing to do with it. Muslims are playing into the enemy's conspiracies that spark unrest among their ranks. In Afghanistan, the enemy strives to alienate Muslims from the *jihad* movement, in Pakistan it creates civil unrest and out-sources the alienation process to people within the society, who go on to urge others to stop waging *jihad*, to pull out of Kashmir, to guard their own country before worrying about the *ummat*... Surely, you have heard this kind of nonsense.

INQUIRER: For the most part, I agree with you, but were you not ob-ligated to make truce between the fighting factions in Afghanistan by neutralizing the enemy's conspiracies before heading off to Kashmir?

MUJAHID: We have tried our best, with the help of Allah, to resolve the various conflicts between Muslims. Sheikh Jamil-ur-Rahman had adopted a similar approach. Salafis have worked very hard to main-tain truce in the region. They gave up their own rights to aid peace efforts. The emirate of *Jamaat-ud-Dawah al-Quran wa Sunnat*, Sheikh Samiullah, and Sheikh Jamil-ur-Rahman's son Inayat-al-Rahman, and various other elders can provide further information on the matter.

104 THE LITERATURE OF *LASHKAR-E-TAYYABA*

Fight the Enemy, Not One Another

INQUIRER: But your efforts seemed fruitless; oppression and barbarism still reign in Afghanistan. It was your duty to combat the aggressors and instil the fear of Allah among them.

MUJAHID: Brother, it is time to fight the enemy, not one another. It is time to break the enemy's back to prevent further conspiracies; this will lead to peace among Muslims.

INQUIRER: Allah commands us to fight the aggressors. I find it strange that you say it is time to fight the enemy.

MUJAHID: Brother, I will present examples from the prophet's life to explain this delicate point for your peace of mind. For those who are naturally inclined to listen, this will be proof enough.

- The hypocrites in service of the prophet tried their level best to create conflict among Muslims, to the point of conspiring with Jews. During the Battle of Khandaq,[6] these traitors sincerely wished Jews and the infidels of Mecca victory. Instead of combatting the traitors, the prophet battled the infidels first, and then the Jews, in order to eradicate the problem at its source so the hypocrites had no one left with whom they could conspire.
- After being defeated in battle by companions of the prophet, the infidels changed their strategy and resorted to conspire against Muslims by creating internal conflicts and misunderstandings. Due to these misunderstandings.
- Muslims formed opposing factions that began fighting one another. One small group of the prophet's companions distanced itself from the infighting and tried to make peace among the rival factions.

Brother, much like the companions of the prophet, and according to the *Hadees*, we cannot allow ourselves to be involved in these conflicts.

Instead, our guns are aimed at disbelievers, and our targets are Hindus, Jews, and Christians. We will expend all our efforts to fight them.

We pray that Allah grant us the capacity to do what is dear to Him. Amen.

'IN DEFENCE OF *JIHAD*' 105

Chapter 3: The Conspiracy to Ensnare Muslims in Civil War

INQUIRER: Is speaking truth to an oppressive ruler *jihad* or not?

MUJAHID: Let us first examine the *Hadees*, stated below, which you reference.

: 'Speaking truth to an oppressive ruler is a great *jihad*.'

: Here, the importance of speaking truth to an oppressive ruler is stressed but this statement cannot be used to foment dissent and rebellion.

INQUIRER: If speaking truth to an oppressive ruler is a great *jihad* then isn't fighting such a ruler prescribed?

MUJAHID: Brother, the truth is what is literally stated in the *Hadees*. If fighting an oppressive ruler were prescribed, the prophet would have said so. On the contrary, consider the following *Hadees*: 'Swearing at a Muslim is debauchery and sin; fighting against one is disbelief.' Jarir reports that during the last pilgrimage, the prophet said, 'After me, do not become heathens by killing one another.'

In light of these statements, we do not target Muslims; instead we try to correct our co-religionists through preaching. Currently, our battlefield is Kashmir and our targets are Hindu disbelievers.

Prohibition on Fighting Evil Rulers

INQUIRER: Some of my friends, who are religious scholars, say that the current regime is oppressive, anti-Islamic, satanic, and acting on behalf of American disbelievers. It is important to fight this regime before dealing with Kashmir.

MUJAHID: Below are listed all the references that keep us from fighting Muslim rulers.

Syedna Auf bin Malik reports that the prophet said the best of your rulers are those whom you love and who love you and who pray for you and for whom you pray; the worst of your rulers are those who make an enemy of you and of whom you make an enemy and whom you curse and who curse you. People said, 'Allah's Messenger, shall we not get rid of such evil

106 THE LITERATURE OF *LASHKAR-E-TAYYABA*

rulers with the sword?' The prophet said, 'As long as they establish prayer among you, and as long as you recognize their wrongdoing in your hearts, do not disobey them' (*Sahih Muslim, Kitab al-Imara*[7]).

A person asked the prophet what the people were to do if, after the prophet's passing, a ruler demands his rights but refuses to acknowledge the rights of his subjects. The prophet said, 'The ruler is responsible for his rights and you are responsible for yours; be submissive and obedient' (Muslim[8]).

The Character of Our Forebears

Our forebears had to deal with unjust rulers as well, but they did not rebel; instead, they endured the most oppressive regimes, preferring proselytizing to fighting. Our history is rife with examples of endurance and patience. Consider the case of Imam Ahmed bin Hanbal.

Imam Ahmed bin Hanbal and the Oppressive Rulers

- Imam Ahmed bin Hanbal suffered all his life.
- Caliph Mamun kept him imprisoned during his entire reign.
- Caliph Mu'tasam had him tortured in jail.
- Caliph Wasiq extended his imprisonment and torture.

Accusation of Treason
During the reign of Caliph Mu'tahwakkal, Imam Sahib was accused of conspiring to overthrow the caliph. The imam's place was raided but no incriminating evidence was found. A messenger read aloud the caliph's message to the imam in which the latter was accused of conspiring with an occult leader to overthrow the government; he was sternly warned against making any such attempt. In response, Imam Sahib claimed to have no knowledge of any such conspiracy. He said, 'regardless of whether it causes me suffering or brings me benefit, I have never entertained the remotest idea of disobeying the Muslim emirate; whether I am demoted from my position or acknowledged for my expertise, I have always begged Allah for stability.'

'IN DEFENCE OF *JIHAD*' 107

Despite the imam's categorical response his house was ransacked, every document and scroll were scrutinized, and women assisting the raid went through the most private areas of his home. The caliph's officers returned without a trace of incriminating evidence because the accusation was false to begin with.

Brother, while I have proven why we should refrain from antagonizing our rulers I will point out that those riling up the public against our leaders are the ones most eager to interact, network, and be seen with said leaders despite accusing them of being oppressive and working for Americans. Some of those who call for rebellion have fallen prey to enemy propaganda and do not have the wits to see what is going on; others babble relentlessly. Then there are those who are opposed to *jihad*; they genuinely want *mujahideen* to turn their guns away from Hindu disbelievers and point them at their own leaders; they want to make a spectacle and a mockery of Muslims by shedding the blood of fellow Muslims.

Brother, why don't these rabble-rousers take up arms themselves? Why don't they fulfil this obligation with their own hands? The fact that they do not practise what they preach is telling enough for anyone with the least bit of perspective.

Fighting Disbelievers is More Redeeming Than Civil War

Instead of rebelling against our own Muslim rulers, we battle oppressive, cruel, polytheistic Hindu rulers because the prophet said:

There are two groups in my *ummat* Allah has protected from hell-fire: one group comprises those who will *jihad* against Hind, and the second comprises those who will join forces with Jesus, the son of Mary (to war against Dajjal).

([Abu Dawood] Ahmed 287:5; *Kitab-al-Jihad*, 43:6)[9]

In light of this *Hadees*, Syedna Abu Huraira used to say, 'I will join the *jihad* against Hind if it begins in my lifetime; if I'm martyred, I will be exalted, and if I return alive, I will be protected from hellfire.'

Brother, according to this *Hadees* and Syedna Abu Huraira's wish, we are at war with the rulers of Hind, in the hope of either dying in the course

108 THE LITERATURE OF *LASHKAR-E-TAYYABA*

of our struggle, or surviving to celebrate our redemption from hell, Allah-willing.

Also, when Muslim rulers are criticized for not implementing Islam, they accept their shortcomings and promise to do whatever they can to uphold the true faith. We ought to convince them to stay true to their word instead of rebelling against them, unless, of course, we see obvious signs of disbelief. This is why we will continue preaching to them instead of taking up arms against them, Allah-willing.

INQUIRER: The *Hadees* commands us to help both the oppressor and the oppressed.

You are responsible for helping the oppressors and the oppressed of Pakistan since they are nearer to you than those in Kashmir. You first ought to fight oppression in Pakistan in aid of the oppressed.

MUJAHID: Brother, the point to note here is this: on one side we have oppressive and cruel polytheistic Hindu rulers, and on the other side, we have oppressive and cruel Muslim rulers. Which of the two sides is more threatening? Which side should be engaged militarily and which one deserves to be forgiven and corrected? Under these circumstances we invite Muslim rulers to fight the polytheists, Allah-willing. This is how we help Muslim rulers in aid of Muslims who are oppressed.

Danger of Fighting Politicians and Government Officials

INQUIRER: *jihad* is urgently needed in Pakistan because of rampant corruption in the country. DSPs (District Superintendent of Police) are corrupt, SSPs (Senior Superintendent of Police) rely on extortion, and even IGs (Inspector General of Police) are busy greasing their palms. Every level of our administration, from the lowest rung of the registrar to the commissioner at the top, is run by corrupt officials. Even our judiciary has been taken over by unscrupulous individuals. It seems enemy agents have infiltrated our armed forces as well. For the past fifty years politicians have been lying to the people while milking the country. It seems odd that in this situation you would leave your oppressed countrymen at the mercy of such traitors to wage *jihad* in a distant land.

MUJAHID: Brother, Islam has prescribed specific penalties for every kind of crime; a thief and a person who accepts bribes are not treated equally. Similarly, if a Muslim commits a crime, he will be punished accordingly but he cannot be declared a disbeliever and consequently killed. In reality, those who oppose the *jihad* in Kashmir would rather *mujahideen* abandon their war against Hindu soldiers and wage their *jihad* in Pakistan against the administration, the judiciary, the politicians, and the armed forces.

INQUIRER: Absolutely! These people explicitly state that *jihad* must first be waged against the oppressive rulers of Pakistan before it is taken abroad.

MUJAHID: *Markaz-ud-Dawah-wal-Irshad* is fulfilling its domestic obligation by proselytizing to local leaders and congregations. If you pay attention, you will note our presence in offices, schools, colleges, and university campuses. We engage the armed forces, the administration, and the judiciary. Politicians are being urged to replace the democratic system with a caliphate and join the dual process of proselytizing and waging *jihad.*

INQUIRER: While Hindus are oppressing Muslims in Kashmir, our grave-worshipping leaders are busy oppressing Muslims in Pakistan. Does it make any sense to help distant victims as opposed to the ones in your own backyard?

MUJAHID: Brother, you must understand that on one hand we're talking about Muslim oppressors and on the other hand we have polytheists as oppressors; this makes all the difference. A Muslim, no matter how depraved, must be dealt with according to his crime, while a disbeliever must be fought as an obligation to Allah. Having determined that the Prophet is a model of excellence worth emulating in every situation, let us consider the prophet's life in terms of our specific dilemma.

Hypocrites among the prophet's followers were constantly conspiring to harm the nascent Muslim community. On various occasions their conspiracies were exposed and the prophet's companions sought permission to kill them. The prophet refused every time, saying he did not want it said that he (the prophet) killed his own people.

110 THE LITERATURE OF *LASHKAR-E-TAYYABA*

Brother, it is obvious that not only did the prophet disapprove of fighting other Muslims, or Muslim rulers, he did not even allow his companions to attack the hypocrites conspiring against Islam.

Jihadi Tactics Against the Enemy

It is essential to devise tactics according to the strength and nature of the enemy. For example:

During the Battle of Khandaq, the pagans of Mecca were the foreign enemy while the Jews of Banu Quraiza were the internal foe. The prophet first defeated the pagans before he turned his attention to Banu Quraiza. Approximately seven hundred Jews were beheaded for their treachery before their wealth was distributed as war booty. There was a third kind of enemy as well. These were the hypocrites within the Muslim camp, but their lives were spared considering there was no one left for them to conspire with, and also because they professed to be Muslims.

Thus, it is important that the Muslim nation unites against the disbelievers and resolutely marches upon the enemy. We must resolve our internal conflicts through mutual understanding, dialogue, and preaching, and we must avoid rebellion and civil war at all cost.

INQUIRER: You are right, to some extent, but your refusal to battle those who exploit the poor is beyond me. Why are you against attacking the oppressors? They are only interested in personal power, they abuse their authority, and they have no regard for the masses. Combatting them is nothing less than *jihad*.

MUJAHID: *jihad* cannot be waged against a fellow Muslim. What we can do is preach more effectively to make the rulers change their ways. In this regard, *Markaz-ud-Dawah-wal-Irshad* is performing its obligation to some extent but institutionalized proselytizing is an objective that has yet to be realized.

INQUIRER: So far, I have concluded that you are unwilling to fight Muslim rulers, but you are hell-bent on continuing your guerrilla warfare in Kashmir as a *jihad*.

MUJAHID: We must employ different strategies when trying to make Muslim rulers honour the rights of Islam as opposed to when we make disbelievers honour the rights of Allah, the rights of Allah's men, and the rights of Islam. Islam has taught us these different methods and we will follow Allah and the prophet's example in the following way:

- Claim our rights from the disbelievers.
- Avenge all the injustices of the disbelievers.
- Free Muslims from the oppression of the enemy.
- Carry out guerrilla warfare.
- Ambush the enemy.
- Target the enemy's military caravans and convoys.
- Destroy the enemy's military supplies.
- Destroy the enemy's military operations.
- Destroy the enemy's communication resources.
- Destroy the enemy's arms manufacturing factories.
- Send every enemy combatant, from the foot soldier to the general, to hell.
- Destroy Bal Thackeray and every member of his organization.
- This war will go on either until the end of perfidious disbelief or until we drink of the elixir of martyrdom and return to our eternal home in paradise, Allah-willing. Allah states in the Quran:

slay the idolaters wherever ye find them, and take them (captive), and besiege them, and prepare for them each ambush. But if they repent and establish worship and pay the poor due, then leave their way free. Lo! Allah is Forgiving, Merciful.

(Surat at-Tawbah 9:5)

Brother, understand that this is the Islamic way to claim your right from the disbeliever. Do not be oblivious to the enemy's exploitations, for life is short.

Chapter 4: Significance of the Sequence of the Meccan and Medinite Periods

INQUIRER: Is *Markaz-ud-Dawah* justly waging *jihad*?

112 THE LITERATURE OF *LASHKAR-E-TAYYABA*

MUJAHID: Thanks to Allah, this *jihad* is being waged according to the Quran and *Sunnat*.

INQUIRER: For the conquest of the true faith the prophet preferred proselytizing which is why he did not wage *jihad* in Mecca. In contrast, you are slaughtering disbelievers in Kashmir and sacrificing the valuable lives of your own men. How can you say your *jihad* is in accordance with the *Sunnat*? Our missionary brothers say it is better to lead a disbeliever into the heaven of faith than kill him and send him to hell, for this is what the prophet did.

MUJAHID: Do you only follow the commandments revealed during the Meccan period?

INQUIRER: No, I follow Islam in its entirety.

MUJAHID: Keep in mind it makes no sense for us to distinguish between the Meccan and Medinite periods in this day and age since Islam has been revealed in its entirety. We are obligated to follow all the commandments. Below are some examples for greater clarity:

- A thief confesses to his crime in court but claims his hand cannot be amputated because he is passing through the Meccan phase of his belief while amputation was enforced as a punishment in Medina.
- A drunkard presented in court claims he is passing through the Meccan phase and alcohol was only prohibited in Medina; he should therefore not be punished under Islamic law.
- A murderer confesses to his crime but claims he only recently accepted Islam so first he must be allowed to live through the thirteen years of Meccan Islam before entering the Medinite period and hence his capital punishment must be postponed.
- A butcher is caught selling mule's meat as food but claims this flesh was legal the first eighteen years of Islam, until it was prohibited at the Battle of Khaybar;[10] so, he only sells it to those who are under eighteen while older people are sold halal meat.
- A fornicator claims that a hundred lashes or lapidation were only revealed as punishments in Medina.
- The one who enters a temporary marriage can also claim that temporary marriages were prohibited after the Battle of Khaybar.
- Usurious traders can make similar claims.

Now, tell me, are these excuses acceptable? Absolutely not! Islam has been revealed in its entirety. If we cater to its chronology the Islamic society will become a moral mess.

Today, if we lived according to the Meccan period of Islam, a number of our treasured obligations would cease. For example:

- Congregational prayers and the call to prayer never occurred in Mecca; hence, this practice would end.
- The Friday prayer was not obligatory in Mecca; this would be optional as well.
- Fasting during Ramazan was not obligatory in Mecca; perfect excuse for those who do not want to fast.
- The pilgrimage was not obligatory in Mecca either; good excuse for the wealthy miser to avoid spending his money on this sacred tour.
- Zakat was only made mandatory in Medina; another good excuse for the wealthy miser to horde his wealth.

Follow Islam in Its Entirety

Brother, if we get caught up in the chronology of the Meccan and Medinite periods, a number of our most binding Islamic obligations will disappear. The truth is that after the revelation of the faith in its entirety there is no concept of a specific period to follow. Consider the following commandment in the Quran:

> O ye who believe! Come, all of you, into submission (unto Him); and follow not the footsteps of the devil. Lo! he is an open enemy for you.
> (*Surat al-Baqarah* 2:208)

Brother, your claim that it is better to lead a disbeliever to paradise through conversion than to slaughter him and send him to hell, sounds very charming but is rooted in your ignorance of the prophet's life. If what you claim was true, the prophet would never have killed a single disbeliever; there would be no commandment to wage *jihad*, and proselytizing would have been our paramount obligation. The blessed companions would never have had to make sacrifices on the battlefield and martyrdom

114   THE LITERATURE OF *LASHKAR-E-TAYYABA*

could have been achieved without raising a finger. But, in contrast, battles were fought, and thousands of infidels were slaughtered and sent to hell. Muslims celebrated the day when Abu Jahl's corpse, along with countless infidel corpses, was dumped in a dormant well after the Battle of Badr.

Brother, your claim that it is better to lead a disbeliever to paradise through proselytizing is also false. We are obligated to proselytize, but guidance is only in the hands of Allah.

Guidance was Beyond the Prophet

The prophet persistently and affectionately preached to his uncle Abu Talib till the latter's last breath but to no avail. Abu Talib died an infidel. The prophet was deeply distraught by this, but Allah said:

> Lo! thou (O Muhammad) guidest not whom thou lovest, but Allah guideth whom He will. And He is best aware of those who walk aright.
> (*Surat al-Qasas* 28:56)

Similarly, to say there was no combat in Mecca is also false. Many blessed companions were attacked in Mecca and those that could defend themselves did so. For example: After Syedna Umar ibn al-Khattab [Umar, Son of Al-Khattab, usually referred to simply as 'Umar']. converted to Islam, a pagan called Jamil bin Muammar Jamhi went through town crying out that Khattab's son has lost his religion. Syedna Umar followed his trail, calling back, 'Not at all! I have accepted Islam!' The pagans of Mecca fell upon Syedna Umar who fought back with all his might. In the course of the scuffle he declared, 'Listen up! I swear upon Allah, if there were three hundred of us, Mecca would be too small for your lot and ours' (*Tarikh Umar bin al-Khattab*[11]).

Syedna Umar's declaration makes clear that if Muslims had the power, they would have taken on the pagans but at the time Allah had not permitted fighting. However, the prophet and the companions had been given portents of future military engagements with the disbelievers that would require Muslims to make unimaginable sacrifices. Allah had yet to reveal the most arduous commandments obligating Muslims to wage a grand *jihad* against the enemy.

strive against them (the disbelievers) herewith with a great endeavour.

(*Surat al-Furqan* 25:52)

Allah informed the prophet of a gruelling life ahead in which there would be no time for rest, in which he was to rise and make the world tremble with fear before god. He was to rise carrying a great burden:

We shall charge thee with a word of weight.

(*Surat al-Muzammil* 73:5)

Brother, in light of Allah's portents, the prophet and his companions eagerly awaited the commandment to wage *jihad*.

People of Quraysh! I Have Been Sent with The Commandment to Slaughter You!

Once, when the prophet was circumambulating the Ka'ba, infidels gathered in the sanctuary and cried out, 'We cannot endure this man's presence here anymore!' After kissing the black stone, as the prophet continued with his rituals the infidels began taunting him. The prophet was clearly upset. Syedna Abdullah bin Amr bin Aas was also present. He reports that when the prophet passed by the infidels a second time, they became more vocal with their aspersions, which upset the prophet further. When the prophet passed them a third time, they continued slandering him. Finally, he stopped, turned to them and said, 'People of Quraysh, listen up! By the one who holds my life in His hands, I have been sent to you (with the commandment) to slaughter (you)' (*Ar-Raheeq al-Makhtum*[12]).

The Prophet Personally Killed Ubay ibn Khalaf

Ubay ibn Khalaf was an influential tribal chief in Mecca, preoccupied with schemes to rid the city of the prophet. He owned a horse that he overfed with a daily supply of seven hundred and fifty kilogrammes of grain. Whenever Ubay ibn Khalaf crossed paths with the prophet, he

116 THE LITERATURE OF *LASHKAR-E-TAYYABA*

would tell the latter that he was fattening a horse called Awad for a direct and fatal confrontation with the prophet.

The prophet would respond, 'Ubay, you cannot kill me. It is I who will kill you.' During the Battle of Uhud,[13] the prophet discharged a spear at Abi who fell off his horse and crawled back to his camp crying, 'By Allah, Muhammad has killed me.' Those who saw him were puzzled because there was neither a wound nor blood but he kept crying out, 'He told me in Mecca that he will kill me, therefore, by Allah, even if he merely spat at me, I would not have survived.' He started bellowing like a wounded bull, 'By Allah, if my current pain was distributed among all the men of Zil Majaz, none of them would survive.' The miserable man finally died on his way back to Mecca (Ibn Hisham, Chapter 2, 48; and *Zad al-Ma'ad*, Chapter 2, 97, as referenced in *Ar-Raheeq al-Makhtum*[14]).

In light of these references, it is evident that in the conflict between truth and falsehood, those within Mecca who could defend themselves, did so, and those who were weak, suffered. In these unfortunate times, the blessed companions sought permission to engage the oppressors, but the prophet said, 'restrain yourselves'.

Chapter 5: Significance of Lack and Abundance in *Jihad*

INQUIRER: *Markaz-ud-Dawah-wal-Irshad* has been criticized for causing countless deaths in Kashmir.

MUJAHID: This kind of thinking is flawed. The time and place of a person's death is predetermined because life and death are entirely in the hands of Allah. The Quran states:

First Proof:

Wheresoever ye may be, death will overtake you, even though ye were in lofty towers.

(Surat an-Nisa 4:78)

Second Proof:

Yet if a happy thing befalleth them they say: This is from Allah; and if an evil thing befalleth them they say: This is of thy doing (O Muhammad). Say (unto them): All is from Allah. What is amiss with these people that they come not nigh to understand a happening?

(Surat an-Nisa 4:78)

INQUIRER: No Muslim denies the fact that life and death are in the hands of Allah; the point is that you dispatch a few moderately trained warriors on suicidal missions to engage seven hundred thousand well-trained Hindu soldiers armed with advanced weapons.

Don't Think Like Disbelievers

Allah has forbidden Muslims from thinking this way for this is the attitude of the disbeliever. The Quran clearly states:

O ye who believe! Be not as those who disbelieved and said of their brethren who went abroad in the land or were fighting in the field: If they had been (here) with us they would not have died or been killed; that Allah may make it anguish in their hearts. Allah giveth life and causeth death; and Allah is Seer of what ye do.

(Surat al-Imran 3:156)

A Challenge: Escape Death

Allah describes those who do not participate in *jihad* as follows:

Those who, while they sat at home, said of their brethren (who were fighting for the cause of Allah): If they had been guided by us, they would not have been slain. Say (unto them, O Muhammad): Then avert death from yourselves if ye are truthful.

(Surat al-Imran 3:168)

118 THE LITERATURE OF *LASHKAR-E-TAYYABA*

These verses state explicitly that it is beneath a Muslim to pity or lament those headed for the battlefield, or, to suggest that had these *mujahideen* not waged *jihad* they would not have died so miserably. Allah describes the glory of a martyr precisely to prevent Muslims from adopting this attitude:

And call not those who are slain in the way of Allah 'dead'. Nay, they are living, only ye perceive not.

(*Surat al-Baqarah* 2:154)

INQUIRER: It is not a fair fight when you have a handful of *mujahideen* take on seven hundred thousand soldiers; it doesn't even make sense to call the ones who die in this battle martyrs. This is equivalent to shedding blood in vain.

MUJAHID: The battle between Islam and disbelief has always been initiated by the prophets. Should the prophets have given up their task simply because there were too many disbelievers?

Similarly, the blessed companions of the prophet never wavered before going into battle, neither did they argue over numbers. Below is a brief but convincing glimpse of the battlefields in which the prophet's followers waged *jihad*.

A Statistical Survey of the Muslim and Pagan Armies

1. Consider the Battle of Badr in which an army of one thousand well-supplied and heavily armed pagans fought a Muslim force of three hundred and thirteen men who possessed only eight swords, six spears, two horses, and seventy camels.

2. In the Battle of Uhud, the Muslim army, fourteen hundred and fifty men strong, was vastly outnumbered by three thousand pagans. Muslims were dealt a heavy blow having lost seventy disciples of the prophet; the hypocrites among them seized the opportunity to demoralize the army by saying they could have prevented the bloodbath had they had more control. Allah admonished them for their ignorance, claiming all control was in His hands.

'IN DEFENCE OF *JIHAD*' 119

Say: Even though ye had been in your houses, those appointed to be slain would have gone forth to the places where they were to lie (3:154).[15]

Listed below you will find some more statistics on the battles waged by the followers of the prophet to remove any and all doubt about when to wage *jihad* and when to hold back.

3. In the Battle of Saif-ul-Bahar,[16] thirty Muslims battled three hundred disbelievers.
4. In the Battle of Ahzab, three thousand soldiers fought alongside the prophet against an army of ten thousand.
5. In the Battle of Khaybar, fourteen hundred Muslims took on an enemy ten thousand strong.
6. In the Battle of Mu'tah, three thousand Muslims fought two hundred thousand disbelievers. Only three Muslims were martyred. The prophet had personally dispatched the Muslim troops. Did the prophet send these men to have their blood spilled in vain? Heaven forbid! No person who fears Allah should raise such issues.

INQUIRER: You are right but when I think of our young men, the beloved sons of the soil, sent thousands of miles away from home to die alone at the hands of Hindu soldiers I cannot help but wish this bloodbath would end.

MUJAHID: In the nascent years of Islam, mothers raised their sons for the sole purpose of sending them into battle to lay their lives for Allah. Today, mothers of our fearless warriors are emulating the women of yore. They themselves send their sons into the battlefield because they have full faith in Allah's promises; they have made a bargain with Allah. In the Quran, Allah describes the glory bestowed upon the tortured body that falls on the battlefield:

Think not of those, who are slain in the way of Allah, as dead. Nay, they are living. With their Lord they have provision. Jubilant (are they) because of that which Allah hath bestowed upon them of His bounty...

(*Surat āl 'im'rān* 3:169–170)

120   THE LITERATURE OF *LASHKAR-E-TAYYABA*

Brother, the martyr's esteemed status is unrivalled. Allah bestows unparalleled glories and honours upon him. In light of this glory, the prophet said:

I wish to die for Allah's cause and to be reincarnated only to die in Allah's cause again, and to be reincarnated again to die in his path again.
(Bukhari, *Kitab-al-Jihad*, *Sahih Muslim*, *Kitab al-Jihad wa'l-Siyar*[17])

Brother when Allah's prophet wishes to bear battle-scars on his body and hopes to die for Allah's cause, isn't it strange for a Muslim to look down upon such a death? Doesn't this attitude stink of hypocrisy?

INQUIRER: In *Surat al-Anfal*, Allah puts in perspective the battle between Islam and disbelief. Consider this verse:

Now hath Allah lightened your burden, for He knoweth that there is weakness in you. So if there be of you a steadfast hundred, they shall overcome two hundred, and if there be of you a thousand (steadfast) they shall overcome two thousand by permission of Allah. Allah is with the steadfast.

(*Surat al-Anfal* 8:66)

In light of this verse, pitting a few *mujahideen* against a Hindu force eight hundred thousand strong is wrong. Clearly, this verse implies we should at least be half as strong as the enemy.

MUJAHID: This verse was revealed in 2 AH; it addresses the nascent Muslim community regarding the initial phases of *jihad*. Before we consider the practical steps taken by the prophet in light of this verse, it is essential to keep in mind he alone is the best interpreter, predictor, and explicator of these verses since the Quran was revealed to him.

A Statistical Analysis of the Prophet's Campaigns

Given the figures in Table 5.1, it is clear as day that in the battle between truth and falsehood, the enemy has always outnumbered Muslims, often, by more than double.

'IN DEFENCE OF *JIHAD*' 121

Table 5.1 lists various battles in which Muslims were outnumbered but victorious.[22]

Campaign	No. of *mujahideen*	No. of Enemy Troops	Analysis
1 A.H Battle of Saif-ul-Bahar	30	300	10 disbelievers per Muslim
2 A.H Battle of Badr	313	1,000	3 disbelievers per Muslim
3 A.H Battle of Uhud	650	3,000	4 disbelievers per Muslim
3 A.H Battle of Hamra al-Assad[23]	540	2,970	Over 5 disbelievers per Muslim
5 A.H Battle of Khandaq	3,000	10,000	Over 3 disbelievers per Muslim
7 A.H Battle of Khaybar	1,400	10,000	Over 7 Jews per Muslim
8 A.H Battle of Mu'tah	3,000	200,000	67 disbelievers per Muslim

At no point did the followers of the prophet ask for an estimate of the enemy's forces before going into battle. In fact, we observe the following:

- The prophet stayed abreast of any given situation; where necessary, he would lead his men into battle himself; at other times he would appoint one of his companions to command the troops. Only later would they discover that... each Muslim was up against three, four, even eight, disbelievers.
- ...in the Battle of Mu'tah each Muslim soldier battled up to sixty-six disbelievers.

Invariably, the enemy turned tail and ran, leaving behind nothing but the dead.

Muslims returned from these wars victorious, self-assured, and wealthy (with loot).

INQUIRER: During the Battle of Khandaq, when the enemy forces were more than double the size of the Muslim camp, the prophet commanded

122 THE LITERATURE OF *LASHKAR-E-TAYYABA*

his men to dig a trench around the city instead of marching out to the battlefield. Has *Lashkar-e-Tayyaba* gathered at least half the number of Indian soldiers in Kashmir before waging *jihad* there? And if not, does this not go against the *Sunnat* of our prophet?

MUJAHID: Cowards look for excuses to avoid war; those who insist on having half the enemy's strength would not go near the battlefield even if we produced twice the men. Brother, your question implies that the Battle of Khandaq was never even fought.

INQUIRER: That is true; due to the steps taken by the prophet, this battle never occurred.

MUJAHID: Then why do we call it the Battle of Khandaq? Let us consider a brief *summary* of this battle.

The pagans of Mecca laid siege to Medina for a whole month until Allah sent them packing with a severe storm that wrecked their tents, put out their fires, and destroyed their camp. Neither man nor beast could bear the freezing temperatures.

Syedna Hazeefa bin Yaman, one of the prophet's spies, brought news of the enemy's retreat. By morning, the siege had ended and the last of the infidels had left.

- Six disciples were martyred in this battle.
- Syedna Saad bin Maaz was severely wounded; later he succumbed to his injuries and died.
- Ten infidels were sent to hell and twenty camels were seized as war booty. How can one say this battle was not fought when the prophet himself prayed for victory?
- Why were the companions nervous?
- Why did the hypocrites avoid battle by making excuses, such as:

'Our homes lie open (to the enemy).'
To which Allah responded:
And they lay not open. They but wished to flee.

(*Surat al-Azhab* 33:13)

- If there was no battle how were twenty camels acquired as loot?
- If this battle never took place how did six disciples lose their lives?

'IN DEFENCE OF *JIHAD*' 123

- In the absence of combat how were ten pagans killed?
- Why did ten thousand pagans from various Arab tribes join forces?

A trench was dug up for this battle under the command of the prophet as part of a military strategy.

Because there was a battle, Allah made Muslims victorious; the Quran says:

O ye who believe Remember Allah's favour unto you when there came against you hosts, and We sent against them a great wind and hosts ye could not see. And Allah is ever Seer of what ye do.

(*Surat al-Azhab* 33:9)

When they came upon you from above you and from below you, and when eyes grew wild and hearts reached to the throats, and ye were imagining vain thoughts concerning Allah.

(*Surat al-Azhab* 33:10)

There were the believers sorely tried and shaken with a mighty shock.

(*Surat al-Azhab* 33:11)

INQUIRER: Given the massive force accumulated by the infidels, the prophet had a trench dug up as part of his strategy to avoid bloodshed in battle. It was due to his foresight that only six Muslims lost their lives.

MUJAHID: Brother, every time the infidels approached the battlefield, they planned to wipe Muslims off the face of the earth. It was Allah who sabotaged their nefarious strategies to make Muslims victorious.

INQUIRER: There is no doubt that, at least in the Battle of Khandaq, the prophet's foresight and military planning saved Muslims from suffering heavily.

MUJAHID: Military planning plays an important role on the battlefield but does not guarantee victory. Victory and defeat are in the hands of Allah. By your reasoning, are you suggesting the prophet's strategizing was inadequate for the Battle of Uhud (May Allah forgive me for saying so)?

124 THE LITERATURE OF *LASHKAR-E-TAYYABA*

INQUIRER: Not at all! But Muslims suffered in that battle because they did not follow his command.

MUJAHID: So, it is obvious that strategy alone cannot win wars; Allah's help and blessings are essential for victory.

INQUIRER: It is true that victory and defeat lie in Allah's hands but for now we are talking about military strategy.

MUJAHID: In the Battle of Mu'tah, three thousand Muslims were up against two hundred thousand disbelievers; that is one Muslim against sixty-seven disbelievers; only twelve Muslims were martyred. Two hundred thousand enemy forces surrounded the Muslim camp. Only Allah's blessings shielded Muslims from heavy losses.

INQUIRER: In the Battle of Khandaq, when three thousand Muslims faced ten thousand infidels, which is one Muslim against more than three infidels, only six Muslims were martyred. In the Battle of Mu'tah, three thousand Muslims battled two hundred thousand disbelievers, and lost only twelve men. These numbers do not add up.

MUJAHID: Precisely! Thus, it makes no sense to believe that military tactics alone won the Battle of Khandaq; would you say the companions' strategies in the Battle of Mu'tah were superior to those of the prophet? Such talk can only come from a devious mind.

INQUIRER: You say that each Muslim faced up to sixty-seven or so infidels; these numbers are staggering. It is possible that the verse that states a hundred Muslims will overcome two hundred disbelievers was revealed after this war.

MUJAHID: Brother, as I have already mentioned, the verse was revealed in 2 AH while the Battle of Mu'tah occurred in 8 AH.

INQUIRER: This means the battle was fought at least six years after the revelation.

MUJAHID: Indeed, this event took place many years after this revelation.

Details of the Battle of Mu'tah

INQUIRER: Please give some details about the historical Battle of Mu'tah.

MUJAHID: The prophet appointed Syedna Zayd bin Harthah the military commander and told the troops that should Zayd be killed, Jafar was to take charge, and should Jafar die, Abdullah bin Rawaha was to be the emirate.

As people bid the troops farewell, Abdullah bin Rawaha started crying. Everyone was shocked to see him in this state; normally, this was considered an auspicious occasion for the companions of the prophet anxiously awaited an opportunity to fight in Allah's cause.

When asked why he was crying Syedna Abdullah said, 'Listen, I swear to Allah I am not crying because I love this world or because I will miss you all. I am crying because I heard the prophet recite the following verse from the Quran:

There is not one of you but shall approach it (hell). That is a fixed ordinance of thy Lord.

(*Surat Maryam* 19:71)

I do not know if, once I approach hell, I will be able to turn back.'

The companions consoled him and said, 'May Allah watch over you, and may Allah return you and your war loot safely to us.'

At this point Syedna Abdullah recited some moving poetry, which translates to:

I seek salvation with Rahman (Allah's name which means merciful); I beg Allah to expose me to a sword that splits a person, or a spear that pierces organs, so when people pass by my grave, they say this grave belongs to a warrior who was guided by Allah.

The prophet gave some last-minute advice to the troops before dispatching them. The military commander sent scouts ahead of the army who reported that the Romans, a hundred thousand strong, had reached a place called Maab, where they were joined by an alliance of Arab tribesmen, also one hundred thousand men strong. The Muslim commander informed his troops about the enemy they were up against; no one was expecting an enemy this size. Many suggested that instead of marching on, they ought to update the prophet about the situation and seek his advice.

For two days, the generals discussed whether to march on or consult the prophet for reinforcements.

126 THE LITERATURE OF *LASHKAR-E-TAYYABA*

One of Two Blessings is Our Destiny

Syedna Zayd bin Harthah addressed his soldiers:

'Listen up!' he said. 'I swear upon Allah, you fear martyrdom whereas we left our homes in search of it.'
'We do not fight the enemy on the strength of our resources or men; we fight in the name of Allah. March on, for one of two blessings is our destiny; either we will be victorious, or we will be martyred, Allah-willing.'

With these words, the generals decided to move forward. They encountered and engaged the enemy ferociously. Three thousand Muslim soldiers battled an overwhelming force of two hundred thousand men.

Zayd bin Harthah, the commander in chief, held high the banner of Islam and fought bravely before being martyred.

The next in command, Syedna Jafar Tayyar, stepped up to the plate; he took hold of the banner and blazed through the battlefield, trampling the enemy every way he went. When, at some point, he lost his right hand, he immediately took up the banner in his left.

When the enemy chopped off his left hand, he positioned the banner between his arms until he was killed in the midst of battle. His body bore ninety battle scars at the time of his martyrdom.

Syedna Abdullah immediately took charge and declared, in verse: O my life, enter the battlefield... aggressively or inadvertently, the flames of war have been blazed... spears will soon be discharged... why do I see you so far from paradise?

His cousin offered him a meal. Syedna Abdullah tore the flesh off a single bone, before grabbing his sword, and plunging into the enemy's ranks. He slaughtered as many disbelievers as he could until he himself was martyred.

News from the Battle Front

The angel Gabriel delivers news of the martyrdoms to the prophet. The prophet repeats the news to his companions: Zayd held the banner but he was martyred. Jafar bin Abi Talib took up the banner but he too was martyred. Abdullah bin Rawaha bore the banner and was martyred as well.

The prophet shed tears as he continued: One of Allah's swords holds up the banner; now Allah bestows victory.

Khalid bin Walid was made commander of the Muslim forces. He launched a terrifying attack in which, he said, 'I went through nine swords until all I had left was a Yemeni machete.'

The Roman troops completely engulfed the Muslims. They were amazed by how such a small army held its ground.

One day, Khalid bin Walid started repositioning his men; the Romans misinterpreted this as a declaration of defeat, but as the Muslim forces withdrew the Romans were convinced this was an attempt to lure them into an ambush. The Romans halted their operations and left the battlefield without pursuing the Muslim troops. Thus, the latter returned to Medina, victorious and safe.

Brother, in light of all these proofs, we believe that statistics regarding resources and manpower do not matter; all that matters is one's sincerity on the battlefield, beyond which both victory and defeat are in Allah's hands. Consider one more example so there is no doubt left in your mind: When the prophet led a sizeable Muslim army in the Battle of Hunayn, many of his men could not contain their conceit over their sheer size. Within moments of the war, Muslims were dealt a terrible blow and they started retreating from the battlefield. Only the prophet remained with a few blessed companions. Sometime later, when the rest of his companions joined him, Allah granted them victory. Allah mentioned this event in the Quran, in the twenty-fifth verse of *Surat at-Tawbah*.

Allah hath given you victory on many fields and on the day of Hunayn, when ye exulted in your multitude but it availed you naught, and the earth, vast as it is, was straitened for you; then ye turned back in flight.

(*Surat at-Tawbah* 9:25)

Brother, keep these facts in mind and remember, a true Muslim never gets bogged down by battlefield statistics because he knows he will be granted one of the following two blessings:

1. The crown of martyrdom in paradise.
2. Bounteous victories that will see him home, laden with war loot.

128 THE LITERATURE OF *LASHKAR-E-TAYYABA*

INQUIRER: Our government is equipped with advanced weapons, trained soldiers, and various other resources, and yet it cannot muster the courage to take on the enemy. On the other hand, you talk of engaging seven hundred thousand Hindu soldiers with a handful of *mujahideen*. This sounds strange and impossible.

MUJAHID: I have already given you proof of how a true *mujahid* is beyond the constraints of statistical analysis for he relies only on Allah's word when entering the battlefield. Similarly, believe it or not, we sacrifice our lives only for Allah's approval. It is obvious that victory does not depend on the relative size of the army but on the will of Allah.

But those who knew that they would meet their Lord exclaimed: How many a little company hath overcome a mighty host by Allah's leave! Allah is with the steadfast.

(*Surat al-Baqarah* 2:249)

INQUIRER: While it is true that victory does not depend on the size of your troops but on the will of Allah, it seems like the *mujahideen* of *Markaz-ud-Dawah-wal-Irshad* have been fighting in Kashmir for ages without even a momentary glimpse of victory on the horizon.

MUJAHID: Through the benefits of *jihad*, Allah is bestowing many victories upon the *mujahideen* but do not blame them if you are unable to perceive this.

- Second, can victory ever be evident before the fight is up?
- Third, did the blessed companions ever ask the prophet to give them a timeline regarding the domination of the true faith?
- Fourth, is it necessary for victory to be evident?

No doubt, no blessed companion ever asked such questions; their task was to follow orders. They marched into battle on command, indifferent to triumph and defeat. In emulation of these blessed men, we too offer our lives and the lives of our children, in Allah's path; when Allah pleases, he will make us victorious, but as long as Allah wishes to keep testing us, battles will rage. The fortunate among us will voluntarily march on, while the reluctant ones will stay back and make excuses, Allah-willing.

'IN DEFENCE OF *JIHAD*' 129

INQUIRER: The prophet was able to make Islam dominant within twenty-three years while *Markaz-ud-Dawah-wal-Irshad* has achieved nothing in so long; is this not proof that you are not waging a legitimate *jihad*?

MUJAHID: Drawing comparisons with the prophet's life and raising such issues is a sign of ignorance and narrow-mindedness. Consider the following examples from the lives of the prophets:

Example 1

The Prophet Noah preached for nine hundred years and only a handful of people accepted his message. Allah says, regarding the Prophet Noah:

> And but a few were they who believed with him.
>
> (*Surat Hud* 11:40)

Given these facts would you dare say the Prophet Noah failed simply because only a few people converted (Heaven forbid)?

Example 2

When the prophet started preaching could anyone have imagined the extent of his success? Could anyone have believed, then, that *jihadi* missions would lead to such glorious victories? No one thought that Muslims would slaughter so many infidels in battle? Absolutely not! Consider the following Quranic verses:

> Ye (Muslims) slew them not, but Allah slew them. And thou (Muhammad) threwest not when thou didst throw, but Allah threw, that He might test the believers by a fair test from Him. Lo! Allah is Hearer, Knower.
>
> (*Surat al-Anfal* 8:17)

Example 3

When the Jews planned to murder the prophet, Allah warned him of their iniquity; as a result, the prophet immediately exited their congregation. Later, the prophet battled the Jews and exiled them from Medina. Details of this event can be found in *Surat al-Hashr*:

130 THE LITERATURE OF *LASHKAR-E-TAYYABA*

He it is Who hath caused those of the People of the Scripture who disbelieved to go forth from their homes unto the first exile. Ye deemed not that they would go forth, while they deemed that their strongholds would protect them from Allah. But Allah reached them from a place whereof they reckoned not, and cast terror in their hearts so that they ruined their houses with their own hands and the hands of the believers. So, learn a lesson, O ye who have eyes!

(*Surat al-Hashr* 59:2)

Brother, the verses above settle the matter regarding one's striving by way of *jihad*. Simpleminded Muslims are being misguided by the comparisons drawn between the Prophet's successes in his twenty-three-year career and our timeline in Kashmir. Allah responds categorically to such misgivings:

1. You weren't slaughtering infidels on the battlefield, Allah was.
2. No one could have imagined exiling the Jews.
3. They themselves could not imagine being exiled, having fortified themselves heavily, but see how Allah threw them out?

Similarly, the fortifications and barricades of the Hindu army in Kashmir do not worry us in the least because Allah is the one who will destroy these fortifications and make the *mujahideen* triumphant. Thanks to Allah, the *jihad* in Kashmir grows stronger every day as we rapidly march towards glory. Very soon, Muslims will receive the glad tidings of victory. No war was ever won with words; triumph comes with making sacrifices, and with Allah's blessings.

INQUIRER: The enemy in Kashmir is equipped with modern weapons, seven hundred thousand men, barracks, and airpower; how can such an enemy be defeated?

MUJAHID: Islamic military history is replete with examples in which the enemy stormed the battlefield with superior firepower only to turn tail and run. The prophet and his companions were often beset by a lack of resources.

'IN DEFENCE OF *JIHAD*' 131

Let us briefly consider the Battle of Khandaq in which Muslims fought with fortitude and courage while the hypocrites were plagued with fear and anxiety; every one of you reading this can identify the camp to which you, the reader, belong.

During the Battle of Khandaq, Muslims faced all kinds of adversity. Due to widespread famine, one companion told the prophet that he tied a stone over his stomach to kill his hunger, to which the prophet replied, he too had done the same. Under these circumstances, when a trench was being dug around Medina, the companions hit upon a boulder that they could not budge. The prophet himself arrived at the spot, axe in hand.

When the prophet struck the boulder, sparks flew. He said Allah-Akbar and told his companions he had been given the keys to Syria and by Allah, he could see its red palaces.

When the prophet struck the boulder a second time, it split. Again, he cried Allah-Akbar and told his companions he had been given Persia and he could clearly see the white palaces of Madain.

Upon the third strike, the boulder disintegrated, and the prophet said, 'Allah-Akbar, I have been given Yemen; by Allah, I can see the gates of Sana from where I stand.'

The hypocrites did not believe in these prophecies. They bickered about the famine, the siege, the fact that no one could leave the city for supplies or rations, and the horror of confronting the superpower of the time. They had no faith in the prophet (Heaven-forbid).

The Quran touches upon their hypocrisy in the following verse:

And When the hypocrites, and those in whose hearts is a disease, were saying: Allah and His messenger promised us naught but delusion.

(*Surat al-Azhab* 33:12)

On the other hand, Allah describes the condition of the true believers in the following words:

And when the true believers saw the clans, they said: This is that which Allah and His messenger promised us. Allah and His messenger are true. It did but confirm them in their faith and resignation.

(*Surat al-Azhab* 33:22)

132 THE LITERATURE OF *LASHKAR-E-TAYYABA*

INQUIRER: But there isn't even a hint of success; every day we hear of losses in Kashmir and our deepest misgivings are affirmed by numerous absentia funeral prayers. All of this reeks of defeat.

MUJAHID: Whether a *mujahid* returns in glory or is martyred in battle, he is always triumphant. Consider what Allah says in the Quran:

> Let those fight in the way of Allah who sell the life of this world for the other. Whoso fighteth in the way of Allah, be he slain or be he victorious, on him We shall bestow a vast reward.
>
> *(Surat an-Nisa* 4:74)

Victory and defeat are neither in the hands of the *mujahideen*, nor did the prophet control them. In fact, adversity and strife are a precondition for *jihad*, as attested in the Quran:

First Example

> Allah hath given you victory on many fields and on the day of Hunayn, when ye exulted in your multitude but it availed you naught, and the earth, vast as it is, was straitened for you; then ye turned back in flight.
>
> *(Surat at-Tawbah* 9:25)

Second Example

Muslims faced grave losses in the Battle of Uhud. Seventy companions were martyred, the prophet was badly wounded, he lost some of his teeth, and there was an overall sense of grief. The hypocrites seized the opportunity to despair in the following terms:

> (They hypocrites say) Had we had any part in the cause we should not have been slain here.
>
> *(Surat al-Imran* 3:154)

> They hypocrites say) Have we any part in the cause?
>
> *(Surat al-Imran* 3:154)

'IN DEFENCE OF *JIHAD*' 133

Allah responds to their negative thinking, and bolsters Muslims' confidence in the following words:

Say (O Muhammad): The cause belongeth wholly to Allah.
(*Surat al-Imran* 3:154)

Brother, the delayed triumph of the Kashmiri *jihad* is not a sign of defeat; in fact, in context of the proofs I have given, we believe that every *mujahid* has, by definition, already won, while victory is entirely in the hands of Allah. A *mujahid* is only responsible for following orders; therein lies his success.

The *Mujahid* Always Wins

- If a *mujahid* is wounded while fighting disbelievers, he is victorious.
- If a *mujahid* returns from the battlefield unharmed, he is victorious.
- Whether *mujahideen* form a large army or a small battalion, they are victorious.
- If a *mujahid* loses a war, he is victorious.
- If a *mujahid* conquers vast swathes of land he is victorious.
- If a *mujahid* comes upon wealth in the form of war booty, he is victorious.
- If a *mujahid* is martyred while battling disbelievers he is, nevertheless, victorious.

His victory is evident to insightful believers. This is the victory the companions of the prophet set out to achieve; this is what drives us as well. A *mujahid* never fails, regardless of the circumstances. For example:

- If a *mujahid* loses an arm in battle, he is victorious like Syedna Talha.
- If a *mujahid* loses a leg and limps for the rest of his life, he is victorious like Syedna Ubaida.
- If a *mujahid* limps, he is victorious like Syedna Amrv bin Jamu.
- If a *mujahid* is blind, he is victorious like Syedna Abdullah bin Umm-i-Maktum.

134 THE LITERATURE OF *LASHKAR-E-TAYYABA*

- If a *mujahid* is martyred soon after getting married, he is victorious like Syedna Hanzlah.
- If a *mujahid* is martyred due to a wound on his chest, he is victorious like Syedna Saad bin Maaz.
- If a *mujahid* dies of exhaustion and bleeding, he is victorious like Syedna Uns, who bore eighty battle scars at the time of his martyrdom.
- If a *mujahid* fights during the day and prays all night, he is victorious.
- If a *mujahid* defers his prayers because he is on the battlefield, he is still victorious, as we saw in the Battle of Khandaq.
- If a *mujahid* loses his teeth on the battlefield, he is victorious like Syedna Abu Ubaida bin Jarah.
- If a *mujahid* dies of injuries to his sensitive parts, he is victorious like Syedna Sumayyah.
- If a *mujahid*'s body is dismembered, he is victorious like Syedna Hamza.
- If a *mujahid* encroaches upon the enemy at night and hides during the day, he is victorious like Syedna Saad bin Abi Waqas who was a spy during in the Battle of Khara.

In conclusion, *jihad* is victory. A *mujahid* is destined to be jubilant and content. Allah, the All-Powerful, protects him from hopelessness and despair.

Whether victory is instantaneous or delayed, it makes no difference to the *mujahid*. He knows that he is responsible for taking up arms, whether he is part of a massive army or attached to a small contingent, for triumph is, ultimately, in Allah's hands.

Chapter 6: The Kashmir *Jihad shariat* and Guerrilla Warfare

INQUIRER: *Lashkar-e-Tayyaba* is currently engaged in guerrilla warfare in Kashmir. *mujahideen* ambush unsuspecting Hindu soldiers before fleeing the region, leaving the local Muslim population to bear the brunt of the Indian Army's vengeance. What is the use of such *jihad*?

MUJAHID: Had you contacted your Kashmiri brothers they would have told you the benefits of our operations. If only you could see the kind of fear and terror we instil in the hearts of our enemies through our guerrilla warfare.

INQUIRER: We are only interested in the Islamic perspective. Tell me, do we find evidence of guerrilla warfare in the prophet's life?

MUJAHID: Plenty. Wars were waged against Mecca even as Muslims resided within the city. The companions also waged guerrilla warfare upon the prophet's command.

Then, when the sacred months have passed, slay the idolaters wherever ye find them, and take them (captive), and besiege them, and prepare for them each ambush.

(Surat at-Tawbah 9:5)*

This verse mentions three types of military tactics that the prophet himself executed. We emulate these tactics in Kashmir; we capture the disbelievers when possible, we besiege them given the opportunity and, when necessary, we ambush them as well.

- The prophet dispatched a group of men to ambush and kill Kaab bin Ashraf in the middle of the night.
- Another time, five *mujahideen* were dispatched to a fortress near Khaybar. The *mujahideen* arrived after sunset, just as the gates of the fortress were being shut. Syedna Abdullah bin Teek strategically managed to slip inside. Once the residents fell asleep, he murdered the Jewish leader Abu Ranay Salaam bin Abi-l-Haqiq before returning safely.
- In 1 AH, during the month of Zilqad, the prophet put together a group of twenty men with Syedna Saad bin Abi Waqas as the emirate, in order to scout out Quraysh's caravans. They were instructed to go as far as Kharar and no further. The guerrilla contingent set out on foot, travelling by night while hiding during the day, until they arrived at Kharar, only to discover the caravan they were pursuing had departed the day before. In Kashmir too, *mujahideen* must often travel by night and take cover during the day.

136 THE LITERATURE OF *LASHKAR-E-TAYYABA*

Guerrilla Attack Upon the Enemy: Two Captured, One Killed

In 2 AH, during the month of Rajab, the prophet dispatched a reconnaissance mission comprising twelve *mujahideen* with Syedna Abdullah bin Jahsh as their emirate. They were given six camels and a letter, which the prophet instructed the emirate to read two days into their journey. After two days, when the contingent stopped to rest, the emirate opened the letter. It said:

When you read this letter, keep on going until you arrive at Nakhla, a place between Mecca and Taif. There, begin stalking a Qurayshi caravan, and bring back information about it.

The emirate gathered his men and explained their mission and its importance. Then, he said:

I am not going to force anyone to continue. Those who value martyrdom should stay while those who despise death should turn back. As for me, I will nevertheless continue in accordance with the prophet's command.

Every one of the men joined the emirate and the contingent took off. Once they arrived in the valley of Nakhla they set up an ambush. When the unsuspecting Qurayshi caravan passed within range, the emirate ordered his men to attack. They released a torrent of arrows upon the caravan, killing one disbeliever and capturing two. They also managed to secure the caravan's merchandise of raisin, leather, and various other goods. The emirate brought the captives and the goods to the prophet.

This operation was executed during a month in which fighting was prohibited. The pagans of Mecca protested vehemently. Allah responded, in the Quran:

They question thee (O Muhammad) with regard to warfare in the sacred month. Say: Warfare therein is a great (transgression), but to turn (men) from the way of Allah, and to disbelieve in Him and in the Inviolable Place of Worship, and to expel his people thence, is a greater (transgression) with Allah; for persecution is worse than killing.

(*Surat al-Baqarah* 2:217)

'IN DEFENCE OF *JIHAD*' 137

Brother, these operations were carried out against the pagans of Mecca even as Muslims resided within their city. *Lashkar-e-Tayyaba*'s guerrilla operations in Kashmir are executed in the manner of the companions of the prophet.

INQUIRER: It is true that Hindus must be expelled from Kashmir and that those dying for this cause are, Allah-willing, martyrs. But the fact of the matter is that your *mujahideen* ambush Hindu soldiers before fleeing into the jungles, leaving local innocent Muslims to face the wrath of the army. Your operations put Muslims in greater peril instead of helping them. Tell me, what kind of *jihad* jeopardizes the lives of innocent Muslims? The Indian Army has always been stationed in Kashmir, but your *jihadi* missions have led them to punish local Muslims collectively.

MUJAHID: What you are saying has no basis in reality. In fact, disbelievers were persecuting Muslims long before we ever showed up. Before the *mujahideen* intervened, the army was accountable to none and acted with impunity. Kashmiris have been relatively safer since we began our *jihadi* missions. To drive home this important point, let us look at the shocking testimony of an Indian *mujahid*. This man has a five-hundred-thousand-rupee bounty on his head. His pictures are flashed on all the media outlets in India and his posters are up at airports, police stations, and train terminals throughout the country.

A journalist asked this *mujahid* if there was any truth to the propaganda about *mujahideen* being the cause for the deteriorating civil order in Kashmir, and about the fact that guerrilla operations, in which *mujahideen* ambush army contingents before escaping, were believed to be directly responsible for the Indian Army harassing, torturing, and oppressing innocent Kashmiri Muslims.

The Indian *mujahid* said, 'Those who disseminate such information are consciously or unconsciously aiding the enemy. Let us set aside Kashmir for now and talk about the way Muslims all over India are being persecuted, so those who want to know the truth can draw their own conclusions. Although the *mujahideen* have yet to begin full scale guerrilla operations in Kashmir, the rampant cruelty and persecution in the region is proof of Hindu barbarism.'

138 THE LITERATURE OF *LASHKAR-E-TAYYABA*

A Cruel Story on the Persecution of Indian Muslims

The Indian *mujahid* said Muslim-owned property was rampantly destroyed with impunity; Muslim factories, fields, orchards, and stores were burnt down through organized pogroms with the express support of government authorities.

He said the Indian infidel government regularly attempts to persecute Muslims throughout the country. It sparks riots in Muslim-majority areas as a pretext to martyr innumerable Muslims and destroy their property. Journalist: Can you name the regions where all this is happening?

MUJAHID: Muslims have been persecuted in countless cities such as Meerut, Muradabad, Maliana, Sambhal, Ahmedabad, Bhagulpur, Ghazi Ehsan in West Bengal, etc., where Muslims were slaughtered, and their markets incinerated. Countless Muslims were stabbed to death. In Ayodhya alone, in a single day, in addition to Babri Mosque, thirty-five mosques were destroyed. Anti-Muslim operations were carried out in Calcutta, Bombay, Maharashtra, UP, and Rajasthan where marble factories owned by Muslims were rendered unworkable through the use of powerful explosives. The barbarians could not have carried out their treachery at such a scale without the support of the government. It is impossible for a civilian to acquire the explosives needed to blow up a marble factory.

For Forty Years We Protested and Passed Resolutions

Journalist: Were Hindus ever harmed in these riots?
MUJAHID: The riots were all planned and executed against Muslims under the supervision of the police. From 1947 to 1988, for approximately forty years, Muslims were specifically targeted. During this period, we organized strikes and protested but when it became obvious these peaceful tactics were futile, we mobilized and armed ourselves and responded in kind.

Next time Hindu mobs entered Muslim areas we were ready for them.

After a number of successful ambushes, the situation in Muslim majority areas changed dramatically. We now want to convince India's

'IN DEFENCE OF *JIHAD*' 139

Muslims that peaceful protests are futile; *jihad* is the only way to keep the enemy in check. *jihad* is the only way to social justice and freedom. Very soon, we will initiate a nation-wide *jihad* within India, Allah-willing.

Today, those who accuse the *mujahideen* in Kashmir of terrorism will levy similar accusations against the *mujahideen* of India, tomorrow. The truth is that these people are ignorant of the benefits of *jihad* and indifferent to the plight of Muslims. If they had to deal with a fraction of the persecution faced by the Muslims of Surat, they would be the first to call for *jihad*. May Allah sharpen their perception and protect their women's honour. Amen.

Another Glimpse of Hindu Barbarity

The information summarized below was gleaned from a well-known Indian gazette titled *Milli Times International*; this information was reprinted on 21 September 1997 in the weekly *Hurmat* (Islamabad-Copenhagen).

- September 1947: In order to annex the state of Hyderabad, Congress gives the green light to the army to carry out Operation Polo in which Indian forces attack the state and slaughter thousands of innocent Muslims.
- From 1961 to 1963, Jamshedpur, Rourkela, and various other cities erupt in communal riots which leave thousands of Muslims dead.
- 1967: Muslims slaughtered indiscriminately in Ranchi and Bahar.
- 1969: Thousands of Muslims slaughtered in Ahmedabad.
- From 1957 to 1967: Indira Gandhi declares emergency rule. Street thugs use this as an opportunity to bulldoze Muslim homes in Old Delhi, castrate Muslim men, and rape Muslim women. When Muslims protest, police respond with the Turkman Gate massacre.
- 1980: Moradabad UP. During the Eid prayers the Provincial Armed Constabulary ruthlessly slaughter thousands of Muslims.
- Maulab Lang tribesmen slaughter over five thousand Muslims.
- 1986: Ayodhya (Faizabad UP): Court orders the appropriation of Babri Mosque. Nationwide protests continued till 1996. 1987

140 THE LITERATURE OF *LASHKAR-E-TAYYABA*

Meerut: the Provincial Armed Constabulary shoots dead thousands of innocent Muslims.

- Hindu extremist L.K. Advani's *rath yatra* between October and December 1990 results in Muslim massacres across the country.
- 6 December 1992: During a *sangh parivar* organized by *Hindu Parishad* (International Hindu Council), Bajrang Dal, and RSS, an incensed mob, storms Babri Mosque in the presence of the police and dismantles the sanctuary brick by brick. The country erupts in anti-Muslim riots. Thousands of innocent Muslims are martyred at the hands of policemen and thugs.
- International condemnation over the Indian government's inability to protect the mosque and the rights of minorities.
- Muslim women collectively gang-raped in Surat; the event, caught on tape, is then played back at various public spots in several Indian cities.
- Police-backed massacre carried out by Shiv Sena thugs in Bombay. Shiv Sena leader Bal Thackeray openly accepts responsibility for instigating the riot and proposes Nazi tactics employed during the holocaust to rid India of Muslims once and for all.

Rectify Your Misperceptions

This terrifying report on Indian Muslims proves that dirty Hindus do not persecute disenfranchised Muslims because of guerrilla warfare waged by *mujahideen* but rather because they are sworn enemies and will never miss an opportunity to spill innocent Muslim blood.

Those who believe that Hindu soldiers target Kashmiri Muslims as a result of *jihadi* operations ought to rethink their position. As of now, *mujahideen* have not even started their full-scale operations. On the other hand, Hindus have been slaughtering Muslims since the bloodbath of 1947, and they have not stopped, in Kashmir or the rest of India, to this day.

The *jihadi* operations in Kashmir have offered local Muslims protection while boosting their confidence. And now, as a result of these operations, things have started to change. Hindu soldiers are more cautious now, whereas in the past they were impulsively violent.

'IN DEFENCE OF *JIHAD*' 141

INQUIRER: The war in Kashmir is being waged for independence. Does the *shariat* allow bloodshed for independence? If, however, this is a fight for the imposition of Islamic principles, then shouldn't we be fighting in our own country first? Why is there no *jihad* in Pakistan?

MUJAHID: Freeing Muslim lands from the occupation of disbelievers is also a form of *jihad*, for as long as disbelievers rule a territory Islam will remain weak, much like that region's Muslim inhabitants. On the other hand, if Muslims occupy a region, Allah will establish Islamic principles through his servants, Allah-willing. Also, *shariat* allows fighting for independence.

INQUIRER: What's the evidence for this allowance?

MUJAHID: Allah states in the Quran:

And slay them wherever ye find them, and drive them out of the places whence they drove you out.

(*Surat al-Baqarah* 2:191)

Allah also states:

Bethink thee of the leaders of the Children of Israel after Moses, how they said unto a prophet whom they had: Set up for us a king and we will fight in Allah's way. He said: Would ye then refrain from fighting if fighting were prescribed for you? They said: Why should we not fight in Allah's way when we have been driven from our dwellings with our children? Yet, when fighting was prescribed for them, they turned away, all save a few of them. Allah is Aware of evil doers.

(*Surat al-Baqarah* 2:246)

The above verse refers to the battle fought by the Prophet Saul to win back Muslim lands.

INQUIRER: You say freeing Muslim lands from the occupation of disbelievers is the same as fighting for Islam, which means your war in Kashmir is being fought for Allah's sake. Be honest, you're not fighting for any personal benefit, are you?

MUJAHID: We are fighting for unbelievable benefits; we sacrifice our lives for unimaginable desires. These include Allah's pleasure,

142 THE LITERATURE OF *LASHKAR-E-TAYYABA*

seventy-two virgins in heaven, one hundred planes of paradise... can there be any greater benefit? Furthermore, consider what the Quran says about desire:

Who forsake their beds to cry unto their Lord in fear and hope and spend of what we have bestowed on them.

(Surat al-Sajdah 32:16)

Think about it! Short of the promise of paradise, why would a person forsake his bed or sacrifice his life? If you're still unclear about this delicate point, answer this:

would you ever sacrifice your son for some earthly gain? Absolutely not! If, however, your Lord reward's you with paradise in return, then, this is obviously a fantastic bargain.

O *Mujahideen!* Celebrate!

Lo! Allah hath bought from the believers their lives and their wealth because the Garden will be theirs: they shall fight in the way of Allah and shall slay and be slain. It is a promise which is binding on Him in the Torah and the Gospel and the Quran. Who fulfileth His covenant better than Allah? Rejoice then in your bargain that ye have made, for that is the supreme triumph.

(Surat at-Tawbah 9:111)

Brother, thanks to Allah, we are fighting in Kashmir for Islam, for the sake of our victimized Muslim brothers, for paradise and for the hope of paradise. On the other hand, sacrificing life and limb for democracy is sheer idiocy.

INQUIRER: If democracy in Pakistan is unacceptable to you, why are you fighting for the imposition of this false ideology in Kashmir? Should your *jihad* be successful, Kashmir, too, will become a democracy.
MUJAHID:
1. We are against any ideology opposed to the Quran and *Sunnat.*
2. You seem to suggest we ought to stop waging *jihad* in Kashmir because it will lead to a democratic Kashmir. How do you know? Are

you some kind of diviner? The future is known only to Allah. We are fighting solely for Allah and for the Muslim victims of Kashmir. We hope that our humble sacrifices will put an end to the treachery of disbelief and win freedom for our Muslims brothers. Islam will reign and we will be closer to achieving our dream of a caliphate and an emirate, Allah-willing. Also, keep in mind, Allah has always blessed Muslims with glory and respect for their sacrifices. History is a testament to this fact.

INQUIRER: The current situation suggests otherwise; what you are saying may well be your wishful thinking.

MUJAHID: What you call wishful thinking is in reality unflinching faith. We take our cue from the life of the prophet.... when the prophet started preaching in Mecca no one could have imagined the impending success of Islam. Just as Allah made Muslims triumphant then, He will, in His beneficence, accept the sacrifices and efforts of *mujahideen* today, and grant Muslims glory and victory, and help establish a caliphate and an emirate.

INQUIRER: The struggle in Kashmir is a regional issue whereas Islam is above regional/national/tribal politics. Does the *shariat* legitimize *Markaz-ud-Dawah-wal-Irshad*'s participation in this war?

MUJAHID: I will cite the Quran and *Sunnat* in a bit but first let us talk about this issue rationally.
Tell me, if someone invades your house, your lands, or your business, will you simply let go of your property?

INQUIRER: Absolutely not! I will apply every effort, strategy, and method within my capacity to reclaim my property.

MUJAHID: What if the invader is stronger than you? Then what?

INQUIRER: I will fight for my right because Islam permits me to fight for what is mine. If I die in the process, I will be a martyr according to the *Hadees*:

'He who is murdered while protecting his property is a martyr.'

MUJAHID: Brother, if you feel this strongly about your personal property, can you not see the relevance of fighting for Kashmir? Kashmir is heaven on earth, the lifeline of Pakistan, and a land occupied by Hindus.

144 THE LITERATURE OF *LASHKAR-E-TAYYABA*

INQUIRER: This means the *jihad* you are waging there is not for the sake of Allah.

MUJAHID: Brother, it is entirely for the sake of Allah; through this struggle we are protecting the lives and properties of Muslims.

INQUIRER: Multiple factions are fighting in Kashmir, as they were in Afghanistan. Supposing Kashmir is conquered, won't these factions start fighting among themselves as they did in Afghanistan?

MUJAHID: Supposing your hypothesis is accurate, answer the following questions honestly:

1. Does *jihad* become obsolete due to the prospect of civil war?
2. Infighting has plagued missionary work as well; does this mean all proselytizing should cease too?
3. If the construction of a mosque leads to conflict, does this delegitimize the house of worship?
4. Does prayer become non-obligatory simply due to a conflict over the running of a mosque or the appointment of an imam? Will propaganda against attendant worshippers be justified?
5. Should madrassas be shut down due to some of the unpleasant things that happen there?
6. Because marital couples have domestic conflicts should the rest of society give up on the *Sunnat* of marriage altogether?

Brother, prayer is mandatory irrespective of the circumstances. Mosques ought to be constructed regardless of potential land disputes. Madrassas must run. The *Sunnat* of marriage will continue to be honoured. It is important, however, to improve our social realities through important reforms. Similarly, *mujahideen*, like any other people, can fall prey to misunderstandings. They too can become victims of greed, desire, and mutual conflict. Allah singles out a situation that occurred during the Battle of Uhud:

Allah verily made good His promise unto you when ye routed them by His leave, until (the moment) when your courage failed you, and ye disagreed about the order and ye disobeyed, after He had shown you that for which ye long. Some of you desired the world, and some of you desired the Hereafter. Therefore, he made you flee from them, that He might try you. Yet now He hath forgiven you. Allah is a Lord of Kindness to believers.

(Surat al-Imran 3:152)

Brother, the verse above refers to the mutual conflicts and worldly desires that plagued *mujahideen* during the Battle of Uhud when they disobeyed the prophet's command only to incur grave losses during the fight. This was a gruelling test from Allah.

Similarly, infighting due to misunderstandings should be expected on the battlefield but these do not mitigate our *jihadi* obligation. Come join the caravan of *mujahideen* and resolve discord wherever it arises... ensure your afterlife and create harmony among your fellow warriors.

Dispersed Factions—Unified *Mujahideen*

INQUIRER: Various independent factions are fighting in Kashmir whereas Allah says:

Lo! Allah loveth those who battle for His cause in ranks, as if they were a solid structure.

(Surat al-Saf 61:4)

MUJAHID: By Allah's grace, the *mujahideen* in Kashmir are like an iron wall; they are in constant communication with one another and they launch joint operations against the enemy.

They collaborate on all operational levels—while planning, during ambushes, while blowing up enemy barracks, and when entering enemy bunkers to slaughter enemy soldiers in cold blood.

They collaborate on reconnaissance and surveillance missions, they travel to targeted areas together, and many times the bodies of martyrs belonging to various groups are discovered in the same location, so even their funeral prayers are offered collectively.

This proves that the *mujahideen* are united. They do not suffer from any major discord; however, some people influenced by enemy propaganda

146 THE LITERATURE OF *LASHKAR-E-TAYYABA*

disseminate rumours about infighting among the Muslim ranks. May Allah guide such people. Amen.

INQUIRER: If the *mujahideen* are united why are they split in factions?

MUJAHID: Ideally, they would not be divided into different groups, and Allah-willing, a time will come when this will change. But there is no harm in associating with various factions either, especially when waging a defensive war. It would be wonderful if, hypothetically, there was a universal movement to unite the Islamic world, but in the course of this effort the enemy may target scattered Muslim populations because the disbelieving nations strive to persecute them everywhere (in which case they will have no option but to fight as factions). Their property is being destroyed, their fields and crops are being burnt, and rivers run red with their blood. All disbelieving nations of the world unite against them, determined to humiliate the believers. How many Muslim lands have been occupied by disbelievers who force the inhabitants to live as slaves? In these circumstances, it makes no difference if Muslims defend themselves as one unified force or as various factions, or even as individuals. In fact, in order to weaken and harm the enemy it is perfectly legitimate to seek the assistance of disbelievers, much like the *mujahideen* in Kashmir employ the help of Sikhs.

Can Disbelievers Be Allies in War?

INQUIRER: What you say is boggling; how can one employ the assistance of disbelievers in a sacred obligation like *jihad*?

MUJAHID: Anyone and anything can be employed for the purpose of *jihad*; disbelievers, Hindus, Sikhs, Christians, Jews, pagans... even animals are legitimate allies.

1. In the early days of Islam, the pagans of Mecca made every effort to hinder the prophet's mission. Abu Talib did his best to assist him to the point of joining the Muslims when they were exiled to She'eb Abi Talib. Abu Talib was an infidel but the prophet accepted his help.

'IN DEFENCE OF *JIHAD*' 147

2. When the prophet returned to Mecca from Taif, his life was in grave danger within the city, so he sought protection from an infidel called Mu'tahm bin Adi.
3. When the prophet migrated to Medina with Syedna Abu Bakr, they employed a tracker who was an infidel to guide them through their arduous journey.
4. During the Battle of Uhud, seven enemy flag bearers were consecutively slaughtered by the prophet's companions. The eighth infidel who reached out to raise the banner was slaughtered by a Muslim called Quzman. Quzman proceeded to slaughter two more infidels who attempted to uphold their flag. Who was this Quzman who displayed such valour in the heat of battle? He was a hypocrite who was badly wounded in the fight. The companions spoke to the prophet of his fortitude on the battlefield; they told him how Quzman slaughtered seven or eight infidels, three of whom were flag-bearers.

Syedna Abu Huraira gives a detailed account of this conversation: Syedna Abu Huraira reports: We were in the presence of the prophet when he said one of the men who claimed to be a Muslim would go to hell. This person was badly wounded in the war. The companions told the prophet that the person he predicted would go to hell fought bravely today and passed away. 'To fire', the prophet remarked. The companions were stupefied. They continued talking about this person when news arrived that he had not died (in battle) but he had killed himself due to the unbearable severity of his wounds. The prophet said: '*Allah-akbar*! I bear witness that I belong to Allah, and I am His prophet.' Then he ordered Syedna Bilal to make a declaration to the people: Look! Only a Muslim will enter paradise; sometimes Allah employs the help of a sinner among us.

5. As the companions were taking stock of the wounded and the dead they came upon the corpse of a Jew from the tribe of Banu Salbah, how did this fellow end up joining the *jihad*? As the clouds of war loomed overhead, this Jew said to his people: O Jews! I swear upon Allah you are aware of your obligation to fight alongside

148 THE LITERATURE OF *LASHKAR-E-TAYYABA*

Muhammad. His people said, 'But it is the Sabbath.' He said, 'for you there is no Sabbath!' As he grabbed his sword he proclaimed: 'If I am killed, my property belongs to Muhammad. He is free to do with it as he pleases.' With these words he headed for the battlefield where he met his end. The prophet said: 'Mukhayyariq was the finest Jew' (*[illegible]* Makhdum).

Brother, in times of war, we are permitted to seek the help and assistance of reliable disbelievers.

Chapter 7: Why Don't You Fulfil the Principle of *Qisas* (Retributive Justice)?

INQUIRER: Allah has used the same prescriptive word for three obligations in the Quran:

1. fasting is prescribed for you... (*Surat al-Baqarah* 2:183)
2. fighting is prescribed for you... (*Surat al-Baqarah* 2:216)
3. the law of equality (*qisas*) is prescribed for you... (*Surat al-Baqarah* 2:178)

Explain why you follow two of these commandments but ignore the third?

MUJAHID: Even though fasting is mandatory there are certain situations that exempt one from fulfilling this obligation. For example:

1. One is allowed to forego fasting if one is ill and too weak to fast.
2. Similarly, if one is traveling one is allowed to waive this obligation as well.

Qisas and *jihad* have similar exemptions even though both are mandatory. Consider the commandments revealed during the Battle of Tabuk:

Not unto the weak nor unto the sick nor unto those who can find naught to spend is any fault (to be imputed though they stay at home) if they are true to Allah and His messenger. Not unto the good is there any road (of blame). Allah is Forgiving, Merciful.

(Surat at-Tawbah 9:91)

Nor unto those whom, when they came to thee (asking) that thou shouldest mount them, thou didst tell: I cannot find whereon to mount you. They turned back with eyes flowing with tears, for sorrow that they could not find the means to spend.

(Surat at-Tawbah 9:92)

The road (of blame) is only against those who ask for leave of thee (to stay at home) when they are rich. They are content to be with the useless. Allah hath sealed their hearts so that they know not.

(Surat at-Tawbah 9:93)

Brother, despite the fact that *jihad* is mandatory, old, infirm, blind, disabled, and ill individuals who lacked the resources were exempt from this obligation; nevertheless, they wept bitterly when they were told there was not an animal for them to ride into battle. Their shortcomings were accepted, and they were declared incapable of waging war. On the other hand, those who made up excuses to stay back despite being fully capable of battle were harshly rebuked.

Mujahideen today are sincere and driven; they want Islamic law within the country as well as the imposition of *hudood* (set of Islamic legal edicts) but they are helpless because they lack the power to impose *qisas*; they are not making any excuses for shirking this obligation. Those who criticize us for ignoring the imposition of this Islamic edict understand if we take the law of the land in our own hands and start handing out retributive justice there would be widespread anarchy. We would be considered renegades for doing so and all the work we have done for Islam so far will be compromised. Instead, we try to convince the government to impose Islamic law as that is in the best interest of everyone concerned. Allah will not forgive anyone for ignoring His commandments. On the other hand, Allah has given us the opportunity, the resources, and the capability to wage *jihad* against disbelievers, leaving us no excuse to shirk this obligation. According to the *shariat*, however, we have a valid excuse to forfeit *qisas*.

150 THE LITERATURE OF *LASHKAR-E-TAYYABA*

INQUIRER: There are documented exemptions from fasting and fighting but we do not find any such exemptions regarding *qisas*. Allah says:

And there is life for you in retaliation, O men of understanding, that ye may ward off (evil).

(*Surat al-Baqarah* 2:179)

This verse clearly highlights the importance of *qisas*, as a result of which society can be cleansed of all kind of crime.

MUJAHID: Only a disbeliever would deny the importance and obligation of *qisas*. The question is: can we, at this time, collectively act upon this commandment? For instance, if you kill a murderer, you yourself will be executed as a murderer; you will be taken to court, you will be testified against, and you will be hanged, and the government will claim to be carrying out Allah's command.

INQUIRER: I find it cowardly that you are more than willing to sacrifice life and limb in the course of *jihad* in Kashmir, but your fear of prosecution and execution makes you wary of *qisas*. This seems like selective observance to me. Allah has condemned this sort of attitude while addressing the Bani Israel (Jews):

Believe ye in part of the scripture and disbelieve ye in part thereof?

(*Surat al-Baqarah* 2:85)

MUJAHID: While it is a crime to observe Allah's commandments selectively, we find salvation in the footsteps and guidance of the prophet. Allow me to present evidence from the Quran and *Sunnat* to highlight the fact that he who does not possess the power to fulfil religious obligations has been exempted from acting upon Allah's command.

First Argument

Allah tasketh not a soul beyond its scope. For it (is only) that which it hath earned, and against it (only) that which it hath deserved.

(*Surat al-Baqarah* 2:286)

Second Argument

So keep your duty to Allah as best ye can, and listen, and obey, and spend; that is better for your souls. And whoso is saved from his own greed, such are the successful.

(Surat at-Taghabun 64:16)

INQUIRER: This means you do not want to confront the government over the imposition of *qisas*.

MUJAHID: In context of the verses above, we refuse to confront a fellow Muslim, let alone the government, in order to avoid perfidy, treachery, civil war, and anarchy. However, the official files of *Mujallah-ul-Dawah* bear testament to our efforts to try and convince the government to impose the Islamic system of justice through *qisas* and *hudood. Jihad* is Being Waged upon the Government's Behest

INQUIRER: It seems you are waging *jihad* upon the government's behest, while iniquitous agencies are using you for their own purposes, which is why you refuse to confront the establishment.

MUJAHID: Brother, Allah has made *jihad* mandatory for Muslims; we are following his command to the best of our capabilities. But even if one assumes your assessment is accurate, so what? Tell me, if the government orders you to pray, or pay *zakat*, will you refuse simply because it was the government that commanded you to do so?

INQUIRER: The government has the authority to enforce *qisas*, much like it has the authority to wage *jihad*. Let the standing army wage wars; why don't you work on having the government enforce Islamic codes of justice like *qisas* and *hudood*.

MUJAHID: We are fulfilling our *jihadi* obligation; the government does not hinder our cause. In this context, assistance from various Muslim agencies is accepted as help from Allah; assistance from reliable disbelievers is also accepted as help from Allah for he may choose whomsoever to assist us in His cause. Also, keep in mind, because the government must publicly declare that it will not engage Hindu forces militarily it is imperative for us to wage *jihad* in Kashmir. In contrast, the government claims to be working on enforcing *qisas*. Hence, we march into Kashmir to fulfil our obligation to fight, while within our borders, we engage our Muslim leaders through criticism, dialogue,

152 THE LITERATURE OF *LASHKAR-E-TAYYABA*

and recommendations, in order to impose Islamic principles such as *qisas*, thanks to Allah!

Chapter 8: How is *Jihad* Possible Without a Caliph?

INQUIRER: Allah says in the Quran:
: Allah loves those who fight in his cause in an orderly fashion, like an iron wall.
: In this context, wouldn't fighting in a disorganized manner incur Allah's displeasure? And wouldn't it be better to wage *jihad* within the country first to rid the nation of divisive rulers in order to create an iron wall of united Muslims?
MUJAHID: Currently, Muslim rulers the world over have forfeited *jihad* altogether. As a collective, we are most certainly disorganized and scattered. Tell me, do you think we should first exert our efforts uniting the Muslim nation or would it be prudent to deflect the enemy's imminent attacks? In this context, allow me to narrate an encounter with a friend.

An Encounter

Once, over a conversation about the *jihad* in Kashmir, a friend told me *jihad* could not be waged in the absence of a caliph. I told him we were involved in a defensive *jihad*; hence no such authority figure was necessary. He said Islam had set limits and rules to every action, and the condition for *jihad* was the authority of a caliph.

For one, this is not true, but even if one is to assume this was accurate, given:

- that every caliphate has been eradicated from the world ...
- Is it permissible to fight the Jews in order to free *Bayt-ul-Muqaddas* from their oppressive occupation in the absence of a caliph?
- In the absence of a caliph, can one fight the Christians who have occupied Spain, which was ruled by Muslims for eight hundred years?

'IN DEFENCE OF *JIHAD*' 153

- Muslims once ruled Hindustan, Assam, Nepal, Burma, etc. Now, Hindus, Sikhs, and Buddhists govern these regions. Tell me, can these disbelievers be militarily engaged?
- If Hindustan attacks Pakistan, may we defend our country in the absence of a caliph?
- If Buddhists attack Bangladesh, can Bengali Muslims defend themselves even though they do not have a caliph?
- If Jews attack Saudi Arabia in the course of Israeli expansion, given there is no caliph, do Arabs have the right to defend the prophet's mosque and the House of Allah?
- I was visiting my friend at the height of the Bosnian war. I said:
- Bosnian Muslims are dispersed and disorganized; they barely have a government to speak of. Should they first take stock of their numbers, organize, set out looking for a caliph, and then defend themselves? And suppose they asked you to appoint a caliph for them so they may start defending themselves; are you in any position to make such an appointment? And suppose you nominate a caliph for them, but no other Muslim accepts his authority, according to you, no Muslim population may ever defend itself even as disbelievers slaughter them en masse. Your rules are neither practical nor religious. They are simply an excuse to avoid *jihad*. Islam is in accordance with nature. It embodies honour and valour. It combines proselytizing and *jihad*. When the times call for it, one is expected to fight the enemy. Depending on the situation, *jihad* can be waged collectively as well as individually. The Quran states:

O ye who believe! Take your precautions, then advance the proven ones, or advance all together.

(*Surat an-Nisa* 4:71)

My friend continued to argue with me about the validity of *jihad* until a gentleman in our congregation told me not to waste my time with him. He accused my friend of being so rigidly anti-*jihad*, that even if the angel Gabriel entered our midst and commanded us to fight, my friend would refuse to budge. Let us continue our dialogue.

Brother, according to you, if fighting as disparate factions incurs Allah's displeasure, then, as a result, all the *mujahideen* in Kashmir ought to lay down

154 THE LITERATURE OF *LASHKAR-E-TAYYABA*

their weapons and the Muslims should happily accept a life of servitude under Hindus. I cannot think of a clearer way to communicate surrender.

Do you think Allah would approve of submitting to Hindustan? Would Allah approve of infighting among Muslims? If so, go ahead and declare war upon our Muslim rulers by practising what you preach?

It is most hateful in the sight of Allah that ye say that which ye do not.

(*Surat al-Saf* 61:3)

Enjoin ye righteousness upon mankind while ye yourselves forget (to practise it)? And ye are readers of the scripture! Have ye then no sense?

(*Surat al-Baqarah* 2:44)

INQUIRER: *jihad* has no concept of differentiated factions; throughout history Muslims have fought as one, under a single banner.

MUJAHID: Does Islam only urge unity in *jihad* or other aspects of life as well?

وَاعْتَصِمُواْ بِحَبْلِ اللّٰه جَمِيعًا وَلَا تَفَرَّقُواْ

And hold fast, all of you together, to the cable of Allah, and do not separate.

(*Surat al-Imran* 3:103)

Despite the Quran's explicit commandment, Muslims are divided into various sects and sub-sects. Is this excusable?

INQUIRER: Beliefs and ideologies vary frequently; variations within sectarian mosques, *madaris*, and publications are not all that serious.

MUJAHID: From another angle this is gravely serious. The Quran and *Hadees* do not allow such variations but the reality that cannot be ignored. Currently, the Muslim *ummat* is dispersed. Enemies have conspired to plunge Muslims into a state of civil war; they planted their agents within the *ummat* to stoke discord among us.

Consequently, we grow weak and disperse into factions.

The enemy occupied Muslim territories, destroyed mosques, raped and plundered, and subjected Muslims to slavery. The enemy is conspiring to destroy Muslim unity again. Understand what the enemy is up to; play your part in strengthening *jihad*, for very soon:

- Through the benefits of *jihad* Muslims will rise to become a force of nature.
- Victimized Muslims will gain freedom and dignity.
- *Jihad* will do away with national and geographic boundaries.
- Muslims will steadfastly grasp the rope of Allah as one.
- Those associated with the Quran and *Sunnat* will unite as one nation under a single caliph and a single banner to carry out their sacred obligations of preaching, learning, and waging *jihad*.

INQUIRER: *Markaz-ud-Dawah-wal-Irshad* and various other *jihadi* outfits are not part of any government. You claim that everything you do is in accordance with the Quran and *Hadees*. Give me an example from the prophet's life or the Quran in which *jihad* was waged without a government.

MUJAHID: Consider the following examples:

1. Syedna Abu Baseer fought the infidels of Mecca without the backing of a government. There are plenty of other such examples.
2. The martyr Shah Ismail waged *jihad* without a government.
3. Maulana Fazl Ilahi waged *jihad* in Hindustan after the creation of the Islamic state of Pakistan; no one can deny his efforts.
4. Imam Ibn Taymiyyah waged *jihad* against the Tartars without the support of a government.

INQUIRER: You mentioned Abu Baseer's *jihad*; kindly elaborate, did he execute his operations independent of the authority of the prophet?

MUJAHID: In 8 AH, when the prophet attempted to make a pilgrimage to Mecca with his companions, they were refused entry into the city. At this point, the prophet made a pact, known as the Treaty of Hudaybiyyah, with the infidels. One of the terms of the treaty stated that should anyone from Mecca defect and escape to Medina, the prophet would return him to the Meccans. After signing the pact, the prophet and his companions returned to Medina. Abu Baseer was a Meccan convert to Islam who managed to escape to Medina. When

156 THE LITERATURE OF *LASHKAR-E-TAYYABA*

the Quraysh of Mecca dispatched two men to retrieve him the prophet immediately handed him over. On their way back to Mecca, when the three stopped to rest, Syedna Abu Baseer disingenuously admired one of his escort's swords. In a moment of vanity, the infidel unsheathed the weapon and handed it over to Abu Baseer so he could have a closer look. Without a moment's hesitation, Abu Baseer struck the infidel with such force the man fell to his death. Terrified, the second infidel ran for all he was worth, with Abu Baseer at his heels, all the way back to Medina.

When he arrived at the prophet's mosque, the Meccan pagan blurted out what Abu Baseer had done to his companion and begged the prophet to protect him.

When Abu Baseer arrived, he said: 'O Messenger of Allah, you honoured your pact by returning me but Allah has freed me.' The prophet responded: 'May your mother perish, if you find a few more partners you will stoke the fires of war.'

Convinced the prophet would return him a second time, Abu Baseer fled Medina for the coast where he pitched his tent near the trade route connecting Mecca and Syria.

From then on, every fresh convert to Islam from Mecca, who managed to escape the city, sought refuge with Abu Baseer. Once they formed a sizeable group of escaped Muslims, they began orchestrating guerrilla operations against the trade caravans of Meccan infidels, independent of the government in Medina. Every passing caravan was attacked and plundered. Seeing that the route became impossible to traverse, the Meccans sent a delegation to the prophet beseeching him to recall Abu Baseer to Medina. Consider the following:

1. Did Syedna Abu Baseer not kill an emissary from Mecca?
2. Weren't Abu Baseer and his companions carrying out guerrilla operations?
3. Weren't Muslims who escaped Mecca seeking refuge with Abu Baseer?
4. The prophet led the well-established government in Medina at the time. Why did the Prophet allow Abu Baseer to escape to the coast instead of returning him to Mecca?

5. Why weren't they forbidden from executing guerrilla warfare against the Quraysh of Mecca?
6. Abu Baseer murdered a man. Why wasn't this murder compensated?
7. Why weren't the goods looted from Mecca's trade caravans by Abu Baseer returned to the owners?

In light of this evidence, it is clear that Abu Baseer was acting outside the authority of the Islamic government of the time. Neither did the prophet take notice of his activities nor did the infidels of Mecca demand retribution or their property back. This is proof that Muslims can wage *jihad* without the backing of a government. The Afghan *jihad* had the full support of Islamic scholars and muftis the world over; in fact, many claimed it was obligatory for Muslims to participate in that struggle. That war was fought without a government, as is the *jihad* in Kashmir.

INQUIRER: It is possible that the prophet disapproved of the operations carried out by Abu Baseer and his comrades.
MUJAHID: How do you know the prophet disapproved?

The Rule

The rule is that the prophet's silence regarding any action or process that occurred during his lifetime must be interpreted as tacit approval, for the prophet and Allah would never ignore any wrongdoing. It was incumbent upon the prophet to guide Muslims. The prophet's silence in the face of these operations is his stamp of approval; this is what the *Hadees* scholars call a declaratory *Hadees*, which means the very act in question becomes a part of *Sunnat*.

INQUIRER: Pakistan has made a pact with Hindustan. *Markaz-ud-Dawah-wal-Irshad* ought to respect its terms.
MUJAHID: While the infidels of Mecca honoured their treatise with the prophet, Hindustan has violated every single pact made with Pakistan. Under these circumstances, it is imperative that we engage them militarily. The Quran says:

158   THE LITERATURE OF *LASHKAR-E-TAYYABA*

And if they break their pledges after their treaty (hath been made with you) and assail your religion, then fight the heads of disbelief Lo! They have no binding oaths in order that they may desist.

(*Surat at-Tawbah* 9:12)

This verse is essential to the logic of the *jihad* in Kashmir for the following reasons:

1. Hindustan violates treaties.
2. It attacks our faith.
3. It destroys mosques.
4. It dishonours us.
5. It spills Muslim blood.

This is why we are fighting Hindustan, and we will continue fighting Hindustan, and according to the Quran and *Sunnat* we are acting in Allah's cause. Indeed, this is *jihad*; this is undoubtedly *jihad*! Allah-willing.

Chapter 9: *Jihad* Upon US Command

INQUIRER: Some friends of mine claim *Markaz-ud-Dawah-wal-Irshad* is waging *jihad* upon the behest of the United States. Is this true?

MUJAHID: This grave accusation is absolutely unacceptable considering our *mujahideen* are inspiring the Muslim nation to rise and wage *jihad* for Allah's cause. This is equivalent to accusing a *muezzin*, who gives the call to prayer so people may wake up and worship, of acting upon the behest of disbelievers; this is sheer nonsense. Like the *muezzin*, *Markaz-ud-Dawah-wal-Irshad* is giving out the rallying call for *jihad*; *mujahideen* respond and proceed to sacrifice their lives solely for Allah's approval. The truth of the matter is that Christian or Jew, every disbeliever wants...

- Muslims to completely disavow *jihad*.
- Muslims to remain unresponsive as *jihad* is revitalized.
- Muslims to forget the lessons of *jihad*.
- Muslims to refrain from repeating the glorious history of their sacrifices. If the spirit of sacrifice is reincarnated US conspiracies will fail.

'IN DEFENCE OF *JIHAD*' 159

- Muslims to not follow the footsteps of their forebears.
- Muslims to remain in a state of subjugation and humiliation by terminating *jihad*.

Brother, consider this: why would Christians ever want us Muslims to follow the footsteps of the prophet, or sacrifice our lives like his companions for the dominance of Islam when this would allow us, as well as other subjugated people, to live with dignity and self-respect?

Why would Christians ever want Muslims to attack and enslave the former and steal their wealth and conquer the world, upending the American world order?

In contrast, this is what the disbelievers want:

Neither those who disbelieve among the people of the scripture nor the idolaters love that there should be sent down unto you any good thing from your Lord. But Allah chooseth for His mercy whom He will, and Allah is of infinite bounty.

(Surat al-Baqarah 2:105)

The Quran mentions their treacherous desires in the following terms:

And the Jews will not be pleased with thee, nor will the Christians, till thou follow their creed. Say: Lo! the guidance of Allah (Himself) is Guidance. And if thou shouldst follow their desires after the knowledge which hath come unto thee, then wouldst thou have from Allah no protecting friend nor helper.

(Surat al-Baqarah 2:120)

In yet another verse, Allah describes their debauchery and greed in the following terms:

Many of the people of the scripture long to make you disbelievers after your belief, through envy on their own account, after the truth hath become manifest unto them. Forgive and be indulgent (towards them) until Allah give command. Lo! Allah is able to do all things.

(Surat al-Baqarah 2:109)

160   THE LITERATURE OF *LASHKAR-E-TAYYABA*

In addition to the three verses above, various descriptions in the Quran of the greed, envy, animosity, and hatred of disbelievers towards Muslims make it clear that they cannot stand us embracing *jihad*, for this rings death for them and spells new life for believers. The Quran states:

> O ye who believe; Obey Allah, and the messenger when He calleth you to that which quickeneth you, and know that Allah cometh in between the man and his own heart, and that He it is unto Whom ye will be gathered.
>
> (*Surat al-Anfal* 8:24)

This means that the instant you hear the call, wage *jihad* without a moment's delay. Most Salafi scholars interpret the verse above as a reference to *jihad* that makes sense in context of the proceeding verse, which warns Muslims of Allah's wrath, and the one after that in which Allah speaks of his special blessings.

> And remember, when ye were few and reckoned feeble in the land, and were in fear lest men should extirpate you, how He gave you refuge, and strengthened you with His help, and made provision of good things for you, that haply ye might be thankful.
>
> (*Surat al-Anfal* 8:26)

These verses make the following points:

- Dignity comes from *jihad*.
- Allah advises us to wage *jihad*.
- Honest livelihood comes from *jihad*.
- *Jihad* is the lifeline of the Muslim nation.
- Allah and the prophet call for *jihad*.
- *Jihad* leads to involution.

The Quran and *Hadees* are replete with the benefits and blessings of *jihad*. Why would the USA ever want Muslims to tread the path to grandeur and paradise?

Even if we assume the USA is coaxing us to wage *jihad*, so what? Sometimes Allah employs disbelievers, sinners, even Satan to do His

'IN DEFENCE OF *JIHAD*' 161

handiwork. Just as the hypocrite Quzman and Mukhayyariq the Jew came handy in Allah's path, the *Hadees* collections mention instances when Satan was also employed for Allah's cause.

It is obvious that American Christians will never dig their own grave by aiding Muslims. They know that once Muslims set out on the path of *jihad*, no power on earth can stop them from wiping infidels off the face of this planet. The fact of the matter is that the people of the scripture do not have the capacity to battle *mujahideen* for the former strive to extend their lives while *mujahideen* long for death. The Quran says:

> And thou wilt find them greediest of mankind for life and (greedier) than the idolaters. (Each) one of them would like to be allowed to live a thousand years. And to live (a thousand years) would by no means remove him from the doom. Allah is Seer of what they do.
>
> (*Surat al-Baqarah* 2:96)

The Quran touches upon the cowardice of the Jews in the following terms:

> They will not fight against you in a body save in fortified villages or from behind walls. Their adversity among themselves is very great. Ye think of them as a whole whereas their hearts are divers. That is because they are a folk who have no sense.
>
> (*Surat al-Hashr* 59:14)

Brother, the Quran has identified truths that cannot be denied. On one hand there are those who want to live a thousand years, and on the other, those who go about seeking death.

When those who hide behind the bolted gates of fortresses come up agains those who ride out into the battlefield, the conflict cannot last too long.

In light of this evidence, it is impossible to imagine the USA aiding *hadi* movements; in fact, it is in the USA's best interest to obliterate all r tions of *jihad* from this world. Americans hire unconscionable Musl as agents to try and create discord among our ranks. These agents put articles, deliver speeches, and hold discussions that delegitimize *ji* They resort to propaganda, rumours, and accusations to confuse r *hideen* into fighting one another in order to distract these noble wa from the real enemy. All these efforts will prove futile, Allah-willin;

162 THE LITERATURE OF *LASHKAR-E-TAYYABA*

The Negotiation Trap and the Termination of *Jihad*

INQUIRER: The facts and proofs you state cannot be denied; neither can anyone deny the successes and achievements of the prophet. Similarly, the prophet's companions' sacrifices and attitudes shape the world to this day. But in this day and age, dialogue is the most effective means of solving problems; therefore, we should try and negotiate on an international platform to avoid bloodshed. After all, why else do international human rights organizations exist? In the past, when there were no such organizations, nations needed to settle their conflicts on the battlefield. Now, we can resolve our problems through negotiations.

MUJAHID: All secular human rights organizations are solely interested in safeguarding the rights of disbelievers as they collaborate with the oppressors to violate the rights of Muslims. The UN was created to trample Islam. Let me offer a glimpse into the character of the dacoits that form such organizations but first, keep in mind, disbelievers the world over are united over the following issues:

Muslims must be kept embroiled in civil war that will ultimately lead to their destruction.

A steady stream of fresh problems must be created for Muslims.

Muslims must be distracted by all means.

Negotiations must be used to trap Muslims in a way that they have time to consider solving their actual problems.

national resolutions must be passed to appease Muslims.

ime by having some countries sympathize with Muslims while others oppose them so when issues are presented before the v Council veto power is used to further delay any kind of n.

nd its Security Council must not resolve a single issue fauslim world.

s have also agreed to conspire to appropriate Muslim enever possible. Hence, disbelievers the world over v looking for, and availing, opportunities to occupy

'IN DEFENCE OF *JIHAD*' 163

9. The prophet once gave his companions a glimpse into this state of world affairs. They were disturbed by his description and asked him why it would come to this. The prophet once said to Suban: 'O Suban! What will your condition be when other nations descend upon you the way you reach out for a morsel of food in your plate?' Suban said: 'O prophet of Allah, may my parents be sacrificed for you; will we be in this state because we will be weak in number?' The prophet said: 'No, in fact you will outnumber the rest, but your hearts will be full of *wahun*.' The companions asked what he meant by *wahun*. The prophet said: 'Love for this world and hatred of death.' (*Masnad Ahmed*, Abu Dawood[18])

Disbelievers Occupying Muslim Lands

The current global state of affairs is a testament to the veracity of the prophet's words. Muslim lands have been occupied by:

1. Jews
2. Christians
3. Hindus
4. Buddhists
5. Communists

INQUIRER: You will need to present some concrete evidence to make your point, as you did earlier.

MUJAHID: Of all the international conspiracies against Muslims, I will briefly document a few:

Syedna Umar conquered *Bayt-ul-Muqaddas* (Dome of the Rock, Jerusalem) in 636 AD. Over the next twelve-hundred-and sixty-years Muslim ruled the region. Christians attempted to take back this sacred city but lost every bloody battle they waged. Finally, in 1917, English Christians succeeded in conquering Palestine. At the time, there were hardly any Jews in the region; the colonizers conspired to use Jews to weaken Muslim control of the land. Christians aided Jewish migration to

164 THE LITERATURE OF *LASHKAR-E-TAYYABA*

the region until there were enough of the latter to attack local Muslims. Riots erupted in 1927, 1929, and 1933 that resulted in Muslim massacres by Jewish migrants under the supervision and with the support of English Christians.

In 1939, a round table conference was organized in London in order to resolve the worsening situation in the region. The British sided with the Jews against Muslims. As a result, the Jews conspired to exile Muslims from their homes. In 1967 alone, over two hundred thousand Muslims were evicted from their lands and forcibly made refugees.

The Establishment of Israel

The British government declared the establishment of Israel in 1939 after which the disbelieving nations of the world began strengthening the fledgling state. As a result, on 5 June 1967, Israel attacked its neighbouring Arab states, annexing large swathes of Muslim territory. Foolishly, Muslims kept trying to resolve the issue through negotiations while the UN kept them running around in circles by making empty promises.

The colonizers continued strengthening Israel, so much so that from 1970 to 1980 this newly found state became an atomic power. The disbelieving nations transformed Israel into a military superpower in order to antagonize Muslims. Consequently, today, Israel bombs Muslims at will.

Israel first attacked Egypt in 1956, and then again in 1967 when it occupied the Sinai desert. In 1969, Israeli Jews set fire to *Bayt-ul-Muqaddas* (Al-Aqsa Mosque) and to this day, they regularly desecrate its hallowed grounds.

The Longest Strike in History Over Palestine

Palestine has become a long-standing source of grievance for the Muslim world. The problem has grown like a cancer. Short of *jihad*, Muslims tried to resolve the problem by every means possible. Muslims have organized strikes, made resolutions, orchestrated protests, argued in the General Assembly, pleaded before the Security Council, and knocked on the

'IN DEFENCE OF *JIHAD*' 165

doors of the UN, but to no avail. They thought Israel and its supporters could be condemned and criticized into giving up the occupation.

Muslims were victims of their own wishful thinking as they organized the longest strike in history in a peaceful attempt to resolve the matter. Consider the report published by the monthly *Bayt-ul-Muqaddas*, Islamabad:

> In 1937–38, Palestinians went on strike for six months; this is considered the longest strike in history. They protested the oppressive military operations of the Jews. In the course of this six-month strike a number of important Palestinian leaders were martyred.
>
> (5 December; Monthly *Bayt-ul-Muqaddas*[19])

To this day, some Muslims believe that resolutions and protests can be productive. Instead, they ought to wise up and fulfil their *jihadi* obligation to insure their salvation in this world and in the world hereafter.

What did the Palestinians achieve through their six-month protest? Did the Jews give up the occupied territories or worsen their aggression?

Was the Al-Aqsa Mosque returned to the Muslims? Was there any resolution to the conflict? Absolutely not! In fact, Muslims' condition worsened, and they remained victims of aggression and oppression, which continues to this day. *Jihad* is the only solution as explicated by Allah and as manifested in the life of the prophet.

The only hope for Muslims in this world is in following the footsteps of the Prophet. Short of this, Muslims are doomed to subjugation, hopelessness, despair, shame, and humility.

Upon the plea of the Saudi Arabian king, Shah Khalid, Muslims observed a day of protest around the world in solidarity with the Palestinian liberation movement, against the desecration of the Al-Aqsa Mosque.

Brother, this brief description of contemporary politics proves that the international community set up the UN as a farce in order to emasculate the *ummat* and deprive Muslims of their rights. Understand this well!

INQUIRER: These eye-opening facts ought to be enough to lay the foundations of global *jihad*.

MUJAHID: Brother, this was only a glimpse of Israeli conspiracies. A cursory glance upon the global stage will reveal that disbelieving

166 THE LITERATURE OF *LASHKAR-E-TAYYABA*

nations, including Christians, Jews, Hindus, atheists and communists, have occupied vast areas of Muslims territory.

INQUIRER: Have the disbelievers actually occupied so many Muslim lands?

MUJAHID: They have not only occupied the land but have subjected Muslims to a life of slavery and submission.

INQUIRER: Describe the conditions in these lands so Muslims can be convinced that *jihad* is the only way forward; prove that if they value their salvation, and hope for their future generations to remain Muslim, they must unite under the banner of *jihad*... that they must follow the prophet's companions by sacrificing their lives in the course of *jihad* in order to preserve their sacred spaces, in order to protect the honour of their women, and in order to uphold the sanctity of their faith. The times and Islam demand this course of action.

MUJAHID: Let us now look into various regions occupied by disbelievers, where Muslims are subjected to humility and strife.

Eritrea Under Christian Control

Islam arrived in Eritrea before reaching Medina. When Muslims migrated from Mecca to Africa, Negus, the kind-hearted king of Eritrea accepted Islam. The famous companion and the first *muezzin*, Syedna Bilal, belonged to this region. Nowadays this land is under Ethiopian control and Christians have made life unbearable for local Muslims.

In 1946, wary of the Muslim freedom struggle in the region, British colonizers employed the assistance of local Coptic Christians. As a result, the biased Christians martyred the president of the Muslim League, Syed Abdul Qadir Muhammad Saleh. In 1950, war broke out between local Muslims and Ethiopian Christians, resulting in a bloodbath in Asmara. Muslims lost a winning battle at the negotiating table. In 1962, religious freedoms were usurped, and Islamic education and Arabic were entirely banned in the region. Muslims were systematically persecuted.

As Muslims fight for independence today, the superpowers of the world side with the greatest oppressor, Ethiopia; consequently, Muslims are forced to live a life of subjugation.

The Plight of Burmese Muslims

Muslim traders brought Islam to the Burmese state of Arakan in 210 AH. Arakan became an Islamic state in 1430 AD. Muslims ruled the region for three hundred and fifty years until 1784 when Rohingya forces occupied the region.

In 1948 Muslims initiated an armed struggle known as the '*mujahid* movement', which would have been successful had they not been lured into negotiations that ultimately cost them their independence. Since then, they have been reduced to sending reminders to Islamic conferences and pleading with international organizations for freedom. The enemy orchestrated an economic genocide against them. They lived a life of poverty and subjugation, constantly appealing to the *ummat* to save them in the name of Islam and humanism. After years of dejection, once again, they have taken up arms and resorted to *jihad*. They are in communication with the *mujahideen* of *Lashkar-e-Tayyaba*, and very soon, Allah-willing, they will reap the fruits of their armed resistance.

Three Hundred Thousand Bulgarian Muslims Slaughtered in the Name of Communism

Muslims ruled Bulgaria for five hundred years. They lost control of the region in the course of battles fought in 1913 and 1940. During 1977–1978, countless innocent Muslims were slaughtered, while one million were displaced, and three hundred thousand died of starvation and cold.

The socialist revolution of 1944 resulted in religious, economic, and educational exploitation of Muslims. Mosques, *madaris*, and Islamic scholars were systematically martyred. It is estimated that approximately three hundred thousand Muslims migrated to Turkey.

Intellectuals, philanthropists, and activists must revitalize the *jihad* movement on a global scale in order to aid our persecuted Muslim brethren.

Thailand

Muslim traders brought Islam to Thailand in the twelfth century AD. Conversion occurred en masse and an Islamic state was soon established. In

168   THE LITERATURE OF *LASHKAR-E-TAYYABA*

1902, the Thai government imprisoned the Muslim ruler Sultan Abdul Kadir and started persecuting his subjects. Thousands of Muslims lost their lives in the course of an independence struggle. In 1968 they began an armed insurgency and started training guerrilla. They appealed to the Muslim world for help but to no avail. The *jihad* was terminated, and once again, Muslims were tricked into negotiating their own defeat. Negotiations and resolutions are pointless; the only solution to the plight of Muslims is *jihad*.

The Massacre of Chinese Muslims

Muslim traders brought Islam to China during the caliphate of Syedna Usman, when Syedna Saad bin Abi Waqas headed a delegation to invite its king to embrace the new faith.

In 251 AH (865 CE) a mosque was erected there, and entire tribes entered the faith collectively. Subsequent skirmishes escalated to five full-scale wars in which hundreds of thousands of Muslims were martyred.

On 17 May 1856, in the province of Yunnan, every Muslim seen in public was executed.

When Muslims protested this atrocity another seventeen hundred were martyred. Tanks were employed to crush a student movement in Peking led by a Muslim.

A Christian general in the Chinese government supervised the Muslim genocide over three years, beginning in 1928, during which 30 per cent of the Muslim population was eliminated.

The cultural revolution of Mao Zedong in 1920 spelled more trouble for Chinese Muslims. Mosques were shut down, *Eid* celebrations were banned, and Quranic learning was prohibited.

Negotiations and resolutions will yield nothing for the millions of Chinese Muslims. Their only solution, as well as the secret to a Muslim's survival, is *jihad* in Allah's cause.

Americans Slaughter Filipino Muslims

The United States bought the Philippines from Spain in 1889. When the USA seized control of Manila in 1900, skirmishes with local Muslims erupted almost immediately. From 1901 to 1903, the skirmishes escalated to an outright war, which left thousands of Muslims dead.

US soldiers massacred Muslims indiscriminately in the Muslim majority regions of Mindanao and Sulu. Until 1924, Muslims pleaded with the international community for justice in the face of an ongoing massacre.

When *mujahideen* of the National Liberation Front began guerrilla operations the enemy cast the net of democracy and trapped them in a so-called referendum.

In 1990, local Muslim were marginally included in administrative affairs and consequently silenced.

To this day, *mujahideen* continue their freedom struggle through *jihad* for undoubtedly *jihad* is the only solution.

Christians Rule Over Muslim Cypriots

Muslims ruled Cyprus from the time of the third caliph Syedna Usman when, in 255 AH (866 CE), the then governor of Syria, Syedna Emirate Muʻawiyah conducted a naval attack and conquered the island. It remained under Muslim control for the next twelve hundred and sixty years.

In 1914 the British colonized Cyprus. To this day, the Turks and the Greeks have battled and negotiated over control of the island while a large local Muslim population is forced to live a life of subjugation under Greek Christians who have been resettled in Muslim majority areas since 1941. Muslims have been dealt a carrot and stick approach in the name of democracy. In 1989, some Muslims took the bait by contesting elections. Plainclothes soldiers abused their powers to sideline and ultimately defeat the Muslim candidates. Only one Muslim candidate was successful.

In 1990, an elected official and an electoral candidate were jailed for eighteen months. Local Muslims have doomed themselves by participating in the democratic process. May Allah make them conscious of *jihad*. Amen.

Chapter 10: Muslim Lands Occupied by Disbelievers

INQUIRER: *jihad* is redundant in the age of international law. Conflicts can be resolved through the United Nations.

170 THE LITERATURE OF *LASHKAR-E-TAYYABA*

MUJAHID: As evident from the brief description of global affairs, to this day the UN and the Security Council have only harmed Muslim interests.

You say *jihad* is redundant in this day and age. If this were true Allah would not have said:

And fight them until persecution is no more.

(*Surat al-Baqarah* 2:193)

Tell me!

1. Has persecution ended?
2. Does Allah's religion dominate the world and subjugate disbelief?
3. Is *jizya* being collected? Are disbelievers being taxed as Muslim subjects?
4. Are innocent Muslims free from persecution or do they continue to be oppressed, tortured, and harassed by disbelievers?
5. Have we successfully stopped Muslims from being massacred and have we avenged the dead?

On the contrary, the enemy has occupied Muslim lands and aggressively carries out expansionist policies to control even more Muslim territory. Are we not obliged to reclaim these lands and free Muslims from oppression?

INQUIRER: Despite sacrificing so many lives in Kashmir there seems to be no sign of victory. It would be better to cease *jihadi* operations and turn to the United Nations for a resolution.

MUJAHID: Dossiers on Kashmir have been gathering dust in UN offices since 1947 but the disbelievers are not the least bit serious about resolving this issue. Millions of rupees have probably been spent on ferrying delegations that disingenuously purport to settle this dispute. Disbelieving nations siding with Hindu aggressors have ignored every resolution that has been signed, refusing to pay heed to the cries and pleas of oppressed Kashmiri Muslims. In fact, it was only after *mujahideen* started taking matters in their own hands that disbelievers gave serious consideration to the Kashmir dispute. Second, you invoke the loss of Muslim life in Kashmir; there is no denying this fact but consider this: Hindus are dying for earthly gains while *mujahideen* are laying down their lives for Allah and His oppressed followers. No doubt, their sacrifice is dear to Allah.

INQUIRER: What you say is true, but news from the frontier gets more distressing by the day.

MUJAHID: No doubt, the Prophet himself was aggrieved by the martyrdom of his men but did he terminate *jihad* because of these losses?

Lives Sacrificed During the Prophet's Times

INQUIRER: Today's losses are far greater than those of the prophet's era.

MUJAHID: Eighty-six battles were fought upon the Prophet's orders. The losses incurred during some of these are listed below:

- The prophet was so profoundly upset to hear of the loss of seventy Muslims in Bir Moina, he execrated the infidels while offering Qanoot-i-Nazla for an entire month.
- During the Battle of Mu'tah, the angel Gabriel informed the prophet that three of his generals had been successively martyred for a total loss of twelve Muslim lives lost.
- The bodies of seventy Muslim martyrs were retrieved from the battlefield of Uhad.
- Despite the losses at Uhad, the prophet continued to wage *jihad* upon Allah's command his entire life; if a battle was won, well and good, if not, the armies returned, but *jihad* was never terminated. The companions were advised to follow this example with determination and fortitude. The companions confronted empires, as they sacrificed life and limb without a second thought.
- During the Battle of Ajnadayn,[20] a hundred thousand Romans fought thirty thousand Muslims of which three thousand were blessed with martyrdom.
- At Qadsiya, thirty thousand Muslims battled one hundred and twenty thousand disbelievers; at the conclusion of this battle

172 THE LITERATURE OF *LASHKAR-E-TAYYABA*

between truth and falsehood, eight thousand Muslims were martyred while the enemy left behind twenty thousand corpses.

- After the bloody Battle of Yarmuk,[21] in which forty thousand Muslims confronted two hundred thousand of Nimrod's men, three thousand martyrs made their way to paradise while the enemy was left mourning seventy thousand miserable deaths.

Jihad continued even after the companions passed away which is why Muslims were blessed with victories and new territories in both East and West.

Despite the losses borne by Muslims, the prophet, as well as his generals, continued *jihad* upon Allah's command. The practical implications of these words have already been outlined while *mujahideen* offer an exegesis in blood.

A Warning to Those Who Avoid *Jihad*

INQUIRER: Thanks to Allah, I fully comprehend your reasoning. To summarize, you state that when necessary:

- *Jihad* can be waged in the absence of a caliph.
- *Jihad* can be waged in the absence of an Islamic state.
- *Jihad* is legitimate even without an emirate.
- You have clearly elaborated the obligation, importance, and necessity of *jihad*.

But what is the penalty for those who do not participate in this struggle?

MUJAHID: Non-participation in *jihad* is a great sin and the underlying cause for disunity. It incurs Allah's displeasure and wrath. Allah says:

If ye go not forth He will afflict you with a painful doom and will choose instead of you a folk other than you. Ye cannot harm Him at all. Allah is Able to do all things.

(*Surat at-Tawbah* 9:39)

Syedna Abu Imama reports that the prophet said whosoever has not waged battle, or has not prepared a *mujahid* for battle, or has not assumed the role of caretaker for the household of a *mujahid* engaged in battle, Allah will embroil such a person in some serious quagmire well before the Day of Judgement.

Abu Huraira reports that the prophet said that whosoever dies without having waged battle or without ever having the desire to wage battle in his heart, has died a hypocrite (*Sahih Muslim*).

Can We Participate in *Jihad?*

INQUIRER: Is it imperative to participate in *jihad* to escape Allah's wrath? How can we participate?

MUJAHID: Anyone who genuinely desires to join the struggle can participate in *jihad* even from the comfort of his or her home. *jihad* can be waged by manufacturing arms, transporting supplies like food, clothes, and medicine, and by guarding the homes of those on the battlefield. Similarly, *jihad* can be waged by inspiring others to join the fight and by countering the negative propaganda against *mujahideen*. *jihad* can be waged through actions, property, and words.

Dedicate Life, Property, and Words to *Jihad*

Syedna Anas reports the prophet said wage *jihad* against the infidels with your wealth, your lives, and your words.

Zayd bin Khalid reports that the prophet said whosoever prepared another for battle in Allah's cause, or offered to be a guardian of the house of one waging battle, it is as if he fought in the battle himself.

INQUIRER: The *Hadees* make clear the various modes in which *jihad* can be waged, but tell me, can one still join the esteemed ranks of the martyrs?

MUJAHID: The Prophet has been explicit about this matter as well. Consider the following *Hadees*:

174   THE LITERATURE OF *LASHKAR-E-TAYYABA*

Sahl bin Hanif reports that the prophet said whosoever sincerely begs Allah for martyrdom will be included among the ranks of the martyrs, even if such a person dies in his bed.

INQUIRER: In that case, this day on, I genuinely intend to participate in *jihad*; one hopes Allah will include me among the martyrs when I die.
MUJAHID: Brother, intentions are linked to actions, for intentions alone are meaningless. At the time of the Battle of Tabuk, the hypocrites declared they fully intended to join the battle but made all sorts of excuses when it came time to fight. Allah exposed them in the following verse:

وَلَوْ أَرَادُوا الْخُرُوجَ لَأَعَدُّوا لَهُ عُدَّةً وَلَكِن كَرِهَ اللَّه انبِعَاثَهُم فَثَبَّطَهُم وَقِيلَ اقْعُدُوا مَعَ الْقَاعِدِينَ

And if they had wished to go forth, they would assuredly have made ready some equipment, but Allah was averse to their being sent forth and held them back and (it was said unto them): Sit ye with the sedentary!

(*Surat at-Tawbah* 9:46)

This verse makes clear that in order to manifest one's sincere desire to participate in *jihad* one must be prepared for battle; hence it is imperative to attend a military training camp.

Brother Journalists! Join the *Jihad*!

Muslims have risen to guard their innocent helpless masses from the aggressive onslaught of disbelievers. This awakening has thrown open the gates of *jihad* in Allah's cause. *jihadi* operations are underway around the globe. From the closest frontier, we receive constant news of the enemy's losses. *mujahideen* are slaughtering officers and foot soldiers alike, as reported by the enemy. The very fact that India's press is up in arms about these operations is a testament to their success.

On our end, *mujahideen* gladly sacrifice their lives for *jihad*. Sisters bid farewell to their brothers and mothers dispatch their sons to the battlefield. What have our journalists done to further our cause in these circumstances?

Brother Journalists!

We invite you to tour the *mujahideen* training camps.

Come! Meet the young warriors, who have pledged their lives for *jihad*, who have returned to us after being embedded in enemy territory. Meet the injured ones who despite being wounded in battle made their way back and live to tell of their operations. Interview these noble men and publish their words.

Once you discover the truth, play your part in this struggle by writing about *jihad*, by publishing exclusive editions on *jihadi* culture, and by running special features on martyrs and their parents. Abandon the traditional gimmicks of journalism.

Expose the enemy's cowardice and failures. Detail the valour of the *mujahideen*; honour their sacrifices. Become an apologist for *jihad* and win Allah's favour.

Respected Scholars!

In this tract, we have detailed the Muslim nation's helplessness, indifference, and humiliation. In today's world, your obligation is not limited to the pulpit or the *madrassah*.

As true inheritors of the prophet's message, you ought to march towards the battlefield in order to exemplify what it means to be a follower of the prophet. Fulfil your obligation to 'rouse the believers to the fight' by offering your own lives on the path of *jihad*. Otherwise, you will have nothing to say when you are presented before Allah Almighty on the Last Day. Have you considered what will become of you then?

6
'The *Mujahid*'s Call' by Naveed Qamar

Here we translate the entirety of a 2001 pamphlet titled *Mujahid ki Azaan* ('The *Mujahid*'s Call'), which is a compilation of various articles by Naveed Qamar, the former spokesperson for the student wing of *Markaz-ud-Dawah-wal-Irshad* Pakistan, which were published in *Zarb-e-Tayyaba*. As we learn in the foreword, the various essays published in this pamphlet inveigh upon numerous issues in the Pakistani education system which have served collectively to lead Muslims astray.

Compared to *Hum Jihad Kyon Kar Rahen Hain* ('Why Are We Waging *Jihad*?') or *Difa-i-Jihad* ('In Defence of *Jihad*'), this pamphlet directly addresses college students who are attending secular schools, and their parents. It describes the social isolation that a student should expect when he decides to live his life 'righteously'. Whereas the previous two pamphlets are proselytization tools, this pamphlet assumes that the consumer of the text is a committed proselytizer himself. This allows the author to dispense with efforts at conversion and instead exposits how the aspiring *jihadi* acolyte should organize his daily life. Shifting from a second-person to a first-person narrative, the author engages the reader thus: 'You must ask yourself: how can I, as an individual, *fulfil* this obligation? First of all, my life must change: a proselytizer cannot maintain a regular routine or hold on to certain friendships and social activities while preaching Allah's word'. Further along, the text explicates the twin obligation of *jihad* and proselytizing: 'The battlefield of truth and falsehood will test our progress in two realms: one is the battlefield of proselytization, which we enter armed with knowledge and evidence; the second is the literal battlefield which we will storm with advanced weapons to wage *jihad*; two civilizations will clash, and one will dominate the other. Allah will aid His followers in humiliating the disbelieving enemy'.[1]

While rhetorically superior to the earlier two titles, this tract clearly addresses a more educated and self-reflective audience, while offering some

178 THE LITERATURE OF *LASHKAR-E-TAYYABA*

cogent critiques of the educational system and the gaps it leaves in character building. 'The *Mujahid*'s Call' draws a direct link between a student, who might be ostracized for a sanctimonious attitude, and the legendary persecution Muhammad had to deal with in Mecca, according to the traditional accounts: 'Arise and Warn! These were the words with which the prophet was instructed to spread the divine message he received at the cave of Hira. It is necessary to inspire every individual at every academic institution to proselytize and wage *jihad* in order to universalize the message of *tawheed* (Oneness of Allah) and *Sunnat*. No doubt, there will be hurdles, for this is the path of humiliation, poverty, and strife but if we tread this thorny road with fortitude, Allah's favour and approval await us in the afterlife.'[2]

This pamphlet has many of the same organizational features of both *Hum Jihad Kyon Kar Rahen Hain* ('Why Are We Waging *Jihad*?') or *Difa-i-Jihad* ('In Defence of *Jihad*') in that most sections do not logically cohere and are poorly constructed. This pamphlet, like the other two translated in this volume, reads more like an annotated list of topics rather than a well-reasoned and well-crafted piece of writing. The reason for this is explained in the Forward authored by Abu Abrar Asif Aziz, who was at the time of publishing the Spokesperson for Student Wing *Jamaat-ud-Dawah-wal-Irshad* Pakistan; there, he explains that this pamphlet is in fact a compilation of various small articles by Naveed Qamar, the former spokesperson for the student wing of *Markaz-ud-Dawah-wal-Irshad* Pakistan, which were published in *Zarb-e-Tayyaba*. It seems to be a fairly common practice for LeT to compose a larger document by assembling speeches or previous articles of LeT activists. Reflecting the role of both men in the student wing of the organization, this chapter aims to address college-age men.

Here, as elsewhere, we retain the organizational structure of the original document. There are six sections of the main treatise. In the first, 'Arise and Warn', the author explains the motivation for this pamphlet: 'to inspire every individual at every academic institution to proselytize and wage *jihad* to universalize the message of *tawheed* (Oneness of Allah) and *Sunnat*'. In the second section, 'The Inauguration of a Movement', the author reiterates his commitment to *jihad* even if he socially outcast for doing so, which suggests that student workers of the organization face considerable opposition to their message if they accept the real likelihood of being social pariahs if they perseverate in spreading the message of *jihad* and *dawah*. In 'An Odyssey of Desires', the author addresses the parents of young man who expect their sons to grow up 'to be a pilot... an engineer... a doctor, maybe a scientist ... [or], he'll be a high ranking official'. The author encourages parents as well as educators to raise train these youth spiritually and physically for *jihad*. He argues, 'Instead of raising them to be Western *sahibs* we ought to train them to be soldiers of Islam', which will also produce more obedient sons who are attentive to the needs of their family and nation.

In 'Who Has Wasted Our Young?', the author first lays out the failure of Pakistan's educational systems to produce opportunities for Pakistani youth. Instead of going to college only to find no decent job without paying ample bribes, the author encourages students to train for *jihad*. While parents and educators may resist this goal, once they see how their characters develop, parents as well as teachers and professor are stunned by the way in which '*jihad* changes every aspect of their existence, from their attitudes to their actions'. In the section titled 'Legalized Gangs', the author denounces secular student unions as legalized gangs which stand in contrast to virtuous Islamic organizations that are banned. In the penultimate section, 'Student Empowerment', is a continuation from the previous. Here takes issues with the equation of student empowerment as being coterminous with participation in the so-called legalized gangs he identified earlier. In the final section, 'The Effects of Proselytizing', the author describes the salubrious effects of proselytizers because of whom 'academic institutions that once supplied the multinationals of disbelief with clerks, bureaucrats, and brown-sahibs, and where hippies and conmen found a nesting place, now produce battalions of young Muslims who are willing to sacrifice their lives for the protection of Islam. These young men have tossed out the myth of a 'bright future' to enlighten the future of their faith for whose honour they are willing to give up their degrees, their salaries, and even their lives.

Foreword

Proselytizers in academic institutions must regularly confront perverse ideologies, mockery, resentment, and Western schools of thought. It is

180 THE LITERATURE OF *LASHKAR-E-TAYYABA*

essential to analyse and refute this multifaceted onslaught in order to guide our young men in light of the Quran and *Sunnat* (actions of the Prophet).

This pamphlet is a compilation of various articles by Brother Naveed Qamar (former spokesperson for the student wing of *Markaz-ud-Dawah-wal-Irshad* Pakistan), published in *Zarb-e-Tayyaba*, on topics including secular educators, materialism in academia, the hypocrisy of democratic student unions, and educational trends that have steered the student body away from true knowledge, which is Islam, and set it adrift in the impassable ocean of mundane ambition; our youth needs to be guided towards the ultimate purpose of existence: obedience to Allah. Many students have compromised their future by falling prey to the politics of their instructors; others have joined the rat race of materialism in service of earthly needs and trivial aspirations; and then there are those who are so utterly Westernized they act more European than the European masters they imitate.

In order to counter disbelievers conspiring against Islam, the times demand Muslim scholars and intellectuals equip themselves with the tools to distinguish right from wrong in every aspect of life according to the standards set by the words and actions of the prophet. Such thinkers can effect social change, obliterate Islam's enemies, and install the true faith of god.

Seekers of truth who wish to proselytize according to the Quran and *Sunnat* in academic institutions will find this text particularly relevant.

Abu Abrar Asif Aziz

Spokesperson for Student Wing *Jamaat-ud-Dawah*-wal-Irshad Pakistan

Arise and Warn

These were the words with which the prophet was instructed to spread the divine message he received at the cave of Hira.

It is necessary to inspire every individual at every academic institution to proselytize and wage *jihad* to universalize the message of *tawheed* (Oneness of Allah) and *Sunnat*. No doubt, there will be hurdles, for this

'THE *MUJAHID*'S CALL' 181

is the path of humiliation, poverty, and strife but if we tread this thorny road with fortitude, Allah's favour and approval await us in the afterlife.

Political organizations are a dime a dozen these days. They promise instant revolutions and overnight change; they produce leaders and guides whose meaningless statements appear as headlines in national dailies as they whip up political storms through rallies and marches and build magnificent castles in the air that have no foundation in reality. Revolutions such as these offer nothing more than pipe dreams. Eventually, the dreams scatter like ocean spray, and the dreamers go back to yearning for genuine transformation, too dazed to notice their own disillusionment.

A movement is not a whimsical whirlwind of emotions that subsides over time; it is neither a castle built on hollow incentives, nor is it the work of reversing certain injustices, only to reconcile others. Movements live well beyond the life span of superficial objectives and mandates, and they are rarely embroiled in mundane rivalries.

The essence of the word 'movement' refers to a consciousness that grips the imagination and conquers hearts; it is an attitude based on knowledge and faith that determines life's purpose and outlives its supporters; it isn't limited by funding (in fact it generates resources), and rather than groping aimlessly in the dark, it progresses in an organized and orderly fashion.

In this respect, Islam is a movement. It breathes life into lives, turning embers of meaninglessness into flames of purpose. It transforms barren wastelands into verdant meadows. It metamorphoses apathy into struggle. We must take note of how Islam has transformed each one of us. How has it impacted our sensibilities and our consciousness? Is every moment of our lives, every aspect of our meditations, and every driving force of our actions a living manifestation of an invitation to Islam? If our educational pursuits and our daily schedules are a testament to the dominance of the Quran and *Hadees* over the infernal subjugation of disbelief, then indeed, we are part of the Islamic movement.

Is it possible for those who profess love for Allah, obedience to the Prophet, and allegiance to Islam, to allow their fellow-citizens to reconcile satanic impulses, sin, and defiance? Righteousness and sin, obedience and rebellion, depravity and dignity can never coexist, but the societies in which we live, these unnatural contradictions persist.

182 THE LITERATURE OF *LASHKAR-E-TAYYABA*

Could it be that our own existence has come to embody and manifest some of these contradictions? No doubt, this must stop. Look around you, pay attention to your environment, challenge the rampant treachery you see everywhere, reignite the Islamic movement in schools and colleges, in your district's neighbourhoods, and on your neighbourhood blocks, and let your character speak for the Quran and *Hadees* that you proselytize; armed with knowledge, sentence disbelief to death and offer peace to all who profess faith.

(Surat al-Muddaththir 74:1–3)

The Inauguration of a Movement

Proselytizing and *jihad* are already underway to guard Islam, like a fortress, in the future.

This objective can only be achieved through personal transcendence supplemented by the rejection of peer-pressure and reinforced by a complete transformation of one's social dynamics. Without letting go of one's individuality, one will stand shoulder to shoulder amidst a disciplined student-body on the path to martyrdom.

Say: Lo! my worship and, my sacrifice and my living and my dying are for Allah, Lord of the Worlds.

(Surat al-An'am 6:162)

This is just the beginning. The sweat and blood of volunteers mingles with the earth as they lay the foundations of a magnificent fortress that will be known as Islam's stronghold, where the destitute and powerless will find shelter, and where infernal aggressors will be punished; this will be a light of hope for the Islamic world. No Hindu thug will dare violate the sanctity of a Muslim woman's chador, no Jew will embroil the Muslim world in another devilish conspiracy, and Satan himself will scour the earth in search of human co-conspirators. Polytheism will be effaced, and religious innovation will end. The light of *tawheed* will permeate a world fragranced by the eternal scent of *Sunnat*.

'THE *MUJAHID*'S CALL' 183

The blood spilled thus far has only cemented the foundational stones. The impending parade of martyrs has just begun. Countless sacrifices have yet to be made to strengthen and mobilize this movement. Our work is not done until Islam's message infuses every aspect of our social and domestic lives. You must ask yourself: how can I, as an individual, fulfil this obligation? First, my life must change: a proselytizer cannot maintain a regular routine or hold on to certain friendships and social activities while preaching Allah's word.

I will have to reengineer my social life. I will have to gauge which friends of mine accept Allah's message and which are defiant. I can only befriend those who live life according to the Quran and *Sunnat* and are willing to support me in my mission. No one else deserves my friendship.

So what if I am isolated at college? A little loneliness cannot shake my confidence. Who knows, those who mock me today may well be the forerunners of my struggle tomorrow. A single flame can pierce enveloping darkness. A single bullet disrupts the line between life and death. What is more, a single Prophet was sent to a tribe in the desert and entire nations rallied around him; on the other hand, there were messengers who failed to garner such support, yet they continued their life's work. My solitude is not a sign of a lost identity; my individuality is not compromised. I will not join hands with the hypocrites who draw up exciting plans and speak with silver tongues, merely to be part of a herd, least of all one that is steeped in idolatry and innovation. I will not give in to any desire to be part of a popular faction at college, even if its members shake the earth with motivational slogans and cover the city in posters and calligraphic graffiti testifying to their dreams of an Islamic revolution. If I feel they bargain their faith for material gain, and alter their ideology for popular support, I will have nothing to do with them. Sometimes, I'm drawn to those who chant 'death to America' in their rejection of Western culture but when I hear the music coming out of their bedrooms and the images displayed on their television screens, I turn my back on them as well. There is no congregation for me in this festering arena of opportunism and factional rivalry.

Indeed, I have no desire to be part of the majority; I must maintain my upright character for I do not need popular support. I am a congregation unto myself. The light with which Allah fills my heart has yet to

184 THE LITERATURE OF *LASHKAR-E-TAYYABA*

reach many more souls. There are countless students who are indifferent to the factions around them as they eagerly await a congregation that will eliminate all doubt and suspicion from their hearts and put them at ease; they need a congregation whose members practice the true and authentic Islam that they preach, who are not plagued by opportunism and popularity, who know how to stop evil by force, who challenge disbelief, and chop the hands off an aggressor but refuse to lay a finger on a brother.

Indeed, how many friends of mine await me? How many upstanding young men of noble character long for a manifestation of *tawheed* and the lessons of purity?

No doubt, I will declare my programme of proselytizing and *jihad* to these people; these are the ones I will pray for and heal, and I will no longer find myself alone. I will mobilize those who accept my preaching in service of Allah's faith.

This is the path to self-reliance and the instalment of Allah's way. The ones who kiss martyrdom and embrace hardship will be my friends. They will spread love and end hatred. As a volunteer of this movement and as a member of this congregation, this is my duty. O Allah, make me steadfast and accept my humble efforts. Amen.

An Odyssey of Desires

My son will grow up to be a pilot... an engineer... a doctor, maybe a scientist... no, he'll be a high ranking official...

These are the objectives students work towards tirelessly. Parents sacrifice their most valuable possessions for this purpose. But desires never end; they twist and convolute endlessly like the devil's intestines.

On the other hand, how long will the next generation continue to be entombed in unending desires and pointless aspirations?

We flood our children with a merciless ocean of desire from the time they leave the mother's womb to the time they begin school. As they accumulate degrees through college and university, and finally, when they set out looking for jobs, they are plagued by our mundane wish to see them enjoy the luxuries we ourselves could not afford. In truth, we lose our precious progeny to such ambition. Even before a child is fully self-aware, we insist on careers in medicine, engineering, and the civil service.

'THE *MUJAHID*'S CALL' 185

Moreover, these programmes are huge financial investments. Success, measured only in certificates, degrees, and test scores, is celebrated, cherished, and lauded. Parents are prone to love a high-scoring child the most, regardless of his character. On the other hand, children who fall behind in this race are resented, humiliated, and harassed. They are constantly snubbed for trumped up character flaws. As a result, perfectly decent youngsters abandon their education due to an inferiority complex only to develop truly reprehensible inclinations to drugs and violence.

One would think the school system might fare better in moulding our young. One would expect schoolteachers, at the very least, to help the next generation realize its true calling and purpose in life instead of pushing it deeper into the quicksand of materialism. But teachers today do not have the strength of character to make an impression on their students. They may know their subjects very well, they may deliver eloquent lectures on Islamic principles and have excellent command over languages, but they have failed to prepare the next generation for what the Muslim *ummat* needs. Instead, a standard of living based on superficial accomplishments like a good job, an enviable salary, an influential post, becomes the standard measure; students who pursue all this successfully are awarded certificates, medals, and trophies, while those who fall behind are labelled failures, idiots, and good-for-nothings.

The question is: are these the ultimate objectives and goals we want our next generation to pursue in life?

We are Muslim. Islam is our faith. In accepting Islam, one must reprioritize life's goals. A Muslim's standard of living is not determined by the quality of his food, the size of his home, or the thread-count of his shirt; he is neither interested in fame nor fortune, although prior to accepting Islam this was the two-headed god he worshipped in his pursuit of recognition and meaning. On the surface, he was satisfied, happy, and content. He blindly followed the theories espoused by every other pop intellectual, jurist, or writer. He was least concerned with his Creator. He had only a vague and tenuous understanding that the universe was the Creator's dominion. In his opinion, these matters were best left to churches and temples. He declared faith a private matter and expunged it from all aspects of public life. But a Muslim is above these base attitudes. A Muslim does not lose his sense of self to the world; rather, multiple universes take shape within his mortal form.

186 THE LITERATURE OF *LASHKAR-E-TAYYABA*

The Quran is the finest and most credible source of jurisprudence, science, knowledge, and ethics. This is the foundation upon which we erect our lives. If our foundational thinking, our actions, and our philosophy are not imbued with the light of the Quran and *Hadees* then no matter how many degrees we earn, we remain ignorant, with nothing to distinguish our so-called Muslim students from their Hindu, Christian, Jewish, Buddhist, and secular peers. Without Islam, all knowledge is useless. Islam guides us in distinguishing truth from falsehood and sin from righteousness. Consider a sophisticated blind man who is well-read, well-dressed, and well-spoken, but cannot see light from dark despite his accomplishments; he may try to walk confidently but he can never be sure of his next step. Instead of making sophisticated blind men of our progeny we ought to try and make them good Muslims for in truth, they are a test from Allah.

And know that your possessions and your children are a test.

(*Surat al Anfal* 8:28)

By raising our young ethically, we invest in our own afterlife. We can mould them into leaders who will save the sinking ship of the *ummat*, restore Islam's dignity, and free Muslims from persecution and treachery as they contribute to an economic, political, and social Islamic revival. But all this is only possible when we forego our personal aspirations and stop trying to ensure happiness for our old age (although no amount of insurance brings joy in one's twilight years). We must forego temporary and superficial rewards to raise our children solely for the ultimate victory and domination of Islam. Instead of planting them before the television screen or sending them off to play cricket, we ought to train them militarily for *jihad*. They need physical training for their bodies and spiritual training for their souls, which must be filled with love for Allah and hatred for disbelief. Instead of raising them to be Western *sahib*s we ought to train them to be soldiers of Islam. When a generation is raised upon these principles, perfidy will be eliminated from this world. Sons will serve their aging parents with the utmost care and affection instead of shoving them into social institutions. When teachers embody these values, the nation will produce men like Khalid bin Waleed, Osama bin Zayd, Abdullah bin Omar, Musa bin Naseer, Muhammad bin Qasim, and Mahmud Ghaznavi.

'THE *MUJAHID*'S CALL' 187

Teachers will be spiritual parents and students will no longer intimidate, harass, and assault them. But this sort of social change is only possible when every professor himself becomes a living manifestation of a proselytizer and a *mujahid*; only then will the godless environment of academic institutions transform into the warm and welcoming atmosphere of Islam.

Armed with knowledge and our beloved parents' and respectful professors' blessings, through proselytizing and *jihad*, we are trying to restore Islam's dignity in this world, in exchange for the gardens of paradise in the world hereafter.

Who Has Wasted Our Young?

As word of proselytizing and *jihad* spreads in academic institutions, countless students enrol in militant training camps across the land; parents, teachers, and the general public feel these students are being pulled out of their classrooms and sent to their deaths as part of a conspiracy.

The following essay refutes these allegations with credible proofs while pointing out the ways in which our student body is being squandered. It is for the reader to decide who exactly is wasting our future!

Who Has Wasted Our Youth ... *Mujahideen*, Student Organizations, or the Academic Environment?

By Allah! The frothing blood of a martyr is hotter than all the passionate speeches of an orator; its scarlet bloom is deeper than all the eloquence of a rhetorician; and it bears more scriptural references than all the citations of a preacher holed up in a mosque. Decades old Islamic movements, centuries old religious organizations, and millennia old institutions are nothing short of barren wastelands unless and until they are irrigated with the fresh blood of martyrs. Organizations, congregations, and institutions cannot withstand the onslaught of falsehood and treachery without the spirit of sacrifice. Once nations forget how to sacrifice their sons and brothers, their politicians and populations accept a life of slavery

188 THE LITERATURE OF *LASHKAR-E-TAYYABA*

and servitude, content to eat crumbs off a disbeliever's boots simply to get through this meaningless existence.

While such a nation is willing to bear every kind of humiliation, the one thing it refuses to accept is *jihad*, sacrifice, blood, and sweat. The masses make all kinds of excuses to delegitimize an armed struggle to avoid *jihad*. They say if students start waging *jihad*, who will care for the old, who will marry the women, there won't be anyone left for learning, the country will fall apart without doctors and engineers, institutions will fail, progress will come to a standstill, academies will become desolate, there will be a shortage of intellectuals, scientists, lawyers, bureaucrats, and economists, there will be a proliferation of arms, etc. But I ask these naysayers: when violent rivalries between student unions in academic institutions result in fatal clashes and unending court cases, who, then, cares for the victims' parents and sisters? How does one cash in on the death of a hardworking student who dies in an accident on his way home from college? As far as administering the state is concerned, any national daily is a testament to rampant fraud, murder, assassination, burglary, theft, and any number of social ills endemic in our country today. Who is responsible for the mass murders in mosques across the land?

Who is Behind the Bombings that Leave Countless Dead? Who is Really Using Students for Nefarious Ends?

Millions of children enrolled in primary schools across the country; thousands make it to college, while only a few hundred manage to get into universities; only a handful graduate; of them, only a few actually secure jobs, that too through influence and bribes. Considering millions enrol in school and only a handful make it through university, what becomes of the rest? What *jihadi* missions do they join?

It is said that only idiots who do not perform well in school join *jihad*. Let us assess the truth of this statement by referencing the academic gazettes of the past fifty years; hypothetically speaking, if twenty-five thousand candidates take the matriculation exam from a particular board, only 10 per cent pass, what *jihadi* congregation do the failures join? What Kashmiri battleground consumes the remaining twenty thousand? These are the statistics for a single board. There are countless such boards in

'THE *MUJAHID*'S CALL' 189

Punjab alone, producing more failures than scholars. What is more, those who are academically successful immediately leave for foreign lands, preferring a life abroad to offering their services to their motherland. Given these facts, who exactly is hindering the country's progress? When the country's finest expend their talents working for foreign institutions and organizations, where do we expect to find intellectuals, politicians, lawyers, bureaucrats, and economists?

Some allege that students who participate in *jihadi* programmes end up wasting their time and losing focus. Let us look at the ground reality to find out who is truly to blame for ruining the lives of our young. When boys are encouraged to play cricket in the name of extra-curricular activities, and they spend every waking moment on the field running aimlessly after a ball, is their time not being wasted? How many young men are lost to trivial pursuits such as these? When students are invited to musical events in the name of entertainment only to be infested with an addiction for the arts and they end up with headphones glued to their ears, banging their heads to rubbish, fancying themselves rock stars... are they not losing focus then?

What academic objectives do our young pursue when they plant themselves in front of the television set and consume all sorts of cable network programming? Thousands of young men waste their most productive years loitering around market squares, joyriding through city streets, flirting, and smoking; when this loses its appeal, they roll over and die in the throes of a drug overdose, while some Casanovas attempt suicide in the face of unrequited love. How many lives are lost to coeducation every year? On the other hand, processions, strikes, demonstrations, riots, protests, and boycotts are orchestrated across colleges and universities in the name of politics. Students have been ensnared by mindless slogans about student rights, voting rights, elections, and freedoms of expression. This kind of political activism shuts down academic institutions for months on end; hostels are sealed, universities are transformed into barracks, classrooms are searched for bombs, departments are locked and even the locks are jammed so they cannot be unlocked. Is this not a waste of students' precious time? The so-called intellectuals among us say this is unavoidable politics. On the other hand, if a single student, having completed his homework, decides to spend merely three weeks of his summer vacation at a *jihadi* training camp, his family and friends lose their minds.

190   THE LITERATURE OF *LASHKAR-E-TAYYABA*

He is criticized and taunted for becoming a terrorist, while the real terrorists are the ones filling the ranks of political student organizations that extort protection money from students across the land, from Sialkot to Bahawalpur, from Punjab University to Agricultural University, from Zakria University to Jamia Karachi, from Lahore to Hyderabad. These organizations harass those who preach the Quran and threaten violence against those who grow a beard and wear their pants above their ankles.

Their members cannot tolerate a difference of opinion; they start rioting if their party's posters are effaced; they act as if they own academic institutions and they view their fellow students as their subjects. Anyone at odds with their politics is banished from the university without a say in the matter. In contrast, consider the behaviour of the students who volunteer for *jihad*.

Before joining *jihad*, almost all students live a life of ignorance, self-indulgence, apathy, and sin. Then, their characters take a U-turn, leaving their teachers and professors stunned. Before their transformation they live meaningless lives, but *jihad* changes every aspect of their existence, from their attitudes to their actions. Our academic institutions fail to produce good human beings, let alone good Muslims. On the other hand, graduates from *jihadi* universities are not only fine human beings but leaders, imams, and guides of the Muslim *ummat*; they are trained to help the Muslim community out of its web of darkness by lighting the lamp of Allah's *kalima* (declaration of the oneness of god and acceptance of the prophet as his messenger) and leading the way. They are living manifestations of the verse أَشِدَّاء عَلَى الْكُفَّارِ رُحَمَاء بَيْنَهُم ('hard against the disbelievers and merciful among themselves', *Surat al-Fath* 48:29); they are full of love and affection for the righteous and full of Allah's wrath for the disbelievers. Nothing about them remotely resembles any feature of the Hindu culture; in fact, they have vowed to spread Islam across the world. Instead of harassing fellow students and professors they have made an oath to slaughter Hindus and Jews. Instead of seizing hostels and academic buildings they have pledged to destroy enemy barracks and camps. Instead of stalking women they seek and destroy enemy hideouts. When they pray, they beg for Allah's mercy with hope in their hearts, and long for peace for the Muslim *ummat* with tears in their eyes.

They are not interested in being popular or collecting votes which is why they don't go around making empty promises. They understand that the solution has nothing to do with the narratives spun by student leaders; instead, they are entirely dependent on their faith in Allah. They know that without the implementation of Allah's commandments, every education system and curriculum is futile for it fosters subservience to disbelief. Hence, all our problems can be solved once we start struggling in Allah's cause. Students are sacrificing their lives for this cause, today; they take time out from their busy schedules to visit training camps in the highlands; they are learning the use of advanced weapons and guerrilla warfare tactics; their journals are not filled with whimsical musings doodled in ink but with a rigorous schedule penned in blood; they are writing the very history of Islam with a passion that will soon illuminate and perfume the entire world. Allah-willing, all members of the student body, regardless of political affiliation, are invited to *jihad* in Allah's cause. This invitation comes to you not from any particular organization or congregation... Allah extends this invitation to you repeatedly in the Quran.

Join these young men who are struggling solely for Allah's approval, not for some mundane earthly benefit. All they want is to end the persecution of Muslims, establish Allah's command across the globe, restore the caliphate, and prosper. Their characters are transparent, their mission is clear, their invitation is universal. Who will step forward and grasp an opportunity to live a life of dignity, with the guarantee of paradise in the afterlife?

> The (true) believers are those only who believe in Allah and His messenger and afterward doubt not but strive with their wealth and their lives for the cause of Allah. Such are the sincere.
>
> (*Surat al-Hujurat* 49:15)

Legalized Gangs

For a while now, secular student unions and so-called Islamic organizations that have been outlawed in academic institutions across the country, are trying their best to have the ban against them lifted.

Even if the ban were lifted, can these organizations guarantee an Islamic character for their respective institutions? Even if these unions

192 THE LITERATURE OF *LASHKAR-E-TAYYABA*

are restored, can they adequately guide the student body? Can they end the rampant violence that pervades universities today?

The following chapter addresses these issues.

Student Unions: Legalizing Gangs in the Name of Freedom and Student Rights

It is important to consider what kinds of rights student unions operating in universities guarantee. After all, high schools, where there are no unions, function just as well; students learn in a peaceful environment, they respect their teachers, there is plenty of character-building, their rhetorical skills are developed, and their talents are recognized. The fact of the matter is that student unions are legalized gangs that operate under the slogan of securing student rights and freedoms. In the name of freedom of expression, students and professors are seen as equals, in fact, at times, the faculty is viewed as subservient to students. The administration is crippled under the authority of inexperienced, ignorant, politically driven students who turn classrooms into dens of cheating, harassment, bribery, and torture; non-partisan students are beaten up, professors are dragged to court, and even the offices of chancellors and principles are attacked. The police and the administration are helpless in the face of such hooliganism.

Various political organizations pump money and arms into these student organizations to further specific political mandates.

Teachers today limit themselves to delivering lectures without giving any mind to the character development of their students because there is no telling when a confrontation with a politically backed student may lead to violence. Every teacher knows that students operate like gangsters; they can have the faculty transferred or fired in a heartbeat.

Student unions are responsible for creating this inverted environment. The expulsion of a disruptive rabble-rouser is unthinkable in this environment. Dedicated solely to their private political agenda, unions encourage disruptive activities, foster violence, and 'train' exceptionally rowdy students to work as activists.

It is unfortunate that despite knowing all these facts, certain faculty members support student unions due to their personal political

'THE *MUJAHID*'S CALL' 193

allegiances. Hence, when the party they support comes into power, they are rewarded for their loyalty, while rival professors are unjustly marginalized. As a Muslim, do you think Islam encourages the kind of freedom that disrupts an academic environment and breeds violence? Absolutely not! Then, why do so-called Islamic organizations act this way? A ban on the very student unions that spread fear, terror, bloodshed, that are responsible for the declining status of professors in academic institutions, is being protested by these so-called Islamic organizations that are making fools of the student body in the name of student rights and freedom.

Ever since the ban on student organizations, their activists have nothing left to do. In the past, elections between rival groups were held merely to keep activists engaged in student politics. Elections provide the opportunity for unions to contest, and consequently, rally, riot, and terrorize. The side that wins literally takes over the university. The side that loses violently reacts to the occupation. And so the cycle of political violence continues, mindlessly, endlessly. Behind closed doors, union leaders admit that only through elections are they able to keep their party active and their leadership relevant. Without an election, they have nothing to fight for. They create an atmosphere in which going to jail is a virtue and assaulting a professor is a sign of confidence. They clash with police, riot, break laws, and harass civilians in order to gain recognition and mark their turf.

Those who support the unions claim that things were better before they were outlawed; they say there were fewer murders and conflicts before the ban. Anyone who was a student in 1989 will recall the number of homicides that occurred before and after student union elections. At the time, academic institutions across Pakistan became war zones.

In 1991, four students were murdered in Taxila's engineering university; another was killed in Lahore's engineering university in 1989; at the science college on Wahdat Road, union president Nasir Baloch was slaughtered soon after winning the election. What kind of democracy breeds such senseless and rampant violence? Four students were slaughtered in Punjab University in 1994 even though one single organization controlled the entire campus; to say the murders occurred because of the absence of unions makes no sense. The aforementioned murders and the ensuing violence were not a result of the absence of unions but rather, everyone involved was somehow associated with some political party or

194 THE LITERATURE OF *LASHKAR-E-TAYYABA*

other, and the tragedies were a direct result of politicians interfering in student life. Through election related racketeering, there was a rabid attempt to maintain control over the student body.

Students are clamouring for an election so they may elect a competent and righteous leader to represent them; one who 'not merely ensures the proper running of the institution but proves to be a guardian of education itself'. But what system will allow such a student to rise among the ranks to a leadership position? Does the current system even deserve such a qualified candidate?

In over half a century our country has been unable to create a leader of such calibre. In fact, even those who had leadership potential soiled their reputation by joining the electoral process. Politics has destroyed the lives of a number of respected scholars and intellectuals who spent much of their careers guarding their reputation. Student unions have never once produced a leader who has worked for strengthening an academic environment. There isn't a single academic institution, from Punjab University to Agricultural University, from Zakria University to Karachi University, from Diyal Singh College to Allama Iqbal Medical College, where Islamic thought suffuses the curriculum. Factions have formed around the politics of Bhutto, and the philosophy of Jinnah; people are being harassed in the name of a so-called Islamic revolution. Name one institution where an Islamic organization won the election and proceeded to Islamize the academic environment. Every hostel is booming with music, television shows, and films.

A democratic process can never produce a godly leader in an environment that is sharply in decline due to the pervading rapidity and scale of media influence. On one hand the majority rejects any mention of piety and Islamic principles; on the other hand, we cannot focus on character building if we must hide our Islamic guidelines to please the majority. As far as the educational system goes, it is obvious to everyone that it is an alien system; everyone, from the minister of education to the individual principals and professors, is helpless before it. Apparently, enslaved nations produce slavish governments that can't be expected to alter such systems.

What is to be done in this environment?
Should we disengage?
Absolutely not!

The prophet's life is a testament to sustainable transformation instead of crisis management. Proselytizing was never done with a majority in mind; in fact, every action and transaction was determined by *shariat*, which guarded the individual as well as the movement from transgression. Islamic standards of conduct and jurisprudence ought to be the backbone of every Islamic student union; proselytizing as a way of being has to be top priority because that is the only way to make Islam manifest. This is only possible if every member is well versed in the Quran and *Hadees*. Foremost, our educational proposal is one of character building that will permeate the entire cross-section of society.

Proselytizing engages our entire being. Its sole purpose is to reproduce model proselytizers who are upstanding manifestations of Islamic principles in areas of education, politics, economics, and culture. Although this cannot be achieved overnight, it need not take half a century, either. We have already wasted fifty years experimenting with democracy; in a few years, the next generation of proselytizers will take over educational outlets. This movement has no need for weapons; all show of strength should be reserved for the frontlines against Jews, Christians, and all nefarious disbelieving forces that puppeteer our governments from afar; those hands, indeed, ought to be chopped for they impose on us an un-Islamic system of governance. Every student is responsible for breaking out of this system. Any student organization that labels itself Islamic and has the capability to provide its members with AK-47s for its own security ought to first, and foremost, pit its strength against disbelievers, in order to benefit the entire community.

Every student has a right to study the Quran and *Sunnat* without being distracted by politics, factional rivalries, and riots. The Quran and *Sunnat* are not meant to be studied in isolation; they must be lived. Student organizations will be expected to do this graciously, without falling prey to sectarianism, in order to create an atmosphere where Islamic values are cultivated. Every student and member will also be required to acquire military training during vacations. Every member will be a model of uprightness within the boarders, and a practical manifestation of divine justice and wrath on the battlefield; in this way Islam must be guarded on the literal battlefields, beyond the frontiers, as well as on the moral battlefields within us. This is the character-building lesson we learn from the life of the Prophet. This is how we will create exemplars of conduct

196 THE LITERATURE OF *LASHKAR-E-TAYYABA*

and justice who will save the sinking ship of our faith. This is how we will produce scholar-warriors whose pens will be as mighty as their swords, and whose sense of justice will foster peace across the globe.

Student Empowerment

To gain the sympathy and attention of the student body, student unions have been bickering about something called student empowerment in which extremely overrated issues are highlighted as serious problems and their resolution is promoted as a crucial victory. What should have been nothing short of a political fad has taken over so-called Islamic parties with utterly short-sighted and superficial agendas. For a better understanding of rights and obligations...

We Do Not Fight for Rights, But as an Obligation to Allah

The following issues and demands have come to define the student struggles of our era: 'Fees are too high... self-finance schemes are selling us short... there is rampant privatization... there is a lack of accountability for *Iqra* surcharge funds... instead of discrediting merit with an entrance policy exam, cleanse the system of all corruption... make the national language the language of education... demand 5 per cent of the national budget for education... demand public universities on every level and women's universities provincially... expand university grants'.

These are the issues for which student organizations will strike, rally, protest, and riot, engineering public opinion to create a sense of unity and brotherhood against the establishment, and more often than not, the rallies end in violence. We intend to transform these rag-tag rioters into skilled volunteers and effective student leaders for their communities. This is how an Islamic revolution will unfold.

The past fifty years have been squandered as millions of rupees were wasted, thousands of workers were killed, countless students were led astray, and countless others were tortured amid senseless rioting. Finally, even when the fight was won and fees were reduced and self-finance schemes were terminated and the budget and the number of schools were increased, even then, we did not manage to produce a godly curriculum ensconced in a worthy educational system.

You cannot glue green leaves to dead branches and pretend it is spring if the roots are rotten. You cannot whitewash a building and pretend it is new if the foundations are weak and its structure is flawed. A sick man can wear new clothes, but he still needs treatment. A waxed car is no good if its engine is broken. It is unfortunate that an Islamic organization would operate on such superficial postulations. It seems like the secular demands were drafted solely for popular support; the Islamic organization could just as well have been a Hindu, Christian, Jewish, or secular organization.

The truth of the matter is that student organizations embroil the student body in meaningless and un-Islamic issues much like the local politicians and city counsellors who promise all kinds of social services in disingenuous displays of civic concern that rarely outlive the election.

Will fixing gutters and mending electric grids produce an Islamic society? Absolutely not, for if the foundation is not based on the Oneness of god, and the model of emulation is not the prophet, all other concerns are meaningless. This is why corruption exists even at the highest echelons of society; in fact, the higher one's rank, the more corrupt one becomes. There is a pervasive sense of debauchery and rebellion; Allah's word has been forgotten, murder is common, burglary is rampant, and no one is safe. As a result, we have some excellent new roads but no civil order. We have evolved in our waste management schemes but we still need to figure out how to cleanse our souls. We have put up brand-new streetlights but as a people we continue to meander in the dark. Our hearts are full of hatred, alienation, and rebellion. We have become so self-centred that human relationships mean nothing to us anymore; sons are at their fathers' throats and marital relationships are falling apart. Why is it so? We have diverted our attention from the real source of the problem to superficial and unnatural causes; we are no longer concerned with Islamic ethics. This is why we have come to resemble a prosperous European nation that has all the hallmarks of civilization but in reality, is nothing more than a society of apes that can measure the efficiency of a machine but cannot gauge the value of a human life.

198 THE LITERATURE OF *LASHKAR-E-TAYYABA*

Students deal with similar issues. Superficial problems distract them from the real task at hand. They waste their energies on futile causes that are portrayed as matters of life and death, without realizing that even if they win their case and, as a result, reduce university fees, or increase the number of schools in a district, they will continue to operate under a system of education imposed upon them by Lord Macaulay, which can never produce anyone worthy of leading the Muslim *ummat* and solving its problems.

Union elections won't cultivate peace. How can a secular educational system give rise to Islamic thinkers and intellectuals? Unless we Islamize all our institutions, we will not produce better politicians, *mujahideen*, officers, or professors.

The petitions listed above, such as fees reduction and increased schools, may garner popular support but have no impact on the system of education itself. Thousands of students graduate without a clue about the purpose of their existence. They have no idea why they earn degrees relentlessly. They have no sense of why they spend the best years of their lives poring over books.

They are made to do all this for a job that pays a few thousand rupees and gives them a fake sense of status and respect. Embodying the true purpose of one's life is much more important than surrendering to the superficial and materialistic aspects of existence; it is imperative to expand one's consciousness. Students have a right to an educational system that doesn't require them to memorize facts but builds their character so they recognize right from wrong; they must be equipped with the tools they will need to counter all forms of religious innovation as they guide the masses towards the true meaning of Oneness in order to foster a peaceful society. Today, the entire Muslim *ummat* is internally fragmented.

Isn't it essential to shield our next generation from divisiveness and factional rivalries?

Disbelievers control the economic and political systems of the Muslim world. Isn't it crucial for students to learn about Islamic economics and politics that they may better lead the nation?

Today, countless Muslims are being persecuted around the world. Isn't it time we made military and *jihadi* training part of the curriculum so our youth can aid their fellow-Muslims?

Instead of entrance exams and elections, wouldn't it more productive to unite under a single banner and mission: the dominance of Islam in the world and an end to satanic forces.

We can say with absolute confidence that if we steered our youth away from petty struggles of empowerment and pointless campaigning, and instead, had them focus on the prestige of their faith and the obliteration of treachery, Allah-willing, within a matter of years we'll be able to produce a generation of students who will apply their education, their degrees, their talent and their strength to helping the *ummat* resolve its problems. These young men will never use force against their peers; instead, they will use their might to destroy disbelief. Friendships will no longer be defined along party affiliations or allegiances but simply by the declaration of one's faith لا اله الاالله محمد رسول الله. Every single student who declares, 'there is no god but Allah and Muhammad is his messenger', will find in us a friend. We see no value in storming hostels, torturing detractors, and harassing those who disagree with us...

Consider the prophet, our model of excellence. Did he convert those around him in this fashion? Did he ever force anyone to join his movement through pain or persecution? Did he guide people to faith, salvation, and enlightenment using the tactics employed by so-called Muslim organizations today? Absolutely not!

What are our foundations?

Keep in mind, peace in academic institutions today cannot be achieved through violence, occupations, or union activities but through knowledge, action, and proselytizing and *jihad*. Change can only come once we replace Lord Macaulay's system of education with that bestowed upon us through the Quran and *Hadees*. This kind of change requires action; merely going on about Islam does nothing until your faith is manifest in every aspect of your life, down to your minutest gestures. Our student organizations have failed us in this respect as well. When it comes to practically embodying faith, activists play down the importance of living life according to the *Sunnat* of the prophet. They insist it is more important to install an Islamic government than live Islam on a daily basis but how can anyone be trusted to follow the *Sunnat* on matters of grave importance if they cannot follow it in their everyday lives?

Those who cannot overcome minor obstacles in their path cannot be expected to climb mountains. If you are unable to incorporate Islam

200   THE LITERATURE OF *LASHKAR-E-TAYYABA*

in your breakfast and your bloodstream, how can you install it across the land?

And who is better in speech than him who prayeth unto his Lord and doeth right, and saith: Lo! I am of those who surrender (unto Him).
(*Surat al-Fussilat* 41:33)

While we are on the subject, it is imperative to understand and accept that no single *Sunnat* of our prophet is any less important than another; as Muslims we are obligated to follow and emulate him as meticulously and holistically as possible.

Not only are we obligated to follow the *Sunnat* of the prophet but therein lies our salvation. Ignoring any aspect of the prophet's way of life is a sign of weakness. Such faith can never achieve anything of worth. This is why we invite those who yearn and fight for an Islamic revolution to start by acting, dressing, and behaving like Muslims but also to actively carry on the dual work of proselytizing among Muslims and waging *jihad* against disbelievers, as manifested in the life of the prophet. If the prophet had wanted, he could have started aid programmes for the poor, or created an organization that battled social injustices. But he did none of that.

The students of *Markaz-ud-Dawah-wal-Irshad* light the lamp of knowledge in a deeply troubled world. Come, join them as they organize their lives around the Quran and *Sunnat* instead of rallying behind ridiculous ten point or fourteen-point referendums. Join the struggle to make the world a better place for mankind.

O ye who believe! Come, all of you, into submission (unto Him).
(*Surat al-Baqarah* 2:208)

Islam's Education Policy

Every incoming government nominally revises and edits the existing national education policy only to be criticized by secular student federations, Islamic student organizations, and educationists, alike; ground realities are rarely factored in; just grievances are summarily ignored. After all, what is knowledge? What is the point of seeking knowledge?

'THE *MUJAHID*'S CALL' 201

How is it to be gained? How is it to be transmitted? These contextual questions are the essence of an Islamic education policy, yet they are categorically denied space in national discussions.

Can we train our youth according to the principles of Islam without altering the Western influences in our local educational system, or re-educating our teachers, or rethinking our curricula?

No doubt, we cannot. Let us consider the solutions offered by the Quran and *Sunnat.*

Our national education policy is a free-for-all with educationists, professors, student unions, and individual students all involved in advising, influencing, and shaping the dysfunctional system we have on our hands today.

In fifty years, we have not been able to determine what exactly we want to teach our future generations. Consider this: there's no end to our discussion about ways to establish more schools and colleges, universalize primary education, develop existing universities, fund private schools and art institutions, expand the education budget, and increase staff wages; while the so-called educated among us welcome this state of affairs, albeit with some reservation, can these superficial gestures really be termed policy?

Policy refers to the strategic process by which certain objectives are to be achieved; any reference to strategy or objectives is inaccurately labelled 'planning'. The question that remains unanswered is this: Are we, by chance, struggling to sustain and execute an education policy imposed on us fifty years ago designed to make slaves of us all?

Our policy makers and educationists constantly bemoan dismal literacy rates but what good has literacy, in of itself, done for us so far? Has literacy led to a more peaceful society? Have we been able to guard our society from cultural dependency in terms of education? Are the policy makers really fulfilling our needs?

Before discussing policy, we must be clear about what exactly is education. Second, we must ascertain what is the purpose of getting an education? And thirdly, we must determine how one is to be educated... how is knowledge to be transmitted? The first two questions deal with policy while the third deals with planning.

We are Muslims. Our education policy must reflect this. Allah led the human race out of the night of ignorance through the appointment

202 THE LITERATURE OF *LASHKAR-E-TAYYABA*

of the greatest teacher of all, the prophet, whose first lesson was: 'Read, in the name of your Lord who created' (*Surat al-'Alaq* 96:1). This was given alongside the universal call to knowledge through 'فَاعْلَمْ أَنَّهُ لَا إِلَهَ إِلَّا اللَّهُ،' ('So know [O Muhammad] that there is no Allah save Allah', *Surat Muhammad* 47:19) in which all humans are to know, by every means possible, that the creator, ruler, king, sustainer, and owner is only Allah, and all other forces or powers that lay claim to any of these qualities are false and unnatural. Thus, in fact, knowledge is that which distinguishes truth from falsehood. Truth can only be proven to be true and falsehood can only be shown to be false, through knowledge.

> That He might justify Truth and prove Falsehood false, distasteful though it be to those in guilt.
>
> (*Surat al-Anfal* 8:8).[3]

And the purpose of this knowledge is to let the truth prevail and let falsehood perish:

> He it is who hath sent His messenger with the guidance and the religion of truth, that He may make it conqueror of all religion however much idolaters may be averse.
>
> (*Surat as-Saf* 61:9)

… And how is this knowledge to be transmitted to our youth? How should this training take shape? This is what the Quran says:

> Allah verily hath shown grace to the believers by sending unto them a messenger of their own who reciteth unto them His revelations, and causeth them to grow, and teacheth them the Scripture and wisdom; although before (he came to them) they were in flagrant error (*despite thinking themselves modern*).[4]
>
> (*Surat al-Imran* 3:164)

This means true knowledge is that which trains a student's mind to discern right from wrong. The methods by which one is trained to make these judgements, serve as the building blocks of one's relationship with the world. This is why in the early days of Islam, when Muslims based

'THE *MUJAHID*'S CALL' 203

their systems of knowledge on the Quran and *Sunnat*, they were at the forefront of development and progress. Europeans fancy themselves at the helm of modernity but at one point in time they were traveling to the academies of Islam to learn. Early Muslim scientists and thinkers produced all the formulae of the modern world employed in technology, sciences, medicine, and various other subjects.

Gradually, Muslims abandoned the teachings of the Quran and *Sunnat* and started following the materialistic ways of the world.

They know only some appearance of the life of the world, and are heedless of the Hereafter.

(*Surat ar-Rum* 30:7)

This is why today we put our entire curriculum at the service of subjects like physics, chemistry, biology, mathematics, engineering, science, medicine and pharmacy, statistics, and political science; we produce doctors, engineers, businessmen, and lawyers, by the truckload but not one of them can distinguish right from wrong. The real tragedy is that anyone who can read or write is considered literate and educated whereas from an Islamic perspective, even a PhD awarded by the current system cannot be considered a testament to knowledge. This is why the Quran lists certain literate people as ignorant. The irony is that the greatest teacher, scholar, and guide sent to the human race, the Prophet, could not read or write but was the wisest and brightest man to have ever lived whose brilliance continues to permeate the greatest intellectuals of our times. This isn't to say modern scientific education is forbidden. Islam elaborates on its stance in the following verse in the Quran:

We verily sent Our messengers with clear proofs, and revealed with them the Scripture and the Balance, that mankind may observe right measure; and He revealed iron, wherein is mighty power and (many) uses for mankind, and that Allah may know him who helpeth Him and His messengers, though unseen. Lo! Allah is Strong, Almighty.

(*Surat al-Hadid* 57:25)

The arts and sciences are not merely useful for inventing gadgets for human convenience, but in fact, they are a test from Allah to see if we

204 THE LITERATURE OF *LASHKAR-E-TAYYABA*

employ all that he bestows upon us, from inventing minds to warrior spirits, towards Allah's faith, His Oneness, and towards making the world submit to the Prophet's divine authority.

'Liya'lam Allah'[5] means that Allah wishes to test to you. As Muslims, should we structure our educational system around the pure materialism of the West or shall we rebuild it in the inspirational light of the divine verses that extol knowledge in order to create a righteous society where everyone is just? Let us begin by making Allah's faith govern the world. ليقوم الناس بالقسط.[6]

If creating a curriculum based on the teachings of the Quran and *Sunnat* was enough, Allah would have delivered His word in a remote wilderness for humans to read and incorporate into their lives. But this goes against human nature. In order for humans to understand the word of god and in order for them to shape their societies according to god's will, the prophet was sent as a teacher and a guide, who not only recited the verses but was also Allah's word manifest. By Allah's command, the Prophet inspired, educated, and guided humans into aligning their lives with nature, creating a congregation that surpassed all other nations, tribes, and states in terms of politics, economics, traditions, and social values, and that will remain a model of excellence for all mankind for all times to come.

Although the government of Pakistan has recommended including translations of Quranic passages in the curriculum, this is analogous to the Quran being revealed in a wilderness, for till now, the ones teaching Islam during *Islamiyat* periods have failed to embody its message or inspire their students.

When teachers themselves fail to embody the spirit of the Quran, how can they be expected to lead the way in more pressing matters?

Second, imagine the confusion when on one hand students are taught Quranic injunctions, while on the other, what they learn in various other subjects directly contradicts the word of god. For instance, in mathematics, they are taught how to calculate interest, in Urdu they are exposed to inappropriate emotions through poetry and literature, in English they are exposed to the Western tradition, in science they learn about Darwinian evolution and theories of countless godless scientists, etc. Students can only benefit if all knowledge is transmitted to them in light of the Quran otherwise the internal contradictions in our curriculum will leave them distraught and they will come to view Islam as just another subject in school.

'THE *MUJAHID*'S CALL' 205

Third, a Quranic curriculum means little without an environment that reflects the values it embodies. Teachers should dress and behave like honourable Muslims; students and teachers ought to offer congregational prayers together at the prescribed times of the day; musical events, fairs, carnivals, and concerts ought to be categorically banned, as should sports that encourage students to waste time without benefiting them in any way; instead of cricket, martial arts should be made mandatory. Our educational policy must incorporate all these changes in light of the Quran and *Sunnat*.

Fourth, a teacher's work is not limited to teaching his subject according to the curriculum; he is responsible for shaping and inspiring his students' character. This concept is lost on today's educationists. This is why, today, teachers refuse to discipline their students on the pretext of being responsible only for teaching their respective subjects. This kind of attitude is steeped in materialistic pragmatism resulting in teachers who are solely interested in duties for which they are paid, with little to no interest in moulding the personalities of those entrusted to them.

We need an education system in which teachers feel responsible for their students' entire lives, twenty-four hours a day. Teachers should not only interrogate their students about homework, but about their prayers, attitudes, company, speech, and the way they conduct themselves in public; additionally, they must also forbid their students from watching television shows and movies. But in an environment where teachers themselves lead conversations antithetical to Islam, how can they be expected to watch over our youth? Despite the fact that this system has corrupted an entire generation, we insist on calling it an education because we have foolishly limited our definition of the term to the ability to read and write.

Teachers who have earned advanced degrees from foreign universities are so awed by the Western tradition they cannot stop praising the advancement and progress of the societies from which they have returned. As a result, their students develop an inferiority complex and try to emulate the cultures they hear about. This is how cultural slaves are produced. Short of rehabilitating such teachers, they ought to be removed from educational institutions, so they stop poisoning our young.

Objectives are the driving force of an education policy. As stated earlier, our current objectives comprise earning degrees, finding work, and making a respectable living. Towards this aim, children go through years of rigorous schooling only to end up begging, bribing, and boot-licking their way into a job. Every year, our schools produce thousands of individuals driven solely by materialistic self-interest. Hence, there's an acute dearth of individuals in the *ummat* driven by Islam's education objectives, which is the conquest of truth and the end to all falsehood. Meanwhile, gradually, we descend into a slavish mindset as a nation. While the most knowledgeable among us ought to be at the forefront of raising the banner of truth and ringing the death-knell for disbelief, they are the most avid supporters and followers of the disbelievers. By our standards, such men are failures.

Similarly, according to our proposed education objectives, we don't aim to send our young women to school merely to earn degrees but to produce worthwhile Muslim mothers. Earning a degree with the mundane objective of acquiring a good job is nothing short of materialism. So long as the Muslim *ummat* produced noble and honourable mothers who made Islam their chief priority, they gave birth to Islamic thinkers, generals, politicians, economists, and scientists; but when they left the sanctity of their homes in emulation of disbelieving cultures, the entire nation devolved into a mess of debauchery and godlessness. Hence, it is important to create a curriculum that specifically caters to the female student body; only then can we hope to liberate and empower 55 per cent of our population.

The battlefield of truth and falsehood will test our educational advances in two realms: one is the battlefield of proselytization, which we enter armed with knowledge and proofs; the second is the literal battlefield which we will storm with advanced weapons to wage *jihad*; two civilizations will clash, and one will dominate the other. Allah will aid his followers in humiliating the disbelieving enemy.

Short of this, if we continue wasting our time on the circus, we call our system of education, the Muslim *ummat* will know neither freedom nor dignity.

***

It is unfortunate that the efforts of various student organizations are limited to trivial pursuits such as conferences, seminars, and rallies;

none of them has been able to provide a radical alternative to the current education policy. Some organizations recommend alterations to the existing framework but much like the dysfunctional framework, these recommendations are not what one might call 'policy'. At best, these are schemes to increase basic literacy rates. Student groups are against the current education policy merely because they oppose the government, which is attempting to ban all kinds of student run democratic (political) and pseudo-religious organizations. In the current stand-off between political student organizations and the government, we side with the government.

We urge the leaders of all student organizations to stop wasting their time on meaningless measures, and instead, to try and play a positive role in the student body. There's no point in sustaining movements on electoral life-support; fame and power are the pitfalls of politics. The Muslim *ummat* needs students who operate beyond this realm. In the past, student organizations have achieved little and, for the most part, have been a nuisance. It is time to look beyond the world of petty politics and focus on problems facing the entire Muslim world; these problems must be solved collectively. The past fifty-three years of experimenting prove that students can no longer be fooled. The world is undergoing a cosmic transformation in which Islam will rise and dominate disbelief through the joint efforts of proselytizers and *jihadi*s. Allah-willing.

We appeal to all student organizations to come join us as we follow the path that guarantees success and salvation, shown to us by the prophet: the path of proselytizing and *jihad*.

Trash your charters, tear up your proclamations, end your personality cults, renounce fame and power, distance yourself from the dirty world of politics; instead, offer sacrifices in Allah's cause with the sole mission of upholding the banner of Islam. Young men must prepare for *jihad*, not petty student elections; we will dispatch our finest to the frontiers to fulfil our obligation to Allah, as we prepare to settle our accounts in the afterlife.

The Effects of Proselytizing

Due to proselytizers, academic institutions that once supplied the multinationals of disbelief with clerks, bureaucrats, and brown-sahibs, and

208 THE LITERATURE OF *LASHKAR-E-TAYYABA*

where hippies and conmen found a nesting place, now produce battalions of young Muslims who are willing to sacrifice their lives for the protection of Islam. These young men have tossed out the myth of a 'bright future' to enlighten the future of their faith for whose honour they are willing to give up their degrees, their salaries, and even their lives.

Effects of Proselytizing on Academic Institutions

The student body is curious about our manifesto; they ask for monograms and membership cards; they want to know our slogans; they want to see the banners we fly; they ask us how they can become members of our congregation.

Brothers, the prophet said:

ترکت فیکم امرین لن تضلو ما تمسکم بهما کتاب اللہ و سنۃ رسولہ

(*Masnad Ahmed*)

'that my *ummat* cannot go astray as long as it adheres to two things'[7]

The two things are Allah's book and the prophet's *Sunnat*; we are the only congregation that embodies these two aspects fully, which is why we are the only ones who have a right to call ourselves the congregation of truth! Brothers, the prophet's words are meant to keep you on the path of righteousness; we have modelled our programme, our proselytization, and our mission according to the Quran and *Sunnat*. Consider the benefits: after all these years in existence, how many institutions or hostels have the students of *Markaz-ud-Dawah-wal-Irshad* occupied? Where have they established a 'hold'? No doubt, these are not the standards by which we measure ourselves. We measure our success in the immortal sacrifices our students sign off with their blood; these testaments flutter in the Kashmiri breeze, from Sri Nagar to Badgam, through Dodha, all the way up to Kupwara.

Brothers, we want as much as anyone else to keep our movement thrive but not through graffiti, or posters, or badges. What makes us endure is the steady stream of graduates from any number of institutions who head for our military training camps, from where they are launched into

'THE *MUJAHID*'S CALL' 209

Kashmir. Our congregation, which is the congregation of the prophet, is alive as long as the guardians of the Quran and *Sunnat* are transforming lives in academic institutions. Consider Punjab University graduate Abu Al-Abrar; he was a second year LLB student when he made his way to Kashmir to crush the aggressors and slaughter Hindus; he learned to embody the Quran and *Sunnat* under *Markaz-ud-Dawah-wal-Irshad.* Consider how Sana-ur-Rahman, a student from Government College Vihari transmitted his message. Brothers, rejoice! Today, there is not a single academic institution where you will not find *Markaz-ud-Dawah-wal-Irshad* at work. Our members wear their *shalwar*s high and their beards long; they style their hair according to *Sunnat...* they are the proselytizers of *tawheed* and they are everywhere, from Agricultural University to International Islamic University, from Government College to Bahawalpur Sindh, and beyond, all the way to Jamia Karachi; and all this, without raising a single weapon or making a single threat. From their ranks, we produce martyrs for Kashmir. Consider the impact of *Markaz-ud-Dawah-wal-Irshad*: half the student body of *Lashkar-e-Tayyaba* comes from institutions where *Markaz-ud-Dawah-wal-Irshad*'s associates operate. Is this not proof that the path we have adopted will lead to certain victory? One day we will attain our goals. Allah-willing. Beyond this, we have no musical programmes, or carnivals, or coeducation seminars, or picnics, or cricket tournaments, or food festivals to offer.

Brothers, we don't need to resort to petty publicity tactics to gain popular support; you yourself make a home for our message in your heart and pledge to make sacrifices for Allah's faith. Today, our growing strength strikes fear in the hearts of disbelievers. Jews and Hindus of the world are still trying to figure out how it happened that the very academic institutions they infiltrated with their syllabi and their professors are now producing fundamentalists who wear their *shalwar*s high and their beards long. Today, the conspiracies of the disbelievers are coming to an end. Israel's end is imminent. The very Europeans who used to produce our syllabi are in a crisis. Hindus are terrified of the kind of strength we have been gaining in our academic institutions. We have been able to achieve all this simply by keeping our message straightforward. This was possible because we never had to resort to silly strategies to win votes, or popular support. Brothers, keep in mind, as long as this message is purely based on the Quran and *Sunnat*, Allah will bestow His blessings and reveal His

210 THE LITERATURE OF *LASHKAR-E-TAYYABA*

favours; He will withdraw His support the second we adulterate our message with personal or political ambition; then, the very institutions that celebrate us for the message we proselytize will cast us out in shame. As it stands, our message has influenced the faculty as well. Professors, who tried to make an impact through their knowledge of technology and science in the past, are now inspiring their students to follow the path of the Prophet, having accepted the message of *Markaz-ud-Dawah-wal-Irshad*. They do not fear terminations or boycotts. By Allah's grace, professors are walking alongside their students, in this procession, shoulder to shoulder.

Brothers, this message cannot stop. We must expend every resource at our disposal to spread it as far and wide as possible. Unlike other student organizations, becoming a member of *Markaz-ud-Dawah-wal-Irshad* will not lead to a stellar job or a high salary once you graduate; we do not offer lucrative positions in high offices; our work is entirely for Allah. Those who wish to join us must do so solely for their desire to serve Allah and make sacrifices in His path. Brothers, now that we have received the message, what are we to do about it? What are our objectives?

Brothers, we must be grateful for the blessing we have received, even though, as of now, our volunteers are not working as hard as those who are working in service of falsehood; no doubt, our activists have a long way ahead of them.

What great movement have we joined? What are our responsibilities? How much time do we spend in Allah's cause? Are we truly producing the force *Lashkar-e-Tayyaba* needs? Are we producing the leadership *Lashkar-e-Tayyaba* could use on the battlefronts? Compared to all the speeches we deliver at education and academic institutions, how much blood and sweat do we expend for this cause? Workers of the student federations spend time in jail, have their legs broken, and take a bullet for their false ideologies; are we willing to make similar sacrifices? We're still double-minded about our capacity to make sacrifices while waging *jihad*. Brothers, we must make a visible show of conviction in all schools and colleges to prove that we are indeed capable of making every kind of sacrifice imaginable. This is only possible when, after we are done with our classes and our homework, we spend all remaining hours of the day inviting every single person we encounter into our fold. Only then can we prove our commitment to the struggle.

'THE *MUJAHID*'S CALL' 211

Countless organizations operate in academic institutions today. Some are politically motivated; others claim to be working for Islam. The latter invite students for meditation circles and chanting sessions. Their impact is growing, and we are to blame for this. Vast swathes of the student body are ignorant about us because we have been lax in delivering our message. We are losing students to contemporary doctrines posing as religion because we haven't knocked on enough doors. We take full responsibility for our lackadaisical attitude that has resulted in a large number of students being led astray.

Brothers, all is not lost. One must plan. We must move forward, not as individuals but as an army. Every academic institution must produce a campaign of its own that marches to the battlefield to obliterate disbelievers. We must seek forgiveness for our sins, and then proceed to gather as many members as possible for our cause by giving glad tidings about the future. Those who have not sacrificed in the past must make sacrifices now. Bear the mockery, the taunting, and the humiliation; family members and friends will accuse you of becoming a '*fundo mullah*', but do not abandon your mission. The point is not to arrive at a military training camp alone; you want to get there as part of a caravan. The Indian Army increases its presence on the battlefield by ten thousand soldiers every few months; we need to match this increase as frequently with warriors of our own. Our academic institutions will provide the fresh blood and leaders we need for this purpose. We pray to Allah to align our attitudes and our inclinations according to the unique programme He has outlined for us, that we may be ready to make every sacrifice necessary. Only then can we mitigate, and ultimately flush out all the iniquities pumped into our educational system by disbelievers. In their place, our message will pervade the halls and corridors of our schools and colleges, while the conspiracies of the disbelievers fall through. This will foster peace in our society, while those who make sacrifices for this cause will gain Allah's favour. We pray that Allah accept our efforts and bless us with the capacity to continue serving Him.

7

We, the Mothers of the Lashkar-e-Tayyaba
by Umm-e-Hammad*

Lashkar-e-Tayyaba (LeT) is distinctive from most of the militant groups in Pakistan in that it dedicates considerable resources to recruiting women and their families. The organization understands that women are responsible for reproducing the *ummat* and raising good Muslims. While LeT encourages women to observe strict *purdah*, it also relies upon women to engage in important social and political activities to engage other women as a means of accessing their families for economic and human resources. A female leader in the wing can achieve significant status within the ranks of the organization and enjoy relative freedom of movement because of the legitimacy and presumed piety that her membership in LeT confers upon her. Participation in LeT's women's wing also affords women a socially acceptable public life and an opportunity to leave their homes to participate in LeT's various women's *ijtema'at* (pl. *ijtema*, meetings), which is also relatively rare in Pakistan.

Perhaps the most well-known member of LeT women's wing is the notorious female propagandist named Umm-e-Hammad. As Haq details, she is a prolific writer of *jihadi* poetry for LeT, as well as the compiler of the three-volume set *Hum Mayen Lashkar-e-Tayyaba Ki* (*We, the Mothers of Lashkar-e-Tayyaba*).[1] The first volume was first published in 1998 and republished in 2001. The second and third volumes were published in 2003.[2] The first and second volumes have prefatory materials followed by several hundred biographies of slain fighters, many of which have been published elsewhere in the organization's various periodicals. The third volume has only a 'Publisher's Note', and contains no biographical accounts of Umm-e-Hammad.

---

* The front matter of this chapter draws from C. Christine Fair, *In Their Own Words: Understanding the Lashkar-e-Tayyaba* (New York: Oxford University Press, 2019): pp. 130–146.

214 THE LITERATURE OF *LASHKAR-E-TAYYABA*

Umm-e-Hammad claims to be the mother of multiple martyrs, which confers upon her considerable credibility among women whom she—and her body of work—hopes to inspire to send their men to wage *jihad*. By extolling Umm-e-Hammad in this way, LeT has conferred to her significant social status not only as a mother of fallen fighters but also as a key leader in its women's league. She also has gravitas among the fighters themselves owing to her poetry and other attributes which are redolent of al Khansa.[3]

Whereas the last three chapters of this volume presented entire translations of pamphlets, this chapter focuses upon three lengthy volumes titled *We, the Mothers of* Lashkar-e-Tayyaba (Volumes 1–3). The bulk of these volumes is comprised of various so-called martyr biographies which are written by their mothers in most cases. Because many of the biographies that are compiled in these volumes have been published in other LeT publications, here we include only excerpts from the series. From the first volume, we present the publisher's note, a memoir of Umm-e-Hammad, and what she calls a preamble. From the second volume, we present the publisher's note and a few illustrative biographies. Due to the repetitious nature of the three-volume set, we do not present translations from Volume 3. We retain the organizing structures of the original.

We, the Mothers of Lashkar-e-Tayyaba: Volume 1

Publisher's Note

By Allah's grace and strength, *Markaz-ud-Dawah-wal-Irshad* continues to launch both proselytizing and *jihadi* expeditions as thousands of *Lashkar-e-Tayyaba* operatives achieve martyrdom by way of *jihad* dispatching countless Hindu soldiers to hell. Meanwhile, the hundreds of thousands who have devoted their lives, heart and soul, to proselytizing are a living embodiment of noble conduct and impeccable character.

The current publication *We, the Mothers of* Lashkar-e-Tayyaba is the result of Sister Umm-e-Hammad's tireless efforts and extensive travels. She is a member of our women's wing as well as a mother of martyrs. She has dedicated her family and her life to *jihad*. Her poetry is popular among *mujahideen*. Her impassioned words have inspired thousands to abandon their homes for the battlefield in search of the gates of paradise.

Umm-e-Hammad has interviewed the mothers, sisters, and relatives and friends of countless martyrs and recorded their sublime emotions in this compilation. Upon reading these biographies one is reminded of the age of the blessed companions (of the prophet) when those who received word of a loved one's martyrdom refused to mourn or lament, but instead celebrated and rejoiced, and offered their consolation and goodwill to the messengers bearing news of the departed.

This book is a testament to the fact that the swelling ranks of martyrs is inspirational in of itself. Every house, clan, and village that loses a member on the battlefield produces many more to take their fallen brother's place. Our volunteers ought to disseminate this publication far and wide such that our women are inspired to dispatch their men to the battlefield.

Umm-e-Hammad has already completed the second volume of this series but due to various complications this has not yet been published. Meanwhile, the second edition of the first volume is before you. Insha'Allah, the second volume is forthcoming.

We pray that Allah accept Umm-e-Hammad's efforts made manifest in this book; may He give her the strength to continue her work such that all Muslim women are inspired to cultivate the spirit of *jihad*. And may Allah give this lowly servant the ability to print the second volume of this series sooner than later. Amen.

Muhammad Ramzan Asri
Masul Dar-ul-Andlus, Lahore

A Memoir

Back in the day, when I thought *jihad* was another word for treachery and I was convinced that *Markaz-ud-Dawah-wal-Irshad* brainwashed our youth into leaving their homes for the battlefield by coaxing them to abandon their education to fight in Kashmir only to be slaughtered like lambs for a few riyals and dollars, my husband Mian Asif Ali Abu Hammad began consorting with Hafiz Muhammad Saeed a little too regularly. Although the two had been friends for some years, when my husband publicly confessed that, by working in a bank, he was raising our children on usurious earnings I was certain the so-called guardians

216 THE LITERATURE OF *LASHKAR-E-TAYYABA*

of the Kashmiri *jihad* had recruited him. As a result, I started taking precautionary measures: I applied for every single loan for which our household qualified in order to entrap my husband in an unending cycle of debt repayment. In short, while his usurious earnings weighed down my husband's conscience, I was trying to protect our future and lifestyle by increasing our debts. I would reassure him that we lived by the sweat of his brow, and that he made an honest and honourable living. Although Satan aided me in my strategy Allah intervened for the sake of my husband; one morning, he went to work, handed his resignation to the manager, and swore never to step inside a bank ever again. Then he went straight to the *Markaz*, and from there, he left for Jaji, *Lashkar-e-Tayyaba*'s pre-eminent training centre in Afghanistan.

All hell broke loose at home. We cursed the *Markaz*'s *emir* to no end, but no amount of venting was enough for me. Upon the insistence of my relatives, I acquired the address of *Markaz-e-Tayyaba*'s training camp in Muzaffarabad and cursed the fraudulent organization the entire way there; the scene I created upon my arrival must have pleased Satan greatly. May Allah forgive my sins for after spending a few days at the training camp observing the *mujahideen*'s lifestyle, their routine, their training, and the passion with which they dedicated their lives to their faith, I was profoundly ashamed to realize that till that point I was the one who had been leading a hollow and meaningless existence. When I heard the sermons delivered to the *mujahideen* I realized that all my life I had been oblivious to the fact that Allah promised us authority, respect, dignity, and dominance on the condition that we wage *jihad* in His cause. There was a time when I wondered why Muslims lived in utter despair and servitude despite the fact that they bore testament to Allah's Oneness, fasted as per His command, prayed, and made pilgrimages to Mecca. I consulted the Quran. When I reread *Surat al-Anfal*, *Surat at-Tawbah*, and various other chapters on *jihad*, I was reminded of that radiant period of Islamic history when mothers bore sons like Salahuddin Ayubi, Tariq bin Zayd, Muhammad bin Qasim, and Mahmud Ghaznavi.

When I took the first step on the path of *jihad*, my heart blossomed instantly. Allah's grace and mercy saved this lowly sinful woman from a grotesque life of luxury, while giving me the strength to boldly dedicate my life to the struggle. May Allah forgive me for warring against Him for

WE, MOTHERS OF THE LASHKAR-E-TAYYABA   217

nineteen years as we lived off the bank's usurious earnings; may He accept our insignificant sacrifices, and may He guide all Muslims who have gone astray. Amen. The only reason I recount this memoir is to inspire other Muslims; I'd be a hypocrite if I said I was fishing for praise.

In this humble publication, I have compiled the testimonies of sincere and honest women from across Pakistan's cities, villages, neighbour-hoods, and communities who have risen in stature, above those who hold advanced degrees and high offices, by becoming living manifestations of the following Quranic verse:

> Lo! Allah hath bought from the believers their lives and their wealth be-cause the Garden will be theirs.
>
> (*Surah at-Tawbah* 9:111)

Abu Sohaib Shaheed's mother is a woman who struck such a bargain with eternity. When *Lashkar-e-Tayyaba*'s *mujahideen* arrived at her door-step to give her news of her son's martyrdom she asked them only one question from behind the door, 'Where did the fatal bullet hit my son?' The *mujahideen* said: 'The enemy pumped multiple rounds into Abu Sohaib's chest; his bullet-riddled body was decked out for the Garden.' Upon hearing this she prostrated before Allah in gratitude with the *Alhamdulillah* (all praise to Allah) on her lips. This brave woman nar-rates, 'When my older son, Abu Habib, who is now a *ghazi* [living war-rior], and my younger son, Abu Sohaib, joined *Lashkar-e-Tayyaba* one after the other, I was deeply aggrieved. One hadn't even matriculated; the other hadn't yet passed his F.A. exams [exams taken after the 12th grade]. I'd weep bitterly on my prayer rug during my midnight prayers. I'd say 'Allah, my sons have dropped out of school, guide them, and show them the right path.' On one of those pitiful nights as I wept and prayed, my heart spontaneously whispered, 'so, you think your sons will bring you a lot of joy if they get their BA and FA degrees, eh? How many years will you live off their earnings? How long do you think you'll live? You fool; they're out there on the battlefield winning palaces in paradise for you by waging *jihad* in Allah's cause, what more could you want?' The minute I realized this I was at peace. From that moment I started praying for their martyrdom. Finally, one morning, my prayer was answered.' The first edi-tion of this book was a compilation of similar inspirational anecdotes,

218 THE LITERATURE OF *LASHKAR-E-TAYYABA*

heart-rending quotations, and enlightened memoirs. By Allah's will and blessings, there will be many more. Allah-willing!

Preamble

Today, *Lashkar-e-Tayyaba* is known the world over, as tyrants fear its power and the persecuted yearn for its assistance. This movement began in Afghanistan's Kunar province at Jaji where certain Afghan and Pakistani Muslims responded to the call of *jihad* for Allah's cause and joined Salafi Afghans in Nuristan in a manifestation of the following Quranic injunction:

> Go forth, light armed and heavy armed, and strive with your wealth and your lives in the way of Allah! That is best for you if ye but knew.
>
> (*Surat at-Tawbah* 9:41)

Together, with very little resources, they looked the Russian Goliath in the eye and brought the bearers of the Red Revolution to kneel; they became a model of emulation and a rallying call for the Muslim *ummat*, so much so that the foul and filthy Hindu enemy that ravaged and persecuted helpless Muslims for the past fifty years suddenly took notice of how the indifferent masses were responding to the call to arms. *Lashkar-e-Tayyaba* gave Muslims a roadmap of *jihad* that led straight to the palaces of paradise and freedom. Kashmiri Muslims welcomed *Lashkar-e-Tayyaba* as the guardians of Islam, protectors of the prophet's honour, and defenders of the *ummat*'s dignity; the *Lashkar*'s caravans left the highlands of Afghanistan for the valley of Kashmir and despite immeasurable obstacles and unwarranted opposition, the miracle of ...

> Ye (Muslims) slew them not, but Allah slew them.
>
> (*Surat al-Anfal* 8:17)

... was not only witnessed by the heavens but also by the *mujahideen*, their friends and their enemies. Fewer than seven hundred *Lashkar-e-Tayyaba* warriors descended into the valley to form an iron wall against over seven hundred thousand of Satan's heavily armed minions. A new chapter of martyrdom and valour was being written in the history of our nation. The unrivalled sacrifices of our women reminded one of Khaula, Hafsa, Ammara, Safia and countless other blessed women whose lives were the embodiment of perseverance and strength. Funerary wreaths consumed more flowers than wedding bouquets. Schools were empty and graveyards were full. Shrines of martyrdom sprung up across the valley like orchards but the women who bore these brave young men did not so much as wince. Their radiant faces effulgent with pride put the terrorizing and terrified tyrants to shame. In a state of panic, cowardly Hindus started fighting among themselves. Some Indian soldiers committed suicide in fear; others gave up their arms to save their lives. For the first time, downtrodden Muslims got a glimpse of the much-awaited dawn of freedom.

This unworthy soul felt the need to lift the veil from the women whose sons and brothers had sacrificed their lives, their hopes, and their dreams in the line of duty. It was an obligation and a debt. I presented my case to *Markaz's emir* Hafiz Saeed who encouraged me wholeheartedly. Some days later, *Lashkar-e-Tayyaba's Emir* Zaki-ur-Rehman Lakhvi and Abdur Rehman al-Dakhil were travelling for *eid* with the *emir* of the occupied valley who is also the contact for the families of the martyrs of Punjab. Once the respected *emir* gave me permission to join them, our caravan first headed for the residence of Imran Majeed Butt Shaheed in district Faisalabad, to interview his mother. There, Maulana Ramzan Asri Sahib and Maulana Abdullah Ubaid-ur-Rehman Sahib joined us, and we continued to Yazman Mandi and travelled all the way up to Sadiqabad. We stopped at over a hundred villages and towns on the way and at every stop, we were led directly to the doorsteps of the esteemed women who mothered the noble martyrs of *Lashkar-e-Tayyaba*; their blood-stained tears fill these pages. On 1st Ramazan 11 January 1996 we returned to our homes.

Although we began our travels the night of 16 December 1995, for the next phase of our project, our Karachi contact Brother Saifullah Mansoor provided us with a car so we could reach the residences of eleven more martyrs in the remote outskirts of the city. Thus, not only did I realize my dream, Allah provided all the support I needed in making it a reality.

In the course of compiling this book, certain interviews could not be included because they were either incomplete or because we were unable

220   THE LITERATURE OF *LASHKAR-E-TAYYABA*

to meet some of our intended interlocutors. We will include the ones we skipped, in upcoming editions. Should Allah extend this unworthy creature's days, I intend to publish a chapter on every single martyr of *Lashkar-e-Tayyaba* as a fulfilment of an obligation and as the repayment of a debt. Allah-willing!

In addition to the mothers of the martyrs, Abdur Rehman al-Dakhil and I also took testimonials from their male relatives and included the opinions and reflections of the *Lashkar*'s *emir* as well as those of serving *mujahideen*; certain details were also gleaned from *Mujallah-ul-Dawah*. Nothing, of course, compared to meeting the women face to face. In the course of my interactions, poetry flowed out of me effortlessly; all the verses I composed in the course of my travels are included in this publication, usually at the end of the very biographies that inspired them.

Start to finish, the honourable and respected Aleem Nasri Sahib provided editorial support in the compilation of this work. He offered his literary expertise to the benefit of both the prose and the poetry included in this publication. He has authored *Shahnamah Balakot*, a historical account of Shah Ismail Shaheed's movement in verse, which is an unparalleled contribution to the world of Urdu literature. I am deeply indebted to him for his attention and dedication in making this work possible. May Allah accept the efforts of all those who aided my humble and meaningless ambition. May Allah sanctify this project with success by making the esteemed and noble women who sacrificed their sons for the glory, preservation, and rejuvenation of Islam a guiding light for all Muslim women.

I apologize to the families of the martyrs, in advance, for any literary and editorial errors in my reporting and compilation. I pray that this unworthy sinner and all those who wage *jihad* in Allah's cause with their wealth, their words, and their person, and those who actively participate in this struggle through their encouragement and support, are worthy of the recommendations the martyrs will give us on the Last Day, Amen. May Allah bless us all with martyrdom. Amen.

There's a wound in every mother's heart, a prayer on every mother's lips
Take the sapling of my dreams, Oh Lord, for the eternal blossoming of my faith

Amen.
The Unworthy Umm-e-Hammad

We, the Mothers of Lashkar-e-Tayyaba: Volume 2

Publisher's Note

The history of Islam is the history of martyrdom and suffering. Since the time of the prophet, the *ummat*'s warriors have displayed such valour on the battlefield and sacrificed their lives with such grace in the slaughter-house, that human history cannot do justice to their tales. Allah describes these valiant men as follows:

> Of the believers are men who are true to that which they covenanted with Allah. Some of them have paid their vow by death (in battle), and some of them still are waiting; and they have not altered in the least.
> (*Surat al-Azhab* 33:23)

The noble character of the martyrs is the pride of Islamic history. But this history is incomplete without mention of the glorious mothers who cloaked their sons in funerary shrouds and dispatched them deep into the valleys of death, with only the following words on their lips:

> Dear Lord, accept the life-blood I offer you as a sacrifice; grant him a martyrdom so magnificent that on the Day of Judgement, I cling to his robes in my attempt to enter paradise, the way he clung to mine in his infancy.

Wa-Allah-al-Hamd! Thousands of mothers continue to add golden chapters to the glorious history of women like al Khansa[4] and Khawlah,[5] in an age of rampant materialism and wanton treachery.

The second volume of Sister Umm-e-Hammad's *We, the Mothers of* Lashkar-e-Tayyaba is a compilation of the strength, forbearance, patience, and magnanimity of these women. It recounts the parting words and wishes with which they bid farewell to their sons, how they endured the years of separation as their sons trained for battle, how they welcomed the dawn of each day and how they bid farewell to the sinking sun at dusk, the prayers they made as their sons confronted the disbelievers on the battlefield, how they prostrated when they heard the news of their martyrdom, the domestic revolutions spurred by the wills left behind by these

222 THE LITERATURE OF *LASHKAR-E-TAYYABA*

martyrs, how every martyrdom inspired another member of the household to seek vengeance who was then dispatched to the battlefield with even more pomp and circumstance than the first, the roles played by the sisters inspired by Safiya, how aged fathers reacted to the martyrdom of their sons, and the lessons learnt from the martyrs' widows.

These are the pearls of inspiration Sister Umm-e-Hammad gathered from the family members of our fallen men as she toured their residences. This is a gift for mothers, sisters, and sons. Read this, and be inspired, for the ultimate victory of Islam will require the blood of a million more stars.

Published by Dar-ul-Andlus, this book is dedicated to the eponymous mothers of our martyrs. May Allah accept this token. Amen.

In need of prayers,
Muhammad Saifullah Khalid
Editor: Dar-ul-Andlus

Abdul Razzaq Abu Abdullah Shaheed (RA)
(Sample Biography from Vol. 2)

Abu Abdullah Thani Shaheed belonged to a religious family from Chak Din Pur Sharif, a rural area in district Bhalwal. His mother entrusted his upbringing to her relatives because of her failing health. She reminisces about the past in the following words:

I had four sons and no daughter. Abu Abdullah Thani was the youngest of the four. From the very beginning he observed his daily prayers regularly. When he found out about *tahajjud*[6] he started offering that as well. He loved playing cricket. As a child he was sick most of the time but by adolescence he was taller and better looking than his older siblings and he had an incredibly attractive personality to match. He was simple by nature; he never fussed over clothes or food. He would eat whatever I put before him and dressed in whatever I gave him to wear. By class seven he even stopped wasting his time playing cricket. His favourite meal was a rice and peas dish he'd prepare himself.

He was studying at Mua'had-ul-Aali when the *jihad* in Kashmir caught his attention. This worried me greatly, so I contacted my brother who was in Mianwali at the time working as the director of the Atomic Energy Commission and asked him to take my son under his wing. My brother had his nephew work such a busy schedule the boy did not have a moment to himself. He would start his day with classes at the Mechanical Training College, then return to baby sit his girl cousins, after which he oversaw running all the household errands. Nonetheless, he spent every moment he could steal studying Quranic exegesis on *jihad*. Once my brother realized my boy was determined to wage *jihad* he was enrolled in the Army. Whenever my son returned home on breaks, he would weep bitterly as he confessed that he had no interest in a career. Also, he could not understand why I wanted to deny myself the esteemed honour of being the mother of a martyr. In order to redirect his attention, we set up a retail store for him and had one of his brothers assist him. He was more interested in reciting the Quran during business hours than managing the store and would often leave his customers in the middle of a transaction to offer his prayers at the appointed hour. Despite this, the business proved to be incredibly profitable and the rest of his siblings joined him as well. Soon enough, he handed over the keys to the store to his brothers and started preparing for battle.

His mother tried holding him back on the pretext of her failing heart, so he asked his aunt to convince her to let him go. Instead, his aunt advised him to stay with his mother, arguing that caring for one's parent was also *jihad*. This angered him greatly. He said: 'Dear aunt, my mother may be ignorant, but you know better; how can you ask me to stay back? Isn't it unfortunate that my mother has four sons to look after her and yet she won't offer even one in Allah's service?' Then he made up his mind and bid us farewell.

His aunt narrates an anecdote:

Once he visited me in the evening and we chatted till late in the night. I retired around midnight but woke up a few hours later to find Abdur Razzaq offering his *tahajjud* prayers. At the time I went back to sleep but in the morning, I asked him how he was able to get up for the night prayers without an alarm despite going to bed so late. He said, 'Dear aunt, when a person is determined to please Allah, Allah bestows him with the capacity to please. Stop worrying about this life and start worrying about the next; you too will sleep like a baby.'

Abu Abdullah Thani Abdul Razzaq bin Khushi Muhammad Shaheed (RA)

Abu Abdullah Thani Abdul Razzaq bin Khushi Muhammad Shaheed was born in Syed Sharif. It was obvious that from an early age he was religiously inclined given his favourite hobby was reciting *na'at* [hymns]. Due to his aptitude, his parents enrolled him in a Quran memorization programme at the local mosque but after a few sessions, he had to abandon the programme because the tutor left. He was then enrolled in a regular school in his village from where he matriculated. He never once missed his prayers, and was mild-mannered, patient, and resilient. Once he set his mind to something he would keep at it; he loved convincing his opponents of his point of view; he avidly read the *Hadees* and Quranic exegesis; he obtained a diploma in mechanical engineering from Mianwali but had no interest in pursuing a career.

In light of his religious inclinations, he enrolled in *Minhaj-ul-Quran*, Lahore but his restless soul found no respite so he headed to *Markaz-e-Tayyaba*'s Muridke headquarters for seminary training where he was gripped with the passion to wage *jihad*; this took him all the way to Afghanistan for a few months of military training. When he returned home it was obvious that he was consumed by the desire to be a martyr. His parents had him enrolled in the Army, but he had no interest in a career in which martyrdom was not guaranteed. Despite his disinclination to work a regular job, a retail store was set up for him but the passion to wage *jihad* and the relentless desire to sacrifice his life consumed him whole. The seed sowed in his heart in Muridke quickly grew into a majestic tree. He constantly mused about going to Afghanistan for more training and never missed an opportunity to preach to his friends, his colleagues, and even his customers, advising them not to incorporate un-Islamic practices into their lives. When it was time to pray, he'd excuse himself even if he was in the middle of a transaction. He refused to sell cigarettes, betel leaves, and snuff at his store for he considered them all *haram*.

When he returned from *Markaz-e-Tayyaba*'s centre in Muzaffarabad he was single-mindedly obsessed with martyrdom. He tried various tactics for the required permission to wage *jihad*. His noble desire finally triumphed over parental misgivings and on 15 August 1997 he set off for Kashmir. Before he left, he asked all his friends and relatives to pray to Allah to grant him martyrdom. Amen.

When news of his martyrdom reached the *Markaz*, members of the organization were dispatched to his house at once, where, upon their arrival they immediately started preparing for his funeral. On 30 May, the day of his funeral, visitors started collecting at the martyr's house in the morning. The funeral was attended by Maulana Aslam Saleem; Ghazi Abu Zayd and Ghazi Abu Abdur-Rehman delivered speeches stressing the importance of *jihad*, while Hakeem Abdul Majeed Sahib's son recited a poem. The funerary prayer in absentia was offered by Habib-ur-Rehman of Jhawariyan. The attendees cooperated with the *mujahideen* during the funeral, and many pledged their own children to the struggle.

After the funeral, the martyr's mother arranged a feast for the attendees.

His Father's Impressions

Now, I also wish to train with the *mujahideen* and like my son, wage *jihad*, and if Allah wills it, I too will be martyred fighting Hindu forces. Allah has blessed me with four sons. Abdul Razzaq was the youngest so naturally he was dearest to me. I wanted him to be a religious scholar; he not only made my wish come true but also attained a station beyond my highest dreams.

Abdul Razzaq was incredibly obedient and hardworking. He was always busy preaching to neighbours and friends and there was invariably someone or the other who wanted to take him home to discuss matters of faith. It is only natural that we miss him but by Allah's grace we are glad that we were able to sacrifice one of Allah's many gifts to us in order to uphold the dignity of His faith. No doubt, in the afterlife, our martyred son will be a source of comfort to us, Allah-willing.

His Mother's Impressions

I had hoped to meet my son before he departed for the hereafter, but this was not what Allah willed. I am blessed that on the Day of Judgement many people will be in a state of panic, but my martyred son will hold my hand and serenely walk me into heaven, Allah-willing.

My dear Abdul Razzaq Abu Abdullah Thani has gained eternal life by sacrificing himself for Islam. He has bestowed me with the honour of being the mother of a martyr. I pray that Allah accept his martyrdom. Amen.

When I recited the Holy Quran, he would sit next to me and listen very attentively and correct me the second I made any error in my recitation. When he returned from training, he was aching to join the *jihad* and constantly begged me to grant him permission. Finally, seeing how eager he was to go, I gave him what he sought. As he left, he asked me to pray that Allah bless him with martyrdom; Allah granted him his wish. May Allah accept his sacrifice and elevate the martyrs. Amen.

My little lion was only twenty years old when he departed this world; I ask that all of you pray Allah accept his sacrifice. Amen.

His Brothers' Impressions

We wanted our brother Abu Abdullah Thani Shaheed to start a business, which is why we set up a store for him in the village. He'd preach to all his customers; after a while he left the store, and this world, and by bargaining his life with Allah, with nothing but a sense of sacrifice in his heart, he confronted the Hindu forces and was martyred in an encounter that led him straight to paradise, leaving us and this mundane world far behind. May Allah give us the opportunity to take his place on the battlefield, Allah-willing.

His Brothers Muhammad Khalid, Muhammad Arif, and Muhammad Al-Haq's Impressions

Our beloved brother fulfilled his purpose in life by attaining martyrdom. He proved to be a success in this world and Allah-willing, in the world hereafter.

May Allah accept his sacrifice; our entire family is proud of his achievement. May Allah accept his martyrdom and bless us with the capacity to follow in his footsteps. Amen.

Since every one of us will die one day, why not devote the few days we have in this world to Allah that we may insure our eternal afterlife.

Shaheed Abu Abdullah Thani's letter to his Family Written from the Valley of Kashmir

Respected Parents!

Assalam-u-Alaikum:

Every day, the sun rises in the east and sets in the west; the moon has traversed its lunar path for thousands of months; countless stars twinkle in the night sky and vanish in the morning twilight, but your prayers, and the love of my well-wishers, have always pierced through the darkest sorrows like a ray of light. By Allah, in moments such as these, prayers are all that come in handy. I am certain you pray for me. Please pray to Allah to grant me success; I have several responsibilities and I am never in one location for too long, hence I cannot send an address.

I constantly move from one district to the next in the Kashmir valley. This winter is particularly brutal and many roads are blocked due to snow but nothing, not even blizzards, can stop us. I send my salaams to all my brothers, sisters, elders, relatives, and friends; I request that they all pray that as long as Allah keeps me alive, I remain a true Muslim, and it is in this condition that I die, and that my death is that of a martyr's. May Allah bless us all and give us the capacity to understand His message and act upon it, for this is the only path to success.

I beg your leave with nothing but sincerity and prayers.

Wa-Salam Alaikum
Your Son,
Abdul Razzaq Abu Abdullah Thani

Abu Abdullah Thani Shaheed's Will

Assalam-u-Alaikum:

Prostrate before Allah with gratitude for His gift and favour (meaning, 'my martyrdom'); never fear life's hurdles for every obstacle is from Allah.

You wanted me to look for employment or start some trade after my education. I did both. I sought employment with the *mujahideen* and traded my life for paradise. I could not have struck a better bargain for Allah's pleasure. I request my respected father grow his beard in emulation of the prophet and offer his prayers communally for the prophet said: I feel like burning down the houses of those who pray at home. Please throw the lewd and demonic television set out of the house for it reeks of obscenities; the prophet has warned us sternly about immodesty; I advise my brothers to be utterly repulsed by song and dance and television-nonsense or else on the Day of Judgement even their prayers will not protect them. Do not turn away from *jihad*; in fact, if you cannot offer your life for *jihad*, make financial contributions; remember what the prophet said about the person who died without participating in *jihad*, or without contributing to *jihad*, or without even considering *jihad* at all. Finally, I request all my friends, relatives, neighbours, and brothers, for Allah's sake forgive me my mistakes, and pray for my martyrdom. I request my parents to pay back anyone I owe money. I hope that as long as Allah keeps you alive, He keeps you on the straight path, and when you die, you die as Muslims with the *kalima* on your lips. May Allah gather me, my brothers, and you, my parents, in paradise, among the martyrs. Amen.

Martyrdom is the destination and the desire
Wealth and conquest mean nothing

Wa-Salaam Alaikum.

Your Son,
Abu Abdullah Thani/Abdul Razzaq

Abu Abdullah Thani Shaheed Speaks of His Kashmiri Sisters
A recent interview with Abu Abdullah Shaheed over a wireless set from occupied Kashmir touches upon the condition of our Kashmiri sisters. It was recorded on a cassette tape. This is what the martyr who dwells in paradise has to say to us:

Trust me, once a person witnesses what's happening in Kashmir, he forgets all past attachments, and feels compelled to fulfil his obligation. Convince my mother on my behalf. No doubt, she loves me dearly, but shirking one's duty is a death knell in of itself; also, one must obey Allah's command. On the Last Day, I want my mother to stand among the mothers of martyrs. Even today, in Kashmir, ruthless Hindu moneylenders carry off any woman they please, when they please, into their camps and no one knows what becomes of the victim as her dignity is torn to shreds. Brothers, if we Muslims don't protect these women who will? How can we stand by silently as Hindus torture them? One woman has this to say to her Muslim brethren: The young men of a nation who have lost all sense of duty and honour ought to wear make-up and hide inside their homes while the women don suits of armour and dive into the battlefield; thus, the Muslim world will know that even if its men lose faith, its women continue to fight injustice and safeguard the religion. However, as long as there remain men who are willing to guard their sisters and their faith, I say:

men who have been on the front lines are the only ones who have earned the right to proselytize. Those who have chosen to stay back in their homes, and have lost all sense of honour and chivalry, should wear their sisters' jewellery and hand over their weapons to the women for we will not shy away from protecting our own. We will never hesitate before shedding blood for the glory of our faith. It is my duty to let my sisters know that never has there been a moment in history when we were so brazenly raped in public squares while our men stood by and silently watched. As the banner of Islam droops in Kashmir, keep in mind, disbelievers, Hindus, polytheists, Jews, and Christians are a growing threat to every Islamic state in the world.

Why is it that in these times of blood and war our youth remain apathetic to what is happening around them? The sons of Islam lack chivalry; they lack the desire for martyrdom that defined the *mujahideen* of earlier times. Sisters keep in mind, if your heart glows with the light of faith, no power in the world can overpower your sons, your brothers, or your husbands. As long as your blood runs wild in the veins of your sons, the love of martyrdom will reign supreme; and as long as our men desire martyrdom, they will strike fear in the heart of the most terrifying foe, Allah-willing.

Tell your brothers we take great pride in men who storm the battlefield and bear battle-scars on their bodies. Tell your sons that if they turn and flee like cowards with their blood dripping at their heels, they will be devoid of the prophet's favours on the Last Day.

230 THE LITERATURE OF *LASHKAR-E-TAYYABA*

We are not prepared to accept such men as our brothers. Our love is only for the brave, not for cowards. He who cannot safeguard our modesty does not deserve to stand among those entering paradise on the Day of Judgement. That day, the daughters of Islam will only know men like Muhammad bin Qasim as brothers.

Final Words Before Martyrdom
By Allah's grace, today that long-awaited hour of virtue has arrived which the Prophet desired for himself; for which his companions left their homes, their wives, their children, and their businesses... which he made tempting for his followers by describing its infinite virtues and blessings in the following words:

'By Allah! I wish to be martyred in Allah's path; then I wish to be re-born so I can be martyred again. And again. And again. And again. And for this to happen repeatedly.'

These were the words of Abdul Razzaq, the subject of this essay. He was indifferent to making a living in this world for he was concerned only with honouring his covenant with god in order to earn an eternal income in paradise, among those, who, according to Allah:

'find their sustenance in the presence of their Lord'.

(Quran[7])

This sustenance is pure, honourable, and halal; it is not acquired by force but eternally earned through blood and sacrifice, Allah-willing.

O' Bird of paradise, death is preferable
To the crumbs that make you stoop.

8
Fighter Biographies

In this chapter, we provide translations of an illustrative sample of so-called *shaheed* biographies, or accounts of the lives of those fighters who died in the service of *Lashkar-e-Tayyaba* (LeT) from the organization's varied periodicals. Until 2007, the organization published these biographies in various print sources which were available in LeT's bookstores and other stores which sold their publications. To the best of our knowledge, the organization has discontinued publishing these sources because it has learned that scholars are using them as sources and because such biographies make it difficult for the Pakistani state to argue that the organization does not engage in *jihad*. In this chapter, we furnish translations from several such sources with an intent to provide variation across time (from the early 1990s to 2007) and across source type while also seeking to provide examples of biographies that exhibit an array of fighter motivations as well as motivations in the families who support them.

The biographies offer several important insights. First and foremost, they serve to promote the notion of the brave and noble warrior taking on a nefarious enemy that ostensibly outnumbers them and which is bent on extirpating the adherents of Islam. In some cases, the biographies narrate miracles that Allah has bestowed upon his fighters on the battlefield. Save a few exceptions, Hindus are depicted as the enemy of the Muslim and each battle is narrated in deeply communalized imagery. In some cases, the biographies are opportunities to persuade Pakistanis that the *mujahideen* are welcomed, trusted and revered by Kashmiris. In some cases, even Hindu Kashmiris bestow accolades upon the *mujahideen*. This is an important propaganda aim because there is a counter-narrative that the locals are exhausted with a conflict that Pakistan insists upon waging on the backs of Kashmiris, who have paid the price for Pakistan's misadventures. By asserting that even Hindu Kashmiris welcome liberation by LeT's fighters, the biographies seek to make a larger point about the predatory nature of the Hindu India state that seeks to subjugate all

232   THE LITERATURE OF *LASHKAR-E-TAYYABA*

Kashmiris, even Hindus. As a part of lionizing the fighters, sometimes the biographies provide absurd battle details of the outnumbered and out-gunned *momin* who, with faith in Allah, nonetheless prevail. This is also a trope used in Pakistan's military publications as well. In both kinds of accounts, frequent reference to historical battles from the time of Prophet are mobilized to sustain morale and to argue that India's numerical might can be vitiated by a handful of dedicated soldiers for Allah. This deeply communalized narrative serves to foster LeT's larger goal of breaking India along this tendentious fault-line. Kashmir is not the end: it is merely a means of achieving this objective.

As Fair has observed previously, this organization makes a concerted effort to recruit the entire family, not just the fighter. It also pays particular attention to women who are the reproducers of the *mujahideen*, both through the physical act of child-bearing but also through child-rearing. The periodicals from which we draw biographies include: *Mujallah Tayyabaat* (*Virtuous Women*); *Mujallah-ul-Dawah* (*The Invitation*); *Mahanah Zarb-e-Tayyaba* (*Strike of the Righteous*).[1] All of the LeT militants included in these biographies died during operations from 1994 to 2007.[2] For this reason, we provide translations of illustrative biographies from the serial publications in chronological order.

For those who are familiar with the portrayal of martyrdom by the Pakistan army, will notice numerous similarities which merit remark here. For both the Pakistan army and the LeT, dying for Islam and dying for Pakistan are co-terminus and thus worthy of the same title: *shaheed*. And for both organizations, two kinds of fighters are prominent: the *ghazi* (the veteran fighter) and the *shaheed* (slain). Neither organization makes great effort to dilate upon the injured as the injured do not have a sancti-fied status. Parents of fighters of both organizations also opine that they told their sons to die valiantly in battle. But we learn nothing from LeT's literature about its combatants who were disabled—either physically or mentally—from participation in LeT-sanctioned production of violence.[3]

Second, the most prominent female family member speaking about the fighter in these biographies is the mother. As Maria Rashid has ob-served, the Pakistan army relies heavily upon the performance of the mother's grief when commemorating its fallen rather than the wife of the fallen. The reasons for this hinge upon the purity and non-sexual na-ture of the mother's love for her son in contrast to physical aspects of the

FIGHTER BIOGRAPHIES   233

husband-wife bond. Just as the family of the army's slain fighters publicly declare that they will send their surviving sons into battle for the army, the family members of LeT's slain fighters make the same proclamation. While the army continues to pay emoluments to the wives of slain soldiers, these emoluments stop should she remarry. The incentives of the Pakistan army are to encourage the widow to remain faithful to husband in death. Here the two organizations differ. LeT actively encourages its widows to remarry. It does so for several reasons. First, it views the social opprobrium against widow remarriage is a vestige of Hinduism which the organization reviles. Second, the organization believes that the wife should remarry, preferably another *mujahid* or the brother of her husband. This is for practical reasons: the wife has economic stability and can produce offspring with her new husband, who she will raise to become *mujahideen* or supporters of the *mujahideen*. Knowing that their wives will be provided for may even make some fighters more comfortable going on missions in which they suspect they will perish. Abdussalam Bin Muhammad in *Hindu Customs Among Muslim*, extolls Muslims to 'marry away widows as early as possible. Islam wishes to see a widow re-settled in society soon after the demise of her husband'. One of the reasons he offers for this advice is practical: 'A true believer never hesitates from participating in *jihad*. He has the assurance that in case of his martyrdom, some of his *mujahid* friends would marry his wife and his family would get instant support.' If Muslims followed these above-noted Hindu customs and abjure widow remarriage, 'would a wife easily let her husband go for *jihad*? She has been living with the fear that after his death, nobody will be there to take care of her.'[4] However, in the various biographies we examine, we rarely hear from the wife. Instead, his parents, siblings, and friends speak of the *shaheed*.

Third, both organizations, manage the performance of grief in similar ways. Whether it is the LeT commander or an army Junior Commissioned Officer or Non-Commissioned Officer who delivers the news of the loss to the family, the families of both organizations are encouraged not to cry; rather, they are encouraged to celebrate because their sons have attained martyrdom. While the mother's sadness is instrumentalized to demonstrate her willingness to sacrifice her beloved child, excessive sadness and weeping undermines the message that the son now resides in Allah's court, surrounded by celestial maidens and other perquisites acquired by virtue of his martyrdom.

234 THE LITERATURE OF *LASHKAR-E-TAYYABA*

Finally, another important objective of these biographies is proselytization of LeT's interpretation of Islam. Through the biographies, the martyr himself in his last will and testament and/or his colleagues who ventriloquize on his behalf often take the opportunity to criticize the practices of Barelvis in particular, including the building of elaborate gravesites such as mausoleums and built-up platforms over the grave. They criticize the popular custom of going to shrines to obtain cures for illnesses, amulets for protection, and special prayers for desired outcomes.

A brief note about the organization of the biographies is in order. These documents do not have a shared structure. Depending upon the ostensible author, different aspects of the slain militant are presented. They often include observations about the slain terrorist from family members as well as from his LeT associates. Sometimes a singular publication will present details on more than one fighter, usually because they perished in the same operation. They frequently include the so-called 'last will and testament' of the fighter, which usually enjoins his family members to embrace LeT's interpretation of the *Ahl-e-Hadees* tradition and to continue supporting *jihad*. These biographies, like the pamphlets translated in Chapters four, five and six of these volumes, are not cogently exposited. The authors—or editors—make heavy use of subject heads as a substitute for logical coherence and clarity of narrative. Given that this is the most common organization for LeT publications, one has to assume that the organization's readers are not terribly annoyed by the seeming illogical structure of their various publications. Here, as elsewhere, we retain the organization and heading formats of the originals.

Amir Hamza, 'Three Captains and Dozens of Soldiers of the Army of Nimrod Sent to Hell in Badgam: Abu Abdullah, Abu Alqama, Abu Jindal and Abu Mu'awiyah are Martyred', *Mujallah-ul-Dawah* (January 1994): 4–10. Translated by Ali Hamza

Jihad, which is the pinnacle of Islam, is reaching new heights in the peaks of Kashmir. The Hindu army is escalating its crackdown, but this urgency has produced more casualties on its side. Now the Hindu soldiers

FIGHTER BIOGRAPHIES   235

are being tricked into serving in Kashmir as they are not told about the gravity of the situation. When they arrive and learn about the developments in the valley, sometimes they even jump out of their trucks and abandon their posts and run. There have been reports of many such incidents.

In this terror, the terror of *Lashkar-e-Tayyaba* is unique. The moment the Hindu Army hears about it, they change course and run. Kashmiri mothers give their children to the *mujahideen* of *Lashkar-e-Tayyaba* so they may train with the Afghans[5] and then fight Hindus. This was narrated to me by Abu Zubair (Muhammad Anwar) who just returned from Occupied Kashmir. He was accompanied by Sajjad, a Kashmiri youth who does not even have a beard yet. Sajjad told me that his mother asked him to go and fight with the Afghans. I was wondering why a mother would dispatch her beloved son to *Lashkar-e-Tayyaba*. The answer to this question lies in those battles of the *Lashkar-e-Tayyaba*'s eagles waged by those who fight only because Allah wills it and because Allah rewards them with respect and honour in this life and with blessings in the hereafter. Now there has been a new battle raging near Badgam, we still have not received the exact details but according to what we know . . .

A village near Badgam was surrounded by the Army because they found out about Kashmiri *mujahideen* and eagles of *Lashkar-e-Tayyaba* there. The Army was annoyed by their constant attacks so when they found out that the *Lashkars* were in the village, some sources claimed that approximately fifty thousand soldiers surrounded the village. When the *mujahideen* found out, they retaliated. The battle started early in the morning at the time of *fajr*[6] prayers and continued for the entire day. In this battle, Abu Abdullah also known as Iftikhar Ahmed bin Nur Mohammed of Samudari was martyred. Along with him, several of his fellow fighters were also martyred including Abu Mu'awiyah (Naeem Iqbal) from Lahore as well as two friends, Mazhar Iqbal Farooqi (Abu Alqama) and Mohammad Sajid (Abu Jandal), both of whom were from a village near Gujrat called Hailaan. The body count of Hindus in this battle has not been confirmed so far, but our sources say that the number is very high. The number is expected to be at least thirty. The people of the area have conveyed that they saw the general collecting the dead bodies of his soldiers and was saying:

236 THE LITERATURE OF *LASHKAR-E-TAYYABA*

'I will never forget this battle with these Afghans'; these words of the General were published on the front page of newspapers of Kashmir.

The Incredible Patience of The Martyr's Mother

When the news of the martyrdom of these *mujahideen* reached their homes, the forbearance displayed by their relatives would never be forgotten by the history of Kashmir. Let us go to the house of Abu Abdullah where the height of his mother's forbearance puts the tallest mountains to shame.

From Faisalabad, the officer *of Markaz-ud-Dawah-wal-Irshad* Maulana Mohammed Ramzan Asari, Maulana Obaidullah Obaid, and the commander of *Lashkar-e-Tayyaba* Azam Cheema along with other companions went to the village of the martyr to convey the news, but first they visited the mosque. When the martyr's mother learned that the *mujahideen* were in the mosque, she paid them a visit and asked about her son's well-being. The companions asked the mother her son's whereabouts to which responded that he went to Occupied Kashmir. They next asked why he went there? 'For martyrdom' the mother responded. Upon hearing this Maulana Yousaf responded that 'then your son has been martyred'.

The mother first said Alhamdullilah [All Praises to Allah] three times and then wiped her teary eyes, which was natural. After several seconds of silence, she said:

So, all of you are companions of my son, and are here to inform me about his martyrdom. Let us go to my home. Prior to leaving, my son implored of me: 'Mother, when my companions come to you with the news of my martyrdom, please make them sit down and offer them fresh milk before they leave.' They responded that this is not appropriate for the time and suggested that they could come again some other time. But the mother insisted that it was her son's last wish and that she would be ashamed if she did not fulfil it. She insisted that that she would not let them go without fulfilling her son's last wish.

There were about thirty companions in two cars. But how could they refuse the hospitality of such a mother? The companions went to the martyr's home and sat on the beds. When the neighbours learned of this, they began gathering and wailing. But the mother said: 'Attention! Do not cry and wail. Instead take this milk as my son wished.'

At last, they collected two buckets of milk. The martyr's mother asked her daughters and daughters-in-law to add sugar to the milk such that they could fulfil the last wishes of their brother. What a scene it was. I do not know if the heavens ever witnessed such an incident before. But, at least, I never read any such account in any book.

That mother was wiping her tears off with the corner of her own scarf while hosting the companions of her beloved son with fresh milk. She then said proudly that she had fulfilled the last wishes of her son.

When Allah observed this event in the presence of all the angels, I wonder how He responded. I suspect that we can find some guidance in the *Hadees* of the prophet. The prophet (PBUH) said:

'When a believer's son dies, Allah asks his angels whether they have confiscated the soul of the believer's son. The angels respond in the affirmative. Then Allah queries whether they have taken what is dearest of him. The angels answer "yes". Allah next asks how the believer responded. Then the angels reply that the believer said: "All Praises be to Allah" and "We surely belong to Allah and to him we shall return." Then Allah commands that they build him a palace in heaven and name it the Palace of Praise.'

Imam Tirmidhi called this *Hadees* a beauty whereas Ibn Habaan deemed it accurate. As narrated by Abu Huraira in *Sahih Bukhari* in a *Hadees* the prophet (PBUH) said: 'When someone, who was selected from the world, dies, the reward for parents is Heaven, provided that they believe in the reward.'

O dear readers, reflect on this: can the person mentioned be anyone other than a martyr? Just imagine! if the death of a mere believer can reap such rewards imagine the blessings reserved for the martyr.

The Martyrdom of Naeem Iqbal Naeem Iqbal (Abu Mu'awiyah)

To notify his mother, Hafez Saifullah asked Hakim Abdul Aziz Ferozpuri, Baba Abdul Rasheed, and myself to his home, where we settled in the

238 THE LITERATURE OF *LASHKAR-E-TAYYABA*

sitting room with the rest of our companions. When we were in the martyr's home, Baba Abdul Rasheed told the mother that our brother and her son, Naeem, was martyred; she took the news with forbearance. Shedding tears is a blessing, but this mother proved to be a mountain of patience. She did not utter a single sound. Indeed, the sons of such mothers are the ones who can really face the enemy on the battlefield, and such mothers are rare.[7]

We all returned to the mosque for the *isha* prayers[8] and waited for brother Naeem's father. By now all the attendees were aware of his martyrdom. After the prayers, the lesson of *Hadees* was postponed. Instead, everyone began asking about Naeem's martyrdom and exchanging stories about him.

Maulana Idrees Hashmi declared that, due to his mannerisms, faith and firmness in his religion, he had a unique stature in the religious community of the neighbourhood.

He explained that while the martyr was a compassionate person, he would stand firmly against anyone when it came to principles. He always offered prayers with the congregation.

Hakim Abdulaziz recalled that when he finished his high school, his father secured him a job as stenographer in the Telecommunications Ministry. For one month he performed this job. But then he declared that he would join a higher cause instead of this insignificant job. When his father tried to talk him out of it, he replied 'Father, all you care about is this world, whereas I am restless because I care about the afterlife.'[9]

His heart was not in his home. So, he spent most of his time in the mosque. Professor Shafqat told us that when he returned home, he would always help his mother and would care for her needs.

Shakirullah Qureshi of Ravi Road and Abidullah Qureshi and other worshippers told us that Brother Naeem contributed considerably to the construction of the Mu'awiyah Mosque, from its foundations to its completion. He was very happy to contribute to it and would go as far as sprinkling its yard with water to keep it clean.

Then we went to Brother Naeem's home. Many people had gathered in Chaudhry Bashir's living room. When the father was told the news of his son's martyrdom, he took it really well displaying incredible patience. Brother Waseem told us that before leaving, Naeem wished that upon his martyrdom his father should forsake the world and follow the path of *jihad* and dedicate himself for the victory of the religion.

Excerpt of Abu Mu'awiyah's Letter to Abu Yazeed
In the name of Allah, the Beneficent and Merciful
Muaskar-e-Aqsa 15 February 1992
Dear Brother Abu Yazeed,
Assalam-u-Alaikum
I am fine here and hope and wish for your well-being and also that of your companions [10]
Today, brother I received your letter. Reading it put my heart at ease. But the things that you wrote about your city and the situation in Oman has saddened me. My companions and I cannot do anything but pray for better days. If Allah wills, we will pray for our Salafi brothers who are in the middle to this adverse situation. In addition to that, I recite *Dua-e-Qunut* everyday with *fajr* prayers and often with *isha* and *maghrib* prayers as well.[11] Furthermore, I will convey the situation of Salafis in the centre. I am currently on a tour, and I will hand over this letter to brother Shakir. He will, if Allah wills, convey the contents of your letter to the centre. Also. I am really missing you. It would have been comforting if you too could have joined me on the frontlines in Kashmir. Anyhow, if your Bosnia plan works out, try to meet me before you leave.
Yours,
Your younger brother,
Abu Mu'awiyah

Abu Mu'awiyah's Last Letter to His Father
In the name of Allah, the Beneficent and Merciful
Dear Father,
Assalam-u-Alaikum
By the Grace of Allah, I am doing well and am constantly praying for your and the family's well-being.
Dear father, I am going to Occupied Kashmir very soon, so it is possible that we shall never meet again. So kindly if you could forgive my transgressions, then Allah will reward you greatly (If Allah wills!). In addition, your and my salvation lies in following the commandments of the prophet (PBUH). You are the head of the family. For this reason, when on

the Day of Judgement, Allah asks you about your family, what will you say? In the worldly affairs, you always have your way. But you don't care that much about spiritual life. So how will you answer him?

Second, you do not offer prayers regularly, nor do you ask others to do so even though the prophet (PBUH) has implored us to offer prayers regularly and has warned us about the hazards of not offering it regularly. The Quran says that when the people of heaven ask the people in hell, why they are there; the people in hell respond that they did not offer prayers. That is why you should offer prayers regularly and also strictly make my mother and sisters and brother offer them regularly too. May Allah reward you well. Amen.

Also pray for me that Allah accepts my sacrifice and grants me the death of martyrdom. Amen.

If you receive the news of my martyrdom, offer prayers of gratitude to Allah and do not wail and cry. I also request kindly that you not listen to songs and music. You do not realize it yet, but you will regret it on the Day of Judgement, and this will not benefit you in any way. The prophet (PBUH) has told us of the sad fate of those who sing and those who listen to music. May Allah show us the right path. Amen.

May Allah accept my sacrifice for His faith. The *Hadees* makes clear that, on the Day of Judgement, molten lead will be poured in the ears of those who listen to music.

Make sure that my mother, my sister and you pay particular heed to *purdah*. If you want to find more information about this, you can read *Surat an-Nur* of the Holy Quran.

Because television is the means of spreading lewdness and nudity, you should toss it of the house. This will be beneficial for you.

If you receive the news of my martyrdom, show courage and patience because this is a boon that is not bestowed upon everyone. Make sure to obey your father and make sure he is happy.

Convey my regards to my siblings and tell them to offer prayers regularly.

May Allah protect us all. I have certainly made many mistakes. But please forgive me, for Allah's sake. Additionally, I hope that my brothers and friends will forgive me too as I will forgive them all as well.

Your son,

Abu Mu'awiyah, Naeem Iqbal.

Care of Hakim Abdul Aziz Ferozpuri, Yunani Davakhana, Al-Madad Pak Colony, near Timber Market, Ravi Road, Lahore

And now let us hear the comments of Abu Mu'awiyah's mother.

My Dear *mujahid* brothers, and *mujahid* sons,

As a mother, I fail to pick the right words to remember my martyred son. I am an insignificant creation of Allah, but due to the great sacrifice of my son, the honour that I am receiving is unmatched. I cannot thank Allah enough. I pray that Allah accepts the sacrifice of my son Abu Mu'awiyah and helps us attain the goal for which so many of our *mujahideen* are martyred. Amen. As a mother, if I have ever hurt my son, I beg for Allah's forgiveness. I was unable to ask him for his forgiveness and this will haunt me for the rest of my life. My brothers and sons, you too should pray for this mother that she finds some solace. I take great pride in the martyrdom of my son. My son was a righteous boy and carried true passion in his heart. He is lucky to have achieved such an honour.

I have so much to say, but I am cutting it short with this prayer for my son: 'Allah, my son was yours and he returns to you. Keep him under the shadow of your blessings and also keep all *mujahideen* under your protection as well'. Amen.

Abu Jandal—Mohammad Sajid

Abu Jandal belonged to the village of Hailaan near Gujrat. An entourage from *Markaz-ud-Dawah-wal-Irshad,* which included Abu Abdul Wahab, Bashir Ahmad Bhatti, Jamil Rahi, Qari Arifullah, and others went to the village of the martyred.

Abu Abdul Wahab narrates that they when they went to the village, they went to the house of the teacher of *mujahideen*, Mr Abdul Qadir. We were spotted by Hakim Mohammad Tariq, the elder brother of the martyred Sajid. So we went to the house, and there they began coming to greet us. We also sent a messenger to inform them that we are here, the messenger met them en route and asked them to join us. The brother figured out the situation and asked if Sajid had been martyred and said that he is coming to meet us. When he arrived, he greeted us with enthusiasm

242 THE LITERATURE OF *LASHKAR-E-TAYYABA*

and received the news of the martyrdom with dignity and started talking about the Jihad in reference to his brother. There was no sign of pain on his face and he said that his brother was pursuing martyrdom and, by the grace of Allah, succeeded. If Allah wills!

Brother Abdul Wahab noted that the brother was smiling; the former asked the brother if he felt no grief. To that the martyr's brother replied, 'He was my brother, I am sad. But this is also a fact that we are Muslims. When a Westerner loses a loved one, they say: "No Problem". We are Muslims and believe in the time and finality of death and we also know that it was our brother's heart's desire. This is a great blessing. Consequently, there is no reason to be sad and there is no problem. Let's pray to Allah that he accepts the martyrdom of our brother. Amen.'

After this we went to meet Mr. Ghulam Qadir, the martyr's father and introduced ourselves. We began talking and he told us that Sajid took him to the centre where he stayed for twenty-one days. It was while he was there that Sajid went to Occupied Kashmir.

Abdul Wahab asked the father whether he gave his consent to which the father said 'yes'. I asked him about the final desire of his son to which he said that he wanted to embrace martyrdom. I marvelled that this means that his final wish was granted. Upon hearing this, the father displayed courage and nodded his head in affirmative and said that death is inevitable even if he would be living here with us. So it is better that it came on the battlefield. May Allah accept his martyrdom. Amen.

And Now Sajid's Last Message to his Parents
My Dear Parents,

Assalam-u-Alaikum, by the grace of Allah, today I leave for Kashmir to spread the message of Allah, because the believers have the right to Allah's Earth, and for that purpose I do not care if I sacrifice my life. If Allah wills and I embrace martyrdom while fighting for Allah's cause, simply praise Allah instead of wailing and crying because doing so is strictly forbidden. Instead, offer thanks to Allah for this great honour. Show patience during the tough times and offer gratitude to Allah during good times. Be punctual in prayers and tell my siblings to offer prayers regularly and to never worship anyone but Allah. Always remember the end of times, and also remember your goal. Do not pay attention to worldly matters as they are worthless. Whatever you achieve in this life, will remain here. Remember

Allah always. Remember me in all your prayers and ask my siblings to pray for me that Allah accepts my sacrifice. If I have ever erred, please forgive me for the sake of Allah. If Allah wills, I will wait for you at the gates of Heaven. If Allah wills!

Requesting your prayers,
Mohammad Sajid Abu Jandal

Abu Alqama Mazhar Iqbal Farooqi

Mazhar also belonged to the Village of Hailaan near Gujrat. Sajid and Mazhar were close friends. Mazhar had graduated high school. Both desired martyrdom in Occupied Kashmir. Two friends from the same village, went on the tour together and fought the Hindus together, and were martyred in the same battle. May Allah grant both of them the highest levels of paradise. Amen.

Brother Abdul Wahab reports that when he reached the house he was received by the martyr's cousin. The martyr's father was in Islamabad at the time. The father is a retired soldier and gave permission to both his sons to wage jihad. After a little while, we were joined by Zafar Iqbal, Mazhar Iqbal's younger brother. We asked Zafar, if his brother ever wrote a letter to him. He responded in affirmative and said that he wrote one letter which basically instructed him to pray for his brother's martyrdom. Then I responded that his brother's wish has been granted. He displayed great patience and courage. He then told the news about martyrdom to the women of the family, and then the women of the neighbourhood came over and started wailing and crying.

The sister of the martyr told the women not to cry so loudly, because her brother has been martyred and this was a great honour. She herself was displaying courage and restraint and asked the other women to do the same.

Then Zafar Iqbal joined us, and we continued to talk. He told us he too wants to walk the same path and wants to go for *jihadi* training.

In short, the great courage, valour and passion displayed by the family of the martyr reminded us of the era of Islam's golden years; once again, one could tell these were a *jihadi* people meant for battles. If this trend continues there will be no place for infidels in India, America, or Europe,

244 THE LITERATURE OF *LASHKAR-E-TAYYABA*

or, as a matter of fact, any place on earth (If Allah wills). And this is exactly the reason why infidels tremble with fear no matter where they are.

May god protect us from the evil eye.

May Allah bless the cause of *jihad*

Long live the *jihad* for the sake of Allah

Amir Hamza, 'The Invasion of *Lashkar-e-Tayyaba* in Occupied Kashmir: Mohammed Idrees and Mohammed Ilyas Butt are Martyred', *Mujallah-ul-Dawah* (February 1994): 4–9. Translated by Ali Hamza

The *Lashkar-e-Tayyaba* has been battling the Hindu Army in Occupied Jammu and Kashmir for about a year and a half. In the fifteenth century of Islam (i.e. now) the *mujahideen* of *Lashkar-e-Tayyaba* are reliving the history of their faith with their blood.

We can also see that Allah has delivered to these *mujahideen* the same help he delivered to the companions of the prophet during the Battles of Badr[12] and the Battle of Uhud.[13] A few months back in January, a story was published in *Mujallah-ul-Dawah* about a fierce battle with the Hindu Army. Now that we have more information about this from different sources, we are publishing the account.

Shahidullah Kalim (Abu Muslim) from Bahawalpur provides a first-hand account of the sequence of events. He has recently returned after fighting the Hindu Army in Occupied Kashmir for many months. He recounts:

Abu Abdul Wahab Sani (Mohammad Idrees) and Mohammad Ilyas Butt (Abu Hafez) from Gujranwala were martyred during the battle. The troops of *Lashkar-e-Tayyaba* are spread throughout Occupied Kashmir. We were in Badgam, and our four friends Abu Ali, Abu Turab, Abu Alqama and Abu Jandal from Supur came to us to replenish our supplies of arms and money. After them Abu Hafez and Abu Khubaib also arrived.

We were together in the jungle at our camp when we hatched a plan. Iftikhar Ahmad (Abu Abdullah), Mohammad Idrees (Abu Abdul

Wahab), Naeem Iqbal (Abu Mu'awiyah), Mohammad Sajid (Abu Jandal), Mohammad Ilyas (Abu Hafez) and Abu Khubaib were all part of this project.

The leader of this unit was Iftikhar Ahmad (Abu Abdullah). They went to the Village Sitharan, and then proceeded to Village Kharian and this is where the battle took place.

Our friends were to stay the night there and then head out the next morning to hunt for the Hindu Army. But the Hindu Army was informed that the hunters were out there tracking them down. Consequently, they surrounded the village, and they numbered in thousands. Because the *mujahideen* were not unaware of the developing situation, they had assigned a watch for their camp. They had to fight the Hindu Army, it made no difference whether did so here or elsewhere.

To break the siege of the Hindu Army, Abu Mu'awiyah and Abu Jandal moved towards Zogo Post whereupon they came face to face with the Army and the battle commenced. The battle was initiated by Abu Mu'awiyah when he threw a grenade at the post and began firing. As a result, a captain of the army was killed and major lost his leg. Many other wounded soldiers began crying in agony. In the meantime, a Hindu soldier, who was hiding behind a tree, fired upon Abu Mu'awiyah and martyred him.

Abu Jandal Mohammad Sajid was also fighting bravely and continued advancing until he too was martyred in the path of Allah.

When Abdul Wahab Sani was trying to break the siege, he came face to face with a few soldiers and he immediately shot them, dispatching them to hell. Now, in the thick of the battle, he continued fighting until his legs were injured after which he continued fighting while seated until he died.

When Fire Refused to Burn the *Mujahideen* of *Lashkar-e-Tayyaba*

Abu Abdullah Iftikhar Ahmad, Abu Hafez Ilyas Butt, and another Kashmiri named Abdul Qayyum advanced towards the river while fighting. They successfully broke the first, second and third circle of siege of the Hindu Army. When they reached the fourth and the final siege, the *mujahideen* confronted a peculiar situation.

246 THE LITERATURE OF *LASHKAR-E-TAYYABA*

There was no place for them to find cover other than a cold flowing stream. So, they took position while sitting inside that cold stream for many hours. The Army was annoyed by them but did not dare to come near them. Finally, the Army used some kind of chemical to set a fire on the water. Even though the water was on fire, when the fire neared the *mujahideen*, it stopped. Fire was on all of the water except that water which was near the *mujahideen*. The infidel Hindus were perplexed.

The fighters of *Lashkar-e-Tayyaba* are monotheist and holy warriors. This was similar to the time when the Prophet Abraham was asked to spread the message of monotheism throughout the infidel country of Iraq and those very infidels threw the Prophet Abraham into a fire. Then Allah commanded the fire:

O Fire, do not burn Abraham and be a blessing for him.

Upon seeing that the fire would not burn the friend of Allah, the Infidels of Nimrod, became perplexed. In this way Allah saved his man.

Similarly, Allah was saving the followers of Abraham from the infidels' fire and the Hindu Infidels became mystified.

It is the greatness of Allah that he helped the *mujahideen* to break three circles of siege and protected them from fire as well. If Allah wills, he could have even helped them escape from this siege. But Allah instead wanted them to reside in Allah's court.

The situation progressed. When the army saw that their chemical was useless, they used the locals as human shields to catch the *mujahideen*. The coward soldiers hid behind innocent people as they sought to arrest each one of the extraordinary *mujahideen*. The *mujahideen* fired warning shots in the air, in response to which the civilians taken as human shields by the soldiers refused to be prodded on, arguing that if they didn't move, the soldiers would shoot them, and if they did move the *mujahideen* would target them.

The army accepted their argument and asked one of the locals to tell the *mujahideen* that if they surrendered themselves, they would not be harmed. But the *mujahideen* of *Lashkar-e-Tayyaba* do not know how to surrender. They asked the messenger to convey to the army that they will fight till their last breath.

FIGHTER BIOGRAPHIES 247

When the messenger returned and informed the army officers of the *mujahideen*'s response, the officer asked the messenger to identify the person with whom he spoke. The messenger said that he had spoken to the company commander of the Afghans. Then the officer asked the messenger to return and say:

> I promise, as Bhagwan as my witness and blah blah as my witness, I just want to see the faces of the Afghans. I will not harm them.

Abu Abdullah responded with a request that he lay down his weapon and come to us. Then we will show him our faces and we will not harm him. Even after this offer, the Hindu commander could not muster the courage to approach the *mujahideen*.

Finally, the three lions emerged from the water, forfeiting their advantage, and began fighting. The battle had begun. They fought gallantly and finally drank from the cup of martyrdom while fighting.

Views from the Battlefield

When the battle began, the Hindu army, which already had thousands of men, asked for reinforcements from Srinagar explaining that they were fighting Afghans. The *mujahideen* of *Lashkar-e-Tayyaba* are called Afghans. There were only six of them and out of those six, five embraced martyrdom and only Abu Khubaib survived.

After the battle, when the Hindu army was collecting the bodies of its dead, there was a bridge which was covered with so much blood it looked as if sheep had been slaughtered there.

A helicopter was called to evacuate the wounded officers. The army boasted in front of the locals that it was their bravery that they fought so gallantly against the Afghans. The dead bodies of the five martyrs were given to the police in front of the locals and the army. The local women, children, and senior citizens were looking at the *mujahideen*'s dead bodies and crying as desperately as if they were their own sons and brothers. The military began charging the locals with batons and demanded that they stop wailing as the dead were unrelated to them. But the locals countered that they were our sons and brothers.

248 THE LITERATURE OF *LASHKAR-E-TAYYABA*

In the meantime, over twenty thousand people gathered there and, as far as one could see, there were cars, buses and jeeps. And then this huge gathering of locals offered the funeral prayers for the *mujahideen*.

There were so many attendees that it took them hours of queuing to get a chance to glimpse at the martyrs' bodies. The leaders of *jihad*, among whom was Abu Khubaib—the lone survivor of the battle, gave speeches about the importance of *jihad* and battle.

The last speech was given by the survivor *mujahid* of *Lashkar-e-Tayyaba*, he said:

> We came here willingly forsaking the comforts of our home and family with a singular objective of spreading the word of Allah and if Allah wills we shall continue this work.

After the speech Abu Khaubaib, people started to hug and kiss him with affection. They were also congratulating him on the martyrdom of the *mujahideen* and the immense loss of the Hindu Army.

A Word on Abdul Wahab Sani

Abdul Wahab Sani toured Occupied Kashmir with the founder of *Lashkar-e-Tayyaba* in Occupied Kashmir Abu Hafez [Hafez Saeed]. He also fought the communists in Afghanistan and for over a year he fought against the Hindu army in Occupied Kashmir. He participated in many fierce battles as well as smaller skirmishes. In many of these instances he was also the commander of his unit.

His mother said that when he was about to leave for occupied Kashmir, he asked us to bring all his photos and pants. When we brought them, he burned them all to ashes. The news of the martyrdom was conveyed by Qari Mohammad Zahid, Master Bashir Ahmad Bhatti, Master Mohammad Khalid and companions from the Center of Dawat-ul-Irshad Gujranwala.

According to Qari Zahid, the news of the martyrdom had already reached the people of the neighbourhood before they arrived. There was a strange vibe in the area, where people were joyous that a person from their neighbourhood was martyred in the path of Allah.

When we arrived at the martyr's home, we were received by his elder brother, Mohammad Ramzan. Our companion, Mr Khalid, began the conversation while the father of the martyr, Mohammad Rafique Ansari, sat listening while exercising great patience and courage. When he heard about the martyrdom, he uttered *Allhamdulliah* three times and then fell silent once again.

After some time, the maternal grandfather arrived and, upon hearing the news of the martyrdom, he proclaimed his thanks to Allah thrice: 'Thanks, thanks, thanks.'

The father of Abdul Wahan Sani said that 'children like Mohammad Idrees are not born every day. Before leaving for Kashmir, he visited all his relatives and also told me that if Allah wills, he will greet us all at the gates of Heaven.'

The mother of the martyr claimed that she herself gave permission for *jihad* in Kashmir to her son because she wanted the honour of being the mother of the martyr in the court of Allah. Now let us go through pieces penned by Abdul Wahab Sani, written during his stay in Occupied Kashmir that detail the situation there and vouch for the courage and patience of Mohammad Idrees.

Dear Parents,

Assalam-u-Alaikum

A million thanks to Allah that I am safe and fighting against the enemies of Islam, and I am certain, that by the grace of Allah, you are doing fine as well. Dear parents, since I have arrived in Kashmir, my companion and I have engaged in many battles against the enemies of Islam. Allah made us victorious in each of those battles. By the grace of Allah, in all those battles, we dispatched many infidels straight to hell by our own hands and, in some cases, we also took their ammunition. Additionally, we collected a lot of other booty. In different battles, a few of our companions also embraced martyrdom while fighting the infidels while others were arrested. But those who were martyred inflicted a lot of damage to the enemy before dying. The consequence of this, by the grace of Allah is that now the enemy fears us. When they come face to face with us, they flee like cowards. Once my companion and I came face to face with an infidel soldier. The distance between us was just five or six feet. When he realized this, he lost all his senses. I took advantage of this and picked up my Kalashnikov and fired upon him, killing two right there. Right after

250 THE LITERATURE OF *LASHKAR-E-TAYYABA*

that, my companions opened fire and the enemy returned fire upon us. Anyways, when the battle was over, we realized that one of our companions had been martyred whereas we sent many infidels to hell. Several days after this battle, we planned another operation. We were nearing our objective when, all of a sudden, someone fired a bullet which wounded me and, thereafter, another companion was wounded. Because the bullet was from a bigger machine gun, it wounded three of us. When the bullet hit me, I fell down and, thinking I had been martyred, I recited the *kalima*. After two minutes, when I opened my eyes, I realized that I was surrounded by my own companions. They told me that the bullet hit my leg and because it was a deep wound, they expected me to die. But they put their trust in Allah and took me to a hospital in Srinagar for recovery. By the time I reached Srinagar, I had lost a lot of blood. So they took me directly to the operation room. The doctor refused to operate on me because he thought I was about to die. But the one Kashmiri person who accompanied me told the doctor that this is a *mujahid* from Pakistan and that he should try. If Allah wills, I will be all right. At any rate, the doctor performed the operation, which began at about 10 o'clock at night and continued until 2 o'clock in the morning. I regained consciousness at around three and learned that the surgery was a success. The next morning, I woke up around ten and offered prayers and had something to eat. After a little while, there was great commotion in the hospital. As the news of the Pakistani *mujahid* had spread, the police raided the hospital. The doctors came to me and told me that someone had ratted me out and it would be difficult for me to escape. But they said that there is one way, namely, if I were to shave off my beard and get a haircut. They sedated me without my consent and then shaved off my beard. When the army arrived, they could not recognize me and that is how I was saved from arrest. Then they transported me to another safe house. By the grace of Allah, now I am healthy and fighting the enemies of Allah in the battlefield again.

Me and my fellow *mujahideen* send our greetings to you.

Wa-Alaikum salaam,

Your son Mohammad Idrees.

Second Letter

Honourable sister Aasia Parveen Mohammad Yasmeen

   Assalam-u-Alaikum,

FIGHTER BIOGRAPHIES 251

Dear sister I am all right by the grace of Allah and because of your prayers. I pray all the time that Allah protects you always.

You may think that I can live without you, but I miss you all the time. I see you before my eyes in the morning and in the evening. When I was in Srinagar, I was accompanied by someone who took really good care of me, but I missed you in those days a lot. Once in the market in Srinagar I saw this young girl returning from school, when I looked at her, I began crying because she looked exactly like you. When I recovered and returned to my companions, I planned to visit you but circumstances wouldn't allow it. If Allah wills, I will visit you but meanwhile, offer prayers, and also pray for me. In particular, offer the morning prayers. Please accept my greetings. Srinagar Badgam.

Your brother Mohammad Idrees.

Mohammad Ilyas Butt Shaheed

Abu Abdul reports that the elder brother and maternal uncle of martyred Mohammad Ilyas Butt said:

I am very happy that I am a brother of one who has been martyred. My brother was deeply in love with the founder and commander of *Lashkar-e-Tayyaba* in Occupied Kashmir and it was due to him that he chose the *nom de guerre* Abu Hafez. We asked our brother twice to return to Gujranwala, once from Afghanistan and once from Kashmir so that he could get married. But he refused both times saying that he has plans to get married in Heaven.

Similarly, when I said hello to the maternal uncle of the martyr, he congratulated me that my companion has embraced martyrdom in the path of Allah. Now let us go through the last message of the martyr.

The Last Message of Abu Hafez Mohammad Ilyas
My dearest Mother,
Assalam-u-Alaikum,
I am doing fine and well, and I hope that you too are fine and doing good. Dear mother, I am leaving for occupied Kashmir. You know very well why I am going to Kashmir, in fact all the Muslims of the world know that infidel Hindus are raping our sisters and mothers there. And

252 THE LITERATURE OF *LASHKAR-E-TAYYABA*

this mutiny against Allah is oppression of the Muslims. They deserve the wrath of Allah and that is why Allah has decreed upon them the wrath of his *mujahideen*. The enemy is afraid to even sleep at night and every waking moment they fear the worst. They are being humiliated at the hands of *mujahideen* and this will continue to happen, if Allah wills!

Dear Mother, it is an unfortunate fact that I can never pay you back for your kindness, even if I serve you for the rest of my life. Please pray that Allah grants me the opportunity to serve His religion the best I can and, when he gives me death, that it should be of martyrdom. Because on the Day of Judgement, when everyone else will be afraid, only the martyrs will have the privilege of feeling relaxed and free of fear. Allah will also allow the martyrs to take seventy people to heaven with them, provided they are not idolaters. Dear mother, how awesome would it be that your son receives such an honour as well? Hence you should pray for my martyrdom. May Allah reward us with goodness.

And when you receive the news of my martyrdom, thank Allah for it. Be patient and do not cry and wail. Make sure others don't either. Now I will beg your leave.

Please convey my regard and love to brother Asghar, brother Saeed Ahmad and Sister Ruqaiyya and Sister Amna Saeed and to the kids and other family members.

Your son

Abu Hafez Mohammad Ilyas.

A Brave Letter from The Battlefield

In the name of Allah, the beneficent and the merciful

Dear brother Saeed Ahmad

Assalam-u-Alaikum

After the greetings, I would like to ask you about your health and happiness. I hope and wish to Allah that you are doing well. In addition to this, I apologize for my laziness for not being able to write to you earlier, which may have led to your worrying about my well-being. I hope that you will forgive me for this slight oversight. And if our Allah wills, then we will meet again in this life and if not, then most certainly we shall meet in heaven. If Allah wills.

FIGHTER BIOGRAPHIES   253

Dear brother as you know, and as every Muslim in the world knows, today infidels are mustering all their strength to eradicate Islam from the face of the planet. Today, the infidel Hindus are trying to rape us and rob us of our honour in Kashmir by slaying our brothers there. The reason for this is that we have abandoned the path of *jihad*. Allah has decreed upon us this state of humiliation in this world because we have forsaken his path. I pray to Allah that he saves us from this humiliation. Amen. And also, I hope that he lets us work for his religion as much as possible. Without the will of Allah, even an insignificant leaf cannot move an inch. It is only because of his blessing that a sinful person such as myself has been saved. As you know, once I was lost and walked on the wrong path, which led me to almost take my own life. But it was the grace of Allah that prevented me from doing so. Indeed, He is the sustainer of the two worlds. Now I believe he saved me because he had another purpose for me: spreading his religion. I too have promised Allah that, for as long as he keeps me alive, I will devote my life to fighting his enemies and will raise his flag wherever possible, Allah-willing. And now I hope that he will use me in best possible way to spread His religion. You too should pray, after every prayer, that I remain determined to serve Him and that Allah grants me success. I also pray that Allah grants this honour to our other brothers as well. There is so much to say that I could go on forever; however, I would like to ask for Asghar's forgiveness too because I did not get to meet him before I left. Please convey my message to him that, as the head of the family, it falls upon him to ensure that the environment of his home more conducive to religious affairs. What else should I say? You know very well this rascal television, against which you used to lecture everyone, is now invading our household as well. And you must remember that you used to consider those who watched television to be without any honour. And, you used to recite the *Hadees* which asserts that no one who lacks honour will enter the gates of heaven. It begs of you to kick this rascal television out of our home so that you may be successful in the eyes of Allah. Try to make our family understand with love. If they resist, then use a baton. Allah has given you the right to beat them if they digress. May Allah help you understand and bless you.

Now promise me that you will get rid of this curse. May Allah be your guide and well-wisher. Now I beg your leave. Goodbye. Please convey my regards and love to Brother Saeed Ahmed, Sister Ruqaiyya, Sister Amna and also to Zil-e-Huma and Iffat Ansa and other kids and to the rest of the family as well.

Your brother,

Abu Hafez Mohammad Ilyas

Comments of Abu Hafez's Mother

In the name of Allah, the Beneficent and the Merciful

Ilyas Ghani was my youngest son. He was my favourite. His father wanted him to be a scholar of Islam. But Allah had other plans for him. He gave my son a bigger honour than being a scholar of religion. When my son asked me for my permission to join the *jihad* of Kashmir, I gave him my blessings happily because this was the will of Allah. When he was about to leave, he requested that should I receive the news of his martyrdom I not wail and cry and instead be happy and congratulate him. This is because it was his wish. I showed a lot of forbearance when I received the news of his martyrdom. I have the great honour of being the mother of a martyr. It is my wish that the mother of the believers should send their sons to fight the infidels everywhere. May Allah accept the martyrdom of my son and other *mujahideen*. Amen.

Expressions of the Brothers

Today, when I received news of the martyrdom of my beloved brother Mohammad Ilyas Ghani (Abu Hafez), I was overwhelmed, and it took me some time to realize that our brother has left us and joined the court of Allah. When he was preparing to leave for *jihad* in Kashmir, he visited my shop and asked me to pray for his success. I kissed his forehead and bid him goodbye. I loved my brother. He was a beautiful youth of twenty-two, strong, fair, with green eyes. When he would shave and wear a jersey, his friends would say that he looked like the film star Shan.[14] But no. Shan is a film actor whose movies spread lewdness throughout our society. Our brother was the hero of the *mujahideen*. He was very brave and even though he was the youngest among us siblings, he has received the greatest honour. He has given his youth and his life in the path of Allah. May Allah accept the martyrdom of our brother and bless him with the highest honours in Heaven. Amen.

Yes, I feel sorrow at this separation. Whenever I think about him, tears come to my eyes. But I am happy with the will of Allah. We can hold our heads high because of his honourable sacrifice. If Allah wills, we too shall follow the same path and achieve success just like him.

Brother of Abu Hafez, Saeed Ahmad Rathore

In the name of Allah, the beneficent and the Merciful

My martyred brother Abu Hafez Ilyas Ghani was my favourite. We used to dote upon him. One day he asked my permission to go for training of *jihad* in Afghanistan. I was more than happy and gave him my permission to go and train for *jihad* for victory of Allah's religion. I wanted him to be steadfast against these vicious powers that are working against our religion. Hence my brother went on a training tour in Afghanistan. Upon his return, we helped him establish a shop in Moti Bazaar. But his heart was not in business. In the worldly business, there is always a chance of profit or loss. He wanted to indulge in a business where there is no chance of loss. What is such a business? What is such a trade where there is no loss? Allah has said:

O You who believe! Shall I guide you to a commerce that will save you from a painful torment. That you believe in Allah and His Messenger (Muhammad), and that you strive hard and fight in the Cause of Allah with your wealth and your lives, that will be better for you, if you but know!

(*Surat as-Saf* 10:11)[15]

My martyred brother was successful in this trade. We fixed his date of marriage and even had the jewellery made but he chose to marry the maidens of heaven instead of the women of earth. Yesterday when our relatives were visiting us after hearing the news of his martyrdom, I was thanking Allah that he has bestowed upon us such a great honour to be related to a martyr.

His actions have made the family proud, and Allah has given us great honour. We too shall contribute to the cause of Allah with our wealth and with our toil and blood.

May Allah be our guide and sustainer. Amen.

Brother of Abu Hafez Shaheed, Abu Abdullah Mohammad Asghar Touhidi Gujranwala

256 THE LITERATURE OF *LASHKAR-E-TAYYABA*

Amir Hamza, 'Attack of the Eagles of *Lashkar-e-Tayyaba* on Hindu Army: *Mujahid* Hamidullah Khan Martyred, Seven Hindu Soldiers Dead', *Mujallah-ul-Dawah* (May 1994): 4–5. Translated by Ali Hamza

Since Pakistan has been taken over by a female head of state, Karachi has fallen into chaos. Daily there is news of robbery, looting and plundering. Some people are protesting on the road just to demand access to food. As for the diplomats, they are secretly negotiating with the Americans to roll back the nuclear programme.

This is how the people of Pakistan are becoming focused upon themselves. There was a time when the people would empathize with Muslims throughout the world. But they now live in such a state of chaos that they can think of little else except their day-to-day survival. As for the media, there is hardly any news about the atrocities in Kashmir and Bosnia. But everyone should mark my words—in particular those who taunt us by calling us fundamentalists—these flames of *jihad* will not be extinguished until they turn the injustices to ashes, Allah-willing.

There is *jihad* going on in Kashmir and the movement is in full swing. By the grace of Allah, *Lashkar-e-Tayyaba* is contributing significantly to it. In the past few days, there was a battle in which a *mujahid* of *Lashkar-e-Tayyaba*, Hameedullah Khan, embraced martyrdom. His *nom de guerre* was Abu Sufian.

The *mujahideen* of *Lashkar-e-Tayyaba* attacked an Indian Army camp near the village of Lassipora, in Tehsil Beerwah in the district of Budgam at night, resulting in the death of seven Hindu soldiers. Additionally, a *mujahid*, Abu Sufian, was struck by a bullet while combatting the enemies of Islam and embraced martyrdom. We surely belong to Allah and to Him shall we return.

Abu Sufian was the only son of a well-to-do family. He attended a *madrassah* for religious education. He was a boy of pure heart and mind. He began working while in school. He would take what he needed and give the rest of the money to charity. Such a noble youth embarked upon the path of *jihad*. He went on a training tour and then attended the yearly festival at the *Markaz-e-Tayyaba* in Muridke. Eventually, he reached Occupied Kashmir. He was indulging in the purity and piety of *jihad*. He

FIGHTER BIOGRAPHIES 257

fought the cruel Hindu *Baniya*[16] for five months before finally embracing martyrdom. Before embarking on this path of righteous *jihad*, let us review the last message of Hameedullah Khan.

In the Name of Allah, the beneficent and the merciful

Assalam-u-Alaikum

I hope that you are doing well. Dear Mother and Father, please do not worry about me. I am a traveller on the righteous path of Allah's *jihad*. Please continue to pray that Allah grants me an opportunity to wage as much *jihad* as possible.

I am writing this last will and testament in the event that Allah should accept my pleas for martyrdom and remove any confusion about the status of my companions. I want to be martyred in the path of Allah, I have worked hard, and now I am leaving for Kashmir.

Dear Mother, Allah has blessed you with grace in contrast to the mothers of Occupied Kashmir who have been robbed of it. Those helpless mothers and sisters are the reason I want to fight. I will fight for their independence, and I am fighting for the victory of Islam. I intend only to please Allah.

Dear Father, do not worry. Once I am martyred, I will ask Allah to grant entry of my family into heaven. Look, worldly life is only temporary whereas the afterlife is eternal. Please be mindful of your afterlife. And, if I have erred, forgive me.

Dear Father, I am sure that you are pleased to donate me in the services of Allah. Father, you must know it is an honour to be martyred and to be the parents of a martyr. On the Day of Judgement, you will be blessed with high grace and honour. Please pray that I stay determined and steadfast in achieving my objective. Amen.

Convey my regards to the rest of the family

Hameedullah Khan Kunya Abu Sufyan

Comments of the Father

When brother Tamiz-ud-Din, Maulana Asghar Aazim Abu Ali and other companions conveyed the news of martyrdom to the martyr's father, he simply praised Allah repeatedly. After doing so, he said, 'it was my desire that my son should attain the honour of martyrdom. Hence Allah has

258 THE LITERATURE OF *LASHKAR-E-TAYYABA*

accepted my prayers. I have eight sons. But even if I had eight hundred thousand sons, and all were martyred while fighting *jihad*, I would not regret it in the least.' He continued: 'In fact, in my opinion, if every Muslims sends one of their sons to fight in Allah's path, there will be no trace of infidels left on this earth.' Amen.

The father of the martyr refused to put a rug in front of his house arguing that if he does, people will come and express their sorrow upon it. Instead, he had a feast prepared and distributed the food among the neighbours letting everyone know that his son had the honour of being martyred.

The funeral prayers in absentia were offered on the school grounds of Cheecha Watani on 6 May. Maulana Asghar Aazim led the prayers whereas Saifullah Kasuri and a *mujahid* from Occupied Kashmir, Ghazi Abu Hunzala, gave a sermon about the importance of *jihad*.

We pray to Allah that he accepts the sacrifice of this *mujahid* of *Lashkar-e-Tayyaba*, Abu Sufian, that he ensconces him at the highest place in Heaven, and that He grants solace to the family of the martyred as well. Amen!

Qazi Kashif Niaz, 'The Whipping of Indian Army by the Wrath of Allah in the Form of a Battle with *Lashkar-e-Tayyaba*', *Mujallah-ul-Dawah* (July 1994): 5–13.

Translated by Safina Ustad

As the snows started to melt in Kashmir, the Hindus also melted before of a mere handful of *mujahideen*. They turned pale at the sight of the *mujahideen*. There were already six divisions of military present, but because they felt helplessness at the hands of *mujahideen*, they requested more back up. To grasp the gravity of the situation, note that the military had ordered helicopter gun ship and air support to fight the *mujahideen*. But for the *mujahideen*, these tactics are nothing new as they have already seen them in the battlegrounds of Jalalabad, Kabul, Ghazni, Khost, and Kunar. The Eagles of *Lashkar-e-Tayyaba* are well trained to counter such tactics as they were the ones who destroyed the world's greatest

FIGHTER BIOGRAPHIES 259

superpower. The roar of these Lions of Allah strikes fear in the heart of infidel Indians. Sopore, Resham Gund, Kupwara, Doabgah, Rashenpura, Budgam, and Jammu are accessible to these *mujahideen*. Every square inch of these places, in fact, invites the *mujahideen*. Now let us take you to one such battlefield.

This is a battlefield in Turigaam (Kupwara). The *mujahideen* of LeT, after fighting multiple battles, busied themselves conducting reconnaissance of new battlefields and areas, searching for a new opportunity to defeat the enemy. The day these lions don't hunt for Hindus, they become restless. In the meantime, a caravan of seven LeT *mujahideen* was travelling from Rajwar to Lolab. They stopped over at the village Teri for the night. Because unpatriotic spies tipped off the clever enemy, the coward military surrounded the entire village at night. But the gallant warriors were not afraid and came out firing their guns. In this chaos, the army shot a *mujahid* named Abu Talha Zayd in the knee. Another *mujahid*, Dr Abu Turab, tried to help his friend and turned around to pick him up, prompting the other companions to stop as well. Clearly, the *mujahideen* could not leave their companion behind like this. Camaraderie is the foundation of their religion....This is their distinguishing quality. They are heirs of the greatest traditions of our ancestors who, during battle, if they were thirsty would give their own water to their companions to quench their thirst while they themselves would wait and drink from the cup of martyrdom. So, these companions without paying mind to their situation, tried to save their wounded companion. In the meantime, the crossfire escalated, and the companions began to fight back with increasing intensity. The *mujahideen* killed many soldiers during this battle, whereas Brother Abu Abdul Rehman, Dr Abu Turab, Abu Talha, Abu Baseer and Abu Ali were martyred by the firing of the Indian Army. Brother Abu Aqasha, who was shot in the shoulder, jumped into the river with the intention of crossing it. Five soldiers also jumped after him to catch him, but vultures cannot compete with eagles: They both fly in this world. But the world of a vulture is different from the world of an eagle. Hence all five cowardly Hindu soldiers failed to capture the eagle and all five of them drowned in the river. Abu Aqasha easily swam across the river. In the battle, some thirty soldiers were killed and five *Lashkar-e-Tayyaba mujahideen* were martyred.

260 THE LITERATURE OF *LASHKAR-E-TAYYABA*

This incident demonstrates Abu Aqasha's prowess at swimming, as well as the importance of training for swimming, which is an integral part of *Lashkar-e-Tayyaba*'s training regimen. But it also demonstrated that Allah was helping the *mujahideen* as well, just as he helped Moses cross the sea when pharaoh tried to drown him.... This blessing is only for those believers who call upon Him with the purity of their heart. And it is only Allah who can help a person in need, not the will of a saint or a prophet. No one else could do it.

And if a wave enshroudeth them like awnings, they cry unto Allah, making their faith pure for Him only. But when He bringeth them safe to land, some of them compromise. None denieth Our signs save every traitor ingrate.

(*Surat al-Luqman* 31:32)

This battle is also a lesson for today's Muslim youth; namely, if they want to indulge in sports, they should learn swimming, archery, shooting or riding. These are the games that were encourage by the prophet (PBUH) who has explained the benefits of them to his companions. There is a famous quote of the prophet (PBUH) about archery:

He who learnt archery and then neglected it, is not from us.

(*Sahih Muslim*)

Archery and target practice were favourite games of the companions of the prophet (PHUB), but they also competed against each other in swimming. In fact, all of these sports prepared them for *jihad*. That is why Islam prefers those sports and games which are not only played for physical fitness, but which are also helpful during war. So much so that if you read *Hadees*, you will discover that the prophet (PBUH) also encouraged those who jogged and raced. In *Sahih Muslim*, there is an account of Salamah bin al Akwa, a companion of the prophet, who was a very fast runner. No one could outrun him. Once the tribe of Ghutfan[17] looted the camels of the prophet (PBUH) and Salamah alone chased them for miles, shooting arrows all the while until they returned the stolen camels and absconded. On this success the prophet said:

FIGHTER BIOGRAPHIES 261

Today, the fastest of the horse rider is Abu Qatada[18] and the fastest man on foot is Salama.

Alas, today cunning infidels have duped our Muslim youth into pursuing sports like cricket, hockey, billiards, cards and video games which are absolutely useless when it comes to learning the skills of war. These are the very sports that the Quran discourages and considers useless. These sports are eroding the talent of Muslim youth.

Tirgam and Roshanpur Incident, In the Light of Fresh Reports

Ghazi Abu Alqama who spent over nine and a half months in Occupied Kashmir narrated the details of this particular incident. He reports that in this battle we lost Abu Al Baseer and Abu Ali along with three other *mujahideen* of LeT in the area of Tirgam.

Dear readers, in the last month's publication it was said that Abu Al Baseer and Abu Ali were martyred in the area of Roshanpur but now that we have updated and verified reports from brother Abu Alqama it is confirmed that they were both martyred in the area of Budgam. He also confirmed that none of the *mujahideen* were martyred in the area of Roshanpur, and that Abu Al Baseer and Abu Ali embraced martyrdom in Tirgam. While no *mujahideen* were killed in Roshanpur a lot of Hindu soldiers were slaughtered in the battle there. Generally, all the reports published here are verified, but sometimes it takes more research to confirm the facts. Just imagine: we are talking about a battlefield which is surrounded by six hundred thousand enemy soldiers and the *mujahideen* live in dark jungles with no proper means of communication, so there is a chance that sometimes the information that reaches us is not hundred percent accurate, and those who think that this is an easy task are either living in a fool's paradise or are enemy agents. It is the work of Satan who wants to confuse people so that people start questioning our *jihad*. But those who love *jihad* are not confused by Satan's propaganda.

According to Ghazi Abu Alqama, the battle in Tirgam continued for about three hours. Two men from *Harkat-ul-Mujahideen* and another

262   THE LITERATURE OF *LASHKAR-E-TAYYABA*

two from *Al-Barq* had embraced martyrdom.[19] Later on, over fifteen thousand people attended the funeral for these martyrs.

Now, some tales of those brothers who were martyred in this battle.

Abu Turab Dr Mohammad Javed Shaheed

This *mujahid* belonged to Mari Bhindraan in the Tehsil of Nowshera Virkaan in the District of Gujranwala. According to Qari Mohammad Zahid, on 4 July, he went to the house of the martyr to deliver the news of his martyrdom, accompanied by Abu Saad Hafez Abdul Hanaan and Qari Khalil-ul-Rehman. 'The moment we entered the village, we realized that the people already had an idea that our *mujahid* had been martyred. We were quite a large entourage; we had Abu Abdul Wahab Anjum, Hafeezullah Baloch, Abdul Hameed from Lahore and quite a few companions from Gujranwala. When we arrived at the house of the martyr we were received by Mohammad Siddique, the father of the martyr. He took us to a small guest room. While we were sitting in the guest room, the father Mohammad Siddique asked everyone to recite Alhamdulilah (All praises to Allah) three times. So, everyone obliged. The father said that death was predetermined and that his son had been martyred, and prayed to Allah to grant him the highest honours in Heaven.

'Then we started conversing. Abu Abdul Wahan Anjum lectured us about the importance of *jihad* and explained the circumstances of the battle in which Abu Turab embraced martyrdom. Everybody listened to him quietly. After that, he began answering the peoples' questions. Hafez Abdul Hanaan and Qari Zahid also narrated a few *Hadees* to highlight the importance of *jihad*. Then Qari Zahid and Hafez Abdul Hanaan went to meet the mother of the martyr. She received us with love and kindness, and she was the embodiment of courage and forbearance. There were other women present who were crying, but the mother instructed them to show courage and have patience and told them that because her son was a martyr they should not wail and cry.

'After this, the martyr's father explained to the people that they were in fact participating in his son's wedding. At his requests, his two sons Shafique and Naveed gave the guests water. After holding discussions with the martyr's father, it was decided that the funeral prayers in absentia should be offered in the high school ground in the village at 4:30pm on Tuesday, 5 July 1994.

'A lot of people attended the funeral. People came all the way from Nowshera Virkaan, Sheikhupura, Lahore Gujranwala, Tutlay Aali and other faraway places. This funeral was the biggest ever in this area. When the people arrived, Maulana Ibrahim Salafi gave a sermon on virtues of *jihad* and then Commander Abdul Wahab narrated the details of the battle. Then Qari Mohammad Tayyab Bhuttwi explained the procedure of offering funeral prayers in absentia, and then led the funeral prayers. Keep in mind that the family of the martyr were Barelvis. After the funeral, around fifty companions visited the family and were offered water; the father apologized he would have preferred to host lunch for us but due to time constraints he was unable to do so.

'The father of the martyr said that people asked him that he should offer the *chaleeswaan* (fortieth day prayer for Barelvis), but he said that he did not need to do so since his son was a martyr. While saying this he was overcome with emotion while the martyr's mother consoled him.'

Dr Javed Shaheed's Last Letter
This letter was written by him to his family, one day before he departed for Occupied Kashmir.

Dear Brother Shafique,

Assalam-u-Alaikum,

Stay happy always and do good deeds and participate in *jihad.*

I am doing well here and hope that you too are doing well. I am thankful to Allah that he picked me for doing his good work and to serve his religion. It was by the grace of Allah that I came across the chance to tour Kashmir and now he has given me another opportunity to serve him even more. Tonight, that is, 25 June 1993, we shall enter Occupied Kashmir. Dear brother, when you receive this letter, I will be in the burnt valley of Kashmir. It is just the blessing of Allah, that he chose a sinner like me to wage *jihad* in Kashmir.

If you want that there should be peace in the world, then you too should wage *jihad.*

Indian dogs are ruining the honour and dignity of our sisters and mothers in Kashmir, while we watch shamelessly. Allah has showed us the path of *jihad*, and now is the time to teach the Indian dogs a lesson.

My brother, this world is temporary; everyone alive will perish one day. And on the Day of Judgement when our deeds will be judged, we do not want to become fuel for hellfire. Do not expect any return from other people, Allah is the only one who can reward us.

The best people in my nation are those, who will wage jihad against Hindustan, and also those who will side with Jesus Christ against the anti-Christ.

My brother, please forgive me for my mistakes. Allah has granted you an opportunity to serve our parents: please do so diligently. This is perhaps the last letter that I will write. I do not know if I will ever write again.

This is because there are many of our companions who are embracing martyrdom in Kashmir. This month *Mujallah-ul-Dawah* published the accounts of about four martyrs. Also, subscribe to the monthly *Mujallah-ul-Dawah*. There is nothing that comes to my mind of any importance at this time, other than that you should pray for me and for my martyrdom. Also do not be sad when you hear the news of my martyrdom and do not wail and cry. After I am gone, you must serve our parents as they will have a difficult time otherwise. Convey my regards to Brother Mohammad Naveed Akbar, Brother Mohammad Nazeed, Master Akram, Mohammad Yusuf Darzi, Dr Tufail Ahmad and to our neighbours and to the people of our village and to our sisters.

Abu Talha Zayd Mohammad Ismael Tahir

Shaheed Abu Talha Zayd's real name was Mohammad Tahir Ismael and he used to live in Shah Faisal Colony in Karachi. His family comprised six brothers and five sisters. Brother Abu Moaz Mohammad Sami-ud-Deen Mohammadi described what happened when he notified the family of Abu Talha's martyrdom.

Abu Moaz Salahudin, Abdul Qayyum, Anees Abdul Rehman of Shah Faisal Colony, Seth Arif Memon, Abu Numair, Abu Arif of Orangi Town and Sheikh Mohammad Hussain, the Amir of Karachi *Jamiat-e-Sindh* of *Markaz-ud-Dawah-wal-Irshaad* Karachi office went to the martyr's home.

FIGHTER BIOGRAPHIES 265

They met with the brothers and the father. Upon hearing the news of his son's martyrdom, the father praised Allah and said that their wishes had been granted. Mohammad Ismael Abu Talha had already had a *nikah*.[20] Last time when Abu Talha came to Karachi, his father asked him if he could write to the *Markaz* to request a leave of four months so that the couple have a *rukhsati*, whereupon the wife would come to the groom's home.[21] Upon hearing it, Abu Rehman blushed and said: 'Father, I do not feel like spending even a single day here and you expect me to stay here for four months. I have to go to Occupied Kashmir and you should not stop me from following in the path of Allah.' Upon hearing this, the father responded that he was satisfied and offered his blessings for him to go and wage *jihad*. Before joining the *Markaz,* Abu Talha would shave off his beard. I was very anxious because I didn't know how to instruct him not to do so. But Allah was gracious and the people from the *Markaz* trained him so well that he started following the right way of the religion. How great is that he chose to walk the path of Allah and chose *jihad* and the battlefield above all else and, during this holy journey, he was martyred. Amen. Ismael waged *jihad* with both his wealth and life.

After the news reached the martyr's fifty-year-old mother, she exclaimed: 'All praises to Allah! Allah has accepted my prayers, and those of my sons and daughters.'

Abdul Hameed of Shah Faisal Colony proclaimed: 'Allah has listened to our prayers; now, god-willing, I will take the place of the martyr to fight the infidels. If Allah wills!'

Brother Abdullah secretly said: 'We trusted the *Markaz* before and we trust it now that it is on the right path of *jihad*. I too will become a companion of LeT and join the battlefield and kill the infidels adding another chapter to what Ismael started. This will continue forever. My knee was injured and as soon as it heals, I will go and take the place of Ismael to avenge the innocent mothers and sisters for the insults and harassment that they have endured. Tyrants always fail and the *mujahideen* always win. If a *mujahid* survives he becomes a *ghazi*[22] and, if he dies, he becomes a martyr. After me, my sons and nephews will follow and, in this way, this shall continue. Now the infidel Hindus will taste the wrath of LeT's *mujahid*. If Allah wills! Everyone by the grace of Allah carried such sentiments.

266 THE LITERATURE OF *LASHKAR-E-TAYYABA*

Last Letter of Abu Talha Mohammad Ismael to his Sister
In the name of Allah, the beneficent and the Merciful

To my beloved sister,

Assalam-u-Alaikum,

I hope that you are doing well, I am doing well by the grace of Allah.

By Allah's grace, I am going to Occupied Kashmir. I pray that Allah grants me success in achieving my goals of liberating the mothers and sisters of Kashmir from the tyrannical rule of these animals and to help those in distress. My dearest sister, while I also sent a letter home, there is one thing that remains to be said. You all should regularly pray five times a day, avoid lying, backbiting and fraud. Also steer clear of gossip and stop attending those useless gatherings. Instead spend your time remembering Allah. Recite the holy Quran in the morning and in the evening. Pray for me and the other *mujahideen* that Allah grants us determination and success. Before going to sleep, hold yourself accountable for the deeds of the day: did you hurt someone? Did you call someone bad names? Did you take something that did not belong to you? Please pass on my suggestions to everyone because these are the things about which the Prophet (PBUH) was very particular. He would forgive everyone and so should you. Also tell my brothers that they should never take someone else's money. Even if you steal a single rupee, on the Day of Judgement this act can send you to hell for eternity. For this reason, according to Allah, all sins can be forgiven except taking someone else's money. Also offer prayers with patience, understanding each and every word that you utter while praying. According to the *Quran,* there are bad tidings for those who do not understand the words they offer during their prayers. A lot of people do not know the meaning and objective of their prayers. We should be mindful of what we offer during prayers and what is right and what is not. If you think my words have any weight, please act upon them. May Allah grant you the courage to do so.

Dear sister, a martyr can recommend seventy people for entry into heaven. If you heed my words, on the Day of Judgement, I will recommend you. I miss you and want to meet you, and I will do so at the gates of heaven. I pray that I achieve martyrdom, and that I am slain by taking, on my chest, a bullet fired from a Hindu's gun. May a bomb blow me up into a thousand pieces, and may those thousand pieces be eaten by a thousand birds. And, on the Day of Judgement, Allah will collect me from the

FIGHTER BIOGRAPHIES 267

stomach of one thousand birds and ask why this happened to me. I will say: 'O Allah! I did it for the victory of your religion.' I pray to Allah that He gives me more opportunities to destroy the Hindus. I pray that you and your family are blessed by Allah, and that He keeps you on the path of righteousness and that all of your sons serve Islam. Also, please pray that Allah uses me to advance the glory of His religion. I am writing this letter from Islampura, which is near the border. Please convey my love and regards to the entire family.

Your brother,

Abu Talha Zayd of Karachi

Mohammad Ismael Tahir

The Last Will and Testament of Abu Talha
Dearest Parents,

If Allah wills, today I will depart for that place where cruel and beastly Hindus butcher small children, mothers, sisters and the elderly. If Allah wills! By the grace of Allah and through your prayers I will destroy the enemy. Please pray for me. In this way you may also participate in my *jihad*. Please pray that if I must die in battle, I should die the death of a martyr.

Dear Father, please pray that after I kill a Hindu soldier, I mutilate his body with my dagger such that other soldiers are terrorized to the core of their being when they see their comrade. His colleagues should be so affected by this experience that they either convert to Islam or quit their path of barbarity.

Dear Brothers, when I am martyred, tell brother Abdul Hameed to join this path immediately because there is a verse in the *Quran* which commands us to do so. The verse reads:

What has happened to you that you do not fight in the way of Allah for those oppressed men, women and children. They say: 'O dear lord, please remove these tyrants from upon us and deliver us from this neighbourhood whose inhabitants are tyrants, and send us someone from your side, who could deliver us from this situation.'[23]

Brothers, take note of this path. It is the path of the holy companions of the prophet (PBUH). According to the Quran, taking part in *jihad*

268   THE LITERATURE OF *LASHKAR-E-TAYYABA*

is obligatory. So brothers, if you choose not to wage *jihad*, then bear in mind that you will be on the losing side.

Brothers and Father, when I am martyred marry my wife off to a fellow *mujahid* who follows the *Markaz-ud-Dawah-wal-Irshad*. They alone are on the right path while all others are on the wrong path. When you hear the news of my martyrdom, praise Allah for it and request that my wife praise Allah as well and be pleased that she has the honour of being the wife of a martyr. Please convey my regards to all our other relatives. Dear Father, also pass on my regards to a fellow named Abu Aqasha in the Karachi Center. And, when my companions come to deliver the news of my martyrdom, please present them with sweetened milk and offer them food.

Brothers, I beseech you once again, when you receive the news of my martyrdom, do not cry; instead, show forbearance. My heart wants to meet you, and I shall meet you at the gates of Heaven. If Allah wills! Please pray that Allah accepts my sacrifice.

Amen

Your obedient son,

Abu Talha Zayd Mohammad Ismael Tahir

Abu Abdul Rehman Hafez Mohammad Deen

Abu Abdul Rehman's real name was Hafez Mohammad Deen. He belonged to a place near Post Office Baldheer, Haripur Hazara. His companions describe him as very hard working, pious, and healthy. According to Amjad Bilal from Gondlaanwala, Maulana Masood-ul-Rehman Janbaz, Molvi Abdullah and Brother Munir delivered news of the martyrdom. The martyr's family received them with love and respect. Upon hearing the news, the grandfather of the martyr said this was an honour not just for the village but for the entire Division as Abdul Rehman was the first martyr in the division.[24] After offering *zuhr*[25] prayers, the visitors begged permission to leave but the hosts insisted that they have food. They were given desi ghee [clarified butter] to drink and also parathas [flat bread fried on a flat pan] made with desi ghee. The locals were so enthusiastic that they came to shake hands with the visitors and vowed to go to Kashmir and get martyred. If Allah wills!

The village folks told stores about the martyr noting how pious and awe-inspiring he was and observed that he never hurt anyone intentionally.

The funeral prayers in absentia were led for brother Abu Abdul Rehman Shaheed. Despite the fact that there was no proper planning, many people attended the ceremony despite the short notice. The entire village congratulated the family for this great honour.

We could not meet the father because he was in Karachi on business. The villagers accompanied us for 7 or 8 kilometres to see us off.

Now let us go through Abu Abdul Rehman's last letter which he sent to his family as his last will and testament.

Dear Parents, brothers and sisters,

Assalam-u-Alaikum,

Allah has said in Quran:

Say: If your fathers, and your sons, and your brethren, and your wives, and your tribe, and the wealth ye have acquired, and merchandise for which ye fear that there will no sale, and dwellings ye desire are dearer to you than Allah and His messenger and striving in His way: then wait till Allah bringeth His command to pass. Allah guideth not wrongdoing folk.

(*Surat at-Tawbah* 9:24)

There are many verses of Quran that would explain to a righteous Muslim the reasons for my actions. As some poet has said:

O Painter, paint something with great art and skill

Here the prophet (PBUH) commands and there I follow it to the word

And this is what Quran tells us as well.

O ye who believe, follow the commandments of Allah and His Prophet and do not waste your deeds.

(*Surat Mohammad* 47:33)

We should think about all these things. The Quran is not a book for mere decoration; rather it guides us in how we must obey Allah and His Prophet. True love is following those commands. For example, if someone hires a servant to do some work and the servant merely pays lip service to the master instead of actually doing the work, is paying him justified? I leave it to you to make your own conclusions. Now if we follow

270 THE LITERATURE OF *LASHKAR-E-TAYYABA*

the commands of Allah, will Allah not love us back? If we do not follow the commands, will Allah send us to Hell? Those who go to hell will be destroyed for all eternity. Hence my last will is that you will not digress from the path of Allah and follow His commandments. Abandon your bad habits and offer prayers regularly. I miss you and want to meet you but now, if Allah wills, I will meet you at the gates of Heaven. If I am martyred, instead of wailing and crying, you should be brave and show forbearance. Allah has honoured those who die in his path. If I am martyred, I will be blessed with the option of recommending up to seventy people for entry into heaven. Hence, I repeat: do not drift away from the righteous path so that I may recommend you. The Prophet (PBUH) has promised as much.

Convey my regards to everyone. May Allah be your guide and sustainer.
Hafez Mohammed Deen

Abu Ali and Abu Baseer

Much has been published about Abu Ali and Abu Baseer in last month's magazine, but we have just received their letters and last wills which are being reproduced as follows:

Abu Ali Shaheed's Letter and Last Will Addressed to his Parents
Dear Parents,
Assalam-u-Alaikum,
I am doing well and am about to leave for Occupied Kashmir. If Allah wills! Dear mother, I need your prayers. I am walking the path that the Prophet (PBUH) has chosen for me, and this path leads to heaven. Dear mother, in previous letters, I have instructed you not to ascribe the qualities of Allah to others.[26] This could be my last letter.

Dear Father, please do not object to what I plan to do. It is Allah's decree that he will not forgive polytheism, even if he forgives other transgressions.[27] A martyr can recommend up to seventy relatives for entry into heaven, provided that they have never committed polytheism and have followed the path of Prophet (PBUH). I want us all to be together in heaven: but you must follow Allah's path as I have explained. It is true, that I gave you nothing in life but sorrow. But rest assured I will be

FIGHTER BIOGRAPHIES 271

there to recommend you for entry into heaven on the Day of Judgement. Allah-willing!

While you wanted to marry me off, this is not what Allah had planned for me. Now I will marry in Heaven. I have one request of Brother Mohammad Khalil: Please, at least once, go to Afghanistan for twenty-one days[28] so you can understand the meaning of being *Ahl-e-Hadees* and enhance your knowledge of other important aspects of religion. Brother, this world is temporary and we may die at any moment without any warning. Please contemplate your afterlife. Dear sister Aasia, I request that you observe *purdah*. Wherever you go, you should observe *purdah*. Please remember my advice because this is what garners women respect. The prophet (PBUH) has said that there will be more women in hell. That is because it is so difficult to stop them in this world. And believe you me, one woman may take up to four men along with her to Hell. Pay heed today so that tomorrow, on the Day of Judgement, you don't accuse me of not telling you. Dear brother Sultan Rehmani, please put your heart and mind into your studies. The objective of being educated is not simply getting a job but also to understand and serve our righteous faith. And brother Jameel Rehmani, I am sure that Allah will use you for the victory of his religion. Please pray five times daily regularly and ensure that your trousers stay above your ankles.[29] This advice is not just for you but for everyone. Little Shakeel, you have to grow up to become a Mohammed Bin Qasim, Tariq Bin Zayad and Khalid Bin Waleed so that you can save Muslims from tyranny. Shazia, Rabia, Nadia, please forgive me my various mistakes. I am sorry that I could not fulfil the responsibilities of being a good brother to you. Instead, I will become a good brother by helping our sisters in Kashmir. Allah-willing, I will build a palace for you all in Heaven. Please pray that Allah makes good use of me for attaining the victory of his religion and that he grants me the death of a martyr. I will wait for all of you at the gates of Heaven. Allah-willing!

Wa-Salam

Dear Parents,

Assalam-u-Alaikum,

Dear Parents

Today, by the grace of Allah, I will leave for Occupied Kashmir to fight the infidels who are oppressing our Muslim brothers and sisters. Why am

272 THE LITERATURE OF *LASHKAR-E-TAYYABA*

I doing this? Simply because Allah has commanded so in *Surat an-Nisa* of the Quran:

> How should ye not fight for the cause of Allah and of the feeble among men and of the women and the children who are crying: Our Lord! Bring us forth from out this town of which the people are oppressors! Oh, give us from thy presence some protecting friend! Oh, give us from Thy presence some defender!
>
> (*Surat an-Nisa* 4:75)

And Quran also says:

> O Prophet ask them if their father, mother, wives, sons, family, tribe, and the business in which they are afraid of loss, and their houses which they like, if they like these things more as compared to Allah and his Prophet, and they do not wage *jihad*, then wait for Allah's curse over them and Allah does not guide the transgressors.
>
> (Quran, citation not given)

In the Quran, Allah clearly states that *jihad* has been made obligatory for all of us.

This is why I go to fight jihad: to perform that which has been made obligatory. My last request of you is you please stay far and clear from polytheism. No one but Allah controls the worlds.

It is his right alone to be worshipped. There is no one else who deserves to be worshiped, neither saints nor holy men.[30] I make the following requests:

Brother does not have a beard. He should sport one.

The sisters who do not observe *purdah*, should observe it

Offer prayers regularly.

Do all of the things decreed by Allah while abjuring those things Allah has deemed forbidden.

Please pray that I fight the infidels with determination, and that Allah uses me in the service of Islam and grants me martyrdom. I also advise you to walk the path of *jihad*. Convey my regards to the rest of the family and love to the children.

Your Son,

Abu Ali Mohammad Ramzan Rehmani

Last Will of Abu Baseer

Dear Parents and Family, please accept my greetings.

I am doing fine and I pray to Allah that you all are doing well too.

You are not unfamiliar with the situation of Muslims today and how badly they are brutalized. It is true that I could not serve you in this world, but I do have the requisite spiritual insight to understand how lucky those parents are who are granted heaven due to their children's actions. This is a gift for those who believe.

Youth of the Muslim nation and dear brothers, please travel the path followed by the prophet (PBUH) for the victory of Islam. That is the path of *jihad* and *jihad* is the correct route to secure the victory of Islam. On this path, Allah will send his help.

When my companions deliver news of my martyrdom, do not say anything that might anger Allah. If you are patient and strong, Allah-willing, I will wait for you at the gates of heaven. Dear father, the prophet (PBUH) said: 'I have been given Quran and *Hadees*.'

My dear father, the lips of the prophet were the source of the Quran and the prophet also detailed for us the righteous path. Dear father, our prophet's life (PBUH) is an example for us to follow. The Quran should be understood only as the prophet himself has described. To interpret the Quran through your specific belief or through your sect is absolutely wrong. Dear father, you were the one who used to educate us. Now reflect upon what you will say on the Day of Judgement. Dear father, if I have ever offended you, please forgive me as children often make mistakes. May Allah forgive us all and give us death while we are on the righteous path.

Your son … Abu Baseer

Ghazi Faheem Ejaz, 'In Memory of Shaheed Abu Sufian', *Mujallah-ul-Dawah* (August 1994): 31–33.

Translated by Safina Ustad

It was a cold night on 28 October, when a caravan of eight *mujahideen* camped in a forest near Roshanpura. We were on our way to help the oppressed Muslims of Kashmir. The night's cold was arduous. We were shivering as we had only thin shawls to warm ourselves and they were

274 THE LITERATURE OF *LASHKAR-E-TAYYABA*

useless on a cold night in the mountains and jungles of Kashmir. Even though we were huddled together, we were still miserable. At long last, the night gave way to morning. We offered the morning prayers. We saw a few houses in Kashmir suffering the tyranny and cruelty of Hindus. These oppressors were the spitting image of Genghis Khan and Halagu Khan. We were waiting for the sun to rise before descending the mountain into the village. Around 9am, we learned the Indian military was conducting searches at Dardpora, Roshanpura and Kachama and five other villages. So, we could not go to the villages. The area commander, Shahnawaz, met up with us and told us that one of our other companions has been in the jungle for the last two days and, due to the ongoing crackdown, he has not been able to go to the village either. Upon asking he told us that the name of our other companion is Abu Sufian (Hameedullah Khan). Around 4:30 in the evening, he brought Abu Sufian to our camp in the jungle. We were very glad to see him, and we had lunch together. We started talking about the hardships of traveling and Abu Sufian told us how his passage was quite uneventful. Then the Kashmiri commander asked us to follow him into the village after the search operation ended. At his request, we picked up our Kalashnikovs and other arms and started down the mountain towards the village.

We had just reached the village of Roshanpura, when women began screaming and children began to cry. Because Abu Sufian, Abu Hafez and Abu Khubaib were wearing commando uniforms, the village folks mistook them for Indian military and became terrified. But when they learned that these are their *mujahideen* guests, the women and children gathered around and began smiling. After having tea with the people of the village, the caravan continued on its path. Now, per our leader's orders, we divided into pairs of two and began moving with a little distance between us. My partner was Abu Sufian, a dignified man. He began telling me about his earlier travels and listened to my stories. Then around Bahipura we joined up with Abu Hafez and Abu Khubaib while there was another raid in progress. So, Abu Sufian and I hid in a room together. Later on, we travelled to Baramulla together. In the village of Kareeri, we spent another thirty-five days together. There, we decided to teach Kashmiri children about *namaz*, how to use weapons, and to instruct the children and elders about Islam accurately.[31] We had class every day because our commander had instructed us to stay there until we received our next orders. Abu Sufian first taught the Kashmiri children the verses of the Quran and asked them

FIGHTER BIOGRAPHIES 275

to explain their meaning. Because Abu Sufian was Afghan, the children and elders alike took great interest. Afghans inspired great pride because they were reputed to give a very tough time to the Indian Army. I would teach the locals about their responsibilities towards Islam and *jihad*. All the Kashmiris would return home afterwards and talk about what I taught them in class. Through word of mouth, more students started attending my class. Sometimes, Abu Sufian would also instruct the children in physical exercise. The Kashmiris were becoming our friends.

One day, a Kashmiri from a village 1.5 kilometres away invited us to lecture in his neighbourhood. We discussed it among ourselves and agreed. We gave a lecture in his village after the *maghrib* prayers. I highlighted the importance of *jihad* and *namaz*. When we were about to leave the participants started to weep, we consoled them and told them that they need not worry about anything as there were thousands of young LeT fighters like us across the border waiting to cross over to help oppressed Muslims like them. They cried for around ten minutes, which made us realize the gravity of the Hindu army's tyranny. When we left the village, Abu Sufian said: 'Brother Ijaz, next time when we run into the Hindu Army, we will teach them a lesson and let them know not to raid places where Afghans hold the fort.' One day I had Abu Sufian's class take a test during which I questioned them about Kalashnikov. They had really learned well and answered all of my questions. One day, the army raided the village but before they could find us, we escaped to the next village. Sikhs lived in the next village, and we took refuge in a Sikh's home. He treated us with courtesy and brought us tea, which neither of us drank even though some of our companions did. Abu Sufian began teaching the host's child about Kalashnikovs, and the child listened with great interest. Abu Sufian was very strict about punctuality in offering prayers regularly and was also very careful about religious traditions. This is the hallmark of a pious man, and Abu Sufian was certainly a pious man. One day we noticed an old woman taking her sick son to the graveyard. She made the ill boy circle a particular grave in the hopes that this would cure the boy. Abu Sufian told the woman and the boy that only Allah could make a child well again. The woman was quite astonished. She remarked that these Afghans are very intelligent and could perceive even small mistakes. One time there was a crackdown in Kareeri and the commander of Al-Barq, Farooq Bilal was arrested. We were saddened about this. Abu Sufian gifted 500 rupees to his son. The family returned the Rs. 500, which hurt Abu Sufian so much he began to cry. The family members tried to console him. They asked why he was crying. He explained that, at first, he had only heard about the tyranny. Now, he was witnessing it first hand and it brought him to tears. One day, the army raided the village again without any notice. We quickly shifted to a safe house. Even though the soldiers were within the range of our guns, Abu Sufian did not fire upon them because our commander had forbidden us from engaging the enemy. The day we ambushed the army Abu Sufian was leading the way. He wanted to serve for one year, then visit him home briefly before returning again to help the innocent mothers and sisters of Kashmir during which he hoped to get martyred while fighting. But Allah had other plans for him. He was unable to go home and was martyred. Abu Sufian used to tell us about his family, which follows the Deobandi sect. His family is very supportive of his *jihadi* endeavours. He told us that when he was living in Dera Ismail Khan, he followed the Hanafi sect; but when he moved to Chicha Watani he began attending an *Ahl-e-Hadees* mosque. It was there that his passion for *jihad* was born. After researching the matter, he converted to the *Ahl-e-Hadees* sect and went for *jihad* training in Afghanistan. His family told him to get a job as well, but he was only interested in *jihad* as that was his true mission. He told us that his uncle was the only family member who opposed his conversion to *Ahl-e-Hadees*. The others were made their peace with it. Now he was spending his life with his *mujahid* companions in the valleys of Kashmir. Because of the snows of Kashmir, for a few months a year, business and everyday life is severely disrupted. Even the roads are closed. During this time, the *mujahideen* go to their hideouts and try to wait it out. But Allah had other plans. Abu Sufian went to the nearby village of Zill to get groceries for the *mujahideen* when someone recognized and reported him to the military. This particular village is full of Shīʿa. They are traitors and frequently sell us out. The army raided the village. In the battle that ensued, Abu Sufian drank from the cup of martyrdom while fighting the enemy valiantly. He went to heaven where over forty-five LeT *mujahideen* already live in close proximity to Allah as green birds. May Allah accept the sacrifice of our brother Abu Sufian and forgive his sins. Amen.

When Brother Abu Sufian was in Muaskar Umm-al-Qura[32] Brother Abu Sakhr sent for him through Abu Hafez Shaheed. When Abu Sufian arrived, I was there too. He asked Abu Sakhr why he'd been called? Abu Sakhr replied: 'Don't you want to go to heaven? Don't you want to get martyred?' To this, Abu Sufian responded in the affirmative. In this way he left four days before our caravan departed and we met him in the jungle later. However, Abu Sufian and I spent a lot of time together in the valley and his memories are still very fresh in my mind.

Whenever someone talked about martyrdom, Abu Sufian became very passionate. He wanted to fight until Kashmir was liberated. He wanted to fight and then visit home and then return and get martyred while fighting.

He would even surprise the young Kashmiri *mujahideen* with his strict adherence to Sunnat. This is the hallmark of every *mujahid* of LeT. Abu Sufian was very much against shaving the beard. Whenever he met a Kashmiri man, he would always advise him against shaving his beards. If the person disagreed, he would ask if the person would like to be a man or a woman. Since the persons always responded that they wanted to be a man, they conceded Abu Sufian's argument and ended up growing a beard. When Zakriya, Abu Dajana, Abu Sufian and I were about to leave for Burgaam with a Kashmiri, the elders and youth of Kreeri insisted that we not go because they had no one else to train them in the proper way to offer prayers or handle weapons. But, because our leader's command was paramount, we were compelled to leave. Clearly, ordinary Kashmiris were saddened by the prospect of losing one of LeT's diamonds. But today, it is a different situation. He has already left us and is in Allah's abode where he is lord of seventy-two maidens. He will also get seventy free tickets for his relatives; his current status is just beneath that of the prophets. It is my prayer to Allah that He accepts his martyrdom. Amen.

Amir Hamza, 'The Lives and Biographies of the Martyrs of the Battle of Bandipura', *Mujallah-ul-Dawah* (October 1994): 4–9. Translated by Ali Hamza

Abu Umair Shaheed

To look at, Abu Umair was a slim boy, but spiritually he was a heavy weight. On the day of the battle, he thrashed the Hindu Army and then looted a lot of booty from them, as he alone was carrying seven guns.

278 THE LITERATURE OF *LASHKAR-E-TAYYABA*

Abu Umair also fought the communists for a long time in Jaji (in Afghanistan). He spent two *eids* there as well. Whenever Abu Umair was in Bahawalpur, he spent most of his time working for the organization. He would write letters to friends inviting them to the cause of *jihad*. He continued doing this even on the battleground. Whenever he wrote letters to his family and friends from the battleground, he would always educate them about Islam, Judgement Day, and the call to *jihad*. Reminiscent of the way in which the prophet wrote to the kings of his time inviting them to Islam, Abu Umair wrote to the followers of the prophet, inviting them to the true cause. Below are the letters of the martyr: Abu Umair.

From Abu Umair Mohammad Amir Shah ... *Bayt-ul-mujahideen*, Ath-Makaam, Azad Kashmir

Dear Brother Farooq Ahmad
Praise to Allah and his prophet (PBUH)

Jihad is ordained for you (Muslims) though you dislike it, and it may be that you dislike a thing which is good for you and that you like a thing which is bad for you. Allah knows but you do not know.

(*Surat al-Baqarah* 2:216)

Assalam-u-Alaikum,
I hope that you are fine. By the grace of Allah, I am doing well. Today (10 May 1994) I received your letter at three in the morning. At that time, I had just woken up for *tahajjud* prayers.[33] Right after I finished my ablutions in the cold water of a stream, a friend returning from Muzaffarabad handed me your letter. Right now, it is ten in the morning, and I am writing to you from the jungle. It is very cold here and there is snow on the mountain peaks. This is the border area and, in a few hours, we shall cross the border, Allah-willing! Because it has begun to drizzle here, I am writing the rest of this letter from my tent.

Today I am very happy because I am going to Occupied Kashmir. Why am I going there? Well, Allah, the Almighty says in the Quran:

And what is wrong with you that you fight not in the Cause of Allah, and for those weak, ill-treated and oppressed among men, women, and children, whose cry is: 'Our Lord! Rescue us from this town whose people are oppressors; and raise for us from You one who will protect and raise for us from You one who will help'.

(*Surat an-Nisa* 4:75)

Kashmir is burning. The cruel Hindus are playing with the honour and chastity of mothers and sisters. They are burning our holy places and they are burning our property. They're raping young girls in front of their brothers. They are slaughtering boys in front of their families. We are going to Kashmir to avenge these atrocities, Allah-willing!

These atrocities, which are being perpetrated upon our spiritual mothers and sisters today, could be perpetrated upon our real sisters and mothers tomorrow. Before it gets to that point, we are going to stop this madness.

My dear brother, a Muslim can be lazy, passive or even cruel, but he is not shameless. History bears witness to the calling of one Muslim woman who wrote to an otherwise cruel ruler, Hajaj Bin Yousaf, because she had been dishonoured. Even that merciless Hajaj sent his own nephew, Mohammad Bin Qasim, to conquer Deebal (an old name for Karachi) to avenge the honour of a Muslim sister. We too are going to avenge our lost honour.

You might wonder why my companions and I chose this difficult path. This path leads directly to heaven. It would appear that this path is treacherous and is full of dangers, but when a believer starts walking along this path it becomes a bed of roses. Death runs away from the person who seeks it. This is why the lucky ones are those who embrace martyrdom.

There is hailstorm outside, so we are gathered inside. Some are reciting the Quran while others were practising on the wireless set. Some are reciting poems referring to *jihad*. Those who come inside immediately change out of their wet clothes. Meanwhile, I, I am writing to you. You can see that in this kind of environment, it is difficult to focus on just one thing. If you find my letter incoherent, please forgive me.

Another Letter of Abu Umair to his friend

Surely you know what *shirk is*? Allah says in the Quran that he will forgive anything but the sin of *shirk* and that there is no bigger wrongdoing than this.

280 THE LITERATURE OF LASHKAR-E-TAYYABA

We should reflect upon the fact that Allah is our sustainer and our creator. He provides for us and sustains us and blesses us with children. He is the Lord of the Day of Judgement. So how can we forsake our lord and turn to tombs and shrines and give them names like Ganj Baksh,[34] which means the provider of wealth and employment, or call someone Ganj Shakr?[35] I ask you is, is this not *shirk*? Let's assume that you keep a hen in your house and you provide for it. But, when it is time for the hen to lay an egg, she goes to your neighbour's house. Would that not infuriate you? Now that is like Allah. He provides for us and sustains us. Why should we worship someone else?

My dear brother Farooq, in the end you wrote that your eyes are hurting because of welding. Ponder this. Your eyes are hurting you merely from looking at fire. How would you fare if, Allah forbid, you were sent into the fires of Hell?

Note the *mujahid's* wise style of writing in this letter from Abu Umair Mohammad Aamir Shah to his brother.

Dear Brother Farooq Ahmad

Assalam-u-Alaikum

I hope that you are well. I am also doing well. Yesterday, 30 March, I received your letter which was full of love. Reading it filled my heart with happiness because not only did you remember me, but you also responded to my letter. I feel honoured. First, I will comment on your letter. You began your letter by writing 786 on the top. Perhaps you wanted to write *Bismillah*, but instead chose to write 786 for brevity. According to Quran and the *Hadees*, this is absolutely wrong. Some people say that they write 786 instead of *Bismillah* because they do not want to be disrespectful as the paper could be trampled underfoot or discarded as trash.[36] But consider this: the prophet (PBUH) wrote letters—even to infidels. He always started his letter with *Bismillah*. One infidel king even tore up the prophet's letter. But the Prophet continued to start his letters with *Bismillah*. In another place, you recited 786 before eating your food instead of *Bismillah*? This is actually a conspiracy of Jews and atheists to keep us away from the blessings that comes from reciting *Bismillah*. Then you write that you hope that by the grace of *'Khudawund Kareem'* that I am doing well. You should have written *'Allah Kareem'* instead because the former comes from the Persian language and *'Khuda'* means god and *'wund'* means like, so it is godlike. This word has been introduced by

FIGHTER BIOGRAPHIES 281

Christians because they think of Jesus as the son of god. They believe Jesus is godlike and they also think of Jesus as god. Additionally, we should not use the word '*Khuda*' because according to Quran and *Hadees*, Allah has never used this word for himself.[37]

My brother, you wrote that you will join *jihad* next year because you have various responsibilities. You should have written '*Inshallah* (If Allah Wills!), next year I will join *jihad*.' Always use the expression '*Inshallah*' to preface everything that you hope or expect to do.

Letter to Mother and Sister

From Abu Umair Mohammad Amir Shah

To my Dear Mother and Sister

Today, it is 10 January 1994. It is around 9 o'clock in the morning and a cool breeze is blowing outside and it is time for breakfast. But I am fasting because it is Monday. I woke up early for *fajr* prayers and after that, by the grace of Allah, I exercised for an hour. Then after the morning prayers and my workout, I had planned to wash my clothes because I have not washed them for a whole month. But then I thought that I should write to you first and apprise you of the situation. I received your letter on Thursday and, by the grace of Allah, I was fasting then too. I was over-joyed when I read your letter between *Asr* and *Maghrib* prayers and learn how our Creator has arranged to pay my debt so quickly. I feel I had a 'Direct Dialling' connection with Allah during which I pleaded for our arrested brothers. Yesterday, our teacher Brother Abdul Qadir, wrote the names of some twenty companions for a task and, by grace of Allah, my name was part of the list. Please pray that our teacher has made the list of pupils to dispatch to Occupied Kashmir and that Allah calls me to the battle front as soon as possible. A *mujahid* far from the battlefield is like a fish out of water. When he is on the battlefield, he is like a shark in the ocean—right at home. When a *mujahid* is away from the battlefield, he pleads to his lord to let him join the battle again because the joy of slaugh-tering the enemy cannot be expressed in words.

It is narrated in a *Hadees*, that when a *mujahid* takes an oath in the name of Allah, then Allah himself comes to the aid of that *mujahid* to fulfil that oath. I am confident that my oath will also be fulfilled with the

282 THE LITERATURE OF *LASHKAR-E-TAYYABA*

help of Allah and he will afford me opportunities which I cannot even imagine. Allah declares in the Quran, 'Who is better at fulfilling their promises than Allah' (*Surat at-Tawbah* 9:111).

Letter from Occupied Kashmir

From Abu Umair Mohammad Aamir Shah
Dear Parents and Siblings,
Praise to Allah and his prophet (PBUH)
Assalam-u-Alaikum. I am by the grace of Allah doing well so far. Today is 9 Dhul-Hijjah,[38] which means tomorrow is *Eid-ul-Fitr* and, if Allah wills, we shall celebrate it in Occupied Kashmir. It is almost 8:15 in the morning and we have walked for two nights. We are now sitting in a jungle after crossing an enemy checkpoint. The mountains are still covered with snow which is why it is still really cold. By the grace of Allah, the sun is shining. I am wearing warm clothes—jersey, jacket, trousers, and long shoes. I also have my Kalashnikov and my dagger. There are still three or four days of travelling ahead. The real provision for our journey, according to the prophet (PBUH), is our virtue. And those who have the virtue do not fear the perils of the journey. When we get tired of travelling, we recite 'حَسْبُنَا اللهُ وَنِعْمَ الْوَكِيل وَنِعْمَ الْمَوْلَى وَنِعْمَ' it makes us fresh again.[39]

By the grace of Allah, last night we travelled along the banks of the river. But it was a very dark night and three of our companions slipped. Abu Waqas of Bahawalpur was walking ahead of the person in front of me. He fell into a pit that was about 14 or 15 feet deep. But, by the grace of Allah, he walked out without a scratch. In fact, we had not even realized someone had fallen. We only figured this out after he began calling out for us from the pit. In short, we travelled in the darkest of nights in heavy rain, and by the blessing of Allah, the journey went smoothly. These are the blessings of *jihad*; otherwise, a weak person like me would not have made it through such a tough journey—not to mention I was also carrying my kit which weighed another 20 to 25 kilogrammes. At times like these, I pray for the people who supported us financially and gave us ammunition and other supplies for our journey.

O Allah, we are weak, but we follow your command and have started walking the path you have chosen for us. Allah has said in Quran:

Go forth, whether [armed] lightly or heavily, and wage jihad with your possessions and persons in the way of Allah.

(*Surat at-Tawbah* 9:41)

O Allah, please make us steadfast and determined to walk this path and help us, like you helped the Muslims at Badr by sending your angels; like you helped those in the Battle of Tabouk. Amen. We pray for all of you, you too should pray for all of us as much as possible.

Letter of Abu Umair's Sister

Dear readers, Abu Umari has four brothers. The youngest, Mubashir, is fighting in Afghanistan. Another brother was removed from school and was enrolled in a *madrassah* in Karachi. Consider the extent of this family's piety. Let us go through the letter that their sister wrote to me:

Dear Mr Amir Hamza,

Assalam-u-Alaikum,

All praises to Allah, the creator of heavens and the Earth, who has blessed us with understanding of the true religion, the greatest blessing in the universe. It is his boon that we embraced and now practise His true religion.

I think, after this blessing, the second greatest blessing would be the honour of embracing martyrdom while walking the path of righteousness. This is a special honour from Allah and he blesses only those whom He chooses.

By the grace of Allah, Allah bestowed this honour upon my brother. It was his greatest desire to embrace martyrdom and Allah granted his wish. May Allah accept his sacrifice. Amen. He only desired martyrdom because he wanted to make Allah's true religion victorious. You can gauge his passion for this desire by how much time he spent in Afghanistan. Allah wanted him to embrace martyrdom in the paradise on earth[40] instead. This martyrdom, as per the saying of prophet of Allah (PBUH) will be—will be successful if Allah wills it.

When we heard about the news of his martyrdom, we immediately praised Allah because we all happily gave him permission for *jihad*. May Allah bless our eldest brother. Allah took upon Himself the load of worldly responsibilities and allowed our brother to leave for *jihad*. It is Allah's blessing that he gave us the patience and courage to embrace this honour. The forbearance of our parents and the way they were grateful for this honour is exemplary.

284 THE LITERATURE OF *LASHKAR-E-TAYYABA*

But when I first read the last will of my brother, my courage gave in and I shed a few tears. But these tears were not of sorrow; they were the tears of happiness and for the temporary separation that we must bear. My last meeting with my brother Aamir while he visited us the day before *Eid-ul-Fitr* flashed before my eyes. We were extremely happy. When he was about to leave, I asked him to stay one more day since we did not know when we'd meet again. He explained that he was granted leave only for this period. I prayed that Allah would make him a Ghazi, but he retorted that I should rather pray that he becomes a martyr. It was my desire to see him at least once more as a *ghazi* but compared to the honour of martyrdom, my wishes were not even worthy enough to be mentioned. I just wanted to hear his battle stories through his mouth, the stories of valour that strengthen faith. But Allah had other plans and he blessed us with his martyrdom too soon. What a wonderful sight it must have been when my brother was raising the holy battle cries and killing the cruel Hindus to calm the fire in his heart. He must have had seven guns just for himself from booty! All praises to Allah! Perhaps Allah was so pleased by this that he blessed him with martyrdom so soon.

My brother was physically strong, and Allah had blessed him with steadfast determination in matters of faith. Such steadfastness of faith in the battlefield is more crucial than physical strength as it promotes deeper love of faith and a greater sensitivity to the cause of *jihad*.

My brother Aamir started his *jihad* from our neighbourhood. The people of our neighbourhood were not acquainted with the right path of religion and did not possess any particular reverence for those who believed. In fact, our brother built the Mohammadi Mosque so the true religion of Allah could spread throughout our community. He used to love the mosque. The heavens and earth bear witness to the struggles and troubles he endured to construct that mosque. He suffered all that grief, but it never diminished any of the passion he had for religion. This was his first *jihad*, as even the strongest winds of opposition could not dampen his courage. If Allah wills, this will be an enduring legacy of His blessings. He spoke of the mosque in every letter he wrote to us as well as in his last will and testament.

He would teach everyone about the commandments of our religion. He would try to bring people to the fold of Islam and sometimes he would ask people to imitate the example of the holy prophet (PBUH). He would

FIGHTER BIOGRAPHIES 285

always work for fulfilling his duty of Amr-Bil-Maroof-wa-Nahi-an-il-Munkir.[41] Allah blessed my brother with infinite patience. He held religion in the highest esteem and valued the bonds of religion. Perhaps, these were the qualities due to which Allah selected him for the honour of martyrdom. (If Allah Wills).

He always asked us to pray for his martyrdom in every letter or recorded cassette he ever sent us. All of his letters quoted the Quran and *Hadees*. Before entering Occupied Kashmir, he wrote a letter to his friends and invited them to *jihad*, thus fulfilling his duty.

Who can escape death, we all have to taste it sooner or later. Some will taste death in a bed in a hospital and some on the battlefield of *jihad*. But if the aim of life is to earn the blessings of Allah—the creator of the universe—then what better way to die than on the battlefield while on Allah's path. A martyr upon embracing martyrdom utters the following:

I sacrifice my life in His honour because my life was a gift from Him
Alas, the truth is that I cannot repay the debt even with my life

It is unfortunate that some parents forbid their children from participating in *jihad* and some young people do not join *jihad* because of their sinful proclivities. I really cannot understand—and I doubt if anyone can make me understand—how parents forbid their children from joining *jihad* and why these younger men do not go for training. It's as if death only afflicts the ones who join *jihad* and those who stay back never die; we all know that every living thing will taste death eventually! It is man's nature to choose for himself what he considers best, but how can someone choose this temporal life over the eternal one? As Quran says:

Death will find you, no matter where you are. It will find you even if you hide behind in the strong castles and fortresses.

(*Surat an-Nisa* 4:78)

The martyr does not feel the pain of death; this is a blessing for the martyrs and a sign of their greatness. According to a saying of the holy prophet (PBUH) at the moment of martyrdom, a vision of his heavenly palace flashes before the martyr's eyes.

The only delay is the time it takes to sip from the cup of martyrdom.

Then you can glimpse the heavenly garden that you have made for yourself.

286 THE LITERATURE OF *LASHKAR-E-TAYYABA*

Our elder sisters also plan to send their children in the path of *jihad*. May Allah give them courage to stay determined and may He answer their prayers. Amen.

It is our desire and the desire of our parents that other men should also train themselves for *jihad* and they should also walk the path of Allah. My other brothers also plan to train themselves for *jihad* and will start at their earliest convenience. If Allah wills. May Allah grant us all the opportunity to serve. Amen.

It is my prayer and wish that my brother Aamir's sacrifice guide other family members. So much so that this small plant becomes a powerful tree and we all are rewarded heavily on the Day of Judgement. Amen.

May Allah accept the sincerity of the prayers of my *mujahid* brothers and grant them martyrdom and admit them to the highest levels of paradise. Amen.

May Allah grant us the determination to be subservient to his true religion so that my brother Aamir could recommend us for entry into heaven on the Day of Judgement. Amen.

My Plea to All Women
It does not matter what your role is: if you are a mother then educate your son, if you are a wife then educate your husband, if you are a daughter then educate your father and if you are a sister then educate your brother about the importance of *jihad*. Therein lies your success. Stand patiently in this path and if Allah wills He will make you successful in the end.
Ukht-e-Abu-Umair Shaheed

Amir Hamza, 'A Terrific Battle Between the Indian Army and the *Lashkar-e-Tayyaba*: Abu Tahir Muhammad Amjad', *Mujallah-ul-Dawah* (January 1995): 33. Translated by Chaudhary Moiz Abdul Majid

Translated by Safina Ustad

He was a tall twenty-three year old, known for his intelligence and academic achievements in Rawalpindi. He was also known to participate in oratory competitions, and he would win them all. He was in the eighth grade when he took the twenty-one-day training course twice. He went back to his family after his first tour and reviewed the Quran and *Sunnat* after which he was ready for *jihad*. One of his siblings said that we are five brothers and now one of us is martyred. Now there are four of us remaining. Once our martyred brother asked one of us why the *mujahideen* don't bring back captured Hindus alive to which he responded that, one day, we will surely bring them back alive and force them to do the bidding of the *mujahideen*. Although this never happened, he did end up killing several Hindus in battle. Abu Tahir was always smiling, and he was never known to become angry. Let us read his last letter.

Respected Brother,

By the grace of Allah, I am heading towards Kashmir to avenge the desecration of Babri Masjid and many other mosques, as well as pay back the cruelty these cowardly Hindus have inflicted upon Kashmiri Muslims. I pray to Allah that he, after my martyrdom, brings mother and father calm and that he gives them the energy to lead a life in accordance with the Quran. Dear Brother, after my martyrdom, you will be responsible for raising my son and teaching him the purest form of faith. Everyone in the house should observe the *purdah*. You have to educate my son in a way that he knows humility but can think freely. His thoughts should be geared towards *jihad* and you too should orient yourself towards *jihad* and guide the other male family members as well.

Tell my wife to forgive me for any pain that I've caused her and that, *Inshallah*, we'll see each other in heaven again. My wife, you know that since I've been an *Ahl-e-Hadees* adherent, I have given you less time. Allah knows that I don't have the temperament to be trapped inside my home along with my family when my Muslim brothers are suffering. If I remain indifferent to this, then how will I show my face to Allah on the Day of Judgement? What will I say when he asks me how I spent my youth? If Allah blesses me with martyrdom, I will have no regrets. I know that he is forgiving and merciful. If your heart is pure, then Inshallah, by the command of god, I will pray for you. But if your heart is not pure then none of these prayers will be useful. Ask the family to pray that I may be forgiven for any sin or trespass that I have committed. After I die, it would be a sin for you to organize any kind of ritual.[42]

Regards,

Abu Tahir Muhammad Amjad.

288 THE LITERATURE OF *LASHKAR-E-TAYYABA*

Muhammad Idrees Shahid, 'Abu Usman Muhammad Ilyas, Mandi Bahauddin', *Mujallah-ul-Dawah* (January 2001): 31–32. Translated by Safina Ustaad

Abu Usman Muhammad Ilyas is remembered as one of the mighty falcons of LeT. He was from Mandi Bahauddin, a well-known village in Rasoolpur Gharbi. He did not make his mark in the world by attaining degrees from universities; rather, he became a prince of this world and the world hereafter by attaining martyrdom.

Before being introduced to LeT Abu Usman was a mere bus conductor while his father made a living as a goat-herder. One day Abu Usman bumped into LeT workers on a bus. He was profoundly influenced by their lifestyle and maintained contact with them. The *mujahideen* convinced him that he ought to consider *jihad*, for Allah did not give him life to merely make a living but rather he was born to serve Allah by spreading Islam across the globe; the purpose of life was to humiliate and degrade the guardians of false gods. The *mujahideen*'s words found a place in Abu Usman's heart. He decided to join their ranks. He made this decision after attending a basic training camp. Once he returned to Mandi, he spent all his time proselytizing with me. During fundraising drives he'd set up a camp and urge people to donate and join the cause. He was an excellent orator and put this skill to good use by narrating the militant campaigns of the prophet's companions. He would often tell me that he became restless when he urged others to join the battle by narrating the atrocities committed in the valley (Kashmir) for his heart would beckon him to join the slaughter personally. Hence, he said, he had decided to fight in the valley. When he sought permission from his mother, she urged him to find work in the village and help out with their impoverished state. But he had burnt all his ships. He said: 'Dear mother, if I work hard and bring you all the joys and comforts of this mundane life what will become of us in the afterlife when I will have nothing to offer you? Would you rather have the temporary pleasures of Rasoolpur or the eternal hospitality of paradise?'

Finally, his mother relented. Without any hesitation the young mujahid overcame all the obstacles laid down by the Hindus and the Jews and traversed the mountains to join the ranks of the *mujahideen*. For six months he extinguished the fires set ablaze by the moneylenders. When the winter snows settled in, a treacherous informant spied on the *mujahideen* resulting in an intense two-hour gun-battle between Indian soldiers and LeT fighters in Dhalgam. The soldiers set fire to two houses and a cowshed and lost two men, while eight were injured. Abu Usman Ilyas and Abu Arqam Abdur Rahman were martyred, Allah-willing.

Soon after Abu Usman was launched, there was a rumour about him having been martyred and about LeT failing to inform the family of his passing. Another source said he had been arrested and was rotting away in an Indian prison. As a result, Abu Usman's father was furious and declared he would slaughter whoever LeT sent to their home. When I heard all this, I immediately went to Abu Usman's home but I was unable to meet his father. In the meantime, news of Abu Usman's martyrdom was confirmed. Some time after this, I was able to see Abu Usman's father at his house. I asked him if it was true that he had vowed to slaughter any *mujahid* from LeT who visited him. He smiled and said people were spreading false rumours about Abu Usman but Allah had guarded the family from propaganda. Then he told me a dream he had the night before: In my dream Ilyas visited me. I saw a compound with lots of rooms. I was worried Ilyas would not be able to find me there but then he showed up and held my arm and said, 'father, where are you going? This is where we belong.' Ilyas took me inside the compound where lots of young men were seated, their faces illuminated with the light of the prophet. I turned to my son and told him that people have been saying my son is lost. Ilyas shook me and said, 'do not pay heed to what they say. God knows how hard it was for me to get here. I wasn't even injured on my journey. The prophet said that when a martyr dies, he experiences no pain whatsoever, not even as much as an insect bite.'

His older brother reports: when Abu Usman was supposed to be engaged, I went to fetch him from the training camp. First, he refused to return but I finally managed to convince him. When he returned, he was told that he was to be engaged and married. He agreed on one condition: that his bride-to-be would be willing to live with him in the mountains. He said he was determined to spend the rest of his days serving the *mujahideen*; if his wife was happy to join him, well and good, otherwise if she had issues with his beard and his devotion then he had no interest in marrying her.

290 THE LITERATURE OF *LASHKAR-E-TAYYABA*

Abu Usman's *jihadi* companion Abu Sunan Mustafa recalls: After completing my basic training I started volunteering in the Mandi office serving the *mujahideen*. At the time I noticed Abu Usman's dedication; he had set up a stall and proselytized with such sincerity and conviction it was obvious to me that he would attain martyrdom soon. Abu Usman was a gentle soul; he would apologize profusely for the slightest of errors. He couldn't hurt a fly. He was honest to a flaw especially when it came to money and accounting. He would say that the funds they raised belonged to the *mujahideen* and he was always concerned about misplacing them. He was always eager to get the funds into the hands of the *mujahideen* as soon as possible.

Abu Usman was not educated; nonetheless, he learnt as many prayers from his friends as possible.

Abu Usman's Will

Dear Parents,

Assalam-u-Alaikum!

I am well and I hope you are well too. Mother, I am on my way to Kashmir; when you hear of my martyrdom, be patient. Advise the rest to maintain their composure as well. god is with those who are patient. Pray that Allah accepts my sacrifice; I will wait for you at the gates of paradise.

Mother, the truth is that life is fleeting. Why not spend it serving Allah? Allah says do not call the martyr dead; the martyr is alive... it is you who do not comprehend. Mother, advise my siblings to be mindful of their prayers, for Allah recommends we remain punctual with prayer. Give my regards to everyone at home. May Allah protect us all.

Your son, Muhammad Ilyas Abu Usman.

Abu Khalid (Younger Brother), 'Abu Marsad Zakaullah, Faisalabad', *Mujallah-ul-Dawah* (January 2001): 40–41. Translated by Ali Hamza

Zakaullah Abu Mursad the martyr, who was the trained younger brother of Abu Zubair Muhammad Yahya the martyr, was born on 19 January

1976 in Ghulam Muhammadabad. The two of us went to the same school for primary education. After passing middle school, brother Zakaullah began to work in power looms with brother Yahya the martyr. After brother Yahya left for Kashmir, brother Zakaullah began to work in LeT's Faisalabad central office, where he became famous for promulgating *jihad* and proselytizing. Later, he was responsible for the Al Dawah guest library; however, his desire for *jihad* made him restless at home, as well as in his office. He sold the library and left for *jihad*. He took the Abdullah bin Um-e-Maktoom course and began to fight the enemies of Allah in the Anantnag area [of Kashmir]. He fought for roughly a year and nine months before he was martyred in a battle in Islamabad [in Anantnag, Kashmir]. May Allah accept the martyrdom of my brother and give us patience. Amen.

Comments by Zakaullah and Yahya's Father

Jihad is a noble path. Sons are the most prized possession in the world, and Allah wants humans to sacrifice what they most value. Allah has commanded believers to sacrifice their most valued possessions, and he has established huge rewards for doing so. I ask why people hesitate; why they find *jihad* to be difficult. It is the only way for the Muslim nation to survive. And it is the most important duty in Islam. There is no greater pleasure for a Muslim than dying as a martyr. Two of my sons have been martyred and one is a *ghazi*. The fourth one is eager to pick up the gun and avenge the death of his brothers. At this moment, it is very important to offer our lives to save Muslims from oppression by unbelievers. I will not hold back. God-willing. I will make all my sons tread the path of *jihad*. God-willing.

Abu Mursad Zakaullah's Will

My dear parents, brothers and sisters,
Assalam-u-alaikum
When news of my martyrdom arrives, do not panic. Mother and father, you must perform the ablution and say a prayer of gratitude. You

292 THE LITERATURE OF *LASHKAR-E-TAYYABA*

must thank Allah and not worry. When the people of the neighbourhood commiserate, tell them there is nothing to be sad about. Allah has given you seven sons. If you sacrifice two for him, what is there to be sad about?

My dear father, please speak for a few minutes at my funeral to encourage all parents to send their children for *jihad*.

Brothers Sanaullah and Shafaullah, consider the words written on this piece of paper my will. You must train for twenty-one days, pray regularly five times a day, grow a beard, and promote *jihad* and proselytize. Cooperate with the *mujahideen* for the sake of Allah. This has been my desire, but I could not see it while I was alive. I hope you follow it after I'm dead. Do not go off the path of *jihad* no matter what situation you find yourself in.

I request brothers Abdur Razzaaq and Saleem to train, support the *mujahideen* and cooperate with them.

My last advice to my sisters is to pray five times a day and to pray for the *mujahideen*. They should ensure that their children are properly instructed in Islam in a pure domestic atmosphere. They should get rid of the cursed television, observe *purdah*, and make their children follow the path of *jihad* and proselytization.

Whosoever had the passion to see Allah

Allah gave him the status of a martyr]

My dear parents and siblings, you must not worry about my martyrdom and you must not make it look like someone in the house has passed away. Allah says a martyr is not dead, so what is there to worry about? If people arrive to condole, sit them down and invite them to the path of *jihad*.

My brothers, the two of us will wait for you at the gates of paradise on the Day of Judgement. When Allah tells us to enter the paradise, we will remind him of his promise. Allah will tell us to take seventy of our relatives along. Then, we will enter paradise with seventy of our relatives.

I apologize to everyone once again. If I have made a mistake, please forgive me for the sake of Allah, god-willing, we will meet in paradise.

Dear young men, I request you to give up television, satellite dish, cable television, and videocassette recorder and follow the path of *jihad*. I swear upon god, we have a huge responsibility. We must seek revenge from these Hindus for 1947. We must free the al Aqsa Mosque.

FIGHTER BIOGRAPHIES 293

God-willing, we must kill the Hindu Army in Kashmir and slice them up like carrots and radishes. First, it will be India's turn, and then America and Israel. The protectors of Islam will raise the slogan of Allah all over the world. My brothers, leave the games of the world and follow the path of *jihad*.

We have nothing to do with the world, our mission is martyrdom. We will be buried in the mountains, the snow will be our shroud.

My brothers! We are the brothers of young men who fight the enemy until their last breath. Let me tell you the story of one of our brothers. He was hit by a burst of bullets that went clean through his stomach. He gathered his intestines and held them to his body with one hand and held his Kalashnikov in the other hand to fight the cruel Hindu. He was soon hit by another bullet and was martyred.

My brothers! We are the successors of such *mujahid* brothers, but we have buried our heads in worldly matters. Let go of the affairs of the world and follow the path of *jihad*, pick up the Kalashnikov and tell the Hindu that we do not fear anyone but Allah. Oh Hindu, *Lashkar-e-Tayyaba* has come to the battleground to eliminate your ethnicity.

In my will, O Sons of Islam
I tell my sons and brothers
The flag of Islam must fly high
Let the head roll before the flag falls
Peace
Abu Mursad Zakaullah

Ghulam Allah Azad, 'Abu Asadallah Intizar Ahmad', *Mujallah-ul-Dawah* (February 2002): 51–52. Translated by Safina Ustad

Life is nature's supreme gift. Lucky are the ones who recognize this gift and still sacrifice their lives in the path of Allah; their lives pave the path of martyrdom and devotion. For the sake of the mission, countless generations of devoted men offer their blood; keep in mind, Allah never forsakes those who sacrifice with sincerity. One such sincere man was Abu Asadallah Intizar Ahmed.

294 THE LITERATURE OF *LASHKAR-E-TAYYABA*

Abu Asadallah was born in 1978 and completed his primary education in his hometown. He completed fifth grade with Master Khushi Muhammad and then enrolled in Government High School. He was in ninth grade when his father died so he proceeded to leave school in order to support his family, which he did with grace and fortitude. His older brother Usman was a regional officer with the *Markaz* and the higher ups knew him quite well. It was because of his brother that Abu Asadallah came to develop a passion for *jihad*. Eventually, with his brother's blessings, he went to Muzaffarabad for basic training in 1997. At this point his second brother took up the household responsibilities and the farming duties. This caused quite a bit of strife for the family, but such sacrifices are needed in order to fulfil the *jihadi* obligation. When Abu Asadallah returned from basic training, he took on domestic duties again but very soon he delegated all his responsibilities so that in 2000 he was able to go for advanced training. After completing the tour of Abu Mursad Ghanwa he was set to launch. After spending some time in the sector on stand-by he returned home for a visit only to learn about the martyrdom of Master Abu Fahadallah. This was tragic news considering Abu Asadallah had completed his tour under Abu Fahadallah's mentorship.

No sooner did he hear the news of his mentor's martyrdom than he set out for Sialkot to be launched.

According to his family members when he heard of his mentor's martyrdom he rushed out of the house as if there was an emergency. He was launched soon after he arrived at the sector. He was dispatched to Jammu on an important mission with Abu Ahsan and Abu Qattal Kashmiri. They were tasked with uncovering more accessible routes into Kashmir.

This was a difficult mission. However, Abu Asadallah was burning with the desire to avenge his mentor's martyrdom. He had abandoned all worldly obligations for jihad so when his own mentor was martyred, he could think of nothing but slaughter. On their way back the three comrades participated in a number of minor battles; then, on 14 May 2001 they were involved in a major firefight in Jammu's Akhnawar region that left eight Hindu soldiers dead and twelve severely injured. Among the hell-bound dead were Major S.K. Daimon, three commandoes, and Sethi Ram and Jank Raj. The injured included Inspector Ramyashurdat

Sharma, ASI Sarjeet Singh, the SDPO's bodyguards Jagjeet Singh Jugga and Ganesh Das, etc. The encounter started at 5.30am and lasted eighteen hours. Both Abu Asadallah and Abu Qattal were martyred while Abu Ahsan managed to make good his escape. Thus, two brave *mujahideen* offered their lives for the sake of their mission.

When regional officer Shafiqur Rahman delivered news of the martyrdom with Baba Aslam, Master Muhammad Ameen, Abu Mu'awiyah Muhammad Azeem Saleh, and Muhammad Yunus, the martyr's mother became a pillar of resilience and strength. She thanked Allah. The funeral was led by JuD *emir* Professor Hafiz Muhammad Saeed.

Important local celebrities as well as the masses attended the funeral. Countless young men registered their names *for jihad*. According to Abu Hanzala, a good friend of the martyr's, Abu Asadallah was an obedient and religious man. In death, he succeeded in his mission. May Allah exalt his status. Amen.

Abu Asadallah Intizar Ahmed's Will

Dear Mother! In following Allah's command, I head to the valley of Kashmir to avenge the blood of my martyred brothers and to avoid hell and make it to paradise. When you hear of my martyrdom do not cry or mourn; one should only mourn a loss! I, on the other hand, have attained eternal salvation by sacrificing my life.

My brother! I advise you to pray five times a day and grow your beard and stop smoking and wear your pants above your ankles. Complete your basic training sooner than later and continue the jihad after I am gone. The world is about to end. All those who came into this world will leave the world as well. Life is temporary. Then why not live with piety and remember Allah and pray for my martyrdom. Brothers, this is a beautiful path. I advise all my friends and brothers to take on this journey. Brothers, jihad is not about training and then sitting at home. Go for advanced training and then launch. There is much success in this realm.

W'Salam
Abu Asadallah Intizar Ahmed

Um-e-Abdul Rab (Mother of Abdul Rab), 'Lamp of Memories: The Martyrdom of Abu-Zubair Rekindled the Spirit of *jihad* in the Family Associated with *Tehreek-e mujahideen*', *Mujallah Tayyabaat*, (November–December 2002): 24 and 44. Translated by Ali Hamza

Our motherland, which was created in the name of Islam, has failed to establish Islamic rule of law. However, certain Islamic phrases have been so excessively used that people have become familiar with the body of Islamic law but not its soul. Beautiful but meaningless and colourless words are just like scentless papier mâché flowers. One such word is the term *shaheed*. Even if one perishes at the hangman's noose, he is called a martyr; if one dies because of regional or linguistic conflict, he is also considered a martyr. If one dies in a sectarian skirmish, they him a *shaheed*. Even if one dies in a road accident, he is still called a *shaheed*. But the true *shaheed* is the one who dies for the will of Allah. And that is the martyrdom that even the King of Arabs and Non-Arabs desired. And that martyrdom hurts less than the sting of an ant. That martyrdom saves one from the horrors of the Day of Judgement. That martyrdom earns one the privilege of being in the court of god. The prophet of compassion (PBUH) prophesized that the martyr will wear the crown of dignity made of pearls each of which is better than the world and eternity.

So whenever one hears news of such martyrdom, the heart desires and the tongue recites 'O Allah make us one of them'. Amen.

Recently, there was news about one such martyrdom in Rawalpindi, which was by the grace of Allah.

I once visited Abu-Zubair Talha bin Abdul Bari for a Quran lesson. As per the will of Allah, my host's family is educated, decent, steadfast, and faithful. They have always been steadfast in their faith and have long had a *jihadi* orientation. Once we heard about the martyrdom of Brother Talha, we set out to visit them. Meanwhile, sister Um-Hamaad also said that she would like to visit as well. So she came along with us. We reached their place in Satellite Town. They usually host a class on the translation of the Quran. Once we arrived, we conducted a light training programme as well. All praises to Allah.

FIGHTER BIOGRAPHIES 297

The family met with us with great composure and courage. The guests were offered dates and fresh water and everyone was seated.

We met with the martyr's paternal aunt. By the grace of Allah, she was a lady of taste. She narrated the tales of *jihad* of her ancestors who contributed to the war of independence of 1857. There was a large basement in the house, which had been a safe house for the *mujahideen* and was the centre of *jihadi* activities. Then she told us about her migration in 1947 when the basement was reclaimed. By the grace of Allah, we trained there for *jihad* and for strength. She was very pleased that she got a chance to revive the traditions of her forefathers and that her nephew became an heir to the rightly guided. Any mother could empathize with the state of Brother Talha's mother. On one hand she grieved over the temporary separation from her son but on the other hand she rejoiced over the glad tidings of eternal reunion. She spoke in detail about what she was feeling.

Talha was born on 14 August 1980. By a sweet coincidence it was also the day of *Eid-ul-Fitr*. She explained that when she thinks about this in retrospect, these two events surely indicated that there was little chance of Talha surviving. Perhaps Allah kept him alive for the purpose of bestowing upon him the boon of martyrdom. So even death could not touch him before his time. At the time of his birth, there was a complication that imperilled both of our lives. But Allah protected us and we both healed rather quickly. Similarly, at the age of five, this naughty boy was leaning outside the window of a moving bus and suddenly fell out. It was a wedding and we had specially taken that bus. The car was travelling nearly at full speed through the mountains and valleys. When Talha fell off, the other kids began making a racket, but the driver assumed that some piece of luggage fell down. In all this commotion, nobody understood what had happened.

By the time the bus stopped, we had already travelled more than a mile and a half. After stopping we reversed the bus. By the grace of the Sovereign over Everything,[43] the driver of the bus behind us, which was going to Peshawar, saw the child falling from the vehicle and picked him up. His forehead was wounded, and he had turned pale. It was Friday and the doctor was not available. Nonetheless we reached Rawalpindi, where the boy was finally examined, and by the grace of Almighty he

298   THE LITERATURE OF *LASHKAR-E-TAYYABA*

was completely safe. Except for the wound on the forehead, there was not a scratch on him.

The mother recounted that from the beginning she hoped that, by Allah's grace, her children would become *hafez*.[44] Despite his best efforts, he failed. He was in the eighth grade when a neighbourhood boy, who was a *Hafez-e-Quran*, passed away in an accident.[45] While offering condolences at their house, Talha became inspired to memorize the Quran. That was a wish come true. We immediately withdrew him from school and sent him to the mosque. Praise to Allah, he memorized the Quran in four years.

Then came the trying time. Talha began engaging in dubious activities. He was watching films on the VCR and hanging around with questionable characters. I cried a lot. I would recite *Surat al-Anfal* and *Surat at-Tawbah* and pray to Allah to bless my family with a *mujahid* and a *shaheed*. My sincere prayers were answered. A boy from our neighbourhood embraced martyrdom and his words and stories inspired Talha. Talha next reached out to Mr Iqbal Salafi, who further motivated him with the spirit of *jihad*, inspiring Talha to volunteer for training. He also lectured his cousins about his decision and whenever he met his friends, he only spoke about *jihad*. He was a completely transformed person over the course of that year, by the grace of Allah. Also, now there was decency in his gaze and a love of religion, which was visible from his conversations. His character had changed.

All praises to Allah, his *jihad* tour went well. These trips and other voluntary services had become an integral part of his life. *Jihad* became the axis of his life and he desperately wanted to battle the infidel and their disbelief. One day he said to me with a sorrowful voice: 'Mother, I don't know how men who trained after me have already gone to the valley and have embraced martyrdom. Whereas I am still waiting for my turn!' I told him that he should look for those shortcomings in his character that Allah may dislike and then seek to redress them. By the will of Allah, he acquiesced.

Then, last year, on 21 August, he visited us for the last time. He stayed with us for two days during which he spoke with us all night long. I prayed to Allah to grant him a life of bliss, and death through martyrdom, and to bestow upon him the blessing of being *shaheed* or a *ghazi*. I also prayed that he not be taken captive by the enemy or become disabled.

FIGHTER BIOGRAPHIES   299

He truly delighted in my hopes for him. He brought along other *mujahid* and asked me to pray for them in the same way. 'And mother, please send them off as you sent me off!' Then that fateful day in September came, when he called for the last time. I told him that his brother-in-law was ill, and that he should pray for his recovery or even come and visit him. He told me that he has prayed often for him, but I should not ask him to return; rather, he asked for my blessing. I told him I hoped that Allah would fulfil his heart's desire. During his last meeting with his father, he said that he wanted to eat the apples of Srinagar. His father reminded him those apples came with flying bullets. Then he told his father that if Allah will's it, he would eat the apples from Heaven.

We never heard from him again. Almost a year later on 21 August, we received the news of his martyrdom. When the news came, I was outside the home taking my Quran lesson. In my absence, a *mujahid* delivered the news. When I returned, Talha's father greeted me with warmth and congratulated me on our son's his greatest desire being fulfilled. All praises be to Allah.

'Abu Quhafa Shaheed Syed Abdul Rasheed bin Tufail ul Rehman Shah', *Mujallah Tayyabaat*, January 2003, 20. Translated by Ali Hamza

Abu Quhafa Shaheed Syed Abdul Rasheed bin Tufail ul Rehman Shah: And the memory of the Martyrs Remains

Every traveller on the path of *jihad* is lucky, but some are luckier than others. The latter do not have to face hurdles in pursuing this path; rather, their mothers encourage and prepare them each step of the way. And when mothers receive the news of martyrdom in the battlefield, they not only bow down with gratitude but also proudly receive congratulations for such an honour. The story that you are reading is about a martyr called Syed Abdul Rasheed Shah bin Tufail ul Rehman Shah aka Abu Quhafa. He belonged to Nazirabad Colony in Bahawalpur. Abu Quhafa's mother herself sent him to the battlefield. She was personally involved in the call for *jihad*, and if someone embraced martyrdom, she would offer support to the mothers of the martyrs. Whether it was Kargil, or the Afghan

300 THE LITERATURE OF *LASHKAR-E-TAYYABA*

campaign, she would go door to door to collect supplies for *mujahideen*. She would distribute *Ghazwa* and *Mujallah-ul-Dawah* among the neighbours at her own expense. The invitation programmes of Ramazan would be distributed from her home. Her passion on such occasions was exemplary. At the end of every programme, she would promote the virtues of *jihad* through monetary donations. And to lead by example, she would be the first to contribute significant sums to the cause directly impacting the *mujahideen*. Anyhow, if I go into details there are countless examples that demonstrate her devotion to the cause of *jihad* and *mujahideen*.

When the news of the martyrdom of Abu Quhafa arrived, she was visiting relatives in Faisalabad. The family gave her the news by telephone. She praised Allah, instructed the family members to stay composed and to serve the messenger who delivered the news of her son's martyrdom proper food. The next day she returned from Faisalabad. The day after that, when we reached her home, we found that her entire house was full of women. She had previously told us that she would conduct an outreach programme at her home for *jihad*. Consequently, a detailed speech was given about *jihad* and martyrdom.

Every guest arriving at her home was greeted with the martyr's mother's smile. At the end of the session, she distributed sweets to the participants, and expressed her joy over her prayers for her son's martyrdom being accepted by Allah. She felt newly invigorated and declared: 'By Allah, not for a second did I think that I have lost a son.' I asked the mother of the martyr whether she had a dream or premonition before her son was martyred. She told me that the night before the news came, she dreamed of a beautiful bride who was wearing a dress made out of gold thread. 'I was certain in that moment that the almighty Allah had accepted my son's sacrifices. I received the news about his martyrdom the day after.' When I asked her about her son's life, she began telling us mesmerizing stories. We marvelled at the Divine Whim and Wisdom of our Almighty creator who picks the gems among us for His cause. The martyred brother was a *Hafez-e-Quran* [one who had committed the Quran to memory]. He also completed the tenth grade in his secular education along with a four-year diploma in medicine from Tayyaba College.

During his studies, he confronted a daunting predicament at the tender age of fourteen. Unfortunately, as soon as he crossed over into India, he was apprehended for border crossing and was sent to jail in Amritsar.

FIGHTER BIOGRAPHIES 301

The family had no clue about his whereabouts and were worried. After a while, he managed to write a letter to his family explaining where he was. Just imagine what any mother would be feeling knowing that her son's life is in hands of the enemy, particularly at such a young age. Subsequently, the mother presented her case in the court of the Almighty while the family continued to struggle. When Abu Quhafa was in jail in India, his mother prayed with the purity of her heart in the court of Almighty and vowed that should her son return, she would dedicate his life to *jihad* for the sake of Allah. At last, her sincere prayers were answered: six months later, her son returned to Pakistan from the Indian jail. Upon his return, he first finished his education and then began his life of *jihad*.

For some time, he served as a guide. Later he was chosen to launch into Kashmir. Prior to being launched, he visited his family at his home during which time he explained the importance of *jihad* to his relatives. He also instructed them not to shed tears and to remain composed when they received the news of his martyrdom. He reminded them not to let his Kalashnikov go cold.[46] He also decided to give a small portion of his inheritance to his sisters and the rest to the *mujahideen*. After spending a few days at home, he left. Time had brought them to this particular point where what followed was separation.

What were the emotional states of the mother and the son? The son begged her for permission to leave. His mother responded with a kiss on the forehead and said: 'Go, may Allah be your Guarding and Helper.' And so he left, wrapped up in the protective shelter of mother's prayers. As soon as he reached the *jihadi* front, he became a beautiful addition to the battlefield. Before finally leaving, he contacted his family. Again, this *mujahid* was before a *mujahida* (feminine form of *mujahid*) mother who instructed him to 'Fight those transgressors bravely, and dispatch as many enemies of Allah as you can to hell. Do not be cowardly. If it comes to it, then take a bullet on your chest[47] because that is what my heart desires.' The mother continued with her suggestions. He replied only, 'if Allah wills'.

Brother Abu Quhafa was still in the valley when the mother asked his point of contact to connect her to her son through the wireless communication set. He asked: 'Why do you want to talk to your son?' The respected mother responded, 'do not think that I want to call him back; rather, I want to implore him to kill as many of those animals as he can and to

302 THE LITERATURE OF *LASHKAR-E-TAYYABA*

busy himself with killing until the moment that your wish for martyrdom is fulfilled. That you should fight with bravery against these sinners and know that my prayers are with you'. This reminded me of the poetic verses used by righteous mothers to instruct their children on death.

When we would inquire about her son, while he was in the valley, she would say she had sent her child on Allah's path and Allah was responsible for him. At any rate, brother Abu Quhafa was a *mujahid*. He went to the valley and finally embraced martyrdom while fighting the infidels. Praise upon Allah.

Hats off to the mother who in the absence of her son, prayed for his perseverance and bowed down to Allah when she received the news of his success in becoming a martyr. Yes, after the martyrdom of Abu Quhafa, there remained one question in the mind of the mother: where had the bullet penetrated Abu Quhafa? But Almighty Allah answered that question as well when another brother from the same neighbourhood was travelling in the same area and met Abu Quhafa's companions. They told him the details of the battle in which Brother Abu Haider of Rawalpindi, a companion of Abu Quhafa, was involved.

Both brothers were recuperating in a village when the Indian Army attacked them. Both engaged the enemy army. Brother Abu Haider embraced martyrdom leaving Abu Quhafa to continue fighting alone. Finally, he threw his gear in the river so that it could not be used by the army. He clutched a grenade in the palm of his hand. As soon as the Indian Army saw the grenade in his hand, they let loose a burst of bullets which penetrated his chest whereupon he too embraced martyrdom.

The mother of Abu Quhafa Shaheed was thankful that he received the bullet on his chest, as this was her wish too. She told us that she prayed to Allah for help as she continues inviting people to take up *jihad* and that, in this way, she would continue with her son's mission.

At the funeral ceremony of the martyr, the mother of the martyr donated a set of gold jewellery to the cause of the *mujahideen*.

Dear readers, these are the events of the *jihadi* life of Abu Quhafa and his mother, which clearly demonstrate that it was the mother who enabled Abu Quhafa to walk this path. After the martyrdom of her son, she is bringing up her grandsons to walk the path of *jihad*. She is educating these young soldiers so that the victory of Islam can be attained quickly. These are the tales of just one mother. Imagine if half of the mothers of this nation began brimming with *jihadi* emotions like this one? It would be very likely that Kashmir would quickly become free allowing us to move on to other battlefields. If Allah wills!

We should amend our own ways and pray that the enthusiasm for *jihad* will take root in the hearts of the mothers of this nation. May Allah accept the martyrdom of our *mujahideen* and the passion of their mothers. Amen.

Aqsa Daughter of Abdul Rasheed, 'A Mention of Martyrs: Abu Ayub Ansari', *Mujallah Tayyabaat* (July 2003): 23 and 22. Translated by Ali Hamza

Abu Ayub Ansari

Death is inevitable. Every being that is alive must die. Thousands of people die every day, some of them die of disease, some by drowning, some die in accidents and some commit suicide. But fortunate are those souls who sacrifice their lives in the path of Allah. One such fortunate person is brother Abu Ayub Ansari. He grew up in an irreligious environment; the aim of life was pursuit of riches and pleasures. But those who are chosen by Allah are given an innate understanding of religion (right way). Since his childhood, he was not one for the life of luxury. He wanted to sacrifice himself as a martyr. Despite his family's opposition, he went to the base camp. Upon his return, he started gunning for permission to pick up a gun and fight. Finally, Allah accepted his prayers and for a year and a half he kept extinguishing the fire in his chest with the blood of Hindu *Bania* (a caste in sub-continent in money lending business, but here used in a derogatory fashion). At last, he embraced martyrdom on 23 October 2002.

Battle of Martyrdom:

On 23 October, in district Baramulla, the *mujahideen* were en route to a special mission targeting a vehicle. In the area of Chak Sirri, the Indian Occupying forces were searching vehicles at a check post. As soon as the *mujahideen*'s car reached the check post, the warriors of Allah opened fire. This unexpected attack on the Indian forces continued till seven in the morning, in which the military lost seven soldiers including a Subedaar

304 THE LITERATURE OF *LASHKAR-E-TAYYABA*

and four soldiers were gravely wounded. In this skirmish, dearest brother Abu Ansari embraced martyrdom.

The News of Martyrdom

The news of martyrdom was delivered by *mujahideen* on the morning of 5th of Ramazan, which unexpectedly the family took with patience and courage. They listened to the news with patience and thanked god for making their family member the first *shaheed* (martyr) from their neighbourhood. May Allah use more and more youth from this neighbourhood for domination of the religion. May they be granted the understanding of religion so they can seek revenge for their brother from Hindu *Bania*. Amen, thousand Amens.

Comments of the Mother

My son Ayub was my favourite among my children. Since childhood he aspired to be a *mujahid*. My heart sank every time he would ask for my permission to go to Kashmir. He would try to convince me by citing verses from Quran, telling me how often Allah has commanded us to go for *jihad*. He would threaten to go without my blessings as well. I would tell him that I would give him permission after he got married. But he would always say he did not want to marry an earthly woman, but heavenly *hoors* (fairy, heavenly maiden) instead. Eventually, I relented and gave him permission to go. My heart was heavy when he left, but then Allah granted my heart peace. And I am thankful to Allah that He gave me the courage to return to Him what was rightfully His. I am proud of my son for choosing the afterlife over this world. May Allah accept his martyrdom. Amen.

Comments of the Father

My son was valiant and brave and was in love with Allah. He wanted to perform *jihad* in the way of Allah. Allah selected him; how could have we stopped him. May Allah accept his martyrdom. Amen.

Comments of Sisters

Our brother was really fond of *jihad*. We hid his luggage when he was about to leave. But he said that a *mujahid* is a traveller and he can survive even without luggage. We are really happy about our brother's martyrdom. He chose eternal life over this temporal one. May Allah accept the martyrdom of our brother. Amen.

Comments of Brothers

Our brother Ayub too could have lived the life of ease like us. But this luxury is temporary and short. He chose eternal life over this. May Allah accept the martyrdom of our brother. Amen.

Will and Last Testament of Abu Ansari

Dear Father, Mother, Brothers and Sisters!

Assalam-u-Alaikum

The time is near, when I shall, according to the commandment of Allah, be participating on the fields of battle in the holy war. You asked for a meeting, but the time that I have will not come again. There is nothing better than Allah accepting my sacrifice. Amen.

We will meet in Heaven, if Allah wills. Everyone writes a will before going to war, and I too think it is pertinent to advise you. I am not sure if I will ever meet you again. Listen to me carefully. A piece of advice from a *mujahid* is not about business or luxury or worldly matters because he himself is a farer on the path to Allah. Consequently, my advice is all about Allah's commandments and his holy prophet's (PBUH) life. It is difficult to say these things in person, but distance allows for more openness. Clearly, being a part of this world of luxury and plenty makes it more difficult to walk on the path of righteousness. But we must remember that we are Muslims. A *momin* (a term for the righteous Muslim) Muslim does not need these things. In fact, a *momin*[48] is a traveller, and a traveller does not require much. His true destination is the Creator's Heaven. I wish and pray that Allah gives you courage to act

306 THE LITERATURE OF *LASHKAR-E-TAYYABA*

upon this. It is not easy to leave this world behind. I could have continued on the worldly path of life. I could have built a business. I too could have gotten married. But my name is Ayub, then how could I have loved this world when I offered myself to Allah since my birth? Maybe I was away from the battlefield because of Satan's ruses? But when Allah commands, then there is nothing in the world that could change His will. My name means 'one who sacrifices in the way of Allah.' I am very close to Allah. Heed my words. Perhaps Allah will grant heaven to you too. I wish that you are all together in Heaven. But Heaven cannot be attained easily. You must sacrifice. I advise you repeatedly to love the religion of Allah. Make it your lifestyle. Your face should have a beard, without a moustache, as the prophet maintained his appearance. If Allah accepts my sacrifice, then people should know that you were my family and followers of the right path. This is a very sacred place to be. Allah gave this opportunity to an insignificant person like me. This is a great boon from Allah for which I cannot thank Him adequately. Please offer your prayers regularly. This is my advice for you and the rest of our extended family. Stay away from the worldly filth, television and all other junk. My Salaam to all the family.

'Abu Abdul Wadood Fidai Rifaqat Ali', *Mujallah-ul-Dawah* (December 2003): 27. Translated by Safina Ustaad

Reported by the Martyr's Father

The world of infidels is hell-bent on snuffing out the light of Islam. Every race of infidels is contributing to this nefarious project. It is the nation of Islam's great misfortune that there is no Salahuddin Ayubi in this day and age. The world is now crawling with traitors like Mir Sadiq and Mir Jaffar who actively conspire with disbelievers against Muslims. The Pharaohs of today bestow all kinds of degrees and gifts upon such conspirators. In particular, after the destruction of the World Trade Center, under the threat of being bombed back to the Stone Age, countless Muslim generals have offered their services in the project to harass and humiliate innocent Muslim populations. However, there is good news wafting in on the morning breeze. When the USA, the so-called champion of human rights, had to reckon with body bags of its own soldiers it declared that it was in a state of mourning. Indeed, Bush is in a state of mourning, but the guardians of the martyrs celebrate, for now Americans realize what it is like to have bombs fall on innocents in Afghanistan and Iraq. O Americans, you claim your enemies seem to have no heart... in truth, you are devoid of a conscience.

You're the ones who drop thermo-barracks, daisy cutter bombs, cruise missiles, and various atomic bombs. You are the criminal and Allah will teach you a lesson soon. All your pride and arrogance will mix with dust. Allah's soldiers will attack you from all sides. The lions of Iraq and Afghanistan have seen the extent of your courage; you have proven yourself to be a wily fox. You lie relentlessly to your people and the hypocrites among us accept your lies as the truth. Your dear friends Israel and India will also have to answer to Allah. Our high-risk fighters will tear your dear friend India apart. Readers, it was important to state all this at the beginning. Now let us turn our attention to a noble warrior known as Abu Abdul Wudood. This young man dedicated his youth to wreaking havoc on infidels.

His Father Reports

Abdul Wudood was the youngest among his brothers but surpassed them all. He loved his siblings dearly. He never returned from a trip without a gift for his younger sister. When he won a declamation competition on the battlefront, he sent his award to his sister as a gift. He respected his elders and was passionate about martyrdom. His love for *jihad* became an obsession. Due to our limited perspective, we spent considerable time trying to convince him to stay back; we told him his elder brothers work all day and that he should stay back to help me, his father. We tried convincing him this too was a kind of *jihad*. He said a son could do no greater service for his parent but wait for them at the gates of paradise. We forced him to take the intermediate exam, which he took half-heartedly, and then headed straight to the battlefront. He proselytized enthusiastically and worshipped late into the night all by himself. Perhaps that's what caused Allah to give me the strength to let him go fight. We are proud of his martyrdom. In this day and age Allah guarded him from all manner of corruption and rewarded him with martyrdom.

THE LITERATURE OF *LASHKAR-E-TAYYABA*

His Sister's Reaction

By Allah's grace, martyrs fight in the name of the true god and sip from the cup of martyrdom. Allah has included my brother among them. I was the only one at home younger than him. He was incredibly intelligent and mischievous. However, once he started associating with *mujahideen* he set out to make the house more Islamic. He dealt with the television in a strange way: he tossed out all the machinery in the television and said the box that remained would prove to be an excellent nesting place for chickens. When he returned from war, he regularly played hide and seek with his nieces and nephews. In the course of the game, he had me hide in the air cooler. No one was able to find me. He loved me dearly. He'd have me pray for his martyrdom regularly. He was still at the base camp when I had a dream in which I found myself performing the ritual ablution with crystal clear water in verdant plot of land. My brother handed me a gleaming sword and told me never to let the weapon fall. Allah-willing, I will never let his sword fall.

Sister; Mother of Athmar

After Rifaqat Ali's martyrdom I prepared a second missile by the name of Athmar Ahmad. My brother kept the noble act of jihad alive with the heat of his blood. We will follow suit. My brother was physically not that strong, but his faith was unwavering. When we wondered how he would fight Hindus given his petite frame he would remind us of Hazrat Ali. Our brother descended into the battlefield with the strength of his faith and valiantly fought Hindus for four straight years. May Allah accept his martyrdom. Amen.

Ukht Abu Hashim, 'A Mention of the Martyrs: Abu Hamza Sayyaf Sani Abdul Rehman', *Mujallah Tayyabaat* (January 2004): 23. Translated by Ali Hamza

O you martyr, it is your favour to us
That today we can stand tall
We have endured injustice too long
But today is our day!

FIGHTER BIOGRAPHIES 309

Temporal life fades away as eternal bliss advances. When I returned home from college, my family broke the news to me about the martyrdom of Sister Salima's brother. As I tried to digest the news, I pondered how a single house had produced so many martyrs. I began reading his last will and testament. It shone with greatness. Every word was so truthful. For a long while, I was mesmerized by the words penned by this *mujahid*. He loved his mother very much as well as his sisters and other family members. But he was not the kind of person to be tied to such love. Once he took a decision, he acted upon it.

Allah picks the martyrs from you.
(author's translation of *Surat al-Imran* 3:140)[49]

He must have loved his parents and relatives dearly. But even that love could not prevent him from answering the call. Haji Rafique, along with other *mujahideen*, broke the news to the *shaheed*'s family. While he was struggling to muster the courage to tell the family, his mother had a kind of sixth sense about the martyrdom of Abdul Rehman. There was no wailing and crying at the house of the martyr. There were tears of happiness and separation. But the mother, who lost a piece of her heart, was determined to be patient and sought the blessing of the Creator of All worlds, for whom she sacrificed two sons. 'All Praises be to Allah' spontaneously emerged from her lips. She proclaimed her desire to see the rest of her progeny sacrificed in Allah's way.

When I visited the martyr's home, a strange kind of bliss was emanating from it. People were distributing sweets. We are afraid of death and we keep our children away from the company of *mujahideen*. Instead, we run after *maulvis*[50] for guidance. But my eyes were beholding a beautiful spectacle. When the *shaheed*'s mother requested that I read the last will, I tried my best not to weep. This martyr, who spent two years of his life fighting the enemy, was so magnificent. He engaged in countless battles, yet he never bragged about any of it as he did not want to seem boastful or proud. He was a youth of just seventeen who refused to indulge in luxury when the infidels were burning the Quran and parading our naked sisters about the markets. He used to record cassettes with his wise words and send them back home.

310   THE LITERATURE OF *LASHKAR-E-TAYYABA*

The *shaheed*'s mother and sisters were so graceful. Even the sister-in-law was very composed. He was martyred on 7 October. The family learned of it on 17 October.

His neighbours remembered him with awe and love. 'One more hero sacrificed himself in the path of Islam' and 'how fortunate was he as he was selected by Allah himself.' Anyhow, everyone who wanted to go to the *shaheed*'s house and offer condolences were apprehensive about the kind of situation they would confront. But as they arrived, the jolly atmosphere of happiness took them aback. There was no sign of sorrow.

The mothers of Kashmir genuinely love and take care of the *mujahideen*. This can be discerned from what Abu Hamza himself has narrated:

I was the commander of my area. I appointed another brother to take my position in my area while I went to another zone for a while even though he was my rival. People would come to him every day and ask about my whereabouts and wellbeing. 'Has he been martyred?' 'Please for the love of god tell us if he is alright.' 'Please tell us the truth, where is he? He loved others because of Allah.'

Even those who were not related to him by blood sensed his absence, for they were related through Islam. Now Kashmiri people could not bear the absence of Abu Hamza because he was the son of Kashmiri mothers, brother of Kashmiri sisters, and the apple of the eye of the brothers. When brother Abu Hamza returned to his own area the people rejoiced. Abu Hamza's replacement admitted to the people that since Abu Hamza returned, he hadn't tasted even a drop of milk.[51] The Kashmiris brought milk for Abu Hamza and asked him to drink his fill. By Allah, their love was pure, and devoid of any expectation of reciprocity or politics. How low are those people who misrepresent the *mujahideen* as those who go to Kashmir and irritate, tease, and insult them? The heart of the Kashmiris beats with the *mujahideen*. But worldly people cannot understand the depth of that relationship. The Kashmiris were in love with Abu Hamza and he loved them back. I do not know how the Kashmiris coped with this loss when they heard the news of his martyrdom. Allah had blessed our brother with intellect. But, he was also mischievous ... [52]

The vacuum that has been left by him cannot be easily filled. It takes centuries to birth a person like him who creates history. No matter how

FIGHTER BIOGRAPHIES   311

dire the circumstances, they sacrifice their blood and their blood writes an eternal message to awaken those who are left behind. They die to become eternal and, in the rooftops of heaven, they enjoy the hospitality of Allah with *hoors*.[53]

O Allah! Grant me martyrdom in your path.

Um-e-Musfira, 'A Mention of the Martyrs: The Blood of a Martyr is Never for Naught: Abu Huzaifa Abdul Waheed Shaheed', *Mujallah Tayyabaat* (April 2004): 32 and 42. Translated by Ali Hamza

There was no news about the whereabouts of Abu Huzaifa Abdul Waheed. His family was worried and struggling to locate him and requesting others to do so as well. After a few days, news of his martyrdom arrived. Fearing the family's ire, everyone was concerned as how to break the news to the family.

But the brave mother of the martyr, the spiritual daughter of al Khansa,[54] displayed such grace and composure that it impressed the onlookers. The messengers of the news had just entered the living room when the mother, after covering herself up, entered and said that she already had a premonition that by the grace of Allah almighty her son had embraced martyrdom. 'I sent him in the path of Allah, may Allah accept his sacrifice. Amen.'

Those who nurture their lions and then send them to the battlefield
O mothers everywhere listen, such women are still among us

The sky witnessed again the magnificence of early period of Islam. The father of Abu Huzaifa died early on, and it was the mother who struggled to take care of him and his siblings. The mother of the martyr told us that she raised animals but instead of selling their milk and butter she'd feed the latter to the kids, so they would grow quickly and grow strong in order to support the family. The kids were very studious, and they worked many jobs. Abu Huzaifa was also very diligent. As soon as Abu Huzaifa came of age, being the second of three brothers, he found himself in a sea of

312 THE LITERATURE OF *LASHKAR-E-TAYYABA*

responsibilities. His brother used to work in a factory where he was introduced to the message of *jihad* by some volunteers. His brother then introduced Abu Huzaifa to the idea of *jihad* and the *mujahideen* and sent him on the training. Then Abu Huzaifa became a farer on the path of *jihad*, so much so that he never wanted to return. For some time, he served as a guide. The Amir (translator's note: Boss) would in the beginning not allow him to go to the valley but later he relented. Before his launch, he was still in Muzaffarabad when his mother went to visit him. When they met, she said: 'I did not travel all this way to ask you to come back home; your destination is those snow-covered mountains of Kashmir, where Hindus are wreaking havoc with their cruelty. Those mothers whose sons have been shot need you more than I do. The infidels have terrified the followers of Islam, so they need your support more than I do. Go ahead, our guardian is Allah Himself.'

Glory be to Allah; such courage is not common. (Translator's note: There is a line misprinted here which should be later on. I am inserting it at the correct place but highlighting it for reference.) This reminds me of an anecdote from the time of the prophet (PBUH).

The husband of Syeda Rabeeh—May Allah be pleased with her—Saraqa Bin Harris—May Allah be pleased with him—died before the migration to Medina. A little after the exodus the mother and her son Syedna Harrisa—May Allah be pleased with him—both converted to Islam. She took great care of her son and never let him feel the absence of a father figure in his life. At the time of the Battle of Badr, Syedna Harrisa was still young, but he was incredibly fond of the idea of participating in battle, and consequently, he participated in the *jihad*. During the battle he was standing next to a pond with the intention of drinking some water, when he was struck by an arrow of the infidel right between his chest and neck that resulted in him being martyred. When the mother heard about the martyrdom of her son, she worried for his afterlife. When the Messenger of Allah, Peace be Upon Him, returned she asked him: 'O Messenger of Allah, do you know how much I loved my son? Obviously, I am saddened by this separation and my heart really feels like bleeding, but I am enduring it with patience without crying. But if he goes to hell, I will cry myself to death.' Upon hearing this the Prophet Muhammad (Peace be Upon Him) responded: 'You have said something strange. He would not only go to heaven but the highest place in heaven.' Upon hearing this response,

FIGHTER BIOGRAPHIES 313

Syeda Rabeeh (May Allah pleased with her) exclaimed joyously: 'Terrific! O Harrisa! Your luck is incredible.' Then she said to the prophet (peace be upon him) that now I will never ever cry, if it be Allah's will.

After living in the valley [of Kashmir, in Indian-administered Kashmir] for three years, Abu Huzaifa returned to visit his mother. His mother was ecstatic. She extolled: 'my son has returned as twice a man since the time when I sent him to *jihad*. His health is much better than before, even though my son told me that, at times, there was nothing to eat in the valley and they would go hungry for days at a time. But the power of faith defeats the weaknesses of human body. Allah specially blesses these *mujahideen*'.

The mother of the martyr narrates that upon his return, he often wept for he had not yet been blessed by martyrdom. The folks who went after him had embraced martyrdom, yet he returned safely. Even though the bullets missed him by a hair's breadth, his desire for martyrdom remained unfulfilled.

While looking at the big lawn, she wished that Allah has blessed her with a big house on this earth, May Allah grant her such a big house in Heaven as well. Amen.

After his return, he took responsibility of the border of Zafarwal. After spending four months, this bird of battle thought about departing for the battleground again. His mother said to him 'Son, I have found a girl for you, and I am planning to get you married.' To this our brave soldier responded, 'Mother dearest, you are after this worldly bride, don't you want those seventy-two maidens for me?'

With a knowing smile she said, 'those who start to walk on this path never really return; flowers mean nothing to those who walk the thorny road. He was the property of Allah and now he has returned to Him. This worldly life is fleeting; we should all worry about our afterlife.'

The younger sister said that when there was life left in his fate, he stood in the path of bullets for three years and returned home safely, but when his time had come, then by the Grace of Allah, he was blessed with the great death of martyrdom.

At the funeral of Abu Huziafa, his sister-in-law made an announcement regarding dedicating her son's life to the life of *jihad*. She said: 'O sisters, bear witness that I am dedicating my son's life to the life of *jihad* just like his uncle. He will grow up and avenge him.' Allah-willing.

314 THE LITERATURE OF *LASHKAR-E-TAYYABA*

The family had arranged for food for the attendees of the funeral. Inside the house, the women ate, while outside, handsome *mujahideen* sporting the *Sunnat* of the holy prophet (translator's note: referring to moustache less beard) gathered. This seemed as if it were the wedding party of the martyr.

Indeed, this was the wedding party of Abu Huzaifa; Allah must have married him to seventy-two maidens in heaven already. If Allah wills!

As long as there are such mothers and sisters who will send their brothers and sons to the battlefield with a smile on their face, it is only a matter of time before the clouds of cruelty and humiliation are lifted from above us. It is like the hope of spring in autumn, and like the light of the morning star which indicates that the dawn is at hand. May Allah give such passion to all the mothers and sisters of Muslim nations so that we can defeat the Pharaohs and Nimrods[55] of our time so that the truth prevails. O Allah! Humiliate the infidel and let the flag of truth fly high. Amen!

On my way back when I bid farewell of the mother of the martyr, she said, lovingly, 'like we the sisters and mothers of the martyrs are together here on this earth, May Allah keep us together after the Day of Judgement. It would be awesome if we all met there.' Upon hearing this, everyone within earshot said Amen. By the grace of Allah, all of them had sacrificed their loved ones in *jihad* and they all prayed: 'O Allah! Please accept these sacrifices. O Allah, please let us bear witness to the change that the blood of these martyrs will bring upon this earth. Let the infidels be humiliated in front of us so that we can rejoice. And on the Day of Judgement accept the sacrifices of our martyrs and bring us all together in the afterlife as well.' Amen!

Abu Asad, 'A Mention of the Martyrs: Abu Hanzala Amjad Shaheed', *Zarb-e-Tayyaba* (April 2004): 33–35. Translated by Ali Hamza

Abu Hanzul Amjad

I still have not forgotten the evening of February 2000. A young man with fair complexion, a broad forehead, and large black eyes came into the

FIGHTER BIOGRAPHIES   315

office and inquired if we send people to Kashmir. I was busy studying; when I lifted my head, I saw in him a hawk whose feathers were not fully grown, and he was asking about his lost destination.

I offered him water and gave a brief introduction of the place and mission. After this the hawk whose name was Muhammad Amjad, interrogated me about launching, Askariat and preaching. He said he had heard Hindus were brutally murdering Muslim women and children. He wished to join the *jihad* and fight against the violence of Hindus before he died. His words traversed my heart.

In March 2000, he had his ninth grade exams. As soon as he completed his exams, he became so inspired by the tales of *mujahideen* and martyrs that be undertook the initial training. Upon returning, he barely spent a month in school. During his summer vacation, he became Muhammad Amjad Abu Hanzul. He began training with another classmate. After successful completion of his training during the summer holiday, he resumed his studies because Ahmed Pur Sharqia High School was near the office, and this made it easier for him to stay in touch. I met Amjad after two months. He was matured with a grown beard. He asked me to send him to Mu'askar in the upcoming season, after which he could directly confront the enemy.

Ultimately, in April 2001, he left for the next phase of training. After he was gone for a month and a half, his parents grew anxious about his return. At the same time, we wanted him to be fully trained. Eventually, his parents brought him home. Amjad was frustrated and upset. However, he was not at all helpful to his father Ghulam Haji Nazir Mehboob. He liked the company of *jihadi*s and wanted to spend his days and nights with them.

His father arranged a job for him in a pharmaceutical company but after some time the boy ran away. When I asked him why, he said: 'I don't like slavery.'

Afterwards, he returned to Muzaffarabad. Within fifteen days, he arrived at Patoki for the procession. Afterwards he returned home. I asked him to finish the training that he had left. Because his parents would not give him their blessings, he asked that he be launched in the new season based on the training he had completed.

In May 2003, he silently left home without telling anyone about his whereabouts. He stayed in Quetta and then spent a night with his friend,

316   THE LITERATURE OF *LASHKAR-E-TAYYABA*

Abu Ans Arshad-ul-Haq, where he talked about hell, heaven, and after-life. He then spent two nights with his uncle, Advocate Bashir Masood. Then he moved in with his younger cousin, Usman Masood, who was very dear to him. He told his cousin about the crisis in Kashmir and the issues faced by Muslims living there.

When he woke up the next morning, he thought of meeting his family for the last time, but he was still two kilometres from his home when he got off the bus and went on to his real journey. He didn't meet his family because they would stop him from launching into Kashmir.

During his training, he met the supervisor of district Bahawalpur. They became friends because they belonged to the same area. Amjad wore a red-coloured shawl on his shoulder and a blue *shalwaar kameez*. The shawl often drifted down his head or shoulder. The supervisor remarked 'your shawl is so restless'. He replied, 'it will calm down when it is stained with warm blood'. He was so desperate to enter the battlefield.

The group was en route to their mission. They were nearing a village when the Indian army, which was hunting for wounded *mujahideen*, encountered this group. Bullets were exchanged in the encounter. Amjad was with the group. He was injured during the skirmish but fought until 1pm. He successfully killed twelve enemy soldiers and injured seven. Three *mujahideen* were also martyred.

When the report of the martyrdom arrived, I was in the office. The following day, Makki Sahab led the Friday prayer.[56] Khalid Hameed Sahab, Aqeel Sahab, Professor Rafiq Sahab and Professor Azam Cheema[57] and Brother Zahid were also present. They were told not to inform the family over telephone. Instead, we decided to visit them and break the news in person.

When we phoned Amjad's home, we learned that the family was at the hospital since his elder brother Muhammad Ajmal was sick. Khalid Hameed went to the hospital and met with his brother where both his mother and younger brother, Muhammad Akmal, were also present. Amjad's father was busy with the relatives. Amjad's mother incessantly requested to meet her son, just once. I had the copy of the martyrdom report. I was worried that if I told her the news of Amjad's martyrdom, chaos would ensue. So we went to Abu Ans Arshad-ul-Haq's home where other members and elders had gathered. While Cheema Sahab advised us against informing the family in the hospital as they are already in duress, the tehsil supervisor, Abdul-Shakoor, had already announced the news of his martyrdom after the Friday prayer sermon.

The elders were worried because they really wanted to inform his family soon. They decided to call his father in person. After offering maghrib prayers, we went to the hospital. When his father arrived, he asked about his son Amjad. I said: 'You must be aware of the news of his launch? We will tell you everything.' He then asked if people who go to Kashmir ever return. I said, 'brother Amjad may not return because he departed with the wish to die like a martyr.'

His father said: 'I connected the dots when I saw you and your car. So we went to the meeting place of Abu Ans where people had gathered. Abu Saad debriefed us about the blessings of a martyr and broke the news of Amjad's martyrdom.'

I was worried; the martyr's father, Nazeer Mehboob, was a heart patient with one son in the hospital and the other one martyred. He may not suffer a heart attack, but Allah gave him forbearance. He patiently listened to his son's will and report. He put the will in his pocket and requested that we be silent and not tell anyone else.

His father wished to announce the news formally and make arrangements for the funeral. The supervisor went to the martyr's home and offered maghrib prayer. Around fifty people gathered at his home where he gave a lecture and read out the martyrdom report. After that, the martyr's uncle distributed sweets among the attendees. Everyone agreed the funeral should take place in the middle school at 4pm. People began gathering at 1pm and by the time of the funeral, there was a flood of people.

Qari Muhammad Yaqoob Sheikh[58] was supposed to lead the funeral prayers but for some reason he could not make it in time. Professor Muhammad Rafiq gave a detailed account on the benefits of martyrdom and the issues faced by Muslims. Sohail Sahib read out the will and led the funeral prayer. Sheikh Sahib arrived during the prayer and gave a sermon after.

After the funeral, the martyr's father Haji Ghulam Nazeer Mehboob shared a dream he had in which he received a letter notifying him of his son's launching from a gentleman he didn't recognize. The next day, when Cheema Sahib arrived and explained that they were there to attend

318   THE LITERATURE OF *LASHKAR-E-TAYYABA*

Amjad's wedding, the martyr's father recognized Cheema sahib as the man in the dream. On the day of his funeral, Amjad's mother said she had arranged for a feast and everyone went to their home to eat.

Will Manuscript

Beloved parents and siblings!
Assalam-u-Alaikum

Certainty we will remember them forever
Keep the garden of their memories alive forever
It is my promise to Allah that no one will dig my grave
For Allah will lay the foundation of my eternal abode

Dear Mother!

Under the blue skies and in the shadow of clouds, among the warriors of Islam, I am writing the last script of my life. Listen to me very carefully. This life is a necessity but it is not the objective. Because the objective explained by our prophet Muhammad (PBUH) and Allah is more important, I have sacrificed everything for their command.

Please adopt the values of Islam as I did. Follow the teachings of the prophet (PBUH) in every respect. This is true faith. If you fail to do so, the never-ending torment of hell will begin after death. Protect yourself from this suffering. Also, please pray for the acceptance of my martyrdom and punctually offer prayers.

Dear Sister and Sister-in-law!

Be modest and advise your children to offer *namaz* on time and learn the Quran. I could not get you nice clothes for the comfort of this life. But remember, do not forget what the Quran and *Hadees* tell us. Success lies in living simply and following Islam rather than chasing the fashionable things life has to offer.

Dearly loved mother and father! I quench the thirst of my anger by slaughtering the heads of the enemy. I want to slay the enemy until Allah calms me down and uplifts Islam throughout the world. Life and death are in the hands of Allah, but the death in the battlefield has no comparison with any other death.

Brothers! There was a time when the Muslim nation was enthusiastic and ambitious and had strength and valour in their blood. Why have we become so ignorant today? They had such high aims and hope that in whatever direction they went, they became successful as conquerors.

Dear brothers! My adolescence has strengthened me. I'm obliged to make it clear to the Hindu enemy that the Muslim child may be young, but not immature. I want to tell apathetic Muslims that they should live with dignity or die.

Our daughters, upon being humiliated by having their veil removed, wait for a *mujahid* to rescue them as do all the Muslims who suffer in Kashmir. Pay my regards to everyone and tell them to follow *jihad*. It is the shortcut to paradise.

Mother! This life is very temporary, and it will end very soon. People come and go from this world that is merely like a flower, which is fragrant and looks beautiful but gradually dies. Tell other people to quit playing games and adopt *jihad*.

Don't grieve over my departure for it is temporary. Real life will begin after death, hence prepare for it by regularly offering *namaz*. Brother, please look after my mother and serve my father. Do not make my absence felt. Learn the Holy Quran. I have committed so many mistakes. Please forgive me. I will meet you in paradise *Inshaallah*. I recommend my family embrace *jihad* for success lies therein.

Brother Ajmal, get rid of the television. Serve my parents and be nice to everyone. Give love to children and pray for me.

Regards,
Your son Abu Hanzul Muhammad Amjad

Mother's Remarks

I never let Amjad out of sight because he was very dear to me among all the children. But when he decided to go to Kashmir, I dealt with it very patiently. When I learned of his martyrdom, Allah gave me serenity. I have performed Umrah on his behalf and, *Inshaallah*, I will perform Hajj too.

Inshaallah I will show my sons and future generations the path Amjad tread because victory lies in it and they will meet Amjad in paradise.

320 THE LITERATURE OF *LASHKAR-E-TAYYABA*

Father's Remarks

My son went for training during the summer holidays. My father was a renowned religious scholar who offered sermons on the Quran and *Hadees* all his life. Now, my son has sacrificed his life for the sake of Islam and left a mark on the world for generations to come.

When I went to the procession, despite my heart condition, I saw my son in every fighter. *Inshaallah*, if I get a chance, I will go for training and, regardless of my age, I will cross the border. *Inshaallah*.

Ghazi Abu Waleed al-Shamil, 'Commander Abul Qasim Muhammad Shakeel', *Mujallah-ul-Dawah* (August 2004): 59. Translated by Safina Ustaad

'Detach yourself from this world and Allah will love you; detach yourself from what people have and they will love you.'

Those who are detached from this world and leave their homes for Allah's approval are, no doubt, loved by Allah and people. Among such men is Abul Qasim Muhammad Shakeel who sacrificed his life in the path of truth.

We were separated once we entered the valley. We could not communicate for six days. When I finally reached a safe space in the forest and started my radio set, I overheard a conversation between Abul Qasim and Abu Noman. I called Abul Qasim and told him we were in a forest; he comforted us and told us not to worry for they will find us soon. He informed me about the region in coded terms. His sweet voice and comforting words put as at ease and by nightfall we were reunited with the *mujahideen*.

It was only after I spent some days with Abul Qasim that I realized how skilled he was. He was a commander in Rajwar and was constantly planning operations. The Rajwar region is scattered with hillocks instead of mountains. Abul Qasim knew this region well and as a result gave the Indian Army a good and constant thrashing. He was the most well-known commander in the area, after Qari Abuzar, Abu Mauz, and Salamat Allah. Every child in the area knew about him.

FIGHTER BIOGRAPHIES 321

According to a narrative about his courage, once, around fifteen to twenty *mujahideen* from various organizations held a meeting in a safe house when the military cracked down on them and ordered them to step out and surrender. *Mujahideen* do not believe in surrender. Abul Qasim positioned the *mujahideen* at various windows and then rushed out of the house, his gun blazing. He managed to take up a position in the front lawn and opened fire. The soldiers panicked while the *mujahideen* jumped out of the windows. Abul Qasim was able to lead all of them to safety. By the end of the 30-minute encounter, apart from two grenades, Abul Qasim had no ammunition left.

Another time, around 9am, Qasim and Abu Ubaida Naeem were trapped in village Dodipur during a crackdown. The villagers love *mujahideen*. When the military started gathering the villagers in the open field, they helped the two *mujahideen* out by having them wear white *kufi* hats, so they appeared to be civilians. Meanwhile the villagers started protesting their treatment by the military. This troubled the soldiers. The villagers formed a procession that began exiting the village; the two *mujahideen* were able to slip out with the locals. This reflects how much the locals love *mujahideen*.

Abul Qasim dealt with Indian soldiers like a true guerrilla. He was known for firing at the military any time he saw them, whether it was a few shots or a full-scale attack. All our time in Kashmir, we hoped to sustain some injury, or death itself, in Allah's path. In April 2002, Qasim sustained a wound on his back when he was hit by a mortar shell in Bhun (Handwara). He convalesced in Srinagar before returning to his post and resuming his attacks. When he returned to his position Abul Qasim started launching strikes more frequently. He was master at planning high-risk missions and ambushes. Below is a list of his operations:

1. 16 July 2001: Kupwara, district Handwara. The warrior Abu Hamza Haq Nawaz entered the Daripura Camp and fights from 1:45 to 3:45 all by himself; he managed to escape with his life after killing eight polytheists and injuring ten.
2. 15 August 2001: Two *mujahideen* entered the parade at Chanarbagh in Handwara dressed like Indian soldiers. In the middle of the parade, they opened fire, killing ten soldiers, injuring

322 THE LITERATURE OF *LASHKAR-E-TAYYABA*

five, and destroying eight trucks; an ambulance and a fire brigade were destroyed as well. Keep in mind, this is a high-security area.

3. 16 October 2001: The *mujahideen* carried out a high-risk ambush at 8am in village Hanga, in district Hanwara, in Rajwar, killing four soldiers. Three *mujahideen* were martyred.

4. 18 October 2001: three *mujahideen* ambushed a convoy of seventy cars on the National Highway, near Baripura Camp, near Baripura's district Handwara at noon. Four soldiers are killed, and nine are injured. A major was injured in the chest. A car was completely destroyed.

5. 4 December 2001: three *mujahideen* arrived at the gate of an RR camp in Bhaagatpura, Handwara. They killed three sentries, entered the camp, and started an hour-long battle. Seven soldiers were killed, while all three *mujahideen* attained martyrdom.

6. 8 January 2002: three *mujahideen* dressed as soldiers and arrived at Trehgam Brigade Headquarters in Handwara, Kupwara. The half-hour battle that started at 9:25pm left thirteen idol-worshippers dead and seven injured, while two *mujahideen* were martyred, and the third was left unscathed.

7. 3 February 2002: The *mujahideen* were in their hideout in Dodipura when the military carried out an operation in the forest. The forest was small. From dawn till dusk, the *mujahideen* played cat-and-mouse with the soldiers. In the course of this, twelve soldiers were killed. This was possible because Qasim was carrying out psychological warfare. There was a lot of chanting and sloganeering that disoriented and frightened the soldiers.

8. June 2002: *mujahideen* opened fire in a military bunker in the high-security zone of Handwara Chowk killing seven soldiers. The *mujahideen* escaped unharmed.

9. 16 August 2002: *mujahideen* took up positions around the bunkers in Hanwara's main chowk at night. The next morning, they attacked, killing eight soldiers, and injuring fifteen. Two *mujahideen* were martyred, Allah-willing.

10. 6 September 2002: *Mujahideen* assassinated Indian agent and independent politician Sheikh Rahman Adil, along with six of his bodyguards, in district Handwara's Butkot area at 11am. Two SLR guns were taken as booty.

11. 21 September 2002: A platoon of *mujahideen* comprising men from various organizations ambushed a camp near the forests of Dodipura. Seven soldiers were killed. The battle continued well into the evening. *Mujahideen* based in other parts of the valley overheard the battle over their radios. Ten soldiers were killed and seven were injured.
12. 8 July 2002: eight soldiers of the thirty RR were killed in various attacks as the soldiers headed to Dodipura to carry out an operation in the forest.

Abul Qasim was the mastermind behind every one of these operations. These are but a few examples of his ingenious strategizing that left the Indian military in tatters. May Allah accept his martyrdom. His family deserves to be congratulated for producing a son that Allah employed in Kashmir's most dangerous territories. He fought for five years before being rewarded martyrdom. *W'Salam.*

Khurrum Shahzad, 'Abu Abdullah Affan Javed Shaheed: A Great *Honour* for Punjab University Report', *Zarb-e-Tayyaba* (April 2005): 64–67. Translated by Hamza Ali

Abu Abdullah Affan Javed was a very senior companion of the *mujahideen*. He was a student in his final year in Bachelor of Pharmacy.

I had the great opportunity of spending a lot of time with him. Before acting, he would think hard. Similarly, before speaking even a single word he would contemplate its implications according to *shariat*. He would gauge his actions and words in the light of *shariat*. When he is proselytizing, he never missed a single opportunity to correct the errant ways of others.

Even when he was in the hostel, he was always busy spreading the message of the true religion. He would visit every person, and truly embodied the virtues of spreading the good message.

Some people tried keep him from spreading the message of *jihad*. There was a so-called religious student organization in the hostel, which always opposed him and tried to sabotage the good work he was doing. But this

324 THE LITERATURE OF *LASHKAR-E-TAYYABA*

soldier of Allah remained steadfast in his objective of spreading the true message of Islam. Following in the footsteps of the prophet (PBUH), he never retaliated.

These people worked as hard as they could to get him expelled from the hostel and even asked the warden to remove him. Groups of these people continued to threaten and harass him and quite a few times Affan was pushed around by them. But this brave man of Allah never lost faith and continued his good work with the same zeal and ardour. All the people around him agreed that brother Affan was very sincere, hardworking, and dedicated. Even though he had a weak body, this did not prevent him from spreading the true message of Islam. He dedicated most of his time to proselytizing. He did not pay too much attention to his studies.

Finally, he entered the battlefield of practical *jihad*. This was incredibly challenging for a person with his puny physique. Even though there were obstacles that loomed like tall mountains in his path, he was determined to achieve his objective because this was the single-most important aspect of his life. His body was feeble and weak. He had asthma and his gallbladder was full of stones. Despite the ailments, he was determined to achieve his objective and he paid little heed to his medical condition. His heart was full of the desire for martyrdom. He served the leader for many years by spreading the message of religion and *jihad*. But he yearned for martyrdom, and he wanted to go to the battlefield. Everyone told him not to do so. How would he traverse those mountain passes with such a frail body? But little did they know that when a person dedicates himself whole-heartedly to the cause of Allah, Allah helps such people. Allah Almighty assisted this young man, and he finished his practical training. After the completion of the training, the leader recommended that he stay back and spread the message of *jihad*. But after he insisted otherwise, the leader acquiesced and granted him permission to leave for *jihad* and follow the example of companions of the holy prophet (PBUH).

Ignoring his infirmity and feebleness, he crossed the glaciers of Kashmir and the high mountainous altitudes where it is very difficult to breath due to a lack of oxygen. But all of these problems could not stop or delay him in achieving his goal of dying the death of martyr. He wanted to meet his creator and wanted to see Him in heaven. He ran into many problems even during the training. The training was not only difficult for him but almost impossible. For a weak person like him it was difficult to complete the tough exercises, which involved long marches and hauling heavy luggage from one camp to another. The instructors knew of his problems and gave him special attention. But even in the face of all these problems, his resolve was unshaken. He was ahead in every task allocated to him. Due to his weak body, he would quite often fall during the marches and was injured a few times. His physical condition was not good during the entire course of training.

They gave him permission to go ahead because everyone thought that once he experienced the difficulties, he would give up by himself. But when one is determined, then these little problems cannot prevent one from achieving their goals.

Even Iqbal praises such youthful determination:

Those who are determined and have faith in god
Never fear the tides rising against them

Even Allah says: 'Those who wage *jihad* in my way, I help them.'

Due to his determination, Allah provided the opportunity for him to launch as a *mujahid*.

Affan frequently requested his companions pray for his martyrdom. Once, during his tour, when he became ill and went to the house of the *mujahideen* to recuperate, he requested the guard, Abu Sobaan, to pray for him, since the latter's prayers were particularly effective. Even though he was physically feeble, this would have been no excuse in the court of Allah for failing to wage *jihad*. His incapacity would not have been an admissible excuse for failing to traverse the snow-covered peaks, which soared, as high as eleven or twelve thousand feet. But he was an embodiment of the Quranic verse that explains there are some people who sacrifice their lives for the goodwill of Allah.

Affan's martyrdom revealed a path for those of weaker spirit to follow. If you want to be a part of our caravan and want your place in heaven, then you have to truly sacrifice and join the battlefield of *jihad* rather than proffer silly and hollow excuses. This is the easier way to heaven. Even though we may be a part of the larger caravan we still make up absurd excuses to avoid *jihad*. We won't be able to claim innocence in the court of Allah. It is our prayer to Allah:

326 THE LITERATURE OF *LASHKAR-E-TAYYABA*

May Allah Almighty choose us for serving his religion and make us follow the examples of those great people who sacrificed their lives in order to make Islam victorious in the world. Amen.

And those who have true faith, they are deeply in love with Allah.

(Quran)

Comments of the Father

Abu Abdullah Affan, who was twenty-five years old, was my second son. He suffered from asthma since he was a child. So we home-schooled him until the fifth grade. He didn't have any of those hobbies which normal kids enjoyed. He wanted to be educated. When he started high school, he seemed to be so much smaller than his classmates primarily because of his physical weakness. He was extremely intelligent. In 1990, he participated in the Golden Jubilee competitions on the national level when he came in third in his division and received a bronze medal from the Minister of Education. Then he participated in another national competition in Islamabad and took sixth place from across all of Pakistan.

Then he was admitted to a science college for his FSc and, despite his respiratory problems, he still managed to pass the exam in high first division before going on to study pharmacy in Punjab University. It was there that he began his *jihadi* activities. I was very worried about him because he did not develop properly physically and was thin and scrawny. For the last two to three years, he was experiencing pain in his gallbladder because it was full of stones. His surgery was scheduled for September 2001, but he went to Kashmir in August 2001. He often used an inhaler for his respiratory allergies. He was such a cute boy since his childhood that I found it hard to ever be angry with him. He was a very innocent and cute kid. During summer vacations, he would tell me that he was going to *jihadi* camps so that he could go and work in dispensaries and medical camps to serve the *mujahideen*. But he also received training there as well and, in this way, he silently became a *mujahid* himself.

He was truly a pious and righteous soul. Despite his physical problems, he set a great example for others to follow—especially those who have some minor physical problems. And he also set an example for those who are highly educated but limit themselves to speeches and lectures instead of joining the *jihad*. Parents should nurture in their children a similar passion for *jihad*. Even though my son was physically handicapped, he managed to cross those snow-covered peaks to reach the Kashmiri *jihad*.

According to initial news, he was wounded a few days before his martyrdom and was resting in the area of Shopian, where he was being treated. But on 23 January the Indian army conducted a crackdown of the place and even though he was wounded he still fought them bravely before drinking from the cup of martyrdom. Now he is a guest in Allah's Heaven.

By the grace of Allah, I now have the honour of being a father of a martyr. Abu Abdullah Affan was deeply and truly in love with his creator and he strictly followed the *Sunnat* of the holy prophet (PBUH). His faith was higher than the highest mountains and deeper than the deepest of seas. The martyrs they never die, it is only due to our limited perception that we cannot perceive their life.

Comments of the Mother

My son was always first in his class. He was extremely intelligent. He only went to school until his eighth standard in order to take the examination, otherwise he would study all the time at home. All his teachers knew about his medical condition and that is why no one forced him to go to school regularly.

During the preparation for his FSc exams, he began mingling with *mujahideen* and grew a beard. He secured a score of 799 in his FSc exams. He did not make it to medical school because he scored a meagre twenty-two points below the requirement. Instead, we got him admitted to the university to study pharmacy. He was a very studious child. There he started to evolve not only in his worldly education but also in religious education. He studied many books of commentary on Quran and concurrently received *jihadi* training during his summer vacations. I used to remind him he was sick, but he would always say he got better in Kashmir and that he had no trouble breathing there. Even though I knew that in truth he had breathing problems in Kashmir as well. If a commander refused to train him, he would cry and beg to be trained. Thus, one day, all of a sudden, he was dispatched to Occupied Kashmir.

Now I regret that I never formally gave my son my permission to join *jihad* and this shall always haunt me. I urge the mothers whose sons want

328 THE LITERATURE OF *LASHKAR-E-TAYYABA*

to join *jihad* to be happy and give their sons permissions. This will both create ease for their sons and diminish any of their regrets later on.

My son was very strict about his prayers. He would frequently fast and twice sat for *itikaaf* in his lifetime.[59] Last year, he pitched his tent in the mosque and sat in *itikaaf*; he wrote a letter to me saying: 'Dear mother please forgive me as I have been in *itikaaf* without telling you. But I may never get a chance to do this again.' He despised the television and was always eager to break it. He implored us to educate his younger brother more extensively in religion. He made his brother offer prayers regularly. Our second son is also a *mujahid*. May Allah accept the martyrdom of my son; may Allah give us solace, and the courage to follow his advice. Amen.

Muhammad Ameen and Ali Manazir Abdul Rehman, 'Martyr Naveed Ahmad Abu Talha Aziz', *Mujallah-ul-Dawah* (February 2007): 22–23. Translated by Ahmad Raza Naseer

Naveed Ahmad Abbu Talha Aziz

It was a clear, blissful Ramazan night in 2004. I was rushing toward Rehman Mosque, only a few yards away from our home. Rehman Mosque was in the middle of open fields and decorated with twinkling lights inside out. When I reached its door, a young guard came up to me and asked, 'Is your home the one across from here?', I said, 'yes', 'What's your name?', 'My name is Ali'. With a smile on his face, he said: 'My name is Talha'. 'Ali, come to the mosque regularly'. His tone was intimate; this was my first meeting with brother Talha.

Talha was portly and cheerful, and had a neatly trimmed beard. I started going to Rehman Mosque with my younger brother Hassan. This was how our friendship began. On *eid*, I took carrot halva for him, which he liked a lot and asked for it time and again later on. He used to ask us how we made the halva as he had never previously had a carrot halva that was so delicious. After *isha* prayers, we would chat in the open fields in front of the mosque, paying no mind to the freezing cold. Talha was just like a member of our family and used to call my mother *Ammi*. Brother Talha used to recite a poem in the mosque:

FIGHTER BIOGRAPHIES   329

You won't be able to find me even if you tried to find my corpse
I'm so completely shattered you can't stitch me back together

Ami used to cry after hearing this and prohibited brother Talha from reciting it. 'It is fine that the only aim of a *mujahid* is martyrdom but I have a very weak heart.' This would make him laugh. It seems like he never lost his temper; he was always calm and composed. Then, one day in the afternoon we received a call. 'It is Naveed's turn. Please tell him to prepare.' Talha was happy even about the thought of going to the battlefield. But we all were sad for being separated from him. The place where we used to sit felt desolate. On *Eid-ul-Azha*, he came to collect the pelts of sacrificed animals. It was the rainy season and he stayed for a long time. This time, we saw each other off happily. He used to call almost every week. We were satisfied with this schedule. He came again in the summer and stayed at our place for two days. On 15 of Saha'aban, he spoke with each of us individually.

On 8 October 2005, there was a deadly earthquake. We were all distraught because we hadn't heard from brother Talha in so many days. My mother and sisters insisted that we ask someone in the mosque about him. That very day he called and, forever cheerful, he told us he was safe and that he would come see us after a few days. He stayed for the next five to six days of Ramazan. He used to recite the Holy Quran throughout the night. We operate a school, and all the students knew him well. They would ask him with curiosity: 'You are a *mujahid*?! You fight infidels?!' Our last meeting was on 12 January 2006. When he arrived on *eid*, his leg was injured, and he sustained a bullet injury in his shoulder. He had that poem read on a loudspeaker on *eid* and my mother said: 'Look, Talha is making me cry even on *eid*.' My elder brother used to tease Talha saying: 'Talha you manage to escape every time. Does the beauty of Heaven want you to stay here in this world?' Talha would simply smile. After three days, brother Talha left for Kashmir again. On 23 January, he called and told us: 'I have been operated upon. Now I am moving ahead. Pray for my martyrdom.' On the twilight of 14 January, someone knocked at our door. It was brother Talha's friend who lived by the Rehman Mosque. He informed us that brother Talha had embraced martyrdom. I instantly asked when it happened. He told me that it was on the night of 13 February. I told everyone at home. We were all stunned. Grimly, I forbade anyone

330 THE LITERATURE OF *LASHKAR-E-TAYYABA*

from crying. My mother loved brother Talha. Talha would make a point of seeing her before leaving. Mother showed great fortitude: even though she used to cry over his poem, she remained very calm about his martyrdom. Women folk are kind and weak at heart. I knew my sisters cried secretly as Talha was their brother too. On my end, I forbade it. Then in the evening there was an announcement in Rehman Mosque:

The soil of Kashmir asks for the blood of my sons
Rivers and deserts cannot quench her thirst

'Naveed Ahmad Abbu Talha Aziz who had been at war with the Indian Army for a long time embraced martyrdom. His funeral will be held in his hometown'.

I could no longer control myself. I lost my calm. The very mosque where we used to sit, pray, and chat, was now announcing his funeral. His village high school was packed with attendees. I met his father and he very much resembled Taha. Everyone present complimented Naveed for looking sophisticated and debonair. Now when we see Rehman Mosque, we miss brother Talha a lot. Now, he is a groom in heaven and he will be awarded with the most noble and high stature there. On resurrection day, when we will see him again, he will be smiling his usual smile, and he will say: 'On earth, I lived in a mosque, in paradise I live among beautiful women.'

The *mujahid*'s striving makes the world turn
The martyr's blood nourishes a nation

'The Faith Strengthening Memoirs of Martyrs who Fought in Indian Occupied Kashmir: Martyr Abu Jibran Naseem Akhtar', *Mujallah-ul-Dawah* (November 2007): 54. Translated by Ahmad Raza Naseer

Martyr Abu Jibran Naseem Akhtar

After leaving the Army, on 5 August 2005, Martyr Abu Jibran Naseem Akhtar bid farewell and took off for the valley with a burning desire for

FIGHTER BIOGRAPHIES   331

martyrdom. But he was sent home after he sustained an injury from slipping on ice. He blamed his family for his injury and became furious with them for not praying whole-heartedly for his martyrdom. After a few days, his mother fell ill and was taken to hospital where she fainted and needed blood. Although he had the same blood type as his mother, she refused and said: 'I cannot take your blood. It belongs to Allah. You must give it in the way of Allah. Your blood is Allah's trust with me to be returned to Allah in full, whether I live or die.' Abu Jibran honoured and cared for his mother. He would often tell his mother that if Allah accepted him as a martyr, her daughter-in-law will be one of the angels of paradise and she will never argue with her.

Now imagine this: Brother Muddasar, one of the companions from the *Markaz*, is sitting on a big rock thousands of miles away from home in the valley on *eid* day, missing his family and crying, when brother Abu Jibran Naseem puts his hand on his shoulder and says, 'look at me, I can't even remember how many *eid* days I've had to spend away from my family. We may not be able to celebrate *eid* with our loved ones in this world anymore, but we will spend *eid* with our loved ones in paradise.'

His Mother's Account
Our son Jibran was very loving and obedient. He had changed for the better in the company of holy warriors. The prince of paradise had totally changed the atmosphere at home. He would rub my feet and forehead, and when I asked him to stop, he would say massaging me brought him peace. He won hearts with his perfect morals and good behaviour. He was made worthy of martyrdom. After his martyrdom, we offered a supererogatory prayer and demonstrated patience.

His Sister's Account
Our brother loved us a lot. He never argued with us, but he strictly enforced recitation of Quran and female seclusion. We miss him but then we hear about how Muslim women have been raped and the oppression of Muslims by the unbelievers, and this makes us restrain ourselves. Only the chosen few are granted martyrdom. His nephews have vowed to go into the valley to avenge their uncle's death. May Allah accept him as a martyr.

332 THE LITERATURE OF *LASHKAR-E-TAYYABA*

His Brother's Account

He was our younger brother and a great man who had a burning passion for martyrdom and who now dwells in paradise. It's impossible to list all his lovely characteristics. Praise and thank Allah, we have all grown beards now as per his instructions in his last will which include, worshipping Allah, caring for parents, calling for *jihad*, abstaining from sin, and preparing his nephews for *jihad*.

'The Faith Strengthening Memoirs of Martyrs who Fought in Indian Occupied Kashmir: Martyr Abu Kaab Ullah Khan Zaman', *Mujallah-ul-Dawah* (November 2007): 54–55. Translated by Ahmad Raza Naseer

Martyr Abu Kaab Ullah Khan Zaman

His Mother's Account

Praise and thank Allah that he granted my son martyrdom and let him dwell in paradise.

My son would cry and beg me to let him go fight on the frontline. He would say, 'wouldn't you want your son to intercede for you so that you can live in paradise? *Insha Allah*.' I didn't want him to go. I told him that I only have two boys and six girls. I told him that he should fulfil his responsibilities towards his sisters first. I could not convince him and now Allah has blessed him with martyrdom; Allah has blessed me with the honour of being a martyr's mother.

His Sisters' Account

Praise and thank Allah that he has given us the honour of being the sisters of a martyr. We will send our sons to avenge their uncle's death. We pray that Allah makes us mothers of martyrs just like al Khans' and Safiya,[60] may Allah be pleased with them.

His Widow's Account

It is my wish that my three boys become holy warriors and go to Kashmir to avenge their father's death. May Allah grant them martyrdom and make me the mother of martyrs and enter paradise.

His Father's Account

When they told me that my son has been martyred, I praised and thanked Allah that he made me the father of a martyr. I offered *nafl*[61] prayers and congratulated my wife and informed her that Allah has made us the parents of a martyr, hence there were to be no tears. She praised and thanked Allah and offered her supererogatory prayer.

9

Highway to Heaven by Amir Hamza

Amir Hamza's 2004 book, *Shahrah-e-Bahisht* (*Highway to Heaven*), aims to undermine local mystical traditions and beliefs.[1] It should be recalled that Amir Hamza is one of the founding ideologues of LeT/JuD and is perhaps second only to Hafez Saeed in the extent of his influence. He currently is the convener of the *Tehreek-e-Hurmat-e-Rasool* (Movement for the Sanctity of the Prophet), which has opposed any reforms to Pakistan's odious 'blasphemy law'.[2] This book is unarguably the most linguistically and referentially rich and textured work included in this compilation. Its audience comprises those who are confounded or offended by local mystical traditions such as the veneration of relics and shrines, typically associated with Barelvi customs which are prevalent among Pakistani Muslims.

Whereas some of the other items translated and included in this anthology allude to these customs obliquely, this volume uses language which is much more direct. The reader gets the overwhelming sense that this volume *intends* to mock these pervasive local traditions, while affirming the readers' biases against these practices, and offering material to argue against 'corrupting innovations' in Islam. The content varies from a 'scholarly' socio-historical analysis of mystical practices, tracing them to Christian and Hindu rituals, to a farcical account of the author indulging in these practices himself only to realize they are hoaxes orchestrated by charlatans and witch doctors to exploit the uneducated masses.

By and large, *Highway to Heaven* does not attack the great mystics of the past themselves whose shrines and mausoleums have a metonymical relationship with the towns and cities in which they stand; rather, the author excoriates those who build and venerate these shrines and organize religious festivals around the venues. This should be seen within organization's adamance about the doctrine of the oneness of god (*tawheed*). In LeT's various writings, the practices of mystics are subject to great criticism because their practices are redolent of those of Hindus,

336 THE LITERATURE OF *LASHKAR-E-TAYYABA*

such as the use of prayer beads, talismans, propitiation of saints and prescribed rituals and potions to heal any variety of physical, mental, and emotional ailments. In LeT's literature such practices are tantamount to shirk (sometimes translated as idolatry, but also includes ascribing the attributes of Allah to others) or even polytheism.

In this chapter we present translations of important excerpts *Shahrah-e-Bahisht* (*Highway to Heaven*), including: The Publisher's note by Muhammad Saifullah Khalid, the editor of Dar-ul-Andlus at the time of publication; the Prologue, authored by the LeT Emir, Hafez Saeed himself; another prefatory note titled 'In the Shade of the Ka'ba', by Amir Hamza; the first chapter of the volume titled 'Mausoleums: From the Prophet's Point of View'; as well as the second chapter titled 'From [*Data Ganj Bakhsh*] Hajveri's Shrine to Allah's Court'. We retain all of the organizational structure of the originals, including the excessive use of headers.

In Chapter 1, the author critiques mystical practices as institutionalizing polytheism. According to the author, this practice was first introduced by Jews and Christians who 'invented monasticism and incorporated grave-worship into their traditions'. The author denounces Sufism as 'religious corruption', which further 'diverges into multiple creeds, that is, Qadria, Suharwardiay, Chishtia, etc. where each creed follows a different tradition, and every tradition produces its own founders and forebears known as mystagogues'. In Chapter 2, the author presents what he alleged witnessed to transpire at one shrine in particular, *Data Ganj Bakhsh Hajveri*, which is one of Pakistan's largest shrines and located west of Bhatti Gate, which is one of the 'gates' to Lahore's famous walled Old City.

Overall, these translated sections represent a relatively small portion of the volume which totals 229 pages and comprises eight sections, each with numerous subsections. Since much of the volume expounds upon similar themes, this selection is adequate to provide the reader with a sense of how the organization seeks to undermine the legitimacy of mystical traditions. What is clear from this volume is that LeT views Sufi traditions similarly to *Deobandi* organizations, which view Sufism as polytheist. *Deobandi* organizations also believe mystical traditions enshrine apostasy because they describe the prophet in terms that are reserved for Allah. While LeT and its Deobandi militant counterparts interpret Sufi traditions similarly as abhorrent, LeT does not advocate murdering Sufis in Pakistan whereas *Deobandi* militant organizations do.

Publisher's Note

Maulana Amir Hamza's *Shahrah-e-Bahisht* deals with the increasing prevalence of polytheism and grave-worshipping rituals as encapsulated by Sufism. The issue is eating the Muslim *ummat* like a cancer. Allah sent countless messengers to eradicate polytheism and maintain the predominance of *tawheed* (monotheism); our Prophet's twenty-three-year career as a messenger was devoted to this very objective. He endured every kind of hardship imaginable to obliterate idolatry. Allah aided him, Mecca was conquered, the sanctuary of the House of Allah was rid of all false gods, and Arabia was ultimately cleansed of polytheism and pagans.

In his book *Shahrah-e-Bahisht*, Maulana Amir Hamza takes on the worst of these practices that have adulterated our faith, in context of the Quran and *Sunnat*, by highlighting *tawheed* as the key to success in this world as well as in the world hereafter.

The irrefutable arguments and evidence presented in this publication make it worth distributing as widely as possible in order to shatter the night of polytheism with the illuminating dawn of *tawheed* and *Sunnat*.

Dar-ul-Andlus has had the honour to publish this remarkable achievement by Maulana Amir Hamza, organized and made accessible by Brother Muhammad Ishtiaq Asghar and Brother Muhammad Yousaf Siraj, and designed and formatted by Brother Abdul Khaliq and Ajmal Toor. May Allah accept the labour put in by all our brothers and grant each one of them martyrdom.

Muhammad Saifullah Khalid
Editor: Dar-ul-Andlus
23 Rajab 1425–8 September 2004

Prologue

Professor Hafiz Muhammad SaeedThe spiritual environment of the subcontinent has always been disposed to Sufism; under its auspices, shrines and grave worship have gained considerable traction in Hindustan and Pakistan. Annual festivals and symbolic ceremonies have become a staple of our culture and people regularly make offerings and distribute oblations at the resting places of various saints.

338 THE LITERATURE OF *LASHKAR-E-TAYYABA*

In truth, Hinduism holds sway over the collective consciousness of the people for while many Hindus converted to Islam, they continued to follow Hindu traditions, practices, and rituals. The devil infused these practices with such allure that people have come to mistake these corrupted rituals for faith, so much so that even certain clerics have sanctioned these customs. Ironically, the very polytheism and corruption that Islam sought to eradicate are now practised under the guise of Islam. In the repugnant master-subject dynamic of Sufism, many people have lost their faith, their wealth, and their dignity. Society is in desperate need of the reestablishment of *tawheed* and the revival of *Sunnat*. Unfortunately, today, those who proclaim *tawheed* and uphold *Sunnat* are so caught up in democratic/political shenanigans that it seems they have either forgotten the spirit of proselytizing or their hands are tied due to political restraints. They are afraid of offending their constituents by speaking against deeply entrenched polytheistic practices. How this can possibly benefit Islam is beyond the rational mind.

This book is a compilation of revolutionary essays presented in a proselytizing format that speaks directly to our times; they are neither polemical tracts nor research essays. By compiling them in a single book, Maulana Amir Hamza Sahib has created an opportunity for those ordinary Muslims who are passionate about proselytizing to read and disseminate these excellent arguments in favour of *tawheed*, to win Allah's favour.

In the Shade of the Ka'ba

This book is a compilation of seven essays that deal with *tawheed* and attempt to make the reader wary of polytheism and religious corruption. Those who are passionate about shepherding their fellow men to paradise like the messengers and prophets before us, should cooperate with us in having this volume republished as many times as possible that we may keep our brothers from going astray. Consider this: those who are trapped in the cycle of polytheism make shrine-offerings worth hundreds of thousands of rupees; shouldn't those among us who adhere to monotheism contribute towards having this work disseminated at such shrines, to make people aware of the truth? Thanks to Allah, this book has had eleven editions. Allah has filled countless souls with the light of *tawheed*. When I was at the House of Allah (Ka'ba) numerous Indian Muslims told me that this book was incredibly popular in India; it had realigned the beliefs of countless individuals, and its photocopies were distributed widely in a number of cities. Thanks to Allah, three new chapters have been added to the current edition and *zaeeif* (weak) *Hadees* have been replaced with *sahih* (authentic) ones. Various other changes have also been made. May Allah bless us with the means to act upon His will. (Amen!)

Amir Hamza

November 1998, Lahore.

Chapter 1: 'Mausoleums' from the Prophet's Point of View

The prophet forbade the making of concrete tombs, the appointment of permanent caretakers over such tombs, and the construction of mausoleums around them.

(Sahih Muslim)

Brothers! Allah has showered you with countless blessings, not least of which is the gift of hearing. Today, we ask that you use this gift to listen to what the One who blessed you with this sense has to say.

Therefore, give good tidings (O Muhammad) to my bondmen.

(Surat az-Zumar 39:17)

Who hear advice and follow the best thereof. Such are those whom Allah guideth, and such are men of understanding.

(Surat az-Zumar 39:18)

According to these verses, those who accept good advice are men of understanding; they are the rightly guided ones who receive the glad tidings of paradise. The discerning reader will immediately ask how is good advice to be identified?

340 THE LITERATURE OF *LASHKAR-E-TAYYABA*

For such discerning minds, Allah says:

Allah hath (now) revealed the fairest of statements.

(*Surat az-Zumar* 39:23)

Allah goes on to describe the one who imparts good advice as follows:

And who is better in speech than him who prayeth unto his Lord.

(*Surat al-Fussilat* 41:33)

Good advice can only come from those who focus on Allah instead of on their personal achievements, lineage, family, or creed. What Allah has revealed through the Quran and *Hadees* to the prophet has been referred to in *Surat Muhammad* as *haqq* (truth), and those who accept this truth are promised atonement and salvation.

Only the Arrogant Reject the Truth

Allah expresses His rage towards those who refuse to accept the Truth in the following words:

Who heareth the revelations of Allah receive unto him, and then continueth in pride as though he heard them not. Give him tidings of a painful doom.

(*Surat al-Jathiyah* 45:8)

Hence, it is to be understood that according to Allah, he who refuses to accept the truth when he hears it is insolent and full of pride. But what is insolence? When the prophet was asked this question, he said:

Prideful is the one who rejects the truth and is condescending towards people, that is, the one who considers those who present the truth to him wretched and denies the truth; such a person is insolent.

(Abu Dawood, *Kitab al-Libas, baab ma jaa fil-kabr* 4092; *Masnad Ahmad* 427:1)

A True Muslim Accepts the Truth

On the other hand, consider the description of those who recognize the truth instantly: they are unconsciously drawn towards Allah, and they guard themselves from hubris:

> When they listen to that which hath been revealed unto the messenger, thou seest their eyes overflow with tears because of their recognition of the Truth. They say: Our Lord, we believe. Inscribe us as among the witnesses.
>
> *(Surat al-Ma'idah* 5:83)

Another place, Allah describes them as follows:

> Only those believe in Our revelations who, when they are reminded of them, fall down prostrate and hymn the praise of their Lord, and they are not scornful.
>
> *(Surat al-Sajdah* 32:15)

The Most Precious Thing in the Universe

Once the truth has been received, Satan tries to replace it with anxieties about death and disgrace, distracting the faithful with countless mundane temptations for the sole purpose of depriving the believer of the most precious thing he has come to nurture; namely, his faith! The Lord Himself has spoken to the prophet's *ummat* about this rare jewel. Abdullah bin Amr bin Aas narrates the Prophet as having said:

> On the Day of Judgement Allah will bring forth one person (at a time) before whom ninety-nine registers will be spread open. Each register will extend as far as the eye can see. Allah will ask, 'Do you deny what is written in these? Were my scribes unfair to you?' The person on trial will say, 'No, my Lord.' Allah will say, 'Do you have anything to plead?' He will respond, 'No, my Lord.' Allah will say:

342 THE LITERATURE OF *LASHKAR-E-TAYYABA*

'One of your virtues will keep you from being dealt harshly today.' A piece of paper will be brought out that will say ،الله إلا إله لا أن أشهد وأشهد أن محمدا عبده و رسوله (I bear witness there is no god but Allah and Muhammad is His servant and His messenger). Allah will say: 'Let us weigh this in the scale.' The person on trial will respond: 'Oh Allah! How will this piece of paper compare to these enormous registers.' Allah will say: 'You will not be dealt harshly.'

Ravi narrates the prophet as saying:

> All the registers will be piled into one scale and the piece of paper will be placed in the other. The scale with the registers will rise under the weight of the piece of paper for nothing can outweigh Allah's name.
> (Tirmidhi, *Kitab al-Iman, baab maja' fiman ya-maut wa hua yash-hada an-la-ilaha-il-Allah* 2639; *Masnad Ahmad* 213:2)

Whosoever adopts faith without hesitation breaks free from Satan's bonds, leaving the wretch to his miserable devices.

But man's eternal enemy is not one to give up so easily. Satan keeps coming back to ensnare the sons of Adam but those who have tasted the sweet nectar of true faith remain undeterred. Hazrat Bilal was one such person who kept saying 'One! One!' even as Umayya, the devil's representative, tortured the prophet's dear beloved in an attempt to rob him of his most precious possession.

Satan's Assault and the Holy Five of the Prophet Noah's People

Satan cast a net over multiple generations to lure Adam's progeny away from the right path. The famous companion Abdullah bin Abbas explains how this strategy was executed by referencing *Surat Nuh* (Noah) in the Quran which mentions the 'holy five' of Noah's people, namely, Wad, Sawa'a, Yaghoos, Ya'ooq, and Nasr:

> These were the righteous men of Noah's nation. When they died, Satan incited the people to erect stones at the spots where these men

HIGHWAY TO HEAVEN 343

meditated and to invoke them by calling out their names. A few generations later, people started worshipping these very stones.

(*Sahih Bukhari, Kitab-al-Tafseer*, Chapter *Wad-a, Swaʾa-a, Yaghoos, Yaʾooq* 492)

Allama Ibn Qeem says: 'Wise men say that when the righteous die, people start out by becoming permanent caretakers of their tombs, they go on to engrave their images, and some generations down the line, they start worshipping these very images.'

Allah sent Noah to inform his nation of Satan's conspiracy and offer them redemption through faith, but his people turned him away and rejected his offer, hence Allah destroyed them all in a violent deluge.

Another Kind of Satanic Trap: The Establishment of Organized Monasteries

A close reading of the Quran reveals that nations destroyed by Allah's wrath were led astray when Satan convinced them to worship saints, both living and dead. On the other hand, one finds that the messengers sent by Allah expended their efforts prohibiting people from these very acts of polytheism. Like the prophets before him, Jesus Christ tried to make the Jews revert to *tawheed*, before he was lifted up to heaven, but unfortunately, even those who followed him and called themselves Christians gave up the *shariat* revealed to Christ and adopted mysticism instead.

Allah refers to this error on their part in the following words:

But monasticism (*Sufism*) they invented. We ordained it not for them. Only seeking Allah's pleasure, and they observed it not with right observance.

(*Surat al-Hadid* 57:27)

Keep in mind, Christians sought to please Allah but instead of using Christ's teachings as a path to enlightenment they invented monasticism. They rejected the world but, ironically, instead of honouring the monastic way of life that they had themselves invented, they donned the garb

344 THE LITERATURE OF *LASHKAR-E-TAYYABA*

of ascetics and mendicants and amassed material wealth, turning their monasteries into dens of vice and sin.

What is worse, these so-called saints were so invested in turning their monasteries into commercial enterprises that when Allah sent them the 'people of the cave', instead of welcoming the opportunity to revert to monotheism they indulged in their pagan practices more wantonly.

> When (the people of the city [*Christians*]) disputed of their (*the people of the cave's*) case among themselves, they said: Build over them a building; their Lord knoweth best concerning them. Those who won their point said: We verily shall build a place of worship over them.
>
> (*Surat al-Kahf* 18:21)

Consequently, the Christian monastics found in these young believers another source of revenue for their spiritual enterprise.

Never forget, these are the kinds of people about whom the prophet warned his *ummat*; Jandab narrates the prophet as having said the following, five days before his death:

> Beware! People before you turned the tombs of their prophets and their saints into centres of worship. Beware! Do not turn tombs into centres of worship; I forbid you from doing so.
>
> (*Sahih Muslim, Kitab al-Masajid, bab al-nahi an bina al-masjid Al-al Qaboor wa itkhaz al-Soor fiha. . . . Alakh* 532)

Despite the prophet's prohibition, members of his *ummat* rampantly indulge in monastic grave-worshipping rituals in emulation of misguided people. Consider what the prophet said about such people, as narrated by Abu Saeed Khudri:

> You will inevitably start imitating nations that came before you, the way one hand looks like the other, and the way the span of one hand is exactly like the span of the other, so much so that if those people (before you) entered an iguana's nest, so will you. The companions asked: 'Oh Allah's prophet! Do you mean Jews and Christians?' The prophet said: 'Who else?'

(Sahih Bukhari, Kitab al-Aetisam bil Kitab wal-Sunnat, baab qaul al-nabi Lataba'n sunan min kaan Qablikum 7320; Sahih Muslim, Kitab al-Ilm, baab Itiba' sunan al-yahood o nisara 2669)

Jews and Christians invented monasticism, and incorporated grave-worship into their traditions. How accurate was the prophet's foreboding given how Muslims today set aside the Quran and *Hadees* and indulge in religious corruption like Sufism, which they have further diverges into multiple creeds, that is, Qadria, Suharwardiay, Chishtia, etc. where each creed follows a different tradition, and every tradition produces its own founders and forebears known as mystagogues. To think, all this is done to gain Allah's favour.

At the forefront of these various mystical traditions are the caretakers to the shrines and the inheritors of their so-called spiritual benefits, which, apparently, are passed on from father to son. The spiritual mafia that runs these monasteries has acquired immeasurable wealth and property, and its godfathers squander their riches in ways that would put royalty to shame. No one has the right to question their moral character for after all, they are the depositories of spiritual perfection. Their so-called 'acts of mysticism', however, appear in newspaper clippings and can be witnessed, first-hand, at their monasteries. They receive offerings worth millions for their annual *urs* (metaphorical wedding) celebrations in exchange for promises of salvation. These are the people the prophet warned us about. Their indecipherable chants fill the cupolas of hallowed mausoleums as they follow the grave-worshipping traditions of Jews and Christians.

The Quranic View of Shrines

Let us now examine how shrines are referenced in the Quran.

Forbidden unto you (for food) are carrion and blood and swine flesh, and that which hath been dedicated unto any other than Allah, and the strangled, and the dead through beating, and the dead through falling from a height, and that which hath been killed by (the goring of) horns, and the devoured of wild beasts, saving that which ye make lawful (by

346   THE LITERATURE OF *LASHKAR-E-TAYYABA*

the death stroke), and that which hath been (*slaughtered at a shrine*) immolated unto idols. And (forbidden is it) that ye swear by the divining arrows. This is an abomination.

(*Surat al-Ma'idah* 5:3)

In all there are eleven things listed in this verse that have been forbidden, and among them is the flesh of an animal slaughtered at a shrine; later in this chapter, in verse 90, Allah uses a term for shrines much harsher than the word *haram* (forbidden); He declares their existence Satanic, strongly urging Muslims to keep away from their filth, and giving His servants glad tidings for successfully doing so.

O ye who believe! Strong drink and games of chance and idols (*shrines*) and divining arrows are only an infamy of Satan's handiwork. Leave it aside in order that ye may succeed.

(*Surat al-Ma'idah* 5:90)

For a better understanding of Allah's warnings, let us analyse the history of these hermitages and shrines. Here, one will find divisive creeds, as well as grime, squalor, and refuse. Notice, whatever is spurred by the devil and labelled Satanic by god cannot be anything short of filthy and foul.

Graven Images

We have already seen that idolatry began to take root among Noah's people when they started preserving pictures of their saints. Similar graven images were rejected by Abraham's monotheism. When the prophet encountered such images in the House of Allah, much like his predecessor Abraham, he obliterated every one of them, including those of Abraham and Ismail, his forefathers and predecessors.

The Cult of Photographs

Historically, pagan traditions encouraged the preservation, decoration, and worship of images but in this day and age, so-called Muslims behave no differently. Details about this are presented later in the book.

The Shī'a of Iran, who claim to have launched an Islamic Revolution, try to enter the Ka'ba with photographs of their dearly departed leader Khomeini (d. 5 May 1990) pressed against their chests, on the apparent instruction of said leader himself. How can the monotheistic people of Saudi Arabia be expected to allow these photographs in the vicinity of the Ka'ba, a sanctuary the prophet cleansed of all images? But the Shiites are bent on polluting the sanctity of Allah's House with their noxious two-dimensional idols.

Consider the ubiquitous image of Sheikh Abdul Qadir Jilani in Pakistan, where he carries to shore a ship that sank twelve years ago. This image, nothing less than an idol, is bought and displayed in countless homes across the country.

Additionally, there are photographs of mystics in loincloths, surrounded by animals. Some of them ride lions with shrines etched in the background.

The Satanic cult of photographs has enveloped the ardent monotheists. They adorn their homes with pictures of their martyrs and their elders, cashing in on the images at processions where they are reprinted and distributed. Verses from the holy Quran are strewn across the images, because falsehood, after all, can have no impact until it is supported by some element of truth.

What tradition is the *ummat* following? What terms does Islam use for these people? Consider the words uttered by the prophet, as narrated by Hazrat Aisha:

> Umm-i-Habiba and Umm-i-Salma told the prophet they saw pictures hanging in Christian churches in Abyssinia. The prophet said, 'When a righteous man among them dies, they build a prayer-house close to his grave in which they install the deceased's pictures. On the Day of Judgement, these people will be the worst of mankind.'
> (*Sahih Bukhari, Kitab al-Salat, baab hal Tabnash Qaboor Mashrakil Jahilia. . . . Alakh* 427; *Sahih Muslim, Kitab al-Masajid wa Mawaze' al-Salat, Baab al-nahi an Bina'l Masjid Al-al-qaboor* 528)

New Forms of Grave-Worship

Every year, Shi'a organize a procession known as '*taziya*' in which they create a mock sculpture of Imam Hussein's shrine, which they carry around town while chanting slogans and showering the sculpture with offerings. Similarly, others adorn their homes with photographs of saints'

348 THE LITERATURE OF *LASHKAR-E-TAYYABA*

extravagant shrines. Grave worship has taken numerous forms and manifests in various traditions that the prophet termed '*wasan*'.

The prophet prayed to Allah to safeguard his own tomb from becoming *wasan* in the following words:

> O Allah! Do not let my tomb become a *wasan* that people start worshipping it. Nations that turn the graves of their prophets into prayer-houses are subjected to Allah's wrath
>
> (Mu'ta Imam Malik, *Kitab Qasr al-Salat fil Safar, Baab Jamia al-Salat*, 85)

As a result, Allah answered the prophet's prayer and guarded his tomb from anniversaries, festivals, carnivals, and offerings.

Allama Iqbal says:

> Having collected revenue from shrines
> You'd even sell your idols if you could.

Indeed, the latest trend of installing images of the prophet's mosque and tomb in houses of worship, as well as in domestic spaces, is nothing short of idolatry. The content of the image notwithstanding, this act directly contradicts Allah's teachings. Much like the Shiite attitude towards '*taziya*' icons, adorning walls with images of the prophet's tomb is very much idolatrous and something the prophet himself strictly prohibited. Iranian Shī'a, on the other hand, have gone so far as to make Khomeini's tomb in the image of the Ka'ba itself. (Allah forbid).

Praying to Allah at Sites of Grave-Worship

No doubt, many will find the aforementioned arguments disturbing, but in truth, our prophet forewarned his *ummat* against every tradition, action, and shrine that has any connection to grave worship. Consider Abu Dawood's *Sahih Hadees* as narrated by Thabit bin Zahhak:

> A person wished to make a votive sacrifice by slaughtering some camels at a place called Bibuwana. He went to the prophet and said: 'I must make a votive sacrifice by slaughtering some camels at Bibuwana.' The prophet asked: 'Was there ever an idol from the days of ignorance erected at that place?' The companions said there wasn't. Then, the

HIGHWAY TO HEAVEN   349

prophet asked: 'Did polytheists ever use that place as a venue for their festivals (*urs*)?' The companions answered that they did not. Only then did the prophet allow the man to make his votive offering.

(*Sunan Abi Dawood, Kitab al-Iman wal-Nazr, baab maa yu'mir bahu min al wafa bal nazar* 3313)

Notice how the prophet forbade the practice of sanctioned monotheistic rituals at sites that may once have been used for polytheistic practices. This was done to keep Allah's worship free from any kind of corruption.

Considering the prophet avoided any kind of contamination by polytheism, how can one imagine worshipping Allah in a place where idolatry is practised in open defiance? This ought to be a profound consideration for those concerned about the afterlife.

At this point, it is worth noting that the prophet specifically referred to festivals (*urs*) when questioning the man who wanted to sacrifice his camels. Festivals were a favourite past time among pagans. They are breeding grounds for vice and immorality and the prophet detested them profoundly. This is why he told his *ummat* in the clearest terms:

Do not celebrate urs (festivals) at my grave.

(*Masnad Ahmad* 367:2)

He further warned:

Do not pray facing graves and do not occupy them like *sajjadah-nashin*.

The prophet has the following to say about *sajjadah-nashin* (*Sahih Muslim, Kitab al-Janaiz, baab al nahi an-al juluus alaa al-Qabr wa Salat Alaihi* 972):

The fire of a burning ember that sets clothes and skin and skin alight, is preferable to becoming a *sajjadah-nashin*.

(*Sahih Muslim, Kitab al-Janaiz, baab al-nahi anal Juluus Al-al-Qabr wa Salaata ilaihi* 971)

The Tragedy of the Idolater

The tragedy of the idolater is that he wants to see and touch his creator the way he sees and touches objects around him. Hence, he visits shrines.

350 THE LITERATURE OF *LASHKAR-E-TAYYABA*

The more beautiful and glamorous a shrine, the greater the number of idolaters it will attract. This is why the prophet uprooted the tradition of decorating and beautifying tombs altogether.

Jabir narrates:

> The prophet forbade the making of concrete tombs, the appointment of permanent caretakers over such tombs, and the construction of mausoleums around them.
>
> (*Sahih Muslim, Kitab al-Janaiz, Baab al-Nahi An Tahsees al qabr wa banaa ilaihi* 97)

Making Tombs Concrete is Inhumane

Some time ago a news report from China declared that due to a shortage of burial grounds, people had started cremating their dead. On 29 June a similar report about Korea was published in *Nawa-i-Waqt*. Urban centres in Pakistan are facing a similar predicament. It has become increasingly difficult to find a burial spot in a graveyard, making the slimmest plot of land prohibitively expensive. This is obviously the result of concretizing tombs.

If graves were made of earth, according to the prophet's *Sunnat*, with time, they would erode. The prediction that on the Day of Judgement seventy corpses will cry out from each grave implies that graves ought to be stacked. This practice will end wasteful spending on burials and remain *shariat*-compliant.

Consider the fact that a hundred and twenty-four thousand messengers were sent to earth, but only fifteen to twenty of their tombs have survived. If the preservation of tombs were important, the tombs of prophets would have been preserved long before any other grave. The fact that this is not so proves that preserving graves and installing permanent caretakers for them contradicts the *shariat* the prophet received. It is an unnatural tradition championed by those who are predisposed to unnatural ideologies.

The prophet had the following to say about tombs (this *Hadees* is narrated by Abul Hiyaj Asadi who heard it from Hazrat Ali):

> Should I send you on a mission that Allah's prophet sent me on? In this mission spare no image, efface every one of them; spare no tomb, flatten every one of them.
>
> (*Sahih Muslim, Kitab al-Janaiz, baab al-Amr ba-Taswiyah tul Qabr* 979)

Religious Advice for the President of Pakistan

The caliph Hazrat Abu Bakr chose an old garment for his shroud. When his daughter suggested something more suited to his stature he said, 'the living are in greater need of respectable clothes than the dead; this old garment is appropriate for me'. Today, if all the ornate fabrics were taken from every shrine, and every brick of every mausoleum were dislodged, there would be enough material to house and clothe countless people in need; additionally, fresh burial grounds will become available, and most importantly, whoever has the good fortune of enacting such a noble enterprise will be loved and commemorated by Allah and His people, for such an undertaking will be both religious and philanthropic. Therefore, the president of Pakistan and various charitable organizations should work to execute such a proposal at once.

Burying a Saint Outside a Graveyard Institutionalizes Polytheism

When a righteous man is buried beyond the perimeter of a graveyard, his tomb is perceived as something extraordinary, laying the groundwork for idolatry. Some devotees arrange such burials insidiously but then there are those who claim to be devout monotheists and resort to this practice inadvertently. For instance, members of the *Jamaat-e-Islami* wanted to bury Maulana Maududi in Mansoora but upon the insistence of the maulana's family members, ended up burying him in his home. Similarly, certain *Ahl-e-Hadees* members buried the Emir *Mujahideen* Maulana Abdullah in his *madrassah*.

Maulana Maududi may have been buried at home with the express purpose of guarding his tomb from being turned into an object of veneration and worship, although chances of the latter are much higher when a graveyard is not employed; not to mention, if we started burying all righteous men this way, very soon the entire world would turn into a necropolis.

Similarly, Maulana Abdullah's tomb has also taken on the aura of something extraordinary because it lies beyond the walls of an ordinary burial ground.

Burial rituals such as these, especially when performed by devout monotheists, set a bad precedence. Only a few years ago, a fresh proselyte to *Ahl-e-Hadees* expressed his desire to be buried within the walls of the very madrassa he founded. When we advised against it, he said he

352 THE LITERATURE OF *LASHKAR-E-TAYYABA*

was only following the example of the madrassa in Mamun Kanjan. He finally changed his mind once we explained the issue to him in light of the Quran and *Hadees*.

As far as the prophet's tomb is concerned, it must be remembered that he is, in fact, extraordinary, and what applies to him does not apply to anyone else in his *ummat*. For example, an ordinary Muslim man is forbidden more than four wives simultaneously, but the prophet had more than four wives. Similarly, as his wives were considered 'Mothers of the Believers' no one could marry them after his death, but this does not hold for any other Muslim widow. Tirmidhi documents a *Hadees* about the subject of the prophet's tomb:

> When the prophet passed away there were disagreements among the companions over his burial. Abu Bakr Siddique said: 'I clearly remember what the prophet once told me; he said that Allah takes the life of a prophet where He wants the prophet to be buried.' Hence the companions buried the prophet right there.
>
> (Tirmidhi, *Kitab al-Janaiz, baab ayn tadfdun al-Anbiya* 1018)

Allama Nasir al-Din al-Albani claims that based on the witnesses, this *Hadees* is disputed.

The prophet passed away in Hazrat Aisha's quarters and hence, according to his *Hadees*, he was buried there. Because his beloved wife Hazrat Aisha, who was also the 'Mother of the Believers', lived in these quarters, the prophet's tomb came to be housed in a building. She explains the wisdom of this particular burial arrangement:

> If the prophet weren't concerned about his tomb turning into a site of worship it would have been out in the open.
>
> (*Sahih Bukhari, Kitab al-Janaiz, Baab Majaa fi Qabr al-Nabi wa Abi Bakr wa Umar zaad* 1388:3)

As far as Hazrat Abu Bakr and Hazrat Umar are concerned, they were buried in the same enclosure because the prophet was already buried there, otherwise, it would have been unthinkable for them to be buried inside a building.

HIGHWAY TO HEAVEN 353

What is a Better Reminder of the Afterlife: Graveyards or Shrines? Some people claim they visit shrines only to pray for the departed; they say they do not petition the dead for anything. These visitors ought to consider the following:

First, the very fact that the shrine is a grave made of concrete, covered with votive fabric, surrounded by clay lanterns, with a tombstone and annual festival rituals means that it stands in contradiction to the teachings of the prophet.

Second, the prophet forbade reciting the Quran around tombs and plenty of people do just that at these shrines. Furthermore, mosques have been constructed in the vicinity of these tombs, an act that has been cursed by the prophet.

Third, women flock to these places, and many of them have their faces covered with make-up, as if they were on their way to the marketplace. This is why the prophet proclaimed that the mosque is the best of places and the marketplace the worst. The fact is these shrines have too much in common with a bazaar.

Fourthly, during festivals, all sorts of vices like singing, ritual dancing, and various other immoral arts are practised here.

Now, if you have the patience and the courage to stop all this by preaching at these shrines then by all means, you most certainly should pay a visit. But if you quietly return in the face of all that goes on there, and justify your visit with prayer, then listen well: your attendance at the shrine is the death knell of your spiritual dignity and you would have partaken in what has clearly been forbidden. As far as praying at a grave is concerned, keep in mind there is only one good reason to do so, and the prophet has explicitly made clear what that is; if that purpose is fulfilled, well and good; if not, then your visit has only burdened your soul with sin.

The prophet explains the purpose of visiting graves in the following *Hadees*:

Visit graves for they keep the memory of death alive.
(Sahih Muslim, Kitab al-Janaiz, Baab Istizan al-Nabi rabbahu,
fi ziyara qabar umuhu)

354 THE LITERATURE OF *LASHKAR-E-TAYYABA*

Notice the prophet used the word 'graves', not 'shrines', for they remind one of the afterlife. A graveyard ought to have tombs made of mud; some ought to be dilapidated while others completely eroded, with loved ones scattered under the earth, and the surrounding trees rustling in the wind; only then will one be inspired to think about the transience of life and the impermanence of this world; only then will one ponder death and the afterlife. The visitor ought to raise his hands and pray for the ones buried in the ground, who, having returned to the creator, are in desperate need of prayer; and when one returns from such a place one ought to feel indifferent to this life and invested in the next, having shed one's sins as tears. This is how one ought to keep the memory of death alive, according to the one who warned us of the afterlife.

Now let us consider the atmosphere at shrines. One is met with the intoxicating fragrance of incense as one approaches a mausoleum made of marble and fitted with electric fans and air conditioners while taps of running milk and cold water and oblations of halva, sweetened rice, and rice pudding are on offer. Women roam freely with all their charms on display, inviting lustful gazes and wanton ogling. Orchestras fire up emotions with their melodies and chants, while nearby hotels installed with videocassette recorders and dish antennae beam in filth from across the world.

Can One Focus on the Afterlife in a Place Like This?
In order to grasp the issue at hand, consider how the prophet referenced a particular traveller in a *Hadees* from Muslim Sharif:

> He has been travelling a long time; covered in filth, he raises his dirty hands towards the sky and cries out, 'Oh god! Oh Lord,' even though what he eats is *haram*, what he drinks is *haram*, what he wears is *haram*, and his wealth is *haram*; why, then, will his prayer be answered?

Much the same way, he who visits a place whose very existence is an affront to Allah's sovereignty and where everything contradicts the teaching of the prophet, where the entombed personage is referred to as *Daata* (the giver), *Dastigir* (the helper), *Ghaus-al-Azam* (the transmitter of prayers), etc. as an insult to Allah's Oneness, where pilgrims are involved in all kinds of immorality, where no one thinks to preach against idolatry, and

HIGHWAY TO HEAVEN   355

where polytheism, the greatest sin of all, is practised openly with absolute impunity, how does one expect to pray in a place such as this?

Fools prostrate when it's time to stand ...

In this marketplace of idolatry Satan is auctioning off people's faith and this poor fool of a visitor claims he is only there to pray for the departed. Keep in mind, praying in such an environment is not only futile, but it is also a crime according to god. The pilgrims there will think you are petitioning the personage buried in the tomb, much like them. It is a crime, for you will not only add to the idolatrous atmosphere of the shrine, but you will also quietly leave the premises without having fulfilled your obligation of preventing others from committing the unthinkable sin of idolatry. If you do not have it in you to publicly denounce the rampant immorality practised at such places, it is best you do not visit them in the first place.

Thus, the prophet has strictly forbidden his *ummat* from visiting any sanctuary that reeks of idolatry or promotes pagan rituals. According to the following *Hadees*, only three places in the world are worthy of pilgrimage:

> Do not pilgrimage to any site other than the following three mosques: Masjid-al-Haram (the Ka'ba in Mecca), Masjid-i-Aqsa (the Dome of the Rock in Jerusalem), and my mosque (Masjid-i-Nabvi in Medina).
> (*Sahih Bukhari, Kitab Fazal al-Salat fi masjid makkah wa medina, baab masjid: bayt-ul-Muqaddas* 1197; *Sahih Muslim, Kitab al-Hajj, baab safar al-Maraa ma'...* 827)

Since these three pilgrimage sites have been identified, and the benefits of travelling to them has been foretold, there is absolutely no reason to pilgrimage elsewhere, and giving any other place a similar status categorically goes against *shariat*. The companions would even steer people away from places associated with former prophets for fear of idolatry. Hazrat Qaz'ah narrates:

> I intended to pilgrimage to Mount Sinai. When I consulted Hazrat Ibn Umar he said, 'the prophet has forbidden making a pilgrimage to any site except Masjid-al-Haram (the Ka'ba in Mecca), Masjid-i-Aqsa (the

356 THE LITERATURE OF *LASHKAR-E-TAYYABA*

Dome of the Rock in Jerusalem), and Masjid-i-Nabvi (the prophet's mosque in Medina). Therefore, do not pilgrimage to Mount Sinai.

(Akhbar Makta til Uzraqi, baab zikr had al-masjid al-Haraam wa fazlahu wa fazal as-Salaat fiha 66:2)

If the companions were alive today, would they have allowed pilgrimages to shrines and mausoleums?

Furthermore, the quote above proves that even if there is no evidence of idolatry or the existence of a tomb, pilgrimages to any place other than the ones mentioned by the prophet, are strictly forbidden. On the other hand, mausoleums erected over the tombs of saints have become dens of idolatry and are not only to be avoided at all costs, but they also ought to be demolished altogether. A pilgrimage to any such place is nothing short of a crime!

Competing with the House of God (Ka'ba)

Creating a fourth site of pilgrimage is tantamount to reducing the status of the three legitimate sites prescribed by the prophet. A concerted effort is underway to challenge the importance of the House of Allah. The prophet used the word *shareef* to describe the Ka'ba but today, due to the proliferation of shrines, the term is being applied to every other town and village and the rites performed at the Ka'ba are being mimicked at countless tombs. According to Tirmidhi and Nisai, the prophet said that circumambulating the Ka'ba was like praying to Allah; today, when devotees circumambulate a tomb one can only conclude they are worshipping the personage buried inside. Devotees kiss tombstones the way pilgrims kiss the *Hajra-e-Aswad* (the Black Stone installed in a corner of the Ka'ba); devotees cling to the pillars of shrines the way pilgrims latch onto the doorstep of the Ka'ba. While a fresh cloth is draped over the Ka'ba twice a year, shrines are draped in garish multicoloured fabrics all year round. Much like the Ka'ba is bathed, Ali Hajveri's shrine is washed in thousands of litres of rose-water. Pilgrims to the Ka'ba announce their approach to the sanctuary by crying out 'Labbaik! Labbaik!', while devotees at shrines chant blasphemous slogans and sing idolatrous songs. In short, every rite and ritual associated with the Ka'ba is mimicked at thousands of shrines scattered across the world by those who blindly follow in Abraha's footsteps.

How Sultan Abdul Aziz Fried the Friars

The Turks popularized idolatrous practices across the sacred land of the Arabs. The tombs of various companions of the prophet, as well as those of righteous men had been turned into shrines and sites of pilgrimage. Then, Allah blessed the Islamic world with two devout monotheists, namely Imam Muhammad bin Abdul Wahab and Muhammad bin Sa'ud. The former was armed with knowledge, the latter with a sword. Together, the two revived the true puritanical Islam in the land of the prophet. Later, the son of Ibn Sa'ud, Sultan Abdul Aziz became the caretaker of the twin sites of pilgrimage (the Ka'ba and the prophet's mosque) and demolished what few shrines remained in the region. Some religious figures from the sub-continent travelled to Saudi Arabia to persuade the sultan to desist and this is what he said to them:

> Show me a single verse from the Quran or a single *Hadees* of the prophet in favour of shrines and I'll plate them all with silver and gold.

The petitioners had no response and silently returned.

A distinguished Muslim leader of the time, Maulana Zafar Ali Khan, offered a tribute to the sultan in his newspaper 'Zamindar' and expressed the sincere hope that the rest of the world would soon be cleansed of similar shrines by upstanding men like the sultan.

The Prophet's Final Moments

In conclusion, I offer two sayings by the prophet. The first was uttered in his final moments, when he was about to cross the threshold between life and death. Whatever is said at that time is the dying person's will, so before you, dear reader, is the prophet's will. Pay attention, for the prophet forewarned us about a terrible disaster. Hazrat Aisha and Ibn Abbas report:

> As the prophet neared death he would cover his face with a chador, and when he felt suffocated (by the chador) he would remove it.

In this state, the prophet said:

> May Allah curse the Jews and Christians for they have turned the tombs of their prophets into places of worship.

358 THE LITERATURE OF *LASHKAR-E-TAYYABA*

(Sahih Bukhari, Kitab Ahadith al-Anbiya baab maazkar An Bani Israel 3453–3454; *Sahih Muslim, Kitab al-Masajid, Baab al-Nahi An Bina al-Masjid min al-Quboor* 531*)*

Armageddon Will Descend Upon Grave-Worshippers
The prophet said that in the final tortuous hours of Armageddon:

Allah will send an incredibly refreshing breeze from Yemen, which will be the cause of instant death in every person who has a kernel of faith in his heart.

This means the slightest bit of faith in Allah will be enough to win His mercy. But as far as the grave-worshippers are concerned, they are entirely devoid of faith for idolatry obliterates belief. This is why Allah makes no mention of it for when something is obliterated it merits no mention whatsoever. Consequently, we pray that Allah protect us from the sin of grave-worship for unfortunate are the ones who will live to experience Armageddon.

Hazrat Abdullah bin Masud reports the prophet as having said:

No doubt, the worst people are those who will live through Armageddon, and those who turn tombs into houses of worship.

(Masnad Ahmad 435, 405:1*)*

Chapter 2: From Hajveri's Shrine to Allah's Court—A True Story

Truth hath come and falsehood hath vanished away. Lo! falsehood is ever bound to vanish.

(Surat al-Isra 17:81*)*

I matriculated with a first division in science from my village's Saini Bar High School. In my home, we religiously practised the ritual veneration of saints. My childhood was steeped in mysticism; from an early age, I was preoccupied with beholding god and becoming a *wali*. To this end, I would spend entire nights at the mosque and put myself through various endurance tests such as standing on one leg, like a heron, or hanging upside down like a bat, but nothing seemed to work. My desire for union (with the divine) took me to all sorts of shrines and sanctuaries; as a result of the constipating aches of love, I would go into trances, and enter wild states of ecstasy but most of the time, I was merely putting on a show.

As the years passed, monasticism took root more firmly in my heart. Upon hearing translations of Quranic verses, my mind was seized with all manner of odd metaphysical contemplations, and I had no room in my thoughts for the real struggles of life. My father would often say, 'Son, the Quran is incomprehensible to ordinary folk like us; only Allah's special friends can understand its meaning.' I had convinced myself he was right; after all, my father was a veteran of this tradition and he was well-respected (and still is) for his devotion. We routinely commemorated the sacred eleventh (and still do) and I considered it a privilege to participate in this oblation. I was well aware that the path of love was full of trials and tribulations and not everyone could endure it; nevertheless, I was determined to take on every challenge this thorny path laid down before me. Before stepping into the valley of sorrow, one must dedicate oneself to another. Hence, I devoted myself to the person to whom those around me were devoted.

Devotees know well that the object of their devotion, the person they profess to follow and love, is everything to them; he is the revealed and the concealed, the present and the presence, the first and the last, forever looming in their consciousness.

I too was deeply caught up in this creed. In my zeal, I would supplicate with the picture of my *murshid* before me (there was always a picture of him in our home). His countenance brought some ease to my worried mind for he was my protector, my saviour, my helper, and my lord. I was always taught that he was the rainmaker, the provider, and the master. (Never mind the fact that now he is a cripple and has been abandoned by his devotees). But I digress. As I was saying, I wholeheartedly took on the impending suffering that accompanies this path. I routinely stayed up all night. I was restless and passionate; I frequented all sorts of shrines, but I was unable to connect with Allah. At the time, I was unaware that Satan courses through human veins like blood:

Love is nothing short of madness

Hence, one day, having decided to renounce all the pleasures and temptations of this world, I headed for the shrine of Daata Ganj Bakhsh. I had

360 THE LITERATURE OF *LASHKAR-E-TAYYABA*

made up my mind that I would not leave his sanctuary until he bestowed me with spiritual authority.

How I Came to Sojourn at Daata Darbar

I was ensnared by what the Quran has termed man's nemesis, that is, Satan. The honest truth is I was also having nightly visions, (Satan's handiwork, no doubt), in which I was convinced that I should hurry to Daata Sahib's sanctuary to collect my spiritual gifts. Because I would stay up all night, people thought I had acquired spiritual insights. My father owned a brokerage firm in Shahkot, Faisalabad. One day, while he was at work, I changed out of my expensive clothes into a mendicant's tattered robes, and much to everyone's amazement sought my mother's permission to leave. First, I headed for my father's workplace. (Family friends always referred to me as 'Prince' because I was a bon vivant of sorts). My father broke down when I told him my intentions. He said: 'Son, are you really going to leave like this?' I said: 'Indeed, this is how a beggar ought to go before a king.' My father started wailing; I wept uncontrollably as well. Soon, everyone around us was in tears. People turned to my father and said: 'Brother Ghulam Muhammad! You are fortunate to have him as a son.'

Finally, when all the weeping was over, my father said: 'Son! We are followers of *wali*s and no doubt, you have been commanded to leave by Daata Sahib himself. I cannot stop you (as I mentioned before I was regularly having night visions which I'd frequently narrate to my elders) but you know I cannot last a day without you.' I said: 'That is true but this mendicant must leave.' I proceeded to pay my respects at the Nau Lakh Hazari shrine in Shahkot and then headed straight for Daata Darbar. This was my first trip to Lahore.

It is said Daata Sahib won't accept your attendance unless you pay your respects at Pir Makki Sahib's shrine first.

At the Shrine

First, I fulfilled the time-honoured tradition of visiting Pir Makki Sahib's shrine. When I finally reached Daata Darbar, I prostrated before his tomb

HIGHWAY TO HEAVEN 361

and started weeping. A sage-like character took my arm, consoled me, and moved me to the side. I sat there in a daze.

Silently, I stared at the sacred tomb. Oh, the hardship one must endure for proximity with Allah. One must wage a '*jihad*' with one's ego; I started practising for this *jihad*. One cannot know the kind of suffering caused by waging such *jihad* in the sweltering heat of July.

The body that endures is the body that knows
Sufis say that only a cup made of pure gold can hold a lioness's milk; a cup made of any other material will break. This is why the heart looking to be filled with spiritual knowledge must first be cleansed and purified. This bag of bones must be rid of all impurities, and the first step in this process is fasting. In this analogy, knowledge of god is the lioness's milk; I had grown up with a living manifestation of this metaphor. A mystic in my village had not consumed a single morsel of food for twelve years, and consequently, had withered away into a mere shadow of a human being. For many, he had achieved a status of godliness. As the saying goes, 'I said Ranjha so often, I became Ranjha myself'; meaning, the one who says Allah all the time will, at one point, take on the appearance of Allah Himself.

The Passion of Remembrance

Those who insist on knowing god know full well that Ali Ahmed Sabir from Kalyar Sharif had achieved an exalted level of godliness. Below is a brief description of a famous incident associated with him:

Ali Ahmed Sabir was known to have fasted for thirty-six years in the jungle while meditating. He was so involved with god that he had no sense of hunger or thirst. It was reported that within a twelve-mile radius around him, his energy was so intense, even birds flying overhead were singed to ashes. Since he meditated in a single spot under a Gular tree for thirty-six years without moving, gradually, the tree's roots enveloped his emaciated body. When he finally returned to the mundane world he was married. On his nuptial night, when his newly wedded wife introduced herself, he said: 'Does Allah have a spouse?' She said: 'Dear, please do not

362 THE LITERATURE OF *LASHKAR-E-TAYYABA*

mock me; I am truly your wife.' He looked at her with divine rage and she went up in smoke before him. (Women who know what is best for them should make sure that the person they are about to wed has not attained such exalted stations of godliness, or else …).

The Height of Asceticism

As I was saying, I too persisted. During the day, I would consume a few lentil beans and have a drop of water. Mind you, there was no shortage of food around me; oblations of sweet meats and rice pudding were always on offer in the sanctuary, but I never touched any of these. As a result, I would only have a bowel movement once every two weeks. I wept away all my tears until my eyes were completely dry, but I refused to give up. The heat and dryness turned me into an insomniac. Many others like me had gathered around the tomb for similar spiritual athleticism but my endurance surpassed theirs and most of them thought of me as a highly accomplished mystic. No doubt, they were impressed to see someone as young as me (I did not yet have a full beard) endure so much. I imagined I was precociously gaining profound spiritual insights. Countless people visited the shrine every day with offerings and prayers.

Hazrat Moin-ud-Din Chishti and the Wench

Oral tradition has it that when Khaja Moin-ud-Din Chishti made a pilgrimage to Daata Sahib's shrine, he too longed to witness the truth, like me. Many days passed but nothing happened, until one afternoon, a neighbourhood wench arrived at the shrine, paid her respects, and cried: 'Oh Daata, let me reunite with my lover! I swear I will not leave this place until our union.' Out of nowhere, the woman's lover showed up at the shrine and carried her away. Shocked, Moin-ud-Din Chishti turned to the tomb and said: 'This woman's prayer was answered in an instant while I've been sitting here for days now, hoping to behold (god). What great sin of mine keeps me from the object of my desire?' A voice from inside the tomb said: 'Moin-ud-Din! This woman's faith was strong, which is why I took care of her in an instant. But you're dear to me… I want you

HIGHWAY TO HEAVEN   363

to stay with me a while longer.' In response, Moin-ud-Din composed the following couplet:

Ganj Bakhsh is a blessing upon the world, and a manifestation of god's divine light
  This flawed soul has found a flawless master; I have found my guide in the Perfect Man

People would come up to me and say: 'Brother, what is wrong with you? Is this about a woman? Are you trying to win a woman's affection? Don't worry! Daata Sahib will answer all your prayers.' I would say: 'No brother, it's got nothing to do with that at all. If that were the problem, I would have solved it myself... I am on a different plane altogether' and the concerned attendees would chuckle and leave. Gradually, I gained considerable fame among the visitors to the shrine. When sage pilgrims wept before me, begging me to pray for them I would say: 'Friends! If my prayers had any weight, do you not think I'd pray for myself?' But nothing I said deterred them. They would say: 'You are among the chosen ones; please pray for us.' I would say: 'I myself am cursed. What could I possibly do for you?' They would take this as a sign of humility and smile as if we had shared an intimate secret.

Until Daata Comes Out of His Tomb and Embraces Me ...

Over time, an elderly man at the shrine befriended me. He told me: 'I've been living here for a number of years now. I too had a vision after which I decided I wouldn't leave until Daata Sahib emerged from his tomb and embraced me himself.' I would unconsciously respond with, 'Vah! Subhan Allah! Nothing like Daata Sahib ... !' and I would start weeping for no reason. Once, that fellow's watch was stolen while he was asleep. When he awoke, he was deeply disturbed. 'You couldn't tell someone slipped it off your wrist?' I asked. 'No,' he replied, 'it all happened while I was snoozing.' (He too was a great *wali*, you see.) I said, 'don't worry, Daata will recompense you', and with that I returned to my meditations. Many people from my village would visit the shrine and pity me. My father regularly brought me money and new clothes but after he left, I would distribute his gifts

364 THE LITERATURE OF *LASHKAR-E-TAYYABA*

among the poor. All I did was sit there and weep. My father would urge me to take care of myself, but I was least concerned about my condition.

One day my brother visited me. Shocked to see the state I was in, he wept uncontrollably. He begged me to go back home with him. I said: 'It is not time yet; you go.' By this time, I was indifferent to worldly ties. My relatives would pay their respects to me, but I paid them no mind. My sole desire was to become the Perfect Man, a manifestation of god. *Wali*s are great human beings and a moment by their side is better than a hundred years of worship. As the popular couplet goes:

A moment in a *wali*'s presence
Is better than a hundred years of worship

My Destination was Near Yet So Far

Most of my time was spent in close proximity to *wali*s; what more could I have asked for? One day, in a sacred dream I was told to pay my respects at the shrine of Makki Shah Sahib. I was certain this was a sign. As I left the sanctuary, I noticed my shoes were missing but without a second thought, I stepped out barefoot into the street blistering under the midday sun without paying my burning soles any mind. When I arrived at the modest graveyard in the back of Pir Makki Sahib's shrine, a stout mendicant called out to me by my name. He said: 'Come to me quickly, I have been waiting for you!' (Later, I discovered secret agents are employed in the business of spiritual promotions).

I walked a thorny path to reach you, my love
Look at the blisters on my feet

I thought to myself, no doubt, mystics know what's in the heart. I went up to the stout mendicant and said: 'What are my orders, respected Baba?' He said: 'It is not time yet. Makki Sahib has told me to stop you right here and not let you come any farther.' I wept bitterly. They say when love burns too intensely the beloved denies proximity regardless of the lover's suffering. I thought to myself, my love must certainly be at its zenith; no doubt Makki Shah Sahib informed the mendicant about me in a dream.

I Had Yet to Sweep the Floor and Swallow Sacred Spit

I said: 'Sir, what should I do now?' He said: 'Grab a broom and start sweeping the graveyard.' It took me a few hours to sweep the place. Then, I went back to the mendicant and said: 'Now what, Master?' He proceeded to spit into a cup until it was half full. Then, he told me to drink it. I was filled with disgust, but I was dedicated to the secret path of 'true knowledge'. I had heard that certain saints had the ability to transform rice into maggots and slime into nectar; I thought this was a test. But nothing of the sort happened and I ended up swallowing his spit (Oh Allah! I have imbibed a concoction from hell. Forgive me!) I felt tired. I wanted to rest but the mendicant told me to fill a clay pot with water and start watering the trees. Satan tried to lure me away by whispering: 'What are you getting yourself into Tariq?' I shook these negative voices out of my head and got to work.

In my ritual worship I stand, then bow, then sit
But in rituals of love, there isn't a moment's rest

With a clay pot of water on my head and fire under my soles, I got to work. My feet blistered but suffering is meaningless in the path of 'love and madness'. I said to myself: 'Tariq, you're blessed to be Makki Shah Sahib's water-bearer!!' (Unlike Sohni's pot made of unbaked clay, mine was as sturdy as my passion). I emptied a few pots full of water within a circle around a tree trunk but none of it stood.

I poured approximately ten more pots of water and every last drop seeped through the earth. I thought this was a miracle of sorts. By now I was utterly exhausted. Baba Jee chortled at me and said: 'Enough!' I put down the pot and said: 'What now, Sir?' He told me to rest. The sun was setting, and I grew afraid of the encroaching darkness. I tried consoling myself; I reminded myself I was Daata Sahib's child, nothing could happen to me. Keep in mind, the graveyard was enclosed by a wall along which ran a sewer and all the water I poured near the tree trunk went directly into this sewer, but I only discovered this later. As the night deepened, I asked Baba Jee, 'is it time yet; do I have permission now?' I was desperate to pay my respects at the shrine. Baba Jee would say, 'helloooo, hellooo', as if he was on a long-distance phone call. I would stand there

366 THE LITERATURE OF *LASHKAR-E-TAYYABA*

waiting, until he would turn to me and say: 'No, it is not time yet.' Waiting is the hardest thing. After a while, I would ask him again; he would pretend to make a phone call, and then turn me away every time.

Do not raise my hopes and let me down
Don't turn my love into your plaything

Deep inside I blamed myself for not being allowed to pay my respects at the shrine. The desire for union and the pain of separation kept me up all night. When I had reached the end of my endurance, I would say, 'Baba Jee, ring Makki Shah Sahib again and ask him to let me through', upon which Baba Jee would lose his temper and yell, 'No one is allowed to approach without permission, who do you think you are? You are going cut me off from my spiritual fountainhead as well!' and I would crawl back to my corner. At Daata Sahib's shrine I had to force myself to stay up through the night but at this spot, I had become an insomniac. Baba Jee told me to sleep between graves, without a mattress or a charpoy. I lay down between two graves but could not sleep in anticipation.

Death could not close my eyes
I had a habit of waiting for you
Early the next morning, my *murshid* had me sweep the graveyard again.

Baba Jee's Commandments

From his throne, Baba Jee would issue all kinds of orders that I would have to follow unquestioningly if I expected to attain spiritual involution.

First Commandment: Bathe Me!
One morning, Baba Jee commanded me to give him a bath. I washed him thoroughly in the morning light. Visitors started arriving at the shrine; they came with all sorts of unanswered prayers. I wept and prayed and although nothing happened my desire for union grew stronger. The visitors would tell me to serve Baba Jee as best as I could and that I'd be rewarded beyond my wildest imagination for doing so. Sometimes they had informal exchanges with Baba Jee who would abuse them with language

that would make grown men blush. But in that environment, shameless-ness was a virtue. Many times, I, too, was at the receiving end of such lan-guage. The more he swore at people, the more certain they were that their prayers would be answered. They would say: 'Baba Jee's curse is a ticket to heaven.' Only later did I find out these people were colluding with the old man. There was, however, one household in the neighbourhood whose members openly detested Baba Jee and he, in turn, despised them as well. I always felt Baba Jee was magnanimous with them in how he chose not to burn them all to ashes with a single death-stare. I imagined these people disrespected *wali*s. Once, around midnight, Baba Jee asked me to give him a bath.

Second Commandment: Return a Kitten to the Lord of Cats
When I was done bathing Baba Jee, a kitten crept into our enclosure. I was told to take the kitten to the Lord of Cats at Bhati Gate. I had no clue how to get there. Baba Jee gave me vague directions before sending me on my way. When I stepped out into the street I was almost hit by on-coming traffic. Convinced I was trying to kill myself, someone grabbed my arm and helped me cross the road. I asked this person how to get to Bhati Gate and he was surprised that as a grown man, I did not know my way around. How could he have known about my eternal struggles and endless suffering? After dropping off the kitten, when I returned to the graveyard, Baba Jee was furious with me. He demanded to know why I had been absent for so long. I told him I was only following his orders. He said: 'Fine! Now you must go to the River Ravi.' I said: 'Murshid! I do not know how to get there.' He said: 'Very well then, lie down between the graves.' No sooner did I lie down, that little snakes started crawling all over my body, as I trembled with fear. Baba Jee turned to the snakes and said: 'Listen, don't bother this one, he is one of us.' I was in awe of Baba Jee, even though this was nothing but an act. One day, I asked: 'Baba Jee, how much farther is my destination?' He answered: 'The matter is in Makki Shah Sahib's hands. I simply follow his command.'

Third Commandment: Pick Up My Shit!
One day, Baba Jee told me to clear the waste that had collected under his throne. I have already stated that Baba Jee was so overweight he could barely walk; he would sit on a wooden plank with hole in it and defecate

368 THE LITERATURE OF *LASHKAR-E-TAYYABA*

right there. A mound of maggot-infested excrement had collected underneath him.

The prophet once said that Satan descends upon filthy places.

At the time I was unaware of this *Hadees*. Nevertheless, I obeyed Baba Jee's command for I had heard that sometimes acolytes are initiated through unimaginable acts of endurance that could lead to a spiritual promotion or demotion, depending on how one fared. I started cleaning out Baba Jee's excrement with my bare hands and, at the time, if asked, I would have eaten it as well. Those who wish to tread the path of mysticism must remember that such trials are not uncommon; they should only dare to wander into this realm if they feel they can endure such filth.

> If you value your life and your heart
> You will not travel down this road

Perhaps Baba Jee acquired his exalted station after abandoning all sense of decorum and dignity. And having attained such heights, see how he sits on his throne altering people's destinies.

An Unusual Relic

Keep in mind, Baba Jee would often sit on his throne in nothing but a shirt although his partial nudity did not offend any of his visitors. In fact, many would bless their food by brushing it against his skin. This is why Allah has said that most people in the world are ignorant and uneducated. Even now, I look around me and feel like crying. As the poet says:

> I wonder if I should weep or beat my breast
> If I could afford it, I'd hire a mourner to walk with me all the time.

Dear Allah, I cannot thank You enough for showing me what *tawheed* really means, or else:

> I'd have found peace neither in this world nor the world hereafter ...
> I would have been cursed in both worlds.

So as I was saying, even if Baba Jee ordered me to eat his excrement, I would not have hesitated for I was determined to attain the station

HIGHWAY TO HEAVEN 369

where there is no difference between *qum bi izni* (stand up by my command) and *qum bi iznillah* (stand up by Allah's command).

I was willing to offer my flesh for spiritual enlightenment. Veterans of this path believe that the one who steers the flying saucer of spirituality controls fate itself; he can alter destinies upon a whim; I was willing to sacrifice my life for this. One day I grabbed a knife lying next to Baba Jee and said, 'Lord, if you command, I'll cut out a piece of my flesh or gouge out my eyes for you; ask me once and see what happens ... ' (I knew that on the true path of ecstatic love dismembering oneself was not unheard of, as we know well from the love tragedy of Laila and Majnun). Baba Jee smiled and said: 'You have found your destination! You have found your destination!' I was overjoyed. I said: 'Baba Jee! Make the telephone call and see if I may enter the shrine and pay my respects now?' In response, he said: 'He sees everything; it is not time yet.'

Fourth Command: Beg Like a Mendicant
One day Baba Jee ordered me to go out begging in the streets. The thought of begging in public made my entire body tremble. I felt nauseous. My eyes dimmed. Nothing in my life had prepared me for this and I started weeping uncontrollably. I said: 'Baba Jee, don't humiliate me so! Feed me to the dogs but please don't make me go out and beg!' I fell at his feet and begged him to take back his command. In response, he said: 'These are the orders I have received from above. This is the last step.' I accepted this as the final hurdle on my path to spiritual enlightenment. By god, that day I took his bowl with my own two hands and went out begging. Because I knew not how to beg I simply roamed the streets with the bowl, weeping. I turned to the heavens and cried: 'Oh Allah! You know what is in my heart; accept me!' Perhaps the Lord heard my plea. When I returned from the most humiliating experience of my life, I placed all that I had collected by way of alms before Baba Jee, and as usual, he swore at me.

Finally—I Returned Despairingly from the Place of Despair

I said: 'Baba Jee, how much further do I have to go?' He said: 'I have not received any sign from above.' I could hold back no more. 'Mister! What

370 THE LITERATURE OF *LASHKAR-E-TAYYABA*

have I not done for you? How have I not suffered? Your whims have been my command, even when it meant hurting myself. Even Ranjha found Heer after slicing up his ears; cut off my ears if you want but I cannot meander around here for the rest of my life. Tell me what is left to be done! I'll make any sacrifice you want me to!' And all he said was: 'It is not time yet.' 'When will it be time?' I asked. 'It may take a lifetime,' he replied. Deep inside I thought: 'Die, you cursed old fart! You want me to spend my entire life in this wasteland?!' He tried to console me: 'You shouldn't shy away from spending your time with the wise and elderly, who knows when the hour of acceptance is upon you.' I yelled back: 'If it is all about sitting around and waiting, I could do that well enough at home. I can cry out to god from the comfort of my bedroom, why would I put myself through hell sitting here? I thought this mystical path was a short cut! If it takes just as long to attain spiritual enlightenment, then what the hell is this for? Give me back my shawl you idiot!' He had taken the new shawl off my back the day I arrived.

This time he did not respond with his usual verbal abuse. He barely raised his head. He sat there in silence as if his mother had just died. I snatched my shawl (for he was not going to give up easily) and said: 'Watch now! I'm going to Makki Shah Sahib's tomb and don't you dare stop me, you wretch! I have gone insane cleaning up your shit! I cannot even think straight!' I stormed off to the shrine where, after paying my respects, I yelled out all my misgivings about the old man. When I had nothing more to say I took off for Daata Sahib's shrine, entered the inner sanctum and once again, I started weeping uncontrollably. I was convulsing like a fish out of water. I kept saying: 'Oh Daata, please let me have one glimpse of you! If I am worthy at least call out my name from within your resting place. Thousands pay their respects at your tomb; you listen to them, you answer their prayers, you converse with them; what am I lacking that you do not heed my call?' Many days passed and I continued bawling at the shrine, to no avail. Finally, exhausted and hopeless, I said: 'Daata Sahib, be blunt with me; tell me in no uncertain terms that you will not heed my prayer. If you are going to turn away a beggar, have the courtesy to tell the beggar you are going to turn him away.' My words seemed to fall on deaf ears. I kept pleading for a response, but I was met with deathly silence. Allah says:

HIGHWAY TO HEAVEN 371

If ye pray unto them they hear not your prayer, and if they heard they could not grant it you.

(*Surat al-Fatir* 35:14)

At this time, I obviously had nothing to do with the Quran. No doubt, my cries went unheard, unanswered. I kept complaining: 'Daata Sahib, there are rules! Rules, I tell you! But here, in your court, nothing makes any sense. You humiliate me in your own home! Why do you treat me this way? Why do you disgrace me? I have sunk to the lowest depth of depravity for your sake. What have you and Makki Shah Sahib ever given me? Say something!' But both Daata Sahib and Makki Shah Sahib slept quietly in their graves, unaware of who passed by their tombs, unaware of all the nonsense and depravity that went on at their shrines. They will discover all this on the Day of Judgement when they themselves will say: 'Did we ask you to bow at our tombs?' Humiliated, dejected, and emaciated, I left the shrine and headed back home.

... And People Thought I Had Journeyed Through the Cosmos ...

I had yet to cleanse my heart of idolatry. Due to my ordeal, I had paled considerably. People looked at me and said: 'Praise be to Allah!' Some would kiss my hands; others would reach for my feet. Some claimed to see a halo around my head. None of them knew of the demented life I had lived. They mistook my pallid complexion for divine glow.

I was received like a martyr. Loudspeakers announced the arrival of a saint, oblations were made to commemorate my divinity, and people flocked to my feet begging me to pray for them. I, poor ignorant I, remained oblivious to my own involution. A young man begged me to help him win the heart of the object of his love. And then there were others.

I wondered if in the world of spirituality this is all one has to do to win people's trust. I will say this, by Allah's grace, not once was I tempted by greed. If I had wanted, I could easily have exploited all the people around me and become incredibly wealthy overnight. Consider this: an educated

372 THE LITERATURE OF *LASHKAR-E-TAYYABA*

well-to-do man held up the Quran before me and announced: 'I accept you as the Perfect Being.' I said, 'trust me brother, I am no such thing', but he took my denial as an affirmation of my status.

A Ray of Hope After Hopelessness

As I mentioned earlier, people thought highly of me even though I had done nothing to earn their respect. Around this time a childhood friend who lived in my neighbourhood and belonged to the *Ahl-e-Hadees* tradition re-entered my life. In the past, whenever I'd offer an oblation for the sacred eleventh, he'd turn down my invitation. This would anger me and I would yell, 'oh Ali! Save me!' just to irk him. I would taunt him and tease him but in response he would simply recite Quranic verses and *Hadees* back at me. He tried to make me see that what I was practising was idolatry and did his level best to instil the fear of Allah in my heart. In the face of my obstinacy, he was always patient and forgiving. I had seen the worst of those who dwell at shrines; compared to them, this young man's superior character and impeccable social graces were genuinely inspiring. I had come to detest shrine-dwellers, but I could not express myself openly for fear of my elders. Gradually, as I reflected on my friend's approach to life and religion, I felt a ray of light pierce my heart and illuminate my being. He had not given up on me even after I returned from my travails. He never missed an opportunity to show me the right path, until one day, by Allah's grace, the fear of Allah filled my soul, replacing the fear of all false gods for good. Allah answered my friend Abdul Latif's prayer. He had prayed for me when we were in Matric, and he continued praying for me even after we parted ways, when I headed to the shrines in search of a 'mystical garden' and he headed to a madrassa to learn about Quran and *Hadees*.

I learned to embody *tawheed* and *Sunnat* and came to detest idolatry and religious corruption. Who would have thought I would see the day when Allah blessed me with the opportunity to wage *jihad* in Afghanistan alongside Maulana Amir Hamza Sahib. The experience opened up my mind and I realized that the spiritual gifts for which I had humiliated myself to no end were all waiting for me on the battlefield.

Constructing the Real Daata's Darbar

Allah is Lord and the mosque is his court. Upon returning from Afghanistan, we started organizing congregational prayers in Abdul Latif Sahib's house. After a few months, we had Professor Hafiz Muhammad Saeed lay the foundation stone for the village's newly constructed mosque. The locals who followed the twisted paths of spirituality and mysticism tried their level best to have this mosque demolished; others conspired to murder my friend and me, but Allah sabotaged their plans. Once the mosque was ready, we organized an elaborate conference in honour of Maulana Muhammad Hussein Sheikhupuri that was presided over by the founder and former chairman of *Jamia Muhammadia Shahkot*, Muhammad Arshad Sahi Sahib. In his opening address, Sahi Sahib narrated the awe-inspiring story of how he joined *Ahl-e-Hadees* and urged the people to reaffirm their faith in *tawheed*.

Now, by the grace of Allah, my compatriots flock to the true god in droves; falsehood withdraws, truth prevails. As the Quran says:

Truth hath come and falsehood hath vanished away. Lo! falsehood is ever bound to vanish.

(*Surat al-Isra* 17:81)

.

10
The Problem with *Takfir* by Abul Hassan Mubbashir Ahmed

In this chapter we present translated excerpts from Abul Hassan Mubbashir Ahmed Rabbani's *Masalah-i takfir aur is ke usul o zavabit* (*The Problem of Takfir and its Principles and Regulations*).[1] This is one of the most important expositions of a significant difference between LeT and other Salafist organizations and between LeT and the other Deobandi militant groups operating in and from Pakistan: the practice of *takfir*, or apostatizing a Muslim, a declaration that can prove fatal to the subject. LeT, as this peculiar document, illustrates has often found itself in conflict with other *Salafi* organizations because LeT rejects the widespread practice of *takfir* and the violence that accompanies such a declaration. In this text, the author describes a conflict with a Salafist scholar who is inclined towards Al Qaeda. What is apparent is that the Al Qaeda-inclined scholar holds LeT in little regards because of its demurral to practise *takfir*. Rabbani repudiates this by mobilizing highly regarded *Hadees*, commentary, and passages from the Quran to defend LeT's position that the evidentiary standards to declare someone to be a *kafir* are very high and few learned persons are in a position to make that judgement.

This intra-Salafi conflict that plays out in this document is an important fissure that derives from the Salafis' rigorous commitment to the doctrine of the oneness of god (*tawheed*) which creates several intractable practical dilemmas. If a believer's ruler does not follow Islam as dictated by *Ahl-e-Hadees*, should the follower concentrate upon education (*tarbiyat*) and spreading the faith through preaching (*dawah*) to create a purified Muslim society? Alternatively, should the believer revolt against the deviant ruler, using violence if need be? This gives rise to an enduring debate within Salafism: is it 'primarily quietist or activist, and to what degree should it be one of these alternatives?'[2] Joas Wagemakers and Peter Mandaville offer a helpful division among contemporary Salafis

376 THE LITERATURE OF *LASHKAR-E-TAYYABA*

according to which one group comprises quietists or purists who shun political action and focus on education (*tarbiyat*).[3] A second group is of Salafi Islamists who engage in political debates and action. A third is the Salafi *jihadis* who embrace the use of violence to bring about a genuine Islamic government in Muslim countries.

There is often considerable animosity among these groups particularly as we expand our aperture to include Salafis beyond Pakistan. For example, in the scholarly debates among the *ulema* of these groups, they tend to use derogatory labels for each other that draw from early years of Islam. One set of such labels are '*Khawarij*' (alternatively neo-*Khawarij*) or '*Murji'i*' (and its variant neo-*Murji'i*). Two of the more important schisms derive from differences in opinion concerning the proper course of action towards Muslim leaders who fail to impose *shariat* and the proper conduct of *takfir* (the practice of declaring a Muslim to be a *kafir* (non-believer) and thus subject to the death penalty). Quietists may label groups who are cavalier in their application of *takfir* to be *Khawarij* or neo-*Khawarij*, referencing the early rebels in Islamic history who believed in violent rebellion against unworthy leaders. In turn, the Salafi jihadists denounce the quietists as *Murji'i* or neo-*Murji'i*, alluding to a defunct group of early Muslims who believed that no matter how horrendous a Muslim leader may be, rebellion is not permitted unless they commit *kufr* (an act of unbelief), and therefore meets their rigorous process of evaluating the facts and concomitant evidentiary standards for being declared a *kafir*. *Khawarij* literally means seceders, derived from the Arabic verb, *kharaja* (to secede or move out), while *Murji'i* literally means one who postpones or defers, derived from *irjah* (to postpone of defer).

Here, as we saw in *Hum Jihad Kyon Kar Rahen Hain*, the organization lays out its strict argument for non-violence against Muslims, defined largely as someone who has said the *kalima* (one who is *kalima-go*) and recognizes Allah as the highest authority and Muhammad as his final prophet. By understanding the organization's rigorous opposition to groups advocating strife within Pakistan, one can garner insights into the precious relationship that the state has with this group. LeT is the only group arguing for non-violence within Pakistan, even as it is a faithful executioner of the state's policies beyond Pakistan's borders.

A note about the author's style of exposition is also in order. Consistent with LeT's other ostensible scholars, Rabbani makes heavy use of direct quotation from other sources including poetry with germane themes. In some cases, he does very little synthesis of his own. The readers will recognize this habit from other materials presented in this volume. Presumably, this author, as well as authors writing for LeT, assume that this is the most authoritative manner with which to handle controversial and tendentious issues even though it does make for difficult reading.

The translated excerpts in this chapter reflect an overall small portion of the 320-page volume; however, we believe these excerpts to summarize the key insights of the text about the problems of declaring one to be an apostate. First, we include the Publisher's Note, written by Javed al-Hassan Siddiqui who was at the time of writing this note the editor of Dar-ul-Andlus. In this note, he introduces *takfir* and some of the key intellectual and practical debates surrounding it. Next, we translate the Foreword which exposits the origins of this volume, namely, a serious rift between LeT and Salafist organizations which castigate LeT for failing to practise *takfir*. This rift is evidenced by an exchange of letters between the author and a Salafi antagonist. We then translate the Introduction which seeks to describe what apostacy (*kufr*) is and how it manifests. It also lays out the rules and regulations which LeT believes should guide the practice of *takfir*. These sections critically identify the key fissures between LeT and Salafi groups which is necessary to understand the fundamental tension between the Islamic State, which embraces *takfir* liberally, and the LeT which does not. A more cynical reading of LeT's opposition to *takfir* and the often-deadly violence which accompanies it is LeT's own pro-state agenda. As previous chapters attest, LeT is a collaborator with the deep state to minimize violence within Pakistan. Here as elsewhere, we retain the organizational structures of the original.

Publisher's Note

Allah's revealed path is grounded in human prosperity, both in this world and the hereafter. The prophet said:

Religion is another name for prosperity. We [the companions] asked: Whose prosperity? The prophet said: the prosperity of Allah, His

378 THE LITERATURE OF *LASHKAR-E-TAYYABA*

book, His Prophet, the noblemen among Muslims as well as common Muslims.

(Muslim 55)

According to Islamic teachings, all humans are to be dealt with courteously, and are to be invited to Islam with affection, equanimity, and inspiring conduct.

When the prophet dispatched his companions to various tribes and regions for the purpose of proselytizing, he would advise them to 'Make (religion) easy; do not make it rigid. Give people glad tidings instead of making them resentful (through fear)' (Bukhari 69).

Islam is the religion of prosperity, peace, and tranquillity, although some mischief-makers and their misguided followers undermine the faith while posing as its advocates. They declare fellow-Muslims infidels and incite murder and mayhem. They bring a bad name to all Muslims by presenting Islam as terrifying, compassionless, and hateful through their malicious and diabolical approach to religion.

In recent decades, there has been a sharp rise in the scourge of *takfir*, that is, the declaration of certain Muslims as infidels. Numerous Islamic countries have had to deal with a growing misguided population of young and ignorant Muslims who have no exposure to the intricate crafts of religious interpretation and who know little about the ways of the early Muslims, so they interpret Islamic injunctions as they please, thereby leading the masses astray.

The early Muslims and the *Hadees* compilers have elaborated the principles that govern the sensitive matter of *takfir*. In the light of these principles, a number of important issues related to *takfir* have long been settled, such as what actions result in expulsion from Islam, when does this lead to a death sentence, who is to judge the case, and who is to carry out the execution. The entire process has been discussed in great detail. The renowned Islamic scholar and Islamic expert Al-Sheikh Abul-Hassan Mubashir Ahmed Rabbani has compiled these principles in the light of evidence from the Quran and *Hadees* into his book titled *The Issue of Takfir and its Principles*, where he elaborates how and when these principles are to be applied. May Allah accept and bless his effort and hard work. Amen.

THE PROBLEM WITH *TAKFIR* 379

This is a Dar-ul-Andlus publication. It has been proofread by Hafiz Sanaullah Khan, Hafiz Mansha Tayyab, and Hafiz Asif-al-Madni and it was composed by Muhammad bin Jaffer and Ata-ur-Rahman Tahir and Tazayyun Abu Khuzima Muhammad Shafique. Zahiruddin Babar prepared the cover.

May Allah redeem all the individuals involved in this publication and may this book guard those who read it from a malicious and dangerous practice. Amen.

Seeking prayers,

Javed al-Hassan Siddiqui
Editor: Dar-ul-Andlus
1st Zul-haj 1436

Foreword

In modern times, perfidy, which has taken many forms, threatens to destroy the Muslim *ummat* in the form of indecency, sexual freedom, exploitation of women, gender bending, fortune telling, murder, and lawlessness. However, the most dangerous and terrifying manifestation of perfidy is *takfir*, that is, the act of declaring Muslims infidels, invariably accompanied by incitement of violence, and gruesome video recordings of beheadings and pillage. Ignorant fools are swept up in this wave of terror while infidels take full advantage of the situation and employ those who appear to be pious, religious, observant, and god-fearing towards their insidious ends.

It is tragic the way people who have neither an understanding of the intricacies of faith-based jurisprudence, nor a working knowledge of the basic principles of ritual and literal hygiene, are appointed to positions of power. Many so-called *mufti*s (one who issues *fatwa*s) fall into this category. Accusing a Muslim of apostasy is serious business that has nothing to do with personal objectives, opinions, suspicion, doubt, religious identity, sectarian affiliation, etc. Such an accusation requires concrete evidence scrutinized in the light of the Quran and *Sunnat* beyond all reasonable doubt.

Apostasy can Only be Proved Through *Shariat*-Based Evidence

Sheikh-ul-Islam Imam Ibn Taymiyyah says: '(Declaring someone an) infidel is a *sharia*-based injunction and can only be proven through *shariat*-based evidence' (*Majmua al-Fatawa Ibn Taymiyyah* 87:17).

In order to declare someone an infidel, the claimant has to have mastered the Quran and *Sunnat* with an expert working knowledge of *shariat*-based injunctions, objectives, and principles, and a clear understanding of how these are to be applied to daily life, with enough compassion to accommodate the general public's general lack of religious knowledge. The claimant must not have any trace of extremism because declaring a Muslim an infidel can have devastating consequences.

Ignorant fools take the delicate matter of issuing *fatwa*s in their own hands and go about declaring Muslims to be infidels thereby threatening life and property. Declaring a Muslim an infidel without rigorously applying the principles of the Quran and *Sunnat* is nothing short of murder.

The great religious scholars, the esteemed jurists, and the expert *mufti*s have consistently warned against the perils of *takfir*.

Qazi Shokani's Warning

Qazi Qatrimani Muhammad bin Ali al-Shokani says:

Know that declaring a Muslim an infidel outside the realm of Islam is not permissible for one who has faith in Allah and the Last Day unless the evidence is clearer than the midday sun. For the authentic *Hadees* that have been passed down by the companions tell us that when someone calls another an 'infidel', one of the two is going to be at a severe loss. Similarly, Bukhari 6103 and Bukhari 6045–Muslim 61, state: Whosoever calls another innocent Muslim infidel, or Allah's enemy, will have his accusations revert back to him. According to another tradition from Bukhari: one of the two has committed *kufr*. The *Hadees* and the revelations have spoken harshly of those who are quick to practise *takfir*.

(*Al-Seel al-Jarrar* 784:3 *tuay. Dar ibn Katheer, Tiba' Awwal* 14611421 AH/2000)

Qazi Qatrimani Muhammad bin Ali al-Shokani further states:

No doubt, Allah says: when *kufr* is exposed it must be rigorously interpreted until one's heart is satisfied and one's conscience is clear. One cannot take an error of belief at face value, especially when this (error) directly contradicts Islam; even the mere performance of a *kufr* act isn't admissible as evidence when the accused has made no attempt to escape to infidel lands; also, a Muslim (witness) cannot be trusted if he testifies but does not fully comprehend (the implication of) his testimony.

(Al-Seel al-Jarrar 784:3)

In certain *Hadees*, the word *kufr* is used for specific actions: 'After me do not behave like infidels, slaughtering one another.' (Bukhari, *Kitab ul Ilm, baab al ansatlil Ilma*, 121) Qazi Yemen Muhammad bin Ali al-Shokani goes on to say:

When there is no other way to interpret (an act) and there is no other path left to take, in context of the aforementioned *Hadees*, then it is mandatory that the *Hadees* be followed exactly as they were revealed. Say: what the prophet has deemed *kufr*, is *kufr*, and those among Muslims whom the prophet termed infidels are the only ones who can be considered infidels and nobody else, except those who join the infidels. Only then will you be free from hardship. Sensitive issues are not to be dealt with hastily nor are futile efforts to be indulged by those eager to honour their faith.

(Al-Seel-al-Jarrar 784–785:3)

He goes on to say:

It is incumbent upon a Muslim to accuse another of *kufr* only when the most rigorous interpretation categorically reveals as much, after which there must be no complication in exercising this right.

(Al-Seel al-Jarrar 785:3)

According to a poet:

The young man rejects everything but his desire
Even though the truth has been revealed.

382 THE LITERATURE OF *LASHKAR-E-TAYYABA*

Imam Ghazali and the Question of Takfir

Imam Ghazali says:

Takfir should be avoided, as much as possible. No doubt, it is wrong to deny the right to life and property to those who pray facing the Ka'ba and who declare '*there is no god but Allah and Muhammad is His Messenger*.' The blood of an innocent Muslim is more important than the extermination of a thousand infidels.

> (*Al-Iqtisad fil Aitiqad, swaad* 143 *tuay, Dar al-Kutab al-Ilmiyya, Beirut*)

Imam Ghazali's words were quoted by Hafiz Ibn Hujr Asqalani in the following title: *Fataha al-Bari ba-Sharah Sahih al-Bukhari, Kitabah Istabah tal-Murtadeen, baab* 192:16, 7 *tuay. Dar-i-Tayyaba, 30012 tuay. Safiyah.*

Imam Abul Hasan Ali bin Ismail al-Ashari's Declaration of Truth

Imam Muhammad bin Ahmed bin Uthman-al-Zahbi (circa 748 AH) says:

I was amazed and perplexed by some of Ashari's writings in which he quotes Imam Baihaqi. He says: Abu Hazim al-Badi reports that he heard from Zahir bin Ahmed al-Surkhasi: When Abul Hasan al-Ashari neared his last moments in my home in Baghdad, he called to me and said: bear witness to the fact that I have never declared anyone an infidel who subscribes to the *qibla* (the sanctuary in Mecca) for they're all oriented towards the same Creator with different modes of expression.

> (*Sair Aelam al-Nubla* 88:12 *tuay*)

Abul Hasan al-Ashari was the imam of Isharah. He was one of the earliest Mu'tazilites and wrote books in support of the Mu'tazila although he later declared all such writings false.

In his final years he raised the slogan of truth and subscribed to the *Ahl-i-Sunnat* and *Ahl-e-Hadees* traditions and conceded that merely

THE PROBLEM WITH *TAKFIR*   383

facing the *qibla* while praying did not grant immunity from *takfir*, however, his followers went astray and today, they ravage the Muslim world by declaring Muslims infidels, inciting murder and bloodshed.

Sheikh al-Islam Imam Ibn Taymiyyah's Last Statement

After quoting Abul Hasan Ashari, Imam Zahbi speaks of his sheikh, Sheikh Ibn Taymiyyah:

> I have adopted this same approach; similarly, our sheikh Imam Ibn Taymiyyah would say in his last days that he does not subject any member of the *ummat* to *takfir*. The prophet said: 'No one can maintain a state of ablution (ritual purity) other than a Muslim.' Hence, whosoever maintains ritual purity and prayer is a Muslim.
>
> (References: *Masnad Ahmad* 60/37, *hay* 22378, 37:109, *hay* 22433; *Sharah ul-Sunnat* 100)

In the final conclusion, it is obvious that both Imam Zahbi and his sheikh Imam Ibn Taymiyyah did not go round declaring Muslims infidels, exercising extreme caution in such sensitive matters. Certain ignorant imams quote Imam Ibn Taymiyyah out of context and subject the general population to *takfir*, thereby distorting Islam's image. Such fools have no qualms about declaring religious scholars and practitioners infidels as well.

Declaring Religious Scholars Infidels: A Sign of Disavowal

According to Imam Ibn Taymiyyah, exercising the authority to declare religious scholars to be infidels is nothing short of a disavowal of faith. He says:

> No doubt, having ignorant individuals subject Muslim scholars to *takfir* is a severe disavowal (anti-*shariat*); the real *Khawarij* and heretics are those who declare Muslim imams infidels.
>
> (*Majmua al-Fatawa Ibn Taymiyyah* 100:35)

384 THE LITERATURE OF *LASHKAR-E-TAYYABA*

Heretics and *Khawarij* accused the earliest Muslims—those who migrated with the prophet from Mecca as well as their Medinite hosts—of *kufr*. Those who cause mischief today by practising *takfir* are the ideological descendants of these wretched souls.

It is tragic and shocking that certain segments of the *Ahl-i-Sunnat* have also succumbed to this epidemic. This issue has been touched upon by Imam Ibn Daqiq al-Ayeed and Allama Ibn al-Wazir al-Yamani.

Imam Ibn Daqiq al-Ayeed's Explanation

Imam Ibn Daqiq al-Ayeed says:

> This is an insidious trap in which certain people who subscribe to the *Sunnat* and *Hadees* are ensnared.
>
> (*Ahkam al-Ahkam Sharah Umdah tal Ahkam* 74:4; *Ithar al-Haq Al-al-Khalq Ibn al-Wazir, swaad* 386)

Allama Ibn al-Wazir Yamani's Explanation

Allama Ibn al-Wazir al-Yamani writes:

> It is astonishing how those who have no knowledge are quick to declare religious scholars infidels without any insight into the beliefs or the arguments of those they accuse.
>
> (*Ithar al Haq Al-al-Khalq, swaad* 408)

There is an extensive process of analysis and interpretation before a religious scholar can even think of declaring a Muslim an infidel; in fact, as much as possible, a Muslim's *kufr* statement ought to be amended instead of banishing him from Islam altogether.

Kufr and its Negation

Allama Badr-ul-Rasheed-ul-Hanafi states, while elaborating the position of Mullah Ali Qari Hanafi:

No doubt, the great knower of secrets (Yusuf bin Umar al-Hanafi) quotes from Al-Zakhirah: when analysing a case, if there appears to be substantial evidence for *kufr* and only a single piece of evidence that negates it, then it is incumbent upon the *mufti* to afford the accused the benefit of the doubt and give weight to the negation.

(*Al-Fazeela bil Riyaz, swaad* 136 *tuay. Dar-u-'Ula Misr*)

He goes on to say:

If the accused intends for the negation of *kufr* then he is Muslim but if he intends to indulge in *kufr* then the *mufti*'s decision will not cause him loss; he will be ordered to repent, reconsider his words, and annul his marriage.

(*Sharah al-Imam Al-al-Qari Al-al-Kitab alfaz al-kufr, swaad* 230 *tuay. Dar-al-Fazeela bil-Riyaz, swaad. Dar-ul-'Ula Misr*)

One Hundred Elements of *Kufr* and a Shred of Faith

Mufti Muhammad Abdah Misri writes:

If someone ends up making a statement that has a hundred elements of *kufr* and one affirmation of faith, then the said person will be assumed to be of the faithful instead of the infidels.

(*Al-Amaal al-Kamil* 273:3 *ba-tahqiq* Dr Muhammad Ammarah, *tuay. Beirut*)

According to the aforementioned statements by various imams and jurists, it is obvious that the practice of *takfir* requires the utmost caution and restraint, and such a practice ought to be avoided altogether. On the contrary, today, the *ummat* churns out ignorant men who recklessly go round branding people infidels from all walks of life such as politicians, soldiers, security forces, teachers, doctors, engineers, judges, and lawyers, thereby unleashing a wave of terror and mayhem.

For a long time now, those with true knowledge have tried to counter this treacherous trend through lectures and sermons. By Allah's grace, JuD has invested in the prosperity and progress of the *ummat* by disseminating knowledge and promoting unity based purely on the

386 THE LITERATURE OF *LASHKAR-E-TAYYABA*

Quran and the *Sunnat* so that we are able to distinguish Muslims from Islam's enemies and neutralize the latter's conspiracies.

When the Jews, Christians, Hindus, and infidels jump into the fray they hatch conspiracies against Muslims to create rifts and disharmony. Certain young and impressionable individuals get caught up in the lure of wealth and dollars and jewels and act as agents of the very forces out to humiliate and disrobe the *ummat*. Today, such imbecilic individuals have infiltrated our mosques, schools, and religious institutions and threaten everyone with the scourge of *takfir*.

A year and a half after our talk in Sialkot in which righteous scholars spoke out against the plague of *takfir*, a virtual book titled *Marja-tul-Asr* surfaced on the Internet. This book gave the supreme infidel USA much cause to celebrate. It also gave the Americans talking points against Pakistan in particular and the Muslim world in general. In an essay by Stephen Tankel titled 'Protecting the Homeland Against Mumbai Style Attacks and the Threat from Lashkar-e-Taiba', published in the magazine *Carnegie*, the very first page links our organization to *Marja-tul-Asr*.

Eventually, this book appeared on *Ahl-e-Hadees* websites. Vast resources were spent on getting this publication to various institutions, organizations, and individual operatives.

This book falsely links certain *shariat* injunctions to interpretations offered by various imams without seriously reckoning with the detailed explanations offered by these imams, while simply referencing their abstracts. Examples of this will be found below, Allah-willing.

For example: The Quranic scholar Hafiz Salahuddin Yusuf was among the many *Ahl-e-Hadees* scholars referenced in this magazine shown to have declared various Pakistani leaders infidels. Intent on hearing his side of the story, the author of this manuscript contacted Hafiz Salahuddin with a questionnaire. Below, is the full text of the Quranic scholar's detailed response. This should help expose the duplicity and ignorance of the compilers of *Marja-tul-Asr*.

Inquiry

From Abul Hassan Mubashir Ahmed Rabbani to the Respected Sheikh Hafiz Salahuddin Yusuf!

Assalam-u-Alaikum!

A book by the title of *Marja-tul-Asr*, compiled by an ignoramus, has been posted to various *Ahl-e-Hadees* platforms and *madaris*. On page 76, after establishing the fact that many Pakistani scholars view the current leadership of the country as heretical, the author goes on to state:

> Similarly, the renowned *Ahl-e-Hadees* scholar and Quran interpreter, Hafiz Salahuddin Yusuf, editor at the institute of research and compilation at Dar-ul-Islam Lahore also declares our current leaders heretics.

In the margin, the above statement is accompanied by references to *Riyaz-us-Saliheen* (Urdu 513/2) *Tiba' Dar-ul-Islam*, new edition. Respected Sheikh!

1. Do you actually believe that Pakistani leaders, as well as leaders of other Muslim countries, are heretics and infidels?
2. As heretics and infidels do they deserve to be executed?
3. What is your opinion about the scholars who declare these leaders sinful, insidious, and insincere, but refuse to label them infidels?

The people behind this publication spread terror and violence across the land by branding individuals infidels. One hopes you will offer a detailed response by way of guiding the Muslim *ummat*. May Allah protect you and include you among those closest to Him. Amen!

Mubashir Ahmed Rabbani

25 Rajab 1436 AH

15 May 2015

From Quran interpreter Sheikh Hafiz Salahuddin Yusuf: A Word on the Leaders of Muslim States in Response to an Inquiry

ANSWER:

The Quran reproaches both infidels as well as sinful Muslims and both are explicitly warned in various parts of the scripture. Obviously, the

388 THE LITERATURE OF *LASHKAR-E-TAYYABA*

meanings vary according to the context; hence, even when the same terms are used for infidels and Muslims their contexts are different.

Similarly, *Hadees* warn both Muslims and infidels of impending hellfire for all kinds of actions, however, the warnings are not identical. Muslims are warned of a temporary punishment while infidels and heathens are given news of eternal damnation, even though the words used for the two groups are the same.

This subtle difference in meaning can be detected by interpreting the tone, the context, and the supporting evidence. As long as one is clear-headed and unbiased, it is easy to understand the meaning and context of every warning issued in the Quran and by the prophet.

The Quran uses the terms 'debauched' and 'oppressive' for polytheism as well as for various other sins, however, a Muslim cannot be declared an infidel simply by virtue of the fact that he is debauched or oppressive, even though Allah has clearly used these words in context of polytheists.

The purpose of this brief preamble is to elaborate on the issue of *takfir*, an issue that plagues our world today. Certain organized youths have displayed alarming rigidity when it comes to this issue. On the one hand, this rigidity can be seen as a manifestation of their passion and zeal for Islam but on the other hand it embodies sanctimony and arrogance. Where the former is worth appreciating, it is important to highlight and condemn the latter.

The 'straight path' is one of moderation, that is, remain steadfast in your faith in the truth of Islam's teachings and be a living manifestation of Islamic learning. Do not look down upon those who appear to be weak in faith and action; guide these people with the strength of your character. Considering the fact that even prophets were not appointed as their people's keepers, how can an ordinary Muslim take responsibility for the faith of those around him or pass judgement on others based on his extremist inclinations.

Casually issuing *fatwas* is socially and politically damaging. From a practical point of view, the current situation is bleak as the masses are generally unversed in Islamic teachings and the ones who have knowledge lack the will to act.

Exceptions notwithstanding, there is a similar crisis with the country's leadership. Allah has bestowed our leaders with power and resources, yet

THE PROBLEM WITH *TAKFIR* 389

they choose to ignore Allah's injunctions and instead import and impose foreign systems.

Based on the verses above, certain youths tend to declare the leaders of various Muslim countries infidels and consequently take on the dangerous perspectives highlighted in the introduction.

Even if we accept the extremist position, the question remains: how is the Muslim population supposed to live? Most Muslims do not live their lives according to the revelations. If we start trying every other person for being an infidel, it's not difficult to imagine the kind of havoc this will cause.

It is for this very reason that the *shariat* insists that if the leaders of a Muslim population defy Allah's commands and are cruel and oppressive, the common folk are to endure the injustice without rebelling. It is only when leaders explicitly encourage *kufr* that action is required, however, it is important to realize that moral shortcomings are not the same as explicitly encouraging *kufr*. It is only when someone explicitly states that they do not believe in the finality of the prophet, or rejects the Quran, prayer, and fasting altogether, that they can be called an infidel and banished from Islam.

Even though the current Muslim leadership is guilty of not applying Islamic laws, and leading the masses away from Islam, their reckoning is with Allah and it is not for us to declare them worthy of death.

It is important for Muslims to call out un-Islamic impulses, while guiding those who have gone astray. Our leaders deserve our criticism the way a Muslim deserves to be corrected by his fellow Muslim, that is, in the spirit of good will and prosperity, but beyond that, guidance is in the hands of Allah. I have elaborated upon this in my interpretation of select *Hadees*, taken from *Riyaz-us-Saliheen*, on the subject of leadership. For brevity's sake, only a few of these *Hadees* are presented below.

A third insight among the insights of one *Hadees*:

A solution has also been offered for the leadership's shortcomings. This does not involve rebellion or processions or protests; on the contrary, in administrative matters, they (leaders) ought to be obeyed, while turning to Allah for help. Sadly, since Western democracy infiltrated Islamic countries, their entire structure has crumbled; peace and stability demand that the state be shielded from mavericks and rebels. Certain monarchies manage this, which is why they experience relative peace and stability...

390 THE LITERATURE OF *LASHKAR-E-TAYYABA*

however, wherever democracy has taken root, the stability of the state is in serious jeopardy. Consequently, most local resources are wasted on managing political unrest, which steadily erodes peace and stability.

(*Riyaz us-Saliheen Mutarajjam, Jild Awwal, swaad* 305–306)

Another insight from a different *Hadees*:

Until a ruler outright champions *kufr* and denies the validity of the chief tenets of Islam such as prayer, any kind of rebellion against him is forbidden, for rebellion has limited benefit and devastating consequences.

(*Jild Awwal, swaad* 609)

The first benefits of another hadith should be discussed:

This *Hadees* demands submission to Muslim rulers while explicitly drawing comparisons between rebellion and *kufr*; before Islam following a single *emir* was considered a sign of weakness and humiliation. Islam ended this attitude and replaced it with disciplined obedience.

(*Jild Awwal, swaad* 211)

The insights of another *Hadees*:

1. The ruler and the ruled have their respective obligations; everyone must bear the burden of his own transgressions on the Day of Judgement, however, if a ruler falters in his obligation, this does not warrant a similar reaction by the public by way of defiance. Two wrongs do not make a right and this attitude is sure to breed further unrest.
2. Instead of rioting and rebelling, in the interest of public order, it is far better to highlight and criticize within the limits of the law for it is better to follow the example of the esteemed one whose path was not of rebellion or desertion.

The insights of another *Hadees*:

1. To disobey and defy a king is to disrespect and condemn him for defiance compromises a ruler's authority. Peace and stability demand

THE PROBLEM WITH *TAKFIR*   391

the explicit rule of law to keep anti-state and lawless elements of society in check. Anyhow, for the greater good, Muslims have been advised to obey their rulers even if the latter prove to be unjust, or indifferent, or cruel, as long as they do not openly encourage *kufr* and as long as they observe prayer and the other key tenets of Islam.

2. This Islamic injunction directly contradicts the principles of Western democracy wherein opposition is essential to the system. The opposition dedicates itself entirely to criticizing the government and inciting people against it to sabotage and humiliate the administration. Islam has no conception of government and opposition; all Muslims belong to the same *ummat* and are in the same ship, with the same objectives and goals. Despite the shortcomings and failures of the government, it is criminal to incite people against the establishment. Similarly, wasting billions of rupees every few years on elections in which political workers go from door to door sowing the seeds of discord and scandal is also in contradiction to Islamic teachings. Islam does not limit the tenure of a ruler; neither does it encourage the rapid dismissal and replacement of existing leaders. The same wisdom calls for the people to be obedient and patient in the face of their leader's shortcomings so he may have as much time as he needs to improve the condition of his people. If only the masses could be freed from the snare of Western democracy that they may set up an indigenous system of government informed by Islamic values.

It is not hard to guess this author's views on the current leadership in Pakistan. Now consider the evidence offered to prove that our leaders are heretics. How can Islam tolerate the uninhibited mixing of the genders that is prevalent in the West and that is televised in Islamic countries? Rulers influenced by the West allow this filth and debauchery in the name of 'culture'. May Allah free Islamic lands of such heretical rulers.

Obviously, in the statement above, 'heretic' has been used figuratively instead of as a *fatwa*. It denotes the state of mind of leaders influenced by the West; sadly, this state of mind is prevalent in the electronic and print media where various pundits, columnists, and intellectual elites embody this kind of thinking. Heretical thinking is not the same as being a heretic worthy of death. This sort of criticism has been elaborated upon already.

392 THE LITERATURE OF *LASHKAR-E-TAYYABA*

For instance, the downfall of Muslims is often ascribed to the prevalence of hypocrisy, but this hypocrisy is not the hypocrisy punishable in the Quran.

The following Quranic verse further elaborates this point:

And whoso disobeyeth Allah and His messenger and transgresseth His limits, He will make him enter Fire, where such will dwell forever; his will be a shameful doom.

(Surat an-Nisa 4:14)*

How terrible is the punishment for disobedience as revealed in the verse above. It is worth noting the context in which this verse was revealed; it comes after a description of the laws governing inheritance, referred to as '*hudood-Allah*', whose breach can lead to eternal damnation.

Consider the fact that most Muslims completely ignore the laws of inheritance, particularly in how they filch women of their rightful share. Should all those who ignore this law be declared infidels and sent to hell or should we let Allah decide their fate ... ?

The case of Muslim rulers behaving un-Islamically is the same. Allah will judge these rulers in the afterlife. In this life, we can criticize and advise but we have no authority to judge their faith and doing so would only serve to spread fear and terror across the land.

Salahuddin Yusuf
Rajab al-Marjab. May 2015

The brief response reproduced above proves that the ignorant authors of *Marja-tul-Asr* will leave no stone unturned when slandering the *Ahl-e-Hadees* scholars in their propaganda. Allah-willing, when our detailed publication reaches the world, it will expose the liars while readers, *mujahideen*, and proselytizers will gain clarity regarding the insidious objectives of those engaged in *takfir*.

For now, a chapter from this publication, based on the principles listed below, is presented:

The word *kufr* has various meanings and implications; sometimes it is used to denote 'Great *Kufr*' meaning those actions or words that banish a Muslim from the *ummat*; other times it is used to refer to the faithlessness and sinfulness of Muslims who have gone astray. Similarly, the word kufr is also used to reference barbarity, polytheism, and depravity; the meaning is by no means constant. The Quran briefly deals with the implications of *kufr* and proceeds to identify defining features of *kufr* in infidels, such as heresy, polytheism, religious persecution, and antagonism towards Allah, the prophet, and the Muslim *ummat*.

Similarly, the protocol that must be employed before declaring a Muslim an infidel has also been outlined in light of the Quran, the *Sunnat*, and exegeses by leading imams. All this to show that declaring a Muslim an infidel is serious and dangerous business that requires the utmost caution, and that issuing *fatwas* is a serious responsibility, not a whimsical exercise.

All references in this book have been cross-checked with the Quran. *Jamia Islamia Medina Tayyaba*'s Sheikh Ibrahim bin Emir al-Rahili's book *Al-Takfir o Zawabita* has been consulted extensively. May Allah bless him for all the effort he put into his work on *takfir*.

By Allah's grace, we continue our work on *Marja-tul-Asr*, which will be made available to readers as soon as it is completed.

Delays in publication have been caused by the author's ill health.

My colleagues Abu Darda Saeed al-Rahman and Abu Usama 'Abdul Hameed have helped me in producing this manuscript. My protégé Rasheed Hafiz Uthman Shafiq has also been extremely helpful in various phases of production. The author is profoundly grateful to all brothers who aided this publication in any way.

May Allah make this book a source of guidance and inspiration for readers, and a cause of redemption and salvation for its author in the afterlife. Amen!

Abul Hassan Mubashir Rabbani
Raees Markaz al-Hassan 2-P, 88 Sabzazar Scheme. Multan Rd, Lahore

Introduction

According to the Quran and *Sunnat* faith comprises three elements: belief, speech, and action. In the absence of sincere heartfelt belief, one cannot enter the realm of Islam: the Jews knew about the prophet's status, Harqal and Abu Talib testified to his honesty and truthfulness, even the hypocrites appeared to follow the prophet's commands... however, none of them can be considered Muslim. The hypocrites lacked sincere belief, the

394 THE LITERATURE OF *LASHKAR-E-TAYYABA*

infidels refused to submit, and the sinners acted in defiance. Three features are absolutely essential to be a Muslim. Once a person recites the *kalima* (declaration of the oneness of Allah and the prophet's status as messenger) he or she becomes Muslim. After reciting the *kalima* the convert must make arrangements for prayer, fasting, pilgrimage, and charity. Pilgrimage and charity depend on one's resources.

The following five rituals form the foundation of Islam. According to Abdullah bin Umar, the prophet said:

> Islam is founded upon five pillars: bearing witness that there is no god but Allah and Muhammad is His Messenger, prayer, charity, pilgrimage, and fasting.

One becomes a Muslim when Islam's radiance overwhelms the heart and inspires one to act accordingly. Faith is founded on six elements, as explained in the *Hadees-i-Gabriel* below. The angel Gabriel asked the prophet:

> Tell me about faith. He (the prophet) said: belief in Allah, His angels, His scriptures, His messengers, in the Last Day, and in the fact that all good and bad is predestined.
> (Muslim, *Kitab al-Iman, Baab Biyan al-Iman wal-Islam wal-Ihsan...* 8)

Faith is a person's most valuable possession. Muslims are obligated to guard and nurture it for just like one's clothes can wear away with time, faith, too, can begin to tear at the seams.

Reviving Faith

Abdullah bin Umro bin al-'Aas reports that the prophet said: 'Indeed, faith can stale the way old fabrics wear away; pray to Allah for your faith to remain restored.' As this *Hadees* points out, faith is not a constant. It varies, and just like the clothes one wears, it can fade or tear. It can evolve into something sublime, but it can also crumble to its most basic form, and at times it can disappear altogether.

Therefore, it is important to restore one's faith continually. This is why the prophet taught us how to ask Allah to restore our faith. Faith is one's most precious possession because not everyone is blessed with this gift; Allah only extends His most cherished and beloved individuals this favour. On the other hand, His material blessings are more universally distributed irrespective of one's relationship with Him.

Religion Is Only Given to Those Allah Loves

Abdullah bin Masood reports the prophet said:

> Undoubtedly, Allah has distributed among you a sense of uprightness. He has distributed among you your livelihoods; no doubt, Allah offers the world as a gift to those whom He loves as well as to those whom He does not love, but faith is only given to those whom He loves.

As it stands, faith is invaluable, its protection is obligatory, and on the Last Day, redemption will only come to those who have faith for without it, all of one's good deeds are laid to waste.
Allah states:

> Then whoso doeth good works and is a believer, there will be no rejection of his effort. Lo! We record (it) for him.
> (*Surat al-Anbiya* 21:94)

It goes to show that Allah only values piety when performed with Him in mind; as for those actions performed without faith ...

> A similitude of those who do not believe in their Lord: Their works are as ashes, which the wind bloweth hard upon a stormy day. They have no control of aught that they have earned. That is the extreme failure.
> (*Surat Ibrahim* 14:18)

Kufr can neutralize all of one's good deeds, rendering them worthless. On the Day of Judgement, they will be like a mound of ash that can blow away with the wind. Something as precious as faith needs to be guarded from *kufr*, polytheism, and heresy, and we should strive to be vigilant about every threat to our faith in order to protect ourselves.

Syedna Huzaifa bin Yaman frequently asked the prophet about evil and perfidy while the other companions were more interested in issues of faith and the deeds that guarantee them paradise. Huzaifa, however, wanted to know how best to guard himself.

With this thought in mind, this manuscript presents the consequences of *kufr* so readers are equipped with the information needed to guard their faith. Further, it will lay out certain rules and principles that must be kept in mind while defending one's faith. May Allah grant us the capacity to comprehend matters of faith, and honour its obligations; may He protect us from *kufr* and polytheism and keep us on the path of Oneness in the way of our prophet. Amen.

The Essence of *Kufr*

Literally, '*kufr*' means to cover up or conceal. In his book *Alfaz-ul-Mutradifa*, Al-Rumani describes the word *kufr* as concealing or covering up. Allama Muhammad bin Abi Bakr al-Qadir al-Razi states that: 'Imam Razi states that *kufr* is the opposite of faith, in how it denies Allah. It has also been defined as the opposite of gratitude, in how it rejects Allah's blessings'. Allama Abul Hussein Ahmed bin Faris bin Zakriya states that *kufr* means to conceal or cover up, which is why the word is also used for farmers since they conceal seeds in the earth, as is stated in the Quran:

> And this word is the opposite of faith for the infidel conceals the truth; similarly, denying blessings is also a kind of covering up.
>
> (*Surat al-Hadid* 20)[4]

Imam Raghib Asfahani has made similar statements in his book *Al-Mufridat Fi Gharib-ul-Quran*.

Summary
In essence, *kufr* is denial, and stands in opposition to faith; it means denying the truth of Islam. Additionally, *kufr* is also understood in opposition to gratitude considering the word *shukr* means 'something being revealed'. Hence, *kufr* means to conceal, and *kuffara* is to conceal the deleterious consequences of wrongdoing.

THE PROBLEM WITH *TAKFIR* 397

It should be kept in mind that every non-Muslim is a *kafir* save those who have not yet been exposed to the word of Allah. Anyone who has been invited to the truth, and despite all evidence denies it, and then despite every kind of effort, refuses to reconsider, can safely be called a *kafir* or an infidel. To deny the truth once it has been made manifest is *kufr*. Those who have not been exposed to the truth are still on the wrong path but they cannot be called *kafir*; they are known as *zalimeen* or 'those who are astray'.

Potential Manifestations of Kufr

Kufr is essentially defined in opposition to faith, hence *kufr* is manifest terms of faith. Faith is based on three non-negotiable factors: The sincere acceptance of faith, the declaration of this acceptance, and the alignment one's actions accordingly. Imam Bukhari has the following to say about faith:

> Faith is the term used for speech and action, and it can grow strong as well as atrophy.
> (Bukhari, *Kitab-ul-Iman, ma' fatah ul bari* 93:1 *tuay. Dar-i-Tayyaba*)

By speech is meant the declaration of faith, and by action is meant the introduction of prayer and moderation into one's life.

Hafiz Ibn Hujr-al-Asqalani says that the early generations of Muslims said faith is moderation, as well as a declaration, as well as the embodiment of action; by the latter he meant faith demands action.

Imam Hussein bin Masood al-Baghvi says:

> The companions, and the early generations of Muslims concur that action is a part of faith, and that faith is speech, action, and belief. Faith is strengthened by submission and weakened by defiance. The Quran speaks of the strengthening of faith, while there are *Hadees* that talk of the weakness of faith in describing female characteristics.

All scholars of *Ahl-e-Hadees wal-Sunnat* define faith as having three essential non-negotiable elements. Similarly, *kufr* also has three corresponding features: 1. *Kufr* belief; 2. *Kufr* speech; and 3. *Kufr* action.

398 THE LITERATURE OF *LASHKAR-E-TAYYABA*

1. *Kufr* Belief

The belief that Allah can be matched in His divinity or authority. Following are a few examples:

1. Belief that Allah and His Prophet's commands are not worth following and the complete denial of their authority.
2. While not outright denying Allah and His Prophet's commands, giving equal or more weight to someone else's word, or denying certain aspects of Allah and His Prophet's message.
3. Believing that someone other than Allah and His Prophet can speak for Allah and His Prophet.
4. Belief that there is room for any authority other than Allah's and His Prophet's.
5. Belief that there is any state law that supersedes Allah's *shariat*, particularly in settling conflicts and disputes.
6. Belief that local laws and customs have more weight than the Quran and *Hadees*, particularly while resolving disputes.

Summary
Kufr belief is the notion that there is any shortcoming in Allah or the prophet, or that they are somehow connected to any kind of belief system that directly contradicts Islamic teachings, such as the belief that angels are Allah's daughters, or the belief that Allah's characteristics are like those of ordinary humans, etc.

2. *Kufr* Speech

Kufr speech comprises slandering Allah, the prophet, the Quran, angels, Islam, or mocking any of the aforementioned regardless of one's intention. The Quran states:

> And if thou ask them (O Muhammad) they will say: We did but talk and jest. Say: was it at Allah and His revelations and His Messenger that ye did scoff?
>
> (*Surat at-Tawbah* 9:65)

THE PROBLEM WITH *TAKFIR* **399**

Make no excuse. Ye have disbelieved after your (confession of) belief. If We forgive a party of you, a party of you We shall punish because they have been guilty.

(Surat at-Tawbah 9:66)

These verses were specifically aimed at the hypocrites who would make fun of the Quran and at times even use inappropriate words for the prophet. When questioned about their behaviour they denied the charge and said all they were doing was having a bit of fun. Allah snubs them for this.

3. *Kufr* Action

Kufr actions include prostrating before an idol, or heavenly bodies, or graves; in other words, all those actions that blatantly contradict the Quran and the authentic *Hadees*. The performance of any action that the Quran or *Hadees* forbid is '*kufr* action'.

Imam Ibn al-Qim and types of *Kufr*

Sheikh Al-Bani cites Imam Ibn al-Qim:

> There are two types of *kufr*: *kufr* action and *kufr* belief. *Kufr* actions directly contradict faith, for instance bowing before an idol, desecrating the Quran, murdering the prophet or cursing him—these actions directly contradict faith, while disobeying Allah's commands or failing to maintain prayer are also *kufr* action.

In another place he states:

> There are two types of *kufr*: of devotion and action. The heart is the palace of devotion while the palace of *kufr* action is the body.
>
> *(Silsila al-Ahadith al-Sahih* 112:6, *Al-Qism al-Awwal)*

Certain ignorant individuals have accused Sheikh Al-Bani, as well as the proselytizing subgroup of the Sahih Salafi tradition, of *irja* (allowing

400　THE LITERATURE OF *LASHKAR-E-TAYYABA*

everyone into the fold of Islam unconditionally), while the *Khawarij* (those who practise *takfir* wantonly), have always accused the *Ahl-i-Sunnat Ahl-e-Hadees* of being *Murjiya* (all-inclusive).

Why Khawarij Accuse Ahl-i-Sunnat of Being Murjiya

Imam Harb bin Ismail Al-Karmani says:

> *Khawarij* accuse *Ahl-i-Sunnat* of being *Murjiya* but the *Khawarij* lie; in fact, it is the *Khawarij* who are *Murjiya* for they believe they are on the path of truth while everyone opposed to them is an infidel.
>
> (*Al-Sunnat Raqam* 117 *swaad* 64)

NOTE: Certain sects that are misguided, such as *Murjiya*, believe that faith solely means heartfelt belief and the declaration thereof; according to them, *kufr* occurs only in the realm of belief. This is wrong! According to this logic, even Pharaoh cannot be termed an infidel considering he never denied Allah's lordship and godliness and only disobeyed His command.

Takfir: Rules and Regulations

Islam, as a religion, is in harmony with nature. Every human is born into Islam, and every person's natural inclination is towards it. Every person who says, 'there is no god but Allah and Muhammad is His Messenger' is Muslim. Such a person cannot be declared an infidel without concrete evidence. If such a person fulfils the conditions of *kufr*, then he or she is no longer in the realm of Islam. The great sheikh, Imam Ibn Taymiyyah has elaborated upon this in his *fatwa*s. At one point he says:

> When a person recites the *kalima* of *kufr*, and is aware of what he says, then, if what he says has weight and intentionality and agency, then such a person is worthy of *takfir*.
>
> (*Majmua al-Fatawa* 14:118)

THE PROBLEM WITH *TAKFIR*   401

At this point, Imam Ibn Taymiyyah delineates three elements:

Ya'lam: meaning the accused is fully aware of what he says and is not ignorant regarding the content of his speech for ignorance negates *kufr*.

Mukhtar: meaning agency, that is, the person is not acting under duress of any kind, for duress negates *kufr*.

Qasid: the person must intend to utter the words spoken, in that his speech is not the result of a mistake or an error.

In the above quotation, Imam Ibn Taymiyyah notes that knowledge (of what is being said) is essential, for ignorance negates the process of *takfir* altogether. Faith demands knowledge of what is being believed. If one is unaware of various aspects of faith and ends up contradicting them in ignorance, then there is no room for *takfir*. Various scholars and jurists established this principle prior to the great sheikh. Below is one example:

> Sawaid bin Saeed al-Harwi reports that when Imam Sufyan bin Ayeena was asked about *irja'* (the conviction that a believer cannot sin) he said: the *Murjiya* (those who subscribe to *irja'*) state that faith is limited to a speech act (a declaration) but we say faith includes declaration as well as action. *Murjiya* claim that a person who bears witness to the oneness of Allah will automatically go to paradise even as he shirks his religious obligations, as long as he is self-aware; they claim that shirking religious duty, much like indulging in what is forbidden, is a mere sin. However, this is not the same; indulging in what is forbidden, knowing full well it is forbidden, is defiance. And to consciously shirk religious duty is *kufr*.
> (*Kitab al-Sunnat tul Abdullah bin Ahmad ibn Hanbal, Raqam* 722; *ba-tahqiq abi Abdullah Adil Aal Hamdan, hay 745, 1:347–348; Ba-tahqiq* Dr Muhammad bin Saeed al-Qahtani)

This shows that if duties and obligations are avoided out of ignorance, *kufr* cannot be established. Imam Ibn Qadamah al-Muqaddisi has the following to say about skipping prayers:

> The person who skips prayer because he denies it is obligatory is considered to have committed *kufr* as long as such a person is not ignorant

402 THE LITERATURE OF *LASHKAR-E-TAYYABA*

about the truth. If he comes from a tribe that does not recognize the importance of prayer, being new to the faith or due to geographical distance from the lands of Islam, then such a person cannot be accused of being an infidel. Such a person will need to be shown the importance of prayer based on concrete evidence. However, if after all the evidence and explanations this person continues to deny the obligation of prayer, he will rightfully be called an infidel.

> (*Al-Mughni* 275:12 *Raqam al Masla, al-masla* 1540
> *tuay. Hijr-al-Qahira al-Mughni Wailiya al-Sharah al-Kabeer:*
> 98–99:12 *tuay. Dar al-Hadees al-Qahirah*)

Imam Ibn Taymiyyah's statement is based on the Quran and *Sunnat* and he has presented evidence for this in his compilation of *fatwa*s (406–413:11).

The second condition for *kufr* is agency. When a person says or does something *kufr*, it is crucial to make sure this person is in complete control of his of speech and actions to make sure he is not acting under duress of any kind. One can only be subjected to *takfir* when there is complete agency without any sort of compulsion. Allah states in the Quran:

> Whoso disbelieveth in Allah after his belief save him who is forced thereto and whose heart is still content with Faith but whoso findeth ease in disbelief: On them is wrath from Allah. Theirs will be an awful doom.
>
> (*Surat al-Nahl* 16:106)

Hence, a person who is forced to act or speak *kufr* cannot be accused of being an infidel.

The third condition that must be met for *takfir* is intentionality; the accused must have behaved or spoken with the intention of committing *kufr* and not as a result of a mistake or an error in judgement. To be declared an infidel, establishing intent is imperative. Allah says:

> Proclaim their real parentage. That will be more equitable in the sight of Allah. And if ye know not their fathers, then (they are) your brethren in the faith, and your clients. And there is no sin for you in the mistakes that ye make unintentionally, but what your hearts purpose (that will be a sin for you). Allah is Forgiving, Merciful.
>
> (*Surat al-Azhab* 33:5)

THE PROBLEM WITH *TAKFIR*   403

There is plenty of evidence in support of the above regulations that will be revealed in good time.

Imam Ibn Taymiyyah says:

> No doubt, I maintain that Allah has forgiven the sins of the *ummat*, and this forgiveness applies in general to speech and action. The older generations of Muslims had a number of disagreements over this issue but despite their differences of opinion they never accused one another of *kufr* or disobedience.
>
> (*Majmua al-Fatawa* 229:3)

Errors in judgement negate *takfir*. A number of other negations have also been outlined, and as long as a person embodies any one of these, he cannot be termed an infidel.

It is imperative to weigh the evidence before labelling a Muslim an infidel. One cannot rely on rumour, hearsay, scandal, or suspicion. Allah says:

> O ye who believe! When ye go forth (to fight) in the way of Allah, be careful to discriminate, and say not unto one who offereth you peace: 'Thou are not a believer'; seeking the chance profits of this life (so that ye may despoil him). With Allah are plenteous spoils. Even thus (as he now is) were ye before; but Allah hath since then been gracious unto you. Therefore take care to discriminate. Allah is ever informed of what ye do.
>
> (*Surat an-Nisa* 4:94)

Imam al-Mufasirin Muhammad bin Jareer Tabri says:

> Do not be hasty in executing the one whose Islam has been tarnished before you. One hopes Allah blesses him with Islam the way He favoured you with Islam, and guides him with faith the way He has guided you.
>
> (*Tafseer al-Tabari* 352:7 *tuay. Dar Aalam ul Kutab*, *ba-Tahqiq* Dr Abdullah)

Sheikh Muhammad bin Abdul-Wahab says:

> Once a man declares his faith in Islam, then restraint is obligatory, unless this person explicitly opposes Islam. Allah says: 'O ye who believe!

404 THE LITERATURE OF *LASHKAR-E-TAYYABA*

When ye go forth (to fight) in the way of Allah, be careful to discriminate'; that is, be discerning. The verse proves that restraint should be exercised before such a person is declared an infidel and it is obligatory to be as thorough as possible in weighing the matter.

(Kashf al Shubhat, majmua tal tawheed, swaad 231
tiba' Ba-Amral Sheikh Muhammad al-Sabikan)

The prophet said:

I have been commanded to slaughter people until they declare 'there is no god but Allah'. When a person says 'there is no god but Allah' his life and property are safe from me. The matter of his faith is for Allah to decide.

(Bukhari, *Kitab al-Jihad wal Sair, Baab Dua,
Ilal Islam o Nubuwwa...* 4946)

Various authentic *Hadees* testify to the sanctity of a Muslim's life, property, and dignity; they can be found in Al-Sheikh Muhammad Yusuf Rabbani's *The Sanctity of Muslims and the Issue of Takfir.*

The one who has uttered the *kalima* can only be subjected to *takfir* after all the conditions have been met and all evidence pointing to the contrary has been negated. How can someone who is ignorant about Islam apply the faith accurately and according to its injunctions? Consider Bukhari's *Hadees*:

Every child is born into Islam but is then raised by parents as Jewish, Christian, or polytheist. Islam is natural and constant; *kufr* is imposed and arbitrary.

(Bukhari 1358)

Usama bin Zayd reports a *Hadees* in which he was sent with a battalion to attack a branch of the Jahina tribe. We attacked them at dawn and defeated them. At one point an *ansar* (Medinite hosts of the Meccan migrants) and I ambushed an enemy combatant and we were about to kill him when he recited the *kalima*. The *ansar* withdrew but I proceeded to slaughter the man. Upon our return the prophet heard about this incident and said: 'Oh Usama, you murdered him after he recited the *kalima*?'

THE PROBLEM WITH *TAKFIR*   405

I said: 'Oh prophet of Allah, he merely recited (the *kalima*) to save his life.' The prophet again said: 'Oh Usama, you murdered him after he recited the *kalima*?' The prophet kept saying this over and over again and I wished I had not converted to Islam before this incident (Bukhari, *Kitab al-Diyyat*).

According to an authentic Muslim *Hadees*:

> On the Day of Judgement when the *kalima* will be heard, what will you do?' The prophet kept repeating this question.

Similarly, when the prophet sent Khalid bin Waleed to the Banu Juzayma and he invited them to Islam, they were unable to enunciate their submission accurately upon which Khalid bin Waleed cried 'we are *sabi*, we are *sabi*!' and started slaughtering and imprisoning them. Khalid bin Waleed handed each one of us a prisoner and then, one day, he commanded us to kill our captive. Abdullah bin Umar retorted: 'By Allah! I will not murder my prisoner, and neither will my comrades!' The matter was taken to the Prophet who raised his hands to the heavens and twice declared: 'Oh Allah! I am not responsible for what Khalid has done.' (Bukhari, *Kitab al-Maghazi, Baab Ba'ith Khalid bin Waleed*).

Imam Khatabi says:

> The prophet objected to the fact that there was no investigation into the causes behind Khalid's actions and the meaning of his statement 'we are *sabi*'.
>
> (*Fatah al-Bari* 472:9 *tuay. Dar-i-Tayyaba*; *Neez daikhain Aylam al-Sunan* 293:2 *tuay. Dar-i-Tayyaba*; *Neez Daikhain Aylam al-Sunan* 293;2 *tuay. Dar-ul-Kutab-ul Ilmiyya*)

The truth of the matter is that in those days '*sabi*' was used to refer to anyone who left his religion for another. The infidels of Mecca would slander the prophet and his companions regularly by calling them *sabi*. The Banu Juzayma were professing their faith in Islam by saying 'we are *sabi*' but Khalid bin Waleed had them slaughtered and imprisoned; the Prophet strongly condemned this. Thus, it is seen that Islam places great value on the sanctity of a Muslim's life. When a person enters Islam, by default, he ought to be considered a true Muslim unless rigorously

406 THE LITERATURE OF *LASHKAR-E-TAYYABA*

proven otherwise through due legal *shariat* processes. Imam Muhammad bin Ishaq al-Maroof babin Mandah al-'Abdi al-Isbahani comments on the aforementioned *Hadees* reported by Usama bin Zayd with the following statement: 'the fact that reciting the *kalima* forbids murder' (*Kitab al-Iman, swaad 73 tuay. Dar-ul-Kutab-ul Ilmiyya*).

Hence, the one who has recited the *kalima* has protected his life, property, and dignity. This protection can only be revoked through the *shariat*. The principles of *takfir* distinguish between labelling words, actions, and beliefs *kufr* and labelling a person responsible for these words, actions, and beliefs, a *kafir*. There is plenty of evidence for this. Generalized *kufr* (*kufr-i-matlaq*) identification is a form of proselytization but even the most learned scholars avoid *takfir* of the specific (*kufr-i-mu'ayyen*). Allah says:

They surely disbelieve who say: Lo! Allah is the Messiah, son of Mary.

(*Surat al-Ma'idah* 5:72)

They surely disbelieve who say: Lo! Allah is the third of three.

(*Surat al-Ma'idah* 5:73)

Various other verses in the Quran talk of general *kufr*, that is, he who says Allah is the son of Mary or that Allah is the third of three. Such a person is categorically an infidel. In other words, he who is prone to altering the words in the Quran or bowing before anyone other than Allah is an infidel.

This kind of *takfir* does not target an individual or a group; in our publication titled *Kalima Go Mushrik* (*Polytheists Who Recite the* Kalima) we have not labelled any specific person or group polytheistic. Rather, this book lays out the various manifestations of polytheism and warns that whosoever indulges in these will not be protected by his *kalima* recitation unless he repents before his demise.

The following verse from the Quran could be considered *takfir* about a specific group or person.

Lo! Thamud disbelieved in their Lord.

(*Surat al-Had* 11:68)

THE PROBLEM WITH *TAKFIR* 407

In this verse Allah specifically calls out Thamud for being infidels. Many ignorant and unintelligent people make the mistake of starting out with general *takfir* but then end up slandering specific individuals. Imam Ibn Taymiyyah says:

> Investigation into this matter reveals that often times words uttered may be *kufr* in nature, such as when Juhayma said that Allah does not speak and will not be seen on the Last Day, but many people seem ignorant of the fact that in such a situation it is the statement and its content that are called out for being *kufr*, in the tradition of the early Muslims who would say that anyone who believes the Quran to be a species, or that Allah will not be visible on the Last Day, is an infidel. However, an individual cannot be subjected to *takfir* until and unless there is concrete evidence against him.

Similarly, Sheikh Muhammad bin Abdul Wahab writes:

> The issues with specific *takfir* are well known: when someone in general says something *kufr*, it is understood that the person who uttered the words is an infidel, however a specific individual cannot be labelled an infidel until there is concrete evidence.
>
> (*Al-Darr-a-ral Sunniya* 244:8 *Ba-Hawala tal Takfir wa-Zawabita, Sheikh Ibrahim bin Emir al-Rahili, swaad* 119)

The purpose of this brief explanation is to highlight the difference between general and specific *takfir* so when subjecting an individual, group, or organization to *takfir* the rules and regulations of the process are properly understood; haste may result in Allah's wrath over the spilling of innocent blood.

So far, in light of the Quran, the *Sunnat*, the traditions of the early Muslims, the imams, the jurists, and the *Hadees*-collectors, we have compiled the rules and regulations imperative for *takfir*. Although it is impossible to exhaust everything written about the subject, readers will find enough content here that references primary materials in our library; the few references that we do not own have been gleaned from highly reputable sources. We have thus laid out a basic framework because before

408 THE LITERATURE OF *LASHKAR-E-TAYYABA*

studying any subject, sacred or mundane, it is important to understand the basics, such as when learning about *tafseer* one first learns the principles of *tafseer*, or the principles of *fiqh* or *Hadees* etc. in order to do justice to the subject matter at hand.

Every subject demands an understanding of its basic principles in order to avoid misinterpretation and misunderstanding. Thus, every learned individual must comprehensively understand the principles of *takfir* in order to understand his own responsibilities and obligations in its context.

He who does not take into account the rules and regulations of *takfir* puts himself at risk of being subjected to *takfir*. Jeopardizing lives in this way will undoubtedly incur Allah's wrath.

Abu Hurairah reports the prophet as having said: 'When a person calls to his brother with the words: "Oh Infidel!" One of the two has indeed committed *kufr*' (Bukhari, *Kitab al-Adab, Baab bin Akfar Akha*... 2103). Similarly, the following *Hadees* comes from Abdullah bin Umar: Thabit bin Dhahaak reports: 'Accusing a Muslim of *kufr* is tantamount to murder' (Bukhari, *Kitab al-Adab* 2105).

From the above *Hadees*, Imam Bukhari concludes that 'He who accuses his Muslim brother of being an infidel without conclusive evidence is himself an infidel.'

Hafiz Ibn Hujr Asqalani further elaborates:

Imam Bukhari has deemed hearsay without rigorous interrogation for evidence null, that is, calling a Muslim an infidel without concrete evidence implies the accuser is an infidel, and if there is clear evidence then the accuser is not an infidel.

(*Fatah al-Bari* 679–680:13 *tuay. Dar I Tayyaba*)

As for the ignorant ones, there is a separate chapter on them in his book titled *Al-Mosu'a tal Fiqhiyya tal Kuwaytiyah*.

It is obligatory upon the people to refrain from subjecting Muslims to *takfir* and to leave this matter to the scholars since this is an extremely sensitive issue.

(*Al-Mosu'a-tal-Fiqhiyya tal-Kuwaytiyah* 228:13)

In listing the *Hadees* on the issue of *takfir*, Imam Ibn Hubban says: 'He who calls a Muslim an infidel is himself an infidel.' This is supported by a well-known *Hadees* from the tradition of Ahmed, reported by Abdullah bin Umar.

Syedna Abdullah bin Umar reports the prophet once said that: 'When a person accuses another of being an infidel, one of the two is an infidel.'

Hence, accusing or judging someone of being an infidel is serious business, even for the scholars of religion; non-experts have no business indulging in this process. We see examples of this in the lives of the companions.

For example, a couple had a baby while travelling. At one point, the husband suckled his wife to aid in her lactation and accidentally swallowed some of her milk. When Abu Musa Ashari was consulted, he said: your wife is now forbidden to you. The husband then consulted Abdullah bin Masood, who said to Abu Musa: reflect on the opinion you are giving this man. Abu Musa said: What is your opinion? Abdullah bin Masood said: infancy only lasts two years. Abu Musa responded, 'As long as there is a scholar (like Abdullah bin Masood) among you, do not come to me with any of your issues.'

During the reign of the righteous caliphs, only a few companions of the prophet had the authority to practise *takfir* even though all of them drew their knowledge directly from the prophet.

Despite witnessing Islam's revelation and application, not everyone practised *takfir*, and if the issue ever came up the prophet was visibly displeased. 'Were you able to cut open his heart and peek inside?'

Summary

This matter can only be presided over by experts who know the subject. They will consider the following three injunctions before any kind of decision:

1. Complete knowledge of the condition of the accused.
2. Observing due process in context of the charge.
3. Observing the protocol imperative for passing a judgement.

410 THE LITERATURE OF *LASHKAR-E-TAYYABA*

First principle

Takfir is a *shariat*-based injunction that can only be exercised by Allah and his Prophet. No one else has any right over the matter regardless of tribal affiliation, personal clout, intellectual superiority, or political bias.

In the past section a clear definition of *kufr* was elaborated upon and the dire consequences of *takfir* were detailed. In order to avoid these consequences, it is important to remember that *takfir* is a *shariat*-based issue over which only Allah and His Prophet can deliberate, as reported by Ibadah bin Swamat:

> The prophet made us pledge that we will not rebel against our leaders whether we are in agreement with them or not, whether it brings us benefit or hardship, even if it means we are discriminated against... except if you witness *kufr* practised defiantly and Allah exposes concrete incriminating evidence.
>
> (Bukhari, *Kitab al-Futan, Bab Qaul al-Nabi*; Muslim, *Kitab al-Amara*: 1709/46; *Masnad Ahmad* 353:37, hay)

Tabrani's report uses the term *kufran saraha* instead of *kufran bawaha* (*Fatah al-Bari* 16:440 *Tuay- Dar Tayyaba*).

'When you see *kufr* out in the open.' In this *Hadees*, the words '*indakum min Allahi fihi burhan*' reveal that personal desires, conflicts, biases, leanings, and suspicion have no role to play in determining whether a Muslim is an infidel; this is solely Allah's domain. Below is a *Hadees* that leaves absolutely no doubt about the issue. Hafiz Ibn Hujr Asqalani writes:

> What is meant by proof from Allah is a verse whose content is an irrefutable *Hadees*.
>
> Imam Baghvi says that: 'A verse from Allah or a *Sunnat* that cannot be disputed.'

Sheikh Muhammad ibn al-Uthaymin says:

> The prophet said: Do not rebel against the sultan or the government except when you see open and concrete *kufr* and there is clear evidence for what you see from Allah. Only then, can we rebel, but even then, consider the conditions:

THE PROBLEM WITH *TAKFIR*   411

1. *Ila an tarwa*: You must yourself witness *kufr* and not rely on hearsay. Often, we hear rumours about various leaders that turn out to be false. Hence, it is important to directly witness or hear the *kufr* being reported.
2. *Kufr*: It must indeed be *kufr*, not mere debauchery; what is more, even if our rulers are debauched, that does not warrant a rebellion.
3. *Bawaha*: The *kufr* witnessed must be explicit and indisputable. If the issue is debatable and we consider their actions or words *kufr* but they do not think so, or in their mind they are not on the path of *kufr*, then one does not have the right to rebel. This is why Imam Ahmed bin Hanbal says:

He who calls the Quran a species is indeed an infidel, and Mamun (the ruler at the time) would say that the Quran is a species and he would also preach this ideology. Despite this, Imam Ahmed referred to him as the *Emir-ul-Mu'minin* (Commander of the Faithful), for he knew that believing the Quran was a species was not tantamount to rejecting it. It is essential for *kufr* to be explicit, without a shred of doubt according to the *shariat*... short of that, rebellion is forbidden
(*Sharah Sahih al-Bukhari* 259:4 *tuay. Dar al Mustaqbil, Misr*).

4. You must have concrete unquestionable evidence that the *kufr* was explicit. The charge cannot be subject to whim or suspicion, and the evidence must be clear and conclusive without the least bit of ambiguity.

NOTE: Consider Imam Ibn Taymiyyah's *fatwa* on what Sheikh Muhammad ibn al-Uthaymin said in reference to Imam Ahmed bin Hanbal.

'The only reason why such luminaries have been quoted is to elaborate the point that to accuse a Muslim of being an infidel the plaintiff must have clear and concrete evidence from Allah that is devoid of any kind of suspicion for to determine if a person is an infidel is the sole authority of Allah.'

Sheikh al-Islam Imam Ibn Taymiyyah says:

No doubt Ali (the fourth caliph) never accused the *Khawarij* of being infidels or hypocrites; some, like Abu Ishaq Asfraini and his followers,

412   THE LITERATURE OF *LASHKAR-E-TAYYABA*

say that 'we will only subject to *takfir* those who subject us to *takfir*' but this principle is flawed for *takfir* is not the purview of anyone other than Allah. It is forbidden to lie about the matter. One cannot injure the family member of a violent offender in retaliation for injury caused to the member of one's own family. Similarly, if someone subjects one to the act of Lot's people that does not permit the victim to commit the same act back in revenge; if someone drugs another and kills him or rapes him, one cannot drug and rape the convict back... all this is categorically forbidden. Just because Christians curse our prophet, this does not permit us to curse Christ, and if the heretics (Shī'a) subject Abu Bakr and Umar to *takfir* that does not mean we can subject Ali to *takfir*.

> (*Minhaj al-Sunnat Ibn Taymiyyah* 244; *Ba-Tahqiq* Dr Muhammad
> Rashad Salim *tuay, Ula* 1406 AH *ba-Mutabiq* 1986)

Another place he says:

This is why learned Muslims do not go round subjecting their opponents to *takfir* even if their opponents practise *takfir* on them, for *takfir* is the purview of the *shariat*. Pursuing it as a form of vengeance is like sleeping with another man's wife because he slept with yours even though adultery and fornication are forbidden; similarly, the authority over *takfir* lies only with Allah and therefore no person can be labelled an infidel until Allah and His prophet determine this to be the case.

> (*Al-Istighatha fil radd Al-al-Bukra Ibn Taymiyyah* 381:1 *tuay. Dar ul
> Watan al-Riyadh*)

Imam Ibn Taymiyyah writes another place:

No doubt, only Allah and His prophet can say what is obligatory, forbidden, meritorious, punishable, or *kufr*. No one else can interfere in this matter. What is obligatory is only that which has been obligated by Allah and His prophet, just as only Allah and His Prophet have the authority to determine what is forbidden.

> (*Majmu-al-Fatawa Ibn Taymiyyah* 554–555:5)

THE PROBLEM WITH *TAKFIR*   413

Another place he says:

No doubt, *kufr* is a *shariat* issue. It is not subject to intellectual scrutiny. An infidel is one whom Allah and His prophet have labelled infidel, and a heretic is one whom Allah and His prophet have labelled heretic.

(*Minhaj al-Sunnat Ibn Taymiyyah* 92:5)

Imam Ghazali writes:

Kufr (the determination of) is a *shariat* issue for to subject a person to *takfir* is tantamount to saying spilling their blood is justified and that they are eternally damned, therefore this determination can only be done through Quran and *Hadees*.

(*Faisal al-Tufraqa Bain al-Islam wal-Zindaqa lil Ghazali* 128)

Allama Ibn al-Wazir says:

No doubt, *takfir* is a *shariat* issue. The intellect has no part to play here. It should be avoided until conclusive evidence is revealed.

In his compilation of poetry, Qasida Nuniyya, Imam Ibn al-Qayyim writes:

Takfir is the domain of Allah and His Prophet, alone . . .
It is based on evidence and not mere hearsay.

(*Qasidah Nonia swaad* 192, *nashir maktaba Ibn Taymiyyah,*
Al-Qasida tal Nonia Ma' sharha 267:2 *tuay. Dar al Kutab*
al Ilmiyya Beirut wa fi Nuskha 633:2 *tuay, Misr*)

Dr Muhammad Khalil Hiras says the following about the subject:

No doubt, no one has the authority to declare another an infidel simply due to a disagreement. In fact *takfir* is the sole jurisdiction of Allah and His prophet, and it can only be proven with conclusive *shariat*-based evidence; it does not apply to what someone said or did... he whom Allah and His Prophet label an infidel is no doubt an infidel.

(*Sharah Qaseedah Nonia* 267:2)

414 THE LITERATURE OF *LASHKAR-E-TAYYABA*

When asked if Al Sheikh Muhammad ibn al-Uthaymin would subject the *Ahl-i-Taveel* to *takfir*, he said:

We do not have the authority to practise *takfir* for this is the purview of Allah and His Prophet. The *shariat* makes clear that beginning to end this issue is related to the Quran and *Sunnat*, which provide the only valid proof. Therefore, do not subject anyone to *takfir* for it must be understood that a Muslim's very existence is predicated on Islam. His faith must not be questioned until conclusive evidence proves otherwise. When we subject an individual to *takfir* we run the risk of 1) associating falsehood with Allah in context of His laws, and 2) subjecting ourselves to *takfir* if the initial accusation turns out to be false. Hence, before applying *takfir*, the following two steps are imperative: a direct reference from the Quran or Sunnat that shows unambiguously that the specific words or actions performed are indeed *kufr*. And for the accused to clearly understand that all the conditions of *takfir* have been met categorically.

(*Al-waid al Mathli fi Saffat Allah wa Isma-tul-Husna Muhammad ibn al-Uthaymin* 87 and 88)

Summary:

Below is a bulleted list of all the important statements by the esteemed and the learned regarding the subject:

1. *Takfir* is the sole purview of Allah and His Prophet.
2. *Takfir* is a *shariat*-based issue, not an intellectual endeavour.
3. *Takfir* has no room for intellectual grandstanding.
4. *Takfir* can only be done when clear indisputable evidence is revealed.
5. Consequences of *takfir*: 1. Associating falsehood with Allah and His Prophet (should the *takfir* prove inconclusive); 2. Wrongly permitting the murder of an individual; 3. An inaccurate *takfir* applies back to the plaintiff.
6. *Takfir* is not an avenue of vengeance; this is expressly forbidden.

Second principle: Establishing evidence beyond doubt

A person cannot be subjected to *takfir* based on his words, actions, and beliefs until concrete evidence clears all doubt about the matter. This evidence has been described in the Quran in the following words:

THE PROBLEM WITH *TAKFIR* 415

We never punish until We have sent a messenger.

(*Surat al-Isra* 17:15)

Allama Abdur Rahman bin Nasir al-Sadi states:

Allah is just; He does not punish a people until they violently oppose His messenger. As for those who submit or remain oblivious to Allah's message, they remain unpunished. It can be concluded from this verse that Allah will not punish the ignorant ones nor will He punish the children of polytheists until they are sent a messenger, for He does not indulge in cruelty.

(*Tafseer Saadi Urdu* 1450–1451:2 *tuay. Dar-ul-Islam*)

In his book titled *Al-Tafseer al-Thameen* (120/5) Sheikh Muhammad ibn al-Uthaymin makes the exact same point.

Imam Qurtabi states:

No doubt, Allah does not annihilate a people until they are sent a messenger and granted enlightenment.

(*Al-Jama al-Ahkma al-Quran* 152:10)

Imam al-Mufsirin Imam Tabri says:

We do not slaughter a nation until it is sent a messenger with revelations to prevent it from sinning.

(*Tafseer Tabari* 526:14 *tuay. Dar Aalam al-Kutab*)

Imam Ibn Katheer says:

He will not punish anyone before sending a messenger and establishing proofs.

(*Tafseer Ibn Katheer* 122:4, *Ba-Tahqiq* Abdur Razzaq al-Mahdi)

Allama Jamaluddin Qasmi says in reference to 17:15, 20:134, 67:9/8, 39:71, 35:37.

'In addition to the aforementioned verses, there are countless more that prove that Allah neither subjects a people to divine punishment nor does

416 THE LITERATURE OF *LASHKAR-E-TAYYABA*

He burn them, until He sends them a messenger.' (*Tafseer al-Qasmi*, 450:6 *tuay. Dar al Kutab al Ilmiy*)

Imam Baghvi says:

> Allah says: 'we are not one to punish until a messenger has been sent.' This is to establish proofs (of god's existence) and put an end to sin.
>
> (*Tafseer al-Bughwi*, 107 ... 3 *tuay. Idara tal Talifat Ashrafiya*)

Imam Abul Ishaq al-Ta'lami says:

> And we are not the ones to unleash wrath even if a messenger were sent with revelations that cleared all doubt.

Nawab Siddique Hassan Khan Qanoji says:

> Allah does not punish His people until He sends a messenger among them with revelations that conclusively end all doubt, thereby Allah has made clear that He has not left His people in the dark and neither will He try them until they have been given proof (of the Truth).
>
> (*Fatah al Biyan fi Maqasid al-Quran*, 113:4 *tuay. Dar al Kutab al Ilmiyya*)

Allama Muhammad Tahir ibn 'Ashur says:

> This verse is testament to the fact that Allah only holds people accountable after they have been guided. This is evidence of Allah's love for humans and of the fact that until a messenger has invited people to the Truth, they will not be held accountable.
>
> (*Al-Tahrir wal-Tanveer* 43:14 *tuay, Muassassatal Tarikh al-Arabiya Beirut*)

Allama Muhammad Ameen Shanqiti says:

> This verse is testament to the fact that Allah does not punish His creation in this life or the afterlife until they are sent a messenger with warnings and they disobey the messenger and remain on the path of *kufr* despite being warned.

(Azwa al-Biyan fi Ayzah al-Quran bil-Quran, swaad 542
tuay. Dar al-Kutab al-Ilmiyya)

Imam Ibn Taymiyyah says:

The conviction with which the ignorant accuse a specific individual of being an infidel is unsubstantiated, unless the plaintiffs can prove they themselves are messengers sent to contradict the prophets that preceded them. Such is the command of all those who have been appointed. Not all religious modification is equally corrupt, and, in truth, some corruption is sincere—no one is permitted to subject another Muslim to *takfir* even if the accused is guilty, for he may have been mistaken or it may have been accidental... one cannot know until there is concrete evidence to prove otherwise.

(Majmua al-Fatawal Ibn Taymiyyah 500–501:12)

Imam Ibn Taymiyyah says:

He who believes in Allah and His Messenger but lacks the knowledge that will guide him to the right path cannot be accused of being an infidel until it is categorically proven that he is an infidel. Many people misinterpret the Quran, and are ignorant of the *Sunnat*. Humans make mistakes ... one can only be labelled an infidel after rigorous investigations and due process.

(Majmua al-Fatawal Ibn Taymiyyah 523–524 ... 12)

Imam Ibn Hazm says:

There is no doubt that a person who accepts Islam but is unfamiliar with its various principles, and believes alcohol is permitted and prayer is optional, having not yet received Allah's word in its entirety, cannot be considered an infidel. There is no notable difference of opinion on this. Such is the case until there is concrete evidence to prove otherwise or if the accused revolts ... then he is unanimously believed to be an infidel.

(Al-Mahla 130:12; Wafi Nuskha 206:11)

418 THE LITERATURE OF *LASHKAR-E-TAYYABA*

Imam Ibn Hazm says:

> Allah says: 'and this Quran has been revealed unto me so that on the strength thereof I might warn you and all whom it may reach' (6:19). Allah also says: We never punish until We have sent a messenger.
>
> (*Surat al-Isra* 17:15)

Allah has explicitly said that His warnings only apply to those who have received His word. Allah never punishes until He sends a messenger. It is true that he who has not received Islam cannot be punished; similarly, the one who is unaware of the rights and obligations of faith is innocent as well.

Imam Ibn al-Qayyim says:

> Undoubtedly, there are two causes for Allah's wrath: first, when the authority of the *shariat* is denied with the intent of disobeying its injunctions; second, when the authority of the *shariat* is antagonized in defiance. The first is *kufr* of denial/omission, the second is *kufr* of defiance/antagonism. Separately, and additionally, there is the *kufr* of ignorance, which Allah will not punish until the messengers have spread the word.
>
> (*Tareeq al-Hijrateen, Ibn al-Qeem al-Juzi, swaad* 413)

In describing the various types of knowledge mentioned in the Quran, Allama Shatabi says:

> Allah Himself says there is no culpability without warning: 'We never punish until We have sent a messenger' (17:15). Regarding creation, He only punishes after sending a messenger whose word has been defied.' 'Then whosoever will, let him believe, and whosoever will, let him disbelieve (18:29)'
>
> (*Al-Muwafiqat* 200:4 *Ba-Tahqiq Abi Ubaidah Mashhur Hasan Aal Salman*)

Another place Allah says:

> It was never Allah's (part) that he should send a folk astray after He had guided them until He had made clear unto them what they should avoid. Lo! Allah is Aware of all things.
>
> (*Surat at-Tawbah* 9:115)

THE PROBLEM WITH *TAKFIR*   419

Imam Bukhari quotes this verse in his book *Kitab Istibabah* in Chapter 6 in order to prove that even *Khawarij* can only be slaughtered once the proof of authority has been established.

Allama Ainee writes:

Imam Bukhari hints here that *Khawarij* cannot be killed until every pretext for being a *Khawarij* is eradicated, and they are invited to embrace the truth and are shown the flaws in their ways; only if they insist on turning away from the truth does slaughter become obligatory based on the verse quoted by Imam Bukhari.

Countless verses have been revealed on the subject. Allah will ask humans did He not send them His messengers? They will respond in the affirmative. This shows that without the messengers and the revelations there is to be no punishment. Therefore, if an individual or a people have not received Allah's word they will be spared on the Last Day. Then there's the matter of the deaf, the deranged, the mentally challenged, and those who lived and died in between periods of prophecy. According to some traditions Allah will send their souls an angel who will tell them to enter hell upon Allah's command—those who enter obediently will find themselves in paradise while those who resist will be dragged into the fire. Consider *Surat Malik* verses 9 and 8, *Surat az-Zamr* verse 71, and *Surat Fatir* verse 37.

Aswad bin Sari' reports the prophet as having said:

Four kinds of men (will not be thrown in hell) on the Day of Judgement: the dead, the deranged, the aged or senile, and those born in intermediary periods between messengers. The deaf will say: Oh Lord! No doubt Islam was revealed but I could not hear it. The deranged will say: Oh Lord! No doubt Islam was revealed but children threw camel-dung at me. The senile will say: Oh Lord! No doubt Islam was revealed but I was unable to comprehend it. And those who died between prophecy will say: Oh Lord! I was never sent a messenger. Allah will then make them all promise to follow His command. He will then send them an angel who will tell them to enter fire. I swear upon Him who holds Muhammad's life in His hands, those who enter the fire will find it cool and peaceful.

(*Masnad Ahmad* 12301. 228:26, 12302. 230:26;
Al-Ahadith al-Mukhtara 1455–1456; Ibn Haban 7357;
Sahih al-Jamia al-Sagheer 881)

420 THE LITERATURE OF *LASHKAR-E-TAYYABA*

This proves Allah will not be cruel to anyone. Neither will anyone be punished until His authority has been established. Abu Huraira, who is included in the chain of narration for the aforementioned quote goes on to say:

> On the Day of Judgement Allah will gather all the spirits; those who were born in the period between prophecy, and the deaf, and the mute, and the senile, and they will be sent a messenger who will tell them to enter the fire. They will say how can we enter fire when we were never sent a messenger. By Allah! Had they followed the order they would have found the fire cool and peaceful. Again a messenger will be sent to them; the ones who are obedient will act accordingly. Syedna Abu Huraira says: If you want, you can read the Quran and we are not one to punish without sending a messenger.
>
> (*Jamia al-Biyan al-Tabar* 526:14, 527 *Ba-Tahqiq* Dr Abdullah bin Abdul Mohsin al-Turki; *Tafseer Abdur Razzaq* 1541)

This narration is sound, and the content is not the result of jurisprudence or discourse; hence, it is binding.

Imam Fatadah explains the Quranic verse in the following words: 'No doubt, Allah will not punish without revealing some concrete evidence and the sinless will not incur His wrath' (*Tafseer Tabari* 526:14). Imam Novi explains the fifteenth verse of Surah Bani Israel in the following statement:

> When Allah will not punish the one of sound mind if he has not received Allah's word, then the mentally challenged will not be punished either.
>
> (*Fatah al-Bari* 179:4; *Sharah Sahih Muslim* 182:12)

There is a difference of opinion when it comes to children. Muslim children will no doubt go to heaven. As for the children of infidels and polytheists, some say they will go to heaven, some say they will burn in hell.

Imam Ibn Katheer says:

> Out in the fields of judgement, there will be a test. Those who follow Allah's command will enter paradise and those who do not will go to hell.

THE PROBLEM WITH *TAKFIR* 421

However, we learn from the compilations of Bukhari that the children of polytheists will also enter paradise.

In detailing the disputes among scholars on the subject, Hafiz Ibn Hujr Asqalani writes:

> He who dies in a state of madness or in the period between messengers will have his case decided in his favour, and this matter has been settled, and Imam Behqi has affirmed this in his book titled *Kitab-al-Aiteqad.*
>
> (*Fatah al-Bari* 179:4)

Summary:

Until an act of *kufr* has been categorically established, the accused will not be labelled an infidel. Imam Bukhari expounds on this principle in his book *Sahih-al-Bukhari.*

Imam Ibn Taymiyyah states:

> The act of *takfir* is punishable, even if the accused has made statements that directly contradict the sayings of the prophet, for it may be that the accused has only recently accepted Islam or he might be from a remote region where Islam has not fully been understood; such a person will not be subjected to *takfir* without categorical evidence. Many times, people are unaware of the *shariat* injunctions regarding specific matters, or if they're aware they are unconvinced, or they are unable to distinguish flawed interpretations from accurate ones... such people cannot be subjected to *takfir.*
>
> (*Majmua al-Fatawal Ibn Taymiyyah* 231:3)

Another place, he writes:

> No one is permitted to subject another Muslim to *takfir* no matter how egregiously they erred, until and unless there is categorical evidence to prove otherwise; He whose admission of faith has been ascertained cannot be subjected to suspicion and hearsay.
>
> (*Majmua al-Fatawal Ibn Taymiyyah* 422:12)

422 THE LITERATURE OF *LASHKAR-E-TAYYABA*

Imam Ibn Qadamah writes in his popular book *Al-Maghni*:

If that person denies what is obligatory because he has only been exposed to a modern version of Islam or because he was exposed to the faith in a region where Islam has not properly flourished, the learned will not subject such a person to *takfir* until he is made aware of the revelations regarding the matter. If he continues to deny their validity, then he is an infidel. However, if he lives in a place where Islam is well established, then the one who denies is an infidel.

From this treasure trove of opinions, it emerges that when Qadamah bin Muz'awan drank alcohol thinking it was permissible, the second caliph Umar punished him but did not subject him to *takfir*.

Imam Zehri says:

Abdullah bin Emir Rabiya told me that his father was at Badr and Umar made Qadamah bin Muz'awan the governor of Bahrain. He was uncle to Syeda Hafsa and Abdullah bin Umar. Jarwad, the leader of the Abdul Qays tribe in Bahrain, visited Umar and said: 'Oh Commander of the Faithful! Qadamah imbibed alcohol and is now drunk. I feel it is important to correct him as Allah has ordained. It was my duty to report this to you.' Umar responded: 'Do you have a witness?' The tribal leader said: 'Abu Huraira.' Umar summoned Abu Huraira, who said: 'What can I say? I did not see him touch alcohol but I saw him drunk.' Umar said: 'You are too cautious with your testimony.' Umar then summoned Qadamah.

Jarwad said to Umar: 'Enforce Allah's command over him (Qadamah).' Umar said: 'Are you an antagonist or a witness?' 'A witness,' replied Jarwad. 'Then you have fulfilled your obligation as a witness,' said Umar. Jarwad fell silent. The next day Jarwad returned to Umar and said: 'Enforce Allah's command over him (Qadamah).' Umar said: 'It is obvious to me that you are an antagonist in this case; what's more, you only have one witness.' Jarwad responded: 'I swear by Allah (regarding the testimony).' Umar said: 'Hold your tongue or else ... !' Jarwad said: 'Either way, I swear by Allah. Is it not strange that your uncle's son drinks but you want to punish me instead?' Abu Huraira added (addressing Umar): 'If you doubt our testimony then ask Qadamah's wife.'

Umar sent Qadamah's wife, Hind bint Waleed, a message, and she proceeded to testify against her husband. Umar said to Qadamah: 'I will absolutely enforce the Quranic law in your case.' Qadamah said: 'If I did in fact consume alcohol, as has been testified, it is still wrong of you to flog me.' When asked why, Qadamah quoted the following verse from the Quran:

There shall be no sin (imputed) unto those who believe and do good works for what they may have eaten (in the past).

(*Surat al-Ma'idah* 5:93)

Umar said: 'Your interpretation is flawed. No doubt, once you enter a state of piety you must abstain from what has been prohibited.' Then Umar turned to the people and said: 'What do you think about Qadamah's punishment?' The people said it was wrong to flog him since he was ill. Umar was silent for a few days. One morning he woke up determined to punish Qadamah and consulted his advisors. They said that as long as Qadamah is weak and frail he should not be punished. Umar said: 'I would rather Qadamah meets his maker having been flogged than have him die with the responsibility of this punishment hanging over me. Get me a sturdy cane.' Qadamah was then flogged and his friendship with Umar ended.

Qadamah was with Umar at hajj. After *hajj*, they stopped at a place called Suqiya where Umar fell asleep. When he awoke, he narrated the following vision: By Allah, I saw the one who will arrive (the prophet), and he told me to restore my friendship with Qadamah for he is my brother. He summoned Qadamah but the latter refused to come. Umar ordered him to be dragged over. When Qadamah arrived, Umar spoke to him and asked Allah to forgive him, and thus they became friends again (*Al-Musannaf al-Abdur Razzaq*: 17076, 240–243:9, *Min Hadd Min Ashab al-Nabi*. *Al Sunan al-Kubra al-il Bihaqi* 312:8; *Al-Asabah*: 323 and 324; *Al-Istiab* 340–341:3; *Asad al-Ghaba* 376:4; *Al-Aqdul Thameen* 72–73). Imam Zohbi says:

He once misinterpreted the Quranic *ayah* 5:93 and consumed alcohol; consequently, Umar enforced the *shariat* punishment and had him resign from his post in Bahrain.

424 THE LITERATURE OF *LASHKAR-E-TAYYABA*

Ayub Sakhtiani says: he was the only combatant from the Battle of Badr to have received a Quranic punishment.

Similarly, Abu Jandal and his companions consumed alcohol in Syria thinking it was permissible based on their interpretation of the following Quranic verse:

There shall be no sin (imputed) unto those who believe and do good works for what they may have eaten (in the past).

(*Surat al-Ma'idah* 5:93)

However, he was not subjected to *takfir*; instead, he was made aware of the injunction regarding alcohol after which he repented and was awarded the Quranic punishment for drinking. However, Ibn Juraij does not say how this news reached him.

Similar examples can be found in the lives of the pious as evidenced in various *Hadees*:

When Syedna Ma'az returned from Syria he sought permission to prostrate before the prophet; in response, the prophet did not subject him to *takfir* but instead explained to him that one must prostrate only before Allah and no one other than Allah deserves genuflection.

(*Kitab al-Nikah* 1853; *Al-Sunan al-Kubra Lil Bihqi* 292:7; *Sahih Ibn Haban* 1290; Muwaridal-Zaman, *Masnad Ahmad* 145:32, hay: 19403; *Al-Masnad al-Thashi* 231:3, hay: 1332; *Silsila tul Ahadith al-Sahih* 1203)

Abdullah bin Abi Awni reports:

When Ma'az returned from Syria he prostrated before the prophet. The prophet said, 'Oh Ma'az, what is this?' He said: 'In Syria, I found the people prostrating before their priests and their lords so I thought we ought to do the same with you.' The prophet said: 'Do not. If I could allow the worship of anyone other than Allah, I would tell women to prostrate before their husbands. By the One who holds Muhammad's life in His hands, a woman cannot fulfil her duty to Allah until she has fulfilled her duty to her husband and, if her husband approaches her, she should not refuse even if she is mounted on the back of a camel.'

(Ibn Majah, *Kitab al Nikah, Bab Ma-Haq al-Zoj Al-al Marah* 1853)

THE PROBLEM WITH *TAKFIR* 425

Qazi Shoqani has the following to say about the *Hadees* regarding Syedna Ma'az:

This *Hadees* is a testament to the fact that anyone who prostrates before anyone other than Allah out of ignorance is not an infidel.

(*Neel al Autar* 341:12, *Ba-Tahqiq* Muhammad bin Hasan Akhlaq, *tuay. Dar Ibn Jozi*)

Similarly, Abu Huraira reports the prophet said:

By the One who holds Muhammad's life in His hands! He who doesn't hear of me, whether he is Christian or Jew, and dies without accepting what I have been sent, will not be of the ones in fire.

(*Masnad Ahmad* 522:13 *hay*: 8203, 261:14, 8209; *Masnad Abi Awana* 104:1)

Qazi Ayaz interprets this *Hadees* as follows:

In this *Hadees* we learn that the sin of not adopting faith is suspended if one lives in distant regions or is separated from the mainland and is unfamiliar with Islam or the prophet's ways; this is so because of the prophet's opening statement, 'he who does not hear of me . . .'.

(*Ikmal al Muallam Ba-Fawaid Muslim* 428:1 *tuay, Dar al-Wafa*)

Imam Abul Abbas al-Qurtabi says:

This *Hadees* is evidence that he who has not received the prophet's message will not be subjected to punishment. This is similar to what Allah says: We never punish until We have sent a messenger (17:15). And the one who has not even heard of the miracle of the prophet is like the one who was not sent a messenger in the first place.

(*Al-Mufham al Maishkal Min Talkhees Kitab Muslim* 328:1 *tuay. Dar Ibn Katheer Beirut*)

Imam Naudi writes:

This *Hadees* is proof that with the arrival of our prophet, all former religions have been annulled and at the heart of it, this *Hadees* is a testament

426 THE LITERATURE OF *LASHKAR-E-TAYYABA*

to the fact that he who has not received Islam is disabled because according to what has been said, no (Islamic) injunction can be enforced before the *shariat* has been made known.

(*Sharah Sahih Muslim* 162:2 *tuay. Dar al-Kitab al-Ilmiyya Beirut*)

These incidents and narrations prove that one cannot be punished for defying Allah's commands until all his misunderstandings have been resolved. What is more, considering the companions themselves made similar mistakes during the period of enlightenment, it is only fair to give people the benefit of the doubt in these strange times.

The life of the prophet presents us with numerous examples of specific individuals committing *kufr* acts before the prophet without being subjected to *takfir*. They were spared due to their ignorance or their misinterpretation. Ma'az's prostration was an example of one such act.

In another example, Rabiya bint Ma'ooz bin 'Afra reports:

The prophet approached me when I was being presented to my husband. The prophet sat next to me just as you sit close to me now. At the time our women were playing the drums and singing verses in honour of the martyrs of Badr. Suddenly, one of the women said: among us is a prophet who can see the future. The prophet said to her: 'stop saying this and go back to what you were singing earlier'.

(Bukhari, *Kitab al-Nikah, Baab Zarb al-Daf fil Nikah wal-Walima* 5147; *Kitab al-Maghazi* 4001)

Syeda Ayesha reports the prophet as having said:

None but Allah knows what will happen tomorrow.

(*Tabr Ani 'Usat* 43425:241)

Hafiz Ibn Hujr Asqalani confirms the authenticity of this *Hadees* (*Fatah al-Bari* 475:11, *tuay. Dar-i-Tayyaba*; *Neez Dikhain*, Ibn Majah 1897). He writes:

When the woman transgressed in her praise of the prophet, he contradicted her for she was associating him with knowledge of the occult whereas this characteristic belongs solely to Allah, as Allah Himself has said:

THE PROBLEM WITH *TAKFIR* 427

'Say (O Muhammad): None in the heavens and the earth knoweth the Unseen save Allah; and they know not when they will be raised (again)'.
(*Surat an-Naml* 27:65)

And Allah said to the prophet:

Say, 'For myself I have no power to benefit, nor power to hurt, save that which Allah willeth. Had I knowledge of the Unseen, I should have abundance of wealth, and adversity would not touch me'.
(*Surat al-A'raf* 7:188)

Allah bestowed whatever insight the prophet had about the future upon him; personally, the prophet did not possess knowledge of the occult. As Allah says:

(He is) the knower of the Unseen, and He revealeth unto none His secret. Save unto every messenger whom he hath chosen ...
(*Surat al-Jinn* 72:26 and 27) (*Fatah al-Bari* 475:11 tuay. Dar-i-Tayyaba)

Allama Ainee says:

Let go of this quote for the treasures of the occult are possessed by none other than Allah and can be known by none, other than Him.

Allama Ibn al-Mulqan writes:

Stop saying this for only Allah can know the occult.
(*Al-Tauzeeh* 452:24, tuay. Dar-ul-Falah; *Neez daikhain Na/am al-Bari fi Sharah al-Bukhari* 572:9; Az-Ghulam Rasool Saeedi, *Sharah Sahih al-Bukhari lil Kirmani* 82:19)

We gather from this *Hadees* that a woman, while eulogizing her forefathers exaggerated her praise for the prophet by claiming he knew what was to come the next day, even though claiming knowledge of the occult for anyone other than Allah is *kufr*; yet, instead of subjecting her to *takfir*, the prophet simply corrected her.

428 THE LITERATURE OF *LASHKAR-E-TAYYABA*

Mulla Ali Qari says:

Then know, the messengers have no knowledge of the occult save that which Allah reveals to them. The Hanafi scholars have subjected the belief that the prophet possessed occult knowledge to *takfir* for it directly contradicts what Allah has said: None in the heavens and the earth knoweth the Unseen save Allah; and they know not when they will be raised (again) (27:65). And this has been stated in *Surat Maidah*.

(Sharah al-Fatahul Akbar, swaad 180 tuay. Qadeem)

Hence, *kufr* speech or action alone do not warrant labelling the subject an infidel; such a label cannot be applied until all the conditions of *takfir* have been met and all the limitations of *takfir* have been transgressed.

Imam Sha'fi says:

Allah's names and characteristics have been revealed in His book, and His Prophet has reported these to his *ummat*, and for one upon whom this has been made evident it is forbidden to disregard them, for with them was revealed the Quran and what the prophet has said about them proved to be true. The one who antagonizes the Quran and *Sunnat* after being convinced (of the Truth) is an infidel. Before being convinced the person is forgiven because of his ignorance; this knowledge is not the function of intellect or reflection and the ignorant cannot be called infidels until they receive the word.

(Al-Arba'een fi Sifaat Rab-al-Alimeen Lahu Aiza 86, swaad: 84, tuay)

Imam Abu Bakr ibn al-Arabi says:

If the ignorant and misguided among the *ummat* do something that belies *kufr* or polytheism they will not be labelled infidels. Such individuals are protected by their own ignorance until the truth is absolutely clear to them. Thereafter, any kind of repudiation or negation deems them worthy of being called infidels but only if the truth is crystal clear to them, devoid of any kind of doubt or illusion.

(Tafseer Muhasin al-Taweel al-Maroof ba-Tafseer al-Qasmi
1307–1308:5)

THE PROBLEM WITH *TAKFIR* 429

Consider the *Hadees* compiled by Bukhari in which a dying man willed for his body to be cremated with half his ashes poured into the river and the other half scattered across dry land for fear that Allah would otherwise catch hold of him and punish him severely. In discussing this *Hadees*, Imam Ibn Hazm says:

Till his dying breath, this person remained unaware that Allah has the power to collect his ashes and bring him back to life; Allah has forgiven him for his declaration, fear, and ignorance.
(*Al-Fasal fil Malal wal-Ahwa wal-Nahl al-Ibn Hazam* 272:2)

Imam Ibn Hazm notes:

The truth of the matter is that once it is proven that a person's belief is Islam, only explicit defiance and a communal verdict can prove otherwise and mere accusations and hearsay will not suffice. Hence, it is mandatory that a person not be subjected to *takfir* simply because of what he says unless his words antagonize the words of Allah and the prophet that the accused has been shown to hold dear, and that this person feels justified in opposing Allah and the prophet, whether this opposition takes the form of belief or opinion and whether this is regarding a *Hadees* the prophet frequently uttered to a congregation or something he said only once.
(*Al-Fasal fil Milal wal-Ahwa wal-Nahl al-Ibn Hazam* 268:2)

And another place:

In any case, if clear evidence is not established against the one who opposes the Truth, then that person cannot be called an infidel unless there is a specific revelation about his *takfir*.
(*Al-Fasal al-Ibn Hazam* 269:2)

Furthermore:

If someone objects and asks, 'what of the man who testifies that Muhammad is the Messenger of Allah but claims he does not know if Muhammad was of the Quraysh or a Tamimi or Persian, and whether

430 THE LITERATURE OF *LASHKAR-E-TAYYABA*

he was born in the Hijaz or Khorasan, or if he's alive or dead, or if he's here in my presence or elsewhere.' Tell him that if this person is ignorant and has no sense of what's going on around him then he has nothing to worry about. It is obligatory to teach him but once he gains knowledge and the truth is proven to him, any kind of negation on his part will justify him being labelled an infidel, and his life and property are no longer protected, and he will be convicted of heresy. We know numerous individuals who are consulted for *fatwas*; there are countless pious and righteous individuals who do not know when the prophet passed away, or where this happened—what's important in all this is that a person testify sincerely that there was a person called Muhammad and that Allah sent him as a Messenger.

(*Al-Fasal al-Ibn Hazam* 269:2)

Similarly, Imam Ibn Hazm states:

Similarly, whosoever says that his god is embodied is innocent if he is ignorant or misguided; it is obligatory to educate this person. Only once the Quran and *Hadees* are exposed to him, and he opposes both defiantly, is he to be labelled an infidel and convicted of heresy.

(*Al-Fasal al-Ibn Hazam* 269:2)

Elsewhere, he writes:

Allah's words about the subject are clearest: 'When the disciples said: O Jesus, son of Mary! Is thy Lord able to send down for us a table spread with food from heaven? He said: Observe your duty to Allah, if ye are true believers.—5:112 (They said:) We wish to eat thereof, that we may satisfy our hearts and know that thou hast spoken truth to us, and that thereof we may be witnesses.—5:113.' These same disciples had been praised by Allah; they only questioned Jesus Christ out of ignorance when they said, 'Is thy Lord able to send down for us a table spread with food from heaven?' But this question did not tarnish their faith. They would have justifiably been termed infidels had they asked this question after the Truth was revealed to them explicitly and categorically.

(*Al-Fasal al-Ibn Hazam* 272:2)

THE PROBLEM WITH *TAKFIR* 431

In discussing the aforementioned *Hadees* in context of a dying man's will, Allama Ibn al-Waiz says:

> According to Huzaifa's *Hadees* the man was a petty thief but Allah's mercy and the fact that he believed in Allah and the Last Day saved him which is why he was guarded from divine wrath. Ultimately, his ignorance regarding Allah's power would not have been considered *kufr*, unless he first recognized that the messengers spoke of Allah's omnipotence and then denied them or denied any one of them. Allah's statement, 'He will not punish anyone before sending a messenger and establishing proof' is the greatest source of hope and redemption for those who misinterpret.
>
> (*Ithar al-Haq Ala-al Khalaq, swaad* 394)

In fact, Abu Hurairah reports an authentic *Hadees* that says that: 'He performed no pious deed short of *tawheed* (declaring Allah's Oneness).' (*Masnad Ahmad* 8040, 408:13). And according to Abdullah bin Masood's transmission, which links all the way back to the prophet: 'No doubt, this person did nothing positive except *tawheed*.'

According to this authentic *Hadees* this person had no other quality to speak of except his faith in Allah's Oneness and yet Allah showed him mercy.

Imam Ibn Qadamah al-Muqdasi says:

> Similarly, an ignorant person cannot be accused of *kufr* until and unless he recognizes his ignorance and all his misunderstandings are cleared; if, however, he continues to believe that he is in the right then he is an infidel.
>
> (*Al-Maghnil Ibn Qadamah* 277:12)

Imam Novi writes:

> Similarly, a man who denies collective and communal injunctions regarding the five daily prayers, fasting in Ramazan, ritual washing, sex, alcohol, incest, will be considered an infidel even if his knowledge is scattered. However, if he is new to Islam and is unfamiliar with its

432   THE LITERATURE OF *LASHKAR-E-TAYYABA*

prohibitions, then, if he denies any of these injunctions out of ignorance, he cannot be considered and infidel.

(*Sharah Sahih Muslim lal Nuwi* 205:1)

Imam Ibn Abdul Barr says:

The scholars are divided over the gist of this *Hadees*. Some say that this person was ignorant regarding some of Allah's characteristics and one of these characteristics is Allah's absolute power; he did not know that Allah has absolute power over everything. These scholars claim that if a man is ignorant regarding one of Allah's characteristics but believes and recognizes all the rest, then he cannot be considered an infidel for an infidel is one who antagonizes god despite knowing better. This is what the leading scholars and their disciples maintain.

(*Al-Tamheed al-Ibn Abdul Barr* 42:18)

Imam Khitabi says:

Sometimes, the mercy shown to the man in this *Hadees* has caused concern; how can someone who denies resurrection be forgiven? It is said that he did not deny resurrection at all. He was ignorant; he believed that if he was cremated and his ashes scattered in the seas and the wind, he won't be resurrected and will escape divine punishment. Do you not know that when Allah collected his ashes and asked him why he did this (the cremation), the man replied, 'Because I feared You.' It is obvious the man believed in Allah and whatever he did, he did out of fear of Allah and in ignorance.

(*Al-Alaam al-Sunan fil Bukhari al-Khatabi* 207:2 *tuay. Dar al-Kutab al-Ilmiyya*; *Fatah al-Bari* 522:6 *tuay*; *Al-Salafiya wa fi Nuskha* 138:8 *tuay. Dar I Tayyaba*)

Imam Ibn Qutibah says:

At times, certain Muslims are mistaken about some of Allah's attributes, but this does not warrant them being declared infidels.

(*Fatah al-Bari* 138:8 *tuay. Dar I Tayyaba*;
Tahat Hadees Raqam 3479)

Sheikh Muhammad bin Abdul Wahab writes:

When we refrain from attaching the label of infidel to those who worship idols erected at the shrines of Abdul Qadir and Ahmed al-Badvi and other similar personalities simply because they (the grave worshippers) are ignorant and also because there is a dearth of monitors, then how can this man be called an infidel when he has not associated anyone with Allah. If anything, he is pure, and this is an outlandish accusation.

> (*Al-Dar Ral-Sunniya fil Ajoobah tal Jandiya* 104:1; *wa fi Nuskha* 66:1; *Masbah al Zalam, swaad* 84)

Sheikh Muhammad Abdul Wahab goes on to say:

In conclusion, when enemies say, 'I exercise *takfir* because I have doubts and suspicions' or 'this ignorant person should be declared an infidel even though he has not been entirely convinced of the truth', then this is a serious aspersion; they want people to be disgusted with the religion sent by Allah through His Prophet.

> (*Majmuat Muallafat Muhammad bin Abdul Wahab* 25:5; *Duawil Manawa'een ad Dawa tal Sheikh Muhammad bin Abdul Wahab, swaad* 22)

For detailed commentary by Sheikh Muhammad bin Abdul Wahab, consult Dr Abdul Aziz bin Muhammad bin Ali's book *Da'awi al-Manawaeen*, volume 1.

Sheikh Abdul Latif bin Abdur Rahman bin Hasan Aal al-Sheikh writes:

When Sheikh Muhammad bin Abdul Wahab forgives people who worship graves in the absence of guides and monitors then how can he accuse someone who visits the Sanctuary in Mecca an infidel. The sheikh followed the tradition of the prophet and the straight path and accorded every station the respect it deserved.

> (*Misbah al-Zalam fil radd Ala man Kazb-ul-Sheikh al-Imam, swaad* 84)

434 THE LITERATURE OF *LASHKAR-E-TAYYABA*

He further writes:

> Sheikh Muhammad bin Abdul Wahab exercised such restrain in prac-
> tising *takfir*, that he even spared the ones who call out to the dead in-
> stead of calling out to Allah for help, especially when there is no guide
> or monitor to advise them, the rejection of whose guidance would con-
> firm their status as infidels.
>
> (*Minhaj al-Tasees wal-Taqdees*, *swaad* 98–99)

Another place:

> Our dear sheikh would never declare someone an infidel simply based
> on something they said or did; instead, he restrained himself until the
> truth was revealed to said individual, who would only be labelled an in-
> fidel if he remained committed to falsehood. This attitude is highlighted
> in various parts of his writings and his reasoning is well known.
>
> (*Misbah al-Zalam*, *swaad* 516)

Another place he writes:

> Our sheikh never subjected anyone from the *ummat* to *takfir*; he even
> spared Sahib-i-Bardah and only commented on what the latter actually
> wrote in terms of style and content.
>
> (*Masbah al-Zalam*, *swaad* 461)

Sheikh Abdullah bin Muhammad bin Abdul Wahab was asked if the
worship of symbolic representations at graves was not categorically *kufr*.
He said:

> The issue requires an explanation: if the one who builds a vault over a
> grave learns about the prophet's attitude towards this act but is defiant
> and disobedient and refuses to let these structures be dismantled, then
> this is evidence of *kufr*; however, the one who does this in ignorance is
> not an infidel but merely ignorant and has not engaged with what Allah
> and His Messenger have said about the matter.
>
> (*Majmua tul Rasail wa Masail al-Najdiyah* 246:1)

THE PROBLEM WITH *TAKFIR*   435

Sheikh Ibn Taymiyyah says:

After receiving and internalizing the prophet's message we can say with certainty that the prophet did not allow his *ummat* to call out to the dead, to the prophets and messengers, the saints, or any other individual...

(*Kitab al-Istighatha fil-radd al-Al Bakri, swaad* 411 *tuay. Maktaba Dar al-Minhaj*; vao 629–630:2 *tuay. Dar-ul-Watan*, 831:2 *tuay*)

Just as the prophet did not allow his *ummat* to prostrate before a dead body. In fact we know the prophet forbade all this, and no doubt this is a form of polytheism that the prophet and Allah prohibited. However, the onslaught of ignorance and lack of knowledge regarding the prophet make it impossible to subject the subsequent generations to *takfir* until they have been guided and they are able distinguish between what is permissible and what is not.

Sheikh Ibn Taymiyyah further states:

I say to the Juhayma of the Halwaliyah and to those who deny that Allah is in the heavens that if I were to confirm what you believe I will be an infidel because I know that what you say is *kufr* but I do not consider you infidels for you are ignorant. He said this to their scholars, their sheikhs, and their noblemen.

(*Al-Istighasa fil rad Al-al-Bakri, swaad* 253 *tuay. Dar-al-Minhaj* 383–384:1 *tuay. Dar-al-Watan*)

Imam Ibn Taymiyyah's dying words were that he does not subject anyone to *takfir*, as mentioned in the preamble to this book. Imam Zahbi and Imam Abul Hassan al-Ash'ari came to the same conclusion.

Hazrat Ayesha reports the following *Hadees*:

The night it was my turn (for a visit) the prophet wrapped his shawl around himself, took both his shoes off, spread the hem of his garter belt across the bed, and lay down. After a while the thinking I had fallen asleep, he quietly took his shawl, slipped on his shoes, and stepped outside, closing the door softly behind him. I took my chador over my head

436 THE LITERATURE OF *LASHKAR-E-TAYYABA*

and followed the prophet. He entered the Baqi cemetery, assumed the standing position of prayer, and stood there for a long time. Finally, he raised his hands three times before returning. I too returned with him. When he picked up pace so did I. When he ran, I too ran. Once he arrived, I too arrived. I entered the house before him and lay down. When he entered the room, he said: 'O Ayesha, why are you short of breath?' I said: 'Nothing, O Messenger of Allah.' The prophet said: 'tell me everything or it will be revealed to me.' I said: 'O Messenger, may both my parents sacrifice their lives for you', and proceeded to tell him everything. When I was done, he said: 'you were the shadow that walked ahead of me'. I said: 'yes'. He then hit me on my behind, which hurt, and said: 'Do you think Allah and His Messenger won't honour your due?' She asked: 'When people hide something, does Allah know?' The prophet said: 'Yes. Gabriel came to me; when I noticed him, he called out to me and I tried to hide you from him. I accepted what he had to say and kept it from you. He did not appear to you because you had undressed, and I thought you had fallen asleep. I did not want to wake you up since I thought he would frighten you. Gabriel said: No doubt, your Lord commands you to go to the Baqi cemetery and beg forgiveness on behalf of those buried there.' She said: 'Oh Messenger of Allah, how should I say this?' He replied ...

Imam Ibn Taymiyyah says:

The mother of the believers, Ayesha, asked the prophet: When people hide something does Allah know? And the prophet said: Yes. This proves that she did not know this, and before coming to know that Allah is aware of everything that people try and hide, she could not be considered an infidel.

(*Majmua al-Fatawa la-Ibn Taymiyyah* 412–413:11)

The aforementioned narrative, coupled with the exegesis of the imams and the early Muslims, makes clear that one cannot be declared an infidel until the truth has been ascertained. If one is not familiar with the *shariat*, or simply ignorant, then all their doubts and queries must first be eradicated. However, if one stubbornly continues to deny the truth, and

THE PROBLEM WITH *TAKFIR*   437

defiantly ignores the command of Allah and His Prophet then this person is an infidel.

Summary

It is important to note that comprehending the truth is as important as establishing it. Some believe that the truth is established simply by virtue of hearing about Allah and His Messenger. However, this is not sufficient for it is imperative to understand and comprehend the meaning of the message. For a non-Arab who does not know Arabic, simply hearing the recitation of the Quran or *Hadees* is not enough. Such a person would need the words explained to him in detail. Allah says: 'And We never sent a messenger save with the language of his folk, that he might make (the message) clear for them.' (*Surat Ibrahim* 14:4).

Imam Ibn Katheer notes:

One of Allah's great favours upon His creatures is that He sends them a messenger from among them who speaks to them in their own language that he may explain to them whatever he was sent with.

(*Tafseer Ibn Katheer* 220:3 *ba-tahqiq* Abdurrazzaq al-Mahdi, *tuay. Dar al-Kitab al-Arabiyya*)

Imam al-Mufsirin bin Jareer Tabri writes:

Allah says: Oh Muhammad, before you and your people there was never a messenger sent to a nation who did not speak their language, 'so he can explain to them everything'. Allah says: So whatever injunction and prohibitions are sent through him, he can elaborate, so Allah's authority is proven to them; beyond that, one's potential and limitations are in Allah's hands.

(*Tafseer ul Tabari* 592:13 *ba-tahqiq* Dr Abdullah bin Abdul Moshin Turki)

Allama Sewati reports:

'And We never sent a messenger who did not speak the language of his people, that he might make (the message) clear for them.' Allah says:

438 THE LITERATURE OF *LASHKAR-E-TAYYABA*

'If a certain people spoke Arabic, they were sent an Arab messenger; if they spoke a language other than Arabic, they were sent to a non-Arab; if they spoke Hebrew, they were sent to a messenger who spoke Hebrew, in order that he may expound and explicate in detail whatever message he was sent with in order to establish Allah's authority over them.'

> (*Al-Dadar al-Manthur fi al-Tafseer al-Mathur* 487–488:8, *ba-tahqiq*
> Dr Abdullah bin Abdul Mohsin al-Turki)

Imam Ibn al-Jauzi writes:

Allah says: that he might make (the message) clear for them. Meaning whatever message was delivered through the messenger could be grasped by the messenger.

> (*Zad al-Maseer fi ilm-al-tafseer* 504:2 *ba-tahqiq* Abdur Razzaq al-
> Mahdi, *tuay. Dar al-Kutb-al-Arabiyya*)

Imam Ibn Adil al-Damishqi writes:

In this verse Allah mentions the rewards he has bestowed: one is in the form of the prophet, in how every messenger before him was sent to a specific nation but he was meant for all of humanity; the second is a favour upon the general population, and that is: And We never sent a messenger save with the language of his folk, that he might make (the message) clear for them.

> (*Al-bab fi ulum ul-kitab* 335:11)

He goes on to quote Imam Qurtabi:

Qurtabi stated: In this verse there is no authority over non-Arabs, for once the prophet's message was translated into other languages Allah's authority, and the recognition of this authority, became obligatory.

> (*Al-bab* 336:1; *tafseer al-jamia al-Ahkam al-Quran* 223:9)

Imam Razi says:

Allah has never sent a people a messenger save one who speaks in their language. Because of this, it is incredibly simple for them to understand the injunctions of the *shariat* and familiarize themselves with their obligations.

(al-Tafseer al-Kabeer 26:7 tuay. Dar Ahiya al-taratul-Arabiya)

Nawab Siddique-al-Hassan Khan Qanoji writes:

We never sent a messenger save one who adopted the language of his nation and spoke to them in their idiom for only then is it possible for those who have received a messenger to understand what the messenger tells them and how he guides them; if Allah had sent them a messenger in another language the people would not understand his speech or his sermons and they would have had to spend a long time mastering his language first.

(Fatah al-Biyan fi Maqasid al-Quran 525:3 tuay. Dar al-Kutab al-Ilmiyya)

Allama Abu Hayan al-Andlusi says:

'And we have not sent a messenger ... ' This verse contains a generality that includes the prophet even though his (the prophet's) message is meant for everyone. Such a messenger's flock includes those who do not belong to his nation and who speak a different language; hence, a lot depends on mastering the language for the sake of comprehension.

(Tafseer al-Bahr al-Muheet 518:5)

Allama Abu Muhammad Makki bin Abi Talib al-Qaisi says:

The gist of this verse is that no people were sent a messenger who did not speak their language so they may understand.

He further states:

And prior to Muhammad we did not send a people a messenger save one who spoke their language so whatever warning, guidance, and message Allah wishes the people to receive is expounded upon with clarity in order to establish Allah's authority and they are left with no excuses.

(Al-Hidaya ila balugh ul-Nihaya 3771–3772:5)

440 THE LITERATURE OF *LASHKAR-E-TAYYABA*

Allama Abu al-Barkat Abdullah bin Ahmed al-Nasfi says:

> ... in order that the messenger can clearly explain the message and establish Allah's authority, and they cannot say that the language in which they were addressed was incomprehensible to them. Now one might say that the prophet (Muhammad) was sent as a messenger for all humans, according to Allah: Say (O Muhammad): O mankind! Lo! I am the messenger of Allah to you all (7:158); in fact, he was a messenger to all *djinn* and humans, even though they speak different languages, so how can Allah's authority be established over non-Arabic speakers? I say this issue has two possibilities: He could either deliver the revelations in all the languages of the world or He could deliver it in one; there was no need of the former because translation delivers the message without modifying it. Hence, it was determined that the message will be revealed in a single language. And the language that was chosen was that of his peoples since they were closest to him.
>
> (*Madarak al-Tanzeel o haqaiq al-taweel al-maruf ba-tafseer ul nafsi*
> 162:2 *tuay. Maktaba Rahmania Lahore*)

Allama Abu Mansoor Muhammad bin Mahmood al-Matareedi al-Samarqandi explains the fourth verse of *Surat Ibrahim* in the following words:

> Accordingly, one is more likely to understand, accept, and be drawn to a message in one's own language compared to a foreign tongue; Allah said: so they (the messengers) are able to explain better to them (the people). Some commentators say this refers to the messengers being more accessible, while others say this refers to the messengers' communication skills in helping people understand what is said to them.
>
> (*Taweelat ahl al-Sunnat* 7:3 *tuay. Mussassa tul-risala*)

Allama Alaud-din-Ali bin Muhammad bin Ibrahim al-Baghdadi al-Maroof bil-Khazin says:

> Allah says, 'And We never sent a messenger save with the language of his folk', meaning in the idiom of his people so whatever he delivers, they can receive. He further states:

THE PROBLEM WITH *TAKFIR* 441

'You could say Allah did not send the prophet solely for the Arabs, that he was chosen for all humanity according to Allah's statement: Say: O People! I am Allah's Messenger sent for all of you.... In fact, the prophet was chosen for *djinn* and humans even though they speak different languages. Allah uses the expression 'in the language of his folk', and 'his folk' were none another than the Arabs. On the surface it would appear that the prophet was sent specifically to the Arabs, so it would be impossible to add anyone else to that category. I say: the prophet was chosen from among the Arabs and because the rest of the people follow Arabs, one can say the prophet was in fact chosen for everyone. The prophet spread his message by dispatching his messengers in different directions who would translate the message for the people and would invite them to Islam in their respective languages.

(*Al-bab al-Taweel fi ma'ani al-tanzeel, al-ma'ruf ba-tafseer al-Khazan* 28:3 *tuay. Dar-ul-Kitab al-Ilmiyya Beirut*)

Another time he says: 'No doubt, when messengers spoke the language of their people, the invitation was specific, the book was revealed in the language the people understood, the words were easier to access, and consequently, more likely to establish authority.'

Qazi Shokani mentions something similar in his book Fatah-al-Qadeer. Allama Abu Abdullah Abdur Rahman bin Nasir al-Sa'adi says:

It is Allah's beneficence and grace that the messenger He sent every nation spoke the language of the people in order that he may explain to them Allah's commandments. Revelation in any other language would have required the people to master the new language first before they could begin to understand what was being said. Once a messenger explains all the commandments, prohibitions, and injunctions and once his authority is established over the people, those who do not submit are led astray by Allah, while those Allah blesses are bestowed with righteousness.

(*Tafseer al-Sadi Urdu* 1336:2)

Muhammad ibn al-Uthaymin said something remarkably similar in his exegesis of the Quran.

442 THE LITERATURE OF *LASHKAR-E-TAYYABA*

Dr Wahb-al-Zarhili says:

It is Allah's grace and favour upon us that He sent to every nation a messenger who spoke the language of his people in order that the injunctions of faith are easily explained by the messenger and understood by the people before being transmitted to others.

(*Al-Tafseer al-Muneer Fil Aqeeda wal-Sharia wal-Manhaj* 205:13)

The aforementioned explanations offered by the *ummat*'s leading scholars and *muftis* make clear that for the establishment of any kind of divine authority it is imperative to fully comprehend the credibility of said authority; this comprehension need not attain the stature of Abu Bakr's comprehension and appreciation, but it is important for the individual to know the essence of what Allah and His Messenger have said and for all misgivings to be categorically resolved. Even if this person has heard Quranic recitation and been exposed to the *Hadees* of the prophet, but is unsure regarding the content, then he is not someone upon whom authority has been established.

Sheikh Muhammad Rasheed Raza al-Misri says:

He who has not comprehended the word is not subject to authority.

(*Hamish Majmua al-Rasail al-Najdiya* 514:5)

Summary:

1. *Takfir* is only the purview of Allah and His Messenger.
2. One cannot be subjected to *takfir* until (Allah's) authority has been established and proven.
3. One cannot be subjected to *takfir* until all of one's doubts have been eliminated.
4. One can only be subjected to *takfir* after one's ignorance has been completely eliminated.

No matter how grave a sin one commits in ignorance, if one admits ones mistake and repents then there is no prosecution, even for the sin of bowing before anything other than Allah.

THE PROBLEM WITH *TAKFIR*   443

Causes for such ignorance may be recent conversion to Islam, flawed understanding of Islamic teachings, commitment to parallel faith traditions, and flawed interpretations of Islam.

Third principle

Takfir is not limited to belief or action. A common misunderstanding regarding the issue of *takfir* stems from the notion that *takfir* only applies to principles of belief and faith.

There is no evidence in the Quran, the authentic *Hadees*, or the lives of the early pious Muslims that indicates *takfir* cannot be applied to actions as well; such a notion has nothing to do with Islam or the pious Muslims. In fact, this attitude belongs to the *Khawarij*, the mu'tazilites, *juhmiya*, *isharah*, etc. Sadly, this nonsensical attitude has become so commonplace when dealing with issues of *takfir* that some respected scholars have also gone astray.

While no imam has ever presented any injunction about labelling a Muslim an infidel based on his actions or based on the fact that he has altered aspects of faith, anyone who says or does something *kufr* has indeed committed *kufr*. Such a person deserves a clear warning but does not warrant the infidel label. Simply because something said was *kufr*, does not mean the one making this statement is an infidel or deserving of *takfir*. In fact, if the speaker is disabled or challenged in any way, it is imperative that all the principles of *takfir* are observed before passing any kind of verdict.

Imam Ibn Taymiyyah said:

> A *kufr* statement does not necessarily mean that the one making it is an infidel since said person may be victim to ignorance or a misinterpretation. Undoubtedly, for this specific individual, evidence of *kufr* is no different from the evidence for the terror of the afterlife. There are conditions and constraints as explained in detail earlier.
>
> (*Minhaj al-Sunnat* 240:5. According to the research of Dr Ahmad Rashad Salim)

He writes, elsewhere:

> Undoubtedly, the person who interprets with the aim of following the prophet cannot be subjected to *takfir* and neither can he be labelled a

444 THE LITERATURE OF *LASHKAR-E-TAYYABA*

sinner, particularly when he commits a mistake while exercising *ijtehad* (personal reasoning) since this error is commonly understood as a technical issue. As for matters of belief, the companions of the prophet, the imams, and the ones who follow them never subjected misunderstanding in faith to *takfir*. This practice was developed by those who tend to modify and corrupt religion, such as the *Khawarij*, the mu'tazilites, and the *juhmiyah*; now, their ranks are joined by the followers of Imam Malik, Imam Shafi, and Imam Ahmed.

(Minhaj al-Sunnat 239, 24:5)

It is possible that the one uttering *kufr* speech has not yet comprehended the injunctions accurately; it is also possible that he has received them but has not fully accepted them, or, he may have doubts... in short, he who makes mistakes in an attempt to reach god will know god's mercy and beneficence.

In context of *kufr*, there is no difference between abstract belief and practical action. The early Muslims and the esteemed imams never distinguished between the two categories, that is, labelling errors of belief *kufr* while letting actions off the hook.

We know this is the case for even the companions (of the prophet) had disputes over theological matters, like the disagreement between Aisha and the companions over whether the prophet had actually seen Allah or not.

Ibn Abbas, Ka'ab Ahbar, and various others believed that the prophet had indeed witnessed Allah, whereas Aisha, Ibn Masood, and Abu Hurairah disagreed.

Ibn Abbas says:

You wonder at the fact that Abraham was offered a gift, Moses was offered direct communication, and Muhammad was allowed to witness Allah.

(Kitab al-Sunnat La Abdullah bin Ahmad ibn Hanbal al-Shiyani 523, 1019, 1020, 1021; *Kitab al-Tawheed La-ibn Manda* 657; *Al-Rad Ala min Qal-al-Quran Makhooq* 59)

In another tradition, Abdullah ibn Abbas says:

Muhammad witnessed his Lord in all His glory.

(Kitab al-Sunnat 1022–1023; Tirmidhi 3280; *Al-Sunnat Ibn Abi Asim* 444, 430; *Sharah Asool Aiteqad Ahl-al-Sunnat wal-Jamat* 817; *Al-Kamil Ibn Adi* 277:6; *Al-Sama wal-Safat* 444)

THE PROBLEM WITH *TAKFIR* 445

Ibn Abbas's words imply a literal witnessing of Allah while in another tradition they are taken to mean, 'witnessing by the heart'; the unrestricted witnessing is dependent on the limited. Imam Ata quotes Ibn Abbas and says, 'Ibn Abbas said that the prophet witnessed Allah with his heart (Muslim, *Kitab al-Iman* 284:176).'

Abul 'Aliyah quotes Ibn Abbas who cites the following Quranic verses, 'The heart lied not (in seeing) what it saw. Will ye then dispute with him concerning what he seeth? (*Surat al-Najm* 53:11 and 12).

Furthermore, consider *Tafseer Ibn Katheer* 6:23–24, according to the research of Abdur Razzaq al-Mahdi:

These verses imply that the prophet witnessed (Allah) twice with his heart.

Masrooq reports his conversation with Aisha:

'Dear Mother, did Muhammad see his Lord?' She replied, 'what you have said is shocking. Where are you with these three verses? Whoever told you this, was lying. Whoever told you Muhammad saw his Lord is lying.' Then Aisha, the Mother of the Believers recited the following verses: Vision comprehendeth Him not, but He comprehendeth (all) vision. He is the Subtle, the Aware (6, 103). And it was not (vouchsafed) to any mortal that Allah should speak to him unless (it be) by revelation or from behind a veil, or (that) He sendeth a messenger to reveal what He will by His leave. Lo! He is Exalted, Wise (42:51). 'Whoever told you that Muhammad knows what is to come tomorrow is lying.' Then, she recited the following verse: No soul knoweth what it will earn tomorrow (31: 34). Then she said, 'whoever told you that he (Muhammad) has concealed a verse, is also lying.' Then she recited the following verse: O Messenger! Make known that which hath been revealed unto thee from thy Lord (5:67). 'However, the prophet saw the angel Gabriel in his true form twice'.

(Bukhari, *Kitab al-Tafseer Surat Najm* 4800 *wa Kitab Bidd al-Khalq* 3234, 3235; *Kitab Tawheed* 7380; Muslim 177:328; Tirmidhi 3278; *Masnad Ahmad* 275:42227/40; *Masnad Abi Yala* 4901 and 4902; *Tafseer al-Tabri Surat al-Maidah* 28; *wa Surat tul-Inam* 103; *Masnad Abi Awana* 154–100:1; *Kitab al-Iman La Ibn Manda* 767 and 768)

446 THE LITERATURE OF *LASHKAR-E-TAYYABA*

Ibn Taymiyyah says:

Whatever was stated by Abdullah bin Abbas in Sahih Bukhari with regards to witnessing Allah proves one thing: he claimed the prophet witnessed Allah in all His glory with his heart, twice, and Aisha denied this. Some people have tried proving both statements to be true in that Aisha denies ocular apperception while Abdullah bin Abbas insists the heart bore witness.

(Majmua al-Fatawal Ibn Taymiyyah 509:6)

Further discussion on this issue can be found in: *Fatawa Ibn Taymiyyah Mazkura bil-Imqam and Majmua al-Fatawa* 3:239 and 242; *Fatah-al-Bari* 10:239–242; *Sharah Sahih Muslim al-Nuuwi, Al-Kashf wal-Biyan lil-Sabli* 140–142, *Waghirhum).*
Whether Allah can be witnessed or not is a matter of belief and the most righteous among the early Muslims had profound disagreements over the matter as evidenced in the aforementioned discussion. However, none of the individuals involved ever subjected their opponent to *takfir.*
Additionally, denying the ritual obligation of prayer, fasting, pilgrimage, modesty, etc. is *kufr.* These are practical issues, yet disagreements over these issues do not warrant *takfir.* For further discussion, see *Majmua al-Fatawa al-Ibn Taymiyyah* 3:229–231.
Imam Ibn Taymiyyah says:

Undoubtedly, speech can be *kufr,* such as declaring prayer, charity, fasting, and pilgrimage non-obligatory, or declaring fornication, alcohol, gambling, and incest permissible. Those inclined to such acts may never have heard the corresponding injunctions which is why the person making such declarations cannot be subjected to *takfir,* for he may be a recent convert, or he may live in a remote territory with little access to Islamic learning. Consequently, when such a person denies what was revealed to the prophet, he cannot be declared an infidel since he is ignorant about the revelations.

Imam Ibn Taymiyyah's aforementioned quote sheds light on numerous issues with *takfir* but also proves that *takfir* is neither limited to abstractions nor specific to rituals.

THE PROBLEM WITH *TAKFIR* 447

It is important to note that for the one who exercises *ijtehad* (personal reasoning), as he strives for proximity with Allah, he will be guaranteed Allah's mercy for such a person structure's his beliefs entirely upon the foundation of the Quran and the *Hadees* of the prophet.

Imam Muhammad bin Abdul Wahab upheld this principle based on the writings of Imam Ibn Taymiyyah and declared that *takfir* could not be exercised without the categorical establishment of authority and faith, regardless of whether the issues at hand are practical or abstract.

Imam Ibn Taymiyyah says:

Our adversaries accuse us of exercising *takfir* by labelling an ignorant person an infidel upon a whim or as a favour; these are serious allegations with no basis in reality aimed only to instil hatred among the people for Allah, His Prophet, and His faith.

> (*Majmua al-Fatawal Ibn Taymiyyah* 220:3; *Dar al-Jeel al-Tib'a tel-Wala* 1997, 1418 AH) (*Muallafat al-sheikh-ul-imam Muhammad Bin Abdul Wahab* 25:6; *Al-Qasm-ul-Khamis al-Rasail al-Shakhsiya, Wafi Nuskha* 14:3; *Al-Rasail al-Shakhsiya*)

In fact, Imam Ibn Taymiyyah also said:

When we refuse to subject the worshippers of Ahmad Badawi's grave for being ignorant and devoid of guidance how can we subject non-polytheists to *takfir*?

> (*Minhaj Ahl-al-Haq wal-Taba: Misbah-ul-Zalam. Al-Dar Rasiniyya*)

He later addresses the allegations against him:

Those who level allegations against me accuse me of labelling saint-worshippers infidels and subjecting them to *takfir* based on Busiri's statement; I am accused of saying that I will topple the prophet's tombstone if I had the chance, and that I would replace the Ka'ba's aqueduct with a wooden one, and that I consider visiting the prophet's grave a sin, and that I deny any need to visit the graves of ones parents, and that anyone who swears by anything other than Allah I label an infidel, and that I subject Ibn al-Fariz and Ibn-al-Arabi to *takfir*, and that

448 THE LITERATURE OF *LASHKAR-E-TAYYABA*

I encourage the burning of *Dalail-ul-Khairat* and *Rawd-al-Rayaheen* and that I call the latter *Rawd-al-Shayateen*... I only have one response: These are serious allegations!

(*Muallafat-ul-Sheikh* 12:6; *Al-Qasm-ul-Khamis* 8–7:3,
Al-Rasala-tul-Aula)

Sheikh Muhammad bin Abdul Wahab adds:

No doubt, those who have passed away will not be branded infidels, even if their writings are littered with polytheism dressed in powerful rhetoric; the only step that needs to be taken in their regard is a compete refutation of their work. It is important to remember that anyone who explicitly follows their belief system (different from Islam) is a polytheist and an infidel and will be handed over to Allah, but it is inappropriate to try the dead for it cannot be known if the deceased repented or not.

(*Davi Manawa'een; saad* 223; *Majmua-i-Rasail-wal-Masail* 48:1)

Polytheists, innovators, and *shariat*-offenders are referenced here with great caution because accusing any Muslim of being an infidel is a grave crime.

The learned can only issue a *fatwa* declaring an individual an infidel after all the rules and regulations for *takfir* have been rigorously satisfied. In this day and age, incompetent souls issue *fatwa*s, throwing open the floodgates of bloodshed and violence.

Summary

Takfir makes no distinction between abstract and practical issues. In certain matters of principle, despite clear disagreements, *takfir* is impossible, much like the disagreements between the companions. While the denial of the obligation of certain abstract and practical injunctions warrants *takfir*, those who live in remote regions cannot be subjected to this practice despite denying said obligations. Commonly misunderstood, *takfir* is not limited to practical issues or specific to abstract issues of faith, as evidenced in the aforementioned discussion.

11

Destination Kashmir is Nigh by Ali Imran Shaheen

Here we present translated excerpts from Ali Imran Shaheen's 2011 book, *Kashmir: Manzil Dur Nahin (Destination Kashmir is Nigh)*.[1] Like many of LeT's historical materials, this volume presents a highly stylized history on the region. Much of the content in *Destination Kashmir is Nigh* depicts purported atrocities committed by the Indian Army in Kashmir. The introductory chapters, which we have translated and included in this volume, provide a deeply problematic outline of the history of the Kashmiri resistance and, more importantly, the alleged enduring relationship between the local resistance and LeT. To lend gravity and legitimacy to his claims, Shaheen adopts a decidedly more eloquent tone in the introductory chapters compared to the language he uses to describe the episodes of violence he posits, for which he employs simpler and colloquial verbiage. In describing the purpose of this title, the author states on page 27: 'This manuscript presents only a fraction of the sacrifices made in the six months from 11 June 2010 to 11 December 2010. If every single instance of aggression were documented, countless volumes would fill endless stacks in the libraries of justice. Every effort has been made to cover all aspects of the struggle; additionally, the history of the movement and the geography of the region have also been examined in considerable depth.'

What makes this book interesting is not that it charts out a different narrative or proposes a different set of facts than those available to Pakistanis in their media, public school curriculum, or even Pakistani military publications; rather, it is that it echoes the same distorted history to which Pakistanis have become accustomed to and which many accept as reality despite the ready availability of peer-reviewed articles and scholarly books which undermine these narratives.[2] Understanding the extent to which ordinary Pakistanis embrace this fundamentally

450 THE LITERATURE OF *LASHKAR-E-TAYYABA*

perverted accounting of the history of Pakistan's security obsession with India, its role in creating the current situation in Indian-administered Kashmir, and its role in undermining security in India and the rest of South Asia should sober those in India and elsewhere that rapprochement or even dialogue with Pakistan can be a useful way forward. After all, how can you have a dialogue on possible futures if the participants have radically different understandings of the past?

This 348-page volume, which comprises seven parts, each with numerous brief chapters, is quite unwieldy. Necessarily we present only representative selections herein. We first provide translations of all of the extensive prefatory material including: the publisher's note authored by Javed-al-Hassan Siddiqui, the then editor of Dar-ul-Andlus; a preface titled 'A few Words' by Professor Hafiz Muhammad Saeed, the *emir* JuD/LeT; another short prefatory piece titled 'Jubilation!' by Amir Hamza,[3] a founding ideologue of JuD/LeT and who is the Convener of the *Tehreek-e-Hurmat-e-Rasool* (Movement for the Sacredness of the Prophet, another LeT front organization); and another preamble titled 'Words of Praise' by Hafiz Saifullah Mansoor, the chairman, *Tehreek-e-Azadi Jammu Kashmir*. Next, we present several other introductory sections by the author including: 'Jammu Kashmir: The Region', 'The Freedom Movement', the 'All Parties Hurriyat (Liberation) Conference', and 'Prominent Political Leaders of Kashmir's Freedom Movement'. We then present an excerpt from Chapter 1 ('Get Out of Jammu Kashmir'), titled eponymously 'Get Out of Kashmir'. That chapter has eleven sections on the title theme. From Chapter 2, 'Every Wound is Kashmir', we translate five sections, namely, 'From All Sides: The Wounded, The Dead, The Blood and Tears', 'Forces Aimed for the Head: Dozens Left Disabled', 'Young Men Forced to Parade Naked', 'Thousands Murdered for Protesting Insults against the Quran', and 'A Habitable Valley or an Open-Air Prison: Tales of Horror'. From Chapter 3, 'We Will Never Submit', we translate several sections including: 'Pakistan's Independence Day: The Valley Runs Red; River Jhelum Runs Green', 'Who Was Ahad Jan?', 'Rs. 500,000 Bounty: Indians Celebrate Musarrat Alam's Imprisonment', and 'Shabir Shah's Release: Hindus Attack Press Conference'. From Chapter 4, titled 'Never Forget the Blood We Spilt', we offer translations of three sections, including: 'Rafiq Bangroo: The Seventh Martyr of His Clan', 'Pretending to Search a Dumped Body', and 'I Will End My Fast in Heaven'. As with other items presented in this volume, the author makes heavy use of section headers to indicate topical or logical transitions. We retain all organizing structures of the original.

Publisher's Note

الحمدُ لِلهِ رَبِّ العالَمِينَ وَالصلوةُ وَالسَّلامُ عَلى أَشرَفِ الأَنبِياءِ وَمُرسَلِينَ
أَأَمَّا بَعدُ!

Over the past sixty-three years, while the freedom struggle for Jammu Kashmir against Hindustan's brutal domination and oppression has seen many highs and lows, never has the Kashmiri Muslim's desire for liberation wavered. On 11 June 2010, the cold-blooded murder of an innocent young man pumped fresh life into a movement defined by the slogan 'Indians! Get Out of Jammu Kashmir'. For the first time in the history of the struggle, people from all walks of life and from every corner of the valley joined this movement and mobilized in a highly disciplined fashion.

Ali Imran Saheen, well-known literary activist and editor of the weekly *Jarrar*, penned the day-to-day progress and challenges of the movement in a single manuscript titled *Manzil dur Nahin (The Destination is Nigh)*. In this book, he situates the freedom struggle within the geopolitical history of the valley and offers a brief introduction to its political founders and their invaluable contributions. His manuscript also compiles the unprecedented sacrifices made by ordinary individuals in the face of indiscriminate Indian cruelty and aggression.

In the course of conducting a meticulous and exhaustive review of the freedom movement, the author proves that this peaceful struggle carries a resounding message for global organizations, international agencies, and societies that value equity and justice.

Furthermore, this manuscript reveals that the peaceful freedom movement has had a positive global impact in how it has been a source of profound embarrassment for India and her diplomats across the world.

The author pays particular attention to the young leadership that has offered the next generation a strong foundation upon which to breathe

452 THE LITERATURE OF *LASHKAR-E-TAYYABA*

new life into the movement; every youth in Kashmir demands to know why Hindustan is bent on depriving the people of the valley their god-given gift of freedom; they want to know why they are not allowed to live and practise their religion in peace, and why they are denied their right to self-determination?

When the youth of a nation begin asking these questions, the destination is never far, and the mightiest obstacles turn to dust. World history testifies that even the most tyrannical regimes cannot deny liberty to nations willing to sacrifice their lives for freedom. Dar-ul-Andlus has the unique honour of publishing the stories of the freedom fighters, foot-soldiers, and leaders of the Jammu Kashmir freedom movement.

Finally, we pray that the author's efforts bear fruit, and he proves to be an instrument of peace and civil activism for those who strive for freedom. Amen.

In Need of Prayers,
Javed-al-Hassan Siddiqui
Editor Dar-ul-Andlus
22 Safar-al-Muzaffar 1432 AH–27 January 2011

A Few Words

The liberation of Kashmir is critical to Pakistan for a number of political, religious, and economic reasons. From a religious perspective, Kashmiris are our nearest Muslim brothers being persecuted and oppressed by India; the Quran commands us, 'It is imperative that you help the Muslim brothers who are close to you' (*Surat al-Tauba*).[4] What is more, the success of this struggle will not only liberate Kashmir but also free the 260 million Indian Muslims who live as untouchables in servitude of Hindu Brahmins.

From another angle, Kashmir's freedom struggle is an existential battle for Pakistan. Pakistan's founder Muhammad Ali Jinnah said Kashmir is Pakistan's lifeline, that is, Pakistan is economically tied to the valley which is the fountainhead of every one of Pakistan's rivers. India controls these rivers with an iron fist through more than sixty-two dams; during monsoons, the floodgates are opened to waterlog our lands, while at the height of the dry season water is held back in order to turn Pakistan into a desert.

In short, the freedom of Kashmir is imperative to preserve Kashmiri Muslims' faith, to guard their Muslim identity, to protect Pakistan's economic and military resources, and to end the oppression of Indian Muslims. Today, India is plagued with over a hundred separatist movements, more than any other country in the world, as testaments to the country's tyrannical regime and the ruthless domination of the Hindu moneylender. To help Kashmiri Muslims succeed is to help countless persecuted nations within India gain their freedom for our assistance can guarantee their liberation. Despite knowing full well that Kashmiris are categorically opposed to Indian rule, the Indian government is bent on maintaining its control over the valley for it knows the day Kashmir is liberated, a hundred other states will immediately declare their independence, and India, as we know it, will fall apart like the scattered beads of a rosary undone. In particular, the civil movement, mobilized in Kashmir over the past three years in which women, children, and the elderly have pushed the Indian Army up against the wall with nothing but sticks and stones, has made India lose all credibility on the world stage; the writing on the wall is clear as day: the centre will not hold! Every Muslim is contributing in some way or another to making this struggle a success. Ali Imran Shaheen is one such individual who has unsheathed his pen for the cause. While the weekly *Jarrar* regularly features his biting editorials, the effort he has put into documenting the movement 'Indians, Get Out of Jammu Kashmir' is unmatched. The dedication with which he reviews the last sixty-three years of the relentless freedom struggle, as well as his superb presentation of various ground realities in Kashmir, compiled in the single manuscript of *Destination Kashmir is Nigh* are proof of his commitment to the region.

The perceptive reader will know that Kashmir's liberation is nigh. India is already on the brink of collapse; it trembles at the prospect of the last straw that will break its back.

I pray that Allah accept the author's efforts and make him a guiding light for those struggling for freedom. Amen.

Professor Hafiz Muhammad Saeed
Emir Jamaat-ud-Dawah, Pakistan

Jubilation!

The author, Ali Imran Shaheen, lives up to his name. He has the spirit of a falcon, he is well versed in Arabic and English, and when he sits at his computer, he soars through the Internet scouring news reports from around the world. I knew his investigative skills well before they were revealed to the world in the weekly *Jarrar*. I have nothing but high praise for him. I was delighted to hear he has made a reputation for himself as a remarkable orator as well. Some time ago, I advised him to expand his horizons and apply his skills to a lengthier writing project and before I knew it, he was breaking new ground in journalism. With Kashmir as his first subject, he collected first-hand narratives from the persecuted and the oppressed while giving context to their condition through a comprehensive history of the Kashmiri freedom struggle. I have seen him work; his efforts inspire tears and hope with a clear message: those who believe in truth must never cower before aggression for the unarmed masses can obliterate the world's mightiest army with determination and resolve.

Indeed, as *Shaheen* the Falcon observes Kashmir from his vantage point in the sky, he fills our hearts with the sorrowful realization that we are not doing enough for our brothers in the valley; at the same time, he is optimistic that our efforts, no matter how trivial, will, one day, make a difference. Today, India is humiliated on the world stage for its treatment of Kashmiris; soon, there will come a time when Kashmiris will be liberated and the falcons of the valley will take to the skies. Regardless, those who dare to dream and those who dare to document these dreams are making invaluable contributions to the struggle. It is only a matter of time before our journalists swoop down into the valley and report back on our victories, Insha' Allah!

It is clear to me this dream is what inspired Ali Imran Shaheen to write *Destination Kashmir is Nigh*. May Allah accept his efforts. Amen.

Amir Hamza
Convener, Movement *Hurmat-e-Rasool*, Pakistan

Words of Praise

Although Kashmiris' endurance is unparalleled in world history, they have been unable to gain their freedom because they are Muslims, and the global forces of the times not only sabotage them, but also conspire to relegate all Muslims to a life of servitude and humiliation. Currently, the Indian government has the full backing and support of the world community; despite this, the people of Kashmir have not once lost hope. Hundreds of thousands of civilians have been slaughtered, and hundreds of thousands of homes and businesses have been reduced to ashes, but not once has the cry for freedom wavered. None can deny the vigour of the movement that started in 2010. Pakistan has played an unforgettable role in the freedom struggle; countless Pakistanis ache to see their brothers win their freedom but our efforts will only bear fruit once we burn with the same passion and resolve with which Kashmiris blaze the path to their liberation.

This book is the result of Brother Ali Imran Shaheen's laborious efforts as a young journalist profoundly concerned with the plight of Kashmiris. His work is a manifestation of the passion that not only consumes Kashmiris, but also everyone sympathetic to their cause. He gives voice to their resistance in an attempt to make their condition known to the world; he inspires us to assist our brothers while ensuring our own protection, for Kashmir is critical to Pakistan's security. May Allah reward his work with freedom for Kashmir. May our dreams of liberation come true, and may we soon see the day when the banner of Islam is unfurled over Srinagar's Laal Chowk, a landmark Kashmiris have guarded, to this day, from India's tri-coloured flag.

Stimulate your emotions with Ali Imran Shaheen's extraordinary achievement and spread the word so we are all fortunate enough to participate in this struggle.

Hafiz Saifullah Mansoor
Chairman, *Tehreek-e-Azadi Jammu Kashmir*

456 THE LITERATURE OF *LASHKAR-E-TAYYABA*

Preamble

Over the past sixty-three years, through undying perseverance and an impenetrable iron will, the people of Kashmir have evolved into the heavenly *ababeel* that stall the Indian Abraha's elephantine tanks dead in their tracks with nothing more than pebbles and stones—the fearless birds of resistance plunge head first into the very firestorms blazed to rout them out, sacrificing their lives in order to extinguish the flames of oppression and injustice. Thousands have died; thousands more are prepared to die. As it stands, Abraha's forces have brought everything to the fight, but the relentless birds of freedom refuse to give up.

Through 2008, 2009, and 2010, Kashmiris stunned the world by resisting the full might of the Indian Army's brutality and aggression with sticks and stones and while civilians were being massacred indiscriminately, they never stopped resisting. It seemed every soul in the valley was possessed; every man, woman, and child was out to lapidate the Indian devil as the world either watched or tried desperately to protect the aggressor.

The book *Destination Kashmir is Nigh* offers background and context to the movement 'Indians! Get Out of Jammu Kashmir', that now consumes every inch of the valley. Fire rains down from the sky to extinguish this movement but nothing seems capable of snuffing it out.

The rising wave of discontent in the valley has shaken the Indian establishment at its core. The very government officials, who, until recently, reassured the world that the situation in Kashmir was under control and that the issue had been resolved, are now forced to reconsider their statements. They find *Lashkar-e-Tayyaba* at the centre of every issue that grips not only Kashmir, but also the rest of their country.

Since 2001, the people of Kashmir have expressed their solidarity, their support, and their undying love for *Lashkar-e-Tayyaba*, which is why Delhi has squarely blamed the organization for the 2008 and 2009 uprisings, as well as the 2010 movement known as 'Indians! Get Out of Jammu Kashmir'. The people first started expressing their solidarity with the *Lashkar* publicly, in 2001; by 2008, the entire valley echoed with the cry, 'India's end is loud and clear... The *Lashkar*'s here! The *Lashkar*'s here!' Today, every Kashmiri heart beats to the rhythm of this death knell.

From the outset, Indians blamed the *Lashkar-e-Tayyaba* for launching the movement that is now known as 'Indians! Get Out of Jammu Kashmir'. In December 2010, official reports stated that Indian authorities in Kashmir held the *Lashkar* responsible for the pelting of stones by young men, children, elders, and women; the taking of lives; and for rendering all of the verdant Kashmir into a disgrace for India. During a press conference, the Deputy Inspector General of South Kashmir announced that, on 5 December 2010, police and intelligence agencies arrested Shaukat Ahmed alias Adnan Basharat resident of Bandipora Bajbhara, who was found in possession of a matrix code, Chinese grenades, and a motorcycle; as the investigation widened, three more men were arrested: Fayyaz Ahmed Talak, Javaid Ahmed Salafi, and Fayyaz Ahmed Daar were charged with inciting potential recruits to take up arms.

What is surprising is that, until recently, India referred to *Lashkar-e-Tayyaba* as a ragtag gang of Pakistani thugs; today, it is widely believed that Kashmiris have collectively sworn allegiance to the organization as it leads every single nationalistic movement and protest in the valley. One can only conclude by the statements issued by the Indian establishment that the entire occupied valley is aligned, in life, and in death, with *Lashkar-e-Tayyaba*.

'Indians! Get Out of Jammu Kashmir!' is the name of an unparalleled and unprecedented show of resistance that encompasses the firestorms of Indian aggression with the deluge of Kashmiri blood.

This is a historical document... a literary manuscript... an eternal tale! This chronicle of martyrs will revitalize one's faith. The end to Indian aggression by one of the most brutally oppressed people of the world is nothing short of a legend; the numerous accounts of heroism and courage will reignite the fires of passion among all those who value Kashmir's liberation.

Readers will concede that considering Kashmiris have never once wavered in the face of terrible losses and persecution, we have no excuse to back down from contributing to their cause; also, given India's persistent failure in maintaining its hold over the valley through brute force backed by superior firepower, it is obvious that occupied Kashmir will soon know freedom (Allah-willing).

This manuscript presents only a fraction of the sacrifices made in the six months from 11 June 2010 to 11 December 2010. If every single

458 THE LITERATURE OF *LASHKAR-E-TAYYABA*

instance of aggression were documented, countless volumes would fill endless stacks in the libraries of justice. Every effort has been made to cover all aspects of the struggle; additionally, the history of the movement and the geography of the region have also been examined in considerable depth.

One might feel a sense of repetition in the events described herein; this is because every single bloody anecdote is the product of a unique form of brutality and injustice. I have tried to present every event as those who experienced it narrated it to me.

I have kept this manuscript clear of any sort of sentimentality or sensationalism; history need not be tainted with literary and artistic flourishes.

The Kashmiri struggle with its various rhythms and immeasurable sacrifices is a light unto all nations that actively seek freedom; this book is an attempt at capturing that light in a single volume. It will speak to all those invested in Pakistan's prosperity and Islam's inevitable rise. I hope that every bleeding heart exposed to these pages will spontaneously cry out: 'Destination Kashmir is Nigh'.

Wa'Salaam
Ali Imran Shaheen
Editor, Weekly *Jarrar*
Spokesperson, Movement for the Inviolability of
the Prophet, Pakistan
26 January 2011

Jammu Kashmir: The Region

Cradled in the Himalayas, Jammu Kashmir has been called A Piece of Heaven, Little Iran, and the Jewel of Asia. When the Mughal Emperor Jahangir viewed this region, he broke out in verse:
This land is a reflection
of heaven on earth
Kashmir is bordered by Pakistan, Afghanistan, China, and India; currently, portions of the region are disputed between Pakistan, India, and China. The Indian occupied territory is geographically divided into three regions: Kashmir Valley, Jammu, and Ladakh. With the changing seasons, the local seat of government shifts from the summer capital in

DESTINATION KASHMIR IS NIGH 459

Srinagar to the winter capital in Jammu. The seasonal shifting the capital began under Sikh rule due to severe snowfall and extreme winters but continues till today for not only does this tradition cater to the Hindu population of Jammu, but it also conveniently feeds the Indian narrative that Hindus have as much of a right over the region as anyone else (since Jammu is predominantly Hindu).

Jammu Kashmir is a fully recognized state of the Indian federation; administratively, it is divided into Jammu and Kashmir, that are further divided into twenty-two districts with ten districts in Jammu, ten in Kashmir, and two in Ladakh.

The districts of Occupied Jammu comprise: 1) Kathua, 2) Jammu, 3) Samba, 4) Udhampur, 5) Reasi, 6) Rajouri, 7) Poonch, 8) Doda, 9) Ramban, and 10) Kishtwar.

Occupied Kashmir comprises the following districts: 1) Islamabad (former Ant Nag), 2) Kulgam, 3) Pulwama, 4) Shopian, 5) Budgam, 6) Srinagar, 7) Ganderbal, 8) Bandipora, 9) Baramulla, and 10) Kupwara.

Ladakh comprises the districts of Kargil and Leh.

Azad Kashmir is divided into the following districts: 1) Bagh, 2) Bhimber, 3) Hattian, 4) Haveli, 5) Kotli, 6) Mirpur, 7) Muzaffarabad, 8) Neelam, 9) Poonch, and 10) Sudhnoti.

Gilgit-Baltistan, formerly a part of Jammu Kashmir, is now a part of Pakistan, and divided into the following districts: 1) Hunza Nagar, 2) Astore, 3) Diamer, 4) Ghizer, 5) Skardu, 6) Gilgit, and 7) Ghanche.

A portion of Jammu Kashmir was occupied during the Indo-China War of 1962 and remains under Chinese control.

According to a land survey in 1846, the total area of Jammu Kashmir is 224,778 square kilometres. Currently, India controls 101,387 square kilometres. Azad Jammu Kashmir, including Gilgit-Baltistan, is 85,846 square kilometres, while China controls 37,555 square kilometres of the region.

The population of Occupied Kashmir is approximately 9.5 million of which, 6 million reside in the valley of Kashmir. Ninety-five per cent of these residents are Muslim, while the rest are Sikh and Hindu.

Jammu hosts a population of 3.5 million of which only 40 per cent is Muslim, 55 per cent Hindu, while 5 per cent belong to various other

460   THE LITERATURE OF *LASHKAR-E-TAYYABA*

religions. Until 1947, this too was a Muslim majority area but after independence, the Indian authorities altered the demographics of the region. (This shall be discussed later, in detail).

Approximately 1.5 million people from Occupied Kashmir have been rendered homeless due to military and state aggression; a large number of them live in refugee camps in Azad Kashmir. Approximately 3.5 million people reside in Azad Kashmir and 1.5 million in Gilgit-Baltistan. The total population of Jammu Kashmir is 14.5 million.

Pakistan-controlled Kashmir is divided into Azad Kashmir and the northern areas, each of which is ruled by distinct governments. Approximately 100 per cent of Muslims in Azad Kashmir are Sunni, while the majority in Baltistan are Shiʿa. A third religious group called Noorbakhshia is also present in the region and its adherents hold a mix of Shiʿa and Sunni beliefs; they form approximately 20 per cent of the population. While Sunnis are in majority in Gilgit, a large number of Ismailis are settled there as well.

Approximately 98 per cent of the people settled in Pakistan-controlled Kashmir are Muslim.

The largest city in the region is Srinagar. The literacy rate in the region is 67 per cent, the twenty-first highest in the world. The world's second tallest peak, K-2, and the region's largest lake, Lake Dal, are located here as well.

The largest river of the region is Indus, which is one of the mighty rivers of the world; additionally, Jehlum, Shevak, Istur, Gilgit, Neelum, Poonch, Chenab, and Ravi also irrigate the region.

While Lake Dal is the most well-known tourist attraction, the region is popular for countless other stunning lakes such as Wooler, Nageen, Anchar, Mansibal, Sheeshnag, Konsarnag, Gangabul, Tarsarmarsar, Krishanwrishan, Sarrama, Rush, Alpathar, Shundur, Bort, Kashura, Sadpara, Sobri, Rama, Pangang, Siransar, Sunasar, Shevsar, Banjosa, and Ratigali.

Srinagar was a prominent city even for the Mughals who built numerous gardens around Lake Dal, such as Shalimar Bagh, Nishat Bagh, Naseem Bagh, and Charchinar Bagh.

(Indians merely pay lip service to Srinagar by calling it India's crown; to date, they have not carried out a single extensive development project in the city worth mentioning).

Numerous passes link Kashmir to neighbouring countries, particularly Pakistan and India, although it is interesting to note that the passes leading to Pakistan are open all year round while those connecting the region to India are blocked due to severe weather conditions in the winter. The most important and strategic road leading to Srinagar via Jammu has been connected at Banihal with the Jawaharlal Nehru tunnel but even this route is completely blocked during the winters due to extreme snowfall, and during the summers due to extreme rains. There is no doubt in anyone's mind that in terms of religion, tradition, politics, geography, language, and demographics, this region belongs to Pakistan, but ...!

The Freedom Movement

Jammu Kashmir has a thousand-year-old history. Muslims ruled the region for hundreds of years. After the English took over the land, they sold the entire region to Maharaja Gulab Singh for 7.5 million royal Sikh coins. At the time of partition, Gulab Singh's great grandson, Maharaja Hari Singh, ruled the region.

During partition, when the English handed over Muslim-majority Gurdaspur to India, allowing the latter easy access to Kashmir, Maharaja Hari Singh took the opportunity to extend his allegiance to India and started persecuting his Muslim subjects. Consequently, Muslim tribal platoons and voluntary *mujahideen* set out to help their Muslim brothers and made it as far as Baramulla via Muzaffarabad. On 26 October 1947, Maharaja Hari Singh escaped from Srinagar to Jammu from where he asked for Indian assistance. The Indians were eager for the popular Kashmiri leader Sheikh Muhammad Abdullah's vote except at the time, Hari Singh had imprisoned him. Upon India's insistence, Hari Singh released Sheikh Muhammad Abdullah who went on to become a pro-Indian politician; thus, Sheikh Muhammad Abdullah proved to be the first, and the worst, of many traitors who were to become the Kashmiri people's greatest misfortune. On 27 October 1947, Indian forces landed at Srinagar airport and took control of the entire valley.

Meanwhile, when Pakistan's founder and first Governor-General Quaid-e-Azam Muhammad Ali Jinnah, ordered his army to march on Kashmir, the English Commander-in-Chief of the Pakistan Army,

462   THE LITERATURE OF *LASHKAR-E-TAYYABA*

General Gracey, categorically refused. The tribal paramilitary forces and Kashmiri militants continued their operations independently, until they were joined in May 1948 by the Pakistan military. That same year, on 15 August, Skardu was won. It was only when Srinagar and Poonch were about to be sacked by the Pakistani forces that India appealed to the UN for help, a manoeuvre that led to a ceasefire agreement. As part of the agreement, a plebiscite was promised to the people of Kashmir. As a result of the ceasefire, Pakistan recalled its tribal paramilitary forces, and a number of areas that had already been won were returned to India.

(Why the *jihadi* paramilitary and voluntary *mujahideen* were unable to go beyond Baramulla or take control of Srinagar's airport, and how they returned, remains a mystery).

India appealed to the UN on 1 January 1948 and the ceasefire agreement, which contained the pledge of a plebiscite, was passed on 5 February 1948, but to date, India has failed to honour any one of its agreements; what is more, not a single country in the world has exerted any kind of pressure on India to do so.

In 1953, Sheikh Muhammad Abdullah was thrown in jail under Pandit Nehru's watch for demanding a plebiscite. He was released in May 1964, a few months before Nehru's death.

In June 1965, Operation Gibraltar was launched to liberate Kashmir; this operation expanded into an all-out war which Pakistan would have won had it not been dragged to the negotiation table where defeat was snatched from the jaws of victory. At this time, Bakhshi Ghulam Muhammad, Ghulam Sadiq, and Sheikh Muhammad Abdullah formed governments in Kashmir. In 1979, the Russians attacked Afghanistan.

When the Afghans beat the Russians out of their homeland with an unprecedented display of valour, Kashmiris were inspired. Through extensive planning and strategizing, in 1982, the first militant base was set up in Occupied Kashmir. In 1984, the popular Kashmiri leader, Maqbool Butt was imprisoned on charges of militancy and hanged in Tihar jail. (Separately, a case was lodged against Maqbool Butt for conspiring to murder the Indian diplomat Ravindra Mehta, in the UK). At the time, the traitor Sheikh Muhammad Abdullah's son Farooq Abdullah was in power; protests against the judicial assassination of Maqbool Butt were met with brute force and, in the face of growing tension and resentment in the valley, the Indian government replaced

Farooq Abdullah with his brother-in-law, G.M. Shah, in a futile attempt to control the situation.

Over the next three years the inhabitants of Occupied Kashmir started declaring their allegiance and support for Pakistan, publicly. On 31 July 1988, two massive explosions that rocked Srinagar caused Indian forces to descend onto the valley and set up a network of spies and military bases across the region as they started arresting civilians indiscriminately. Seventeen days later, General Zia-ul-Haq was assassinated in a plane crash that plunged Kashmir into an abyss of despair and mourning. For many days after General Zia's death, Kashmiri cities turned into ghost towns, a testament to Kashmiris' attitude and feelings towards Pakistan, General Zia, and *jihadi* movements.

'We're going to cross the border / to get us some Kalashnikovs!' This was the rallying call of the era. Soon enough, every Kashmiri who was formerly a sitting duck, headed to the border to arm himself. Shopkeepers shuttered their stores and students put away their books; the freedom struggle was in full swing.

Guerrilla attacks against military personnel caused the Indian government to increase the number of troops stationed in the valley. On 19 January 1990, when Jagmohan took control of Kashmir as governor, he ordered a series of extra-judicial raids and assassinations. Everyday dozens of bodies piled up as thousands of homes were burnt to ashes. On 20 January, the first day of Jagmohan's rule, at least a hundred Kashmiris were martyred on Gawakadal Bridge in Srinagar. On 1 March 1990, when a million Kashmiris protested Indian aggression and marched for their freedom, forty were shot dead. Jagmohan came to be known as Jagu the Butcher. In May 1990, Indian forces fired upon the funeral procession of the martyr Mirwaiz Maulana Muhammad Farooq, killing dozens of mourners. Despite the wanton aggression by Indian forces and authorities, Kashmir was out of control.

Over the past twenty-two years Indians have tried every strategy imaginable to snuff out the freedom movement in Kashmir but all their efforts have been in vain for although the struggle has seen a number of ups and downs, it never fully stalled. The greatest testament to the ongoing vitality of the struggle is the fact that every year, the number of Indian forces in the valley continues to rise, and yet, over the past twenty-two years, they have not been able to unfurl the Indian flag over Srinagar's Lal

464 THE LITERATURE OF *LASHKAR-E-TAYYABA*

Chowk. Even today, there isn't a single public square where the Indian flag can fly for a day. In twenty-two years, 93,544 Kashmiris have been martyred; 6,982 have been martyred in captivity. 108,874 ordinary Kashmiris have been thrown in jail of which ten thousand remain 'missing'. In this same time period, 22,749 women have been widowed, and 107,400 children have been orphaned. 105,900 properties, including homes, businesses, and stores, have been razed to the ground. Indian forces have martyred and damaged mosques indiscriminately.

Current figures suggest that for every Kashmiri male there is an Indian soldier holding a gun to the civilian's head, but the freedom movement cannot stop.

Kashmir has the unfortunate distinction of enduring the highest density of security personnel in one single region for the longest duration in human history. India commits human rights abuses, violates UN resolutions, and breaks international law on a daily basis with the full support of the United States, Israel, Russia, and various European nations... but the freedom struggle continues.

(Various historical facts and events regarding the movement are recounted throughout the book).

All Parties Hurriyat (Liberation) Conference

In addition to armed resistance, the Kashmiri people have been engaged in various sorts of political struggles, not least of which is a constant attempt at reminding the UN of its promises and resolutions. Their aim: defeat India on the world stage, win freedom, and establish an Islamic government in Kashmir. Towards this end, on 10 March 1993, twenty-six religious and political organizations in Occupied Kashmir laid the foundations of a united front called All Parties Hurriyat (Liberation) Conference. The following organizations are currently part of this alliance:

Aawami Action Committee, *Ittihadul Muslimeen, Anjamani Auqafi Jama Masjid, Anjaman-e-Tablig-ul Islam, Ummah Islami, Auquaf Jama Masjid*, Employees and Workers Confederation (both groups), All Jammu & Kashmir Employees' Confederation, *Jamiate Ulama-e-Islam, Jamiat-e-Hamdania*, Jammu and Kashmir People's Conference, Jammu Kashmir

Liberation Front, Jammu and Kashmir Human Rights Committee, Jammu and Kashmir People's Basic Rights (Protection) Committee, Liberation Council, *Kashmir Bazme Tawheed*, Kashmir Bar Association, *Muslim Khwateen Markaz*, Muslim Conference, Political Conference, *Tehreek-e-Huriati Kashmiri*, People's League, Islamic Students League, Imam Ahmad Raza Islamic Mission, *Saut-ul-Aliya*, Jammu and Kashmir People's Freedom League.

In 2002, with the announcement of state elections, the Hurriyat Conference split in two factions: one faction comprised organizations that boycotted the election under the leadership of Syed Ali Shah Geelani whose politics was considered relatively extreme; the other faction was led by the relatively moderate Mirwaiz Umar Farooq. With the rise of the 'Indians! Get Out of Jammu Kashmir' movement in 2010, Mirwaiz Umar Farooq's incendiary remarks shook the Indian parliament and now, the establishment considers him as much of a threat as Syed Ali Shah Geelani.

Currently, almost all differences between the two groups have been resolved. As it stands, the largest nationalist party in Occupied Kashmir is Syed Ali Shah Geelani's *Tehreek-i-Hurriyat* while Mirwaiz Umar Farooq is the most popular orator and preacher in the valley; he is the imam of Kashmir's largest mosque, *Markaz-e-Jamia Masjid Srinagar*, and for centuries his family has held the title '*Mirwaiz*'. He is the fourteenth Mirwaiz of Kashmir; Indian forces martyred his father, Mirwaiz Muhammad Farooq in May 1990, as he led a procession of four hundred thousand Kashmiris from Jamia Masjid. His funeral was attended by hundreds of thousands of Kashmiris, approximately fifty of whom were martyred that day when Indian soldiers opened fire.

Prominent Political Leaders of Kashmir's Freedom Movement

Despite the fact that numerous popular Kashmiri leaders have been martyred in assassination ploys while waging a political battle for freedom, the world continues to support India. Following are short biographies of the most popular political leaders of Occupied Kashmir's freedom movement.

466 THE LITERATURE OF *LASHKAR-E-TAYYABA*

Syed Ali Shah Geelani

Born on 29 September 1929, in district Bandipora, in northern Kashmir, Syed Ali Shah Geelani is now one of the oldest and most prominent leaders of Kashmir's freedom struggle. Not only does he want freedom for Kashmir, but he also supports its annexation with Pakistan. He received his early education in Sopore and graduated from Oriental College, Lahore before returning to Occupied Kashmir to join the struggle.

He has dedicated his entire life to the liberation movement. A profound admirer of the work of the Islamic thinker Allama Iqbal, he has spent approximately twenty-seven years of his life in Indian prisons. On 7 August 2009, he laid the foundation for an independent movement known as *Tehreek-e-Hurriyat*. By conservative estimates, the inaugural convention of Tehreek-e-Hurriyat was attended by fifty thousand Kashmiris. Currently, he is the chairman of both Hurriyat Conference and *Tehreek-e-Hurriyat*.

Tehreek-e-Hurriyat's Secretary General is Muhammad Ashraf Sehrai. Syed Ali Geelani has had to face all kinds of abuse for his clear and consistent stance on Kashmir. Pervez Musharraf once called him an 'aged lunatic' for his categorical opposition to any kind of dialogue, friendship, or economic relationship between Pakistan and India.

Geelani considers any such relationship a betrayal of Kashmiri blood.

Indian authorities confiscated his passport in 1981, which was only returned to him once, in 2006, so he could perform *Hajj*. Short of the pilgrimage, he has never been allowed to travel outside India. Some years ago, he was due to receive a kidney transplant in the USA but was denied a visa. After a lifetime of dodging assassination attempts and baseless trials, he is currently under house arrest in Hyderpura, Srinagar.

Mirwaiz Muhammad Umar Farooq

Muhammad Umar Farooq was born on 23 March 1973 and assumed his role as Kashmir's fourteenth *mirwaiz* (chief preacher) immediately following his father's martyrdom. He received his early education at Burn Hall School Srinagar; in his youth, he was interested in becoming a software engineer, but circumstances landed him squarely at the heart of the freedom struggle. Currently, he is the president of the Kashmiri organization Action Committee, and chairman of the moderate Hurriyat Conference. He has had a crucial role in highlighting the Kashmir problem in the global consciousness. *TIME* magazine included him in its list of Asian heroes. He has the unique distinction of becoming chairman of Hurriyat Conference at the tender age of twenty. He holds a doctorate from Kashmir University.

Shabir Ahmed Shah

Shabir Ahmed Shah, now fifty-six, started working for Kashmir's liberation at the tender age of fourteen when he was thrown in prison and he experienced Indian brutality first-hand. He has spent twenty-six years of the forty-two-year struggle in prison. He was born in the Karipura district of Islamabad. In 1982, he was among the Kashmiri leaders who purged alcoholism from Kashmiri society at a time when Indian authorities conspired to sabotage the newly burgeoning freedom movement by making liquor readily available and excessively cheap in order to distract the youth of the region.

Because of the long years Shabir Ahmed Shah has wasted in prisons, he is known as the Nelson Mandela of Kashmir. In 1978, the traitor Sheikh Muhammad Abdullah visited Shabir Ahmed Shah in prison and tried to win him over by calling him his son. Shabir Ahmed Shah retorted, 'My father is Ghulam Muhammad Shah; how can I be your child?' At the time, Shabir Ahmed Shah was the president of the Democratic Freedom Party. He was released on 3 November 2010. His father was tortured to death in an Indian prison.

Muhammad Yasin Malik

Yasin Malik is one of the most prominent leaders in Occupied Kashmir. He is part of Jammu Kashmir Liberation Front, founded by Amanullah Khan and Maqbool Butt in Birmingham on 29 May 1977. Yasin Malik was born in 1966 in Srinagar's Maisma region. His father was a government bus driver who worked the extremely dangerous route between Srinagar

468   THE LITERATURE OF *LASHKAR-E-TAYYABA*

and Ladakh. Yasin Malik was first imprisoned in 1987 and freed in 1994. Six attempts have been made on his life. He has toured the Unites States, the United Kingdom, and various other countries in order to alter public opinion about Kashmir. In 2007, he organized an elaborate campaign called '*Safr-e-Azadi* (Freedom's Journey)' during which he toured three thousand five hundred cities, villages, and towns in Occupied Kashmir and collected one hundred thousand signatures petitioning for freedom. He sent copies of the signed petition to the Indian authorities as well as to various governments across the world. He is profoundly influenced by Allama Iqbal's poetry.

Syeda Asia Andrabi

One of the most notable women in Occupied Kashmir's freedom struggle is Syeda Asia Andrabi, president of the women's organization *Dukhtaran-e-Millat* (Daughters of the Nation).

She was born in 1962 to Dr Syed Zia-ud-Din Andrabi and completed her Home Science degree from Kashmir University in 1981. Although she was interested in traveling to Himachal Pradesh to pursue an advanced degree in the sciences, destiny had other plans for this dynamic woman.

Rumour has it, after reading a book titled *Khwateen Kay Dilon Ki Batain (The Inner Life of Women)* from her father's library, she was inspired to bring about a religious revolution among Kashmiri Muslim women. Deeply moved by the plight of her people she laid the foundation for a women's organization. Towards this end, she married a well-known *jihadi* commander Dr Muhammad Qasim Faktu. Soon after their union, her husband was arrested on charges of attacking Indian soldiers and sentenced to life in prison; most recently, this term was extended from fourteen to seventeen years.

Over the years, Asia Andrabi has been imprisoned numerous times. Her dynamic personality inspired Bollywood producers to make a film about her, but she threatened them with a lawsuit if they went ahead with the project. Nevertheless, a film loosely based on her life and her struggles was ultimately produced and released. Countless Kashmiri women have been inspired by her to start taking the formal veil. She has confronted her Indian oppressors fearlessly and has worked desperately to counter the spread of alcoholism and vulgarity in the valley.

From 2008 to 2010, Asia Andrabi was imprisoned on multiple occasions. Currently, she is in jail, with numerous cases pending against her. Her two sons, Muhammad bin Qasim and Ahmed bin Qasim, spent their adolescent years in prison with their mother. She is very open about the fact that she doesn't want her sons to grow up to be engineers or doctors; rather, she wants them to be like Osama bin Laden and Mullah Muhammad Omar. On more than one occasion she has expressed her desire for her husband to take three more wives, not only to give Kashmiri widows a home but also to produce more Osama bin Ladens and Mullah Muhammad Omars.

Musarrat Alam

The greatest threat to India today comes from thirty-seven-year-old Musarrat Alam, who was arrested, yet again, on 18 October 2010. He received his primary education from Basko School and holds a science degree from S.P. College. He began his political career by laying the foundations of *Muslim Muttahida Mahaz* (United Muslim Front). Formerly, he has served as a commander in Hizbullah, and so far, he has spent ten years in prison. In 2008, during the nationalist movement, he introduced the slogan *ragdra* (quash) against Indians, much to the consternation of the Indian authorities; in time, *ragdra* became a favourite rallying call of Kashmiri youth.

Alam embodies the very spirit of the movement 'Indians! Get Out of Jammu Kashmir'. He popularized the slogans 'Go India! Go Back!' and 'Get Out of Jammu Kashmir.' In the past, he's acted as president of Jammu Kashmir Muslim League as well as Deputy Secretary General Hurriyat Conference (G). Seventeen cases have been filed against him with the aim to keep him imprisoned. He is known as 'Shahbaz of Kashmir' (Hawk of Kashmir). From 11 June 2010 to 18 October 2010, he led the movement while in hiding. His mother and wife are the only members of his family left in his house.

Among the numerous important leaders in Jammu Kashmir is the president of *Jamiat Ahl-e-Hadees* Maulana Muhammad Shaukat who was

470   THE LITERATURE OF *LASHKAR-E-TAYYABA*

made President of Coordination Council during the nationalist movement in 2008. In addition, President of *Sut-al-Haq*, Hafeez-ur-Rehman Butt, leader of Muslim Women's Center, Zamruda Habib, President of Kashmir Bar Association Mian Abdul Qayyum, Secretary General Ghulam Nabi Shaheen, as well as Bilal Ghani Loan, Farooq Ahmed Dar alias Bitta Karate, Shakeel Ahmed Bakhshi, Agha Fareed Hassan Budgami, Mukhtar Ahmed Waza, Ghulam Ahmed Mir of Rajwari, Mushtaq-ul-Islam, and Maulana Abdullah Tahiri are among the notable leaders of the freedom struggle.

Chapter 1: Get Out of Jammu Kashmir

'Get Out of Jammu Kashmir'

In the face of Indian brutality, the Hurriyat Conference distributed protest schedules across Kashmir as mosques erupted in protest anthems and freedom chants. After evening prayers, protestors cried out for their liberation over loudspeakers across Srinagar, and in some cases, protestors even dared to step outside the houses of worship. In Sopore, Indian forces fired live ammunition and tear gas on a procession headed to Main Chowk. Hurriyat Conference (G) called for a civil curfew that left the streets desolate as an eerie silence took over the valley.

To mobilize the population against Indian aggression, Hurriyat Conference launched the 'Indians! Get Out of Kashmir' movement and convinced the public that one decisive battle was better than dying a little every day. To this end, anti-government programs were distributed in which state-wide strikes were scheduled for 25 June, and 2 and 3 July, with specific formats for women and students.

In a press conference, Musarrat Alam, a central figure of Hurriyat Conference, along with Zamruda Habib, Advocate Muhammad Shafique Raishi, and Nisar Hussein Rather, stated that Hurriyat Conference had been in session for two days, and had decided to launch the 'Get Out of Kashmir' movement until the last Indian soldier was evicted from the valley.

India took control of the region in 1947 and since then, Kashmiris have been sacrificing their lives in pursuit of their freedom. Musarrat Alam announced that this time, everyone had united under one slogan: 'Go India Go Back!' As a protest calendar was put together, it was announced that starting that day, 25 June, there was to be a state-wide strike, and on 26 June, every mosque in the valley was to organize a formal prayer for the end of Indian occupation.

On 27 June, Kashmiris were to graffiti 'Go India Go Back' on every visible surface in the valley so every Indian soldier, agent, and tourist realized that Kashmir was in no way a part of India. This tag line was to go viral on the Internet as well so the world could know that all Kashmir wants is freedom. On 28 June, students were to tie black armbands and yell 'Go India Go Back!' On 29 June, female students were to do the same. On 30 June, from the evening prayers at dusk, till the evening prayers at night, this same slogan was to be blared over loudspeakers in mosques; black flags were to be hoisted on houses, stores, and buildings.

On 1 July, according to the 'March to Pathar Mosque' programme, women were to collect in Pathar Mosque and in an open congregation they were to pledge to keep the movement alive. The congregation was to be presided over by Dukhtaran-e-Millat leader Asia Andrabi and Hurriyat Conference leader Zamruda Habib and Sister Fareeda. On 13 July, *Yom-e-Shuhada* (Day of Martyrs), after praying for salvation at the graveyard of martyrs in Naqshband Sahib, there was to be a public meeting titled *Eid-gah Challo* (March to the Eid House).

Chapter 2: Every Wound is Kashmir

From All Sides: The Wounded, The Dead, The Blood and Tears

Friday, 30 July, Kashmir. The wounded and the dead were scattered across the streets. The hospitals of Srinagar were full. Sadr Hospital echoed with anguished cries. Ambulance sirens filled the sky as victims of police and CRPF (Central Reserve Police Force) brutality were brought in. Oblivious to the ensuing chaos, people went around helping the wounded.

In Sopore, the bodies of two martyred youths were kept in police custody inside the hospital for two hours as their family members and friends protested against the puppet government of Kashmir.

472 THE LITERATURE OF *LASHKAR-E-TAYYABA*

An eyewitness recounts,

As soon as I stepped inside the hospital I saw men, women, and children weeping helplessly all around me. I discovered that two men wounded in Sopore, had died on their way to Sadr Hospital. I tried to reach the room where the bodies were stored but the hospital staff had blocked its entrance as a mob collected outside. After a half hour of waiting, people started breaking down the door so the staff finally gave up the dead. At this moment, cries of freedom rang out in the hospital... the bodies were brought out into the courtyard. Everyone was crying relentlessly. The bodies were transferred into an ambulance, which wasn't allowed to leave the premises because the police had locked the gates and refused to let anyone out; for two full hours the bodies decomposed inside the ambulance. People were afraid the bodies would be taken into police custody again, and their suspicions were confirmed when a police ambulance appeared on the scene. People were on the verge of rioting; sensing their anger, the police finally opened the hospital gates. As the ambulance carrying the dead left for Sopore, multiple ambulances rushed in from Patan and Tiral, carrying dozens of wounded protestors. Once again, the hospital turned into a site of mourning. Due to shortage of space, many of the wounded were laid out on the blood-spattered floor. The hospital administration had never imagined it would have to deal with so many injuries at once. Despite the misery, the pain, the blood, and tears, thousands of men and women continued chanting slogans for freedom.

Forces Aimed for the Head: Dozens Left Disabled

Protestors were shot directly in the head and chest; the bodies of the martyred were a testament to this policy. Sura Hospital in Srinagar admitted dozens of young men and women in critical condition; it was obvious that even if they survived, they would remain bed-ridden for the rest of their lives.

Thirty-five-year-old Hanifa Vani from Kreeri Pattan struggles for her life on a ventilator. Her chest has been pumped with bullets. Even if she survives, she will live the life of an invalid. Unable to move anything

DESTINATION KASHMIR IS NIGH   473

but her eyes, she lies still on bed number fourteen of the Cardiovascular Thoracic Surgery Department. Her spine has been severed.

Hanifa was not the only one. This very hospital was host to numerous other patients in a similar state. According to doctors, dozens of people were brought in with gunshot wounds to the head and chest. The situation in Medical Institute was unthinkable; of the thirty-one patients admitted, twenty-five were hit with live ammunition, fourteen of which had bullets lodged in their skulls.

According to doctors, the situation in the hospitals was deplorable. The wounded were struck with bullets to the head, chest, and abdomen, and their treatment required time, medicine, and resources that were simply not available. Reporting on the condition of anonymity for fear of police reprisal, one doctor testified that it was clear the forces in the valley were not merely dispersing protestors but deliberately targeting them in order to wipe them off the face of the earth. Many of the wounded were half-dead by the time they reached the hospital, and even those who survived were permanently disabled.

Twenty-five-year-old Iqbal Ahmed Khan from Chanapora and Bilal Ahmed from Panpur were shot in the head. When they were rushed to the surgical ward in critical condition, four of the thirty-one patients who had been brought in had already attained martyrdom. The police and the CRPF had shot them from 30 July to 1 August.

According to doctors, it was apparent that the protestors were being targeted in specific parts of their bodies in order to disable them permanently. Shabir Ahmed from Amr Garhath Sopore, and Mashooq Ahmed Khan and Mudassar Ahmed Malik from Pattan were shot in the chest. Their vital organs had been hit and they were in critical condition. Fourteen-year-old Umar Farooq from Kakapura Palwama had been shot in the right shoulder.

Fifteen-year-old Aqib Vani from Panpur and fourteen-year-old Mian Irfan from Pattan were shot in the head while the young Muhammad Iqbal Rathar from Sangrama Sopore had been shot in the arm. Aqib Rathar, and nineteen-year-old Meraj-ud-Din Butt from Sopore were shot in the legs. Aqib was struggling to stay alive on bed number sixteen. Muhammad Hussein Kabli, an elderly man from Islamabad had been shot in the face and was admitted into the plastic surgery department. Manzoor Ahmed Butt, Malik Zubair, and Asif Riaz Mir from Pattan,

474 THE LITERATURE OF *LASHKAR-E-TAYYABA*

Sheikh Ashiq Hussein and Akhtar from Palwama, and Shaheen Khan from Bimna were shot in the most sensitive areas of their bodies. The aforementioned were admitted to Sura Hospital after 30 July.

Young Men Forced to Parade Naked

The world is blissfully unaware of the kind of treatment meted out to Muslims, particularly Kashmiri Muslims, in Indian prisons. Their torture commences with forced nudity immediately after their capture. No one truly knows their plight, for not a single journalist or so-called human rights organization is allowed inside Occupied Kashmir and no one has access to the bowels of Kashmiri prisons. Prisoners are tortured in a variety of ways: they are electrocuted, and then shoved into prison cells completely naked, without any access to the outside world. This is why a video released from Pulwama in which Indian forces interrogated and cursed a bunch of Kashmiri youth, after stripping them naked, caused a global scandal. The world was stunned by how Kashmiri prisoners were treated, although this was a mere fraction of what Muslim captives have to endure. Indian Interior Minister P. Chidambaram said the video circulating online in which Kashmiri youth were being paraded naked by Indian forces had not yet been authenticated. Meanwhile, a spokesperson for the CRPF announced that the video was a hoax, stating the security personnel would never commit such a crime, and neither could such an event be kept under wraps in a place like Kashmir. It's been some months since this issue exploded but India has swept the entire incident under the rug.

Thousands Murdered for Protesting Insults Against the Quran

On 11 September 2010, on the ninth anniversary of the September 11 attacks on the World Trade Center, Pastor Terry Jones announced he would burn copies of the Quran in Florida to express his hatred of Muslims. In anticipation of Muslim rage and inevitable *jihad*, the US government tried to convince the pastor to alter his plans; Quranic pages were, nevertheless, torn up and desecrated in a number of locations. Muslims across the world protested these deplorable acts and declared *jihad* on the perpetrators. Some of the most organized and awe-inspiring processions were held in Occupied Kashmir and the Indian forces turned out to be more aggressive than they had been against the freedom marches in the past as thousands of Kashmiris were shot indiscriminately. The very first day seventeen Kashmiris were martyred while thousands were critically wounded. Outraged by the unwarranted aggression, protestors attacked police stations in Humhama, Tangmarg, and various other cities and set dozens of government buildings on fire.

The administration had imposed a curfew in anticipation of Hurriyat Conference (G)'s 'March on the Chamber' rally. The masses openly defied the curfew as they cried out in support of Islam and freedom while cursing the USA and those insulting the Quran.

Fifty protestors were shot dead in Tangmarg. The wounded included Tariq Ahmed Ganai, son of Abdul Ahad Ganai from Thilagam Pattan, twenty-six-year-old Mudassar Ahmed Para, son of Ghulam Rasool from Krisha Hama Pattan, and Abdul Majeed Dar from Bingham Kunzar. All three died before reaching the hospital in Tangmarg. Three other youths died in the hospital: Muhammad Iqbal Malik, son of Bashir Ahmed from Timbar Hama Tangmarg, Abdul Qayyum Wani, son of Muhammad Iqbal from Gangabal Tangmarg, Ikhlaq Ahmed Khan, son of Muhammad Azam Khan from Iqbal Colony Tangmarg. Gunshots rang through Panpour throughout the day, leaving nine injured and two dead.

Protestors assembled in Budgam around midnight and continued protesting the desecration of the Quran till Monday evening. During this period, the police and CRPF shot dead four people, including one woman, and injured over thirty protestors, many of whom were in critical condition.

Processions in Islamabad came under indiscriminate fire; after shelling the protestors with tear gas, forces chased them down the streets and alleys firing at them relentlessly. Four men jumped into the river, three of who were rescued by locals but the fourth Raju, son of Mukhtar from Khanabal, drowned. Many locals risked their own lives in searching for his body but in vain. The following day, countless protests spontaneously erupted in Islamabad.

476 THE LITERATURE OF LASHKAR-E-TAYYABA

The following day a state-wide curfew was declared to control the deteriorating condition. People were imprisoned in their own homes. There had been so much bloodshed in the valley that this was the second time (the Kargil War being the first) when Srinagar's airport was shut down for three consecutive days. Three wounded protestors from the day before lost their lives. The Quran's desecration was protested across Jammu as well.

A Habitable Valley or an Open-Air Prison: Tales of Horror

While every Kashmiri is paying the price of demanding freedom, the kind of atrocities unleashed upon thousands of residents of Palhalan for the movement 'Indians! Get Out of Kashmir', is unparalleled in human history. Nearly every house in this town has been damaged or destroyed, month long round-the-clock curfews have been enforced, water systems, electrical grids, telephone lines, in short, the entire infrastructure has been dismantled. Below, are first-hand accounts of the atrocities civilians have had to endure.

Meet Ghulam Hassan (name changed for fear of police retaliation), a seventy-year-old storeowner who nearly lost his life to the curfew. The curfews, crackdowns, killings, and arrests of the 1990s are still fresh in his mind, but according to him, the current state of affairs is unimaginable. He claims it's impossible to lead a normal life when attending a funeral is a crime. After the twenty-seventh day of Ramazan, a Special Forces unit was stationed at the entrance to the village along Srinagar's Virmal Avenue, so the police and CRPF could keep constant watch over the villagers. For twenty-five days, the curfew kept every single man, woman, and child locked indoors. 'For the past twenty-eight days we have not been allowed to meet one another; at most, we can only talk on the phone, that too if we're lucky enough to get through. Just across the road, in Gori Mohalla, a woman passed away but not a single neighbour was able to pay their respects.'

Ghulam Hassan goes on:

When the forces arrived in the village after 27th Ramazan, and shot dead four people, we knew no one was safe. Anyone or anything that

DESTINATION KASHMIR IS NIGH 477

came in their path was crushed even though there hadn't been a single demonstration in the village at the time. Every house is shot through with bullet holes. In those twenty-eight days, all three hundred houses of a single neighbourhood were severely damaged; even sawmills in wood factories were destroyed. The forces shot up four transformers, cutting off power to the village. (Around this time a journalist managed to slip into the village to speak directly to the victims. At one point, the neighbourhood dogs started barking and all those gathered to speak to the journalist started running for shelter. He asked why everyone was running. He was told the dogs started barking every time soldiers approached the village, so every time they barked, people instinctively ran for cover. Even the journalist was afraid of what would become of him if the forces found out he had slipped through. Soon, it was discovered the dogs were merely fighting among themselves and the journalist resumed interviewing us).

Ghulam Rasool (name changed), a retired schoolteacher, states that when soldiers broke into his house, he hid inside the animal barn with his wife and children as the soldiers ransacked his property and took whatever they pleased.

A worker at the Department of Health tells a similar tale. He recalls when soldiers marched through the village, he gathered his family and ran straight up to the second floor of the house, letting the soldiers loot and destroy whatever they pleased.

Ali Muhammad says: 'As we were harvesting the rice, soldiers dragged us out of our fields and took seven of us captive; we had to bribe them heavily to let us go.' Muhammad Subhan (name changed) says: 'The fruits in our orchard are rotting away but we are not allowed to pick them. At this point, soldiers stationed along the railway tracks have assumed complete control of our orchards and help themselves to whatever fruit they like, whenever they want, and however much they please, with impunity.' All local government and private schools have been shut down. For twenty-eight days, children have not been able to attend school. It is unthinkable to step out of the village for an education. Any student that dares step outside the village for tuition is sent home with broken bones.'

Ghulam Ahmed says that conditions are much worse than what he'd seen at the height of the anti-occupation demonstrations. The curfew is

478   THE LITERATURE OF *LASHKAR-E-TAYYABA*

never relaxed and there is no leniency whatsoever. Muhammad Subhan claims that Pattan police does not hesitate to arrest medical patients and their attendants. 'Pattan's hospital is only 3 kilometres away, yet no one can access it. In an emergency we must go to Sumbal Hospital 13 kilometres away, from where patients are transferred to Srinagar.' Since 27th Ramazan, Jamia Mosque, which is located on the main road, has not hosted a single congregational prayer.

Palhalan has become an annual site of Indian aggression against Kashmiris. No resident is given government employment, or verification or a passport to travel abroad; as a result, highly educated people in the village must resort to menial labour to make a living, and gradually, that too is being restricted. Some have taken bank loans to buy jeeps to get to work but the forces do not allow them to leave their homes; consequently, they are unable to make the monthly payments on their loans. There is only one, basic, dispensary in the village, which offers nothing more than first aid. During the curfew, Major Sharma of Hyderbeg Camp would take roll call every morning.

All the doors and windows of Abdul Jabbar's (name changed) house have been destroyed. Cars have been totalled, and tractors have been dismantled. Ghulam Ahmed says they have been cut off from the outside world. 'We somehow help one another get by; there are homes without any food. Without mutual help the residents would have starved to death.' (At this point, the journalist wrapped up and took off, managing to slip out of the village undetected).

The following day when Chairman Kashmir Liberation Front, Yasin Malik, attempted to pay his condolences to the family members of martyrs, he and his workers were arrested.

Chapter 3: We Will Never Submit

Pakistan's Independence Day: The Valley Runs Red; River Jhelum Runs Green

As always, on 14 August, Kashmiris celebrated Pakistan Day under the leadership of Syed Ali Geelani. There were fireworks and crescent flags as people prayed for Pakistan. There were demonstrations in various cities in which two protestors were martyred and dozens were wounded. That same day Bal Mosque was attacked during prayers and its windows were smashed.

In addition to the bloodletting Kashmiris had to suffer on Pakistan's Independence Day, they also expressed their love for Pakistan in a heart-breaking show of solidarity by sending thousands of Pakistani flags floating down River Jhelum, all the way into our territory. They dispatched these flags amidst firecrackers and chants. The flags arrived in Pakistan, but alas... the Pakistani media and politicians paid them no mind. Their gesture of love and solidarity did not cause as much as a ripple, even though they risked their lives preparing and dispatching the flags.

That evening, just after *iftar* (end of fast), a band of CRPF personnel fired upon seventeen-year-old Muhammad Umar Dar, son of Muhammad Abdul Ahad Dar, resident of Bazar Mohalla Narbal in the Narbal area of Srinagar, for no apparent reason. The teenager died on his way to the hospital. Umar used to sell vegetables with his father. Protests erupted in the region and went on throughout the night.

The following day, police stopped worshippers from entering the premises of Hazrat Bal mosque upon which the worshippers started agitating; they were met with tear gas and batons which left over twenty-five protestors injured. According to local eye-witnesses, police and CRPF personnel stormed the premises, smashed all the windows and beat up the worshippers inside. They proceeded to attack the female congregants and attempted to tear off their clothes. Loudspeakers strung up on minarets, in and around Srinagar, blared with chants of freedom through the night.

Who Was Ahad Jan?

On 15 August, Abdul Ahad Jan threw a shoe at Umar Abdullah, the puppet prime minister and the latest in a long lineage of traitors, at India's Independence Day festivities. Overnight, Abdul Ahad Jan became a celebrated hero of the struggle. But who was Abdul Ahad Jan? What circumstances compelled this ordinary government worker to take such an extraordinary step?

480 THE LITERATURE OF *LASHKAR-E-TAYYABA*

Despite all the sacrifices fifty-five-year-old Abdul Ahad Jan made for the puppet government of Kashmir, he had been the victim of a string of injustices. Not only had he been the target of police brutality, *ikhwan* (literally: brothers; reference to government employed thugs) had also been sent to burn down his house; his sons barely escaped with their lives. When Abdul Ahad protested this barbarism, he was declared insane and forcibly admitted to a mental asylum where he remains locked to this day, permanently sedated in an unending stupor. In 1992, Abdul Ahad was in the service of Director General Police, Mr Siskina when *mujahideen* boldly attacked the DG's office with explosives. Abdul Ahad risked his life by carrying DG Siskina on his shoulders out of the building. Greatly impressed with this rescue, police officials announced they would give Abdul Ahad two out-of-turn promotions. DG Amrpur promoted him once, but the promise of a second promotion remained unfulfilled. Abdul Ahad submitted a writ in 1995, petitioning the High Court to resolve the matter; it has been sixteen years since the petition was filed but a decision has yet to be made.

Abdul Ahad had to pay a heavy price for petitioning the High Court against the police. Officers routinely harassed him and his son Shaukat Ahmed, who reports that the abuse was so intense it took a toll on his father's health.

On 5 May 1996, *ikhwan*, the government employed thugs, assassinated Retd. VLW Ghulam Ahmed Vani, schoolteacher Gulam Nabi Loan, his older brother police Hawaldar Abdur Rasheed Loan, and a student called Farooq Ahmed Sheikh, in addition to a landowner Muhammad Abdullah Rather. The latter was murdered simply because he had a beard and was respected in the village. Abdul Ahad Jan was loud and clear in his condemnation of the thugs and tried his level best to stop them as well. As a result, they burnt down his house and went after his family. His older son, Shaukat Ahmed ended up joining the *mujahideen*; he was wounded and arrested during a clash between *mujahideen* and Indian forces in Garora, Bandipora. He was ultimately released, a cripple, after many years of being tortured in prison that left his right arm disabled. Abdul Ahad Jan's ageing mother lives with him. He has two sons and two daughters as well, and their family has no source of income.

Abdul Ahad Jan has a profound sense of honour and dignity. Three years ago, while stationed at Budshah Chowk in Srinagar, he slapped a

CRPF officer for catcalling a woman. He also got into an altercation with an Indian major in Ajas.

Abdul Ahad's recent transfer was also an exercise in intimidation. On 21 May 2010, he was arrested at Parampore Police Station for public drunkenness only to be released on bail, later that day, proving the case against him was a sham.

While serving on the security detail of a puppet political leader he was transferred for three months on trumped up charges, but when news of him throwing a shoe at the prime minister reached Ajas, he became a hero overnight. People chanted, 'Ahad Jan is dear to you... Ahad Jan is dear to us!' (*jan* means dear). He was declared a hero of the Kashmiri freedom struggle. There were fireworks in Kupwara, Trehgam, Karalpura, Shamnag, and Lolab. After the evening prayers, there were massive demonstrations in Chachi and Magam in which Abdul Ahad Jan's gesture of defiance was celebrated.

Rs. 500,000 Bounty: Indians Celebrate Musarrat Alam's Imprisonment

When Muslim League's Vice-President and Hurriyat Conference's Deputy Secretary General Musarrat Alam was arrested on 18 October 2010, India rejoiced. The Army had been engaged in a desperate manhunt, offering up to Rs. 500,000 for information leading to his arrest. After four months in hiding, on Monday evening, after Isha prayers, around 7:55pm, a Special Operations group arrested him from his relative's residence in Elco Colony, Tulbul. his aging mother was with him at the time. He was immediately transferred to S.O.G. Quarter Cargo. At the time of his arrest, a laptop, four mobile phones, and cash were confiscated from him. The Indian establishment declared Musarrat Alam's arrest a victory for peace in the valley. Earlier, Musarrat Alam had been arrested in 2008 during the Shrine Board movement in Aluchi Bagh under the Public Safety Act. The High Court declared his arrest under the Safety Act null and void seven times but instead of being released, the Safety Act was used to confine him.

When his confinement under the Safety Public Act was declared null and void an eighth time, he was held for twenty-one months under the

482 THE LITERATURE OF *LASHKAR-E-TAYYABA*

Enemy's Ordinance Act after which he was released on the condition that, every three days, he report to the police station and provide details about where he had been and his upcoming plans. When Syed Ali Shah Geelani was arrested with his followers in Kupwara on 20 June 2010, Musarrat Alam held a press conference at an undisclosed location on 24 June in Srinagar's Payeen area, in which he gave the world the slogan, 'Indians! Get Out of Kashmir', and 'Go India Go', before going into hiding.

During his four months in hiding, Musarrat Alam only appeared before the public twice; on 27th Ramazan, he addressed a crowd of protestors outside Mosque Butt Malo, and a few days before that, he addressed a crowd in Qamarwari. During this period, in addition to remaining active online, Musarrat Alam also released video recordings of himself. Since Syed Ali Shah Geelani was under arrest at the time, Musarrat Alam managed the resistance. He was arrested three days after he got married and immediately transferred to Kot Balwal Jail.

To curb the expected backlash, India's puppet government in Kashmir imposed a state-wide curfew in the region. Despite the clampdown, there were demonstrations throughout the valley that left 30 protestors severely injured. The following day, when Musarrat Alam was presented in court under tight security, many lawyers and supporters showed up to register their solidarity. According to journalists, Musarrat Alam was extremely composed; he assured his supporters of his wellbeing and asked them to pray for him.

Shabir Shah's Release: Hindus Attack Press Conference

On 3 November, the leader of Democratic Freedom Party, Shabir Ahmed Shah, was released after nine months in prison. Some days before his release he was offered amnesty if he agreed to sign an agreement based on specific conditions; he said he would sooner sacrifice his life and his family than sign an agreement with the Indian government. Shabir Ahmed Shah (who is currently fifty-six years old) has spent over twenty-six years of his life in jail. He was fourteen at the time of his first incarceration. When Farooq Abdullah visited him in jail, the politician said Shabir Ahmed was like his son, but Shabir Shah refused to sign a plea deal, leaving the politician speechless.

DESTINATION KASHMIR IS NIGH   483

Shabir Ahmed Shah was arrested during the Shrine Board movement on 27 August 2008 and released after ten months, on 2 June 2009. Six days later, on 8 June 2009, he was arrested yet again, and released four months later on 21 October 2009. He was arrested again on 3 February 2010 and released after nine months. He was initially kept in Kathua Jail and later transferred to Kot Balwal Jail. During this period, he was held under PSA (Public Safety Act) seven times, and all seven times the High Court dismissed his incarceration under PSA and ordered his release but every time the police came up with a new excuse to jail him.

The day after his release, a press conference was organized at a hotel in Jammu but the moment Shabir Shah arrived at the venue it was attacked by terrorist Hindus who ransacked the stage, broke the microphone, and tried assaulting him. Shabir Ahmed Shah reiterated he would stop at nothing until Kashmir was liberated. The following day, he was put under-house arrest at his residence in Srinagar.

Chapter 4: Never Forget the Blood We Spilt

Rafiq Bangroo: The Seventh Martyr of His Clan

Rafiq Bangroo was the seventh member of his family to be martyred; he was killed while protesting the murder of Tufail Ahmed. The freedom movement in Occupied Kashmir cost the Bangroo family many precious lives. What is interesting is that none of the martyrs of this family was ever in the direct line of fire of the Indian forces.

Ghulam Rasool Bangroo was the first to fall in 1990 when he was shot dead by soldiers. Javed Ahmed Bangroo, Rauf Ahmed Bangroo, Bashir Ahmed Bangroo, Muhammad Rafiq Bangroo, Abdul Hamid Bangroo, and then Muhammad Rafiq Bangroo, son of Abdul Ahad Bangroo, followed, one by one, as Indian aggression ran amok in the valley. According to the Bangroo family, their only crime was a desire for self-determination and an alliance with the freedom movement.

Rafiq Ahmed Bangroo's family members had started preparing for his funeral even before he lost his final battle with death on the night of 19 June since there was little chance of his survival. His first cousin from his father's side reports that when Rafiq Ahmed was martyred, his father

484 THE LITERATURE OF *LASHKAR-E-TAYYABA*

Abdul Ahad Bangroo gathered us in one room and forbid us from protesting his death because he did not want anyone else's child murdered in the process. Instead of burying his son in the Graveyard of Martyrs, where the funeral procession ran the risk of swelling into a full-blown demonstration, he wanted to bury his son in his ancestral graveyard in Dana Mazar to avoid further bloodshed.

The cousin reports: 'We mourned his death for three days. His father refused to register a case against the oppressors; instead, he said he would present his case before god on the Day of Judgement, for the courts around him did not serve justice.'

Rafiq Ahmed Bangroo passed his Matriculation exams before working as a handicraftsman. He worked tirelessly to improve the economic condition of his household and pay off their debts. He and his brother Halal Ahmed worked ten to twelve hours a day. Halal Ahmed recalls, 'Rafiq's right leg was weak which is why he couldn't run very fast. When the security personnel came after us, Rafiq tripped and fell, and the soldiers beat him to a pulp without letting any of us close. We were crying hysterically. Some women from the neighbourhood helped us load Rafiq into a car. Even as we lifted his lifeless body his right hand was in his pant pocket.

'After Rafiq's beating, I was getting constant phone calls from relatives and friends. When my phone's battery died, I slipped my SIM into my brother's phone in order to take calls but within an hour my SIM registration was cancelled by the service provider and my phone stopped working. We are stunned by Rafiq's martyrdom. We're trying our best to make sense of the tragedy.'

Pretending to Search a Dumped Body

At seventeen, despite having a father and an older brother, Muzaffar Butt was the sole breadwinner in the family. This young man from Bugam would study as well as work as a farmer. One day, he was in the fields till one in the afternoon, after which he had lunch with his mother and then napped for a bit. No one knew this would be his last meal.

When the puppet government's State Minister toured the area that afternoon, every man, woman, and child pelted his convoy with stones. Once the minister left, some of his security personnel returned to the area to apprehend a group of teenagers playing cricket. Most of the boys were thirteen and fifteen years old. Muzaffar Butt was the eldest among them. As the CRPF soldiers and police came after them, the younger ones escaped over the open sewer, but Muzaffar Butt was apprehended. He tossed his mobile phone, wallet, and cap towards his friends and told them to take the items to his mother.

Despite the testimony of an eyewitness who clearly saw the Deputy Superintendent of Police beat Muzaffar Ahmed to the ground, the police refused to register an F.I.R. (First Information Report) to cover-up the incident. The same eyewitness reports that 'after the police beat up Muzaffar, they took him with them; many people from the area searched for him in various police stations. Around five in the morning, the police returned to disperse the people protesting Muzaffar's arrest. In the fiasco, as protestors fled from the scene, the police dumped Muzaffar's body in the Doodh Ganga sewer and then pretended to search for it in boats. At 8am they 'retrieved' the body from the sewer and returned it to his family.'

Muzaffar's brother Nisar Ahmed says, 'Muzaffar's body was found 200 metres upstream from where he was beaten up; if he had actually drowned in the sewer his body would have travelled downstream. When we were given his remains there was fresh blood trickling out of his nose and there were no signs of drowning. There are rumours going round that we are upset because we were given government aid, but this is not true. We would never bargain our brother's life; all we want is for our brother's killers to be brought to justice.'

Muzaffar's mother reports that she was at the market purchasing bread. 'From a distance I saw the police harassing someone; had I known it was my child they were harassing I would have rushed over and offered my life for his. I would have begged and pleaded with them; perhaps they would have spared my boy's life.

'Muzaffar Ahmed Butt was in eleventh grade in Higher Secondary School Budgam. We suggested he apply to Batamaloo but he refused saying that things there were always unstable and that this was not conducive to an education. This is why he and all his friends continued their education in Budgam.'

Muzaffar's childhood friend Wahid is severely depressed due to Muzaffar's death. When a local journalist tried asking him about Muzaffar, Wahid remained silent, and then wept, without uttering a word.

I Will End My Fast in Heaven

On 14 August, Kashmiris celebrated Independence Day in solidarity with Pakistan. By dusk, Indian soldiers decided to exact revenge for this 'transgression' with the full backing of their superiors.

After 'Asr prayers, as Kashmiris prepared to conclude their fast, forces started attacking them in their towns and villages across the valley. In Islamabad, Irshad Ahmed was shot dead in the street as he returned home from the market with groceries. People risked their lives by carrying him to the hospital. There was still some time until the end of the fast. They tried giving him water for he had lost a lot of blood, but he said: 'Today I'll conclude my fast in heaven.' Before long, the light in his eyes faded and he passed away. When Irshad's body was brought home, the entire village erupted with rage. At his midnight funeral prayer, fifteen thousand people saw him off to heaven, with the hope of freedom in their hearts.

12

Noble Warriors and Battlefronts
by Muhammad Tahir Naqqash

In this chapter we present translated excerpts from Muhammad Tahir Naqqash' 2001, 590-page volume titled *Ghaziyan-i-Saf-Shikan* (*Noble Warriors and Battlefronts*),[1] which is a collection of various tales of LeT's various operations, including the 2000 *fidayeen* attack on the Red Fort in New Delhi and the attack on the airport in Srinagar in October 2001. This volume aims to provide, in vivid action-packed detail, the life and adventures of various LeT *mujahideen* stationed in Kashmir and elsewhere in India. These accounts deftly mix fact with braggadocio to aggrandize the purportedly heroic feats of LeT operatives. As we saw in the various biographies of slain martyrs, the content is decidedly communalized to emphasize simultaneously the heroism of Muslim *mujahideen* and the incessant victimized subject position of Muslims in Kashmir and elsewhere in India. Hindus are depicted as both craven but also violence-prone perpetrators.

What makes this volume particularly interesting is the forward that was written by Zaki-ur-Rehman Lakhvi, LeT's chief of operations and supreme commander of operations in Kashmir. Lakhvi was the mastermind behind the November 2008 attack in Mumbai. However, this is not the only outrage to his credit. As noted earlier in this volume, Lakhvi was a founding member of LeT when, in Afghanistan in the late 1980s, he merged his *Ahl-e-Hadees* militant group with *Jamaat ud Dawah* (JuD, Organization for Proselytization), founded by Hafiz Muhammad Saeed and Zafar Iqbal. The ensuing organization was known as the *Markaz-ud-Dawah-wal-Irshad* (MDI, Centre for Preaching and Guidance); however, within a few years of MDI's founding, Hafiz Saeed established LeT as MDI's armed wing.[2] Like many of the items included in our compilation, this text also belies any of Pakistan's claims that LeT (or any of its other operational names) does not engage in the production of violence.

488 THE LITERATURE OF *LASHKAR-E-TAYYABA*

In the Foreword he has penned, Lakhvi asserts: 'Our *jihad* is by no means limited to Kashmir; we intend to take this fight to every region of the world where Muslims are being persecuted and oppressed.' Consistent with this vision, Lakhvi is also accused of internationalizing LeT's *jihad*, beyond the comfort zone of the organization. For example, Lakhvi was the one who pressed for the attacks on non-Indians in the November 2008 assault on Mumbai. He also pushed the organization to undertake operations in Afghanistan. This has led some analysts to suggest that Pakistan's intelligence agencies happily made Lakhvi the 'fallguy' for the attack, justifying his detention. By detaining him, both the Pakistani deep state and LeT were able to limit his influence upon the rest of the organization while exerting tighter control over his activities. He has since been released and quietly removed from Pakistan's terrorist watch list.[3] This sprawling volume contains forty-one chapters in addition to several prefatory sections, each of which has varying numbers of subsections. Here we present translations of all prefatory materials including a foreword by Zaki-ur-Rehman Lakhvi, the emir *Lashkar-e-Tayyaba* Jammu Kashmir; an author's note by Naqqash himself; and a preamble by Dr Manzoor Ahmed (a central leader of LeT/JuD described herein as a 'commander'.). We in entirety Chapter 9, 'A Hindu Idol's Tribulations'; Chapter 12, 'Hunting Israeli Commandos'; Chapter 28, 'Indian Forces and Mujahideen Play Hide-and-Seek During Elections'; Chapter 30, 'The Hospitality of Kashmiri Muslims'; Chapter 35, '*Lashkar-e-Tayyaba*'s Popularity Among Hindus'; Chapter 37, 'Slaughtering Shiv Sena's Thugs'; Chapter 38, 'The Inter-Connected Issue of Kashmir and Sindh'; Chapter 39, 'Can India be Shattered'; Chapter 40, on 'The Red Fort Attack'; and Chapter 41, 'The Finest Investment'. As with all of LeT publications presented in this volume, excessive use of headers substitutes for logical coherence in exposition. Necessarily, we have retained the structure of the original.

Foreword

The prophet trained his followers to march upon the Caesars of the world without paying this mundane existence any mind. In their love for Allah and the prophet, these men challenged social orders, confronted their own clansmen, and sent the most formidable armies packing. This was entirely the result of the prophet's training. Crushing titans like the USA and Russia are easy, if one's belief in the prophet is absolute and one's bond with his teachings is strong.

In the publication 'Noble Warriors and Battlefronts', the discerning reader will notice that a warrior's understanding and internalization of the prophet's message is directly proportional to his resolve on the battlefield. Our *jihad* is by no means limited to Kashmir; we intend to take this fight to every region of the world where Muslims are being persecuted and oppressed. We will travel to these lands with our heads on silver platters the way Tariq bin Ziyad landed on the shores of Spain to defend the honour of a Christian girl.

Brother Tahir Naqqash has successfully revitalized the militant spirit of our struggle through his pen. Even a cursory reading reveals the value of this publication.

It not only introduces the militant aspect of the *Lashkar's jihadi* operations but also explicates the *jihadi* imperative so those who are apathetic to the cause are ultimately inspired to take up arms and join the cavalries and campaigns heading to Kashmir, paving the way to India's destruction. May Allah accept his contribution and make his efforts a source of salvation for him in the afterlife. Amen.

Zaki-ur-Rehman Lakhvi
emir *Lashkar-e-Tayyaba* Jammu Kashmir
10 March 2001. Lahore.

Author's Note

Islamic history is testament to the fact that through *jihad*, Muslims garnered respect, upheld their dignity, and spread Islam; they confronted infidels with the reins of their stallions in one hand and unsheathed swords in the other; they spent their days on horseback and their nights in humble prostration, begging Allah for mercy; their militant lives had one single objective: to spread Allah's *kalima* ('There is no god but Allah and Muhammad is His messenger) across the globe. Today, much like their noble forebears, the *mujahideen* of *Lashkar-e-Tayyaba*, embody their militant heritage as they confront disbelievers on the battlefield.

490 THE LITERATURE OF *LASHKAR-E-TAYYABA*

Lashkar-e-Tayyaba's *jihadi* services in Kashmir are no secret; their high-risk missions in the region are part of a grander *jihadi* operation that views Kashmir merely as a gateway. Once we march into India with the full might of our armies, we will rescue sixty million persecuted Muslims and aid the numerous states engaged in separatist struggles across the land, Allah-willing. Our *jihad* is by no means limited to Kashmir. By Allah's grace, *Lashkar-e-Tayyaba* does not pay lip service or play politics; we follow the path mapped out by the prophet fourteen hundred years ago as he dispatched cavalries from Medina to the four corners of the world, to obliterate every manifestation of disbelief and paganism on the way. Today, the *Lashkar* is dutifully acting upon the example of our prophet by aiding our Kashmiri brothers according to the Quran, and by offering life and limb in fulfilment of the prophecies regarding Hind in numerous *Hadees*. Kashmir has proven to be the gateway to India; our *jihad* will continue until the end of oppression and persecution. There is no doubt that Pakistan's ideological and geographical boundaries can only be fortified by continuing the Kashmiri *jihad*. Today, *mujahideen* continue a fourteen-hundred-year-old tradition by waging *jihad* across the globe, much like the *mujahideen* of yore.

Powerful kings and mighty kingdoms emerge and die... While time grinds everything to dust, there are those whose immortal influence is untouched by temporality. They illuminate the fragile pages of history only to light up the world through the ages. They are never forgotten for they bestow upon the world their eternal words of wisdom, their tales of determination and fortitude, and their memories.

This manuscript is a compilation of events that will not erode with time or wither with age; in fact, these events will be told and retold as inspiration for future *mujahideen* who will seek wisdom and support from these very pages. Our history, immortalized by the valour and courage of our soldiers and their victories, will outlast us, as it revitalizes the *mujahideen* of tomorrow.

Countless *jihadi* movements from the past have proven to be a great source of inspiration but once the men who embodied the heart and soul of these movements passed away, future generations of writers and historians could only speculate about them through conjecture; as a result, historical tracts fraught with inaccuracies and made-up ideas about *jihad*

NOBLE WARRIORS AND BATTLEFRONTS 491

and *jihadi* ideology, emerged. The compilations explicated ideologies that had little to nothing to do with the actual movements they documented; Shah Ismail Shaheed's *jihadi* movement is a classic example of such misrepresentation. With Allah's blessings, I have attempted to document the rise of *Lashkar-e-Tayyaba* as this organization ravages disbelief through fire and sword. I have done this precisely so our narrative does not befall the same fate as the other movements, and so future generations won't have to speculate or debate the truth of this struggle for they will have a reliable resource and a ready reference at hand; subsequently, they will be able to identify and counter all manner of propaganda immediately.

Only Allah knows how successful I have been in my endeavour; may He accept my efforts. I had hoped to present this book to Vajpayee as a gift from *Lashkar* when he visited Pakistan upon Nawaz Sharif's invitation, that he may better understand the philosophy behind Islam's *jihadi* imperative, but due to certain unavoidable issues, this was not possible. After one hundred and fifty years, Allah has bestowed *Lashkar-e-Tayyaba* the opportunity to launch *jihadi* operations from inside the Red Fort. All diplomatic efforts by the Vajpayee administration have failed to curb *jihad*; in truth these efforts were nothing more than a conspiracy by disbelievers to lock Pakistan in a chokehold by sabotaging the Kashmiri *jihad* and restricting *mujahideen*. Praise Allah, their efforts have failed miserably.

Through this book, we wish to inform Pervez Musharraf and all those invested in diplomacy that Kashmir's problems cannot be resolved through dialogue for conniving Hindus cannot be dealt with at the negotiating table.

The cunning but cowardly and usurious Hindu only fears the flashing glint of the *jihadi* sword. Mark our words: Kashmir can only be liberated through confrontation and revolt, not through condemnation and resolutions.

Musharraf Sahib! Fan the flames of *jihad* with the resolve you showed in Agra in order to free Kashmir and subdue the usurious Hindu so the latter may submit to your will. I present this manuscript to my brothers to commemorate the joyful and blessed continuation of *jihad* in the face of countless unsuccessful attempts to have it terminated. I hope that in the future this book proves to be a milestone in understanding

492 THE LITERATURE OF *LASHKAR-E-TAYYABA*

Lashkar-e-Tayyaba, and is a foundational text for those compiling the *Lashkar*'s origins and history, Allah-willing.

I am deeply indebted to *Lashkar-e-Tayyaba*'s *emir*, Brother Zaki-ur-Rehman Lakhvi for making this book possible; he suggested the title and offered invaluable advice and mentorship, in addition to authoring its foreword. Also, I must offer my sincerest thanks to the respectful commander of *Lashkar-e-Tayyaba*, Dr Manzoor Ahmed, for his editorial contributions.

I am also indebted to my dear brother Amir Hamza, brother Abu Habib of Shahdarah, Lahore, and brother Abdul Qadir, the master of *mujahideen*—all three were incredibly generous with their advice and helped revise this manuscript. May Allah give these brothers greater opportunities to put their skills at the service of their faith, and may Allah accept their efforts, as well as mine; may we be guarded from the afflictions of pretence and sanctimony and may we attain the honour of martyrdom only while fighting for Allah's pleasure.

Muhammad Tahir Naqqash
Lahore, 2001

Preamble

Lashkar's Nights and Days

On the frigid winter morning of 27 December 1979, Russians announced that they had exiled the god of the extremists from their country as they landed their forces in Kabul's airport and dispatched their tanks across the Amu Darya[4] into Afghanistan. Drunk with power and backed by a powerful military, they began what would become a saga of relentless cruelty and unparalleled aggression against Afghans. News of this tragedy provoked the Muslim world's honour and dignity. After long years, the dormant passion of martyrdom was stirred to life, once again.

مَّا لَكُمْ لَا تَرْجُونَ لِلَّه وَقَارًا

What aileth you that ye hope not toward Allah for dignity.

(71:13)

As the Quranic verse above started knocking on the collective conscience of Muslims, a Salafi youth by the name of Abu Waleed Zaki-ur-Rehman was dividing his time between *Jamia Salafia, Mamun Kanjan* and *Jamia Muhammadia*, Gujranwala, to quench his thirst for knowledge. He was a staunch believer in Allah's greatness, with an insatiable appetite for *jihad*. His prayers were answered when, one day, he was introduced to a *jihadi* commander who led him directly into the firestorm of war.

From the start, Allah bestowed Abu Waleed with tremendous responsibilities; he siphoned *mujahideen* to various training camps in Jaji (Afghanistan)—such as *Markaz-e-Mecca, Markaz-e-Medina*, and others—from where they were dispatched to confront Russians on numerous battlefronts. It was here that he encountered Arab fighters, who trained him in developing a sound argument in favour of *jihad* and bloodshed. He was intimately involved in *jihadi* missions in Kabul from August 1987 to January 1990; during this time, he also travelled to Nuristan and developed contact with regional Arab fighters.

Around the same time, after a series of *jihadi* operations Sheikh Jamil-ur-Rehman announced the formation of an Islamic emirate at a place called Tango in Kunar. On 22 February 1990, the young Abu Waleed, with the assistance of some empathetic Pakistani religious scholars like Professor Hafiz Muhammad Saeed, etc. laid the foundation of the militant training camp *Muaskar-e-Tayyaba*. Graduates from this esteemed military academy started showcasing their skills and their valour in various battlefields in Afghanistan. Among their ranks were martyrs like: 1) Abdul Rauf Janbaz, Okara; 2) Nazir Abu Bakr, Bahawalpur; 3) Muhammad Aslam, Karachi; 4) Khalid Saif, Lahore; and 5) Muhammad Qasim Sajid, Faisalabad.

Over ten years of relentless warfare, Allah blessed thousands of Afghans with martyrdom; their sacrifices finally bore fruit on 14 February 1989, when Russian forces withdrew over the same Amu Darya they crossed a decade earlier as conquerors; this time, however, Russian generals pleaded for safe passage during their retreat.

The great superpower of the time, notorious for never withdrawing from a land it conquered, was thrown out of Afghanistan after a humiliating defeat. Its catastrophic obliteration won Afghans honour and dignity on the world stage and inspired persecuted nations to dream of freedom; so it was with Kashmir. The occupied valley had been agitating for freedom for quite some time and the Muslims there had kept up their *jihad* against all odds.

On 25 January 1990, Squadron Leader Ravi Khanna and four of his fellow Indian Air Force pilots were shot dead at a bus stop in Rawalpora. All five victims were members of an air force that had landed thousands of Indian soldiers over 704 flights, from 27 October to 17 November 1947 at Srinagar's airport in order to occupy and subdue Kashmiris. The slaughter of the pilots was an outstanding act of rebellion that sounded the drums of war and sparked a conflict with India that will only be settled by the sword, Allah-willing.

Multiple operations were launched against Indian soldiers, simultaneously. As a result, on 11 February 1984, Jammu Kashmir Liberation Front's founding leader Maqbool Butt was sentenced to death by Justice Ganju and hanged in Delhi's Tihar Jail.

Startled by the repeated acts of rebellion, the Indian government appointed Jagmohan the Butcher, Governor of Kashmir. He believed the greatest threat to Kashmir was war and set about fortifying military bunkers in the region before unleashing hell upon unarmed civilians; this bloodthirsty governor slaughtered dozens of Kashmiris, and thus began an era of bloodshed and brutality.

Around 1990, as *mujahideen* started arriving at *Muaskar-e-Tayyaba*, Afghanistan for military training, *Muaskar-e-Aqsa* was set up in the neighbouring mountains in order to customize training for specific terrains; meanwhile, the recruitment centre *Bayt-ul-Mujahideen* was established in Muzaffarabad in order to recruit potential fighters. A fraternal environment of *jihadi* camaraderie was fostered as Kashmiri and Pakistani *mujahideen* were disciplined and trained side by side, according to the Quran and *Sunnat.*

Muaskar-e-Aqsa's Earliest Graduates

Towards the end of 1990 and the beginning of 1991, the first *jihadi* contingent arrived at *Bayt-ul-Mujahideen* Muzaffarabad in order to inspire potential *mujahideen* by way of proximity to the battlefield. Badr Post and Umm-al-Qura were set up as bases for *mujahideen* to carry out their operations. In Occupied Kashmir, the brutality of the Indian forces was at

NOBLE WARRIORS AND BATTLEFRONTS   495

its peak and the Indian government erroneously believed that to some extent it had curtailed the rebellion brewing in the valley.

Finally, the long-awaited hour of reckoning arrived when, in August 1992, a contingent specifically trained by *Muaskar-e-Aqsa* crossed the border into Occupied Kashmir.

On the morning of 12 August 1992, as Indian forces approached Guzriyal in the Rashi Ghund district of Kupwara for a crackdown, Abu Khalid Aftab Ahmed fired a rocket from an RPG-7 that annihilated an entire military unit; the Indian Army in Kashmir had never before been challenged with such deadly force.

The Indian government admitted losing one captain, two JCOs, and five NCOs among the nineteen soldiers killed that morning... the demoralized freedom-fighters of Kashmir regained their morale, and the people of the valley breathed a sigh of relief; 'Allah's help has arrived!' they cried. The Indian government publicly admitted this was the first time it had been confronted in the valley; meanwhile, Abu Khalid Aftab Ahmed of Bahawalpur, Abu Muhammad Akram of Sheikhupura, and Muhammad Sharif of Lahore achieved martyrdom.

The aforementioned *mujahideen* had been picked from the battlefields of Afghanistan; they were unfamiliar with Kashmir; the valley was a completely new terrain for them. These men cannot be replaced; may Allah reward them for their duty, Allah-willing.

In order to keep abreast of the changing situation in the valley, Kashmir's first *emir* Lala Abu Hafs headed to *Bab-al-Jihad* in Muzaffarabad and appointed Abrar Khan as his substitute. Abrar Khan was martyred in an encounter with Indian forces as they conducted a crackdown in an area known as Hangi Kot, in Rajwar, Kupwara.

When Lala Abu Hafs returned to the valley, he was martyred in an encounter on 8 May 1993 on Tangmarg Road in Baramulla while travelling to Srinagar to establish contact with other organizations.

After these martyrdoms, *mujahideen* conducted a raid on the Vilgam Police Station and confiscated a large number of weapons as booty, as well as an idol made of silver... after this success, the *mujahideen* spread across the breadth and width of the valley under Allah's protection. On 8 June 1993, *mujahideen* ambushed a party of BSF soldiers travelling from Toosh Maidan Camp and beheaded two soldiers with daggers. The entire operation lasted three minutes and yielded

496 THE LITERATURE OF *LASHKAR-E-TAYYABA*

twenty-five LR guns, a wireless set, two watches, and various other valuables.

Around the same time, *mujahideen* ambushed Indian forces at Dhalan, on Tarapur Road, Kupwara, killing thirty soldiers. Three vehicles were completely destroyed. The targets included a variety of soldiers from three different camps; the martyrs involved in the operation were:

1. Abu Hanzala Mudassar Saeed, Gujranwala
2. Abu Mugheera Tilawat Khan, Peshawar
3. Abu Ahmed Muhammad Aslam, Faisalabad

This encounter was reported in the international media, including the BBC, as a gruesome battle. After the success of these brilliantly coordinated attacks, *mujahideen* of *Lashkar-e-Tayyaba* announced their permanent presence in the valley as an independent organization; at the same time, two new training camps were established in Muzaffarabad Kashmir, namely, Abdullah bin Masood and Umm-al-Qura. In 1995, *Lashkar-e-Tayyaba* infiltrated Jammu and faced off with Indian forces in the region for the first time.

During the formative years, numerous commanders sacrificed their lives in the struggle; Kashmir's history is incomplete without the chapters these exemplary martyrs and noble rebels wrote with their blood. They include Abu Emir Harun-al-Rashid (Swat), Abu Abdullah Iftikhar (Faisalabad), Abu Sangar Yar Shams-ur-Rehman Afghani, Abu Mursad Hafiz Abdur Reham (Sheikhupura), Qari Abu Zar Ata-ur-Rehman (Gujranwala), Abu Mansur Shoaib Najeeb (Sahiwal), Abu Abdullah Arshad Javed (Faisalabad), Zulqarnain Muhammad Akhtar Sajid (Bahawalnagar), and Abu Awais Ghazanfar Abbas (Khanewal). Each one of these men presided over numerous operations across the valley.

Countless district and divisional commanders also sacrificed their lives in order to open up the pathways of *jihad* including: Abu Saeed Tanvir (Gujranwala), Abu Muhammad Asim (Rawalpindi), Abu Walid Hafiz Abdur Rehman (Sahiwal), Abu Baseer Hafiz Abdur Rehman (Faisalabad), Abul Qasim Muhammad Younis (Faisalabad), Abu Salman Mahmood Alam (Gujranwala), Abu Bilal Muhammad Zahid (Gujranwala), and Abu Abbad Zawar Ahmed (Sahiwal).

And so, the *jihadi* years continued until one day, the movement took a new turn... *mujahideen* took control of a vast area of land in Kargil, much to India's shock and horror. This area instantly drew the world's attention as it became the site of heroic and historical encounters; nine Indian jets were shot down, one pilot was captured alive, many Indian helicopters were destroyed, thirty-five thousand Indian soldiers were besieged, and the area was cut off from the mainland while most of India's forces were stuck on various other fronts. Kargil was the ideal opportunity to avenge the debacle of East Pakistan, when ...

The prime minister of Pakistan fell to his knees grovelling before Bill Clinton and lost the war to dialogue; it was a dark day in Kashmir. The valley was plunged into despair. Consequently, the Indian government and forces made life hell for the civilians. There were rampant crackdowns and raids and every single person in the valley was treated as a suspect; soldiers went around taunting Muslims; 'Where is your Pakistan now?' 'So much for the beloved *mujahideen*!' After consulting with various religious scholars, the *emir* of *Lashkar-e-Tayyaba* announced the launch of state-wide *fidayeen* (high-risk; literally, sacrificial) missions in retaliation.

Thus, began a second wave of attacks by *Lashkar-e-Tayyaba*. On 12 July 1999, BSF's Madar Camp (brigade headquarters) in Baramulla Bandipur was attacked; the encounter, which went on till the morning of 15 July, claimed the lives of D.I.G (Brig.) S.A. Chakarvarti, Deputy Commandant Mohan Raj, as well as eleven security personnel.

Three days into the attack, when the military was unable to reclaim its headquarters from the daring Abu Salman Muhammad Akmal (Multani) despite reinforcements, it resorted to blowing up its own building, martyring Abu Salman in the process.

As soon as reports of this operation were aired on the radio, the citizens of Kashmir broke out in jubilation, proud that the very *mujahideen* the army claimed to hunt in the forests of Kashmir had hunted the army down in its own camp.

Then, on 3 November 1999, *Lashkar-e-Tayyaba's* fearless warriors stormed into 15 Core Headquarters in Srinagar's Badami Bagh and eternally silenced military spokesman Major Parshutum, who was known for his public anathemas against the *mujahideen*.

498 THE LITERATURE OF *LASHKAR-E-TAYYABA*

Colonel Bhattia, Major Parshutum, Major Kumar, Subedar B.T. Sharma, Deputy Subedar S.K. Shakla, Naik Hawaldar P.K. Merana, Officers M.R. Haq and Radha Kashan, and Sentry Jogandar Singh were among the forty-three Indian security personnel who were slaughtered in what was, according to the Indian Army, an incredibly sensitive but secure location. It turned out that *mujahideen* wreaked havoc on this installation; Abu Maooz Muhammad Ameen from Bahawalpur was martyred in the encounter.

On 1 January 2000, as the Christian world celebrated the New Year and its brutal domination over Muslims, *Lashkar-e-Tayyaba*'s *mujahideen* executed a *fidayeen* attack against an Indian Army camp in Poonch that left thirty-five soldiers, including two officers, dead; two *mujahideen*, Abul Qasim Muhammad Arshad from Bahawalnagar and Abu Siraqa Muhammad Amjad from Vihari, were martyred in the encounter.

On 21 March 2000, *mujahideen* attacked a BSF camp in Srinagar Chanpura; the attack lasted eighteen hours and despite the Indian Army's armoured vehicles the camp was destroyed, and eighteen soldiers were killed. News of this attack was aired on international radio channels; gunshots could be heard during BBC's live coverage of the event. Abu Muhammad Imran Butt of Gujranwala and Abu Harith Muhammad Niazi of Sialkot were martyred in the encounter.

Eleven *fidayeen* missions were launched in 1999 in which 258 soldiers and officers were killed. The dead included one D.I.G. (Brig.) S.A. Chakarvarti, one Deputy Commandant Mohan Raj, Colonel Bhattia, and army spokesman Major Parshutum as well as three majors, a deputy superintendent, three officers, and two I.G's; in addition, three camps were completely destroyed. All this was achieved by eleven valiant *mujahideen* who sacrificed their lives and attained martyrdom during the attacks.

By Allah's grace, *mujahideen* executed forty-eight *fidayeen* attacks in 2000, in which 891 soldiers were killed; among the dead were three colonels, ten majors, one commandant, one captain, three engineers, and numerous JCOs; two camps were obliterated, five cars and four military trucks were destroyed, while seven cars were rendered useless; two LMGs and three SLRs were acquired as war loot.

Of all the *fidayeen* missions and brazen attacks, the most memorable one is *Lashkar-e-Tayyaba*'s attack on Delhi's Red Fort on the night of 22 December 2000 at 9:07pm.

For the longest time, Muslim kings ruled India from Delhi's Red Fort. English pirates disguised as East India Company traders overthrew the last Muslim king Bahadur Shah Zafar and made him a mere pensioner within the walls of his ancestral palace. On 15 August 1947 India announced its independence from the steps of the Red Fort in Delhi; on 22 December 2000, *Lashkar-e-Tayyaba*'s militants stormed into this fort and shook the very foundations of the Indian establishment; the city was plunged into mourning and despair; Kashmir became a distant unattainable dream for the Pharaohs of India who scampered at the resounding march of the *mujahideen*.

What's most impressive about this attack is the fact that *mujahideen* slaughtered twelve Indian soldiers and returned to their bases safely after accomplishing their mission, by Allah's grace and blessings. Meanwhile, Indian authorities tried to cover up the security breach by killing civilians and presenting their bodies as those of the so-called terrorists.

In 2000 alone, *Lashkar-e-Tayyaba*'s *mujahideen* carried out 370 operations against India's terrorist soldiers, which included:

46 operations raids on military installations. 454 Indian soldiers were killed, and 132 were injured. 33 ambushes led to the death of 226 soldiers and left 42 wounded.

On eight occasions Indian soldiers ambushed *Lashkar-e-Tayyaba*'s men but every time, the *mujahideen*, by Allah's grace and blessings, counter-ambushed the Army, leaving forty-seven soldiers dead and seven wounded.

Lashkar-e-Tayyaba remotely attacked army installations at twelve different locations, killing forty-six soldiers and injuring forty-four, in addition to destroying six vehicles, two power-stations, and one television station.

Cumulatively, in 2000, over 370 attacks, *Lashkar* sent 2,599 Indian soldiers back to Delhi in body-bags, in response to the Indian government's brutal and oppressive control over Kashmir. Nine hundred and seventy-four Indian soldiers have been permanently disabled by *Lashkar*'s *mujahideen*; these men will spend the rest of their days licking their wounds; they are a reminder to all that the hand that dares tarnish the dignity and honour of Muslims will be chopped off by the noble sons of Islam, Allah-willing!

500 THE LITERATURE OF *LASHKAR-E-TAYYABA*

This past year, 289 noble warriors honoured their promise to their Lord and attained martyrdom, Allah-willing.

In the eleven-year struggle for Kashmir, 14,369 Indian soldiers have been wiped off the face of this earth while 1,016 *mujahideen* have re-written the history of the valley's ice-capped peaks, verdant meadows, fertile fields, frothing springs, serene lakes, and bustling cities with the steaming heat of the martyrs' immortal blood that will inspire generations to come, Allah-willing.

From Madar Camp in Bandipur to 15 Core Headquarter in Badami Bagh, from Delhi's Red Fort to Srinagar's New Airport, *Lashkar-e-Tayyaba's mujahideen* have proved to the world, through their actions and their sacrifices, that we will continue fighting the Pharaohs of disbelief and the governments of oppression until all injustice and treachery is eradicated from this world, and Allah's true religion reigns.

This is our method and our *jihad*; this is our core message, and our objective, Allah-willing.

Dr Manzoor Ahmed

27 January 2001

Chapter 9: A Hindu Idol's Tribulations

Mujahideen took off with a Hindu 'god'; Indian soldiers and their 'god' were helpless.

When Mahmud Ghaznavi's heirs—*Lashkar-e-Tayyaba's* valiant and fearless *mujahideen*—attacked Srinagar's police station and overpowered the officers, they took off with one of the 330 million gods of the idol-worshippers, dragging the idol behind them; Indian soldiers stationed all around were unable to free their helpless 'god'... the soldiers looked on as their 'god' was abducted by *mujahideen*... and humiliated in public... and despite all the advanced firepower the soldiers were helpless... even their 'god' could do nothing but suffer its own desecration.

Sultan Mahmood Ghaznavi asserted Allah's Oneness by repeatedly attacking the Hindu polytheists and destroying their idols. Historians say that in Mahmood's mosque in Ghazni, when the imam said *walad-duwaleen* (a verse from prayer) the entire mosque would call back with a resounding *Ameen*! Syed Badi'-ud-Din Shah Rashidi declared Sultan Mahmood a true monotheist according to the definitions of the Quran and *Sunnat*. Afghanistan's Hanafi king *emir* Abdur Rehman had the following epitaph engraved on Mahmood's tomb:

محی السنۃ قاطع شرک و بدعت

He who keeps *Sunnat* alive and obliterates polytheism and religious innovations.

Sultan Mahmood Ghaznavi destroyed the golden idol in Somnath and earned the title of Idol-Wrecker for himself. The falcons of *Lashkar-e-Tayyaba* keep the memory of this brave warrior alive by obliterating polytheism and eradicating religious corruption according to *Sunnat*.

Bizarre Form of Revenge

In September 1993, when Abu Abdul Wahab Anjum, Commander of *Lashkar-e-Tayyaba* in Occupied Kashmir gave details of attacks by *Lashkar-e-Tayyaba*'s dedicated fighters in context of the importance and glory of *jihad* while addressing the *Jihad-e-Kashmir* and Bosnia Seminar in Lahore, the audience was moved to tears. He said:

When our founding commander Brother Abu Hafs was martyred in June 1993, our men were deeply aggrieved and desperate for revenge. Every one of my warriors wanted to execute an elaborate attack on the life and property of the enemy that would make the latter think hard before ever attacking our *mujahideen* again. I told my men we needed to be patient because our resources were depleted but they refused to back down. Their thirst for revenge trumped all my arguments; putting all our faith in the hope that Allah will help us through every ordeal, we prepared for battle. We were short of ammunition so first we devised a plan to restock. A party of ten *mujahideen* broke into the Vilgam Police Station and an ammunition depot located between the Border Security Forces and the Vilgam Camp. I had stationed three of my *mujahideen* on either

502 THE LITERATURE OF *LASHKAR-E-TAYYABA*

side of the depot, while the rest of us crawled through barbed wires; normally, these wires are electrified but by Allah's grace, that day there was a power outage. We made our way through the barracks to the main gate. I knocked on the door and said:

'Brother, please open the door.'

'Who is it?' someone responded.

'I'm one of your own,' I said, in Kashmiri.

The guard called the clerk and told him someone was here to see him. At this point it is important to note that by Allah's grace, due to the valour and courage of *Lashkar-e-Tayyaba*'s *mujahideen*, all the fighters in general, and their *emir*s in particular, are well known throughout the valley. When the clerk saw me, I asked, 'Do you know who I am?'

'Yes, I know you,' he said.

I ordered him to open the door. I said, 'I know you have wireless sets here that you use to inform the Army about the whereabouts of the *mujahideen*. You have my brothers attacked, captured, tortured, and martyred. I'm here to investigate the matter so open the door.'

He opened the door, and we entered the premises. After surveying all the rooms, we arrived at the depository. I told the clerk to hand me the keys to the room.

The clerk said, 'Sir, I'm responsible for what's deposited here.'

I yelled at him to hand over the keys.

The coward relented. The room was full of arms and ammunition. When I flashed my torch inside, I noticed an eight-armed idol hanging from the ceiling. It was made entirely of silver, with red gems for eyes. I pulled the idol down and told one of my men to take it out. Again, the clerk protested.

'Are you Muslim?' I asked.

'Yes,' he answered.

'Then shut up!' I yelled. 'You're willing to take responsibility for a Hindu idol! We're going to take it back with us.'

After exiting the room, I told him to lock up all the workers in the building in the large hall.

Once we had transferred all the ammunition, I turned to the men locked up: 'Listen up!' I said. 'Muslims are being oppressed the world over. Women, men, old, and young are being slaughtered indiscriminately.

Men are being dragged into the mud by their beards and tortured to death while hypocrites like you shamelessly betray your brothers.'

The Charge

One might ask why we took weapons from Muslim police officers. We did so for a very good reason; in those days, the police of numerous districts including Srinagar, Pulwama, Bandipora, Lar, Kanganpura, Islamabad, Anantnag, Sopore, and Budgam, was on strike. During the strike, officers of Srinagar's Central Jail dug underground tunnels and supplied *mujahideen* with vast quantities of arms and ammunition. The Indian Army had to besiege the central jail and ultimately had to tear its walls down with tanks. When it was discovered that officers had been smuggling weapons to *mujahideen*, they were thrown in jail, along with their families. During all this, Vilgam's police station was the only station where the officers not only refused to cooperate with *mujahideen* but actively betrayed them by spying on them and hunting them down.

Beg For Mercy

I berated and shamed the officers bitterly. I said: 'The Muslim *ummat* is in despair yet you're bent on harming your brothers instead of helping them out. You're the ones who ought to be behind bars; you do not deserve to live. We ought to throw you in the very cells you use to imprison us. Now, you're going to crouch down in submission and hold your ears and beg for forgiveness.'

The presiding officer seemed confused. So I yelled at him: 'I COMMAND YOU ALL TO BEND OVER AND HOLD YOUR EARS!'

Everyone bowed down and gripped their ears. Next, I told them to let go of their ears and crawl under the charpoys.

They followed my orders. The presiding officer stuck his head out from under the charpoy and said: 'Now what?'

I said: 'We're taking off with all our loot. When we exit there will be some gunfire. As soon as the firing stops, you are to sever all telephone

504 THE LITERATURE OF *LASHKAR-E-TAYYABA*

lines and set this post on fire so never again can you launch any kind of operation against *mujahideen* from this cursed place.'

Abducting an Idol

As we took off, each one of us was carrying over ten guns stolen from the depository, but nothing filled us with greater joy than to have made off with the silver idol, which was like a mother to Hindus that they worshipped like a god; that day, every Hindu money-lender was made to realize that every Muslim man is a Sultan Mahmud Ghaznavi, and that as long as we maintain our relationship with *tawheed* and *jihad*, we will continue exposing the false gods for what they are by smashing them to pieces.

The idol was displayed in November 1993 at *Markaz-e-Tayyaba*'s annual convention in Muridke during which thousands of congregants attacked the idol with hammers and rods as they relived the noble actions of Sultan Mahmud Ghaznavi, Victor of Somnath, Destroyer of Idols. Among those who smashed the idol in a public display of faith were Sheikh Abdul Aziz, Commander Muslim Forces of Bosnia, Abu Abdul Wahab Anjum, and the martyr Sheikh Jameel-ur-Rehman's son, Sheikh Samiullah Afghanistani.

We had some trouble carrying all the weapons we had acquired, not to mention, there was the threat of three army units behind us with a BSF barrack only a short distance to the north. At this point Allah aided us in His infinite mercy and unleashed a heavy downpour that kept the Indian soldiers inside their camps. We exited the post firing into the air, while the police officers remained faithful to their Muslim faith and emptied the petrol from their jeeps and used it to set the station on fire; within seconds, all the police records and files, as well as the vehicles parked at the station were engulfed in flames. Soldiers surrounded the inferno; some tried coming after us, but thanks to Allah, we escaped unscathed. This operation was a serious boost to our morale; subsequently, my men started craving more action.

I said: 'Now that we have sufficient ammunition, there will be blood, Allah-willing.'

... And Then We Sorted the 'Gurus'

At the time, we were unaware that an entire brigade was assembling in Kupwara's Tharth Camp; a brigadier had called a meeting to discuss methods with which to deal with Afghan guerrillas. Keep in mind, *Markaz's mujahideen* were known as Afghan guerrillas throughout Occupied Kashmir. When the meeting officially commenced that evening, our guerrillas approached the venue on a reconnaissance mission, only to discover that many high-ranking 'gurus' of the Indian armed forces were assembled there.

The martyr brother Abu Saria declared: 'Today, let's sort out all these so-called "gurus".'

Brothers, there was a time when Kashmiris were afraid to take up arms against their oppressors for fear of death. Thanks to Allah, since the *Markaz's mujahideen* entered the fight, and taught the locals about *jihad* and faith, and convinced them we are not fighting for freedom, or land, or Kashmir, but solely to raise the banner of Islam across the globe, things in the valley have changed. Kashmiris are now willing to offer their life's savings for ammunition; they are eager for us to conduct operations in the valley; they take comfort in the echoes of our gunfire. We prayed to Allah before attacking the assembly and proceeded to destroy the camp. Someone who lived close to the venue later told us: 'The howls emanating from the camp sounded like humans were being skinned alive.'

I said: 'But we only fired guns and lobbed grenades; no doubt, Allah's angels must have descended to help us.'

One hundred and fifty 'gurus' were dispatched to hell in this operation; not a single one of our men was remotely injured. After this glorious victory, Kashmiris begged us to carry out similar operations and offered their full support. They have undying love for our *mujahideen*; if we show up at their doorstep in the middle of the night, they immediately offer us a meal and a bed. I was personally hosted by an old couple that kept vigil over me as I slept and woke me up at *tahajjud* for the midnight prayer. By Allah, why would we not help those who love us so dearly, especially when this is what Allah commands?

506 THE LITERATURE OF *LASHKAR-E-TAYYABA*

'I Commend This Afghan *Mujahid*'s Valour!' Hindu General

This brazen attack shook the Indian Army to its core. Military units proceeded to lay siege to the entire area while locals begged us for another operation so the Indian soldiers would not dare harass Muslims again. Consequently, the very next day we left our hideouts in the mountains and forests and set up an ambush in the square in Dhaman. After the operation, a Hindu General said: 'I commend the valour of the young warrior who did not yet have a proper beard but staved off thousands of Indian soldiers while guarding his injured comrades.'

Thanks to Allah, during this operation we destroyed four vehicles while the authorities themselves reported they lost fifty-seven soldiers (this is a very conservative estimate).

Brothers, although these anecdotes are from Kashmir, today, Europe, America, in fact the entire world is terrified of *mujahideen*. Our terror rocks the very foundations of parliaments and presidencies. The Israeli prime minister himself announced, 'If the Afghan *mujahideen* aren't stopped, *Jihad-e-Kashmir* will succeed.' It is abundantly clear that disbelievers see their own demise in *jihad*; this is the only aspect of Muslims that terrifies them; Allah-willing, this *jihad* will inevitably succeed.

Chapter 12: Hunting Israeli Commandos

Mujahideen make short work of elite Israeli commandos sent into the valley.

Israeli commandos... approached *mujahideen*... with speed and stealth... when all at once... Abu Waleed raised his LMG gun ... squeezed the trigger... gunshots... in an instant, three Israeli commandos... collapse, dead.'

I, Brother Abu Qatada, was a plant operator for an air-conditioning manufacturer in Karachi when I read an essay on the martyrdom of

Zia-ul-Hafeez, whose father Qari Abdul-Hafeez had also been martyred at Jalalabad; this essay moved me deeply. I regularly attended the sermons delivered by Maulana Abdullah Nasir Rehmani at the mosque on Court Road; soon, I was inspired to join the *jihad*. Consequently, I quit my job in 1990 and headed to Samarkhel, Afghanistan. I received basic training from my mentors Shabbir and Brother Nasr Javed at *Muaskar-e-Tayyaba* after which I received special training before being dispatched to Kashmir.

When Hindu Soldiers Dragged Their Own Dead

Brother Abu Qatada from Karachi describes his *jihadi* tale as follows:

> There were eight of us and I was the *emir*. After a night in Bandipora, as we concluded our *fajr* prayers, we discovered we were surrounded by Hindu soldiers. We managed to escape into the mountains and opened fire as the Hindu soldiers headed towards us. The encounter lasted seven hours; while the soldiers were distracted, three of our men who had been unable to escape with us earlier made it out alive. By Allah's grace, we sent fifteen Hindu soldiers to hell without incurring any loss.

> During the encounter we spread across the mountainside and brazenly communicated with one another over our wireless sets in order to intimidate the enemy. I'd say something like, 'Go control Sopore Road,' into my radio and one of my men would respond, 'Sir, we've taken over Sopore Road already ... we've cut down the trees so they can't leave the area ... ' or 'we've taken control of Baramulla Road, you should go for Bandipore road... don't let these cowards escape with their dead.' Our chants of *takbeer* (Allah Akbar) echoed through the mountains and sent chills up the enemy's spine ... we settled down and shot at the soldiers as they eavesdropped on our exchange over their wireless sets.
> We proceeded to sit back and watch the Hindu soldiers run; they dragged their dead by the feet and tossed them into their vehicles like trash. They left behind four cars that we promptly set ablaze.

508 THE LITERATURE OF *LASHKAR-E-TAYYABA*

Israeli Commandos

There were eight of us bathing in Bandipora's canal when a spy informed the army of our presence. We joked that if soldiers showed up, we would have to run and assume position without our clothes. One of my men said: 'Hazrat Zarar used to fight without his shirt on; today, we'll fight like him.'

We were chatting among ourselves when suddenly a shot rang out. When I turned my wireless set on, I discovered that *mujahideen* were trying to warn us; five minutes later there were three more shots. *Harkat-ul-Mujahideen*'s fighters informed us over the radio that Hindu soldiers were headed in our direction and that they were only thirty to forty metres away. We immediately put our clothes on and started hiking up the mountain; soldiers were ascending the same mountain from the opposite side. We assumed our positions while brother Abu Waleed went up to the summit with his LMG. I ordered the rest of my men to fan out. When there were only ten meters between the soldiers, and us there was a gunfight. We were surprised to see their commandos scale the slopes with such speed and stealth. Nevertheless, brother Abu Waleed opened fire and shot three commandos dead. We could hear soldiers talk among themselves; they were saying, 'These are Afghan fighters; they are not going to give up; we are going to have to fight them!' Once they called in the mortars, we noticed that among the Hindu soldiers there were commandos who moved much more efficiently than the rest and transported and installed artillery from one mountain to the next with alarming speed; a mortar round exploded only five metres from brother Abu Waleed but he was protected by Allah's grace. In response, Abu Waleed fired his LMG at the artillery and all three of its operators were instantly killed. The rest of the soldiers abandoned their positions and were descending the mountain when we fired a rocket and killed two more of them. The rest kept running for their lives. We went after them but by the time we got down they had fled, leaving behind two SLR rounds as war loot for us. None of our men was even remotely injured. Allah's greatest gift to us that day was the death of eight commandos. Their distinct uniforms, their highly efficient movements, and their faces were a dead giveaway; these weren't Hindus, they were Jews sent into the valley as a result of a pact between India and Israel. *Lashkar-e-Tayyaba*'s *mujahideen* had not only killed Hindus, but Jews as well, thanks to Allah. This was all by the grace of Allah for we are but mere *jihadis* in His path. We pray that Allah keep us devoted to this path. If all Muslims united for *jihad*, we could free *Bayt-ul-Muqaddas* very quickly, Allah-willing. Allah is ready to hand it over to us as long as we are prepared to follow the footsteps of the prophet in how he exiled the Jewish tribes of Banu Nazir and Banu Qaynuqah.

Conversations with Abrar Khan

Vazirabad's Afzal Ahmed Abu Ali narrates: I received basic training in Samarkhel Afghanistan. After my advanced training, I was dispatched to the valley with a contingent of six men. When we arrived in the valley on 15 October 1992, some Kashmiris joined our group. By Allah's grace, I have been involved in numerous large-scale encounters. I consider it an honour to have fought alongside Brother Abu Hafs when he was martyred in June 1993; I was also with Brother Abrar till his last breath in May 1993 at Hangnikot.

Once, in May 1993, as ten of us entered a village for Friday's congregational prayer, it started raining lightly. Brother Abrar said it was a good opportunity for us to bathe. As some of us took off, I discovered, via my wireless set, that Hindu soldiers had ambushed some *Hizb-ul-Mujahideen* fighters. I informed our commander who said it was crucial for us to go and help our brothers. 'But it's time for the congregational prayer,' I protested but he insisted helping our brothers was more important than offering our prayers in that moment.

As we approached the ambush, we discovered that the Hindu soldiers were done with their operation and had already left the village.

The following day, we stopped in a village to rest. Brother Abrar used to take care of us like a father. He told us to nap while he went to the bazaar, bought some meat, and cooked for us. He woke us up when dinner was ready. Many times, he would watch over us as we slept even though he was our commander. That day, as usual, he prepared breakfast for us after *fajr* prayers and fed us with his own hands. After breakfast, we were preparing to return to our base when a Kashmiri came running towards us, yelling: 'There's a crackdown in the neighbouring village; I barely escaped with my life!'

510 THE LITERATURE OF *LASHKAR-E-TAYYABA*

Brother Abrar told us to prepare for combat, Allah-willing. As we proceeded to the neighbouring village, he told me to collect five more men from a specific location and meet him with the reinforcements. He said we were going to open fire at 1pm. Once I collected the five men and arrived at the agreed upon location, I discovered a full-blown gunfight was already underway. When the soldiers saw us, they mistakenly thought they were surrounded and started fleeing. I was unable to make contact with brother Abrar, so I decided to look for him. As I descended into the village, a Kashmiri with a first aid kit told me brother Abrar had been injured. Both of us made a dash for the forest where we found him gravely wounded. He turned to me and said, 'Abu Ali! I am freezing; take me some place warm!' We started carrying him away, but he had already been martyred!!

My companions informed me that when Brother Abrar was hit, he spontaneously cried out, 'All praise to Allah! I've been hit!' As Abu Bilal tried carrying him to a safe location, he was again hit on the calf, at which point he said, 'Is there any hope for my survival? There's so much I have to do for Islam.'

Readers, brother Abrar was the model *mujahideen* commander; only a commander of his calibre can say, 'Praise Allah' when he's hit for he's fully aware of the glory of his wounds which, on the Last Day, will ooze blood the colour of saffron and the scent of musk; his dying thoughts were about how much more service he owed the faith... Kashmir had yet to be conquered, India had yet to be destroyed, Pakistanis had yet to be awakened from their slumber, and Israel had yet to be sorted. May Allah grant him a glorious place in heaven, Allah-willing.

Hafiz Ghazi Abd-ur-Rehman Took a Bullet with Paradise in His Eyes

From early childhood, I had an inclination towards *jihad*; even as a primary school student I dreamt of becoming a soldier. When Maulana Abd-ur-Rauf of Sahiwal was martyred, I became more serious about joining the *mujahideen*. After receiving my mother's permission, which she granted wholeheartedly, I headed for Kunar, Afghanistan. I received most of my training in Jalalabad. During my advanced training my mentor was Shabbir. In October 1992, I was dispatched to the valley.

We Will Have Our Grapes in Heaven

I had the good fortune of participating in two encounters in Kashmir the first of which occurred under the leadership of Abrar Khan. There were sixteen of us; we were to attack Magam Camp. On our way when we stopped to buy some grapes our commander said: 'We will have these grapes in heaven.' About five hundred metres from the camp, we split up into smaller groups where Abrar Khan divided the grapes among us before we offered our *maghrib* (evening prayer) and *isha* (night prayer) prayers.

Brother Abrar led one contingent himself; fifty metres from the camp, he fired a rocket straight through a window that exploded inside the room. Later reports confirmed that every soldier in that room was killed. Then, brother Abrar told the rest of us to give his party cover fire, as he and his men returned to safety. As we were heading back a mortar round fell exactly where we had been standing moments earlier; by Allah's mercy, not one of us was even remotely injured. Long after we left the site, the Hindus kept firing and wasting their ammunition.

Apart from numerous other skirmishes, my second major encounter was alongside Tilavat Khan.

Once, we were resting in a village for the night and had barely fallen asleep when our sentinel woke us up to inform us of the presence of Army vehicles. We immediately left the village for the mountains. It was two o' clock at night. Hindu soldiers were headed for a crackdown in the neighbouring village of Rafiabad as we crossed their path under the cover of darkness. All of a sudden, one of our men sneezed; the soldiers immediately opened fire; later, we found out there were thousands of soldiers; it seemed all of them were firing indiscriminately, yet we made it out without a single injury. Meanwhile, a new batch of Hindu soldiers descended into the village and thought they were being fired upon by *mujahideen*, so they returned fire and shot dead seven of their own men. Locals told us about this the following day; they said the Hindus cremated the soldiers they had accidentally killed in the village.

512 THE LITERATURE OF *LASHKAR-E-TAYYABA*

Brother Abd-ur-Rehman narrates that during a certain encounter he mistakenly believed that a bullet that had merely grazed his ear had actually hit him in the temple; he thought he was going to die. Consequently, he recited the *kalima*, and lay down to welcome, what he thought was, his impending martyrdom. He had been told that when a martyr dies he feels nothing more than a pin-prick, so he was certain that because he felt no pain, despite the fact that a bullet had hit him in the head, he was undoubtedly on his way to martyrdom. After staying down for a long while, he stood up and realized he hadn't been hit at all. Keep in mind, this man is now a martyr, and having a fantastic time in paradise, Allah-willing.

Brother Zafar Iqbal bin Syed Muhammad narrates I was overjoyed when finally my number was called in the lottery that determined who would head to Kashmir from Muzaffarabad, but my fellow *mujahideen* and I had to turn back halfway because of inclement weather and landslides. I was not chosen in the next lottery; I was so upset I could not hold back my tears. Abu Dajana took pity on me and gave me his number. This is how I came to be a part of Fahadullah and Tilavat Khan's group.

Run! Run!

Wular Lake in Bandipora is known for its majestic beauty and size. Often, we would sail out into the middle of the lake for a nap. One morning, after spending the night on the lake, as we washed ourselves and said our *fajr* prayers in our boat, we spotted an army vehicle and discovered there was a crackdown in the neighbouring village. We immediately got to shore, disembarked, went up the mountain, assumed our positions, and attacked. By Allah's grace, we killed seven Hindus. In the course of our attack, we could hear them yelling: 'Run! Run!'

Allah's Assistance

Often, we recite the following verse from the Quran:

وَجَعَلْنَا مِن بَيْنِ أَيْدِيهِمْ سَدًّا وَمِنْ خَلْفِهِمْ سَدًّا فَأَغْشَيْنَاهُمْ فَهُمْ لَا يُبْصِرُونَ

And We have set a bar before them and a bar behind them, and (thus) have covered them so that they see not.

(Quran 36:9)

While we uttered this prayer numerous times, once, during a crackdown in Bandipora, we actually lived it personally. According to our coded signals, in the face of a crackdown, three rounds are fired to warn *mujahideen* of an imminent threat. We were in Bandipora when we heard three gunshots, so we immediately left the village and made our way into the night. As we walked in the dark, we saw five soldiers walking towards us. One of our men asked the approaching soldiers: 'Who are you?'

One of the soldier's responded: 'Arath Singh. Who are you?'

Our man said: 'We are just on our way to our post.'

They mistook us for soldiers and didn't bother us. Allah quietly led us out of the area without anyone raising an eyebrow; as we moved away, we saw thousands of soldiers moving in the night.

Chapter 28: Indian Forces and *Mujahideen* Play Hide-and-Seek During Elections

Lashkar's fearless *mujahideen* were fighting valiantly... they had been surrounded on all sides by the Indian Army... forty Hindu soldiers lay dead ... in a panic, the soldiers called in reinforcements... commandos poured out of helicopters... on the other hand... policemen were embracing the *mujahideen*... saying: 'Are we not brothers? We have been waiting for you... if the soldiers fire at you we'll provide cover.'

Meet martyr Abu Abd-ur-Rehman who has been battling Hindu beasts for quite some time now. Here is the story he has to narrate about Kashmir:

In 1997, in an attempt to fool the people of Kashmir in particular, and the world in general, India pulled a democratic stunt by holding elections in the valley, in an attempt to establish a puppet government in order to show the world that the Indian government had the situation in the region under control.

514 THE LITERATURE OF *LASHKAR-E-TAYYABA*

Election Operation

Just before the elections in 1997, villagers from Turkpora begged us to attack the military camp in their village so soldiers wouldn't force them to vote; it was common knowledge that areas where *mujahideen*'s presence was strong were less likely to be harassed by the military. *Mujahideen* were already actively involved in 'election operations'; hence, they put together a force comprising men from *Lashkar-e-Tayyaba, Harkat-ul-Ansar, Al-Fatah,* and *Hizb-ul-Mujahideen* that proceeded to launch a full-scale attack with rockets and grenade-guns on the military camp in Turkpora. The soldiers were caught off guard and lost fifteen men; countless more were wounded. As a result, the military not only pulled out of Turkpora but also withdrew from Malangam; the residents of the region were able to breathe easier after that. Another time, *mujahideen* attacked a camp at Dardpora in which fourteen Hindu soldiers were sent straight to hell. By the time the soldiers figured out what was going on the *mujahideen* had long escaped. *Mujahideen* operate with such efficiency and stealth that by the time they are done with an attack, the soldiers are left with the wounded and the dead. This is why families of young soldiers sent into Occupied Kashmir despise the Indian government.

Once, during an encounter, one of our men was severely injured by shrapnel. Abu Talha Hazarvi (martyred) managed to transport the wounded fighter to a safe location even as the fighting continued. Later, we collectively operated on our brother's wounds; very quickly, the injured fighter was well enough to get back on his feet and join us in our operations. We were amazed how such deep wounds that required two surgeries healed so quickly; undoubtedly, when fighting in Allah's path, there is divine assistance every step of the way. One night, we were returning from the border region with some fresh arrivals when we heard the voice of a soldier cry out: 'Who goes there?!'

One of the *mujahideen* responded: 'Who are you?'

Without another word, the soldiers opened fire but not one of us was injured. The soldiers had set up an ambush, but we had prepared a counter-ambush. The fighting was hard; our chants of Allah Akbar mingled with their anguished cries... by the end of it all we managed to slaughter a major and six of his men; after setting their vehicles ablaze, by Allah's grace, we merrily went our way without any loss of life or limb.

Commandos Descend from Helicopters

Once, the army got wind of a group of *Lashkar-e-Tayyaba*'s men on their way to receive fresh arrivals and surrounded the forest for a crackdown. The army wanted to arrest all of us alive, or at the very least, corner us in an attack; we discovered, through our own sources, that the soldiers were on our trail, so we changed our path and scaled the mountain close to where they had set up an ambush. When the soldiers were unable to corner our two groups, they opened fire on the group coming in from Pakistan. The battle lasted from 9am till late at night; under Abu Zar Basri's leadership the men fought back valiantly. After losing forty soldiers the military called in reinforcements and commandos began pouring out of helicopters into the valley; the encounter between the military and the new arrivals from Pakistan lasted a number of days during which five *mujahideen* were martyred (Azizullah, Abu Zeeshan, Abu Qaizan, Abu Abdul Qahar, Abu Zar Basri). One night, as the *mujahideen* from Lolab returned to their base through the forest they heard the sound of a boot striking a tree. Everyone stopped. After some time, they heard the crack of a whip. They understood there was an ambush up ahead and that a Sikh soldier was risking his life to warn them. Thanks to the Sikh soldier, they altered their course and safely reached Lolab.

Sikh soldiers in Occupied Kashmir are sympathetic to our cause and often cooperate with us; they never miss an opportunity to undermine Hindus for they know that the success of the separatist movement in Khalistan is intrinsically linked to Kashmir's liberation.

Terrorized Soldiers

One day before the election, we launched a concerted attack in collaboration with Al-Barq, on Dardpora's camp with fifty-seven missiles and rockets. There were three camps in the village, two of which had been recently installed to force the people to vote. Our attack was so efficiently executed, soldiers were caught off guard and their horrified cries filled the valley. Within no time, twenty-two soldiers were slaughtered along with two Indian agents while eight were left wounded as we safely made our way back to our base. The following morning, on Election Day, we surveyed

516 THE LITERATURE OF *LASHKAR-E-TAYYABA*

the village from our binoculars and noticed that not a single person went out to vote. Then, we saw Indian soldiers forcing people out of their homes and dragging them to the polling station, so we decided to launch another attack. We descended from the mountainside into the village and when the soldiers were within range we attacked. They ran into their camp leaving two of their wounded and three of their dead behind. Throughout the day we exchanged light fire with the soldiers holed up in the camp as a result only one vote was cast and the army's farcical election turned out of be a flop. At the end of the day, even the soldiers were looking for an excuse to stay holed up in the safety of their camp. When they stepped out into the open, they cursed their own government for putting them in harm's way for they didn't know when a bullet might have sent them to hell.

Once, soldiers of a camp near Dardpora, got a thrashing from their superiors for not doing their job: '*Mujahideen* are driving everyone mad while you all are too scared to step out of your camps! Go attack the *mujahideen* bases now!' Soldiers know full well where our bases are located in the forest, but they are too afraid to inform the High Command because in an attack, they will be on the frontline facing our wrath. That day, soldiers went around violently interrogating villagers, but no one gave up any information about us despite being tortured. When we heard of this, we formed a contingent of twenty-five men (fifteen from *Lashkar*, four from *Hizb-ul-Mujahideen*, and six from *Al-Barq*) under the leadership of brother Abu Hafs from Khanewal. We attacked the military camp with RPG-7s, grenade guns, and AK-47s, killing fifteen soldiers, and wounding ten; the rest turned tail and ran in so many directions no one knows how many of them survived.

Police and *Mujahideen*

Psychologically, the Indian Army has lost the battle for Kashmir as the local police force lends its full support to *mujahideen* and sympathizes with our cause. Once, *Lashkar's mujahideen* needed to cross a bridge that was being guarded by approximately twenty-five policemen. They stopped us and embraced us, saying, 'Are we not brothers? We long for you. If the Army attacks you, we will always give you cover.' We will never forget their words of support and affection.

A *Mujahid* Addresses the Indian Army

Two of *Lashkar-e-Tayyaba*'s bases were located close to each other in Rafiabad. Once, our men were travelling from one hideout to the other when they were ambushed by soldiers from four different camps. During the attack, a bullet grazed Brother Abu Rehan's head while another went right through his arm. We launched a counter-ambush and the *mujahideen* from the second base aimed their guns at the sky, cutting off any chances of reinforcements joining the fight from helicopters; thus, the soldiers were trapped. The encounter lasted from 9am to 2pm in the afternoon; one by one, Indian soldiers were being slaughtered on the battlefield when all at once, Abu Mujahid from Khushab made his way to the mountaintop and looking down on the battlefield, he addressed the polytheists and enemies of Islam. The firing ceased and an eerie silence took over the terrain. In his rant, our brother taunted the infidels, and warned them Allah was on our side; at one point he recited the famous poem that begins with:

> Yesterday, the world saw Russia disintegrate
> Today, we'll witness India's collapse
> And:
> Bitter enemy, do you have any clue whom you've provoked?
> Infidels! Hindus! Do you have any clue whom you've provoked?

For half an hour, our brother launched a fiery tirade against our enemy. The fighting started again; *mujahideen* had the upper hand in terms of their positions on the mountain. Every time the chant *'Allah Akbar'* rose from one of our positions, the enemy cowered and withdrew; soldiers stopped obeying their superiors out of fear. When a major ordered his men to charge, they refused. On the other hand, *mujahideen* taunted the soldiers, by yelling 'Blasted Hindus! With Allah's help we will only rest once we have chased you off the battlefield.' To boost the morale of his troops, the major yelled, 'Bastards! I'll personally deal with you and your god!'... but the minute his head emerged from behind his cover, in a fitting display of honour and valour, one of our men shot at the skull that housed such blasphemous thoughts, blasting all his hubris to smithereens. Later, we saw this blasphemous wretch being dragged by his feet

518 THE LITERATURE OF *LASHKAR-E-TAYYABA*

through the dirt by his own men as they tried to salvage his body. We chanted '*Allah Akbar!*' as they kept running.

We were at a vantage point; they were too afraid to come out of the bushes. Their officer told them to charge; they said: 'We have little kids; we can't afford to die.'

We could hear their conversation clearly. We lobbed a grenade that exploded behind them. Fearing an attack from the rear, they immediately got up to run and we mowed them down. There were seven of them; all seven were slaughtered. By Allah's grace, we killed thirty-three Hindus in all, including a lieutenant colonel, a major, and a captain.

The Headless Captain

Once, in Nabarda, when the Army attacked *mujahideen*, one of our men managed to decapitate a captain by shooting straight at his neck. Three days later, as the soldiers were passing through a village with their dead, the captain's head rolled out and fell to the ground. The villagers chanted slogans in favour of Pakistan and the *mujahideen*. In the encounter two *mujahideen* from Harkat-ul-Ansar were martyred while twelve soldiers were sent straight to hell.

Bastard! It's Me

Once, *Lashkar-e-Tayyaba*'s *mujahideen* had a surprise encounter with Indian soldiers in which Abu Mujahid, the man who delivered a diatribe from atop a mountain against disbelievers, was injured. His clothes somewhat matched the Indian Army uniform. Wounded, he quietly lay down to the side. When soldiers passed by him, they could not tell if he was one of them or one of us. Taking advantage of his camouflage Abu Mujahid shot one of the soldiers who leapt and cried: 'Bastard! It's me! Why are you firing at me? I didn't expect any better from the likes of you.' Abu Mujahid proceeded to murder four soldiers before escaping, despite his wounds. This incident shows how divided the Indian Army actually is and how little soldiers trust one another. The common Hindu soldier does not trust his officers because he knows that the officers are Brahmins

NOBLE WARRIORS AND BATTLEFRONTS   519

while he belongs to a lower caste and Brahmins see him as nothing more than vermin.

Chapter 30: The Hospitality of Kashmiri Muslims

Kashmiri children said to us... our mothers have granted us permission... take us to Pakistan ... !! What a sight ... !! Indian soldiers slept in one room of the house... while we were having a meal in the next ... hosted by Kashmiri Muslims ... !!! An old man cried out... this is the first time we've seen *mujahideen* since 1965 ... '

Sector Commander brother Abdullah narrates: We were on this side of River Tavi when we stopped at a house to rest. We were about to take our shoes off before sitting on the lush carpets spread out for us when the old lady of the house said: 'Sons! Don't worry about your shoes. I've been waiting for you since yesterday. I had them pull twice as much water from the stream today to cook for my sons.' We told her we did not have enough time to eat. She said, 'But this is nothing. What I really wanted to do was roast some chicken for you. Never mind, if you don't have time to sit and eat just take the food with you and have it when you get the chance.' We said: 'Mother, we already have a full meal with us from the last house we last visited.'

After an encounter near Mohre, when we sought shelter in a house, the residents welcomed us with open arms. Old women kissed our foreheads and said: 'While you were fighting, we begged Allah to keep you safe.'

Once, after a quiet meal in a house in Mohre, as we were leaving, we were told that some Indian soldiers were sleeping in one of the adjacent rooms; apparently, they had forced their way in for a rest. How courageous were the residents; they welcomed us and fed us despite knowing full well that had we been discovered all of them would have been tortured and at the very least, their home would have turned into a battlefield between the *mujahideen* and the soldiers; despite all the risks, they hosted us with utmost courtesy.

Another time, five of us were making our way past a house when we feared someone was spying on us, so we settled down some distance from

520 THE LITERATURE OF *LASHKAR-E-TAYYABA*

the residence. After a while, some girls exited the house to collect water from a stream. They spotted us and started crying out in their local language. We asked our Kashmiri brother what they were saying. He told us they were calling out to the men in the house, saying: 'Brother! Father! These men are our guests. We must welcome them into our home.' The residents proceeded to host us for the night.

Every now and then children would stop us in the streets and compete among themselves to see who could host us and offer us more food. As we would eat, they would take our AK-47's on their shoulders and tie a turban around their heads and say: 'Look at me brother, am I not a *jihadi* now? Take me to Pakistan will you, my mother says I can go with you.'

Another time, an old man started crying when he saw us. We asked him what was wrong. He said: 'After the 1965 war, this is the first time I am seeing *mujahideen* walk among us again. Thank Allah that in my lifetime I've had the opportunity to witness the resurgence of *jihad*.'

We stopped in a forest near Bir; we were still figuring out how we'd eat and where we might cook when suddenly an old Kashmiri man emerged from behind the foliage with steaming hot parathas and halwa; an old woman stumbled after him with more food. It turned out they were siblings. We asked the old woman why she inconvenienced herself so.

She said, 'I thought to myself, why should my brother be the only one to win Allah's favour by helping *mujahideen*?'

Another time, after getting caught in the rain, the locals fed us while their women, our Kashmiri sisters, dried our mantles over a fire. In short, people offered us their lives, their wealth, everything they had in return for the simple promise that we would never abandon them.

I Will Never Let You Go

Abu Sumama narrates the following encounter: After the pre-fast morning meal, as we set off from Rajouri, I turned to my brother, a member of *Hizb-ul-Mujahideen*, and said I did not have a good feeling about the road we were on.

Shahbaz said there was nothing to worry about and volunteered to walk ahead.

A few short steps ahead we were ambushed. I spontaneously jumped and hid behind a boulder. In the ensuing gunfight Shahbaz was wounded. I was left alone battling the Hindu enemy and tending to my brother Shahbaz. He had been hit by four bullets. He kept saying to me, 'I'll keep them engaged until I'm martyred; you ought to take off; don't worry about me.'

But how could I have abandoned my brother? I said: 'As long as you are alive, I will never let you go. If I am martyred as well, we will go meet our Lord together.'

In his final moments, Shahbaz handed me his wireless set and his belongings, and said his final prayer before departing this world for the next. May Allah accept my brother's martyrdom. I shot my way out of there and returned to my companions at our base. The following day, Indian radios aired news of our skirmish and claimed both of us had been martyred, although by Allah's grace, here I am talking to you. We sent fourteen soldiers to hell during this encounter.

Capture and Interrogation of a Hindu Soldier

Lashkar-e-Tayyaba's *mujahideen* have had the distinction of isolating an entire Army unit and slaughtering its colonel, beheading a Hindu soldier and taking his head back to Pakistan, and taking a Hindu soldier captive from a post in Jammu sector near Traran Wali. (Since then, we have taken many more Hindu soldiers captive).

Three of *Lashkar*'s *mujahideen*, namely, Hafiz Abu Baseer, Abu Sa'ad, and brother Qadhafi, were passing through a settlement when they noticed an Army post in the distance. They tried contacting headquarters to ask their *emir* Hafiz Abd-ur-Rehman what to do but they were unable to connect; meanwhile, they had gradually come very close to the post.

It was a dark night. A sentry was positioned atop the post. A soldier stepped out from inside, probably to use the bathroom, when he flashed his torch in our direction and caught us in the light, he cried: 'Who are you?' 'Who are *you*?' we responded; at the same time, we ordered him to lower his flashlight. We engaged the soldier in conversation while Brother Qadhafi quietly went around the back and grabbed him by the

522 THE LITERATURE OF *LASHKAR-E-TAYYABA*

neck. When the sentry noticed what was going on he ran inside. The *mujahideen* took the soldier captive and moved on.

The *mujahideen* contacted their Emir and asked him what to do with the soldier. The Emir told them to take the soldier further away from the post and then contact him again for further instructions.

The soldier was from UP; he started pleading: 'Brother, please don't take me too far from the post or I'll lose my way coming back.'

'Don't worry my friend, we will put you on a path where you will never lose your way again,' the *mujahideen* responded.

Once the soldier had been transferred quite some distance from the post the *emir* contacted them and told them to interrogate him. During the interrogation, one of the questions they asked the soldier was: 'Why have you come all the way from UP to Occupied Kashmir?'

He said: 'I swear to god I was forced to come here. We're all forced to come here. We are helpless. Let me go; soldiers have spread throughout the region. I'll tell you a secret way out so all of you can escape.'

The *mujahideen* said: 'Well aren't you sly; do you have any idea how many of us there are? Do you know we've got your entire Army surrounded?'

Upon hearing this, the soldier started crying hysterically: 'Oh I'm a dead man! Oh Brother! Why did I ever come to Kashmir? I was supposed to get married soon! What will become of my fiancée? That bastard colonel convinced me to stay; he asked me to stay one more night; I did not want to stay another night. I was forced to be here tonight. Oh god, I'm dead now. Why did I come to Kashmir? Why did I take this post? That bastard colonel!'

The *mujahideen* said: 'Listen; stop making a scene. Convert to Islam; come with us, live with us, we won't hurt you.'

When he refused their offer, the *mujahideen* said: 'Tyrants! There are eight hundred thousand of you in Kashmir... you have unleashed a reign of cruelty and oppression throughout the valley... you have martyred countless Kashmiris... including children... you have raped and plundered... you take away our sisters on the pretext of interrogating them only to have your way with them... now you are crying out for your wife... we have come to this valley primarily to deal with the likes of you!'

With these words the *mujahideen* killed the soldier and dumped his body in the forest. They retrieved Rs. 5,700 from his pocket, two month's pay, and a Titan watch; later, this watch was sent to the *Markaz* in Lahore. The soldier's flashlight was also taken as loot.

His fellow soldiers minding the post did not find their missing comrade. When he did not return by dawn they started accusing him of desertion. When their colonel heard of his absence, he cut off his men's ration until they located the deserter. The soldiers pleaded; they said they had searched the entire region but couldn't find him; they were convinced he had long deserted them.

The colonel said: 'Rubbish! He was about to get married, and I had approved his leave; he was going to go back the very next day, he had no reason to run away. I want that man now!'

But their man was lying dead in the forest, and they would not dare enter a forest where *mujahideen* have set up their bases for the soldiers know death around every corner.

Readers, there was a time when India bemoaned the fact that the Afghan *mujahideen* carry out lethal close-quarter encounters without the fear of dying; now, Indians ought to know that in the future we will also abduct soldiers, arrest them, interrogate them, and, one by one, kick them out of Kashmir, Allah-willing!

Summer

It is 1997... as the summer begins to thaw the valley, fighting resumes. Summer strikes fear into the hearts of Hindu soldiers, although in the winter of 1997, *mujahideen* were just as brazen in their attacks against the army despite the freezing temperatures. Jammu sector's brother Abu Sumama narrates:

It was so cold that when one of our men melted some snow in order to wash himself after using the bathroom, the man who went in after him couldn't use the leftover water for it had already frozen.

The extreme weather conditions in the valley never weakened the *mujahideen*'s sense of honour, decorum, shame, and dignity. Once, a group of them arrived at a house only to discover that all the resident males were out and only their women were present. The *mujahideen* refused to step inside. The two sisters present kept insisting: 'You are our brothers. Let us offer you a meal. Our brothers and husbands will return shortly.'

524 THE LITERATURE OF *LASHKAR-E-TAYYABA*

The *mujahideen* did not think it appropriate and begged leave when the sisters said: 'May Allah forgive us for turning away our *mujahideen* brothers without feeding them; this is unacceptable to us!'

Then, convinced that the *mujahideen* would not accept their hospitality, one of them cried out: 'Listen! See that house down there; that's my brother's house. I believe he is home. Settle down there and we will send some food over.'

Chaste Kashmiri women wait for their Pakistani brothers to save them from Hindu aggression; *Lashkar's* warriors will sacrifice themselves to guard their sisters' honour.

Readers, when you are ethically secure and your character has been honed to resemble that of the (prophet's) companions, then Allah offers assistance every step of the way. Abu Sumama continues:

A Bed of Snow

Once, three of us were on our way to stash some of our equipment by burying it but when we arrived at the allocated spot and started digging, the sun started to come up, so we abandoned our project and headed back. As we were returning it started to snow but very quickly, what started as a flurry turned into a snow blizzard; it became pitch dark. At one point, we had to scale a near vertical cliff with over a hundred-foot drop. The slightest misstep would have plunged us to our deaths, so we settled down where we were. Our hands and feet became brittle, like ice. We prayed to Allah and fell asleep; when we awoke, the day had risen and by Allah's mercy the sun was shining. Soldiers were spread out across the region but as we started our journey clouds enveloped us and offered cover. Hence, we safely arrived at our base, concealed by Allah's grace. By the time we reached our destination our boots had turned to wood.

Readers, in context of these *jihadi* anecdotes, we are obligated to be more determined in our *jihad*. We witness its benefits across the valley, across Jammu, increasingly, across all of India; we ought to match these blessings with our resolve. Support the *mujahideen* with your actions, your words, and your pen, for . . .

نَضْرٌ مِّنَ اللّه وَفَتْحٌ قَرِيبٌ

Help from Allah and victory is nigh.

(61:13)

We are already seeing this divine help manifest in countless ways; our victory in Srinagar and Jammu is, indeed, nigh, Allah-willing!

Chapter 35: *Lashkar-e-Tayyaba*'s Popularity Among Hindus

When Indian soldiers dug up the earth... they discovered the remote control planes we had buried there... the soldiers were amazed... they were terrified... they were afraid to touch the planes... god knows what these things were... "what if something happens the moment we touch them"... when they discovered those were mini remote control planes... that we fly into their camps... they realized they were looking at the angels of death...!

'Preetam! Ram! Careful now, keep watch! Don't fall asleep or nap! Keep your eyes open! Don't nod off... be vigilant! Keep an eye out in all directions. If you see anything suspicious or unusual... any sign of the Army, let us know at once; *mujahideen* are resting so don't make any noise either; do you understand what I'm saying?' the old Hindu man said to his sons.

'Yes father, don't worry, we understand. We'll risk everything to protect our *mujahideen* brothers,' said the sons.

Then the old Hindu man called out to his daughters, 'Listen up girls! Hurry up and wash the *mujahideen*'s clothes, they need to leave soon.'

'Yes Baba, here, we're done. Now we're going to go cook for them. We're as concerned for them as you are; don't go round yelling instructions lest someone hears you and reports us to the military,' whispered the girls.

The old man is silent. He considers what his daughters have told him. He realizes he should not use words like '*mujahideen*' out loud. Silence invades the house and in this silence this Hindu family hosts, serves, and watches over the *mujahideen*. The night deepens and my thoughts

526 THE LITERATURE OF *LASHKAR-E-TAYYABA*

wander out into the darkness… the most recent events flash before my eyes…

The Marketplace of *Jihad*

We've been dispatched from Abu Alqama's Emirate on a 'special mission' to Jammu's Banihal region. When we arrive, after crossing impossible borders and enduring bloody encounters, Taya Rafiq, Chief Commander of Jammu, receives the following message:

'Abu Yasir and Abu Janbaz are headed your way. Send them to Abu Alqama (commander of the special mission). A *jihadi* marketplace has been set up there. These two want to make an offer as well.'

This was a coded message from *Lashkar-e-Tayyaba's emir* in Pakistan. It meant that very soon, there was going to be a major operation in Jammu; both the brothers named were keen on participating.

The special mission involved blowing up the Banihal Tunnel, the only land-link between Jammu and Kashmir.

Not only does this tunnel provide a supply route for the military but Jammu and Kashmir's entire transportation system runs through it as well. We were given this mission to isolate the Army in Kashmir. This was to be a large-scale operation. The tunnel is strategically relevant; every day, 250–500 military vehicles pass through it with weapons, ammunition, food rations, petrol, and various other goods.

Once we reached brother Abu Alqama upon the orders of our *emir*, we traversed the General Highway Road in Banihal and entered the valley.

The very sight of the tunnel made our blood boil; we felt like blowing up our intended target right there and beheading all the Hindu soldiers present but we had to be patient.

Among us were Abu Yasir of Bahawalpur, Abu Khalid of Dir, and Abu Darda of Faisalabad. We mingled with the locals in the settlements around the tunnel. When Abu Darda fell ill, Abu Haider of Multan took his place. For a few days we scouted the area in parties of two, surveying the tunnel for ideal spots to plant the explosives and attack the army. One day, as we were cooking food out in the open Abu Yasir noticed that he couldn't spot a single Indian soldier through his telescope. It turned out, the army had descended to where we were and soldiers were going door to door looking for us. We immediately left the village of Doligam for the woodland.

Conspiracies against *Mujahideen*

We returned from the forest around 1:30am and spent the night at the residence of a Law Ministry clerk whose house was only a half hour away from the General Highway. The following day, we visited the residence of a reporter associated with the popular Hindu daily Hind Samachar. Earlier, Indian soldiers shot dead some of *Lashkar*'s local civilian assets and blamed *Hizb-ul-Mujahideen* for the massacre in order to spark a feud between us. Brother Abu Yasir told Hind Samachar's reporter that the Indian government and Army were trying to sabotage the unity of the *mujahideen*; he said the propaganda about infighting was patently false, and in reality, the two groups coordinate their attacks against military installations. He went on to name the various camps our groups had attacked collaboratively. Thus, Abu Yasir nipped the conspiracy in the bud.

The Vow

When we left the reporter's residence, we discovered we were completely surrounded by the military. At this point, brother Abu Khalid of Dir made me vow that whether we make it out alive or not, we will stay together; 'if we are killed we will enter paradise together and if we are not, we will leave this battlefield together.' As I tried crawling through a barbed wire fence my shalwar got caught and I tripped; my gun fell beyond my reach. A soldier noticed me and fired. The spray of bullets tore through my clothes. As I patted myself down for wounds, I kept my eyes locked with the soldier's for had I taken my eyes off him even for a moment he would have escaped. There was neither blood nor pain. Meanwhile, Abu Khalid contacted me and told me Allah had given him a second chance at life for a bullet blew his hat off but barely grazed his head, neatly parting his hair without even touching his scalp. I told him how a burst of bullets had ripped through my clothes but not one of them hit my body. Then,

528 THE LITERATURE OF LASHKAR-E-TAYYABA

I asked him to give me cover so I could retrieve my gun. My brother came to my assistance, and I retrieved my gun before we escaped with our lives into a sewage tunnel. The place was crawling with soldiers, but they had no clue where we were.

Later that evening, soldiers descended to Abu Yasir and Abu Haider's hideout so the two they launched a surprise attack; the soldiers turned tail and ran back to their base, begging for reinforcements.

Approaching the Target

We had lost our shoes and our feet were bleeding. It seemed like soldiers were repeatedly firing at one single spot; we knew it was the spot where Abu Yasir and Abu Haider were hiding, and we imagined they had both been martyred. In the morning, when we surveyed the area through a telescope our suspicions regarding our brothers were confirmed when we saw local Kashmiris preparing two graves. Around sunset, as we returned to the village, a Gujjar who offered us a meal told us that two *Lashkar mujahideen* had been martyred but two had managed to escape the ambush. We did not tell him we were the two who escaped. We headed towards General Highway; on the way, an old Kashmiri man told us he made sure our martyred companions were buried in shrouds made of new fabric. We asked him for a pair of shoes and paid him despite himself. We were welcome with offers of fresh milk into every house on the way to General Highway.

After surveying the area around our intended target, we concluded that to blow up the tunnel we would need many more explosives than what we had on hand.

Since we could not blow up the tunnel immediately, we decided to attack the Hindu soldiers guarding the place, instead.

We moved forward with the intention of destroying the military camps Bazla, Tarna, and Neel.

Saifullah Askari went for Bazla Camp, Abu Alqama for Tarna, and Abu Musa of Gujranwala for Neel; we launched a simultaneous attack around 7pm. First, Abu Alqama fired a rocket that hissed its way past the camp without hitting its intended target. Bewildered soldiers started pouring out of their base wondering what had happened, crying out 'Who is there?

What do you want?' Abu Alqama yelled back, 'Hang on a second... I'll tell you all what's going on,' and fired a second rocket straight at them. Cowardly Hindu soldiers scattered like a colony of ants under attack. We proceeded to fire rockets on Bazla and Tarna. After the onslaught we escaped to our hideouts, leaving the Hindu beasts squirming and writhing in the mud. This was an historical event in Banihal for in one single night *Lashkar*'s men simultaneously attacked and destroyed three military camps.

After the operation, local *mujahideen* informed us that the region we had attacked was normally so militarily secure that for the most part, *mujahideen* operated defensively there. As we headed back to our bases after the operation Kashmiris received us like heroes; some offered us cups of milk, others held out bowls of yogurt, and still others offered us fresh spring water; we quenched our thirst and carried on. The next day, when we observed the camps from our telescopes, we noticed they had been completely abandoned. Soldiers from a different camp arrived, cleared out the corpses of their fallen comrades, and tried fixing up the place. During this process no civilian was allowed anywhere near the carnage. Later, the official report aired on radio claimed the Bazla Camp, Tarna Camp, and Neel Camp respectively lost twenty-eight, thirty-two, and twenty-six Hindu polytheists, while one hundred and fifty soldiers had ended up in Banihal's hospital. Only Allah knows how much loss the military actually suffered.

'Please, Do Not Tell on Us'

Once, Abu Shadakh of Multan (shaheed) and I were on a mission when we stopped in Sonamarg only to discover a new military post had been set up in Ghoragali. We asked the locals if the Hindu beasts had been harassing them.

The locals said: 'No, they don't harass us at all; they're simply doing their job so don't attack them. Some days ago, they met with the village elders and told them they would not harass any of us; they requested we not tell on them to the *mujahideen*.'

We scaled the mountainside to our base and sent one of our civilian operatives to buy rations from the village. On his return, the civilian claimed that while shopping he overheard an Army officer say to the

530 THE LITERATURE OF *LASHKAR-E-TAYYABA*

storeowner: 'I heard *Lashkar*'s men were here recently; I wanted to see them but they left before a meeting could be arranged.'

After consulting with Abu Shadakh, we sent the officer a letter telling him to call us between noon and 1pm on a particular number.

The officer received the letter but never called, much to our indignation. We left the area for a few days and upon our return, our civilian contact informed us that the officer had a message for us; the officer said, 'I'll meet you anywhere in the forest; I'll come alone and you should come with only a few men but don't tell anyone about this.'

We wrote back: 'You failed to respond to our earlier communication; this time, if you fail to honour your commitment, you'll receive much more than a letter from us.'

In response, he said: 'It was overcast at the time you wanted me to contact you (meaning there were soldiers all around). Some days ago, one of your men was martyred in district Mawar; we retrieved his wireless set as well as his notebook with details of all the frequencies you use to communicate. I suggest you alter your frequencies immediately, or at the very least communicate in code. Two of your sets are in Mawar's police station; your communications are being tapped.'

We responded: 'If you want to live, give us all the information of X camp.'

The officer delivered all the confidential information from said camp to us through our civilian contact. When we double-checked his information later, it turned out to be accurate. The officer sent us another message: '*Mujahideen* are free to come to the mosque nearby; they're free to offer Friday's congregational prayers, as well as their daily prayers; no one will bother them.'

Nevertheless, we were cautious; we attacked the camp whose information the officer had disclosed and slaughtered twenty-five Indian soldiers.

Immediately after the attack, our Emir transferred us to an area where one of our brother's had recently been martyred.

The Long-Haired Warriors

Beaten down by *Lashkar*'s repeated attacks, the Army tried a new tactic against *mujahideen*; they started making their soldiers wear long beards, grow out their hair, and don red caps to look like us except it seems they did not realize *mujahideen* do not chew tobacco or smoke cigarettes; not to mention, their boots always gave them away.

Mini-Planes

We were staying at a Muslim residence in sub-district Kalakote, district Rajouri when we received a shipment of mini-planes from *Lashkar-e-Tayyaba*'s camp in Pakistan. These small remote-control planes pack a powerful punch when loaded with explosives; they also allow us to attack without risking our lives. When the shipment arrived, we were in an area where 80 per cent of the population was Hindu, which meant we could not test fly them for they would be reported immediately. All things considered; we buried the planes in the forest. Meanwhile our host was picked up by the military; they tortured him until he was forced to tell them that *mujahideen* had been staying in his house and that we had taken a shovel with us into the forest to bury something. Soldiers fanned out across the region and soon found the site where we had buried our two remote-control planes. Needless to say, the soldiers were shocked by what they discovered. Despite themselves, they managed to disinter the planes and take them back to their base but when they fully realized that these were angels of death that could potentially crash into their military camps and their check-posts at any moment, they were horrified. The officer who led the mission in confiscating them was promoted, while much was made of this case in the media. The military and government were shaken; Vajpayee and Advani lodged their protest on the world stage over the kind of technology *mujahideen* were being supplied to attack Indian forces. Government and military leaders put their heads together to figure out how to arm their soldiers in order to counter such an offensive from the sky. Air force jets and civilian planes started flying at higher altitudes in the region, and since the discovery of our remote-controlled angels of death, vast swathes of land had to be cleared and surveyed before supply helicopters dared land.

I was lost in thought when suddenly I heard Preetam cry out: '*Mujahideen* brothers! Food is ready, and so are your clothes.' Then, after a brief pause: 'I've been watching you for a few minutes now; you

532　THE LITERATURE OF *LASHKAR-E-TAYYABA*

seemed lost in thought. Perhaps you were thinking of your family and friends in Pakistan?'

I said: 'Preetam, my friend! Even though you're very close to us, you will not understand what occupies my mind; I was playing back all the operations I have been involved in, in my head. As far as siblings go, when we cross the border, we leave behind our loved ones; we don't carry them over with us. Besides, when one finds loved ones like you, it's easy to forget old friends.' Meanwhile, the rest of the *mujahideen* also awoke; we ate, changed our clothes, and then bid farewell to our dear Hindu friends.

A Conversation with an Elderly Hindu

In Kalakote, District Rajouri, we would stay with Hindu civilians who hosted and fed us although some of our men did not like eating their food. No doubt, there is something odd about Hindu civilians aiding us in our attempts to destroy the Hindu Army. Once, we asked the aging patriarch of a Hindu family: 'Baba Jee! Why do you welcome us into your homes? Why do you feed us, wash our clothes, let us rest, and protect us from the Indian forces?'

The old man fell silent for a while; then, he took a deep breath and said, 'It is true you are Muslims, and we are Hindu and religiously, we are worlds apart, but with regard to human values, we are one; besides, you only aim your guns at those who confront you. On the other hand, we feel that you are not here solely to protect Kashmiri Muslims; rather, you're here for every one of us who is oppressed, irrespective of religion or creed. Your presence here not only protects Muslim girls but Hindu girls as well. Indian soldiers and Shiv Sena[5] thugs used to march into our villages and carry off our poor little girls to rape and torture them as they pleased; this had become routine. Since the *mujahideen* have shown up, we feel your presence offers some degree of protection. (Sighs deeply.) Who would've thought we'd see the day when our co-religionists would threaten our lives and our property, and indiscriminately rape our wives, sisters, and daughters? If we try and stop them, they torture us... they'll even kill us. On the other hand, those we considered our enemy simply because they were Muslim have turned out to be our guardians and pro-tectors. Therefore, we welcome the *mujahideen*; they would lay down

NOBLE WARRIORS AND BATTLEFRONTS 533

their lives to protect us. This is why our women cook meals for you and wash your clothes, while our young men watch over you when you rest. You and I are joined by our empathy for the oppressed; that is all.'

The elderly man's words made us realize that whenever Muslims have taken up arms against oppression, irrespective of religion, caste, or creed, Allah has provided help and assistance from within enemy ranks. Our history shines with the likes of Tariq bin Ziyad and Musa bin Nazeer; *Lashkar's* lion-hearted *mujahideen* are inheritors of a great tradition as they collude with Hindu civilians to obliterate the Indian Army.

We said, 'Baba Jee! We are happy to hear how you feel about us. We're probably not worthy of your estimation of us but rest assured, your daughters are our sisters; protecting their honour is not a favour we do to you but an obligation we fulfil, for this was the way of our warrior prophet; he said a daughter is a daughter, regardless of whether she's a polytheist or a believer. Every Muslim is obligated to internalize this for the prophet himself laid his mantle before a polytheist's daughter once. We are the *ummat* of such a man. We will sacrifice our lives to guard your daughters' honour. If ever a soldier harasses you again, let us know; we will do everything within our means to teach him a lesson.'

We were safer in Hindu residences than in Muslim ones for no one ever suspected a Hindu would give us shelter. Many times, when soldiers raided a village, they only searched Muslim homes.

Ratan Laal and an Invitation to Faith

Once, after spending a night at the residence of a man called Ratan Laal, we gradually introduced him to Islam. We told him about life after death and Allah's judgement. Taya Rafeeq was with us. We kept proselytizing to him all day. Finally, based on the evidence we provided, he declared:

Allah will welcome the pious into heaven and send the bad to hell; Hindu deities are nothing. After death, one will have to answer for one's actions.

We invited him to recite the *kalima* but he refused. This greatly angered some of our companions, but we told them Islam is not something that

534 THE LITERATURE OF *LASHKAR-E-TAYYABA*

can be imposed. If someone accepts it willingly, well and good, otherwise we cannot force anyone to convert; we can only give evidence and arguments to win a person over; it is Allah who opens hearts and minds to Islam. There were three idols in Ratan Laal's house: Krishna, Brishna, and Kali. We told him: 'Look! Those you consider gods cannot even dust themselves; they cannot even wave a fly off. If they are so obviously helpless, how can one believe they run the universe? How can they be gods?' These questions put him in deep thought and he started reflecting. We encouraged him to think about the matter as we left his home.

The last few pages tell the awe-inspiring story of the warrior Abu Janbaz of Lahore; he completed three tours of duty. This was his last mission in Kashmir.

Chapter 37: Slaughtering Shiv Sena's Thugs

When a Hindu CRPF [Central Research Police Officer[6]] officer... found the decapitated heads... of Shiv Sena thugs... arranged in a line... he fainted... and died on the spot... Meanwhile, after a thrashing from *Lashkar's mujahideen*... Shiv Sena's thugs... were making good their escape ... ... they stopped by a stream... to wash their pants... for they had soiled themselves out of fear... they were washing the shit out of their clothes... 'untouchables' watched and laughed ...

Because the Indian Army is being defeated on multiple fronts in Jammu and Kashmir, the militant Hindu party BJP (Bharatiya Janta Party[7]) has taken to training thugs from organizations like 'Shiv Sena Hindu Parishad' and 'RSS' so they may be dispatched to Kashmir to confront *Lashkar's mujahideen* and harass the local Muslim population.

The following report appeared in the Indian newspaper *Sunday Tribune* on 5 October 1997:

In a recent constitutional amendment, the government has established defence committees in seventy villages, with a thousand armed men trained to counter militants.

What the newspaper reported as 'one thousand armed men' was actually many thousands of armed thugs. They were brutal in oppressing and harassing Muslims living in the Hindu majority region of Jammu until *Lashkar's mujahideen* arrived and slaughtered them, one by one. Following is a detailed account by Ghazi Muhammad Shafiq Abu Sa'ad of how this strategy by the Indian establishment was completely neutralized and disabled. Ghazi Muhammad Shafiq Abu Sa'ad is from Lahore and has spent three years fighting Shiv Sena's operatives in Jammu. This fearsome warrior reports:

You Have Brought Joy to Our Lives!

When we arrived in Jammu's Doda region, the locals welcomed us with great fanfare and aplomb. The villagers wept about how Shiv Sena's thugs, backed by the government, had been brutalizing them.

'They raped my daughter before my eyes,' an elderly man cried.

Another young man reported, 'Shiv Sena thugs and Army soldiers gang-raped my wife; you cannot know how happy we are now that you're here to protect our dignity.' (Allah-willing.)

Mujahideen! Crush These Hindu Thugs

One of the elderly gentlemen who hosted us said: 'I have four daughters… Shiv Sena and army thugs have been coming to my house every night for a few days now. I am old, what can I do?? For Allah's sake, attack their camps; slaughter these hounds that I may rest in peace.'

One of the *mujahideen's* mother invited us for a meal. We were about to cook the goat she slaughtered in our honour when soldiers arrived accompanied by Shiv Sena's thugs. We immediately hid the meat and lured the thugs away from the residential area after which we engaged them in a four-hour gun battle in which we sent nine of their men to hell, only to slaughter eight more in a skirmish the following day. We did not lose a single fighter in either battle.

536 THE LITERATURE OF *LASHKAR-E-TAYYABA*

Avenging Muslim Blood

Two Muslims would regularly sell milk in a village in Bhaderwah with a sizeable Hindu population that hosted Shiv Sena's men. Every day, the thugs would take the Muslims' milk and money and send them back empty-handed. One day, the Muslims stood their ground; Shiv Sena's thugs found the excuse they were looking for and stabbed the two to death.

When we heard of this we were outraged. We located the Shiv Sena gang-leader and two of his men. One of the men managed to escape but we shot the remaining two dead. The Hindu villagers stayed holed up in their homes with their doors bolted although they had nothing to fear because we were only there to kill two thugs to avenge the two Muslim murders; at the end of the day, we do not target ordinary civilians.

A Female Shiv Sena Operative

Shiv Sena's operatives are battling Muslims on every front. A Hindu lady doctor serving in an Arab country in the Gulf regularly transferred funds to Siv Sena's account in India. Once, when she transferred twenty thousand dirham (approximately two hundred thousand Indian rupees), the Muslim cashier at the bank recognized the recipient and informed intelligence; various investigations revealed that she not only transferred funds, but, as a gynaecologist, she was actively engaged in infanticide against Muslim babies. In her confession, she stated: 'I did so to reduce the number of Muslims in the world so in the future we'd have less of them to deal with; even though this was only a drop in the ocean, it was still better than nothing.'

Brother Shafiq narrates: Once, I was traveling with Abu Abdullah Kashmiri and Abu Zubair Shaheed from Kishtwar to Thathri when, after a gruelling journey, we stopped at a house for shelter, only to discover the resident were not only Hindus but Shiv Sena operatives. When they realized we were *mujahideen*, they refused to let us in. We told them it was bitter cold and we desperately needed a place to rest for a while but the residents went up to the roof and opened fire. We returned fire and the gun-battle went on through the night. One of the three attackers was a woman. By morning we had injured one of the men. We took them hostage and were making our way back to our base when local Muslims negotiated their release.

They Fought Us for Rs. 1.5 Lakh

Shiv Sena's thugs were promised Rs.1.5 lakhs for every militant they killed; their greed drove sixteen of these thugs to stalk us as we returned to our base. When we were very close to our base, three of our companions who had been basking in the sun noticed the thugs on our tail and opened fire. Two were killed instantly, while one was injured. Abu Abdur Rehman Ashraf walked up to the injured man and slit his throat with his extraordinarily large dagger that, up until now, has beheaded ten Hindus. Later, Abu Abdur Rehman Ashraf had a poisoned dagger forged in district Rajouri; anyway, after the throat slitting, we took the fallen men's belongings, including their 303 guns, and deposited them in the *mujahideen* centre in Muzaffarabad. Abu Abdur Rehman Ashraf's hands were spattered with the Hindu's impure blood.

The Hindus who escaped went straight to the CRPF battalion and asked for assistance. The soldiers said, 'You yourself provoked them, now suffer them yourselves! There's a reason why we don't mess with them, we value our lives. As far as the bodies of your comrades are concerned, go to the *mujahideen* camp with some local Muslims and you might be able to retrieve the corpses.'

Consequently, escorted by some local Muslims, they were able to take back the bodies of their Hindu compatriots. When an officer in the CRPF camp saw the slit throats of the Shiv Sena thugs, he had a heart attack and died on the spot. His body was transferred immediately while the corpses of the Shiv Sena thugs were cremated right there.

When Shiv Sena's thugs turned tail and ran after attacking *Lashkar-e-Tayyaba*'s *mujahideen* they were spotted near a stream washing their clothes. Apparently, they had urinated and defecated in their pants out of fear. Keep in mind, all the attackers were high-caste Brahmin and Kshatriya men; they were ridiculed by the Shudra (untouchables) onlookers who said: 'Check out our 'fighters!' They went to battle militants but couldn't even dislodge their '*shooti*'.

538 THE LITERATURE OF *LASHKAR-E-TAYYABA*

Kashmiris call the tiny filter attached to the opening of a barrel of a gun to keep out dust, a '*shooti*'. What the onlookers meant to say was the thugs were unable to fire a single round and returned with nothing but shit in their pants.

The Murder of Three Shiv Sena Leaders

Lekh Raj, Shadi Lal, and Robil Singh were three notorious Shiv Sena gang-leaders. They routinely looted Muslim property and raped Muslim women. They publicly declared that they would not spare a single Muslim soul. Consequently, we had been pursuing them for a while. Finally, one day, in Doda, we executed a crackdown in a place called Jura and captured all three from their residence.

Once we were some distance from the village, we said to them: 'Why are you hell-bent on engaging us when we're not out to fight you. We're only fighting the Indian Army. Stay out of our way and let us fight our war; we'll protect you as well.'

They said, 'We are fighting to protect our religion; we will sacrifice our lives but we will not stop; we know you will murder us but we will not give in.'

We tried to reason with them: 'Never mind all that; just recite the *kalima* and we'll forgive you all your sins.'

They refused. Abu Abdur Rehman Abid proceeded to slaughter them with his dagger. Even as their throats were being slit, they kept crying 'Ram'; they were staunch Hindus but they got what they deserved for their aggression.

Bhagat Singh's Murder
Bhagat Singh was a Shiv Sena gunman. We took him hostage during an ambush and in his interrogation, he confessed he was a salaried operative with Shiv Sena. He also confessed he had spied on us. Hafiz Abid strung him upside down and slit his throat.

Puran Chand's Murder
In Darai, some Muslim girls were out in the forest grazing their cattle when a dozen Shiv Sena thugs attacked them. The men had started raping

NOBLE WARRIORS AND BATTLEFRONTS **539**

the girls when we came upon the scene. Most of the thugs managed to escape but we got hold of one Puran Chand. We lay the pig on the ground and slaughtered him right there.

Crackdown on Baddhi
When we found out that Shiv Sena operatives were actively training in a village, we conducted a crackdown of the area and recovered four guns and two ammunition belts. We also captured six thugs. We would have slaughtered them had it not been for some local Muslims who intervened.

War Booty of 2.5kg of Silver and 0.25kg of Gold
Once, we found out that BJP workers were openly assisting Shiv Sena thugs in a particular village, so we immediately raided the area and ended up with 2.5kg of silver and 0.25kg of gold as war booty for which we thanked Allah.

Twenty-five Shiv Sena Leaders Killed in Single Missile Attack

The *yatra* (pilgrim march) in Pahalgam is an incredibly popular spiritual procession attended by hundreds of thousands of Hindu devotees. Ahead of the event, we distributed flyers advertising our plans to stage attacks against Shiv Sena's leaders in attendance, hence approximately fifty thousand soldiers were deployed to protect the pilgrims although we were only interested in targeting Shiv Sena operatives.

We had long been in possession of a powerful missile we called '57' which we had never gotten the opportunity to fire. We felt an attack on Shiv Sena would be an appropriate use of this firepower. Four *mujahideen* were selected for the operation: Abu Ayub, Abu Saeed Jilani Kashmiri, another Kashmiri, and me. The four of us collected our weapons and the missile and took off on a long arduous journey towards Pahalgam. When we passed through Ladakh where the snow-covered mountains were so cold, we came across the frozen carcasses of cows, buffaloes, wolves, goats, horses, and donkeys. After six arduous days, we arrived at a village called Aru. Our scouts immediately went about identifying the hotel hosting BJP and Shiv Sena's leaders. We set up our equipment in

540 THE LITERATURE OF *LASHKAR-E-TAYYABA*

a stream from where we had a clear view of the hotel. The crystal-clear water channel was lined with numerous fruit-bearing trees. The spot we had selected was strikingly paradisiacal. We prostrated before god and wept and prayed:

'Oh Allah! In the past we have travelled with this missile to multiple battlefronts but never had the chance to use it. Dear Lord, today, yet again, we have transported this missile to use against particular enemies. We have come here after a hard journey. Dear Lord, do not shame us, let us succeed!'

We aimed the rocket at our target, turned on the switch, and left. Around *fajr*, when we stood up to pray, we wept uncontrollably as we begged Allah for our plan to succeed. We were in the seated phase of our supplication when the missile fired, and an explosion rocked the region. We uttered our final invocations and thanked god for His assistance; our prayers had been answered. Later, we found out the missile shot through a window and exploded inside the hotel. Twenty-five leaders staying in the hotel were instantly killed and countless more were injured.

Our operation shocked the Indian government and the military alike; the establishment could not have fathomed that we could stage such a brazen attack despite the presence of fifty thousand soldiers. Shiv Sena operatives staged demonstrations in which they accused their own military of colluding with us.

Readers consider how far we have come in our struggle. Once, there was a time when the Indian military was notorious for its crackdowns against locals but today, *Lashkar-e-Tayyaba*'s valiant warriors are the ones cracking down on the Army and Shiv Sena's thugs. Only a handful of *mujahideen* confront a military eight hundred thousand strong and yet we cannot be contained; is this not proof enough of the military's failure? The task forces the Indian government set up with Muslim traitors failed, and the very Hindu militants these traitors were spying for are now being slaughtered. Very soon, Kashmir will be liberated, Allah-willing.

'Let Me Consume My Mother's Flesh!'

Brother Salamat Allah reports that in Occupied Kashmir, certain Indian soldiers are beginning to sell their arms and ammunition to *mujahideen* in order to desert the army and return to their homes in mainland India.

NOBLE WARRIORS AND BATTLEFRONTS 541

Once, when a Gorkha soldier discovered his mother was deathly sick he asked his commanding officer for leave to return to his village and consume his mother's flesh. He was denied leave, so he approached the *mujahideen*, handed us his gun for some travel money and left. We asked Brother Salamat Allah why the soldier wanted to eat his mother's flesh instead of taking her to a hospital. The incredibly knowledgeable Salamat Allah told us that instead of cremating or burying the dead bodies of their loved ones, Gorkhas prefer to consume their flesh; this particular soldier was sure his mother was going to die.

The Sound of Footsteps
Brother Salamat Allah reports that after *mujahideen* attack a military camp, the military personnel posted there refuse to emerge from their barracks for months. Apparently, BSF personnel are the worst; they scamper at the very sound of our footsteps. Our brother narrates that when fresh *mujahideen* recruits cross the border and first enter the valley, they are particularly cautious with regards to the military. Once, to eliminate their fears, we took them to a military camp and the very sound of our footsteps sent the soldiers and sentries running inside. Exposing the so-called 'might' of the army proved to bolster the new arrivals' confidence.

Brother Salamat further tells that during the winter months, soldiers deliver messages through civilians, pleading with us not to bother them in the freezing cold. According to brother Salamat, he was free to go wherever he wanted in the valley, whenever he pleased.

Awaiting the Season of Martyrdom

Ghazi Abu Basir Nasir Ahmed reports that three months into 1998, when not a single brother had been martyred, the *mujahideen* started praying: 'Oh Allah! Make me the first martyr of 1998!' Similarly, every time there's a new moon, they pray to Allah to make them the first martyr of the lunar cycle. While most people are out to save their lives, *mujahideen* are reckless with theirs; this is the greatest difference between a *mujahideen* and regular civilians. For a normal person, survival is the most important thing in the world, while for *mujahideen*, nothing is more important than martyrdom.

542 THE LITERATURE OF *LASHKAR-E-TAYYABA*

On the night of 7 July 1998, a party of *Lashkar-e-Tayyaba*'s *mujahideen* that included a sizeable contingent of Nuristani fighters who had been launched in Occupied Jammu and Kashmir on *Lashkar-e-Tayyaba*'s platform was traveling through Pir Panjal's Sanglakh mountain range, led by Commander Abu Abid Swati and Abu Hamza Manjakoti. After a night's rest, as they continued at dawn, they were attacked by Indian security forces. Brother Abu Abid returned fire while the rest of the *mujahideen* crawled into position to launch a counterattack. Abu Abid Swati and Abu Hamza Manjakoti launched multiple grenades at a trench from where there was heavy fire; after sixty to seventy grenades exploded in and around the trench the firing stopped. As our men approached the site two soldiers manning another trench immediately opened fire. From their uniforms and action, it appeared that they were Rashtriya Rifles commandoes. Abu Abdullah Abd-ur-Rehman and various Nuristani *mujahideen* resisted the commandoes. *Mujahideen* were being fired upon from all directions. Nuristani *mujahideen* characteristically stood their ground with tremendous fortitude. Commander Abu Abid and Abu Hamza wanted to move forward to help their men escape but they were being fired upon relentlessly. Meanwhile, *mujahideen* started crying out 'Allah Akbar!' Abu Hamza Manjakoti handed over all his belongings to Abu Abid and said he was going to teach the infidels a lesson. As brother Abid gave him cover fire, brother Abu Hamza exposed himself to a hail of bullets as he ran towards the commandoes and launched four hand grenades one after the other. The commandoes screamed in terror as Abu Hamza cried out 'Allah Akbar' and emptied an entire magazine of bullets into their filthy bodies. A Nuristani fighter called Abu Shadgul started banging the butt of his gun into the skulls of the murdered commandoes in anger until his comrades stopped him. The *mujahideen* took the commandoes' baggage as war booty; it included two magazines, a wireless set, and a helmet. They searched the area for their weapons but were unable to find any. *Mujahideen* stood on the corpses of the commandoes and cried out 'Allah Akbar!' when suddenly eight more soldiers appeared from another trench and opened fire. *Mujahideen* immediately took up their positions again and returned fire, killing four soldiers on the spot. Commander Abu Abid and Abu Hamza decided to leave the area since military units in the surrounding region were beginning to mobilize. As Abu Abid and Abu Hamza provided cover fire Abu *Jihad* Nuristani led *mujahideen* through a secret passage to safety. Brother Abu Abdullah was martyred in this encounter, but we were able to retrieve his ammunition.

The Underground Trench

Before returning from Occupied Kashmir, *Lashkar-e-Tayyaba*'s *emir* Salamat Allah wished to bid the Indian soldiers farewell with one last attack; to this end he gathered a contingent of *Hizb-ul-Mujahideen* fighters and attacked the Tiray Makha camp in the Lolab region of Kupwara. *Mujahideen* used rocket launchers and machine guns in this offensive; one of our contingents managed to break into the camp and started slaughtering Hindu soldiers indiscriminately. *Mujahideen* were able to confiscate ten enemy weapons as war loot while dispatching twenty-five soldiers to hell. Of the 120 soldiers inside the camp at the time of the attack only three managed to escape. Unable to access an underground tunnel, as the *mujahideen* exited the camp three of them, namely, Asad, Nawaz, and Shafqat were martyred. A local ten-year-old fighter, who had proven to be incredibly effective during the attack, was also martyred in this operation.

Fire Protects *Mujahideen*

In 1998, international media houses, especially BBC London, All India Radio, and various Pakistani newspapers, claimed that the Indian Army had burnt four *Lashkar-e-Tayyaba mujahideen* alive. Before me sits Abu Talha of Hafizabad; he is one of the people BBC London and All India Radio claimed had been reduced to cinder. He is living proof of the fact that the entire news report was nothing but a hoax. He himself will narrate the miraculous help bestowed by Allah during his *jihad*. He infiltrated Kashmir in 1997 after completing his advanced training. He narrates:

This is a story of how we were ambushed soon after we crossed the border into Occupied Kashmir. As per our training, right after crossing the border we made our way to a house for the night because as the evening grew darker, we feared the rising moon might expose us. By morning, we transferred to a new house but soon after we moved, Indian

544   THE LITERATURE OF *LASHKAR-E-TAYYABA*

soldiers laid siege to our latest residence. We had the residents vacate the premises, so they were not caught in the impending crossfire, when a little girl wandered in to pick up her friend on her way to school. The little girl noticed us and said, 'I know you are *mujahideen*; no doubt you are hungry.'

She put her books down and left, only to return sometime later with flatbread, butter, and rice concealed in her shawl. When she initially wandered in, there were only two of us in the house but by the time she returned with food for us, there were two more. While handing us our breakfast, she said, 'Brother *mujahideen*! Don't leave; I'll be right back. I thought there were only two of you but now I see there are four.'

When she returned a second time, she brought apples along with the flatbread and butter concealed under her shawl.

We were amazed at how this little girl cared nothing for the soldiers surrounding us. We gently warned her not to come back, 'Little sister, you must not come back here; we are surrounded by soldiers and if they catch you, they might hurt you.'

With the confidence of an adult, she said, 'My *mujahid* brothers, you must roast those Indian hounds... you're to shoot down each one of them... pile up their corpses! My older brother was a *mujahid* as well... those beasts martyred him; you must avenge his death. So, what if he's been martyred!! I have brothers in all of you. My *mujahid* brothers! With you around, I don't feel my brother's loss.'

The noble sister of a *mujahid* left us mesmerized by her courage, zeal, valour, and wisdom. Around noon, the little girl sent her mother our way with dry fruit, who beckoned us to cut the Hindus into pieces. 'These thieves have made life on earth hell for Muslim mothers and Muslim sisters.'

We had hardly finished eating when an old man, sent as a messenger by the army, informed us that soldier had laid siege to Dandipur and Roshanpura and had dispatched Black Cat commandoes our way. Then he repeated a clear message verbatim: 'We have you completely surrounded; surrender and save yourself.'

We told him, 'Go back! Our Lord will watch over us; we will never surrender, in fact we will continue fighting in Allah's path; do whatever you can, we will either die in Allah's path or kill you.'

NOBLE WARRIORS AND BATTLEFRONTS 545

The old man went back and told the soldiers, 'These are *Lashkar*'s men; they will never surrender.'

The soldiers opened fire. We fired back for a while, and then stopped. After three minutes of silence, the soldiers assumed we were either dead or wounded. That's when we started shooting soldiers one by one, like snipers. In response, they started launching mortars at us, completely destroying the rear wall of the house, causing the roof to cave, but by Allah's grace, no one was injured. They kept raining mortars down on us until the house caught fire and we were trapped inside a room full of smoke. We started suffocating due to smoke inhalation. Kashmiri men, women, and children pleaded with the soldiers to get us out of the blaze alive.

The house was in flames with the *mujahideen* inside; perhaps this sight led BBC, All India Radio, and the Pakistani press to report that *Lashkar*'s *mujahideen* were being burnt alive.

Due to the dust and smoke kicked up by the mortar fire we were unable to see one another. We prayed to Allah to help us get out of the place, when almost instantly, one of the *mujahideen* backed into a window that flew open. The four of us jumped out of the window only to land utterly exposed to Indian soldiers. In that moment of vulnerability, Allah's help arrived in the form of a thick curtain of smoke that miraculously engulfed us in a cloak of invisibility. Suddenly, the sky burst and there was a heavy downpour. The rising smoke billowed towards the soldiers and stung their eyes. When we jumped out of the window and started running, we were inadvertently heading straight towards a military camp; we went through a gutter where there is a permanent ambush and broke through two checkpoints, all without being noticed. Surely, this was nothing short of Allah's favour.

We arrived at a house in Dandipur where we bathed, prayed, and slept. Three days later we contacted the rest of our men and returned to Pakistan. Various newspapers published reports about our safe return.

Here, I would like to draw the attention of those who claim Kashmir's civilian population does not cooperate with *mujahideen* to the little girl who risked her life to bring us food. Do not fall prey to the insidious propaganda of disbelievers. Instead, we ought to try our best to counter this nonsense that we may destroy India through *jihad*, for Kashmiri Muslims are eternally devoted to *mujahideen*. In this day and age, we

546 THE LITERATURE OF *LASHKAR-E-TAYYABA*

must counter all anti-Islam conspiracies and storm the battlefields of *jihad* to win back the *ummat*'s lost glory.

Avenging the Insult to the Prophet's *Sunnat*

While delivering Ramazan's final Friday sermon at Mochi Darvaza in 1999, *Emir Markaz-ud-Dawah-wal-Irshad*, Hafiz Muhammad Saeed said, 'It is Ramazan in Kashmir... before the crack of dawn, an Islamic scholar goes round crying out:

"It's time for the pre-dawn meal before the fast begins ... ! Wake up Muslims ... ! Eat!' There is a military camp nearby. Soldiers tell him to stop disturbing them; obviously, they don't want Muslims waking up for their pre-dawn meal. When the Islamic scholar cries out again, Hindu soldiers assault him by tearing at his beard! When no one can stop the Hindu soldiers, the victim makes his way into the forest and tells the *mujahideen* what happened.

"Task Force soldiers tore at my beard (the prophet's *Sunnat*). They dragged me and beat me... simply because I committed the crime of waking up Muslims for the fast.' *Lashkar-e-Tayyaba*'s *mujahideen* are enraged; their blood begins to boil. Their eyes are hot with vengeance. Instinctively, they reach for their AK-47's and prepare for battle. First, they pray to their Lord:

"Oh Allah! The beard of a man who serves your religion ... Alas! This beard! This is not only the beard of an Islamic scholar; it is the honour of Islam! Oh Allah! We are here to lay down our lives for your last prophet and for the dignity of Islam; help us!'

'With Allah's praises on their lips, the fearless *Lashkar-e-Tayyaba* warriors set off for the military camp; normally, *mujahideen* carry out their operations at night but this time their sense of honour doesn't permit them to wait for nightfall. They disregard all threats to their lives to exact a swift and immediate revenge. In broad daylight they attack the enemy. In one quick manoeuvre, the beastly Hindu soldiers are taken out of their holes, and lined up ...

'The *mujahideen* proceed to ask the Islamic scholar which one of the soldiers attacked him. They say, 'which one of these men insulted the *Sunnat* of our esteemed prophet, the Mercy upon Both Worlds?'

'The Islamic scholar points to a few soldiers. The *mujahideen* slit their jugulars with daggers, like goats in a slaughterhouse, as a fair warning to the disbelievers and a reassurance to the *ummat* that among our ranks are lion-hearted men who will do whatever it takes to guard the honour of prophethood.'

Chapter 38: The Inter-Connected Issue of Kashmir and Sindh

The Kashmir Struggle will Resolve the Problems in Sindh

The infidels of the world are focused on Sindh, eager to separate this region from Pakistan once and for all to gain control of the port city of Karachi. Russia had similar ambitions but failed. Today, the disbelieving power brokers of the world offer India all manner of resources to destabilize the region to cut it off from the rest of Pakistan; a global conspiracy ensues. India is investing heavily in this operation by sponsoring terrorism and injecting its agents into the area to collaborate with Pakistani traitors solely to breach the Islamic fort of Karachi. The following statement delivered by the Israeli prime minister ought to give a clear idea of their interest in Sindh, and their eagerness to sabotage the *jihad* in Kashmir.

Jewish Interest in Sindh

In 1995, while being interviewed by *Hindustan Times*, the Israeli prime minister said:

The Islamic movement has spread through Central Asia and North Africa; the situation is getting increasingly dangerous for non-Muslims. The Islamic wave has taken over Sudan. We are also afraid of a *jihadi*

548 THE LITERATURE OF *LASHKAR-E-TAYYABA*

success in Kashmir. Japan and China need to recognize the threat from Islam.

In August 1968, a Jewish journalist wrote in the *Jewish Post*:

The global Zionist movement should take the threat posed by Pakistan seriously; Pakistan should be our primary goal and we must use India as a base. India itself has much to gain from this in addition to the support of global powers; the purpose of separating East Pakistan was to turn Pakistan into one of the many smaller nation states surrounding India, like Bhutan, Sri Lanka and Nepal, so Pakistan cannot look at India as an equal and the movement in Kashmir can be silenced forever.

Despite the separation of East Pakistan, India fears us. The dormant Kashmir movement has been reinvigorated, and there's nothing anyone can do about it. Consequently, in an attempt to distract from this struggle, India is sponsoring a separatist movement in Sindh.

All Indian Writers, Yogis, and Journalists Visiting Pakistan are Spies

Undercover agents from India and Sindh routinely exploit various seminars and symposiums organized between Pakistan and India; literary, journalistic, and yogic delegations from India use these convocations to deliver commands and covert information.

o According to newspaper reports, spies routinely disguise themselves as yogis in Hindu temples in Pakistan. During the Babri Mosque riots in India, when young men in Lahore tried to attack the temple in Neela Gumbad Chowk, Anarkali, Lahore, police arrived at the scene and frisked the yogi inside the temple only to find a wireless set and a map of sensitive areas as well as various other important documents on his person.

o Hindus use *urs*, religious festivals, and mysticism etc. to establish their network.

o A *pir* in Hyderabad runs an international business with a Hindu partner. Many of his disciples are Hindus as well. Hindu devotees from Hong Kong and various other countries travel to Sindh to kiss his feet.

o A Sindhi Hindu by the name of Sant Gobind Ram receives Hindu delegates from India every year.

o Hindus regularly visit Sindh for a number of Sufi ceremonies such as Sukkur's Sadh festival, Dero Lali's *urs*, ceremonies at Shadani Darbar in Mirpur Mathelo, Hayat Patani's festival, Sachal Congress, Bhitai's *urs*, Lal Shahbaz Qalandar's *urs*, Pathoro's festival, etc.

o In 1990, during Sachal Congress, various Hindu writers and journalists were given the opportunity to make a pilgrimage to Sindh. They included Narain Parthi, Goband Malhi, Dr Murlidar Chataili Qeemat Jai Singhai, Veena Sharangi, and Krishan Kotwai. Later it was discovered that the female writer Veena Sharangi is a RAW agent.

How Is *Jihad-e-Kashmir* the Solution to the Sindh Problem?

It is essential to remember that the Muslim *ummat's* prosperity and longevity lies not in India but in Mecca and Medina. The stronger our alliances with our Muslim brothers, the clearer our recognition of the threat of Indian and Hindu culture, the surer our prosperity and collective survival. On the other hand, the closer we are to India, the more we expose our jugular to the Brahmin's poisoned dagger.

Full-blown participation in the Kashmiri *jihad* is the only way to stop the separation of Sindh from Pakistan. Those who cannot fight ought to contribute financially while the rest are obligated to train for the battlefield. The Indian government is forced to spend billions of rupees in Kashmir daily solely because of the Kashmiri *jihad*. If this *jihad* stops, this expenditure will no longer be necessary; however, as long as we continue our struggle Kashmir will continue to bleed India's resources until the national economy collapses and the country goes bankrupt at which point India will be forced to withdraw from both Kashmir and Sindh.

550   THE LITERATURE OF *LASHKAR-E-TAYYABA*

Keep in mind, Russians pulled their forces out of Afghanistan only when their economy was in tatters; if the Russians had enough resources they would never have surrendered. The Sindh solution depends on the *jihad* in Kashmir, and we can save Sindh by providing financial support as well as manpower to *mujahideen*. Be warned, if we lose Sindh, nothing can stop the rest of Pakistan from disintegrating.

In Pakistan we have a real opportunity to strengthen the *jihad* in Occupied Kashmir, which will not only solve the Sindh issue in Pakistan, but will allow us to annex vast swathes of Indian Sindh as well, for Muslims across the border are as weary of Hindu aggression as our brothers in Kashmir. When the Kashmiri *jihad* gains momentum, Khalistan will also declare independence and Muslims in occupied Sindh will welcome our forces and our *mujahideen* as liberators; they have declared as much in the face of Hindu oppression. There is overwhelming evidence to support this claim. Consider the following report:

Indian Sindhis Demand Occupied Kashmir and Sindh Accede to Pakistan

Sindhis in India have demanded that the geographical borders of Hind and Sindh return to the Prachin era, and for areas of Sindh under Indian control to accede to Pakistan for permanent peace and stability in the subcontinent. The solidarity front working towards Sindh's liberation held its annual liberation day gathering on 23 March 1996 demanding the accession of Sindh, Marwar, Kuch, Kathiawar, Gujrat, and Junagadh. The gathering was attended by six thousand delegates from various cities including Maharashtra, Bhopal, Gandhidham, Gujrat, Jaisalmer, Bikaner, Jodhpur, Jaipur, Nagpur, Alwar, Bharatpur, Mewat, Rajkot, and Koli. While paying tribute to Raj Gopal Kothari, the founder of this movement, Pakistani Sindh's Chief Minister Syed Abdullah Shah said: 'We will win Kashmir as well as liberate Buj Rajasthan, Gujrat, and Junagadh, which, for centuries, have been a part of Sindh.'

In his address, Raj Gopal stated:

56 years ago, to the day, the misgivings expressed by Muslim leaders in Lahore regarding religious and linguistic minorities across India have

proved to be well-founded. Gandhi and Pandit Jawaharlal and company unsuccessfully tried to solve the 'Muslim problem' upon Lord Mountbatten's command through violence and aggression; they sowed the seeds of hatred between the subcontinent's Hindus, Sikhs, and Muslims.

'In the current political climate, we will not participate in the national elections because these elections create new problems for the various language groups in India.'

In the recent past, Pakistan extended India the status of 'most favoured nation'; this gesture was akin to sprinkling salt over the wounds of our warriors and a betrayal of the blood of our martyrs. Even the Muslim World League proposed a resolution to economically boycott India over Kashmir, but we were too busy 'favouring' our nemesis; how can we expect justice from Europe or other non-Muslim nations, or expect to go through with a boycott, given our attempts at strengthening ties with India?

Many wonder what we plan to do once Kashmir is liberated. From the start we have been clear: we have no political aspirations in Kashmir. When Russians invaded Afghanistan and our brothers there called out to us, we fought by their side until the Russians were pushed back beyond the River Amu. After this victory, we did not know where we would reap the fruits of *jihad* until Allah offered us an opportunity in Kashmir; like Afghanistan, we are here solely to follow Allah's command to help our Kashmiri brothers. Second, our goal is not limited to Kashmir's liberation; we intend to make Kashmir a base camp from where we will free the two hundred million Muslims living in servitude in India, Allah-willing.

It was abundantly clear that after Russia's collapse, India was going to be next. So, India trembles at its imminent collapse.

At an annual '*jihad*' conference it was decided that the subcontinent was to be divided into three zones; Western Bengal would be annexed with Bangladesh; Eastern Punjab, Kashmir, Rajasthan, Gujrat, Junagadh, Kuch, Bhuj, and Maharashtra would go to Pakistan, and what was left in the middle could remain Hindu. In this way, the ancient Prachin era borders of Hind and Sindh are to be restored, leading to a more equitable balance of power in the subcontinent, commencing a period of peace and stability in the region.

552 THE LITERATURE OF *LASHKAR-E-TAYYABA*

Dear readers! While India was busy trying to foment dissent and separatism in Pakistani Sindh, residents of Indian Sindh betrayed their own country and demanded accession to Pakistan. This baffled the Indian government. Strengthening the *jihad* in Kashmir will not only resolve the Sindh crisis but will also lead to territorial gains for Pakistan along its border with India.

Lashkar's Sindh Policy?

In the past, *emir Lashkar-e-Tayyaba* Jammu and Kashmir Zaki-ur-Rehman Lakhvi has publicly stated *Lashkar's* policy regarding Sindh and Occupied Kashmir as follows:

We guarantee that if we strengthen the *jihad* in Kashmir, we will not only liberate Kashmir but also India's 200 million Muslims.

Regarding Sindh, he stated, on behalf of *Lashkar*:

As long as *jihad* continues, all threats to Pakistan will be neutralized, and if we collectively work towards this *jihad* with clear intentions, Islam will ultimately dominate the entire subcontinent (Allah-willing).

Mujahideen and various other separatists have become ulcers for India; infected organs need to be cut out and removed in order to save a patient's life. The *jihad* in Kashmir has spurred numerous freedom movements across India; the metastasis eats away at India's body like a cancer; we aim to force India to cut these organs away from itself in order to survive.

Readers, these are not hollow statements; rather, these are facts that haunt the Indian establishment night and day. The seeds of these fears were sown by the *jihad* in Kashmir. As Indian leaders peer into the future they see the flames of this *jihad* spread to other states, gradually consuming India whole.

Chapter 39: Can India Be Shattered?

The Startling Revelations of an Allegedly Impossible Hypothesis in Light of Ground Realities

Many believe India's ultimate collapse is nothing but wishful thinking while others, influenced by the propaganda of disbelieving powers, express their reservations regarding the success of *jihad* by drawing attention to the fact that this *jihad* has been going on for ten years during which time *mujahideen* have constantly talked about India's disintegration and the grave losses to the Indian Army but to date, there seems to be no evidence supporting the prediction that one day India will fall apart. The sceptics need to get one thing straight: victory and defeat are entirely in Allah's hands; the faithful are required to pursue victory and glory by following Allah's command and His prophet; we are not in any way responsible for what is beyond our control.

First, all the commandments in the *shariat*, including that of *jihad*, need to be obeyed as diligently as possible regardless of the outcome for results are entirely in Allah's hands. Anyone who does not subscribe to this does not trust in Allah and his or her faith is defected.

Second, there is no such thing as 'defeat' in *jihad*; one is either victorious or martyred, in either case, it's a win. In the first instance, one succeeds in this world and in the world hereafter, while in the case of martyrdom, one succeeds in the afterlife. Therefore, anyone who succumbs to the fear of any notion of defeat in terms of *jihad* has, in truth, not comprehended Islam's philosophy regarding *jihad*.

Now, let us consider *jihad-e-Kashmir*, in particular:

Until recently, people considered a confrontation with a superpower like Russia mere insanity. It was commonly believed that once the Russians sank their talons into a region, nothing could repel them. But soon, the world witnessed not only Russia's withdrawal but also the collapse and disintegration of the vast and powerful Soviet Union. Today, the Muslim *ummat* is nurturing similar misconceptions about the power and might of India in context of the *jihad* in Kashmir. This *jihad* is being viewed as the work of a few isolated, reckless, and delusional individuals.

554 THE LITERATURE OF *LASHKAR-E-TAYYABA*

Confessions of *Hindustan Times*

An editorial in India's widely circulated *Hindustan Times* states that 20 per cent of Indian soldiers are suffering from fatal diseases and the Indian Army has the highest rate of war crimes in the world. The newspaper reports that these conditions coupled with the loss of manpower and unsustainable military expenditure have veritably left the Indian economy in tatters. The paper describes the country as an elephant being torn in multiple different directions at once. The editorial notes that in addition to Kashmir, seven other states are dealing with separatist struggles that are gradually gaining momentum. India is losing control of Kashmir, and Kashmir's ultimate liberation will pave the way for the seven other states to gain their independence as well; it seems India will end up no differently than Russia. The newspaper squarely holds Congress responsible for this mess by sticking to antiquated policies instead of adopting a more contemporary approach to the issues plaguing the nation. The editorial further states that Congress's leaders are on their last political breath. While declaring Indian control of Kashmir illegal, unethical, and unsustainable, the paper states the valley has not only ruined the country's economy it has also severely weakened one of the mightiest armies in the region. Industry is running on government subsidies and the fact that the country survives on foreign loans and aid does not bode well for its future. Militarily, Pakistan is fully equipped to completely obliterate India's armoury. The editorial was also critical of India's latest atomic tests.

The cartoon published alongside this editorial shows an enormous elephant attacked by eight ants; the paper openly states that Kashmir has slipped from India's control, and much like the former Soviet Union, India's disintegration is inevitable (Roznama Pakistan, 28 February 1996).

Lt. General Sharma Predicts India's Disintegration

Indian Army's East Command's Operational Chief Lt. General M.R. Sharma has said that in India's north-eastern states, rebels, separatists, and bandits have made conditions much worse than they are in Kashmir. On 9 February 1996, he told the BBC: 'In this region there are at least twelve armed separatist groups that want independence from India. In order to crush these groups, 400,000 regular soldiers and roughly the same number of paramilitary forces have been deployed.'

Mr. Sharma further stated, 'Increasing cooperation between the separatists has been a huge problem for the armed forces. In the past, these groups were rivals but now they have bandied together, and they are armed with the latest weapons. They execute brazen attacks against soldiers in broad daylight. India shares a border with five different countries and there is a heavy flow of arms and ammunition through these borders.'

Mr Sharma advised the government to combine the regular forces and the paramilitary forces under a single permanent command to counter the separatists (*Nava-i-Waqt*, 25 February 1996).

India Tops List of Nations at Risk of Collapse

CIA Report

According to the CIA, India leads the top 16 nations in the world that run the risk for collapse. In 1995, former Vice-President Al Gore asked the CIA for a report on various nations around the world at risk of falling apart; in response the CIA created a task force comprising well-known intellectuals and seasoned diplomats who analysed 113 cases of failed states based on events in 1994–1995. After this initial analysis, over twelve states were singled out for being at high risk of collapse with India right at the top. In addition to India, this list includes Armenia, Central Africa, Haiti, Kyrgyzstan, Mali, Nigeria, Brazil, Turkey, Zambia, Madagascar, Benin, and Bolivia etc. The most prominent reasons given for the potential collapse of a nation were black market economy, security threats, lack of justice, failing healthcare, human rights violations, inflation etc. (Pakistan, 27 February 1996).

India Panics: Military Budget Increased by Rs. 2.3 Billion

The numerous separatist movements in India are a major reason why military spending in the country is perpetually on the rise. The nation's either busy preparing missiles like Prathvi, Nag, and Trishul, or testing its atomic capabilities in an attempt to intimidate its enemies with potential annihilation; consequently, according to a reliable report, the military expenditure for 1997 was raised by Rs. 2.3 billion. In parliament, the transitional budget for the military for 1996–1997 was a

556 THE LITERATURE OF *LASHKAR-E-TAYYABA*

staggering Rs. 207, 990,000, 000, which was a 10 per cent increase from the previous year's budget, making it a Rs. 2.3 billion increase, while additional increases are expected. god knows when this madness will end. *Mujahideen* will settle the score long before India is done throwing money at the problem.

Fourteen Indian States Rebel

While the Indian government is panicking in the face of a deteriorating security situation fourteen states have rebelled and taken up arms against the establishment. Kashmir alone draws 800,000 soldiers while hundreds of millions of rupees are being spent daily in order to snuff out the *mujahideen*. Narasimha Rao told his generals: 'The government will provide as much as is needed for necessities but there has to be a limit.' However, the Army keeps demanding more, to the consternation of the political elite.

Areas afflicted by separatist movements are labelled emergency zones. In response to extended *jihadi* campaigns in Kashmir, Indians have created the Rashtriya Rifles, a unit specially trained in counter-insurgency tactics; so far the government has set up thirty such battalions but expect to create many more. This was in 1996; god knows how many operate today.

Khalistan

Recently, the Ninth Division spent eighteen months in Eastern Punjab slaughtering Sikhs who demanded independence. From 1986 to 1996, the army has murdered one hundred and ten thousand Sikhs and imprisoned seventy thousand; as a result, Sikhs too are now thirsty for Hindu blood and desperate to see India's demise.

Nagaland

When the people of Nagaland expressed a desire for freedom banks were shut down and the search for oil in the region was immediately stalled.

Gorkhaland in Assam

The freedom struggle to establish Gorkhaland has gained considerable momentum. Gorkha fighters attack Indian soldiers at every opportunity. ZTV reports:

Posters demanding the establishment of Gorkhaland have sprung up all over Assam. The resurgence of the Gorkhaland movement has adversely affected the local tourism industry for an annual loss of Rs. 200 million to the government.

Manipur

An armed resistance is already underway in Manipur that the government has been unable to control, despite itself. A Christian state is being carved out of India in the North-East with the full backing of the Christian world. After Pope John Paul's recent tour of India, and the rampant Hindu–Christian riots in the country, Europeans and Americans have publicly declared their support for the struggle. There is also a concerted missionary effort in the region. Indian newspapers report that 90 per cent of the population in Nagaland, Mizoram, Meghalaya, and Manipur has converted to Christianity and a similar trend is noticeable in Himachal Pradesh. The Nationalist Socialist Council of Nagaland is on the rise; the council controls the entire Nagaland region while the Indian government is helpless there. Keep in mind, Nagaland Council already has a well-established embassy in New York with branches in the Hague, Geneva, Dhaka, Islamabad, Kathmandu, Bangkok, and Rangoon.

Bihar

The Jharkhand freedom struggle in the Indian state of Bihar has recently gained incredible momentum. The Indian government has agreed to offer Jharkhand in the northern state of Bihar the right to self-determination. Over 20 million people reside in Jharkhand's forests and mountains. These people have been fighting for their independence for quite some time now. Multiple political parties have announced the right of these people to self-determination.

The Establishment of a New Kind of Military

Due to the rise in separatist movements across India, the government has had to establish a new kind of military unit trained specifically in counterinsurgency tactics. At this point, it has become nearly impossible for the regular army to contain the insurgencies. The former interior

558 THE LITERATURE OF *LASHKAR-E-TAYYABA*

minister has been involved in creating a reserve battalion known as IRB for this purpose; in addition, Punjab, Andhra Pradesh, Assam, Rajasthan, Manipur, Mizoram, Himachal Pradesh, and Sikkim have been given official approval to establish fifteen such battalions of their own. Indian officials are on record for saying the objective of these battalions is to relieve the standing army of the endless 'work' it has put into places like Kashmir.

In short, since the collapse of Russia and the subsequent liberation of various Muslim states in Asia, India has been engulfed in a firestorm of separatism and rebellion with multiple states and nations demanding freedom.

India is not only dealing with *mujahideen* in Kashmir, but also countless insurgencies and rebellions inspired by *mujahideen* across the country. On the eastern front we have the Khalistan movement in Eastern Punjab, on the other end are the separatist movements of Assam, Nagaland, Tirupur, Mizoram, and Jharkhand. These regions sit precariously on India's border with China; geographically, they do not even appear to belong to India. On one end of this border is Bangladesh and Burma while on the other end is Bhutan, Sikkim, Nepal, and China. A minor sliver of land connects these states to India, and they seem removed from the rest of the country. This is why the states in this region are known as the Union. From the start, the inhabitants of these regions never fully accepted their accession to India. They are deeply divided along ethnic lines resulting in violent and bloody riots.

Over 70 per cent of the people living in Andhra Pradesh, Karnataka, and Tamil Nadu are Harijan who have begun to call for the establishment of a 'Harijanland' or 'Shudraland' in these regions. The militant movement of the Harijans is called Dalit Mahasabha. At the start of 1992, Dalit Mahasabha openly demanded a separate homeland and independence from India for the first time.

These reports make one wonder why so many nations and people in India are demanding independence. A comprehensive survey of these separatist struggles reveals that all of them are being waged by non-Brahmins against a Brahmin establishment. Non-Brahmins are finally standing up to centuries old oppression. They are finally beginning to question the poverty, subjugation, and humiliation that have become their fate. They want to know why, despite being only 5 per cent of the population, Brahmins hold almost all the top positions in the country while 95 per cent of the population lives deplorably even though 70 per cent of these people are Hindu themselves. Apparently, being Hindu isn't good enough if one belongs to one of the lower castes. Despite being a minority, Brahmins hold 70 per cent of all government positions in the country while the lower castes fill only 5 per cent of the seats despite being a majority. The lower castes include Yanadi, Badi, Gujjar, and Harijan. Among them, Harijan are the first to have demanded equal rights after partition. They form 28 per cent of the Hindu population and are unanimously despised. Responsible for cleaning gutters, disposing the dead, and various other menial jobs, they are barred from important government positions and systematically pushed to the bottom of the social ladder in a rigidly hierarchical system. They are the most persecuted of all minorities, which is why they are inclined to accept Islam as well as demand liberation. Not only do Harijan despise upper caste Hindus, especially Brahmins, but they have also started banishing their oppressors from states where they are in a majority. Their militant wing, Dalit Mahasabha, regularly executes attacks against the military, police, and upper caste Hindus. It is expected that in the next few decades, these people will accept Islam.

Harijan Leaders Announce: 'If Exploitation Does Not End, All Shudras Will Convert to Islam.'

In August 1992, Harijan leaders announced in no uncertain terms: 'If the exploitation of Harijan does not end, all Harijan in India will simultaneously convert to Islam.' Short of Morarji Desai every Indian leader has been Brahmin. This caste has not only held an absolute monopoly over Indian politics, it has had complete legal immunity as a result of which it has unleashed a reign of terror against Muslims and Harijan, alike. During Narasimha Rao's government, for instance, Babri Mosque was martyred; during the same period, Harijan who voluntarily converted to Islam were forced to convert back to Hinduism; after centuries of oppression and persecution the lower-caste Hindus had had enough and started demanding separate homelands. Thus, a country that has been posing as a secular state is about to face imminent defeat and humiliation. India was never one country; neither is its people a single nation. The only time

560 THE LITERATURE OF *LASHKAR-E-TAYYABA*

in history that this vast territory was held together as a single nation was when Muslims ruled the subcontinent. This was only possible because Muslims did not subscribe to the oppressive caste system; Islamic values of humanism, friendship, and cooperation allowed the locals to live in peace and prosper collectively under Muslim rule.

To protect India from its inevitable and terrifying doom, militant organizations under the patronage of upper caste Hindus have spontaneously sprung up across the land. Organizations like Bharatiya Janata Party, Shiv Sena, and Rashtriya Swayamsevak Sangh are quite public about their agenda to convert all non-Hindus in India to Hinduism, and patronize Hindu extremists in order to guard the nation. But it seems the more these organizations gain strength, the more they guarantee the imminent collapse of India. Brahmins want all nations in India to convert to Hinduism so they may rule over them the way they have ruled over Shudras for thousands of years. Hinduism comprises four castes in which Brahmins rule over Kshatriya, Vaishnavas, and Shudras. In today's world, lower castes are conscious of their institutionalized persecution and humiliation. Attempts by upper caste Hindus to unite the lower castes and forge a collective identity are only worsening the situation and fanning the flames of discord.

Table 12.1 is a chart displaying the insufficient numbers of junior officers enrolled in the Indian Army, Navy, and Air Force.

India's former Prime Minister Chandar Shekhar stated: 'They (Brahmin) want to rewrite the history of India by wiping out all non-Hindu symbols and landmarks in the country. They are trying to homogenize India whereas Hindu society was never homogenous; it was always scattered. Their unsuccessful attempts will alienate many Indians.'

The Cure Made Matters Worse

As we analyse the separatist struggles of India, we must keep in mind that these movements are not a new phenomenon; they have been erupting since India gained its independence, although for the longest time the iron fist of the Hindu moneylender suppressed them. It was only when a handful of *mujahideen* challenged the might of India's armed forces that separatists across the land found the inspiration and the courage to resist.

Table 12.1 Numbers of junior officers enrolled in the Indian Army, Navy, and Air Force.

ARMY		
Rank	Approved Nos	Actual Nos.
General	1	1
Lieutenant General	53	57
Major General	196	196
Brigadier	796	796
Colonel	3,794	3,686
Major	13,889	10,832
Captain and under	22,604	13,832
Total	44,643	32,369
NAVY		
Admiral	1	1
Vice-Admiral/Air Admiral	52	52
Captain/Commodore	371	357
Commander	1,191	1,057
Lieutenant Commodore and under	5,577	5,311
Total	7,192	6,778
AIR FORCE		
Air Chief Marshal	1	1
Air Marshal	23	21
Air Vice-Marshal	48	47
Air Commodore	152	154
Group Captain	587	562
Wing Commander	1,791	1,640
Squadron Leader	3,645	2,941
Flight Lieutenant and under	4,622	4,513
Total	10,869	9,897

Allah-willing, when India collapses, and *mujahideen* march into Kashmir as victors, all the oppressed nations that have been struggling for freedom will voluntarily accept Islam much like all the infidels of Mecca converted simultaneously when the prophet marched into Mecca as a conqueror, even though in the fifteen years preceding the conquest only a

562　THE LITERATURE OF *LASHKAR-E-TAYYABA*

few hundred people embraced the new faith. Similarly, when Sultan Muhammad Al-Fateh conquered Bosnia, the Yugomeli (a persecuted sect of Christianity) accepted Islam, collectively. Such conversions will become commonplace again due to the benefits of *jihad*, Allah-willing.

Gorkhas Join the Battle
In January 1997, Gorkha Liberation Front officially announced the commencement of its freedom struggle in Darjeeling. The Marxist member of the Indian Parliament, Ratna Bahadur addressed all Gorkha organizations striving for liberation with the following words:

'You must unite towards a common goal. The government of Western Bengal is exploiting Gorkhas; funds allocated to Darjeeling are being used for development projects in other areas. Gorkha Liberation Front has announced that on 26 January, on India's Independence Day, they will launch their freedom struggle; we hope that freedom-loving nations of the world will support us. We will fight until we are victorious.'

Indian Youth Abhor Military Service: Eighty Thousand Positions Empty
India's former Junior Minister of Defence, N.V.N. Somu announced in Lok Sabha:

Over 80,000 positions remain empty in the Indian Army, Navy, and Air Force; 15,000 of these positions are at the officer level, while the rest are for lower ranking soldiers. In size, the Indian military ranks fourth in the world. Experts believe that young men are wary of joining the armed forces due to the rebellions in Kashmir, Assam, and Punjab. What's more, due to the aggressive way in which separatist movements are being put down, Indian soldiers are no longer viewed positively in the world, or even in their own country. Indian soldiers often engage in unethical tactics, which is why many people despise the Army. As a result, the Indian government is having a tough time convincing people to join its armed forces (Pakistan 27 February 1997).

Despite India's Military Budget, Separatists Spread Across the Land
India presents itself to the world as a superpower when it comes to missiles and armament but in truth, its military lacks even the most

NOBLE WARRIORS AND BATTLEFRONTS 563

traditional and basic weaponry. According to an investigative report in a weekly magazine:

India's military budget has left its economy in tatters, creating an unprecedented surge in unemployment, crime, theft, and prostitution. The army is 4,120,000 strong but despite being allocated 20 per cent of the national budget its expenses are still not met. Military officials keep demanding more. Due to poor economic conditions, the government has failed to provide a twelfth of its soldiers with AK-47's despite promises made ten years ago. Many soldiers still use weapons from the Second World War. Due to these conditions, no one is particularly interested in joining the Army, which is why 80,000 positions remain vacant. Numerous militant struggles in the country have managed to gain a foothold because of the military's decline. The militants are relentless. There are five kinds of militant organizations in India: upper caste militant organizations, lower caste militant organizations, anti-upper caste militant organizations, Sikh organizations, anti-state/anti-Hindu organizations, various separatist movements as well as numerous groups working for personal, political, and religious gains.

These organizations have been trained and mobilized like military units and many have their headquarters in foreign countries. These groups are drawing India into a protracted civil war. India is now economically, militarily, politically, and socially crippled. It is likely to collapse very soon (Pakistan, 5 March 1997).

India Will Split Into Twenty-Eight Zones
According to former Indian Minister Arjun Singh, sectarianism, regional loyalties, and caste divisions will lead India to collapse much like the Soviet Union. According to him: 'India will split into numerous zones.'

Indian Government and Armed Forces Plead for Mercy
Day by day, the oppressive Indian regime is sinking deeper into the grave it has dug for itself. The more harshly it deals with its minorities and separatists, the sooner it will collapse, like Russia. The greater the ferocity with which it brutalizes Muslims and various other minorities, the greater their resolve in fighting back with everything they have got. BJP's unreliable puppet government, led by Vajpayee, is beginning to have to deal

with the separatists head-on. In April 1997, India's Interior Ministry reported that at least ten states are embroiled in political turmoil, of which seven are publicly demanding independence. The Army has had to intervene in Andhra Pradesh, Maharashtra, Madhya Pradesh, Orissa, Assam, and Occupied Kashmir due to political upheavals. The report made special mention of Kashmir.

India's imminent collapse at the hands of separatists was noted in the British magazine International Review in an article that analysed India's internal and external defence situation:

India's greatest threat is not Pakistan or China but the numerous separatist struggles brewing within. According to Indian commandoes, instead of preparing for a traditional war with Pakistan or China, the Indian Army must prepare for alternative military tactics in order to deal with insurgencies; to this end, a special task force comprising 20,000 men should be set up at once. In addition, it has been decided that a special battalion of former soldiers will be stationed at Doda to counter the *mujahideen* in Kashmir. Recruitment efforts to establish twenty such companies are underway.

Indians are forming task forces every day to crush the numerous separatists in their midst. Kashmir alone has drawn eight hundred thousand men from the Indian Army and yet they have not been able to contain mujahideen; on the contrary, the Army continuously loses its own men in battle. The two new forces being proposed will face the same fate as all the other Indian soldiers who have fallen in Kashmir. *Jihad-e-Kashmir* and The Ummat's Responsibility.

It must be duly noted that the *jihad* in Kashmir is more challenging than the *jihad* in Afghanistan. The world community, including the USA and Europe fully backed the *jihad* in Afghanistan whereas the *jihad* in Kashmir not only lacks international support, but Pakistanis themselves are also wary of providing military or financial assistance for this cause. During Benazir's government, the *jihad* was actively being suppressed. Those who express reservations about the *jihad* in Kashmir should realize that despite the full backing of the global community, the *jihad* in Afghanistan took fourteen years to land a conclusive victory, on the other hand, with very little support, *mujahideen-e-Kashmir* have driven India to the brink of dissolution in a relatively short period of time. Indian sources themselves predict India's imminent collapse. It's evident that

India cannot last long. When Russia collapsed, it happened suddenly; no one saw it coming, no one predicted it. Internally, India is falling prey to all kinds of crises, but the fissures are being concealed; all we need, to deliver the final blow to the sinking ship that is India, is the full support of the Muslim *ummat*. As it stands, even a little support for the *jihad* in Kashmir will allow us to deliver the final blow, Allah-willing. Not only will we liberate Kashmir, but numerous Pakistani will also emerge from India, and Muslims who have suffered Indian aggression for the past fifty years will finally breathe a sigh of relief with the freedom to practice their religion and live according to the values of Islam.

Our misguided intellectuals continue to regurgitate the script fed to them by infidels; they say the *jihad* in Afghanistan was meaningless because once the *jihad* succeeded the various *jihadi* factions started warring against one another and that Kashmir is doomed to a similar end. We must remind such 'thinkers' that the Afghan *jihad* was waged, first and foremost, for the survival of Pakistan, then, for the liberation of Afghanistan as well as for the defence of the gulf region; the conquest of Central Asia turned out to be a bonus. The *jihad* in Kashmir is being waged for the protection of Muslims and Pakistan for if we lose this war due to our foolishness, Pakistan's very existence will be threatened. Even those opposed to *jihad* are invested in the survival of Pakistan but have no clue how to ensure this survival. Regardless, *mujahideen* are resolute and shall remain so; this extract from an essay that appeared on 18 April in *Nawa-e-Waqt*, reprinted in *India Abroad*, is testament to their determination:

> Since 1947, India has refused to accept the two-nation theory. Nehru believed that even if Pakistan were created, it would collapse within a few months and re-integrate into India, but alas, this did not happen. Next, we split up Pakistan but unfortunately, despite the creation of Bangladesh, Pakistan emerged ever stronger. When we tried to interfere with Sindh, we received a resounding response in Eastern Punjab as a result of which we were forced to be on the defensive. We even failed to gain control of the northern areas via Siachen, which put us entirely on the back-foot. We were unable to destroy freedom fighters' training camps in Occupied Kashmir and Pakistan; it seems we are incapable of preventing Kashmir's liberation.

Readers, even the Hindu moneylender must reckon with the *mujahideen's* success. It was due to the *jihad* in Kashmir that Vajpayee rushed to make amends by touring Pakistan when he saw there was no other way out. During his visit, he accepted Pakistan's existence, agreed to talks, and recognized Kashmir was a problem that needed to be resolved. He resorted to flattery by complimenting the people of Pakistan and assured us that we ought to forget about Kashmir altogether and instead focus on increasing trade between India and Pakistan.

Readers, look how the moneylender spins the narrative. Because he is being exposed in Kashmir, he goes around proposing increased trade without putting a stop to the brutality of his own forces in the region; to the contrary, he recently announced a surge in troops in the valley; the more soldiers in Kashmir, the more target practice for us. The hunting grounds are full, the hunters are ready; we will pick them off one by one. Behold, the moneylender is about to flee, he has admitted as much himself.

Oh People of Pakistan! Oh People of Kashmir!
This is a golden opportunity, for heaven's sake do not waste it! Advance the *jihad* in Kashmir with your words, your wealth, and your muscle. If you let this opportunity go, the Hindu moneylender, who has spent the past fifty years trying to create a Greater India, will double his efforts only to put you on the defensive whereas right now, we are on the offensive. The enemy has been put to flight. Henceforth, never talk about terminating *jihad* in Kashmir; instead, talk about how, once the Hindu moneylender has been driven from Kashmir, we will take over the valley and turn it into a base camp from where we will pursue every Hindu in India, via Kathua Road, to exact our revenge. We must deliver the message of freedom to the two million Muslim brothers in India so when *mujahideen* enter Delhi, Bombay, Ayodhya, Calcutta, Madras, Jaipur, Bangalore, Hyderabad, and Junagadh, heads bowed in humility, Muslims shower us with rose petals and garland us with marigolds. These are the images for which we live and die. Be patient, stay focused on *jihad*; by all means, let your heart fill with pride and joy at the success of the Afghan *jihad*, and guard yourself from all kinds of toxic and negative premonitions.

Chapter 40: Red Fort Attack

Sri Nagar Airport: A Battlefield

The cowardly Hindu moneylender is insidious and innovative in his oppression of Kashmiri Muslims. To maintain control of the piece of heaven known as Kashmir, Sri Nagar's airport has been constructed on reinforced foundations so when needed, it can be used by fighter jets to bomb freedom fighters and *mujahideen* as well as to invade Pakistan's airspace. Because *Lashkar-e-Tayyaba*'s *mujahideen* are fighting the battle between disbelief and Islam, they are cognizant of the enemy's every move.

On 15 January 2001, six *Lashkar-e-Tayyaba mujahideen* dressed in police uniforms got hold of an official car belonging to the Department of Forestry, and sailed through the gates of Sri Nagar's airport. Our brothers first lobbed a few grenades and then opened fire on the soldiers before two *mujahideen* entered the reception area inside the building, and pumped bullets into the guards standing next to the X-ray machines. Two others made a dash for the runway and opened fire on military planes as a result of which one jumbo jet was severely damaged. The remaining two stormed their way through the officers' mess, firing indiscriminately. One of the *fidayeen* broke into the airport canteen, bunkered down, and started sniping soldiers one by one. The operation started at 2:15pm, Pakistan Standard Time. After three and a half hours of relentless fighting, one by one, each one of our brothers was awarded martyrdom. In this attack, eighteen soldiers were killed, including one officer, while fifteen to twenty soldiers were wounded.

Two kinds of police operate in Kashmir. The local police force comprises local Muslims responsible for preventing crime, much like Punjab police or Sindh police in Pakistan. The second is what is known as the Task Force; this comprises traitors who have sold out to Indian authorities. *Mujahideen* never attack the local police for they cooperate with us, but we show no mercy to the Task Force. It was the Task Force's uniforms that the six *fidayeen* had on when they attacked Sri Nagar's airport. Before the operation, Brother Abu Hanzala went on an extensive reconnaissance mission inside the airport gathering as much information about the offices and sensitive spots on the premises. Keep in mind, Brother Abu Hanzala has spent seven years in the air force himself. For the most part,

568 THE LITERATURE OF *LASHKAR-E-TAYYABA*

international airports are similar in design and structure. This is why he was able to map out the airport in great detail. Two more of our men had collected as much information as possible about the network of roads and buildings surrounding the airport. In total, three men had been involved in planning this attack.

Why was the Airport Attacked?

The airport in Sri Nagar was not attacked simply because it was an airport but because it was used for military purposes. According to one of our senior *mujahideen*, two years ago (February 2001), five to seven gunship helicopters hovered over the airport all night long. Since then, the situation has worsened considerably and numerous bunkers have sprung up around the airport.

Despite having a sizeable air force base in Koel, in southern Kashmir, vast parts of Sri Nagar's airport are used for militaristic purposes. In 1998, the airport was closed off to civil aviation for a period of six months on the pretext of repairing the facility. But in truth, the airport was closed from 8 June 1998 to 31 December 1998 not merely for repairs but to restructure it so Russian jets could utilize it. According to India's military experts, in any potential conflict, Sri Nagar's airport is far more important than the air force's base in Koel because approximately thirty Russian jets can land and take off from this facility. Thus, this airport was, in effect, a military post, which made it an important and legitimate target.

While admitting to strategic failures and accepting *mujahideen*'s superior strength, state police confessed that they knew beforehand that *mujahideen* would carry out a *fidayeen* attack on the airport and despite taking all sorts of precautions, they were unable to prevent the assault. The spokesperson for the police said: 'We had verified reports about an imminent attack on the airport by *mujahideen*. We had also prepared ourselves for such an attack. We set up barriers across every road leading to the airport. But despite our best efforts, *mujahideen* were successful in carrying out this operation.'

Indian media tried their best to prove that *mujahideen* were unable to enter the airport and were killed at the gates. If the Indian authorities were interested in the truth they would have allowed journalists and

NOBLE WARRIORS AND BATTLEFRONTS **569**

photographers inside and shown them exactly where the martyrs' blood was spilled; instead, media personnel were briefed a kilometre away from the airport in an unsuccessful bid to cover up the military's shortcomings.

The fact that the attack lasted three and a half hours is testament to how valiantly and determinedly the *mujahideen* battled the military. Allah had predetermined martyrdom for them that day but in the course of achieving this esteemed status, they set an unprecedented example of valour and fortitude.

Demonstrations and protests were held in Sopore, Bandipora, Kupwara, Islamabad, and Pulwama demanding the return of the blessed bodies of the martyrs killed in the attack. In Budgam, thousands gathered beyond police lines and proceeded in a single grand procession to the local Eid-centre where they chanted 'Death to India!' and 'Long Live Pakistan!' and 'Long Live *Lashkar-e-Tayyaba*'. Kashmiri leaders paid tribute to the martyrs and demanded India return their bodies so that the people may offer their funeral prayers and give them a proper burial. In Sri Nagar, thousands of markets were shut down, strikes were organized, and there were massive assemblies in which people refused to budge until the bodies of the martyrs were returned. The Indian forces responded with characteristic brutality by attacking peaceful protestors with batons and tear gas, while confiscating loudspeakers from mosques in an attempt to silence the dissenters. Tens of thousands of were out in the streets, and large portions of these people were women and children.

How the Airport Attack was Reported in the Media

Below are a few news reports as samples of how the attack was presented in the media:

Flights to Sri Nagar Not without Peril—BBC

In analysing the operation the BBC reported that the attack on the airport was the most brazen attack executed so far, second only to the one on the Red Fort. This attack could have many negative consequences, one of which is the increased risk of flying to Sri Nagar. The Security Committee in the Indian Parliament will review the situation on the ground before deciding upon a ceasefire (BBC-Pakistan).

570 THE LITERATURE OF *LASHKAR-E-TAYYABA*

Media Offices' Telephone Lines Disconnected to Cover
up Military's Failure

To cover up the losses dealt to the military during the attack on the airport, the authorities in Kashmir disconnected the phone lines of the
various media outlets with offices in Sri Nagar, as a result of which communications were severely hampered and it became virtually impossible
to verify reports.

Sri Nagar Airport was the Most Heavily Fortified Airport in India: International News Media

'One plane damaged; flights suspended; unannounced curfew.'

The *fidayeen* of *Lashkar-e-Tayyaba* broke through all the precautions
the Indian Army had taken and boldly attacked the airport and slaughtered fifteen Indian soldiers and two civilians within the first hour; all
six *fidayeen* were martyred while nine security personnel were severely
wounded. According to detailed reports, on Monday, after 2:30pm, a
green jeep carrying men in Special Operations (commandoes) uniforms
tried entering the airport. They were stopped at a certain checkpoint beyond which arms are strictly prohibited even for security personnel but
the *fidayeen* carried on and soon thereafter gun battles broke out between
them and the paramilitary CRPF. Indian soldiers immediately responded
to the violence and took up positions. The gunfight continued for a full
hour during which four soldiers, a sixteen-year-old girl, and a bank manager, and all six *mujahideen* were martyred; nine soldiers, including three
lady-officers, were wounded. According to Voice of America, two of the
mujahideen had their names written on their arms with ballpoint pens;
one was Talha and the other Abu Habeeb. According to a police spokesperson in Kashmir, *mujahideen* successfully went through the first checkpoint. According to AFP, Sri Nagar's airport was the most secure and
heavily fortified airport in all of India and it was used for both civil and
military aviation. According to AP, the airport is some distance outside
Sri Nagar and the road leading to the airport is perpetually jammed due to
security checkpoints; passengers are frisked at least four times before they
even enter the premises. The attack happened on 26 January, during India's
Independence Day preparations. *Mujahideen* usually attack around this

time. According to KMS, the attack created havoc in the government and military sectors. According to Indian television, *mujahideen* attacked the airport's Gate No. 1; under the leadership of Commander Salahuddin, *fidayeen* stole a military vehicle and used this to enter the airport before they instantly launched a grenade at CRPF personnel and stormed through the high security zone to take up positions for a gunfight.

According to *Voice of Germany*, one of the attackers took cover in an airport store from where he continued firing for a long time; another one entered an x-ray room and started targeting security personnel. The paramilitary, called in for reinforcements, set fire to a number of stores on the premises during the operation. When the external gates were attacked, two civilian airliners, one of which was Indian Air, were on the runway. In the panic, airport authorities dispatched both planes to New Delhi (AFP, AP, Radio V Report, and Jang; 17 June 2001).

Eighteen Soldiers Killed in Attack on Airport in Sri Nagar; *Kashmir Times* Reveals Indian Cover-Up

The widely circulated daily, *Kashmir Times*, printed in Occupied Kashmir, has revealed the facts the Indian Army was desperately trying to cover-up: in the attack on the airport in Sri Nagar, *Lashkar-e-Tayyaba's mujahideen* slaughtered eighteen Indian soldiers. It turns out *Lashkar's* claims were true, after all. According to details, the widely circulated and highly respected *Kashmir Times*, published in Occupied Kashmir, revealed that in the attack on the airport by *Lashkar's mujahideen* eighteen soldiers were killed. This revelation has caused a stir in the puppet government and military circles. At the time of the attack Jet Airways and Indian Airlines planes had just landed from New Delhi but the raid upset the entire system; passengers present on the runway were crammed into military planes and the airport was instantly evacuated (*Kashmir Times*, Pakistan, 18 January 2001).

Lashkar-e-Tayyaba Acquires Chinese Anti-Aircraft Artillery

In order to destroy Indian jets, buildings, and bridges, *Lashkar-e-Tayyaba's mujahideen* have acquired Chinese anti-aircraft artillery. According to the Press Trust of India, the 60mm rocket launchers can easily hit their intended targets; China and *Lashkar* have denied the transaction.

572 THE LITERATURE OF *LASHKAR-E-TAYYABA*

Extremist Attacks Will Be India's Undoing

Former Chief of Indian Navy, Retired Admiral Vishnu Bhagwat says that extremist operations will be India's undoing. While talking to journalists in Bombay, he said that nowadays, the creation of Ram Mandir is being talked about much the same way that the martyrdom of Babri Mosque was instigated years earlier. The government encouraged the crisis in Ayodhya to distract the public. The central government conspired to demolish Babri Mosque because all avenues of prosperity had been sealed off. Now, once again, the country faces unprecedented levels of unemployment and in addition, it must deal with indefensible borders; the situation is out of control while extremists operate openly. Fanning the flames of Ayodhya will further weaken Vajpayee's government.

Beyond The Red Fort

The Muslim king abandoned the world-renowned Red Fort that, for centuries, had been a chronicle of Islamic history in the subcontinent and a witness to the glory and supremacy of Muslims and *mujahideen*... the fort's gates and towering walls were a testament to Islamic power, dominance, and might... the lives of infidel kings depended on the commands issued here as they'd cower and grovel before the Muslim king who occupied its throne... they licked the boots of the Muslim rulers who ruled from within its walls... they'd pay jizya, taxes, tributes... they'd humiliate themselves and their women at its doorstep... our powerful Muslim kings once ruled the world, humiliated disbelievers, defeated infidels in battle, upheld the supremacy of Islam, spent their days waging *jihad* against disbelievers and spent their nights praying for mercy... but when these kings abandoned *jihad* for the luxuries of their court, and welcomed ignorance into their midst... and replaced the call to prayer with the seductive and intoxicating songs of courtesans... and traded the grit and grime of battle for the meaningless metaphysics of mysticism... even as dedicated men like Shah Ismail Shaheed and the *mujahideen* of Balakot and warriors like Emir Maulana Vilayat Ali kept insisting that Muslim kings like Bahadar Shah Zafar ought to realign their lives and their projects with the Quran and *Sunnat*... their words fell on ears poisoned with melodies... *jihad* was terminated... and we were subjected to Allah's humiliating and terrifying

NOBLE WARRIORS AND BATTLEFRONTS 573

wrath. When Muslims stopped warring against disbelievers, infidels, in the guise of the English, overcame Muslims ... bloodied and bloated bodies of Muslim men, women, and children were left rotting across the land... those who survived, scattered, like a colony of ants under attack ... there was chaos... carnage... cannon fire... hooves of stallions trampled the innocent... the last Muslim king Bahadar Shah Zafar hid in the back alleys of Delhi like a petty criminal... the courtiers had already fled... the legacy of Muslim prestige was in tatters... the very fort where maharajas, rajas, cunning Hindu moneylenders and worthless Thakurs bowed before Muslim kings in veneration and paid their tributes and respects... that historical bastion the world knew as the Red Fort was occupied by Christians. The Muslim king was finally captured, and accused of mutiny! He was charged, tried, convicted, and deported by a Christian judge like a petty thief and left to rot in a prison in Rangoon, Burma, thousands of miles away.

Five captions detailing the timeline and targets (right to left):

1. 9:05pm: *Lashkar fidayeen* enter through Lahori gate and open fire on soldiers stationed in their barracks.

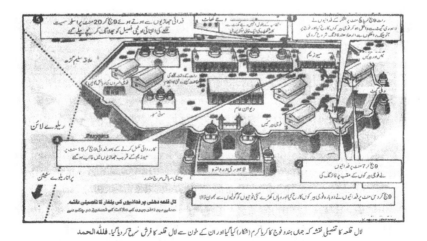

Picture 1. Detailed map of the Red Fort where *mujahideen* hunted down Indian soldiers and flooded its hallways with their blood, thanks to Allah!.
Source: Muhammad Tahir Naqqash, *Ghaziyan-i-Saf-Shikan*, p. 563.

2. 9:07pm: *fidayeen* open fire on rear barracks.
3. 9:10pm: *fidayeen* return to first barrack and slaughter a number of soldiers.
4. 9:15pm: after completing their intended mission, *fidayeen* hide in bushes near the museum.
5. 9:20pm: *fidayeen* scale extremely high rear wall, jump over, and escape.

Thus, began the humiliating phase of the history of the Red Fort during which attacks meant to obliterate Muslims were launched from within its walls. For almost a century, the fort had to endure this indignity... during this time, every brick, stone, and passage inside the fort waited patiently, longingly, for the noble warriors to demolish enemy lines, and for their footsteps to echo through its corridors again, and for their chants of '*Allah Akbar!*' to fill its halls, and for their foreheads to graze its floors as they bowed before Allah... finally, when Christians scurried back to England, the Red Fort was glad to be rid of their filth and rancour, overjoyed at the prospect of being inhabited once again by the chaste Muslims who once roamed its halls and corridors and dispatched *jihadi* caravans to the far corners of the land... but what is this?... alas!... monkey and pig worshippers invaded its sacred spaces... with their putrid doctrines and their filthy bodies... instead of invocations of Rehman and Rahim, Ram Ram echoed through its halls... once again, the Red Fort was despondent as it was populated by those who worship idols and stones and animals instead of those who worship Allah... was this to be its fate?... forever sealed off to the *mujahideen* who demolish enemy lines... forever waiting in vain... it had waited a century and a half... from 1857 to 2001... it is said waiting is harder than death... the waiting brought on the dark clouds of despair... then, one day, *mujahideen* who demolish enemy lines sent the fort a message of hope... we were on our way to rid its grounds of the filthy Hindu beasts, and rekindle its glorious history; we were going to breathe new life into its environment... we promised that devoted sons, relentless defenders, courageous youth, and fearless warriors were on their way to restore its dignity... the Red Fort was surprised... it wondered... how will you manage when countless infidels hold me hostage with their canons and armies... how would the sons of Islam break through these defences, when my boundary wall stretches over a mile and a half and my body is

NOBLE WARRIORS AND BATTLEFRONTS   575

spread across an area 3,000ft long and 1,800ft wide. On River Jumna's side my walls are 20ft high, while towards land, my walls are 75ft (from the bottom of the moat to the top of the wall)... the moat is 30ft deep and 75ft wide... every single step of the way some Hindu soldier/occupier is keeping watch over me... he blasts anything that moves against his will... in such circumstances who is insane enough to try and reach me... I have been so heavily barricaded behind security checks that even birds are wary of flying over me... anyone approaching me is shot dead... Hindus have shackled me and torture *mujahideen* deep within my bowels... who are these men who claim they will reach me one day to unfurl the banner of Islam over me and blast these dreaded Hindus to hell? Indeed, these men are strange!

Then, one evening, two *fidayeen* enter the Red Fort through Lahori Gate, past the armed guards and vigilant watchmen; they walk right by a contingent of oncoming soldiers, but Allah blinds the soldiers who went by the *fidayeen* without least suspecting them of being angels of death. Families of these soldiers are filing in to audition a light and sound show but what do *mujahideen* who demolish enemy lines have to do with entertainment... they're preparing to put on a show of their own... a suicidal show. As the filthy Hindus are dazzled and awed by the lights and sounds, Allah's warriors are busy surveying the area... they look upon the walls of the Red Fort with longing... after a century and a half the Red Fort and *mujahideen* greet each other with a mixture of melancholy and joy... every aspect of the fort was delighted to see us... it had been too long since *mujahideen* tread its walkways... they looked upon the fort one last time before hiding in its bosom, waiting in ambush... the civilians begin exiting the premises, having watched their show, but the *fidayeen* are about to start theirs... suddenly, a soldier appears out of nowhere, glaring directly at the *mujahideen* with his filthy eyes... one of the *mujahideen* squeezes the trigger and a burst of bullets blasts holes through the soldier's eyes and chest... gunfire... the soldier's anguished cry... more gunfire... the fort echoes with gunshots... a horrifying scene begins to unfold... the soldiers are baffled... they run every which way in fear and panic... *fidayeen* chase them down with guns and grenades... one filthy idol-worshipping Hindu soldier is chased into the parking lot... he runs around like a chicken with its head chopped off... finally, one of the *mujahideen* puts him out of his misery and shoots him dead... his blood-spattered corpse collapses to the ground... the *fidayeen* proceed to storm

576 THE LITERATURE OF *LASHKAR-E-TAYYABA*

the residential barracks... wild with fury, one of them lobs a grenade, another opens fire; one by one, Allah's enemies are dispatched to hell... Then, the *fidayeen* go hunting... two civilians appear before them but their lives are spared for we are at war only with Hindu soldiers... the occupiers and oppressors... as soon as the civilians disappear a military car arrives on the scene; the two soldiers inside are instantly shot dead... a sentry runs across the grounds; a *fidayeen* chases him for ten meters before shooting him dead... the Hindu Army is stunned... *mujahideen* are now being attacked from all sides... a hail of bullets... a shower of steel... but those who demolish enemy lines continue their operation... Allah guards them from the bullets raining down on them... a soldier emerges from the museum... a *fidayeen* takes aim and shoots him dead... this is how they keep picking off Allah's enemies ... one... by... one... the blood of Kali's worshippers floods the grounds of the Red Fort... every act of brutality is avenged... twelve monkey-worshippers... Hindu soldiers... sent to hell... as *fidayeen* go after soldiers they are separated... and by Allah's grace, due to their superior militant training, both of them manage to escape, alive!... leaving behind Indian soldiers armed with the latest weapons, wringing their hands... as the *fidayeen* exit the fort they spot a solider inside an office and shoot him dead ... soldiers fan out across the region in search of the *fidayeen* like bloodhounds, but all glory to Allah who blinds the soldiers, and allows the *fidayeen* to escape.

That evening, the Red Fort filled with pride as monkey- and cow-worshippers lamented their dead. No one could believe such an attack was even possible. The Indian Army was bewildered. In the sample news reports below, notice how soldiers describe the attack on them by those who demolish enemy lines. Newspapers, radio stations, and television channels, reported the event as follows:

Both *Mujahideen* Entered Through a Gate Under 24-Hour Surveillance

After the attack on the Red Fort, the Indian capital is on red alert. Every single car leaving the city is being thoroughly searched; Uttar Pradesh is also on red alert. On Saturday, the Red Fort was completely shut down; even workers employed in the various government offices located on its premises,

NOBLE WARRIORS AND BATTLEFRONTS 577

as well as tourists, were barred entry. Police found twenty bullet shells. Both *fidayeen* entered the fort with spectators attending the light and sound show at the venue. The *fidayeen* proceeded to cut off power, and target soldiers. Police authorities termed the attack a grave security breach. Investigations are underway about how the *fidayeen* entered through a gate under 24-hour surveillance. Police and soldiers raided numerous guesthouses in New Delhi and claim to have found a cell phone number and a Rs. 500 note that may be of interest. BBC reports that this attack proves that *Lashkar-e-Tayyaba* can strike anywhere in India, not only in Kashmir. While this attack has stunned authorities, it also reveals that Pakistan cannot control *Lashkar-e-Tayyaba*. According to Radio Tehran, all public spaces and sensitive areas in Uttar Pradesh have been cordoned off and are under heavy surveillance (radio, television report, AFP, Jang, 24 December 2001).

Further Attacks Expected; Increased Security Around Fifteen Airports
After the attack on the Red Fort in Delhi, fearing further attacks by *mujahideen*, all airports in Eastern India have been on red alert. Civil Aviation's Security Bureau spokesperson stated that 15 airports, including the one in Calcutta, are on red alert on the recommendation of the Interior Minister. Meanwhile, BBC reports that after the attack on Delhi's historical fort, authorities are admitting to serious gaps in the city's security (AFP, *Nawa-e-Waqt*, 25 December 2000).

Embarrassed and Indignant, Army Seeks Mujahideen
After the attack on the Red Fort in India's capital, the military is raiding the entire city in search of the perpetrators. At the time of the attack, Rajputana Rifles and Jat Regiment were stationed at the venue.

According to the newspaper *Hindu*, Military Intelligence (MI) and Intelligence Bureau (IB) are headquartered on the premises of the Red Fort. *Mujahideen* engaged the soldiers for 45 minutes before the searchlights were turned back on; soldiers immediately armed themselves and exited through Lahori Gate, in search of the attackers. Archaeological Survey of India's offices are also located in the Red Fort. When police arrived at the scene, they were not allowed to enter the premises.

Indian media were highly critical of the security agencies, more so because *mujahideen* had warned Indian authorities of just such an attack. Despite this, Indian security forces were unable to prevent it. Apparently,

578 THE LITERATURE OF *LASHKAR-E-TAYYABA*

Delhi police were fully aware that *Lashkar-e-Tayyaba* planned to carry out an operation in the capital on Monday or Tuesday; despite extensive police search operations the *mujahideen* could not be located.

According to *Times of India*, an embarrassed and indignant Indian Army is searching for *mujahideen* inside the fort. The bullet shells recovered from the attack have been submitted for chemical analysis.

According to Zee News, *fidayeen* shot dead two soldiers from Rajputana Rifles and one from Jat Regiment; three locations were attacked and numerous soldiers were injured. According to Radio Tehran, various security measures were being taken to secure the State Assembly.

9:20pm The Red Fort in Delhi was not attacked by three *mujahideen* but two, both of whom were from Occupied Kashmir and have been associated with *Lashkar-e-Tayyaba* for quite some time. Their names are Basheer Ahmed Vani and Syed Muhammad Ali. They entered the fort at 9:20pm and before starting the operation they cut the power supply. The *mujahideen* were not interested in attacking civilians; their targets included Rajputana Rifles headquarters as well as the prison where, according to the Indian Army, high value terrorists and *mujahideen* are interrogated. The *fidayeen* did not carry any heavy artillery; they were armed with nothing but AK-47s. This is the first proper attack by *mujahideen* in India. Earlier, Harkat-ul-*Mujahideen* carried out an unsuccessful attempt at freeing Masood Azhar, leader of the newly formed *jihadi* organization Jaish-e-Muhammad (Khabrain, 24 December 2000).

Delhi Police Refuses Duty at Red Fort

Delhi police refused to guard the Red Fort on the pretext that it was the duty of the Department of Antiquities to provide security. The police will return to duty once the guards have been trained (16 December 2000).

According to Zee TV, in the annual police press conference, while reporting on his department's performance, Ajay Sharma revealed that during the past year, forty-three terrorists were apprehended in Delhi, seventeen of whom were allegedly Muslim. According to the police, the most active operatives in Delhi belong to *Lashkar-e-Tayyaba*. Additionally, organizations like *Hizb-al-Mujahideen*, Khalistan Zindabad Force, and Al-Badr also maintain a presence in Delhi. The police also admit its criminal intelligence unit is weak.

Prime Minister's Security Detail Poorly Armed

After *Lashkar-e-Tayyaba*'s attack on the Red Fort, India's Prime Minister Atal Bihari Vajpayee planned to attend the great Hindu festival Kumbh, in order to bathe in the waters of the Ganges and wash away his sins (according to Hindu beliefs). According to an official source, the newspaper Statesman reports that Vajpayee's specific security detail is responsible for his protection but due to a lack of advanced weaponry everyone involved is being extremely cautious. Vajpayee's Ganges-wash has become a nightmare for everyone concerned, especially since *Lashkar-e-Tayyaba* has specifically threatened to sabotage the Kumbh festival (AFP, *Nawa-e-Waqt*, 14 January 2001).

Indian Government Did Not Expect a Large-Scale Operation in Delhi—BBC

Specialized planes can conduct surveillance operations; the navy has always been sidelined—Indian authorities. Police and various other security agencies have been put on high alert around the country's largest oil field, situated near Mumbai, in anticipation of an attack by *Lashkar-e-Tayyaba*. According to the Indian newspaper The Statesman, police officers investigating the attack on the Red Fort report that *Lashkar-e-Tayyaba mujahideen* are actively planning an attack on the oil field on the western coast. Meanwhile, the Indian Navy, responsible for protecting the oil field, states that patrols around the area have been increased. According to the naval command, all boats and ships in the region are being checked; in case of a threat, fighter jets can also be deployed for surveillance purposes. Keep in mind, the oil field in Mumbai provides 40 per cent of the country's energy needs.

According to ANN, after the attack on the Red Fort, Indian police and secret services are in shock. In anticipation of future attacks, all secret service agencies have been put on red alert (Statesman, AFP, Jang, 7 January 2001).

Indian Defence Minister George Fernandez has stated that every Indian government till now has completely sidelined the navy, leaving gaping holes in the nation's security. While addressing a naval ceremony, he stated that in the past fifty years, not once did anyone even consider the possibility of a sea-attack, which is why India's coastal security was severely compromised. He further stated that because the Andaman and

580 THE LITERATURE OF *LASHKAR-E-TAYYABA*

Nicobar Islands have been duly ignored, they are now a hotbed of terrorist activity (KPI, Insaf, 6 January 2001).

Fear of Fidayee *Operation*

India has publicly declared a conditional withdrawal of its troops from Occupied Kashmir in the next five years. According to a report quoting a high-level source in the Indian newspaper *Hindustan Times*, if the Liberation Conference can guarantee the Indian government a cessation of terrorist activity by *mujahideen* in Jammu and Kashmir, it will withdraw its troops. According to the report, a delegation from the Liberation Conference will tour Pakistan for a week to discuss this proposal with various *jihadi* organizations. If the Liberation Conference can come out of these talks with the guarantee that all *jihadi* organizations agree to end their activities in Occupied Kashmir, the Indian government will begin withdrawing its troops from the region (*Hindustan Times*, Ummat, August 2001).

After the Defeat of 800,000 Indian Soldiers, Extremist Hindus Form Lashkar-e-Hind *in Response to* Lashkar-e-Tayyaba

Having lost all faith in their army, Hindu extremists announced the creation of *Lashkar-e-Hind* with an initial contingent of twenty-five trained men equipped with advanced automatic weapons. It was founded by BJP's former Member of Parliament and current president of Kisaan Mazdoor Party, Ganga Charan Rajput, on the banks of River Gormuti in Uttar Pradesh. Ganga Charan stated that it was impossible to counter militancy without the presence of an armed counter-terrorist organization. Ganga Charan appealed to young Hindus to join *Lashkar-e-Hind* in order to wage an armed struggle against militancy. He said *Lashkar-e-Hind* operatives would be stationed at the borders to resist anti-India elements (Internet, Insaf, 16 January 2001).

Oh Pakistanis, Oh Youth of the Nation, Oh *Jihadis*... notice the wishful thinking of the enemy. By successfully storming through the impenetrable walls of the Red Fort and sending the Indian Army packing, *mujahideen* have proved that if we keep the lamp of *jihad* burning, and continue attacking the enemy, and slaughter Allah's opponents, Allah will continue to shower us with victories and assistance, Allah-willing. Countless mosques have been dismantled and martyred even after the martyrdom of Babri Mosque, countless mosques long to hear the call to prayer again. Hindu moneylenders are crushing millions of mosques, indeed, millions of mosques, even today. The enemy is out in the open flashing his sword in order to intimidate, slaughter, and horrify innocent Muslims yet again... enemy swords will behead the heads that bow before Allah, and silence the tongues that sing Allah's praise... Oh Youth of the Nation, Young Warriors of Islam, Sons of Muhammad bin Qasim and Tariq bin Zayd... how many mosques in India lay barren and destroyed... they call out to you and your honour... the arrows of disbelief pierce our hearts and souls... can you hear the anguished cries... infidels are hell-bent on annihilating us... is anyone listening? Is anyone out there? Who will care for our wounds and heal our injuries? Who will free us from the disbelievers and their oppression? We are crying out... we are tired... is there not a single son of Muhammad bin Qasim who will respond with 'z!!' when we cry out...?

Oh Muslim *ummat*! Where are the living symbols of your honour, dignity, and courage? Where is the pride of the nation? Where are the warriors who can obliterate the battlefronts of Jews, Christians, and Hindus? The names of those who laid the foundations of the Red Fort were Izzat Khan and Ghairat Khan. Today, in a grand display of honour and dignity, much like the honour and dignity in the foundations of the Red Fort, fearless *fidayeen* attacked the Red Fort as a signal to downtrodden Muslims and dilapidated mosques... we will cry '*Labbaik*!!' to the cry of every mosque in India that is destroyed, and we will turn all of India into the Red Fort. The *fidayeen* missions will continue... the Red Fort is not our ultimate goal... it is merely a milestone... the destination is still far... our journey continues well beyond the Red Fort. Our objective is justice for every Muslim, mosque, and persecuted minority in India... regardless of race, caste, or creed... we will carry out *fidayeen* operations in every corner of India where there is persecution, oppression, and injustice... Indian soldiers will fall dead... armed forces will be attacked... we will sit in ambush... we will cut off every limb of the aggressor... we will behead and slaughter... we will slit throats with daggers... the Red Fort attack will be emulated and repeated over and over, all over India... Allah-willing... through an esteemed and noble *jihad* we will give the oppressed, the weak, and the downtrodden reasons to rejoice... and this *jihad*... in the prophet's words... ماض الى يومالقيمة will never end... in fact, it will continue till the Last Day! Allah-willing!

لال قلعہ کی دیو ہیکل تاریخی دیوار کہ ظالم ہندو فوج کے لاشے گرانے کے بعد مجاہدین اس دیوار سے نیچے اترے اور ہندو درندوں کو بلکتا سسکتا چھوڑ کر اپنی ہائیڈوں اور کچھاروں میں فدائیوں کے پاس جا پہنچے

Picture 2. The towering wall surrounding the Red Fort from where, after throwing off the bodies of Indian soldiers, mujahideen escaped to their *fidayeen* hideouts, leaving the Hindu beasts licking their wounds.
Source: Muhammad Tahir Naqqash, *Ghaziyan-i-Saf-Shikan*, p. 575.

Chapter 41: The Finest Investment

A Lucrative Investment for the Traders and Businessmen of the World

A Lucrative Investment
Dear, Readers! Let me tell you about an investment that will not only pay dividends in this world but will also give a hefty return in the world hereafter. Its guarantor is the holy prophet himself!

Seven Hundred Sins Forgiven

مَّن ذَا الَّذِي يُقْرِضُ اللَّه قَرْضًا حَسَنًا فَيُضَاعِفَهُ لَهُ أَضْعَافًا كَثِيرَةً وَاللَّه يَقْبِضُ وَيَبْسُطُ وَإِلَيْهِ تُرْجَعُونَ

    Who is it that will lend unto Allah a goodly loan, so that He may give it increase manifold? Allah straiteneth and enlargeth. Unto Him ye will return.

(2:245)

Those who spend in Allah's path are like a kernel with seven ears with each ear containing one hundred more kernels for Allah bestows upon whom He wills and Allah is expansive and most knowledgeable.

Syedna Khareem bin Fatik reports the prophet said: 'He who contributes any amount in Allah's path (*jihad*) will be rewarded seven hundred times his contribution.'

Seven Hundred Harnessed She-Camels
Syedna Abu Masood reports that a person brought a harnessed she-camel to the prophet and said: 'Accept this for *jihad*.' The prophet responded: 'On the Last Day, Allah will bless you with seven hundred harnessed she-camels in exchange for this one she-camel' (Muslim: *Kitab al-Amara*).

Spending In Allah's Path Is the Finest Sacrifice
Syedna Suban reports the prophet said: 'The greatest dinar that a man spends is that which he spends on his family and friends and what he spends on his travels in Allah's path and what he spends on his companions in Allah's path' (Muslim: *Kitab al-Zakat*).

جہادِ کشمیر میں پوری پاکستانی قوم شامل ہے بلکہ عالم اسلام بھی مختلف ذرائع سے شامل ہے۔ اسی لیے بیت اللہ شریف میں امام کعبہ" الشیخ عبداللہ بن سبیل نے کشمیر کا نام لے کر اس کی آزادی اور وہاں کے مسلمانوں کے حق میں دعا کی کہ جس میں شاہ فہد بھی شامل تھے۔......... الغرض عالم اسلام جہت نظیر جدت جلد از جلد آزادی کے لیے بیقرار ہے۔...... لشکر طیبہ بھی اس کی آزادی کے لیے عملی جہاد میں شامل ہے اور اپنا گرم خون پیش پیش کرنے میں پیش پیش ہے۔ اسی بناء پر پاکستانی قوم اس کے ساتھ جہاد فنڈ کے سلسلہ میں دل کھول کر عطیات اور فنڈ دیتی ہے۔......... یہ بات عالم کفر کو بہت ناپسند ہے کہ پاکستانی قوم اور دنیائے اسلام مجاہدین کی پشتیبانی کرے۔ اسی مقصد کے لیے وہ جہاد اور مجاہدین کے متعلق ہر وقت زہریلا پروپیگنڈا کرنے میں مصروف رہتے ہیں۔ زیر نظر تصویر بھی ہندوستانی ذرائع ابلاغ نے جاری کی ہے کہ دیکھو لوگ کس طرح دھڑا دھڑا لشکر طیبہ کو چندہ دے رہے ہیں اور پاکستان قوم کس ولولہ انگیز جذبات سے مجاہدین کو سپلائی لائن مہیا کر رہی ہے۔ ہندوستانی 'میگزین' اخبارات اور دیگر ذرائع ابلاغ نے لشکر کے خلاف پروپیگنڈے پر مبنی جہاد فنڈ کے اسٹالز کی ایسی تصاویر شائع کر کے اپنی قوم کو پیغام دیا ہے کہ تم بھی اپنے دفاع کے لیے کچھ کرو ورنہ یہ لوگ اگر اسی طرح جہاد کو مضبوط سے مضبوط کرتے رہے تو پھر کشمیر کے بعد پورا ہندوستان کشمیر ہی کی طرح مجاہدین کا ہدف ہو گا اور یوں ہندوستان کا وجود ختم ہو جائے گا اور اب امریکہ کے پیٹ میں بھی مروڑ اٹھ رہے ہیں اور ہمارے حکمران اس کی خواہش کو عملی جامہ پہنانے کے لیے جہاد فنڈ کو روکنے کے پیغامات جاری کر رہے ہیں۔

Picture 3. All of Pakistan is involved in the *jihad* in Kashmir; in fact, the entire Muslim world contributes in some form or another towards this struggle. The Imam of the Ka'ba in the House of Allah al-Sheikh Abdullah

God Punishes the Hoarder

Allah speaks of those who hoard their wealth instead of spending it on Him in the following words:

يَا أَيُّهَا الَّذِينَ آمَنُوا إِنَّ كَثِيرًا مِّنَ الْأَحْبَارِ وَالرُّهْبَانِ لَيَأْكُلُونَ أَمْوَالَ النَّاسِ بِالْبَاطِلِ وَيَصُدُّونَ عَن سَبِيلِ اللَّهِ وَالَّذِينَ يَكْنِزُونَ الذَّهَبَ وَالْفِضَّةَ وَلَا يُنفِقُونَهَا فِي سَبِيلِ اللَّهِ فَبَشِّرْهُم بِعَذَابٍ أَلِيمٍ

يَوْمَ يُحْمَى عَلَيْهَا فِي نَارِ جَهَنَّمَ فَتُكْوَى بِهَا جِبَاهُهُمْ وَجُنُوبُهُمْ وَظُهُورُهُمْ هَـٰذَا مَا كَنَزْتُمْ لِأَنفُسِكُمْ فَذُوقُوا مَا كُنتُمْ تَكْنِزُونَ

O ye, who believe! Lo! many of the (Jewish) rabbis and the (Christian) monks devour the wealth of mankind wantonly and debar (men) from the way of Allah. They who hoard up gold and silver and spend it not in the way of Allah, unto them give tidings (O Muhammad) of a painful doom. On the day when it will (all) be heated in the fire of hell, and their foreheads and their flanks and their backs will be branded therewith (and it will be said unto them): Here is that which ye hoarded for yourselves. Now taste of what ye used to hoard.

(9:34–35)

bin Sabeel specifically mentioned Kashmir in his prayer for the Muslims of the region; King Fahad was present at this momentous occasion... In short, the entire Muslim *ummat* is eager to see Kashmir, Heaven on Earth, liberated. *Lashkar-e-Tayyaba* is actively working towards Kashmir's liberation by sacrificing life and limb. The Pakistani people contribute generously to the *jihad* fund set up for this struggle... Disbelievers are irked by the fact that Pakistanis and Muslims world over support *mujahideen*, which is why there is a constant stream of propaganda against *mujahideen* and *jihad*. The picture above was printed in an Indian newspaper to show the people how generously Pakistanis contribute to *Lashkar-e-Tayyaba* and support its *mujahideen*. By running these images, Indian magazines, newspapers, and various other media send a clear message to the Indian people: contribute to your own defence as well for if these people continue to support the *jihad* so generously soon *mujahideen* will set their sights beyond Kashmir, at all of India, and soon there will be no India. Today, the USA has begun to worry about *mujahideen* as well; in order to appease it, our leaders are issuing warrants against contributing to the *jihad* fund.

Source: Muhammad Tahir Naqqash, *Ghaziyan-i-Saf-Shikan*, p. 581.

586 THE LITERATURE OF *LASHKAR-E-TAYYABA*

هَاأَنتُمْ هَؤُلَاءِ تُدعَونَ لِتُنفِقُوا فِي سَبِيلِ اللَّه فَمِنكُم مَّن يَبخَلُ وَمَن يَبخَلُ فَإِنَّمَا يَبخَلُ عَن نَفسِهِ وَاللَّه الغَنِيُّ وَأَنتُمُ الفُقَرَاءُ وَإِن تَتَوَلَّوا يَستَبدِلُ قَومًا غَيرَكُم ثُمَّ لَا يَكُونُوا أَمثَالَكُم

Lo! ye are those who are called to spend in the way of Allah, yet among you there are some who hoard. And as for him who hoardeth, he hoardeth only from his soul. And Allah is the Rich, and ye are the poor. And if ye turn away He will exchange you for some other folk, and they will not be the likes of you.

(47:38)

وَأَنفِقُوا فِي سَبِيلِ اللَّه وَلَا تُلقُوا بِأَيدِيكُم إِلَى التَّهلُكَةِ وَأَحسِنُوا إِنَّ اللَّه يُحِبُّ المُحسِنِينَ

Spend your wealth for the cause of Allah, and be not cast by your own hands to ruin; and do good. Lo! Allah loveth the beneficent.

(2:195)

What Does It Mean To 'Be Not Cast By Your Own Hands to Ruin'?

Few people are familiar with the exegesis on وَأَنفِقُوا فِي سَبِيلِ اللَّه وَلَا تُلقُوا بِأَيدِيكُم إِلَى التَّهلُكَةِ; brothers who are constantly preoccupied with worldly affairs and driven solely by profit should listen carefully:

Syedna Abu Ayub Ansari reports: The verse وَلَا تُلقُوا بِأَيدِيكُم إِلَى التَّهلُكَةِ was revealed regarding us, the Ansar. Once Allah blessed the prophet with victory and made Islam dominant, we asked the prophet (since we were done waging *jihad*) if we could return to our businesses and get them running again. In response, Allah revealed: 'Spend your wealth for the cause of Allah, and be not cast by your own hands to ruin.' '... be not cast by your own hands to ruin' meant we should not allow ourselves to be consumed by making money at the expense of *jihad*.

(Abu Dawood: *Kitab al-Jihad*)

The Commandment Against Hoarding

Syedna Jabir reports the prophet said: 'Save yourself from oppressing, for on the Last Day oppression will form layers of darkness; save yourself from hoarding for hoarding was the end of nations before you; (due to hoarding) they spilled innocent blood and made legal what was prohibited' (Muslim: *Kitab al-Bar wa Salat Raqm, 2578*).

The One Who Spends Quietly Will Be in the Shade of His Lord
Syedna Abu Huraira reports the prophet said: there are seven men who will be given shade by Allah on the day when there will be no shade to be found. 1) A just leader. 2) A young person who was raised to worship Allah. 3) He whose heart is in the mosque. 4) Two men who love one another merely for Allah's pleasure, who meet and part for Allah's pleasure. 5) A man who thwarts the advances of a powerful and beautiful woman by saying, 'I fear Allah!' 6) A man who spent in the way of Allah so covertly that his right hand remained unaware of what his left hand distributed. 7) A man who remembered Allah in solitude and wept (Muslim: *Kitab al-Zakat*).[8]

Angels Pray for Those Who Spend
Syedna Abu Huraira reports the prophet said: 'There is not a single day that goes by without two angels descending to earth with one angel praying, "Oh Allah! Reward the ones who spend in your path," while the other prays, 'Oh Allah! Confiscate the wealth of the miser"' (Muslim: *Kitab al-Zakat*; Bukhari: *Kitab al-Zakat*).

A Little Spending Can Free You from Hell
Syedna Adi bin Hatim reports the prophet said: 'Save yourself from fire! Even if all you can sacrifice is half a date' (Bukhari: *Kitab al-Zakat*).

Reward for Guidance
Syedan Abu Masood Ansari reports that once a man came before the prophet and said: 'I have lost my ride (horse, camel), give me a ride that I may join the *jihad*.' The prophet said: 'I do not have a ride.' Another man said: 'Oh Prophet! I know of a person who can give this person a ride.' The prophet said: 'Anyone who guides another towards good will receive as much reward as the person doing the good deed' (Muslim: *Kitab al-Amara*).

Money Best Spent
Syedna Thuban reports the prophet said: 'Your money is best spent on family and friends, and horses and people (*mujahideen*) waging *jihad* in Allah's path' (Muslim: *Kitab al-Zakat*).

588 THE LITERATURE OF *LASHKAR-E-TAYYABA*

Double Reward for Spending in Allah's Path

Syedna Abdullah bin Amr reports the prophet said:

> He who sets out to wage *jihad* will be rewarded for *jihad* and he who sponsors another person's *jihad* will be rewarded for spending on *jihad* and will also be rewarded for the *jihad* of the person being sponsored.
>
> (Abu Dawood: *Kitab al-Jihad*)

Allah-has-willed-it! Imagine being rewarded for *jihad* as well as being rewarded for spending of one's wealth.

Prosperity Awaits

While wealth is both a test and a trial for humans, it can also be a source of prosperity. For example, if a wealthy man spends on things like televisions, video players, dish antennae, and various other profanities prohibited by Allah then no doubt, his wealth will be his doom, but should he spend it on good then his wealth will be a source of reward and salvation.

There are so many among us, who are blessed with immeasurable wealth by Allah, yet they are deprived of the esteemed status of a *mujahid*; on the other hand, unknown men from remote villages who have little to no wealth or land manage to attain the glorious heights of martyrdom. There are those who desperately wish to join the *jihad* but are unable to do so because of their financial and social responsibilities; for them the prophet has offered a solution.

Hear this solution issued directly from the prophet's mouth, and realize the blessings and benefits Allah is so eager to bestow:

The Sponsor's Reward

Abu Saeed Khadri reports the prophet sent the following message to Banu-l-Hiyan: 'Send one of every two men for *jihad*; the reward will be distributed equally between them' (Muslim: *Kitab al-Imara*).

Mujahid's Reward Is Not Reduced

Syedna Zayd bin Khalid Aljhani reports the prophet said: 'He who prepares a warrior for *jihad*, it is as if he himself waged *jihad*, and he who looked after the family of a warrior waging *jihad*, it is as if he himself waged *jihad*' (Bukhari: *Kitab al-Jihad*; Muslim: *Kitab al-Imara*).

NOBLE WARRIORS AND BATTLEFRONTS **589**

Syedna Zayd bin Khalid Aljhani reports the prophet said: 'He who gives *iftari* (provisions to end a fast) to one who fasts will be rewarded as much as the one who fasts without reducing the reward of the one who was fasting, and he who prepared a *mujahid* for *jihad* in Allah's path will be rewarded as much as the *mujahid* without any reduction in the *mujahid*'s reward' (Tirmidhi: *Abwab al-Siyam*).

He Who Cannot Wage *Jihad*

Syed Anas bin Malik reports that once, a young man from the Aslam tribe came to the prophet and said: 'Oh prophet of Allah! I want to join the *jihad*, but I do not have enough resources.' The prophet said: 'Go to this other person who had completed his preparations for *jihad* but fell ill.' The young man went to the ill person and said: 'The prophet sends his greetings and suggests you give me all that you have prepared for *jihad*.' The sick man called his wife and said: 'Give this man all that I had put together for *jihad*. Make sure you don't hold back anything for whatever you hold back will be of no benefit to us' (Muslim: *Kitab al-Imara*).

Assisting a Warrior in Difficult Times

Syedna Sahl bin Hanif reports the prophet said: 'He who assists a *mujahid* fighting in Allah's path or assisted in freeing schools will be given shade by Allah on the day there will be no shade' (Masnad Ahmad 3:487, Ibn Abi Shayba, *Kitab al-Jihad* 5:351).

A Remarkable Display of Cooperation with the Household of a *Mujahid*

Syedna Zayd bin Aslam's father reports: I went to the marketplace with Emir-ul-Mu'minin Syedna Umar. There, we encountered a young woman. She said: 'Oh Emir-ul-Mu'minin! My husband has died and left behind two young children. By Allah! I even afford to cook them goat's hooves. They have neither land nor milk-giving cattle. I fear they might starve to death. I am Khaffaf bin Aima Ghaffari's daughter. My father was with the prophet during Hudaybiyyah.' The moment Syedna Umar heard these words he stopped dead in his tracks. He said, 'Welcome! Your family is close to us.' He proceeded to load two heavy bags of grain on a powerful camel along with other basic necessities and clothes, and as he handed the woman the reins, he said, 'Take it; before this finishes Allah will provide more, and better' (meaning, she would have a share in the impending war

لشکر کا ایک صف شکن فدائی....... انڈین آرمی کیمپ کے پرخچے اڑانے اور اس کو ملیا میٹ کرنے کے بعد...... اس کے ملبے کو اپنے پاؤں سے روندتے ہوئے..... آگے بڑھ رہا ہے...... جبکہ آگ کے ساتھ ساتھ دھوئیں کے بادل...... چھائے ہوئے ہیں...... اور ہندو ظالم زندہ فوجیوں نے چیخوں سے آسمان سر پر اٹھا رکھا ہے۔

Picture 4. A *Lashkar-e-Tayyaba fidayeen* demolishing enemy lines... after obliterating an Indian military camp... walking over its rubble... moving forward... thick clouds of smoke gather overhead... the tortured shrieks of surviving Hindu soldiers... rise into the sky...,

Source: Muhammad Tahir Naqqash, *Ghaziyan-i-Saf-Shikan*, p. 591.

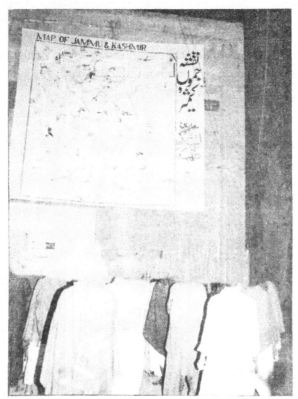

Picture 5. Resolutions will not free Kashmir until Hindus are sorted.
Source: Muhammad Tahir Naqqash, *Ghaziyan-i-Saf-Shikan*, p. 592.

booty). Someone said: 'Oh Emir-ul-Mu'minin! You gave this woman too much.' This angered Syedna Umar greatly and he said: 'May your mother find you lost! By Allah! I saw this woman's father and brother lay siege to a fort belonging to infidels until the fort was conquered. In the morning we helped ourselves to the wealth of the fort they had sacked' (Sahih Bukhari, *Kitab-al-Maghazi*, Ghazwa Hudaybiyyah).

Notes

Notes on Transliteration and Translation

1. Nor do we use the expression 'Peace Be Upon Him (PBUH)' after the mention of the Prophet Muhammad (or its Arabic variant *ṣallā Allāhu 'alayhi wa-ala ālihi wa-sallam* (abbreviated as SAWS) or its calligraphic equivalent ( ), as is the custom of Muslim writers. This is not intended to offend Muslim readers; rather, I find the use of such expressions to be inappropriate in a book authored by a non-believer.

Acknowledgements

1. C. Christine Fair, *In Their Own Words: Understanding Lashkar-e-Tayyaba* (London: Hurst, 2018).

Chapter 1

1. PTI News Agency, 'Pakistan Supported, Trained Terror Groups: Musharraf', *The Hindu*, 2 September 2016, https://www.thehindu.com/news/international/south-asia/Pakistan-supported-trained-terror-groups-like-Lashkar-e-Taiba-Pervez-Musharraf/article60516617.ece; and News Desk, 'Pervez Musharraf u-turn: ISI Trains Lashkar-e-Taiba, Jaish-e-Mohammed, Says Former Pakistan President Ex-Army Chief General Parvez Musharraf Admitted that ISI Trains LeT and JeM Terrorist and Encourages Terrorism Against India', *India Today*, 16 February 2016, https://www.india.com/news/india/pervez-musharraf-u-turn-isi-trains-lashkar-e-taiba-jaish-e-mohammed-says-former-pakistan-president-939367/.
2. Notable exceptions include C. Christine Fair, *In Their Own Words: Understanding Lashkar-e-Tayyaba* (London: Hurst, 2018); C. Christine Fair, 'Lashkar-e-Tayiba and the Pakistani State', *Survival* 53 (August 2011): 1–23; Mariam Abou Zahab, 'I Shall be Waiting at the Door of Paradise: The Pakistani Martyrs of the Lashkar-e-Taiba (Army of the Pure)', in *The Practice of War: Production, Reproduction and Communication of Armed Violence*, ed. Aparna Rao, Michael Bollig, and Monika Böck (New York: Berghahn Books, 2007), 133–158; and Samina Yasmeen, *Jihad and Dawah: Evolving Narratives of Lashkar-e-Taiba and Jamat ud Dawah* (London: Hurst, 2017).

594 NOTES

3. This section draws from C. Christine Fair. *In Their Own Words: Understanding the Lashkar-e-Tayyaba* (New York: Oxford University Press, 2019): 4–16.
4. See Yoginder Sikand, 'The Islamist Militancy in Kashmir: The Case of the Lashkar-e-Taiba', in *The Practice of War: Production, Reproduction and Communication of Armed Violence*, ed. Aparna Rao et al. (New York: Berghahn Books, 2007), 215–238; Abou Zahab, 'I Shall be Waiting at the Door of Paradise'; Saeed Shafqat, 'From Official Islam to Islamism: The Rise of Dawat-ul-Irshad and Lashkar-e-Taiba', *Pakistan: Nationalism Without a Nation*, ed. Christophe Jaffrelot (London: Zed Books, 2002), 131–147; and Zaigham Khan, 'Allah's Army', *The Herald Annual*, January 1998, 123–130.
5. See C. Christine Fair, *The Counterterror Coalitions: Cooperation with Pakistan and India* (Santa Monica, CA: RAND, 2004); and Peter Chalk and C. Christine Fair, 'Lashkar-e-Tayyiba Leads the Kashmiri Insurgency', *Jane's Intelligence Review* 14, no. 10 (December 2002): 1–5.
6. Stephen Tankel, 'Lashkar-e-Taiba: Past Operations and Future Prospects', *New America Foundation*, National Security Studies Program Policy Paper, April 2011.
7. US Embassy, 'US Embassy Cables: Lashkar-e-Taiba Terrorists Raise Funds in Saudi Arabia', *The Guardian*, 10 August 2009. https://www.theguardian.com/world/us-embassy-cables-documents/220186.
8. See US Department of Treasury, 'Recent OFAC Actions', 27 April 2006. https://www.treasury.gov/resource-centre/sanctions/OFAC-Enforcement/Pages/20060427.aspx.
9. US Department of State, 'Addition of Aliases Jamaat-Ud-Dawa and Idara Khidmat-E-Khalq to the Specially Designated Global Terrorist Designation of Lashkhar-E-Tayyiba', 28 April 2006. https://2001-2009.state.gov/r/pa/prs/ps/2006/65401.htm.
10. See US Department of State, 'Secretary of State's Terrorist Designation of Falah-i-Insaniat Foundation', 24 November 2010. https://www.state.gov/j/ct/rls/other/des/266648.htm; and United Nations, 'Security Council Al-Qaida Sanctions Committee Adds Four Names to Its Sanctions List, Amends One Entry', 14 March 2012, http://www.un.org/press/en/2012/sc10578.doc.htm.
11. C. Christine Fair and Ali Hamza, 'The Foreign Policy Essay: Whether or Not Pakistan Will Join the War in Yemen May Depend on a Group You've Probably Never Heard Of', *Lawfare*, 12 April, 2015. https://www.lawfareblog.com/foreign-policy-essay-whether-or-not-pakistan-will-join-war-yemen-may-depend-group-youve-probably.
12. Stephen Tankel, *Storming the World Stage: The Story of Lashkar-e-Taiba* (London: Hurst, 2011).
13. PTI News Agency, 'Hafiz Saeed's JuD Launches Political Party in Pakistan', *The Quint*, 8 August, 2017. https://www.thequint.com/news/hafiz-saaed-jud-launches-political-party.
14. C. Christine Fair, 'The Only Enemy Pakistan's Army Can Beat Is Its Own Democracy', *Foreign Policy*, 9 August, 2017. http://foreignpolicy.com/2017/08/09/the-only-enemy-pakistans-army-can-beat-is-its-own-democracy/.

NOTES 595

15. Web Desk, 'A-120 By-Polls: JUD Fields Candidate', *The Nation*, 13 August 2017. http://nation.com.pk/national/13-Aug-2017/na-120-by-polls-jud-fields-candidate.

16. Shahid Kunwar Khuldune, 'A Win for All: Pakistan's NA-120 By-Election', *The Diplomat*, 21 September, 2017. https://thediplomat.com/2017/09/a-win-for-all-pakistans-na-120-by-election/.

17. Maria Abi-Habib and Salman Masood, 'Military's Influence Casts a Shadow Over Pakistan's Election', *The New York Times*, 21 July 2018. https://www.nytimes.com/2018/07/21/world/asia/pakistan-election-military.html.

18. C. Christine Fair. *In Their Own Words: Understanding the Lashkar-e-Tayyaba* (New York: Oxford University Press, 2019): 19–17.

19. 'About', *Online Computer Library Center*, Dublin, Ohio. https://www.oclc.org/en/about.html

20. Regrettably, Ms. Vega even ate one of them. There is no accounting for taste.

21. US intelligence official who must remained unnamed for reasons of the obvious.

22. Fair, *In Their Own Words*.

23. Abdussalam Bin Muhammad, *Hum Jihad Kyon Kar Rahen Hain* [*Why Are We Waging Jihad?*], trans. C. Christine Fair and Safina Ustaad (Lahore: Dar-ul-Andlus, 2004), 15.

24. Ubaidurrahman Muhammadi, *Difa-i-Jihad* [*Defence of Jihad*], trans. Safina Ustaad (Lahore: Dar-ul-Andlus, 2003), 34. This is nothing but a lame attempt to excuse oneself from the kind of *jihad* waged by the prophet, in which your friends attain martyrdom all around you. Critics demoralize those who wish to follow the prophet's *Sunnat*. We ask those who seek the truth to compare the lives of those who ramble against *jihad* to the lives of those *mujahideen* who have dedicated themselves to this struggle; visit the training camps and assess the curriculum; observe the way these young warriors live; see how they spend their days and how they manifest their dedication; meet the ones who have spent years camped out in Kashmir. Then, decide for yourself which path you would rather take.

25. Muhammadi, *Difa-i-Jihad*, 25: Today, Muslims are obligated to proselytize and wage *jihad* simultaneously. Let's take a cursory look at some successes in the prophet's life. There was a time when the infidels of Mecca considered the prophet too weak to be paid any mind. When they forced the prophet to migrate, he left Mecca for Medina where he launched proselytizing and *jihadi* missions to the four corners of the world in service of the true faith. Within a mere decade, Mecca was conquered, after which followed a series of military triumphs. The prophet personally led twenty-seven military expeditions... he bore battle scars on his body... his companions wrote the history of Islam with their blood. Allah blessed the companions' sacrifices in war and made Muslims victorious; in a short duration, the banner of Islam waved over a large portion of the world. This brief sketch reveals that *jihad* was the solution then, and it is the only solution now.

26. Bin Muhammad, '*Hum Jihad Kyon Kar Rahen Hain*' 12.

596 NOTES

27. Bin Muhammad, '*Hum Jihad Kyon Kar Rahen Hain*' 15 and 43; and Muhammadi, *Difa-i-Jihad*, 13–14.
28. Naved Qamar, *Mujahid ki Azaan* (Lahore: Dar-ul-Andlus, 2001), 72.
29. Qamar, *Mujahid ki Azaan*, 11.
30. Umm-e-Hammad, *Hum Mayen Lashkar-e-Tayyaba Ki* [*We, the Mothers of Lashkar-e-Tayyaba*], Vols 1–3 (Lahore: Dar-ul-Andlus, 1998), 17.
31. Umm-e-Hammad, *Hum Mayen Lashkar-e-Tayyaba Ki*, 19.
32. Umm-e-Hammad, *Hum Mayen Lashkar-e-Tayyaba Ki*, 2 and 38–39.
33. Arif Jamal, 'Analyzing the Role of the Top LeT Ideologue: A Profile of Amir Hamza', *Jamestown Militant Leadership Monitor* 3, no. 6 (June 2012): 6–7. https://jamestown.org/wp-content/uploads/2012/06/Militant_Leadership_Monit or_-_Volume_III__Issue_6.pdf. Also see Anon., 'Taseer Killer's Case Should be Decided as per Shariah Law: JuD', *The Indian Express*, 7 January 2011. https://indianexpress.com/article/news-archive/print/taseer-killers-case-should-be-deci ded-as-per-shariah-law-jud/.
34. Abul Hassan Mubbashir Ahmed Rabbani, *Masalah-yi takfir aur is ke usul o zavabit* (*The Problem of* Takfir *and its Principles and Regulations*), trans. Safina Ustaad (Lahore: Dar-ul-Andlus, 2015), 15.
35. Ali Imran Shaheen, *Kashmir Manzil Dur Nahin* [*Destination Kashmir is Nigh*] (Lahore: Dar-ul-Andlus, 2011).
36. Muhammad Tahir Naqqash, *Ghaziyan-i-Saf-Shikan* [*Of Noble Warriors Demolishing Enemy Lines*: Jihadi *Tales of* fidayeen *Missions from Delhi's Red Fort to Srinagar's Airport*] (Lahore: Dar-ul-Andlus, 2001).
37. Jamal, 'Analyzing the Role of the Top LeT Ideologue'. Also see Anon., 'Taseer Killer's Case Should be Decided as per Shariah Law: JuD'.
38. Bin Muhammad, '*Hum Jihad Kyon Kar Rahen Hain*' titles include: 'Jihad with Assistance of Polytheists' and 'The Prophet Sought Help from Polytheists', 39–42.
39. Naqqash, *Ghaziyan-i-Saf-Shikan*, 475.
40. Naqqash, *Ghaziyan-i-Saf-Shikan*, 491.
41. Tariq bin Ziyad was the general who conquered Gibraltar in 711 for the Umayyad caliph Al-Walid I.
42. Naqqash, *Ghaziyan-i-Saf-Shikan*, 25
43. Naqqash, *Ghaziyan-i-Saf-Shikan*, 567 and 570.

Chapter 2

1. This section draws from and compresses Chapter 4 of C. Christine Fair, *In Their Own Words: Understanding the Lashkar-e-Tayyaba* (London: Hurst, 2018), with permission from Hurst.
2. It is impossible to adjudicate which version—if any—of this history is accurate given that these studies tend to rely upon interviews with militants and Pakistani

NOTES   597

officials who may not be truthful and/or who may remember events incorrectly. Indeed, scholars who have interviewed LeT militants find that they often disagree with one another on key dates, pivotal events, and even on the important personalities involved in the group's history and operations. Pakistani officials, moreover, have their own incentive to dissemble the role of the state in supporting the organization. See Yoginder Sikand, 'The Islamist Militancy in Kashmir: The Case of the Lashkar-e-Taiba', in *The Practice of War: Production, Reproduction and Communication of Armed Violence*, ed. Aparna Rao, Michael Bollig, and Monika Böck (New York: Berghahn Books, 2007), 215–238; Mariam Abou Zahab, 'I Shall be Waiting at the Door of Paradise: The Pakistani Martyrs of the Lashkar-e-Taiba (Army of the Pure)', in *The Practice of War: Production, Reproduction and Communication of Armed Violence*, ed. Aparna Rao, Michael Bollig, and Monika Böck (New York: Berghahn Books, 2007), 133–158; Saeed Shafqat, 'From Official Islam to Islamism: The Rise of Dawat-ul-Irshad and Lashkar-e-Taiba', *Pakistan: Nationalism without a Nation*, ed. Christophe Jaffrelot (London: Zed Books, 2002), 131–147; and Zaigham Khan, 'Allah's Army', *The Herald Annual*, January 1998, 123–130.

3. In Pakistan there are five major sectarian traditions, referred to as *maslak* (school of Islamic thought, which derives from the Arabic *salaka*, which means 'to walk' or 'to walk on a path'): four are Sunni and include Barelvi, Deobandi, *Ahl-e-Hadees*, and *Jamaat-e-Islami* (JI); and the fifth is Shi'a, which also includes several distinct traditions. Most Sunnis in Pakistan follow the Hanafi school of Islamic jurisprudence (*fiqh*). For example, even though Deobandis and Barelvis have many differences, they are both Hanafi. *Ahl-e-Hadees* rejects all *fiqh* and self-identify as *ghair-muqallid* (those who do not follow *taqlid*, which is guidance that has been historically given). *Ahl-e-Hadees* proponents see the various schools of jurisprudence as being tantamount to personality cults surrounding their various founders. As such, they are even more zealous than Deobandis in establishing a singular standard of piety and behaviour, and even more unrelenting in extirpating the various customary practices that they understand to be *bid'at*. *Bid'at* literally translates as innovation, but it carries the valence that it is heretical and displeasing to Allah. They also propound a rigorous doctrine of the oneness of god (*tawheed*). *Ahl-e-Hadees* followers are frequently confused with Wahhabis; however, Wahhabis follow the Hanbali school of jurisprudence. See Mariam Abou Zahab, 'Salafism in Pakistan: The Ahl-e-Hadees Movement', in *Global Salafism: Islam's New Religious Movement*, ed. Roel Meijer (London: Hurst, 2009), 126–139; and Barbara Metcalf, *Islamic Contestations: Essays on Muslims in India and Pakistan* (New Delhi: Oxford University Press, 2004).

4. The Geneva Accord which brought the conflict to a close was signed in 1988. See Stephen Tankel, *Storming the World Stage: The Story of Lashkar-e-Tayyaba* (New York: Oxford University Press, 2011); and Stephen Tankel, 'Lashkar-e-Taiba: Past Operations and Future Prospects', *New America Foundation*, National Security Studies Program Policy Paper, 27 April 2011.

598 NOTES

5. In total, about seventeen persons helped found the MDI, one of whom was Abdullah Azzam, an associate of Osama Bin Laden who was affiliated with the Islamic University of Islamabad and the *Maktab ul Khadamat* (Bureau of Services for Arab *mujahideen*). Azzam was killed in a bomb blast in 1989 in Peshawar. See Khan, 'Allah's Army'. Yasmeen's timeline is somewhat different. She says that linkages between JuD and Lakhvi's militia happened in 1995. See Samina Yasmeen, *Jihad and Dawah: Evolving Narratives of Lashkar-e-Taiba and Jamat ud Dawah* (London: Hurst, 2017).

6. See Sikand, 'The Islamist Militancy in Kashmir'; and Abou Zahab, 'I Shall be Waiting at the Door of Paradise'; and Shafqat, 'From Official Islam to Islamism'.

7. As noted above, Wahhabis follow the Hanbali school of *fiqh*, and the latter reject *fiqh* altogether. See note 2.

8. Tankel, 'Lashkar-e-Taiba'.

9. Khan, 'Allah's Army'. There are various unconfirmed rumours that bin Laden contributed 10 million Pakistani rupees to help build the mosque and residential area at the *Markaz*. There are also rumours that, until 1992, when he was ostensibly 'banned' from travelling or staying in Pakistan, bin Laden regularly attended rallies at the *Markaz*. See Yosri Fouda and Nick Fielding, *Capture or Kill: The Pursuit of the 9/11 Masterminds and the Killing of Osama bin Laden* (New York: Arcade Publishing, 2012); and Wilson John, *Caliphate's Soldiers: The Lashkar-e-Tayyaba's Long War* (New Delhi: Amaryllis and the ORF, 2011.

10. Azmat Abbas, 'In God We Trust', *The Herald (Pakistan)* (January 2002): 45–49.

11. See Tankel, *Storming the World Stage*, which says that this happened in 1990; and the other sources which suggest it happened later in 1993: PTI News Agency, 'Hafiz Saeed Asks Govt to Curb Foreign Bid to Bolster IS in Pakistan', *Indian Express*, 17 October 2015. http://indianexpress.com/article/world/world-news/hafiz-saeed-asks-govt-to-curb-foreign-bid-to-bolster-is-in-pakistan/; Sikand, 'The Islamist Militancy in Kashmir'; Abou Zahab, 'I Shall be Waiting at the Door of Paradise', 'Salafism in Pakistan'; and Shafqat, 'From Official Islam to Islamism'.

12. Tankel, 'Lashkar-e-Taiba'.

13. Cited in Tankel, *Storming the World Stage*.

14. See Tankel, *Storming the World Stage* and 'Lashkar-e-Taiba'; and Cathy Scott-Clark and Adrian Levy, *The Siege: 68 Hours Inside the Taj Hotel* (New York: Penguin, 2013).

15. V.S. Subrahmanian, Aaron Mannes, Amy Sliva, Jana Shakarian, and John P. Dickerson, 'A Brief History of LeT', in *Computational Analysis of Terrorist Groups: Lashkar-e-Taiba* (New York: Springer, 2013), 23–68.

16. Emir Rana Muhammad, *The A to Z of Jehadi Organizations in Pakistan* (Lahore: Mashal Books, 2004).

17. Tankel, *Storming the World Stage*, 116.

18. Tankel, *Storming the World Stage*, 116.

NOTES 599

19. See Tankel, *Storming the World Stage*; and Sean Noonan and Scott Steward, 'The Evolution of a Pakistani Militant Network', *Stratfor*, 15 September 2011. https://www.stratfor.com/weekly/evolution-pakistani-militant-network.
20. Tankel, *Storming the World Stage*.
21. Author work with the UN Assistance Mission to Afghanistan from June to October 2007.
22. C. Christine Fair and Peter Chalk, *Fortifying Pakistan: The Role of US Internal Security Assistance* (Washington, DC: United States Institute of Peace, 2006).
23. See C. Christine Fair, 'India and Iran: New Delhi's Balancing Act', *The Washington Quarterly* 30 (Summer 2007): 145–159; and Tankel, *Storming the World Stage*.
24. Author work in Afghanistan in 2007 with the UN Assistance Mission to Afghanistan; see also American Foreign Policy Council, 'Lashkar-e-Taiba'; Tankel, *Storming the World Stage*; Brulliard, 'Afghan Intelligence Ties Pakistani Group Lashkar-i-Taiba to Recent Kabul Attack'; and Swami, 'Kabul Attack'.
25. Scott-Clark and Levy, *The Siege*, 52.
26. Manjeet Pardesi, 'The Battle for the Soul of Pakistan at Islamabad's Red Mosque', in *Treading on Hallowed Ground: Counterinsurgency Operations in Sacred Spaces*, ed. C. Christine Fair and Sumit Ganguly (New York: Oxford University Press, 2008), 88–116.
27. Subrahmanian et al., 'A Brief History of LeT'.
28. PTI News Agency, '2008 Indian Embassy Attack in Kabul Sanctioned by ISI, New Book Claims', *The Times of India*, 23 March 2014. http://timesofindia.indiatimes.com/india/2008-Indian-embassy-attack-in-Kabul-sanctioned-by-ISI-new-book-claims/articleshow/32545791.cms.
29. Mark Mazzetti, 'A Shooting in Pakistan Reveals Fraying Alliance', *The New York Times*, 12 March 2011. http://www.nytimes.com/2011/03/13/weekinreview/13lashkar.html.
30. PTI News Agency, 'LeT Responsible for Attack at Indian Consulate in Herat: US', *The Times of India*, 25 June 2014. http://timesofindia.indiatimes.com/world/us/LeT-responsible-for-attack-at-Indian-consulate-in-Herat-US/articleshow/37205339.cms. See also American Foreign Policy Council, 'Lashkar-e-Taiba', in *The World Almanac of Islamism* (Lanham, MD: Rowman and Littlefield, 2011); andTankel, *Storming the World Stage*; and Karin Brulliard, 'Afghan Intelligence Ties Pakistani Group Lashkar-i-Taiba to Recent Kabul Attack', *The Washington Post*, 3 March 2010. http://www.washingtonpost.com/wp-dyn/content/article/2010/03/02/AR2010030202427.html; and Praveen Swami, 'Kabul Attack: US Warning Was Accurate', *The Hindu*, 3 August 2008. http://www.thehindu.com/todays-paper/Kabul-attack-US-warning-was-accurate/article15271791.ece.
31. Sebastian Rotella, 'Four Disturbing Questions About the Mumbai Terror Attack', *ProPublica*, 22 February 2013. https://www.propublica.org/article/four-disturbing-questions-about-the-mumbai-terror-attack.
32. Sebastian Rotella, 'Mumbai Case Offers Rare Picture of Ties Between Pakistan's Intelligence Service, Militants', *ProPublica*, 2 May 2011. https://www.propublica.

600   NOTES

org/article/mumbai-case-offers-rare-picture-of-ties-between-pakistans-intel
ligence-serv.

33. Scott-Clark and Levy, *The Siege*.

34. Scott-Clark and Levy, *The Siege*.

35. Sebastian Rotella, 'Four Alleged Masterminds of 2008 Mumbai Attacks Are
    Indicted in Chicago', *ProPublica*, 25 April 2011. https://www.propublica.org/arti
    cle/four-alleged-masterminds-of-2008-mumbai-attacks-are-indicted-in-chicago.

36. Scott-Clark and Levy, *The Siege*.

37. Scott-Clark and Levy, *The Siege*.

38. Bruce Riedel, 'Al Qaeda 3.0: Terrorism's Emergent New Power Bases', *Brookings
    Institution*, 3 December 2012. https://www.brookings.edu/opinions/al-qaeda-3-
    0-terrorisms-emergent-new-power-bases/.

39. See Fair, C. Christine, *The Counterterror Coalitions: Cooperation with Pakistan
    and India* (Santa Monica, CA: RAND, 2004); and Peter Chalk, and C. Christine
    Fair, 'Lashkar-e-Tayyiba Leads the Kashmiri Insurgency', *Jane's Intelligence
    Review* 14, no. 10 (December 2002): 1–5.

40. See US Department of Treasury, 'Recent OFAC Actions', 27 April 2006. https://
    www.treasury.gov/resource-centre/sanctions/OFAC-Enforcement/Pages/20060
    427.aspx.

41. Author's field work, December/January 2004.

42. US Department of State, 'Addition of Aliases Jamaat-Ud-Dawa and Idara
    Khidmat-E-Khalq to the Specially Designated Global Terrorist Designation of
    Lashkhar-E-Tayyiba', April 28, 2006. https://2001-2009.state.gov/r/pa/prs/ps/
    2006/65401.htm.

43. See US Department of State, 'Secretary of State's Terrorist Designation of Falah-
    i-Insaniat Foundation', 24 November 2010. https://www.state.gov/j/ct/rls/other/
    des/266648.htm; and United Nations, 'Security Council Al-Qaida Sanctions
    Committee Adds Four Names to Its Sanctions List, Amends One Entry', 14 March
    2012. http://www.un.org/press/en/2012/sc10578.doc.htm.

44. C. Christine Fair and Ali Hamza, 'The Foreign Policy Essay: Whether or Not
    Pakistan Will Join the War in Yemen May Depend on a Group You've Probably
    Never Heard Of', *Lawfare*, 12 April, 2015. https://www.lawfareblog.com/fore
    ign-policy-essay-whether-or-not-pakistan-will-join-war-yemen-may-depend-
    group-youve-probably.

45. Lakhvi, in particular, was perturbed by Saeed's blatant nepotism in making these
    appointments because he believed that he was being sidelined in the organiza-
    tion. Given that Lakhvi was a foundational member of MDI as well as the founder
    of the militant group that combined with JuD to form MDI, these developments
    were intolerable. Lakhvi briefly parted ways with Saeed and formed the *Khairun
    Nas* ('Good People', a reference to the so-called companions of the prophet).
    Tankel, *Storming the World Stage*.

NOTES 601

46. PTI News Agency, 'Hafiz Saeed's JuD Launches Political Party in Pakistan', *The Quint*, 8 August 2017. https://www.thequint.com/news/hafiz-saaed-jud-launc hes-political-party.

47. Kunwar Khuldune Shahid, 'India Dictating Terms to Pakistan' Claims Jamaat ud Dawa', *Asia Times*, 24 November 2017. http://www.atimes.com/article/india-dictating-terms-pakistan-claims-jamaaat-ud-dawa/.

48. 'Hafiz Saeed's JuD to Contest 2018 Pakistan General Elections', *Economic Times*, 3 December 2018. https://m.economictimes.com/news/international/world-news/hafiz-saeed-to-contest-pakistan-general-elections-next-year/amp_articles how/61897257.cms.

49. Susannah George and Shaiq Hussain, 'Pakistan Hopes Its Steps to "Eradicate" Terrorism will Keep It Off a Global Blacklist', *Washington Post*, 20 February 2020. https://www.washingtonpost.com/world/asia_pacific/pakistan-fatf-terrorism-blacklist/2020/02/20/df67602c-51e4-11ea-80ce-37a8d4266c09_story.html; International Monetary Fund, 'IMF Executive Board Completes the First Review of Pakistan's Extended Fund Facility', *Press Release* 19, no. 447, 19 December 2019. https://www.imf.org/en/News/Articles/2019/12/19/pr19477-pakistan-imf-execut ive-board-completes-review-of-pakistans-extended-fund-facility; and Rezaul H. Laskar, 'Pak Gets 4 More Months to Deliver on Terror Financing Watchdog FATF Plan', *The Hindustan Times*, 29 April 2020. https://www.hindustantimes.com/world-news/amid-covid-19-crisis-pakistan-gets-4-more-months-to-implement-terror-funding-watchdog-fatf-s-action-plan/story-bC4OsMf7oduz821RSmG 1rO.html .

50. Laskar, 'Pak Gets 4 More Months to Deliver on Terror Financing Watchdog FATF Plan'.

51. Husain Haqqani, 'FATF's Grey List Suits Pakistan's Jihadi Ambitions. It Only Worries Entering the Black List', *The Print*, 28 February 2020. https://theprint.in/opinion/fatfs-grey-list-suits-pakistans-jihadi-ambitions-it-only-worries-enter ing-the-black-list/372524/.

52. Leshon Wani and Sidhant Sibal, 'New Name, Same Terror Group: LeT Becomes TRF to Save Pak from FATF Axe', *DNAIndia*, 29 April 2020. https://www.dnain dia.com/world/report-new-name-same-terror-group-let-becomes-trf-to-save-pak-from-fatf-axe-2823051.

53. Gibran Naiyyar Peshimam, 'Pakistan taken off global watchdog's "grey" list for terrorism financing', Reuters.com, 21 October 2022. https://www.reuters.com/world/asia-pacific/pakistan-taken-off-global-watchdogs-grey-list-terrorism-financing-2022-10-21/.

54. Described in Milos Popovic, 'The Perils of Weak Organization: Explaining Loyalty and Defection of Militant Organizations Toward Pakistan', *Studies in Conflict & Terrorism* 38, no. 11 (2015): 919–937; and Fair, *In Their Own Words*.

55. See C. Christine Fair, 'Militant Recruitment in Pakistan: Implications for Al-Qa'ida and Other Organizations', *Studies in Conflict and Terrorism* 27, no. 6 (November/December 2004): 489–504; C. Christine Fair, 'The Militant Challenge

602 NOTES

in Pakistan', *Asia Policy* 11 (January 2011): 105–137); Amir Mir, *True Face of the Jehadis* (Lahore: Mashal, 2004); Nicholas Howenstein, 'The *Jihadi* Terrain in Pakistan: An Introduction to the Sunni *Jihadi* Groups in Pakistan and Kashmir', University of Bradford, Pakistan Studies Research Unit, 1 (2008). https://bradscholars.brad.ac.uk/handle/10454/2224); Arif Jamal, *Shadow War: The Untold Story of Jihad in Kashmir* (New York: Melville, 2009); and Shehzad H. Qazi, 'Rebels of the Frontier: Origins, Organisation, and Recruitment of the Pakistani Taliban', *Small Wars and Insurgencies* 22, no. 4 (2011): 574–602); Syed Manzar Abbas Zaidi, 'The Taliban Organisation in Pakistan', *The RUSI Journal* 154, no. 5 (2009): 40–47; and Muhammad, *The A to Z of Jehadi Organizations in Pakistan*.

56. C. Christine Fair, 'Insights from a Database of Lashkar-e-Taiba and Hizb-ul-Mujahideen Militants', *Journal of Strategic Studies* 37, no. 2 (2014): 259–290.

57. Muhammad Ismail Khan, 'The Assertion of Barelvi Extremism', *Current Trends in Islamist Ideology*, 19 October 2011, https://www.hudson.org/research/9848-the-assertion-of-barelvi-extremism.

58. Summarized in Fair, *In Their Own Words*.

59. Abul Hassan Mubbashir Ahmed Rabbani, *Masalah-i takfir aur is ke usul o zavabit* [*The Problem of Takfir and its Principles and Regulations*], trans. Safina Ustaad (Lahore: Dar-ul-Andlus, 2015), 32.

Chapter 3

1. F.M. Donner, *Narratives of Islamic Origins: The Beginnings of Islamic Historical Writing* (Princeton, NJ: The Darwin Press, 1998), 61.

2. Donner, *Narratives of Islamic Origins*, 72.

3. Also see Abdullah Saeed, *Islamic Thought: An Introduction* (New York: Routledge, 2006); Jane McAuliffe, *The Qur'an: What Everyone Needs to Know (R)* (New York: Oxford University Press, 2020).

4. Saeed, *Islamic Thought*.

5. Donner, *Narratives of Islamic Origins*, 3.

6. Saeed, *Islamic Thought*.

7. Stephen J. Shoemaker, *The Death of a Prophet: The End of Muhammad's Life and the Beginnings of Islam* (Philadelphia, PA: University of Pennsylvania Press, 2012), 80.

8. W.B. Hallaq, 'The Authenticity of Prophetic Hadees: A Pseudo-Problem', *Studia Islamica* 89 (1999): 84.

9. Hallaq, 'The Authenticity of Prophetic Hadees', 87.

10. J.A.C. Brown, 'Did the Prophet Say It or Not? The Literal, Historical, and Effective Truth of Ḥadiths in Early Sunnism', *Journal of the American Oriental Society* 129, no. 2 (2009): 281; although, as Brown explicated, this probably had less to do with malice or incompetence and more to do with a different understanding of epistemic knowledge.

11. Brown, 'Did the Prophet Say It or Not?', 284.

12. Shoemaker, *The Death of a Prophet*, 80.

NOTES 603

13. Donner, *Narratives of Islamic Origins*, 48.
14. Z. Sardar, *What Do Muslims Believe? The Roots and Realities of Modern Islam* (Tandem Library, 2007); Suleyman Sertkaya, 'A Critical and Historical Overview of the Sīrah Genre from the Classical to the Modern Period', *Religions* 13, no. 3 (2022): 196.
15. Shoemaker, *The Death of a Prophet*.
16. Michael Bonner, *Jihad in Islamic History: Doctrines and Practices* (Princeton, NJ: Princeton University Press, 2006), 37.
17. Abdussalam Bin Muhammad, *Hum Jihad Kyon Kar Rahen Hain* [*Why Are We Waging Jihad?*], trans. C. Christine Fair and Safina Ustaad (Lahore: Dar-ul-Andlus, 2004), 3.

Chapter 4

1. Abdussalam Bin Muhammad, '*Hum Jihad Kyon Kar Rahen Hain* [*Why Are We Waging Jihad?*]', trans. C. Christine Fair and Safina Ustad (Lahore: Dar-ul-Andlus, 2004). In this work, the author frequently draws upon historical sources described in Chapter 3. The author frequently does so without complete sentences or even complete references. This fosters the impression that the speaker is simply drawing upon these sources casually during conversation but with authority. We have retained this feature of the text as it seems to be an important aspect of the author's intent. This document is translated in entirety.
2. *Takfir* is the 'Pronouncement that someone is an unbeliever (*kafir*) and no longer Muslim'. *Takfir* is used in the modern era for sanctioning violence against leaders of Islamic states who are deemed insufficiently religious; see John Esposito ed., 'Takfir', in *The Oxford Islamic Studies Online*, 2017. At http://www.oxfordislamic studies.com/article/opr/t125/e2319).
3. '*Wajib ul qatal*' literally means worthy of being killed. However, this translation does not do the phrase justice because it also implies that those who kill persons so deemed will actually receive a boon for doing so.
4. From the earliest years of Pakistan's existence, Islamists bleated adamantly to have Ahmadis declared 'non-Muslim' because they do not recognize the ordinal finality of the prophet and recognize a living prophet. Nearly twenty years after these agitations began, Zulfiqar Ali Bhutto—an ostensible liberal—declared them to be non-Muslim in 1974 by constitutionally redefining their status. Prior to this move, Pakistanis considered Ahmadis to be as a sect of Islam even though they do not accept the ordinal finality of the prophet. With Bhutto's move, the Ahmadis became a non-Muslim minority overnight despite their prominent role in the movement to secure an independent Pakistan. This constitutional provision also expanded the legal and extra-legal justifications for killing Ahmadis with wanton impunity. See Sadia Saeed, 'Pakistani Nationalism and the State Marginalisation of the Ahmadiyya Community in Pakistan', *Studies in Ethnicity and Nationalism* 7, no. 3 (2007): 132–152.

604 NOTES

5. It has been my experience in dealing with Pakistan various journalist that they are often unable to accurately describe violence perpetrated against Ahmadis because they lack acceptable verbiage to describe, for example, a massacre at a place of worship without using the word '*masjid*'. The word that is often used by Ahmadis in lieu of '*masjid*' is '*ibadat gah*' (literally 'place of worship'), although it is not widely known among journalists.

6. Here and elsewhere, we use the translation of the Quran offered by Muhammad Marmaduke Pickthall (born Marmaduke William Pickthall), at https://www.islam101.com/quran/QTP/index.htm.

7. Here, we translate '*fitnah*' as 'civil conflict'.

8. Note that this text is identical to the quote that precedes it. This is not an error. The Quran frequently repeats prose albeit in different political contexts and with different follow-on text. A learned reader is supposed to understand this.

9. This battle, also known as the Battle of the Ditch or Battle of the Trench, occurred in 627 CE. The Muslims' victory at this battle compelled the Meccans to recognize both the political and religious power of the Muslims in Medina.

10. This battle took place in September 629 CE near the village of Mu'tah between those forces commanded by the Prophet Muhammad and those under the command of the Byzantine Empire and their Arab Christian Ghassanid vassals. In sources such as the one translated here, this battle is usually described as Muslims' efforts to punish Ghassanid chief for murdering a Muslim emissary.

11. This battle is the last battle that Prophet Muhammad fought. It took place in October 630 CE in the region of Tabuk which is in contemporary Saudi Arabia, near the Gulf of Aqaba. This battle is notable as it took place between the Roman and the forces of Muhammad. During this battle, so-called '*munafiqeen*' [hypocrites] refused to join the ranks. Prior to undertaking the expedition, the prophet appointed Imam Ali as his successor in Medina while he was away. However, fighting did not actually take place and Muhammad's men returned to Medina without confronting the Romans. Some verses in the Quran use this episode to dilate upon and expose the *munafiqeen*.

12. This battle was fought in 624 by the forces of Muhammad against a larger Mecca-based army under the control of Abu Sufyan. This battle often symbolizes Islam's triumph over polytheism and unbelief and evidences Allah's guidance and intervention on behalf of the out-numbered Muslims. Pakistan's defence journals frequently describe this battle with the intent of encouraging Pakistan's armed forces to believe that they can defeat the much larger armed forces of Pakistan's primary nemesis: India. See C. Christine Fair, *Fighting to the End: The Pakistan Army's Way of War* (New York: Oxford University Press, 2014).

13. The *shalwar* is a kind of lose pyjama-like pants worn by men and women in South Asia. Its looseness derives from the fact that waist is very large and is tied with a draw-string. Long, loose shirts, such as a *kameez*, are frequently worn with them.

14. Al-Nasai (829–915 CE) was a noted collector of *Hadees* and the author of one of the six canonical *Hadees* collections recognized by Sunni Muslims.

NOTES 605

Chapter 5

1. This 152-page volume comprises introductory material such as a table of contents, a foreword by Hafiz Muhammad Saeed himself, a justification by the author for writing the book as well as ten chapters. We present a translation of the complete work.
2. Ubaidurrahman Muhammadi, *Difa-i-Jihad* ['In Defence of *Jihad*'], trans. Safina Ustad (Lahore: Dar-ul-Andlus, 2003).
3. These are two of the organization's original training camps which were founded in the near-end of the so-called anti-Soviet *jihad* in Kunar, a province in Afghanistan. After the Soviets withdrew and Afghanistan became mired in internecine fighting among different armed groups, the organization relocated to Kashmir. This is consistent with the organization's commitment to avoiding conflict among Muslims.
4. While the reference for this *Hadees* in the original text is illegible, it can be traced to the *Hadees* collection of Abu Dawood Ahmed, Book 24, *Hadees* 47.
5. Bajaur is one of the seven Tribal Agencies in Pakistan. Bajaur shares a border with the Afghan province of Kunar.
6. This battle, also known as the Battle of the Ditch or Battle of the Trench, occurred in 627 CE. The Muslims' victory at this battle compelled the Meccans to recognize both the political and religious power of the Muslims in Medina.
7. The original text does not offer a complete citation for the *Hadees;* this particular *Hadees* appears in the collection of Muslim, Book 20, Chapter 17, *Hadees* 4573.
8. This *Hadees* can be found in the collection of Muslim, Book 20, Chapter 12, *Hadees* 4551.
9. While the original text presents this *Hadees* with a full citation, it appears to have been referenced incorrectly. This particular *Hadees* can be found in the collection of Nasai, Book 25, Chapter 41, *Hadees* 91 (https://sunnah.com/nasai/25/91).
10. This battle took place in 628 CE between Muslims and Jews who were living in an oasis of Khaybar, which is about 150 km from Medina in contemporary Saudi Arabia.
11. Umar bin al-Khattab, also known as Umar Farooq, is an important figure in the life of Muhammad and in early Islam. After the deaths of Muhammad and the first caliph Abu Bakr, Umar became the second of the four so-called 'righteously guided caliphs' of Islam, and is credited with expanding the Islamic State into an empire. However, before becoming a statesman, when Muhammad started proselytizing in Mecca, Umar, a powerful man in both status and stature, brutally opposed the new faith. Legend has it that one day Umar was on his way to assassinate Muhammad when he was told his own sister had accepted Islam. Upon hearing this news he changed course and headed straight for his sister's house intent on slaughtering her, but when he heard her recitation of the Quran the verses had a profound impact on him, and he converted there and then. His conversion was seen as a major boost for Muhammad, and a blow to Mecca's infidels.

606 NOTES

12. *Ar-Raheeq al-Makhtum* (*The Sealed Nectar*) is a modern biography of Muhammad written by the Indian Islamic scholar Safi-ur-Rahman Mubarakpuri (1942–2006). This is considered a complete and authoritative work on the life of the prophet.

13. This confrontation took place in 624 CE in the Hejaz region of the Arabian peninsula. It was fought between the early Muslims commanded by Muhammad and another army led by the Mecca-based Abu Sufyan (see Battle of al Badr).

14. *Ar-Raheeq al-Makhtum* (*The Sealed Nectar*) references earlier biographies of Muhammad, such as Ibn Hisham's (d. 833 CE) work as well as the biography written by Ibn Qayyim al-Jawziyya (1292–1350 CE) titled *Zad al-Ma'ad* (*Provisions for the Hereafter*).

15. It should be noted that Pakistan's army in its various publications also present such statistical tabulations of orders of battle. See C. Christine Fair, *Fighting to the End: The Pakistan Army's War of War* (New York: Oxford University Press, 2014).

16. This battle (better described as an expedition) occurred in 623 CE. The eponymous platoon, comprised of thirty fighters who had emigrated from Mecca to Medina, was led by Hamzah bin 'Abdul Muttalib. This expedition was tasked to intercept a Quraish caravan of three hundred people, among whom was Abu Jahl bin Hisham. While the sides prepared for battle, fighting was averted by the presence of Majdi bin 'Amr, who was known to both combatants. This non-battle is remembered because, on this occasion, Muhammad is believed to have accredited the first white Muslim flag.

17. Note that the original text provided an incomplete reference.

18. The original text provided an incomplete reference.

19. This seems to be a magazine about Palestine, however, we have been unable to locate it or information about whether or not this is a *Lashkar-e-Tayyaba* publication.

20. This battle was fought in July or August 634 CE in a location which, while unknown precisely, is thought to be in contemporary Israel near Beit Guvrin. It was the first major conflict between the Byzantine Empire and the Arab Rashidun Caliphate, in which the Muslims decisively won.

21. This conflict occurred in 637 CE between Muslim forces, led by Khalid ibn al-Walid, and Byzantine forces led by the Byzantine emperor Haraclius. The Muslim forces decisively won and forced the Byzantine forces to withdraw from Syria and Palestine which were subsequently surrendered to the Muslims within the decade after the conquest. In 648, Jerusalem was also surrendered to the Muslims.

22. It should be noted that Pakistan's army in its various publications also present such statistical tabulations of orders of battle. See Fair, *Fighting to the End*.

23. This battle was fought in 624 CE, after the Battle of Uhud, when the Quraysh were returning to Mecca. The Quraysh hoped to extirpate the Muslims, commanded by Muhammad, after weakening them in Uhud. They were thwarted.

NOTES 607

Chapter 6

1. Naveed Qamar, *Mujahid ki Azaan* (Lahore: Dar-ul-Andlus, 2001), 72.
2. Qamar, *Mujahid ki Azaan*, 11.
3. This is the only place in the text that Yusuf Ali's translation has been used instead of Marmaduke Pickthall's for purposes of flow.
4. The italicized phrase is a parenthetical borrowed from the source document added to the translation.
5. 'Allah knows best.'
6. This expression, ليقوم الناس بالقسط, appears in the Quran in 57:25; it means, 'that the people may maintain their affairs in justice'.
7. This *Hadees* appears in the *Hadees* collection of Imam Malik, one of the earliest compilers of prophetic tradition; it can be traced to Book 46, *Hadees* 1628.

Chapter 7

1. Umm-e-Hammad, *Hum Mayen Lashkar-e-Tayyaba Ki* [*We, the Mothers of Lashkar-e-Tayyaba*], Vol. 1 (Lahore: Dar-ul-Andlus, 1998); Umm-e-Hammad, *Hum Mayen Lashkar-e-Tayyaba Ki* [*We, the Mothers of Lashkar-e-Tayyaba*], Vol. 2 (Lahore: Dar-ul-Andlus, 2003); and Umm-e-Hammad, *Hum Mayen Lashkar-e-Tayyaba Ki* [*We, the Mothers of Lashkar-e-Tayyaba*], Vol. 3 (Lahore: Dar-ul-Andlus, 2003).
2. While there was news of a fourth volume, we have yet to locate it or even confirm whether or not it has been published.
3. Al Khansa (575–645 CE) was a female poet who was a contemporary of the Prophet Muhammad who is revered both for her poetry but also her sacrifices, which often formed the subject of her writings. When al Khansa's brother, Mu'awiyah, was murdered by members of another tribe, she insisted that another brother, Sakhr, avenge his death. Sakhr was wounded while doing so and succumbed to his injuries a year later. She mourned his death by writing poetry for which she became famous. In 629 CE, she met the prophet and converted to Islam. She had four sons, all of whom also converted to Islam as well and subsequently perished in the famed 636 CE Battle of Qadisiyah in which the Muslims conquered Persia. Reportedly, when al Khansa learned the news of her sons' demise, she did not grieve; rather, she exclaimed: 'I consider it an honour that they died for the sake of Islam. I ask only that god allow me to meet them in paradise.' She is revered for being the finest poet of classical Arabic and even the Prophet Muhammad is known to have requested her to recite her poems frequently, most of which were elegies on her two brothers and slain sons. She is also venerated among *jihadi* circles for her willingness to dispatch her loved ones into battle. For example, Islamic State named a brutal, all-female police squad after her (al-Khansa Brigade) which ensure that female members are fully covered in public, do not wear inappropriate attire (such as high heels), and

608 NOTES

are accompanied by a male in public. See Loulla-Mae Eleftheriou-Smith, 'Escaped Isis Wives Describe Life in the All-Female al-Khansa Brigade who Punish Women with 40 Lashes for Wearing Wrong Clothes', *Independent*, 20 April 2015. http://www.independent.co.uk/news/world/middle-east/escaped-isis-wives-describe-life-in-the-all-female-al-khansa-brigade-who-punish-women-with-40-lashes-10190317.html. Al Qaeda also produced an internet-based women's magazine under the title of al Khansa which aims to help them become better fighters. There are numerous accounts of her on the internet and other *jihadi* publications. See Caron E. Gentry and Laura Sjoberg, *Mothers, Monsters, Whores: Women's Violence in Global Politics* (New York: Zed Books, 2007). See also Suzanne Evans, *Mothers of Heroes, Mothers of Martyrs: World War I and the Politics of Grief*, Montreal: McGill-Queen's University Press, 2007, 34; and Abdullah Al-Udhari, *Classical Poems by Arab Women* (Bilingual Edition) (London: Saqi Books, 1999).

4. Al Khansa (575–645 CE) was a female poet who was a contemporary of the Prophet Muhammad who is revered both for her poetry but also her sacrifices, which often formed the subject of her writings. When al Khansa's brother, Mu'awiyah, was murdered by members of another tribe, she insisted that another brother, Sakhr, avenge his death. Sakhr was wounded while doing so and succumbed to his injuries a year later. She mourned his death by writing poetry for which she became famous. In 629 CE, she met the prophet and converted to Islam. She had four sons, all of whom also converted to Islam as well and subsequently perished in the famed 636 CE Battle of Qadisiyah in which the Muslims conquered Persia. Reportedly, when al Khansa learned the news of her sons' demise, she did not grieve; rather, she exclaimed: 'I consider it an honour that they died for the sake of Islam. I ask only that god allow me to meet them in Paradise.' She is revered for being the finest poet of classical Arabic and even the Prophet Muhammad is known to have requested her to recite her poems frequently, most of which were elegies on her two brothers and slain sons. She is also venerated among *jihadi* circles for her willingness to dispatch her loved ones into battle. For example, Islamic State named a brutal, all-female police squad after her (al-Khansa Brigade) which ensure that female members are fully covered in public, do not wear inappropriate attire (such as high heels), and are accompanied by a male in public. See Eleftheriou-Smith, 'Escaped Isis Wives Describe Life in the All-Female al-Khansa Brigade who Punish Women with 40 Lashes for Wearing Wrong Clothes'. Al Qaeda also produced an internet-based women's magazine under the title of al Khansa which aims to help them become better fighters. There are numerous accounts of her on the Internet and other *jihadi* publications. See Gentry and Sjoberg, *Mothers, Monsters, Whores*. See also Evans, *Mothers of Heroes, Mothers of Martyrs*, 34; and Al-Udhari, *Classical Poems by Arab Women*.

5. Khawlah bint al-Azwar is a legendary female warrior and contemporary of Muhammad who was trained in archership, sword combat and horseback riding. She is the sister of another celebrated military commander, Dhiraar bin al-Aswar, who commanded the Rashidum army during the Muslim conquest of the seventh

NOTES   609

century. She led a rescue mission to free her brother who had been captured while fighting the Byzantines under the banner of the first caliph, Abu Bakr al-Siddiq. Despite being captured, she and other female fighters escaped after killing at least thirty enemy combatant and injuring many more. She is noted for her leadership in battles of the Muslim conquests in parts of what are today Syria, Jordan, and Palestine, and in particular one battle in which she is said to have led a group of women against the Byzantine army. Tradition holds that she fought alongside her brother in numerous battles, including the Battle of Yarmouk against Byzantine forces. She along with al Khansa is venerated by Salafi *jihadis* and is often mobilized in *jihadi* literature to attract female recruits. Accounts of these and other historical female combatants are also used to shame men who lack the courage of these women to fight for Islam. See Sara Jul Jacobsen, 'Calling on Women: Female-Specific Motivation Narratives in Danish Online *Jihad* Propaganda', *Perspectives on Terrorism* 13, no. 4 (2019): 1–26.; and. Tomasso Previato, 'A Neglected Genealogy of the Martyred Heroines of Islam:(Re)-Writing Women's Participation in *Jihad* into the History of Late Imperial Gansu', *Journal of Muslim Minority Affairs* 38, no. 3 (2018): 301–325.

6. This is an optional prayer offered in the middle of the night, which signifies particular devotion above and beyond the required five daily prayers.

7. This phrase can be found in the Quran 3:169; the full verse reads: Think not of those, who are slain in the way of Allah, as dead. Nay, they are living. With their Lord they have provision.'

Chapter 8

1. *Mujallah-ul-Dawah* (renamed *Al-Haramain*) has been *Lashkar-e-Tayyaba*'s and *Jamaat ud-Dawah*'s most important publication. The first issue of the magazine was published in March 1989, and it is currently edited by Maulana *Amir* Hamza, the founding ideologue of the JuD. Qazi Kashif Niaz is also believed to have been an editor of *Mujallah-ul-Dawah* for a period. Typically, every issue carries articles on what being a Muslim should mean to every Muslim, drawing especially on the *Ahl-e-Hadees* school of Islamic jurisprudence. *Mujallah-ul-Dawah* also usually carries reports of *jihad* (particularly in Indian-administered Kashmir), information about fallen militants, and updates about the workings of all JuD departments. *Mujallah-ul-Dawah* reportedly has a circulation of one hundred and forty thousand. Other LeT linked magazines include: *Ghazwa Times* (renamed *Jarrar*), *Tayyabaat* (a bi-monthly magazine for women, which has been renamed *Al-Saffat*), *Voice of Islam* (an English-language magazine, which has been discontinued), *Nanhe Mujahid* (a monthly now released under the name *Rozatul Atfal*), and *Al-Ribat* (a monthly magazine in Arabic, which is now titled *Al-Anfal*). Umm-e-Hammad is the compiler of the three-volume series *Ham Mayen Lashkar-e-Tayyaba Ki*, and is the editor of *Tayyabaat*, LeT's magazine for women, the head of LeT's Women Wing, and a mother of two LeT militants. For background, see

610 NOTES

C.M. Naim, 'The Mothers of the Lashkar', *Outlook India*, 15 December 2008, www.outlookindia.com/article.aspx?239238; and Humeira Iqtidar, *Secularizing Islamists: Jama'at-e-Islami and Jamat'at-ud-Da'wa in Urban Pakistan* (Chicago, IL: University of Chicago, 2011), 106–107.

2. In principle, later data exists but I am unable to acquire these materials for data extraction, assembly, and analysis.

3. Maria Rashid, *Dying to Serve: Militarism, Affect and the Politics of Sacrifice in the Pakistan Army* (Stanford, CA: Stanford University Press, 2020).

4. See Abdussalam Bin Muhammad, *Hindu Customs Among Muslims*, trans. M. Saleem Ahsan, (Lahore: Dar-ul-Andlus, 2007); and the discussion of this text by C. Christine Fair, 'The Milli Muslim League: The Domestic Politics of Pakistan's Lashkar-e-Taiba', *Current Trends in Islamic Ideology* (July 2018): 33–44.

5. The LeT, like many in South Asia, systematically refer to the Afghans as 'Afghanis'. This is incorrect. The proper term for the citizens of Afghanistan is 'Afghan' or 'Afghans'. The currency of the country is 'Afghani'.

6. *Fajr*, which means 'dawn' in Arabic, refers to the first of the five daily prayers (*namaz* or *salat*) performed by observant Muslims.

7. In the original, several lines are illegible. For this reason, we skipped to the next section of this slain fighter.

8. This is one of five daily prayers, offered in the evening. It is the last of the five obligatory prayers of the day.

9. The next three lines are not legible.

10. Note that much of this text is illegible. For this reason, we have only translated excerpts of entire letters.

11. This is an additional supplicatory prayer offered while standing in the course of offering other prayers.

12. This battle was fought in 624 by the forces of Muhammad against a larger Mecca-based army under the control of Abu Sufyan. This battle often symbolizes Islam's triumph over polytheism and unbelief and evidences Allah's guidance and intervention on behalf of the outnumbered Muslims. Pakistan's defence journals frequently describe this battle with the intent of encouraging Pakistan's armed forces to believe that they can defeat the much larger armed forces of Pakistan's primary nemesis: India. See C. Christine Fair, *Fighting to the End: The Pakistan Army's Way of War* (New York: Oxford University Press, 2014).

13. This confrontation took place in 624 CE in the Hejaz region of the Arabian peninsula. It was fought between the early Muslims commanded by Muhammad and another army led by the Mecca-based Abu Sufyan (see Battle of al Badr).

14. Shan is a popular Pakistani film star.

15. Translator's note: the original did not provide a reference for the Quran citation. We believe the one we provide is correct.

16. *Baniya* is literally a Hindu caste which describes a group of occupations that include bankers, moneylenders, and merchants (such as those who sell grains or spices or other more contemporary commercial ventures). While this is the strict

NOTES 611

definition of this term, many in Pakistan and India associate the *baniya* with being cheap, stingy, and cheats. This is the context in which the author is likely using this term here.

17. This is one of several Arab tribes which had been the subject of the Roman Empire, but ultimately allied with state of Medina and converted from Christianity to Islam.

18. Abu Qatadah was a horseman of the prophet.

19. These two groups are associated with the *Jamaat-e-Islami*.

20. Note that *Nikah* refers to the formal religious ceremony in Islam, which is the signing of the marital contract. But the language implies that their marriage was not consummated.

21. *Rukhsati*, which occurs after the contracting of the marriage through *Nikah*, is when bride comes to the home of bridegroom.

22. A *ghazi* is a veteran of a conflict.

23. The original provides no source for this quote, merely a translation of it in Urdu.

24. In Pakistan there are several levels of administrative divisions. There are four provinces: the Punjab, Sindh, Balochistan, and Khyber Pakhtunkhwa. Below the level of the province is the division and below this level is the district.

25. The *zuhr* prayer is the fourth of the five obligatory prayers for observant Muslims. It begins after the sun reaches its zenith.

26. This likely suggests that his mother is a Barelvi. Barelvis often attribute to the prophet qualities that are reserved for Allah himself.

27. This also suggests that his father is a Barelvi who garner criticism for worshipping the prophet as well as Allah and viewing the prophet as having non-human attributes. This is considered *shirk*, or polytheism in LeT's ideology.

28. This most certainly refers to *daura-e-aam*, the twenty-one-day basic training tour offered in one of the organization's camps in Afghanistan. He is not merely asking him to travel around Afghanistan for a few weeks.

29. *Ahl-e-Hadees* prescribe men to wear their pants such, so the hem falls above the ankles.

30. This is further evidence that the young man's families are Barelvis propitiating saints, amulets, graves, etc.

31. This likely refers to proselytization of LeT's interpretation of *Ahl-e-Hadees*.

32. This is one of the LeT training camps in Pakistan-administered Kashmir.

33. This is not one of the five mandatory prayers. It is an optional prayer which is offered during the night upon waking up from sleep. It is derived from 'hujud' which means sleep in Arabic. Thus, 'tahajjud' literally means to give up sleep. This is usually a mark of particular piety.

34. Again, the author is critical of his associates who appear to be Barelvi. Ganj Baksh refers to the largest shrine in South Asia (Datta Banj Baksh in Lahore) which houses the remains of Abdul Hassan Ali Hujwiri (commonly referred to

612 NOTES

as Ganj Baksh), a mystic who is believed to live at the site in the eleventh century CE.

35. The author here refers to another revered mystic in Pakistan. Fariduddin Ganjshakr, popularly known as Baba Farid, is a thirteenth-century Sufi mystic who was based in Pakpattan (Punjab). Like Datta Ganj Baksh, this shrine is one of the most revered in Pakistan. Sikhs also revere the shrine and the mystic whose poetry is included in the Guru Granth Sahab, the compilation of sacred writings which Sikhs consider to be the eternal Guru.

36. This again is referencing Barelvi practices pejoratively. *Bismillah* literally means 'in the name of Allah'. Muslims use it as an invocation before commencing a new undertaking (such as a new job, marriage, a move to a new location, etc.). The expression '786' is often used as a shorthand for this expression to avoid inscribing language on a piece of paper that would make its disposal a form of blasphemy. This number is derived by adding up the numeral order of all characters in the full expression '*Bismillah al-Rahman al-Rahim*'. In contrast, Barelvis believe that if they write out the full expression in Arabic, ordinary disposal of that document would be blasphemous.

37. Khuda is the Persian word for 'god'. This expression can reference any god, whether Christian, Hindu, Muslim, Jewish, Bahai etc. Because LeT, like Salafists, emphasize the oneness of god, this implication of multitude is anathema. For this reason, they champion jettisoning expressions like '*Khuda Hafez*' (said while departing) for '*Allah Hafez*'. Moreover, Salafists more generally embrace expunging Persian expressions such as '*Ramadan Mubarak*' for Arabic expressions and Arabic translations such as *Ramazan Kareem*.

38. This is a date in the Islamic calendar that roughly corresponds to May 1994.

39. This is a *wazifa* or *zikr*, which is a saying derived from the Quran used by persons who are seeking help. This particular *wazifa* or *zikr* is offered when one is facing difficulties or hardships. What is curious about this in this text that the particular version of this is often used by Sufis (Barelvis) whose practices this author otherwise repudiates. The phrase is drawn from two parts of the Quran. The first part (حَسْبُنَا الله وَنِعْمَ الْوَكِيل) is from *Surat al-Imran* (3:173) and is used widely by Sufis as well as more orthodox Muslims. The second part (وَنِعْمَ الْمَوْلَى وَنِعْمَ النَّصِيْر) is from *Surat al-Anfal* (8:40). I am thankful to Dr Mohammad Taqi for his patient explanation of this.

40. This refers to Kashmir.

41. To ask people to do what is good, and to stop them from doing what is evil.

42. This biography implies that the *mujahid* was not always an adherent of *Ahl-e-Hadees* and was likely a Barelvi, who are known for various rituals. He is instructing his wife to abjure from such rituals in the event of his demise. This suggests that, on her own, she would.

43. One of the ninety-nine names for Allah.

44. One who memorized the Quran in entirety.

NOTES 613

45. One who has memorized the Quran is known as a *Hafez-e-Quran* or protector of the Quran.

46. This likely is used as a metaphor, instructing them that they should not let his mission fail and implying that someone from among them should follow in his stead.

47. The actual expression is 'eat a bullet on your chest'. This is an Urdu expression of extreme bravery.

48. A faithful Muslim.

49. Note that the author provides a non-standard translation for this verse. The author's translation renders as 'Allah picks the martyrs from you'. Other translations, such as that of Pickthall, is 'Allah may know those who believe and may choose witnesses from among you'. We have retained the author's original.

50. A popular expression for 'clerics' of varying quality and qualification. It is often used pejoratively to describe an unlettered cleric.

51. In other words, this brother who was competing with him did not enjoy the support of the locals as he did. Sharing milk is a sign of hospitality for those who are respected.

52. The next several lines of the text were illegible.

53. A *hoor* or *hoori* refers to the celestial maidens in heaven.

54. In these biographies, writers favourably compare mothers and other women who enthusiastically encourage their sons and menfolk to embrace shahadat to al Khansa (575–645 CE), a female poet who was a contemporary of the Prophet Muhammad, and is revered both for her poetry but also her sacrifices, which often formed the subject of her writings. When al Khansa's brother, Mu'awiyah, was murdered by members of another tribe, she insisted that another brother, Sakhr, avenge his death. Sakhr was wounded while doing so and succumbed to his injuries a year later. She mourned his death by writing poetry for which she became famous. In 629 CE, she met the prophet and converted to Islam. She had four sons, all of whom also converted to Islam as well and subsequently perished in the famed 636 CE Battle of Qadisiyah in which the Muslims conquered Persia. Reportedly, when al Khansa learned the news of her sons' demise, she did not grieve; rather, she exclaimed: 'I consider it an honour that they died for the sake of Islam. I ask only that god allow me to meet them in Paradise'. She is revered for being the finest poet of classical Arabic and even the Prophet Muhammad is known to have requested her to recite her poems frequently, most of which were elegies on her two brothers and slain sons. She is also venerated among *jihadi* circles for her willingness to dispatch her loved ones into battle. For example, Islamic State named a brutal, all-female police squad after her (al-Khansa Brigade) which ensure that female members are fully covered in public, do not wear inappropriate attire (such as high heels), and are accompanied by a male in public. See Loulla-Mae Eleftheriou-Smith, 'Escaped Isis Wives Describe Life in the All-Female Al-Khansa Brigade who Punish Women with 40 Lashes for Wearing Wrong Clothes', *Independent*, 20 April 2015. http://www.independent.

614 NOTES

co.uk/news/world/middle-east/escaped-isis-wives-describe-life-in-the-all-fem ale-al-khansa-brigade-who-punish-women-with-40-lashes-10190317.html. Al Qaeda also produced an internet-based women's magazine under the title of *al Khansa* which aims to help them become better fighters. There are numerous accounts of her on the internet and other *jihadi* publications. See Caron E. Gentry and Laura Sjoberg, *Mothers, Monsters, Whores: Women's Violence in Global Politics* (New York: Zed Books, 2007). See also Suzanne Evans, *Mothers of Heroes, Mothers of Martyrs: World War I and the Politics of Grief* (Montreal: McGill-Queen's University Press, 2007), 34; and Abdullah Al-Udhari, *Classical Poems by Arab Women* (Bilingual Edition) (London: Saqi Books, 1999).

55. Nimrod is a biblical figure described as a king in Mesopotamia. In extra-biblical traditions, he is believed to have built the Tower of Babel as defiant king on earth rebelling against god.

56. This likely refers to Abdul Rehman Makki, the second in command of LeT and brother-in-law of Hafez Muhammad Saeed.

57. This likely refers to Azam Cheema, one of the LeT masterminds of the November 2008 Mumbai attacks and the July 2006 Mumbai train bombings.

58. The Qari Muhammad Yaqoob Sheikh referred to here likely refers to a member of LeT's central advisory committee who held various leadership positions in the group since 2006, including deputy director of political and foreign affairs between 2008 and 2009. As of mid-2008, he was in charge of Islamabad's office, including LeT's general operations in the capital area. Clearly something is important about this particular fighter that so many high-value persons were involved in his funeral.

59. This is a special Muslim practice which involves of a period of retreat in a mosque for a certain number of days in accordance with the believer's desires. Usually, persons do this during the month of Ramazan.

60. Safiya refers one of the prophet's aunts who wielded a sword in the Battle of Khandaq in 627 AD. Reportedly, she decapitated an enemy fighter who was trying to climb the city walls and threw his head back to his fellow soldiers. For more details, see Christine Sixta Rinehart, *Sexual Jihad: The Role of Islam in Female Terrorism: Agency, Utility, and Organization* (Lanham, MD: Lexington Books, 2019); and David Cook, 'Women Fighting in *jihad*', in *Female Terrorism and Militancy*, ed. Cindy Ness (New York: Routledge, 2008), 37–48.

61. This is a supererogatory prayer.

Chapter 9

1. It was first published in 1998.

2. Arif Jamal, 'Analyzing the Role of the Top LeT Ideologue: A Profile of Amir Hamza', *Jamestown Militant Leadership Monitor* 3, no. 6 (June 2012): 6–7. https:// jamestown.org/wp-content/uploads/2012/06/Militant_Leadership_Monit

NOTES 615

or_-_Volume_III__Issue_6.pdf. Also see 'Taseer Killer's Case Should be Decided as per Shariah Law: JuD', *The Indian Express*, 7 January 2011. https://indianexpr ess.com/article/news-archive/print/taseer-killers-case-should-be-decided-as-per-shariah-law-jud/.

Chapter 10

1. Abul Hassan Mubbashir Ahmed Rabbani, *Masalah-yi takfir aur is ke usul o zavabit* [*The Problem of Takfir and its Principles and Regulations*], trans. Safina Ustaad (Lahore: Dar-ul-Andlus, 2015).
2. Roel Meijer, *Global Salafism: Islam's New Religious Movement* (New York: Columbia University Press, 2009), 9.
3. Joas Wagemakers, '"Seceders" and "Postponers"? An Analysis of the "Khawarij" and "Murji'a" Labels in Polemical Debates between Quietist and Jihadi-Salafis', *Contextualising Jihadi Thought*, ed. Jeevan Deol and Zaheer Kazmi (New York: Columbia University Press, 2012), 145–164; and Peter Mandaville, *Global Political Islam* (Abingdon: Routledge, 2007).
4. Note that this is the source provided in the original; however, it bears little resemblance to the actual verse in the Quran.

Chapter 11

1. Ali Imran Shaheen, *Kashmir Manzil Dur Nahin* (*Destination Kashmir is Nigh*) (Lahore: Dar-ul-Andlus, 2011).
2. Iftikhar Ahmed, 'Islam, Democracy and Citizenship Education: An Examination of the Social Studies Curriculum in Pakistan', *Current Issues in Comparative Education* 7 (Dec ember 2004): 39–49; K.K. Aziz, *Murder of History: A Critique of History Textbooks Used in Pakistan* (Lahore: Vanguard, 1998); Marie Lall, 'Educate to Hate: The Use of Education in the Creation of Antagonistic National Identities in India and Pakistan', *Compare* 38 (January 2008): 103–119; A.H. Nayyar and Ahmed Salim, *The Subtle Subversion: The State of Curricula and Textbooks in Pakistan—Urdu, English, Social Studies and Civics* (Islamabad: Sustainable Development Policy Institute, 2003); and Rubina Saigol, *Becoming a Modern Nation: Educational Discourse in the Early Years of Ayub Khan (1958–64)* (Islamabad: Council of Social Sciences, 2003), at http://www. cosspak.org/mono-graphs/monograph_rubina.pdf.
3. Arif Jamal, 'Analyzing the Role of the Top LeT Ideologue: A Profile of Amir Hamza', *Jamestown Militant Leadership Monitor* 3, no. 6 (June 2012): 6–7. https:// jamestown.org/wp-content/uploads/2012/06/Militant_Leadership_Monitor_-_ Volume_III__Issue_6.pdf. Also see'Taseer Killer's Case Should be Decided as per Shariah Law: JuD', *The Indian Express*, 7 January 2011. https://indianexpress.com/

616 NOTES

article/news-archive/print/taseer-killers-case-should-be-decided-as-per-shar iah-law-jud/.
4. Note that, despite the quotations, this does not come from any verse in *Surat al-Tauba*.

Chapter 12

1. Muhammad Tahir Naqqash, *Ghaziyan-i-Saf-Shikan* [Of Noble Warriors Demolishing Enemy Lines; *Jihadi* tales of *fidayeen* missions from Delhi's Red Fort to Srinagar's Airport] (Lahore: Dar-ul-Andlus, 2001). All the images used in this chapter were sourced from this book.
2. See Yoginder Sikand, 'The Islamist Militancy in Kashmir: The Case of the Lashkar-e-Taiba', in *The Practice of War: Production, Reproduction and Communication of Armed Violence*, ed. Aparna Rao, MichaelBollig, and Monika Böck (New York: Berghahn Books, 2007), 215–238; Mariam Abou Zahab, 'I Shall be Waiting at the Door of Paradise: The Pakistani Martyrs of the Lashkar-e-Taiba (Army of the Pure)', in *The Practice of War: Production, Reproduction and Communication of Armed Violence*, ed. Aparna Rao, Michael Bollig, and Monika Böck (New York: Berghahn Books, 2007), 133–158; Saeed Shafqat, 'From Official Islam to Islamism: The Rise of Dawat-ul-Irshad and Lashkar-e-Taiba', *Pakistan: Nationalism without a Nation*, ed. Christophe Jaffrelot (London: Zed Books, 2002), 131–147; and Zaigham Khan, 'Allah's Army', *The Herald Annual*, January 1998, 123–130.
3. See discussion in C. Christine Fair, *In Their Own Words: Understanding the Lashkar-e-Tayyaba* (New York/London: Hurst/Oxford University Press, 2018/ 2019). Also see 'Bailed Mumbai Suspect Lakhvi's Luxury Jail Time', *BBC.com*, 10 April 2015, https://www.bbc.com/news/world-asia-31606798; Taha Siddiqui, 'Why Is Pakistan Reluctant to Bring Lashkar-e-Taiba to Justice?', *Al Jazeera*, 26 November 2018. https://www.aljazeera.com/indepth/opinion/pakistan-reluct ant-bring-lashkar-taiba-justice-181121143620490.html; Hugh Tomlinson, 'Pakistan Cuts Thousands From Terrorist Watch List', *The Times*, 22 April 2020. https://www.thetimes.co.uk/article/pakistan-cuts-thousands-from-terrorist-watch-list-mjxc8vfg8.
4. This is the river which forms part of Afghanistan's northern border with Tajikistan, Uzbekistan, and Turkmenistan.
5. The Shiv Sena (lit. Army of Shiva) is a Maharashtra-based Hindu nationalist/chauvinist party founded by Bal Thackeray in Mumbai in 1966. See Sikata Banerjee, 'Warriors in Politics: Hindu Nationalism, Violence, and the Shiv Sena in India', *Nations and Nationlism* 7.2(2001): 257–258.
6. According to Vinay Kaura, the Indian government 'has raised seven Central Paramilitary Forces (CPMFs) which are regularly deployed for law and order duties along with the police forces of respective states.[3] These seven CPMFs

NOTES 617

are the Central Research Police Force (CRPF), Border Security Force (BSF), Assam Rifles, Central Industrial Security Force (CISF), Indo-Tibetan Border Police (ITBP), Seema Surksha Bal (SSB), and the National Security Guard (NSG), founded in 1986 in the aftermath of Operation Blue Star. While the Indian army has about 1.2 million personnel, all seven CPMFs number more than 1.3 million. CRPF, the most important of the CPMFs, performs a wide range of duties including management of law and order, counter-insurgency and counter-terrorism all over India'. See Vinay Kaura, 'India's Counter-Terrorism Policy against Jihadist Terror', *Connections* 16, no. 4 (2017): 54.

7. The Bharatiya Janata Party is Hindu chauvinist political party in India. See Christophe Jaffrelot, *Modi's India: Hindu Nationalism and the Rise of Ethnic Democracy* (Princeton, NJ: Princeton University Press, 2021).

8. The text isn't clear whether the author is Bukhari of Muslim. Upon searching, the author appears to be Muslim.

References

Abbas, Azmat. 'In God We Trust'. *The Herald (Pakistan)* (January 2002): 45–49.

Abi-Habib, Maria, and Salman Masood. 'Military's Influence Casts a Shadow Over Pakistan's Election'. *New York Times*, 21 July 2018. https://www.nytimes.com/2018/07/21/world/asia/pakistan-election-military.html.

Abou Zahab, Mariam. 'I Shall be Waiting at the Door of Paradise: The Pakistani Martyrs of the Lashkar-e-Taiba (Army of the Pure)'. In *The Practice of War: Production, Reproduction and Communication of Armed Violence*, edited by Aparna Rao, Michael Bollig, and Monika Böck, 133–158. New York: Berghahn Books, 2007.

Abou Zahab, Mariam. 'Salafism in Pakistan: The Ahl-e Hadith Movement'. In *Global Salafism: Islam's New Religious Movement*, edited by Roel Meijer, 126–139. London: Hurst, 2009.

Ahmed, Iftikhar. 'Islam, Democracy and Citizenship Education: An Examination of the Social Studies Curriculum in Pakistan'. *Current Issues in Comparative Education* 7 (December 2004): 39–49.

American Foreign Policy Council. 'Lashkar-e-Taiba'. In *The World Almanac of Islamism: 2011*. Lanham, MD: Rowman and Littlefield, 2011.

Anon. 'Taseer Killer's Case Should be Decided as per Shariah Law: JuD'. *The Indian Express*, 7 January 2011. https://indianexpress.com/article/news-archive/print/tas eer-killers-case-should-be-decided-as-per-shariah-law-jud/.

Aziz, K.K. *Murder of History: A Critique of History Textbooks Used in Pakistan*. Lahore: Vanguard, 1998.

BBC News. 'Bailed Mumbai Suspect Lakhvi's Luxury Jail Time'. *BBC.com*, 10 April 2015, https://www.bbc.com/news/world-asia-31606798.

Bin Muhammad, Abdussalam. *Hum Jihad Kyon Kar Rahen Hain [Why Are We Waging Jihad?]*, translated by C. Christine Fair and Safina Ustad. Lahore: Dar-ul-Andlus, 2004.

Bin Muhammad, Abdussalam. *Hindu Customs Among Muslims*, translated by M. Saleem Ahsan. Lahore: Dar-ul-Andlus, 2007.

Bonner, Michael. *Jihad in Islamic History: Doctrines and Practices*. Princeton, NJ: Princeton University Press, 2006.

Brown, J.A.C. 'Did the Prophet Say It or Not? The Literal, Historical, and Effective Truth of Hadiths in Early Sunnism'. *Journal of the American Oriental Society* 129, no. 2 (2009): 259–285.

Brulliard, Karin. 'Afghan Intelligence Ties Pakistani Group Lashkar-i-Taiba to Recent Kabul Attack'. *The Washington Post*, 3 March 2010. http://www.washingtonpost.com/wpdyn/content/article/2010/03/02/AR2010030202427.html.

Cook, David 'Women Fighting in *jihad*'. In *Female Terrorism and Militancy: Agency, Utility, and Organization*, edited by Cindy Ness, 37–48. New York: Routledge, 2008.

620 REFERENCES

Donner, F.M. *Narratives of Islamic Origins: The Beginnings of Islamic Historical Writing*. Princeton, NJ: The Darwin Press, 1998.

Eleftheriou-Smith, Loulla-Mae. 'Escaped Isis Wives Describe Life in the All-Female Al-Khansa Brigade who Punish Women with 40 Lashes for Wearing Wrong Clothes'. *Independent*, 20 April 2015. http://www.independent.co.uk/news/world/middle-east/escaped-isis-wives-describe-life-in-the-all-female-al-khansa-brigade-who-punish-women-with-40-lashes-10190317.html.

Esposito, John. ed. 'Takfir'. *The Oxford Islamic Studies Online*, 2017. http://www.oxfordislamicstudies.com/article/opr/t125/e2319.

Evans, Suzanne. *Mothers of Heroes, Mothers of Martyrs: World War I and the Politics of Grief*. Montreal: McGill-Queen's University Press, 2007.

Fair, C. Christine. *The Counterterror Coalitions: Cooperation with Pakistan and India*. Santa Monica, CA: RAND, 2004.

Fair, C. Christine. *Fighting to the End: The Pakistan Army's Way of War*. New York: Oxford University Press, 2014.

Fair, C. Christine. 'India and Iran: New Delhi's Balancing Act'. *The Washington Quarterly* 30 (Summer 2007): 145–159.

Fair, C. Christine. 'Insights from a Database of Lashkar-e-Tayyaba and Hizb-ul-Mujahideen Militants'. *Journal of Strategic Studies* 37, no. 2 (2014): 259–290.

Fair, C. Christine. *In Their Own Words: Understanding the Lashkar-e-Tayyaba*. London: Hurst, 2018.

Fair, C. Christine. *In Their Own Words: Understanding the Lashkar-e-Tayyaba*. New York: Oxford University Press, 2019.

Fair, C. Christine. 'Lashkar-e-Tayiba and the Pakistani State'. *Survival* 53 (August 2011): 1–23.

Fair, C. Christine. 'The Militant Challenge in Pakistan'. *Asia Policy* 11 (January 2011): 105–137.

Fair, C. Christine. 'Militant Recruitment in Pakistan: Implications for Al-Qa'ida and Other Organizations'. *Studies in Conflict and Terrorism* 27, no. 6 (November/December 2004): 489–504.

Fair, C. Christine. 'The Milli Muslim League: The Domestic Politics of Pakistan's Lashkar-e-Taiba'. *Current Trends in Islamic Ideology* 23 (July 2018): 33–44.

Fair, C. Christine. 'The Only Enemy Pakistan's Army Can Beat Is Its Own Democracy—Foreign Policy'. *Foreign Policy* 9 (August 2017). https://foreignpolicy.com/2017/08/09/the-only-enemy-pakistans-army-can-beat-is-its-own-democracy/.

Fair, C. Christine, and Peter Chalk. *Fortifying Pakistan: The Role of US Internal Security Assistance*. Washington, DC: United States Institute of Peace, 2006.

Fair, C. Christine, and Peter Chalk. 'Lashkar-e-Tayyiba Leads the Kashmiri Insurgency'. *Jane's Intelligence Review* 14, no. 10 (December 2002): 1–5.

Fair, C. Christine, and Ali Hamza. 'The Foreign Policy Essay: Whether or Not Pakistan Will Join the War in Yemen May Depend on a Group You've Probably Never Heard Of'. *Lawfare* 12 (April 2015). https://www.lawfareblog.com/foreign-policy-essay-whether-or-not-pakistan-will-join-war-yemen-may-depend-group-youve-probably.

Fouda, Yosri, and Nick Fielding. *Capture or Kill: The Pursuit of the 9/11 Masterminds and the Killing of Osama bin Laden*. New York: Arcade Publishing, 2012.

REFERENCES 621

Gentry Caron E., and Laura Sjoberg. *Mothers, Monsters, Whores: Women's Violence in Global Politics*. New York: Zed Books, 2007.

George, Susannah, and Shaiq Hussain. 'Pakistan Hopes Its Steps to "Eradicate" Terrorism will Keep It Off a Global Blacklist'. *Washington Post*, 20 February 2020. https://www.washingtonpost.com/world/asia_pacific/pakistan-fatf-terrorism-blacklist/2020/02/20/df67602c-51e4-11ea-80ce-37a8d4266c09_story.html.

Hallaq, W.B. 'The Authenticity of Prophetic *Hadees*: A Pseudo-Problem'. *Studia Islamica* 89 (1999): 75–90.

Hamza, Maulana Emir. *Shahrah-e-Bahisht* [*Highway to Heaven*]. Translated by Safina Ustaad. Lahore: Dar-ul-Andlus, 2004.

Haqqani, Husain. 'FATF's Grey List Suits Pakistan's Jihadi Ambitions. It Only Worries Entering the Black List'. *The Print*, 28 February 2020. https://theprint.in/opinion/fatfs-grey-list-suits-pakistans-jihadi-ambitions-it-only-worries-entering-the-black-list/372524/.

Howenstein, Nicholas. 'The *Jihadi* Terrain in Pakistan: An Introduction to the Sunni *Jihadi* Groups in Pakistan and Kashmir'. University of Bradford, Pakistan Studies Research Unit, 1 (2008). https://bradscholars.brad.ac.uk/handle/10454/2224.

International Monetary Fund. 'IMF Executive Board Completes the First Review of Pakistan's Extended Fund Facility'. *Press Release* 19, no. 447, 19 December 2019. https://www.imf.org/en/News/Articles/2019/12/19/pr19477-pakistan-imf-execut ive-board-completes-review-of-pakistans-extended-fund-facility.

Iqtidar, Humeira. *Secularizing Islamists: Jama'at-e-Islami and Jamat'at-ud-Da'wa in Urban Pakistan*. Chicago, IL: University of Chicago, 2011.

Jacobsen, Sara Jul. 'Calling on Women: Female-Specific Motivation Narratives in Danish Online *Jihad* Propaganda'. *Perspectives on Terrorism* 13, no. 4 (2019): 1–26.

Jamal, Arif. 'Analyzing the Role of the Top LeT Ideologue: A Profile of Amir Hamza'. *Jamestown Militant Leadership Monitor* 3, no. 6 (June 2012): 6–7. https://jamest own.org/wp-content/uploads/2012/06/Militant_Leadership_Monitor_-_Volu me_III__Issue_6.pdf.

Jamal, Arif. *Shadow War: The Untold Story of Jihad in Kashmir*. New York: Melville, 2009.

John, Wilson. *Caliphate's Soldiers: The Lashkar-e-Tayyeba's Long War*. New Delhi: Amaryllis and the Observer Research Foundation, 2011.

Khan, Muhammad Ismail. 'The Assertion of Barelvi Extremism'. *Current Trends in Islamist Ideology*, 19 October 2011. https://www.hudson.org/research/9848-the-assertion-of-barelvi-extremism.

Khan, Zaigham. 'Allah's Army'. *The Herald Annual*, January 1998, 123–130.

Kunwar Khuldune, Shahid. 'A Win for All: Pakistan's NA-120 By-Election'. *The Diplomat*, 21 September 2017. https://thediplomat.com/2017/09/a-win-for-all-pakistans-na-120-by-election/.

Kunwar Khuldune. Shahid. 'India Dictating Terms to Pakistan' Claims Jamaat ud Dawa'. *Asia Times*, 24 November 2017. http://www.atimes.com/article/india-dictat ing-terms-pakistan-claims-jamaaat-ud-dawa/.

Lall, Marie. 'Educate to Hate: The Use of Education in the Creation of Antagonistic National Identities in India and Pakistan'. *Compare* 38 (January 2008): 103–119.

Laskar, Rezaul H. 'Pak Gets 4 More Months to Deliver on Terror Financing Watchdog FATF Plan'. *The Hindustan Times*, 29 April 2020. https://www.hindustantimes.com/world-news/amid-covid-19-crisis-pakistan-gets-4-more-months-to-implem

622 REFERENCES

ent-terror-funding-watchdog-fatf-s-action-plan/story-bc4OsMf7oduz821RSmG
1rO.html.

Mannes, Aaron, John. P. Dickerson, Amy Sliva, Jana Shakarian, and V.S. Subrahmanian. 'A Brief History of LeT'. In *Computational Analysis of Terrorist Groups: Lashkar-e-Taiba*, 23–68. New York: Springer, 2013.

Mazzetti, Mark. 'A Shooting in Pakistan Reveals Fraying Alliance'. *New York Times*, 12 March 2011. http://www.nytimes.com/2011/03/13/weekinreview/13lashkar.html.

Meijer, Roel. *Global Salafism: Islam's New Religious Movement*. New York: Columbia University Press, 2009.

Metcalf, Barbara. *Islamic Contestations: Essays on Muslims in India and Pakistan*. New Delhi: Oxford University Press, 2004.

Mir, Amir. *True Face of the Jehadis*. Lahore: Mashal, 2004.

Muhammad, Emir Rana. *A to Z of Jehadi Organizations in Pakistan*. Lahore: Mashal Books, 2004.

Muhammadi, Ubaidurrahman. *Difa-i-Jihad* ['In Defence of *Jihad*'], translated by Safina Ustad. Lahore: Dar-ul-Andlus, 2003.

Naim, C.M. 'The Mothers of the Lashkar'. *Outlook India*, 15 December 2008. www. outlookindia.com/article.aspx?239238.

Naqqash, Muhammad Tahir. *Ghaziyan-i-Saf-Shikan [Of Noble Warriors Demolishing Enemy Lines]*. Lahore: Dar-ul-Andlus, 2001.

Nayyar, A.H., and Ahmed Salim. *The Subtle Subversion: The State of Curricula and Textbooks in Pakistan—Urdu, English, Social Studies and Civics*. Islamabad: Sustainable Development Policy Institute, 2003.

News Desk. 'Pervez Musharraf u-turn: ISI Trains Lashkar-e-Taiba, Jaish-e-Mohammed, Says Former Pakistan President Ex-Army Chief General Parvez Musharraf Admitted that ISI Trains LeT and JeM Terrorist and Encourages Terrorism Against India'. *India Today*, 16 February 2016. https://www.india.com/ news/india/pervez-musharraf-u-turn-isi-trains-lashkar-e-taiba-jaish-e-moham med-says-former-pakistan-president-939367/.

Noonan, Sean, and Scott Steward. 'The Evolution of a Pakistani Militant Network 2011'. https://www.stratfor.com/weekly/evolution-pakistani-militant-network.

OCLC. 'About'. *Online Computer Library Center*, Dublin, OH. https://www.oclc.org/ en/about.html.

Pardesi, Manjeet. 'The Battle for the Soul of Pakistan at Islamabad's Red Mosque'. In *Treading on Hallowed Ground: Counterinsurgency Operations in Sacred Spaces*, edited by C. Christine Fair and Sumit Ganguly, 88–116. New York: Oxford University Press, 2008.

Popovic, Milos. 'The Perils of Weak Organization: Explaining Loyalty and Defection of Militant Organizations Toward Pakistan'. *Studies in Conflict & Terrorism* 38, no. 11 (2015): 919–937.

Previato, Tomasso. 'A Neglected Genealogy of the Martyred Heroines of Islam:(Re)-Writing Women's Participation in *Jihad* Into the History of Late Imperial Gansu'. *Journal of Muslim Minority Affairs* 38, no. 3 (2018): 301–325.

PTI News Agency. '2008 Indian Embassy Attack in Kabul Sanctioned by ISI, New Book Claims'. *Times of India*, 23 March 2014. https://timesofindia.indiatimes.com/ india/2008-Indian-embassy-attack-in-Kabul-sanctioned-by-ISI-new-book-cla ims/articleshow/32545791.cms.

REFERENCES 623

PTI News Agency. 'Hafiz Saeed Asks Govt to Curb Foreign Bid to Bolster IS in Pakistan'. *The Indian Express*, 17 October 2015. https://indianexpress.com/article/world/world-news/hafiz-saeed-asks-govt-to-curb-foreign-bid-to-bolster-is-in-pakistan/.

PTI News Agency. 'Hafiz Saeed's JuD to Contest 2018 Pakistan General Elections'. *Economic Times*, 3 December 2018. https://m.economictimes.com/news/international/world-news/hafiz-saeed-to-contest-pakistan-general-elections-next-year/amp_articleshow/61897257.cms.

PTI News Agency. 'Hafiz Saeed's JuD Launches Political Party in Pakistan'. *The Quint*, August 2017. https://www.thequint.com/news/hafiz-saaed-jud-launches-political-party.

PTI News Agency. 'LeT Responsible for Attack at Indian Consulate in Herat: US'. *The Times of India*, 25 June 2014. http://timesofindia.indiatimes.com/world/us/LeT-responsible-for-attack-at-Indian-consulate-in-Herat-US/articleshow/37205339.cms.

PTI News Agency. 'Pakistan Supported, Trained Terror Groups: Musharraf'. *The Hindu*, 2 September 2016. https://www.thehindu.com/news/international/south-asia/Pakistan-supported-trained-terror-groups-like-Lashkar-e-Taiba-Pervez-Musharraf/article60516617.ece.

Qamar, Naved. *Mujahid ki Azaan*. Lahore: Dar-ul-Andlus, 2001.

Qazi, Shehzad H. 'Rebels of the Frontier: Origins, Organisation, and Recruitment of the Pakistani Taliban'. *Small Wars and Insurgencies* 22, no. 4 (2011): 574–602.

Rabbani, Abul Hassan Mubbashir Ahmed. *Masalah-yi takfir aur is ke usul o zavabit* [*The Problem of Takfir and its Principles and Regulations*], translated by Safina Ustaad. Lahore: Dar-ul-Andlus, 2015.

Rashid, Maria. *Dying to Serve: Militarism, Affect and the Politics of Sacrifice in the Pakistan Army*. Stanford, CA: Stanford University Press, 2020.

Rinehart, Christine Sixta. *Sexual Jihad: The Role of Islam in Female Terrorism*. Lanham, MD: Lexington Books, 2019.

Riedel, Bruce. 'Al Qaeda 3.0: Terrorism's Emergent New Power Bases'. Brookings Institution, 3 December 2012. https://www.brookings.edu/opinions/al-qaeda-3-0-terrorisms-emergent-new-power-bases/.

Rotella, Sebastian. 'Four Alleged Masterminds of 2008 Mumbai Attacks are Indicted in Chicago'. *ProPublica*, 25 April 2011. https://www.propub-lica.org/article/four-alleged-masterminds-of-2008-mumbai-attacks-are-indict-ed-in-chicago.

Rotella, Sebastian. 'Four Disturbing Questions about the Mumbai Terror Attack'. *ProPublica*, 22 February 2013. https://www.propublica.org/article/four-disturb-ing-questions-about-the-mumbai-terror-attack.

Rotella, Sebastian. 'Mumbai Case Offers Rare Picture of Ties Between Pakistan's Intelligence Service, Militants'. *ProPublica*, 2 May 2011. https://www.propublica.org/article/mumbai-case-offers-rare-picture-of-ties-between-pakistans-intelligence-serv.

Scott-Clark, Cathy, and Adrian Levy. *The Siege: 68 Hours Inside the Taj Hotel*. New York: Penguin, 2013.

Saeed, Sadia. 'Pakistani Nationalism and the State Marginalisation of the Ahmadiyya Community in Pakistan'. *Studies in Ethnicity and Nationalism* 7, no. 3 (2007): 132–152.

624 REFERENCES

Saigol, Rubina. *Becoming a Modern Nation: Educational Discourse in the Early Years of AyubKhan (1958–64)*. Islamabad: Council of Social Sciences, 2003. http://www.cosspak.org/monographs/monograph_rubina.pdf.

Shafqat, Saeed. 'From Official Islam to Islamism: The Rise of Dawat-ul-Irshad and Lashkar-e-Tayyaba'. In *Pakistan: Nationalism Without a Nation*, edited by Christophe Jaffrelot, 131–147. London: Zed Books, 2002.

Shaheen, Ali Imran. *Kashmir Manzil Dur Nahin [Destination Kashmir is Nigh]*. Lahore: Dar-ul-Andlus, 2011.

Shoemaker, S.J. *The Death of a Prophet: The End of Muhammad's Life and the Beginnings of Islam*. Philadelphia, PA: University of Pennsylvania Press, 2012.

Siddiqui, Taha. 'Why is Pakistan reluctant to bring Lashkar-e-Taiba to justice?'. *Al Jazeera*, 26 November 2018. https://www.aljazeera.com/indepth/opinion/pakis tan-reluctant-bring-lashkar-taiba-justice-181121143620490.html.

Sikand, Yoginder. 'The Islamist Militancy in Kashmir: The Case of the Lashkar-e-Tayyaba'. In *The Practice of War: Production, Reproduction and Communication of Armed Violence*, edited by Aparna Rao, Michael Bollig, and Monika Böck, 215–238. New York: Berghahn Books, 2007.

Subrahmanian, V.S., Aaron Mannes, Amy Sliva, Jana Shakarian, and John. P. Dickerson. 'A Brief History of LeT'. In *Computational Analysis of Terrorist Groups: Lashkar-e-Taiba*, 23–68. New York: Springer, 2013.

Swami, Praveen. 'Kabul Attack: US Warning was Accurate'. *The Hindu*, 3 August 2008. http://www.thehindu.com/todays-paper/Kabul-attack-US-warning-was-accur ate/article15271791.ece.

Tankel, Stephen. 'Lashkar-e-Tayyaba: Past Operations and Future Prospects'. *New America Foundation*, National Security Studies Program Policy Paper, 27 April 2011.

Tankel, Stephen. *Storming the World Stage: The Story of Lashkar-e-Tayyaba*. New York: Oxford University Press, 2011.

Tomlinson, Hugh. 'Pakistan Cuts Thousands From Terrorist Watch List'. *The Times*, 22 April 2020. https://www.thetimes.co.uk/article/pakistan-cuts-thousands-from-terrorist-watch-list-mjxc8vfg8.

Al-Udhari, Abdullah. *Classical Poems by Arab Women* (Bilingual Edition). London: Saqi Books, 1999.

Umm-e-Hammad, ed. *Hum Mayen Lashkar-e-Tayyaba Ki [We, the Mothers of Lashkar-e-Tayyaba]*, Vol. 1. Lahore: Dar- ul-Andlus, 2001 (1998).

Umm-e-Hammad, ed. *Hum Mayen Lashkar-e-Tayyaba Ki [We, the Mothers of Lashkar-e-Tayyaba]*, Vol. 2. Lahore: Dar- ul-Andlus, 2003.

Umm-e-Hammad, ed. *Hum Mayen Lashkar-e-Tayyaba Ki [We, the Mothers of Lashkar-e-Tayyaba]*, Vol. 3. Lahore: Dar- ul-Andlus, 2003.

United Nations. 'Security Council Al-Qaida Sanctions Committee Adds Four Names to Its Sanctions List, Amends One Entry'. 14 March 2012. http://www.un.org/press/en/2012/sc10578.doc.htm.

US Department of State. 'Secretary of State's Terrorist Designation of Falah-i-Insaniat Foundation'. 4 November 2010. https://www.state.gov/j/ct/rls/other/des/266 648.html.

US Department of Treasury. 'Recent OFAC Actions'. 27 April 2006. https://www.treas ury.gov/resource-center/sanctions/OFAC-Enforcement/Pages/20060427.aspx.

REFERENCES 625

US Embassy. 'US Embassy Cables: Lashkar-e-Taiba Terrorists Raise Funds in Saudi Arabia'. *The Guardian*, 20 August 2009. https://www.theguardian.com/world/us-embassy-cables-documents/220186.

Wagemakers, Joas. '"Seceders" and "Postponers"? An Analysis of the "Khawarij" and "Murji'a" Labels in Polemical Debates between Quietist and Jihadi-Salafis'. In *Contextualising Jihadi Thought*, edited by Jeevan Deol and Zaheer Kazmi, 145–164. New York: Columbia University Press, 2012.

Wani, Leshon, and Sidhant Sibal. 'New Name, Same Terror Group: LeT Becomes TRF to Save Pak from FATF Axe'. *DNAIndia*, 29 April 2020. https://www.dnaindia.com/world/report-new-name-same-terror-group-let-becomes-trf-to-save-pak-from-fatf-axe-2823051.

Web Desk. 'A-120 By-Polls: JUD Fields Candidate'. *The Nation*, 13 August 2017. http://nation.com.pk/national/13-Aug-2017/na-120-by-polls-jud-fields-candidate.

Yasmeen, Samina. *Jihad and Dawah: Evolving Narratives of Lashkar-e-Taiba and Jamat ud Dawah*. London: Hurst, 2017.

Zaidi, Syed Manzar Abbas. 'The Taliban Organisation in Pakistan'. *The RUSI Journal* 154, no. 5 (2009): 40–47.

Index

For the benefit of digital users, indexed terms that span two pages (e.g., 52–53) may, on occasion, appear on only one of those pages

Abbas, Abul, 36
Abbas, Ibn, 64
Abdullah, Farooq, 462–63
Abdullah, Sheikh Muhammad, 461, 462
Abdullah, Syedna, 125, 126
Afghan *jihad,* 95–96, 97–104
   bounties of, 98
   fight against aggressors, 104
   fighting the enemy, 104
   restoration of prayer-houses, 100
   Russian invasion of Afghanistan
     and, 102–3
   silence of, 100
   valour of Afghan *Mujahid',* 506
Ahl-e-Hadees, 1–2, 19, 28
Ahmadis, 9, 44
   antagonism against, 44–45
   to be *kalima-go,* 44–45
   as *wajib ul qatal,* 44–45
Alam, Musarrat, 469–70
   imprisonment of, 481–82
al-Ayeed, Imam Ibn Daqiq, 384
Al Badr, 28–29
al-Dakhil, Abdur Rehman, 219
Ali, Hazrat, 73–74
al-Kashmiri, Maula Abdul Wahid, 21–22
al-Khattab, Syedna Umar ibn, 114
All Parties Hurriyat (Liberation)
   Conference, 464–65, 470
   factions, 465
   organizations participation, 464–65
Al Qaeda, 2, 22–24, 25, 30
Al Shams, 28–29
al-Shokani, Qazi Qatrimani
   Muhammad bin Ali, 380–81
al-Uthaymin, Sheikh Muhammad ibn, 410

Al-Walid I of Umayyad dynasty, 5
al-Yamani, Allama Ibn al-Wazir, 384
Andrabi, Syeda Asia, 468–69
Asbab al-Nuzul, 32–33
asceticism, 362
Asri Sahib, Maulana Ramzan, 219
Aziz, Abu Abrar Asif, 178
Aziz, Maulana Abdul, 23
Aziz, Sultan Abdul, 357

Baba Jee's Commandments, 366–69
Bangroo, Rafiq, 483–84
Barelvi, 28
   militancy, 28–29
Baseer, Abu, 40–42, 59–60, 89
   jihad of, 155–57
   operation against infidels, 59
   prophet's disapproval, 157
Battle of Ahzab, 119
Battle of Ajnadayn, 171
Battle of Badr, 72–73, 113–14, 118, 244, 424
Battle of Khandaq, 104, 110, 121, 122–
   23, 131
Battle of Khaybar, 112, 119
Battle of Mu'tah, 119, 121, 124–25, 171
Battle of Saif-ul-Bahar, 119
Battle of Tabuk, 174
Battle of Uhud, 116, 118, 123, 132, 144–
   45, 147, 244
Battle of Yarmuk, 172
Bayt-ul-Muqaddas, 163–64, 165
Bharatiya Janta Party (BJP), 534
Bihar, 557
Bosnian Muslims, 153
Bush, George W., 2, 25
Butt, Maqbool, 462–63

628 INDEX

Chabad House attack, 24–25
Chinese Muslims, massacre of, 166
Chisti, Khaja Moin-ud-Din, 362–63
Christ, Lord, 343
Christian monastics, 343–44

Daata Sahib's sanctuary, 360, 363–64
Dar-ul-Andlus, 5–6
dawah. See proselytization *(dawah)*
Day of Judgement, 419, 420
deaths
  escaping, 117–18
  in Kashmir, 116
  time and place of person's death, 116,
    117
Deobandi, 4, 28, 30, 43–44
Difa-e-Pakistan Council, 3, 26
Difa-i-Jihad (Ubaidurrahman
    Muhammadi), 79, 80–81
  Afghan *jihad*, 97–104
  chapters, 80–81
  follow Islam, 113–14
  foreword, 83–84
  geographic significance of Muslim
    regions, 92–93
  jihad in Kashmir, 134–48
  jihad waged in Allah's cause, 82
  lack and abundance in *jihad*, 116–34
  occupation of Muslim regions, 163–
    64, 169–75
  overview, 87
  principle of *qisas* (retributive justice),
    148–52
  prohibition on fighting unjust rulers,
    83–84, 108
  publisher's note, 81–82
  rise and fall of Islamic Nation, 87–97
  significance of Meccan and Medinite
    Periods, 111–16
  targeting Hindu disbelievers, 105,
    107–8, 170
  without caliph, 152–58

Emir, Abdullah bin, 72–73
excuses for not waging *jihad*, 70–77
  absence of caliph or emir, 70–71, 88
  Battle of Badr, 72–73

  government assistance to victims,
    74–75
  help from polytheists, 71–72
  provoking of Hindus to rape and
    plunder, 75
  Quranic interpretation, 70

faith, 394, 395, 403–4
  elements of, 392–93
  non-negotiable factors, 397
  reviving, 394–95
Falah Insaniat Foundation (FIF), 3, 21–22,
    25–26
Farooq, Mirwaiz Muhammad Umar,
    466–67
farz-i-ayn (compulsory for every
    individual), 47–53, 61–65, 66–67
  Quranic interpretation, 62–63, 67
farz-i-kifaya, 53, 61–65, 66–67
Federally Administered Tribal Areas
    (FATA), 2, 19, 25
fighter biographies, 10–11
Financial Action Task Force (FATF), 27
forebears, 106
Foreign Terrorist Organization (FTO),
    2, 25

Geelani, Syed Ali Shah, 466
  celebration of Pakistan Day, 478–79
ghair muqallid, 28
Ghazali, Imam, 382
Ghazi, Abdul Rashid, 23
Ghaziyan-i-Saf-Shikan, 13–14
*Ghaziyan-i-Saf-Shikan (Noble Warriors
    and Battlefronts)*, 487
  abduction of idol, 504
  about Hindu civilians, 532–33
  Allah's assistance, 512–13
  author's note, 489–92
  consumption of mother's flesh,
    540–41
  destruction of Hindu temples,
    500–6
  election operations, 513–19
  foreword, 488–89
  hospitality of Kashmiri Muslims,
    519–25

INDEX 629

hunting of Israeli commandos,
506–13
killing of Gurus, 505
lucrative investments, 583–92
operations against India's soldiers,
501–4, 507, 511–12, 513–19
preamble, 492–500
Red Fort attack, 572–76
sale of arms and ammunition to
mujahideen, 540
shattering of India, 553–66
Sikh soldiers, 515
Sindh problems, 547–52
slaughtering of Shiv Sena's thugs,
534–47
Sri Nagar's airport attack, 567–72
good advice, 340
Gorkhaland movement, 556–57
Gorkha Liberation Front, 562
grave-worship, 347–48, 434
burial of saints outside graveyard,
351–52
concrete tombs, 350
final tortuous hours of Armageddon,
358
praying to Allah at, 348–49
guerrilla warfare
in Kashmir as *jihad,* 110–11, 134–48
in valley of Nakhla, 136–37

Habib Allah, 38
Hadees, 8, 31, 34–36, 38, 59, 82, 99, 104,
107–8, 154, 155, 157, 160–61, 345,
425–26
authenticity of, 426
Battle of Badr, 72
in context of a dying man's will, 429,
431, 435–36
discrepancies between Quran and,
35–36
faith in Allah's Oneness, 431
founding fathers of, 34
'*indakum min Allahi fihi burhan*', 410
isnad and *matn,* 34
on *jihad,* 63, 64, 66, 105
narratives, 34
prophet's tomb, 352

punishment, 425
purpose of visiting graves, 353
recital of *kalima,* 404–5, 406
sahih (sound), 34
sin of not adopting faith, 425
zaeef (weak), 34
Hanafi school of Islam, 28
Hanbal, Ibn, 35
Hanbal, Imam Ahmed bin, 106–7
accusation of treason, 106–7
Hanbali school of *fiqh,* 28
Hanif, Sahal Bin, 64
Haqqani Network, 22–23, 27
Harijan in India, 559–60
Harthah, Syedna Zayd bin, 124, 126
Headley, David Coleman, 23–24
Mumbai mission, 23–24
Hezb-e-Islami, 101
Highway to Heaven, 12
Hindu Army *vs* LeT. *See Lashkar-e-*
Tayyaba (LeT)
Hindu barbarity, 139–40
persecution of Indian Muslims,
138–39
Hindu Customs Among Muslim, 232–33
Hisham, Ibn, 37–38
Hizb-ul-Mujahideen, 28–29
House of Allah (Ka'ba), 338–39
Hum Kyon Jihad Kar Rahen Hain, 79,
376
Huraira, Abu, 63, 173
Huraira, Syedna Abu, 107–8, 147
Hurairah, Abu, 65
Hypocrites, 109–10

Idara Khidmat-e-Khalq (IKK), 3, 25–26
idolater, tragedy of, 349–50
Imama, Syedna Abu, 173
Inayat-al-Rahman, 103
Indian military
budget, 555–56, 563
junior officers enrolled in, 561*t*
new kind of military unit, 557–59
Indian soldiers, 554
Hindustan Times report on, 554
sale of arms and ammunition to
mujahideen, 540

630 INDEX

Indian Youth Abhor Military Service, 562
India–Pakistan partition, 461
India's disintegration, 563, 564
   CIA report, 555
   Gorkha movement, 562
   Harijan exploitation, 559–60
   Hindustan Times report, 554
   Lt. General Sharma's prediction, 554–55
   state's separatist movements, 556
India's parliament attack, 2
infidels
   children of, 420
   jihad against, 55–56, 59, 60, 73, 89, 104, 115, 147
   operation against, 59
   prophet against, 115, 123
   Quranic warnings to, 388
   religious scholars as, 383–84, 447–48
International Security Assistance Force (ISAF), 22
Inter-Services Intelligence Agency (ISI), 4, 20–21, 23–24, 26–27
Iqbal, Zafar, 1–2, 19, 21–22
Ishaq, Ibn, 37–38
Islam, 7–8
   in Eritrea, 166
   as movement, 181, 182
   rituals, 394
   in Thailand, 167–68
Islamic historical sources, 31
   Hadees, 31, 34–36
   Quran, 31–33
   Seerat, 31, 36–38
Islamic State, 30, 102
Islamic state
   alcohol, prohibition of, 57
   azaan (call to prayer), praying, and congregational prayers, 56, 57
   charity tax, 56, 57
   extra-marital sex, prohibition of, 57
   fasting in month of Ramazan, 57
   temporary marriages, prohibition of, 57
   usury, prohibition of, 57

Islam's education policy, 200–7
   battlefield of truth and falsehood, 206
   education objectives, 205–6
   free-for-all policy, 201
   strategy or objectives, 201
   teacher's work, 205
   teachings of Quran and *Sunnat*, 201, 203, 204
   true knowledge, 201–5
Israel, establishment of, 164

Jahsh, Syedna Abdullah bin, 136
Jaish-e-Muhammad (JeM), 2, 20–21, 25, 27, 28–29
Jamaat-e-Islami (JI), 28–29
Jamaat ud Dawah (JuD), 19, 44–45. *See also Lashkar-e-Tayyaba* (LeT)
   militant groups merged with, 4
   profit-making activities, 20, 21–22
   umbrella organizations in, 26
   umbrella organizations under, 3
Jamaat-ud-Dawah-wal-Irshad, 178
Jamil-al-Rahman, Sheikh, 101–2, 103
Jan, Abdul Ahad, 479–81
Jews of Banu Quraiza, 110
Jharkhand freedom struggle, 557
jihad, 7–8, 29, 40, 43, 114, 115, 149, 165, 166, 171, 372, 488, 489–92
   in absence of Islamic state, 56–58
   Allah's cause, 144, 170, 173, 196–200, 209–10, 218
   for avenging Muslim murder, 49–51, 54
   benefits of, 155
   for breaching treaty, 51, 54
   consequence of non-participation in, 117–18, 172
   creation of Islamic state and caliph, 60–61
   for defending the defenceless, 49, 54, 93–94
   against ego, satan and worldly desires, 75–77
   excuses for not waging, 70–77
   by factions and groups, 88
   farz-i-ayn (compulsory for every individual), 47–53, 61–65

INDEX 631

farz-i-kifaya, 53, 61–65
fighting infidels, 55–56, 59, 60, 73, 89,
    104, 115, 147
fighting politicians and government
    officials, 108–10
fight in self-defence, 52, 55
for freeing occupied lands, 52–53,
    55–56
impact of termination of, 91–92
for *jizya* collection, 49, 54
in Kashmir, 80–81, 83, 128, 130, 132,
    140, 143, 150, 152, 158, 170
as mandatory, 151
in matters of faith in Islam, 48–49, 53
military planning, 123
modes of waging, 173–74
objections to, 86, 98–100
in Pakistan, 68–69, 73–74
pamphlet related to, 46–47
participation in, 173, 174–75
path of, 89, 94–95, 96–97
preparations, 88
rationale for waging, 47–56, 86, 87,
    160–61, 172–73
for removing obstacles to accepting
    Islam, 48, 53
student participation in, 188–91
in *Surat at-Tawbah,* 66
tactics against enemy, 110–11
termination of, 171
till Day of Judgement, 58–60
unity in, 154
USA aiding, 158–69
without caliph, 152–58
without government support, 155
without organized congregation, 89
jihad-e-Kashmir, 553
Jihad-e-Kashmir, 549–50
jihadi assets, 2–3
Jinnah, Muhammad Ali, 461–62

Kadir, Sultan Abdul, 167–68
kalima, 73–74
kalima-go, 44–45
*Kashmir: Manzil Dur Nahin (Destination
    Kashmir is Nigh),* 449
    Ali Imran Shaheen's views, 454

appreciation, 455
atrocities in the valley, 476–78
chapters, 450–51
content, 449–50
Hazrat Bal mosque attack, 479
imprisonment of Musarrat Alam, 481–82
'Indians! Get Out of Kashmir'
    movement, 470–71
Kashmiri martyrs, 463–64, 483–86
Kashmir's freedom struggle, 452–53,
    461–64
murder of protesters, 474–76
Pakistan's Independence Day
    incident, 478–79
preamble, 456–58
publisher's note, 451–52
Shabir Shah's release, 482–83
treatment of Kashmiri Muslims in
    Indian prisons, 474
wounded and dead, 471–74
Kashmiri *jihad,* 549–50, 564–65
Kashmir *jihad,* 80–81, 82, 83, 128, 130,
    132, 140, 143, 150, 152, 158, 170,
    244–55, 584*f*–85
rationale for, 84–87
shaheed Kashmiri *mujahideen*s, 234–36.
    See also martyrs and martyrdom
Kashmir Manzil Dur Nahin, 13–14
Kashmir region, 458–61
Azad Kashmir, 459, 460
cities, 460
Gilgit-Baltistan, 459
Jammu, 459–60
lakes and rivers, 460
literacy rate, 460
Occupied Jammu, 459
Occupied Kashmir, 459, 460
Pakistan-controlled Kashmir, 460
passes in, 461
police forces operating in, 567–68
Kashmir's freedom struggle, 452–53,
    461–64
guerrilla attacks against military
    personnel, 463
history, 461–63
Kashmiri martyrs, 463–64
prominent leaders of, 465–70

632 INDEX

Kashmir's freedom struggle, 452–53
Khadri, Abu Saeed, 65
Khadri, Muhammad Saifullah, 80–81
Khairun Nas, 4
Khalaf, Ubay ibn, 115–16
Khalid, Muhammad Saifullah, 79
Khalid, Zayd bin, 64
Khalistan movement, 556
Khan, Abrar, 509–10, 511
Khan, Imran, 4–5
Khaubaib, Abu, 248
Khawarij, 30, 73–74, 376
    accusation against *Ahl-i-Sunnat* of
        being *Murjiya,* 400, 411–12
Kitab al-Maghazi, 37–38
kufr, 392–93, 395, 396, 412, 413, 421,
    426, 443
    action, 399, 428
    belief, 398
    elements of, 385–86
    manifestations of, 397
    meaning of, 396–97
    as *shariat* issue, 413
    speech, 398–99, 428, 444
    statement and its negation, 384–85
    types, 399–400
Kumar, T. Raja, 27–28
Kunar, 19–20

Laal, Ratan, 533–34
Lakhvi, Zaki-ur-Rehman, 1–2, 4, 19, 21–
    22, 23–24, 219, 487, 488
Lashkar-e-Jhangvi/ Sipah-e-Sahaba, 21,
    28–29, 30
Lashkar-e-Tayyaba (LeT), 1, 7, 31, 210,
    213, 218, 487, 489–92, 590*f. See also*
    operations against India's soldiers
    acquisition of Chinese anti-aircraft
        artillery, 571
    Afghan insurgency, 22–23
    anticommunal and anti-sectarian
        nature of, 29
    ban of, 2–3, 21–22
    fidayeen missions, 498–99
    fidayeen operations, 21, 23, 24–25
    formation, 1–2
    guerrilla warfare in Kashmir, 134–48

    against Hindu army in Occupied
        Kashmir, 14–15, 21, 244–55,
        256–58
    Hum Kyon Jihad Kar Rahen Hain, 43
    martyrs, 496
    martyrs of. *See* martyrs and
        martyrdom
    'moderated *jihad*' strategy, 22–23
    Muaskar-e-Aqsa's earliest graduates,
        494–500
    mujahideen, 10–11, 15–16, 75, 83, 90
    nights and days, 492–94
    obligation of *jihad* and *dawah,* 7–10,
        29–30, 38, 45–46
    in Pakistan, 28–30, 376
    popularity, 525–34
    practice of *takfir,* 30, 43–44
    Red Fort attack, 2000, 16, 572–76,
        573*f,* 582*f*
    Sindh policy, 552
    Sri Nagar's airport attack, 567–72
    student body of, 208–9
    Tirgam and Roshanpur incident,
        261–62
    use of Quran, *Hadees* and *Seerat,* 32–33,
        38–42
    vow, 527–28
'Liya'lam Allah,' 204

Makki, Hafiz Abdul Rehman, 21–22
Malik, Muhammad Yasin, 467–68
Manipur, 557
    Hindu– Christian riots in, 557
Mansoor, Saifullah, 219
Markaz-ud-Dawah-wal-Irshad, 97, 101,
    109, 110, 116, 128, 129, 155, 157,
    158, 200, 208–9, 215–16
Markaz-ud-Dawah-wal-Irshad (MDI),
    1–3, 46, 487
    headquarters, 20
    militant mission in Kashmir, 20
    Muaskar-e-Tayyaba, 19
    obligation of *jihad* and *dawah,* 19, 20
martyrs and martyrdom, 11, 219–20
    Abdullah, Abdul Razzaq Abu, 222–24
    Abdullah, Abu, 235
    Ahmed, Abu Asadallah Intizar, 293–95

INDEX 633

Akhtar, Abu Jibran Naseem, 330–32
Ali, Abu, 270–73
Ali, Abu Abdul Wadood Fidai Rifaqat, 306–8
Amjad, Abu Hanzul, 314–19
Amjad', Abu Tahir Muhammad, 286
Ansari, Abu Ayub, 303–6
Aqasha, Abu, 258
Aziz, Naveed Ahmad Abbu Talha, 328–30
Bari, Abu-Zubair Talha bin Abdul, 296–99
Baseer, Abu, 270–73
Butt, Mohammad Ilyas, 251–55
Butt, Mohammed Ilyas, 244–55
Dr Javed, 262–64
Farooqi, Abu Alqama Mazhar Iqbal, 243–44
Farooqi, Mazhar Iqbal, 235
Hamza, Abu, 308–11
Idrees, Mohammed, 244–55
Ilyas, Abu Usman Muhammad, 288–90
Iqbal, Naeem Iqbal Naeem, 237–40
Jandal, Abu Jandal Mohammad, 241–43, 245
Javed, Abu Abdullah Affan, 323–28
Khan, Hamidullah, 256–58
Mu'awiyah, Abu, 235, 245
Muhammad, Abu Abdullah Thani Abdul Razzaq bin Khushi, 224–30
Mursad, Zakaullah Abu, 290–93
news of, 248, 304
noble character of, 221
path to martyrdom, 182–84
portrayal of martyrdom, 232–33
to prophet, 126
Quhafa, Abu, 299–303
Rehman, Abu Abdul (Hafez Mohammad Deen), 268–70
Sajid, Mohammad, 235
Shah, Abu Umair Mohammad Amir, 278–86
Shakeel, Abul Qasim Muhammad, 320–23
Sufian, Abu (Hameedullah Khan), 273

Umair, Abu, 277–78
Waheed, Abu Huzaifa Abdul, 311–14
Zaman, Abu Kaab Ullah Khan, 332–33
Zayd, Abu Talha (Mohammad Tahir Ismael), 264–68
Masnad Ahmed, 72–73
Maududi, Maulana, 351
Meccan and Medinite periods, distinguish between, 111–16
Allah's portents and guidance, 114–15
examples, 112–13
Islamic obligations, 113
murder of Ubay ibn Khalaf, 115–16
People of Quraysh, 115
Messenger of Allah, 429–30
Milli Muslim League (MML), 4–5, 27
Misri, Mufti Muhammad Abdah, 385
Mohammad, Bin, 43
monasticism (Sufism), 336, 337–38, 343, 345, 359
movement, 181
path to martyrdom, 182–84
Muaskar-e-Aqsa, 84
Muaskar-e-Tayyaba, 84
Muhammad, Abdus Salam bin, 45–46
Muhammad XII of Nasrid dynasty, 5
Mujahid, Yahya, 2–3
Mujahid ki Azaan ('The *Mujahid*'s Call'), 177
effects of proselytizing, 207–11
foreword, 179–80
Islam's education policy, 200–7
life of youth and students, 187–88
message of proselytize and wage *jihad,* 180–82
motivation for, 178–79
new generation, desires and aspirations, 184–87
path to martyrdom, 182–84
peace in academic institutions, present times, 199
structure, 178–79
student empowerment, 196–200
student unions, 191–96, 206–7
target population, 177
teachers, present times, 192
topics, 180

634 INDEX

mujahid/mujahideen, 10–11, 15–16, 75, 83, 90, 91, 97
about human rights organizations, 162–63
allies in war, 146–48
appearance, 530–31
awaiting martyrdom, 541–43
battle between Islam and disbelief, 118, 120
battle life, 119, 121, 121*t*, 122–25, 126–33
Battle of Khandaq, 131
Battle of Mu'tah, 124–25
benefits of *jihad,* 141
choice of afterlife, 10, 77, 145, 177–78, 180–81, 186, 191, 207, 225, 226, 238, 257, 271, 288, 304, 312–13, 314, 315–16, 349, 353–56, 393, 416, 443, 489, 553
consequence of non-participation in *jihad,* 117–18, 172
conspiracies against, 527
debauchery and greed of Jews, 159
distinction between Meccan and Medinite periods, 111–16
escaping death, 117–18
exempted from acting upon Allah's command, 150–52
on fasting, 148–49, 150
fighting in Kashmir, 144, 145–46
freeing Muslim lands from occupation of disbelievers, 141
guerrilla warfare in Kashmir as *jihad,* 110–11, 134–48
jihadi obligation, 151
lives of prophets, 129–30
Markaz-ud-Dawah-wal-Irshad, 110
martyr's status, 120
military tactics, 135
Muslim oppressors *vs* polytheists as oppressors, 109
persecution of Indian Muslims, 138–39
present times, 149
reason for fighting Hindustan, 157–58
time and place of person's death, 116, 117

true, 128
victory and defeat for, 132, 133–34
waging *jihad* for Allah's cause, 158–59
'*The Mujahid's Call*', 9–10
Mujallah-ul-Dawah, 151
Murji'i, 30
murjiya, 13
Musharraf, Pervez, 1, 2, 25
Muslim regions
disbelievers occupying, 163–64, 169–75
geographic significance of, 92–93
Muslims
acceptance of truth, 341
being a Muslim, 185–87
conditions after Prophet's death, 90–91
education level, 88
freedom struggle in Eritrea, 166
importance of unity, 154–55
international conspiracies against, 163–64
kufr statement and its negation, 384–85
persecuted in different countries, 138
sects and sub-sects, 154
standard of living, 185
ummat, 56, 60–61, 66, 79–80, 83, 103, 107, 154, 165, 167, 185, 186, 190, 198, 199, 205–6, 207, 208, 213, 218, 344, 347, 385–86, 428
Muslims, atrocities against
in Bulgaria, 167
in China, 166
in Cyprus, 169
in Eritrea, 166
plight of Burmese, 167
slaughter of Filipino Muslims in USA, 168–69
in Thailand, 167–68
Muslim *ummat,* 154
Muta'am, 72
mystagogues, 345
mysticism, 343
acts of, 345
criticism of, 336
prophet's prohibition of, 344

INDEX   635

Nagaland, 556
Nationalist Socialist Council of
    Nagaland, 557
new generation, desires and aspirations,
    184–87
    education, 184–85
Noble Warriors and Battlefronts, 14–16

Operation Gibraltar, 462
operations against India's soldiers,
    494–500, 501–4, 513–19, 520–21,
    543–46, 562–63
    Abu Mujahid's encounter with Indian
      soldiers, 518–19
    approaching target, 528–29
    capture and interrogation of Hindu
      soldier, 521–23
    commandos descending from
      helicopters, 515
    discovery of military posts, 529–30
    election operations, 513–19
    execution of operations, 515–16
    local police force and, 516
    murdering of captain, 518
    places of encounter, 526–27
    at Rafiabad, 517
    revenge for insulting prophet's
      Sunnat, 546–47
    during snow, 524–25
    during summer, 523–24
    use of mini-planes, 531–32
    use of rocket launchers and machine
      guns, 543
Operation Silence, 2007, 23

pagan traditions, 346
    festivals, 349
    hinder prophet's mission, 122
    against Muslims, 110, 114, 118, 136,
      137, 146
    Satanic cult of photographs, 346–47
Pakistan, 2
    defence of *jihad*, 79–80
    international scrutiny, 27–28
    militant groups, 26–27
    war on, 30
Pakistani Taliban, 28–29

Pakistan People's Party (PPP), 4–5
Pakistan Tehreek-e-Insaf, 4–5
Palestine struggle, 164–66
Pasban-e-Harmain-Sharifain, 3
'*Pasban-e-Harmain-Sharifain*', 26
Pasruri, Basim Sharif, 47
Pasruri, Rana Iftikhar Ahmed, 47
People of Quraysh, 115
piety, Islamic notion of, 32
pilgrimages to shrines and mausoleums,
    356
pious, lives of, 424
PL-480 programme, 6–7
polytheism, 182
*Problem of Takfir and its Principles and
    Regulations* (Mubbashir Ahmed
    Rabbani), 375
    act of *takfir* as punishable, 421–24
    al-Shokani's warning, 380–81
    al-Wazir Yamani's view, 384
    application of *shariat*-based evidence,
      380
    application to principles of belief and
      faith, 443–48
    authority to practise, 414
    content, 377
    Daqiq al-Ayeed's view, 384
    established evidences, 414–37
    first principle, 410–14
    flawed principle of *takfir*, 411–12
    foreward, 379–86
    Hadees insights, 388, 389–91
    Imam Ghazali's view, 382
    important statements, 414
    inquiry, 386–87
    limitations of *takfir*, 428
    perils of *takfir*, 380–81
    publisher's note, 377–79
    rebel against sultan, 410–11
    references to *Riyaz-us-Saliheen*, 387,
      389
    response to inquiry, 387–93
    rules and regulations, 400–48
    shariat-based injunction, 386, 410
    Sheikh Ibn Taymiyyah's view, 383
    third principle, 443–48
    Uthman-al-Zahbi's view, 382–83

636 INDEX

The Problem with Takfir, 12–13
prophet
about tombs, 350
campaigns, 120–24
on faith, 394
final moments, 357–58
guerrilla warfare, 135, 136–37
importance of Ka'ba, 356
against infidels, 115, 123
lives of, 129–30
lives sacrificed during times of,
171–72
martyrdoms to, 126
on mausoleums, 339–58
murder of Ubay ibn Khalaf, 115–16
prohibition of monastic grave-
worshipping rituals, 344
Prophet Abraham, 246
purpose of visiting graves, 353
on registers, 341–42
rejection of graven images, 346
successes and achievements of, 162
tomb of, 352
wasan tradition, 348
proselytization *(dawah)*, 7–10, 29–30,
38, 45–46, 88, 113–14, 177–78
in academic institutions, 179–80,
208–11
effects of, 207–11
next generation of proselytizers, 195

Qadamah, Ibn, 61
qisas (retributive justice), principle of,
148–52
Quran, 31–33, 44, 97, 113, 120, 136, 150,
154, 155, 179–80, 186, 195–96,
208–9, 345
about desire, 142
alcohol, prohibition of, 57
attitude of disbeliever, 117
cowardice of Jews, 161
Day of Judgement, 32, 56
elements of faith, 392–93
extra-marital sex, prohibition of, 57
fighting for independence, 141
'holy five' of Noah's people, 342–43
on hypocrisy, 131, 132, 391–92

monotheism and salvation, 32–33
obligations in, 148
oneness of god, 32
against polytheism, 388
precondition for *jihad,* 132–33
revelation, 32–33
straight path, 388
temporary marriages, prohibition
of, 57
traditional form, 32
transgression, prohibition of, 85
treacherous desires, 159, 160
usury, prohibition of, 57
view of shrines, 345–58
warnings to infidels, 388

Rabbani, Abul Hassan Mubashir
Ahmed, 386–87
Rawaha, Abdullah bin, 125
Red Fort attack, 2000, 16, 572–81, 573*f,*
582*f*
Rehmat-al-il-Alameen, 38
The Resistance Group (TRF), 27–28
rights of Allah, rights of Allah's men, 110

sabi, 405–6
Sabir, Ali Ahmed, 361–62
Saeed, Abu, 64
Saeed, Hafiz Muhammad, 1–3, 4, 14, 19–
20, 21–22, 24, 26–27, 79, 337
Salafi groups, 30
Salafi *jihadi*s, 375–76
Saleh, Syed Abdul Qadir Muhammad,
166
Samiullah, Sheikh, 103
Samurah, Jabir bin, 58
Sani, Abdul Wahab, 248–51
Satanic cult of photographs, 346–47
Seerat (Muhammad's biography), 8, 31,
36–38, 90
Abu Baseer's story, 40–42
hijra (migration) to Medina, 37, 39–
40, 72
Ibn Ishaq's manuscript, 37–38
military campaigns, 37–38
threat from residents of Mecca, 72
11 September 2010 attack, 474–75

INDEX 637

Shah, Shabir Ahmed, 467
  release of, 482–83
shaheed biographies, 231–32
  brothers's grief and perspective, 226,
    254–55, 305, 332
  father's grief and perspective, 225,
    257–58, 289, 291, 304, 306–7, 320,
    326–27, 333
  in Kashmir, 234–44
  mother's grief and perspective, 232–
    33, 236–37, 249, 254, 304, 308, 319,
    327–28, 331, 332
  objectives, 234
  performance of grief, 233
  portrayal of martyrdom, 232–33
  sisters's grief and perspective, 305,
    308, 331, 332
  widow's grief and perspective, 332
Shahrah-e-Bahisht (Highway to Heaven),
  12, 335
  audience, 335
  connecting with Allah, 358–73
  content, 335–36
  criticism of mystical practices, 336
  forms of grave-worship, 347–49
  Hinduism, 338
  'holy five' of Noah's people, 342–43
  House of Allah (Ka'ba), 338–39
  idolater, tragedy of, 349–50
  organized monasteries, 343–45
  prologue, 337
  prophet's view on mausoleums,
    339–58
  publisher's note, 337
  Quranic view of shrines, 345–58
  religious advice, 351
  reminder of afterlife, 353–54
  Satanic cult of photographs, 346–47
  Satan's interventions, 341–43
  Sufism, 336, 337–38
Shi'a, 9, 347–48
  Islam, 28
  of Iran, 346–47
Sharif, Nawaz, 4–5
Sharma, Chief Lt. General M.R., 554–55
Sheikh, Muhammad Yaqoob, 4–5
Shiv Sena, 534–47

atrocities of, 535, 536
  female operative, 536–37
  murder of leaders, 538–39
  slaughtering of, 534–47
Shiv Sena Hindu Parishad, 534
Shokafi, Imam, 67
shrines and mausoleums
  cleaning of, 365–66
  Daata Sahib's sanctuary, 360, 363–64,
    370, 371
  pilgrimages to, 356
  Pir Makki Sahib's shrine, 360–61, 364
  Quranic view of, 345–58
Sindh, 547–52
  demand of Sindhis in India, 550–52
  Jewish interest in, 547–48
  LeT's policy, 552
  solution to problems of, 549–50
  spies of, 548–49
Singh, Maharaja Hari, 461
South Asia Cooperative Acquisitions
  Program, 6–7
Sri Nagar's airport attack, 567–72
  LeT modus operandi, 567
  media report, 569–72
  reason for, 568–69
  soldiers killed in, 571
student empowerment, 196–200
  follow *Sunnat,* 200
  military and *jihadi* training, 198
  overcoming minor obstacles, 199–200
student unions, 191–96, 206–7
  character-building, 195–96
  leadership potential, 194
  proselytizing, 195
  right to study Quran and *Sunnat,*
    195–96
  violence and homicides, 193–94
Sufyan, Abu, 72
Sunnat, 8, 33–34, 97, 143, 150, 157, 179–
  80, 195–96, 200, 208–9, 372
  conventional sense, 33
  of marriage, 144
Sunni *masalik,* 28
Surat al-Anfal, 120
Surat at-Tawbah, 127
Surat Muhammad, 86

638 INDEX

Talib, Abu, 71, 114
Talib, Jafar bin Abi, 126
Taliban, 2, 22–23, 25
tawheed, 10, 12, 32, 177–79, 180–81,
   182, 208–9, 335–36, 337, 338, 343,
   372, 375–76, 431, 504
Taymiyyah, Sheikh al-Islam Imam Ibn,
   383, 407, 411, 435, 446, 447
   rules and regulations of *takfir,* 400–48
Tayyar, Syedna Jafar, 126
taziya, 347–48
Tehreek-e-Hurmat-e-Rasool, 12, 335
Tehreek-e-Tahafuz-e-Hurmat-e-Rasool,
   3, 26
Tehreek-e-Tahafuz Qibla Awal, 3, 26
tombs, 350
Treaty of Hudaybiyyah, 40
truth, acceptance of, 340–41

Ubaid-ur-Rehman Sahib, Maulana
   Abdullah, 219
Umar, Syedna, 163–64
Umm-e-Hammad, 11, 213–15.
   See also We, the Mothers of
   Lashkar-e-Tayyaba
   Markaz-e-Tayyaba's training, 216
   path of *jihad,* 216–17
UN Security Council Resolutions 1267
   and 1989, 3
US military operations in Afghanistan,
   2, 22, 25
Uthman, Hazrat, 73–74

Uthman-al-Zahbi, Imam Muhammad
   bin Ahmed bin, 382–83

Wahab, Sheikh Muhammad bin Abdul,
   403, 407, 433, 434, 448
'*wajib ul qatal*' 3 status, 44
Walid, Khalid bin, 127
We, the Mothers of Lashkar-e-Tayyaba,
   213, 214
   Abu Mu'awiyah's mother, 241
   Abu Sohaib Shaheed's mother, 214–15
   patience of martyr's mother, 236–37
   preamble, 218–20
   publisher's note, 214–15
   second volume, publisher's note,
   221–22
   Umm-e-Hammad's contribution,
   214–15
We Are the Mothers of Lashkar-i-
   Tayyaba, 10
women's wing of LeT, 213
   Hum Mayen Lashkar-e-Tayyaba
   Ki. See We, the Mothers of
   Lashkar-e-Tayyaba
WorldCat, 5–6

Yaman, Syedna Hazeefa bin, 122
Yaman, Syedna Huzaifa bin, 396
Yusuf, Hafiz Salahuddin, 386, 387–93

Zaki-ur-Rehman, 101
Zia-ul-Haq, General, 463

The manufacturer's authorised representative in the EU for product safety is
Oxford University Press España S.A. of el Parque Empresarial San Fernando de
Henares, Avenida de Castilla, 2 – 28830 Madrid (www.oup.es/en or product.
safety@oup.com). OUP España S.A. also acts as importer into Spain of products
made by the manufacturer.

www.ingramcontent.com/pod-product-compliance
Lightning Source LLC
Chambersburg PA
CBHW071833290825
31867CB00003B/129